Fatoumata Jawara and Aileen Kwa

Behind the scenes at the WTO: the real world of international trade negotiations

lessons of Cancun – updated edition

Zed Books
LONDON · NEW YORK

in association with

Focus on the Global South
BANGKOK

Behind the scenes at the WTO: the real world of international trade negotiations was first published by Zed Books Ltd, 7 Cynthia Street, London N1 9JF, UK and Room 400, 175 Fifth Avenue, New York, NY 10010, USA in 2003

Behind the scenes at the WTO: the real world of international trade negotiations/lessons of Cancun – updated edition was first published by Zed Books Ltd, 7 Cynthia Street, London N1 9JF, UK and Room 400, 175 Fifth Avenue, New York, NY 10010, USA in 2004

www.zedbooks.co.uk

in association with Focus on the Global South, c/o CURSI, Chulalongkorn University, Bangkok 10330, Thailand

www.focusweb.org

Cover designed by Andrew Corbett
Set in Monotype Dante and Gill Sans Heavy by Ewan Smith, London
Printed and bound in the United Kingdom by Cox and Wyman, Reading

Distributed in the USA exclusively by Palgrave Macmillan, a division of St Martin's Press, LLC, 175 Fifth Avenue, New York, NY 10010

A catalogue record for this book is available from the British Library
Library of Congress cataloging-in-publication data: available

ISBN 1 84277 532 4 cased
ISBN 1 84277 533 2 limp

Six British development organizations – ActionAid, CAFOD, Christian Aid, Oxfam, Save the Children, and the World Development Movement – co-funded the authors in the research and writing of this book because of the importance they attach to all future negotiations on international trade issues being fully transparent and democratic. Responsibility for all points of view and any errors of fact in the book, however, remain solely with the authors.

Contents

Figures, tables and boxes

Acknowledgements

Fatoumata Jawara I would like to thank David Woodward for giving me the wonderful opportunity to work on this project, for doing the editing, and for support, friendship and encouragement throughout. Many thanks to Aileen Kwa, Shefali Sharma of IATP Geneva, Sabrina Varma (formerly of the South Centre) and all the Geneva-based South Centre staff for advice, support and kindness. Thanks to the Geneva Missions and WTO Secretariat staff for granting interviews, at very short notice in some cases.

My heartfelt gratitude to my friends and my wonderful family, especially N'jaimeh (Baby), Mariam, Aunty Jarra, Kawsu, Nadua, Toulie, Baby Chilel, Mama N'jaimeh, Haddi Secka, Nace Marenah and all the rest! Very special thanks to my parents Sir Dawda and Lady Chilel Jawara – for unstinting love and support always.

Robert Molteno of Zed Books, thanks for unflagging enthusiasm and interest in the project. Last but not least, thanks to the funders of the project, who include David Woodward, Save the Children (UK), Oxfam (GB), Christian Aid, CAFOD, World Development Movement and ActionAid. It should be noted, however, that the views expressed in this book are not necessarily theirs.

Aileen Kwa Sincere appreciation and thanks go to David Woodward, who has worked very hard on both editions, carefully editing and pulling together the different strands into a coherent whole. If not for your unwavering commitment to the 'larger cause', the book would most likely not have been completed. To Fatima Jawara, your humour and energy carried us through a long way. Robert Molteno, Anna Hardman, and the superb Zed team, including Farouk Sohawon whom we overworked last year, I cannot thank you all enough for your efforts in helping us bring our message to the world. The publicity the book has received must also be credited to the hard work of John Hilary and Hannah Crabtree; Dave Timms and Peter Hardstaff; Maud Johansson (Forum Syd); Tim Anderson (Attac Australia and Aid/Watch); Federico Cuello, and many others. John Hilary was also a tremendous help in pulling together financing for the book. Launches and the timely distribution of the book to Southern government delegates were possible only with the generous contributions of NOVIB, ActionAid and the WDM.

This work could never have taken form if not for the generosity and trust of many Geneva-based developing country delegates over the last few years. I have learnt much from you, and admire your determination to keep fighting, despite constant frustrations.

My gratitude and appreciation go to the entire South Centre staff, for welcoming me into the family, the infrastructural support, as well as for the invaluable inputs into this work – Branislav Gosovic, Caroline Menang, Guadalupe Quesada, Jacqueline Barmine, Kwame Quansah, Luisa Bernal, Maria Jordan, Martine Julsaint, Paul Morejon, Rashid Kaukab, Sisule Musungu, Someshwar Singh, Sabrina Varma, Vicente Yu and Gale Raj. Sincere thanks to Vasanthan Pushparaj for being always available, even at the shortest notice!

To the Focus family, you have been a source of inspiration more than you realize – Nicola Bullard, Shalmali Guttal, Chanida Bamford, Minar Pimple, Meena Menon, Raghav Narsalay, Joy Chavez, Marylou Malig, Jacques-chai Chomthongdi, Herbert Docena, Anoop Sukumaran, Nok Ruechakiattikul, Soontaree Nakaviroj, Praphai Jundee and Walden Bello, who did not dodge the falling debris.

To Shefali Sharma, I'll never forget our time together in Geneva – you are sorely missed. Special mention and thanks must also be accorded to Tan Li-Anne, Charulata Prasada, Clare Lim, Sandy Sim, Angela and Tito Issac and the Leos.

To all my family – for making so many accommodations while the writing was underway – Aimee, Vissia and Xavier Gonzales, Ruth Alimohamed, Michelle and Edwin, Lucia and the Magnificat Community, and Gonzalo. I am above all grateful to my wonderful parents Jane and Vincent, for your unstinting love and generosity, but also for being co-parents, not merely grandparents! This work – carried out sometimes at the expense of motherhood – is dedicated to Maria, with love.

Chronology

1947	Geneva Round of Multilateral Trade Negotiations; signing of General Agreement on Tariffs and Trade (GATT)
1948	General Agreement on Tariffs and Trade (1947) comes into effect
1949	Annecy Round of Multilateral Trade Negotiations
1951	Torquay Round of Multilateral Trade Negotiations
1956	Geneva Round of Multilateral Trade Negotiations
1960–61	Dillon Round of Multilateral Trade Negotiations
1964–67	Kennedy Round of Multilateral Trade Negotiations
1975–79	Tokyo Round of Multilateral Trade Negotiations
1986–94	Uruguay Round of Multilateral Trade Negotiations
1994	*April*, signing of the Uruguay Round Agreements and the Marrakesh Agreement
1995	*January*, establishment of WTO
1996	*December*, First WTO Ministerial Conference, Singapore
1998	*May*, Second WTO Ministerial Conference, Geneva, Switzerland
1999	*July*, selection of Mike Moore and Supachai Panitchpakdi as directors general
	September, Mike Moore takes office as director general
1999	*November/December*, Third WTO Ministerial Conference, Seattle, USA
2001	*August*, Mexico mini-ministerial Meeting
	October, Singapore mini-ministerial Meeting
	November, Fourth WTO Ministerial Conference, Doha, Qatar
2002	*January*, establishment of the Trade Negotiations Committee (TNC); appointment of director general as *ex officio* chair of TNC
	February, appointment of Stuart Harbinson as Agriculture Committee chair
	September, Supachai Panitchpakdi takes office as DG; appointment of Stuart Harbinson as *chef de cabinet*
	November, Sydney mini-ministerial
2003	*February*, Tokyo mini-ministerial
	September, Fifth WTO Ministerial Conference, Cancun, Mexico

Abbreviations

ACP	Africa, Caribbean and Pacific
AGOA	African Growth and Opportunity Act
AoA	Agreement on Agriculture
APEC	Asia Pacific Economic Co-operation
ARV	antiretroviral
ASEAN	Association of South East Asian Nations
ATPDEA	Andean Trade Promotion and Drug Eradication Act
AU	African Union
BWTD	Bridges Weekly Trade Digest
CAFTA	Central America Free Trade Agreement
CAP	Common Agricultural Policy
CARICOM	Caribbean Community
COMESA	Common Market for Eastern and Southern Africa
COW	Committee of the Whole
CSO	civil society organization
DDG	deputy director general
DG	director general
DSB	Dispute Settlement Body
EC	European Communities
ESM	emergency safeguard mechanism
FAO	Food and Agriculture Organization
FDI	foreign direct investment
FTAA	Free Trade Area of the Americas
G77	Group of 77
GATS	General Agreement on Trade in Services
GATT	General Agreement on Tariffs and Trade
GDP	gross domestic product
GSP	Generalized System of Preferences
HIPC	Highly-Indebted Poor Countries
HIV	Human Immunodeficiency Virus
ILO	International Labour Organization

IMF	International Monetary Fund
IPR	intellectual property rights
IT	information technology
LDC	least developed country
LMG	Like-Minded Group
MEA	Multilateral Environmental Agreement
MFA	Multi-Fibre Arrangement
MFN	most favoured nation
MNC	multinational company
NAFTA	North American Free Trade Agreement
NAMA	Non-Agricultural Market Access
NCC	National Cotton Council (USA)
NEPAD	New Partnership for Africa's Development
NGO	non-governmental organization
OECD	Organisation for Economic Co-operation and Development
PhRMA	Pharmaceutical Research and Manufacturers of America
R&D	research and development
SACU	Southern African Customs Union
SADC	Southern African Development Community
SAP	structural adjustment programme
SDT	Special and Differential Treatment
SPS	Sanitary and Phytosanitary Measures
TBT	Technical Barriers to Trade
TIFA	Trade and Investment Framework Agreement
TNC	Trade Negotiations Committee
TRIMs	Trade-Related Investment Measures
TRIPs	Trade-Related Aspects of Intellectual Property Rights
UK	United Kingdom
UN	United Nations
UNCTAD	United Nations Conference on Trade and Development
USA	United States of America
USTR	[Office of the] United States Trade Representative
WAEMU	West African Economic and Monetary Union
WHO	World Health Organization
WTO	World Trade Organization

Preface

This book represents a valuable contribution to the study and understanding of current multilateral politics and North–South relations, as played out in the WTO. It depicts the 'lopsided playing fields' on to which the developing countries were thrust by the North after the conclusion of Uruguay Round Agreements and the establishment of the WTO.

It is a sober and sobering book for all those who believe in a prosperous world economy anchored in a rule-based system in which North and South co-operate and equitably share the gains from global economic expansion. The WTO (or, more accurately, its predecessor the GATT) has been the chief rule-making body for international trade in manufactured products. It is now increasing its reach by bringing under its disciplines not only manufacturing trade but also agricultural products, services and intellectual property rights, as well as issues such as investment, competition policy, government procurement; and so on.

In this carefully researched, unique book the authors lift the veil on how decisions are actually taken. They conducted structured, in-depth interviews with a large number of Geneva-based missions to the WTO and WTO Secretariat staff members. While some of the interviewees understandably chose to remain anonymous, this does not in any way detract from the authors' analysis or conclusions. Interviewees are named wherever possible, and their views are quoted directly to the extent possible, or else indirectly to reflect their judgements. The sample of missions was chosen from right across the spectrum of the WTO membership.

What emerges is a fascinating story that would do credit to the best kind of investigative journalism. However, the authors have a more serious intent and they are able to demonstrate with their research the kind of arm-twisting and bullying of developing countries that routinely occurs in the negotiating process, through which developing countries are obliged to accept agreements that they know are not in their long-term interests.

Instead of the far-sighted approach adopted by the USA after the Second World War to help build up European economies through non-reciprocity (for example, providing market access to Japanese and Italian goods without insisting on reciprocal access to the Italian and Japanese markets), today's rich countries seem to be guided entirely by narrow, short-term mercantilism rather than the long-term interests of the world economy as a whole. The WTO Secretariat, instead of being a neutral and essentially administrative body, aids and abets this process and thereby violates its own mission statement, which is contained in the very first paragraph of the preamble to the WTO Agreements. This preambular paragraph makes it clear that the purpose of the organization is not free trade in itself but the fostering of sustainable long-term economic development and improvement of living standards in rich and poor countries alike.

The authors find that the culture of the Secretariat has internalized concepts of market access and liberalization to a degree that it cannot but act as essentially the agent of advanced countries rather than seek to redress the balance for poor countries. A fundamental change in this culture would be required for the Secretariat to appreciate that liberalization does not always promote economic development, and that it may even retard it. The recent appointment of a developing country public figure as the head of the organization is unlikely to change this deeply ingrained culture.

The study depicts the hostile, threatening and biased negotiating and institutional environment that the developing countries have to face in the WTO. It is thus a wake-up call for all those who understand and share developing countries' aspirations and sensitivities, or who still hold illusions about the democratic nature of multilateral processes and organizations, or about the need to make development a priority and to provide the developing countries with appropriate support and fair treatment.

The book also makes painful reading to those familiar with the manner in which trade and development figured on the international agenda, including in the GATT, following the creation of UNCTAD in 1964, by showing how the gains achieved at that time have been eroded and forgotten.

The volume will indubitably lead to an outcry and denials from concerned quarters. On the other hand, the developing country negotiators, familiar with the WTO scene, will no doubt welcome it as providing a broad-brush description of the reality in which they have to survive and operate.

Developing country leaders and citizens need to understand the nature of the institutions and processes through which their future is being decided, and the process by which their development options are rapidly being reduced. It is up to them to resist and change the institutional status quo, which is unfair and prejudicial to the South. In view of the realities of the distribution of world economic and political power, developing countries can succeed only by working and acting together.

The challenge now is to proceed with systematic and sustained empirical analysis of the workings of the WTO, and of similar global power-wielding international organizations, which have emerged as a key tool in the hands of Northern governments and corporations, *inter alia*, to control and manage developing countries. It is to be hoped that the Jawara and Kwa study will be followed by studies from other researchers from the South, as well as independent-minded scholars from the North. Such research should probe in depth the political processes, structures, institutions and underlying premises that underpin the unequal relations between the North and the South in the contemporary multilateral setting.

The authors have done a signal service to the international community with their important study, which deserves to be widely read and its conclusions acted upon.

Professor Ajit Singh, University of Cambridge, Cambridge, UK
Branislav Gosovic, South Centre Secretariat, Geneva, Switzerland

Introduction: Cancun and its aftermath – 'multilateralism' without goodwill

The remainder of this book recounts what happened before, during and after the Fourth WTO Ministerial Conference in Doha, Qatar, in November 2001. It tells how developing countries were bullied and coerced into acquiescing with an 'agreement' with which most of them profoundly *dis*agreed. The process culminated in a Ministerial Conference which continued through the night and after its scheduled end (and the departure of some developing country delegations) until the developing countries were finally beaten into submission and the major powers got their way.

All that the developing countries achieved for their strenuous efforts was the label 'The Doha *Development* Agenda' attached to the new round of trade negotiations; a Ministerial declaration on TRIPs and Public Health; and agreement that negotiations on the 'Singapore' issues (expanding the WTO's remit to cover investment, competition, transparency in government procurement and trade facilitation) would begin only on the basis of 'explicit consensus' on the modalities of negotiations at the Fifth WTO Ministerial Conference in Cancun, Mexico, in September 2003. The events surrounding the Cancun Ministerial demonstrated that all three were worthless.

This Introduction tells the story of the Cancun Ministerial. Until the last day, the process was strikingly similar to the deeply flawed Doha process, except for the emergence of a new coalition of developing countries – the G20[1] (then comprising Argentina, Bolivia, Brazil, Chile, China, Colombia, Costa Rica, Cuba, Ecuador, El Salvador, Guatemala, India, Mexico, Pakistan, Paraguay, Peru, the Philippines, South Africa, Thailand and Venezuela) – and the re-emergence of the G90, comprising the least developed countries (LDCs), the African, Caribbean and Pacific (ACP) group and the African Union (AU).

Most delegates also expected a similar end-game, with the major players again prolonging the Ministerial and negotiating into the early hours, relying on last-minute brinkmanship to ram through their agenda. But to the shock of developed and developing government delegates alike, the Ministerial came to an abrupt halt without an agreement at 2.30 p.m. on the final scheduled day (14 September), as Mexican Foreign Minister Luis Ernesto Derbez, as conference chairman, pulled the plug.

The final hours of Cancun

At 2 p.m. the previous day, Chairman Derbez had finally issued the long-awaited revised draft of the Ministerial Declaration – supposed to reflect the views of the entire WTO membership as expressed at the conference. The immediate reactions were disbelief, acrimony and anger, as it entirely disregarded the positions of the developing country majority in all the critical areas: agriculture, the Singapore issues, cotton, industrial tariffs and development issues. Far from bringing positions together, the draft widened the differences still further, and developing country ministers, incensed at having been so arrogantly brushed aside, fought back.

At the Heads of Delegation (HOD) meeting which followed, delegation after delegation spoke up, tearing the draft to shreds for ignoring the strong and repeated messages the developing world had sent throughout the previous three days (see Box In.1). As the European Communities (EC) Trade Commissioner, Pascal Lamy, later recalled: 'Delegation after delegation took the floor to denounce the text as a travesty of justice, as an affront to every developing country, as a heresy of enormous magnitude. At the end of Cancun, the 13 September text looked dead and buried' (Lamy 2003c).

Nine ministers (from the USA, the EC, Mexico, Brazil, China, India, Malaysia, Kenya and South Africa) were invited to a mini 'green room'[2] meeting on the Singapore issues from 1 a.m. to 3 a.m., but it yielded no results. A larger 'green room' meeting, attended by the same nine plus more than twenty others (Argentina, Australia, Bangladesh, Benin, Botswana, Canada, Chile, Colombia,

BOX In.1 Developing countries' comments on the 13 September text

General comments

India: 'We are disappointed that the draft text ignores several concerns expressed by us and many developing countries. I note that the pretence of development dimensions of the Doha Agenda has finally been discarded confirming the apprehension expressed by me at the plenary session that this is mere rhetoric ... '

'We have to express our disappointment that the revised text brought out by you has arbitrarily disregarded views and concerns expressed by us ... We wonder now whether development here refers to only further development of the developed countries. This text does not lend itself to any meaningful dialogue.'

Antigua and Barbuda: 'We do not recognize in this text the consensus we heard articulated in those groups on the development issues, small economy issues and Singapore issues. What we see in this text is unsatisfactory and disappointing. And on cotton we believe the response in para. 27 to the arguments put forward by Africa is insulting and unworthy of this organization ...

'My government has a duty to care for its people. Were we to accept this document we would deserve our people's condemnation. For we would not only have gained no relief for them, we would have condemned them to a life of perpetual underdevelopment. And that my delegation will not do. I have to advise that this draft does not enjoy the support of my government.'

Bangladesh, representing the LDCs: 'We are told that this is a development round. We are yet to see concrete manifestation of the desire of the Membership to meaningfully help the LDCs.'

The Singapore issues

Malaysia, whose written statement was mostly written in large font and in bold:

'MALAYSIA CANNOT SUPPORT ANY TEXT TO IMPLY THE COMMENCEMENT OF NEGOTIATIONS ON MODALITIES ... MALAYSIA'S POSITION IS NON-NEGOTIABLE REGARDLESS OF ANY MOVE or development IN THE OTHER ISSUES being discussed in the Cancun Ministerial.'

Botswana, representing the G90: 'What [the draft] represents is unacceptable to us since it is not based on explicit consensus. Therefore there cannot be negotiations on these issues. Further, the linkage to other issues is surprising and also totally unacceptable to us.'

Bangladesh, representing the LDCs: 'We are unable to agree to negotiations ... The experience of the Uruguay Round has left us with bad memories, which we do not want repeated.'

India: 'It would appear that the views expressed by a large number of developing countries on the need for further clarification have been completely ignored. This is yet another instance of the deliberate neglect of views of a large number of developing countries. It represents an attempt to thrust the views of a few countries on many developing countries.'

Agriculture

India: 'We are compounding the Uruguay Round distortions by adding some more to them. The heightened ambition on the market access pillar, which ironically provides Special and Differential treatment in favour of developed countries, is utterly incomprehensible and extremely insensitive to the large number of people living in poverty in these countries. How can we expect developing countries to reduce tariffs on a number of items to 0% and 5% when the distortions against which such tariffs are supposed to compensate are sought to be enhanced?'

Sources: Khor (2003a); India (2003); WTO (2003b).

Egypt, Guyana, Hong Kong, Indonesia, Jamaica, Japan, Korea, Mauritius, Morocco, New Zealand, Nigeria, Pakistan, the Philippines, Singapore, Switzerland, Thailand) was held at 8.30 a.m., again on the Singapore issues.

Realizing that he could not get consensus on all four Singapore issues, Lamy finally offered to drop two or three of them – although he had no mandate to do so without approval from the EC's Council of Ministers. Developing countries repeated their opposition to negotiations on any of the Singapore issues, while Japan, Korea and Switzerland continued to support the launch of investment and competition negotiations.

By 12.30 p.m. it was clear that they were at an *impasse*, and Derbez suspended the meeting, to enable the ministers involved to consult with delegations outside. At a stormy G90 meeting during the break, delegates asked why Africa, barely coping with existing WTO obligations, should allow the launch of *any* of the Singapore issues; why Lamy was parading the dropping of three issues as a concession, when there was clearly no consensus on any of them; and what African countries were getting in return for accepting trade facilitation, which represented yet another slate of obligations, when the Doha promises on development had not been delivered.

Ugandan delegate Yash Tandon captured the spirit of the meeting.

The delegate of Malawi said, 'Why are we discussing the Singapore issues which are their issues. Our issues are developmental issues, commodities, prices, financial development, protection of farmers, protection of our industries' ... Zambia said, 'What are we taking home for the poor? No deal is better than any deal.' And then someone said, 'Maybe if we don't agree to Singapore issues the WTO will close down!' So the Zimbabwe delegation said, 'We are not here to be blackmailed.' The mood was incredible.[3]

According to Senegalese delegate Moussa Faye: 'Minister Nkate of Botswana [who represented the G90 in the 'green room'] requested the other delegates to accept one of the Singapore issues in return for an agreement on agriculture. African and Caribbean countries emphatically asked what part of "NO" they didn't understand' (*Pambazuka News* 2003).

The G90 did not give Nkate the mandate to agree to negotiations on any of the Singapore issues. Nkate responded: 'Well, I have heard you. I am going to represent what you have said' (ibid.).

When the 'green room' meeting reconvened at 1.30 p.m., Botswana reiterated the G90's opposition to negotiations on any of the Singapore issues. The EC offered to drop investment, competition and transparency in government procurement in exchange for immediate negotiations on trade facilitation. But Korea and Japan, still taken aback by Lamy's move, stuck to their insistence on retaining these issues.

It was at this point that Derbez – to the surprise of many ministers, including Lamy – closed the meeting and the conference. Brazilian Foreign Minister Celso Amorin requested that the Singapore issues be set aside and negotiations moved to agriculture; but Derbez stood by his decision, and the meeting was adjourned at 2.30 p.m. (South Centre 2003), while the EC Council of Ministers was still discussing Lamy's mandate. At the 4 p.m. HOD meeting, Derbez tabled a one-page final Ministerial statement, merely urging officials to continue working on outstanding issues 'with a renewed sense of urgency', 'taking fully into account all the views ... expressed in this Conference'. He said he would not negotiate further and, after taking two reactions from the floor, he closed the meeting.[4]

Reactions to the collapse – shock, anger, blame ... and elation

Reactions to the collapse of the Ministerial were strikingly different. As civil society representatives broke out in song and dance in the convention centre, US Trade Representative (USTR) Robert Zoellick, clearly sulking, threw a tantrum in his final press conference.

> Too many were spending too much time pontificating, not negotiating. Whether developed or developing, there were 'can do' and 'won't do' countries here. The harsh rhetoric of the 'won't do' overwhelmed the concerted efforts of the 'can do' ... Demands and tough rhetoric are easy; negotiations require commitment and hard work. And some countries will now have to decide whether they want to make a point or whether they want to make progress ... Many spent too much time with tactics of inflexibility and inflammatory rhetoric before getting down to negotiate. (USTR 2003a)

> A number of countries just thought it was a freebie – they could just make whatever points they suggested, argue, and not offer and give. And now they're going to face the cold reality of that strategy, coming home with nothing. (Associated Press 2003)

US Under-Secretary of Commerce for International Trade Grant Aldonas made an even more colourful attack on developing country trade negotiators, insinuating that some countries' reluctance to launch negotiations on government procurement reflected personal corruption. 'When I look at the developing world and I look at decision makers in the room who are wearing an awful lot of expensive jewellery and then don't want to negotiate about transparency in government procurement ... I have a very different perspective about whether they want an agreement' (Reuters 2003b).

US business interests seemed inclined simply to walk away. Frank Vargo, vice president for international economic affairs for the National Association of Manufacturers, said: 'American industry wants market access. If we can't get a level playing field in the WTO, we are going to take our poker chips out of this game and start dealing in free trade agreements where we know we can get a fair deal' (*International Trade Daily* 2003a).

Pascal Lamy's reaction was more measured than that of his US counterpart: 'I do not want to beat about the bush: Cancun has failed. This is not only a severe blow for the World Trade Organization but also a lost opportunity for all of us ... We will not play the blame game and we will remain open to reviving this process' (Lamy 2003a). He later acknowledged that the outcome of the Ministerial 'has been a major shock, there is no point in denying it', adding that the negotiating programme 'if not dead [was] certainly in intensive care' (Lamy 2003b). He also appeared to develop a sudden zeal for institutional reform: 'The WTO remains a medieval organization ... The procedures and rules of this organization have not supported the weight of the task. There is no way to structure and steer discussions amongst 146 members in a manner conducive to consensus. The decision-making needs to be revamped' (Lamy 2003a). However, what he had in mind was a still more undemocratic 'security council' decision-making structure in the WTO – anathema to most developing countries.

Developing country delegates formally registered their disappointment at a missed opportunity. Privately, though, many – particularly members of the G20 – were jubilant. Philippine Trade Secretary Manuel Roxas captured the sentiment being expressed by many developing country negotiators, saying: 'We are elated that our voice has now been heard' (Lannin and Waddington 2003).

The G20 chair, Brazilian Foreign Minister Celso Amorin, took a similar view: 'It was not possible to get a concrete result ... But we think that we have achieved some important things. Firstly, the respect for our group' (Waddington 2003). 'Not only were we able to keep our unity; but we were also permanent actors in the negotiations' (King and Miller 2003).

He later wrote: 'The voice of the developing world was taken into consideration ... I am convinced that Cancun will be remembered as the conference that signaled the emergence of a less autocratic multilateral trading system' (Amorin 2003).

Even South African Trade Minister Alec Erwin – previously

close to the developed countries, but a visible player in the G20 in Cancun – congratulated the developing world: 'This is the first time we have experienced a situation where, by combining our technical expertise, we can sit as equals at the table ... This is a change in the quality of negotiations between developing and developed countries' (Elliott et al. 2003).

Ecuadorean Minister Ivonne Juez de Baki described Cancun as 'historic' and setting the stage for greater co-operation among developing countries at the WTO. 'It's not the end. It's the beginning ... of a better future for everyone' (*International Trade Daily* 2003b). 'No deal is better than a bad deal' has since become a common phrase among Southern diplomats.

The issues – roads to nowhere?

The rot set in well before Cancun, as the major powers consistently blocked progress on issues of importance to the developing country majority, drew back from pledges made in Doha, ignored deadlines and pushed their own agendas heedless of all resistance. As usual, they got their way, and the draft declaration submitted to the Ministerial almost entirely reflected their positions on all the key issues: the Singapore issues, agriculture, cotton, TRIPs and public health and the development issues.

The Singapore issues

On the Singapore issues, most developing countries, including the G90, wanted the study programme to continue rather than negotiations to begin. However, the developed countries remained deaf to their concerns. The EC wanted immediate negotiations on all the issues as a single package, while the USA preferred unbundling them, with immediate negotiations on government procurement and trade facilitation, and a continued study process on investment and competition.

A key issue was what constituted 'modalities' (which had to be agreed by explicit consensus in Cancun as a basis for future negotiations) in the terms of the Doha Minsterial declaration. As Richard Eglin, Director of the Trade and Finance Division, acknowledged:

'The language you see from Doha was written by the Secretariat but it was deliberately ambiguous. We are experts at finding the most ambiguous words. For instance, what does "modalities" mean? It doesn't mean anything. But we need to find words that will bridge the differences so that both sides can see their position in the language.'[5]

Developing countries interpreted 'modalities' as 'substantive modalities', including the scope of each new agreement. The EC, however, wanted agreement only on procedural modalities, for example, how often meetings should be held. One developing country negotiator summed up the situation before Cancun:

> We are told to accept the launch of negotiations and then negotiate the details later. Once we accept the negotiations, it is difficult for developing countries to determine the contours of the negotiations – like what happened in TRIPs [where an agreement on counterfeit goods became an all-encompassing intellectual property rights agreement]. They [the developed countries] know how to outdo us and get what they want ... If you want me to cross the river, and I am not able to swim, then you should tell me how deep the river is.

The draft declaration produced in Geneva for discussion in Cancun contained two options on the Singapore issues. The first stated that negotiations would begin on all four issues, setting out 'modalities' for each in annexes; the second, without annexes, stated that the study process would continue.

A week before Cancun more than forty countries (led by Malaysia) submitted a proposal objecting that the draft

> gives a distorted view, that the Annexes have been discussed by Members. It would be recalled that the text on transparency in government procurement was introduced by the proponents in a small group meeting. We are not aware of any text having been put forward by the proponents on trade facilitation. The text on competition policy was discussed only in a small group meeting. Only the proponents' paper on investment was introduced

and discussed inconclusively in the HOD level meeting. Thus, Members did not have an opportunity to discuss the modalities identified by the proponents in all the Annexes to the Draft Ministerial text. (WTO 2003d)

The proposal included annexes detailing how the clarification process (rather than negotiations) should proceed on each issue. The stage was set for a bitter fight in Cancun.

The first shot was fired at a crowded press conference on Day 2 of the Ministerial, when sixty-nine developing countries announced their rejection of negotiations on the Singapore issues, and of any link between these issues and agriculture. Malaysian Minister Rafidah Aziz firmly stated: 'If any country looks at it from this standpoint, to link progress in agriculture with what they can get from new issues ... it doesn't want the Round to be completed' (Khor 2003b).

Asked about US and EC efforts to change countries' positions during the Ministerial, Aziz replied: 'They can't do that. All these years they've told us yes, and we told them no. We have become much wiser. In the Uruguay Round only a few countries knew what it was about. Now we have learnt our lessons. No more will we sit in the corridors and be given sweeteners' (ibid.)

The following day, the sixty-nine countries submitted a letter to Canadian Minister Pierre Pettigrew, as chair of the Singapore issues working group, expressing their 'doubts on the benefits of WTO frameworks on the new issues', their concern about the 'process through which these issues have been brought to this Ministerial without any prior discussion on the modalities', and their 'firm view that there is no option to pursue other than the continuation of the clarification process'.[6]

The agriculture impasse

Agriculture negotiations were blocked for months after Doha by disagreement between the USA and EC about how markets should be liberalized. The USA preferred an ambitious Swiss formula approach (cutting high tariffs more than low tariffs), while the EC

– reluctant to reduce its tariffs in sensitive sectors such as dairy, sugar and meat – preferred a Uruguay Round formula (cutting all tariffs by the same percentage), and lobbied about seventy-five developing countries to support this position.

Washington, however, spurred on by its commodity lobby groups, was adamant. On 1 July, fourteen major US commodity groups, led by the American Farm Bureau Federation, criticized Agriculture Committee chair Stuart Harbinson's approach, particularly in countenancing smaller tariff reductions for 'special products' in developing countries. They warned Zoellick that if this approach proceeded, 'the ultimate outcome of the negotiations will not be acceptable' (*Congress Daily* 2003).

For most of 2003, the talks were also held hostage by the EC's Common Agricultural Policy (CAP) reform. When this was finally completed, only on 26 June 2003, however, it was an anti-climax, leaving subsidies unchanged and allowing them to increase with the addition of ten new members. The only difference was that part of these payments would be decoupled (delinked from production). This gave the EC slightly more flexibility in the discussions, since the Commission argued vehemently that decoupled payments were less trade distorting. From developing countries' viewpoint, however, this difference was merely cosmetic (Kwa 2003).

The USA and EC finally released a 'framework' agreement incorporating both their interests on 13 August – later described as 'a transatlantic alliance for perpetual agricultural protectionism' (Zedillo 2004). This suggested a 'blended' tariff formula disastrous for the developing world,[7] only cosmetic changes in domestic support, and no end-date for phasing out export subsidies. 'Blue box' subsidy payments,[8] which developing countries wanted eliminated, were expanded to include increased US subsidy payments under the 2002 Farm Bill. This 'framework approach' was a major departure from the Doha Declaration requirement for agreement on 'modalities', because it contained only general formulae without actual numbers. Developing countries were thus being asked to agree to an ambitious tariff reduction formula, without knowing the extent of developed country subsidy cuts.

The Cairns Group – previously the third force in agriculture negotiations – made no effective response to the US/EC framework. It had been undermined by deep splits between those who wanted major tariff reductions, and others (such as the Philippines and Indonesia) who prioritized defending their domestic markets against imports. In its place, an informal coalition of countries, including India, Brazil, South Africa and China, submitted a joint response on 20 August. This marked the birth of the G20.

The G20 proposed a less ambitious tariff reduction formula, greater reductions in domestic support, and an end-date for export subsidies. While the proposal gave much room for continued US and EC subsidies, it proved more than they were willing to concede. According to an African LDC ambassador:

> The US and EC wanted to give the illusion of progress in agriculture when no real progress [or concessions from them] was being made. And that is why they came up with their framework without figures. If not for the G21 standing firm and saying 'There is no progress', we would have been told that these are concessions and now you should move on new issues, etc. The framework would have been portrayed as a breakthrough. Then there would have been pressure on many of us to accept it. The firm position of the G21 relieved the pressure on many of us.

At a press conference on the eve of the Ministerial, the G20 clearly rejected the Geneva draft text – largely a reproduction of the US/EC position – as failing to reflect divergent positions, and made it clear that their proposal should have equal status in the negotiations. The following day, they warned agriculture working group chair George Yeo not to deliver a revised text as a *fait accompli* right at the end of the talks, but to make the text available early enough to allow members to make amendments (ICTSD 2003a).

By Day 3 of the Ministerial, agriculture was at the forefront of the negotiations, discussion centring on the USA, the EC and the G20. The USA and EC publicly attacked the G20 for not being 'flexible' or constructive, predicting its disintegration once the new text came out and negotiations began in earnest. In their meeting with Zoellick the evening before, Deputy USTR Peter Allgeier said the G20 were 'articulating their wish list ... but not offering much in negotiations'.[9]

An Asian delegate also felt that the meeting with Zoellick 'went very badly'. Zoellick 'was completely rude and arrogant. That's how he is – he is downright rude.' After listening to the G20, he recalled, Zoellick said: '"This is a very good wish-list you have given me. Anybody else have anything to add to it?" We kept quiet. "And what are you giving me in return?" Nobody had an answer for that.' Zoellick's position was that 'to have any more concessions [beyond the US/EC paper] is impossible'. However, G20 chair Celso Amorin was equally forceful.

The EC's meeting with the G20 went little better, EC Agriculture Commissioner Franz Fischler saying derisively: 'We also expect the G21 that they stand ready to address farm protectionism on their side. And to be frank, there the G21 has shown no ambition at all' (Fischler 2003).

A Latin American delegate was equally unimpressed with the EC delegation:

> Lamy says, first, he didn't make any commitment on phasing out export subsidies. He said that EU has never committed to that. Apparently he has another reading of the Doha Development Agenda. Then he says, 'I don't know what you are going to do with *your* farmers, but the EU has to preserve the way of living of farmers.' So our reading was, your farmers can be killed and harmed, but ours, no, because they are *European* farmers.

EC spokesperson Gregor Kreuzhuber 'explained' Lamy's position: '"A view to phasing out" [the wording of the Doha Declaration] doesn't mean phasing out, doesn't mean eliminating. The European Union position has been very clear' (*WTO Conference Daily* 2003c).

Cotton: the *Cancun development issue*

How can we cope with this problem? Cotton prices are too low to keep our children in school, or to buy food and pay for health. Some farmers are already leaving. Another season like this will destroy our community. *Brahima Outtara, a small cotton farmer in western Burkina Faso, quoted in Oxfam 2003*

Increasing publicity about the suffering caused to West and Central African (WCA) cotton farmers by US and EC subsidies made cotton the mascot of development in Cancun. More than 10 million people in the region depend directly on cotton production and millions more indirectly. Over-production as a result of global subsidies estimated at US$6 billion in 2001/2[10] (mostly from the USA, China and the EC) has led to world cotton prices collapsing over the past decade. While the WCA countries' production – among the most efficient in the world – increased by 14 per cent between 1999/2000 and 2001/02, their export earnings fell by 31 per cent.

In May 2003, Benin, Burkina Faso, Chad and Mali submitted a formal proposal on cotton, pointing out that:

> The subsidies given to American cotton producers are 60 per cent more than the total GDP [national income] of Burkina Faso, where over 2 million people depend on cotton production. One half of cotton subsidies to American producers (around US$1 billion) goes to a few thousand farmers who cultivate around 1,000 acres of cotton and are thus well above the poverty threshold. In the WCA countries, on the other hand, these subsidies penalize one million farmers who only have five acres of cotton and live on less than US$1 per person per day. (WTO 2003a)

They therefore proposed a stand-alone agreement in Cancun to eliminate all forms of subsidies for cotton over time, and to create a US$250 million compensation mechanism within the WTO framework to address the dysfunctions of the international trading system. The special place of cotton in their economies, they said, meant that this was their only specific interest in the Doha Round. Additional market access in other products would not help, as they had few other export products, some of which already received preferential access. Therefore, 'Any outcome of the negotiations that does not help to ensure respect for the principles of free trade and competition in global trade in cotton will be seen by the WCA countries as unbalanced, unfair and contrary to the objectives approved by all the Member countries at Doha' (ibid.).

The cotton initiative was supported by the entire African Group and the G20. However, they were pitted against the US National Cotton Council (NCC) – perhaps the most effective agricultural lobby in the world, as demonstrated by the generous treatment of cotton under the various US farm bills. Cotton farmers receive more subsidy per capita than any other US producers in the USA, and five times as much per acre (Watkins 2003).

Rather than dealing with the proposal, however, the USA preferred to avoid the issue and silence its opponents. On 9 September, US delegates told the WCA countries that they should instead diversify their economies away from cotton and towards textiles, for which the USA would grant them preferential market access under AGOA (the African Growth and Opportunity Act) (ICTSD 2003a). The African countries were unimpressed.

The USA also tried to block broader African support for the initiative. An African official said that, before Cancun,

> We were told not to talk so loudly on the cotton issue. Let the four of them [Benin, Burkina Faso, Chad and Mali] fight it. It was portrayed to be a war against the US. There was some pressure to quieten some countries. I don't think it worked. It was like you were trying to fight against the US, which you know is not acceptable in this setting. It is like you are committing a sin or a crime.

On Day 1 of the Ministerial, a separate negotiating group was created on cotton. Since ministers approached to chair this group had declined in view of US sensitivities, WTO Director General Supachai Panitchpakdi himself took on this role – a step analysts saw as 'unwise', as it put the 'neutral' Secretariat into an extremely sensitive political situation. Responding to Mali and Chad's call for an 'early harvest' decision on cotton, Supachai underlined the importance of the issue, and risked angering the US delegation by observing that they were not seeking special treatment but a solution based on a fair multilateral trading system (WTO 2003e).

On Day 3, all hell broke loose, with what a Latin American negotiator described as 'the hottest exchange in Cancun, between Zoellick and some other people'. According to an African ambassador, Supachai was 'heavily criticized' by the Americans in front of the working group. According to an African negotiator:

> Supachai was told [by Zoellick] that he is the Chair of the entire WTO system. He is not a chair of a particular sector. He has no business to chair a sub-sector of the WTO. As Chair of the cotton working group, he was pleading with the US and EU to move. I don't think the US liked that. He was told, 'it is not your business to involve yourself in any one particular sector. What you are trying to portray is that you place a lot of importance on cotton, which is wrong. You should not show that you have an interest in something and not another.' So I hear he was in a corner.

Though widely recognized as having genuinely sought a positive conclusion on cotton as a stand-alone issue, Supachai was swept along by the political currents and eventually backed down under intense US pressure. According to an Asian delegate: 'In Cancun, we were told that the US said to [Supachai], "If developing countries' demands are met, you'd better watch out." That is why he came up with this basically American text on cotton.' As a Bangkok official observed, 'in the end, [Supachai] has to give in to the US, because it is like that'.

While the proposing countries held firm to their position that cotton should be dealt with separately, Supachai suggested that members had started to converge on an approach where it could be linked to overall agricultural discussions, and that financial assistance to the WCA countries should involve other international organizations (ICTSD 2003b). After Cancun, Supachai was 'more concerned about getting talks back. He is no longer making prominent statements on cotton as he used to. And you can see to a certain extent now, there has been an attempt to merge the issue of cotton with agriculture' – that is, to adopt the US position.

TRIPs and public health – patents before patients

Discussions on TRIPs and public health were also blocked for most of the year before Cancun, and the decision on how members without manufacturing capacity could access generic drugs, pending since Doha, became a symbol of the WTO's intransigence. Just days before the Ministerial, however, under the pressure of publicity and opprobrium for single-handedly holding up a solution for almost a year beyond the December 2002 deadline, Washington showed a sudden rush of enthusiasm to clinch a deal.[11]

On 20 December 2002, a temporary decision (the 'Motta text') had been agreed by everyone except the USA. This was already a deeply flawed compromise. By stipulating burdensome terms and conditions for the export and import of generic drugs, it fell short of the Doha promise that the TRIPs Agreement 'can and should be interpreted and implemented in a manner supportive of WTO Members' right to protect public health and, in particular, to promote access to medicines for all' (WTO 2001a). US opposition reflected the desire of the US pharmaceutical industry – a major contributor to the 2002 congressional elections – for yet more obstacles. Zoellick himself acknowledged the key role of industry interests when he suggested to African ministers at the July 2003 Montreal mini-ministerial that they negotiate directly with with the major pharmaceutical transnationals.

When a deal was finally sealed on 30 August 2003, US pharmaceutical interests again prevailed. A chairman's 'Statement of Understanding', drafted with the help of US patent lawyers and the pharmaceutical industry, was appended to the Motta text, applying the procedures outlined to active ingredients as well as formulated pharmaceuticals. It also mandated the WTO's TRIPs Council to review the implementation of the decision annually, so that members importing generic drugs under the agreement could be challenged through the WTO.

TRIPs expert Carlos Correa described this 'solution' as 'largely symbolic in view of the multiple conditions required for its application' (Correa 2004), while James Love of the Consumer Project on Technology said that the decision puts the WTO into uncharted waters. The WTO secretariat, the TRIPS Council and the Chair of the TRIPs Council will now begin to routinely review the issuance of individual licenses, and the WTO will now, as a matter of expected practice, oversee the use of compulsory licensing in the most intimate terms, looking at the terms of individual licenses, evaluating the basis for deciding if manufacturing capacity is insufficient, or reviewing or second guessing any of the new terms and obligations that the new implementation language introduces into the regulation of compulsory licensing of patents on medicines. The persons who have negotiated this agreement have given the world a new model for explicitly endorsing protectionism. (Love 2003)

According to D. G. Shah of the Indian Pharmaceutical Alliance, the statement was 'so designed that no generic manufacturer would be able or willing to comply with its provisions' (Correa 2004). The painful two-year exercise thus amounted to no more than another cosmetic attempt by the USA to appear sympathetic towards development and deflect international criticism, while in reality protecting its own commercial interests.

To secure this unworkable 'solution', the USA offered a US$15 billion Emergency Plan for AIDS Relief in fourteen African and Caribbean countries, which critically weakened the resolve of many African countries. Zoellick also sought to divide the Africans from Brazil, China and India by warning that the production-for-export system could be 'abused' by their generic drug industries (Baker 2003). Despite these pressures, however, developing countries maintained their insistence that the solution should be applied to *all* public health needs at all times, not only to named diseases or emergency situations.

The final deal was negotiated under a shroud of secrecy, with only four other members (Brazil, India, Kenya and South Africa) privy to the US-prepared chairman's statement. When it was finally issued, the press gave the strong impression that the four had already agreed to it, while, according to an African LDC ambassador, 'pressure was put on people not to talk. In the capital, pressure was intense.' As a result, only one or two African countries openly criticized the US deal.

In fact, as Kenyan WTO negotiator Nelson Ndirangu made clear at the Geneva launch of the first edition of this book, Kenya did *not* willingly agree to the text:

> We did not want a statement that added an extra burden on developing countries, beyond the 20 December text. On the night of August 28th, Kenya said that it was not comfortable with the statement. Kenya went into consultations till midnight. When the sense of reason got to the edge, other methods were used. Those methods were used and Kenya threw in the towel ... A developing country member can reason out the arguments, but the behind-the-scenes strategies come into play. The Minister gets called and new instructions are issued from the capital. On the night of the 28th, neither Philippines, Argentina, Cuba nor Venezuela, which earlier had reservations, raised those issues. When you are dealt with singly, the pressure is too much. Information that gets to the capital [conveyed by others] also makes the Minister think that you are embarrassing him by being rigid. The Minister was told that Kenya was alone in blocking the solution that promised to save lives in Africa.[12]

Eventually, delegations which had reservations were picked off one by one; in the end, they reluctantly acquiesced. Nevertheless, some strong statements were made in the final session adopting the decision, various delegations giving *their* understanding of the decision.

The USA made the maximum mileage from this 'benevolence', aided by Supachai, who hailed the decision as a 'historic' one, bearing 'testimony to [the] goodwill' of the major powers (WTO 2003c). For those who understood the technicalities of compulsory licensing, however, the cumbersome decision was not about to deliver relief to the poor. Its only positive feature was that it removed the item from the Cancun agenda, so that ministers would not feel pressured into offering a *quid pro quo* for something that was essentially empty.

Development issues – no headway

No progress was made before Cancun on the development issues (Special and Differential Treatment for developing countries and implementation issues arising from the 1994 Uruguay Round Agreements). In the Geneva draft, to the anger of the Africa Group and other developing countries, the priority of the implementation issues was downgraded, and the twenty-four Special and Differential Treatment (SDT) provisions included were of little or no economic value (WTO 2003f). Most were just more non-binding 'best endeavour' language that offered no improvement on the status quo, or, according to one African expert, were even worse. Some sixty commercially more meaningful SDT proposals tabled by the Africa Group had fallen off the agenda, 'destined for a never-never-land at the WTO' (Raghavan 2003a).

In Cancun, despite repeated objections by the Africa Group and other developing countries, the text on SDT hardly changed from the Geneva draft.

The process – more of the same

Before Cancun, developing country delegates were left groping in the dark, guessing each step along the way how the preparatory process would unfold. Driving the process was the WTO Secretariat, working hand-in-glove with the Quad (the US, EC, Japan and Canada) and Uruguayan ambassador Perez del Castillo, then General Council chairman. Members attended the various meetings (when they were invited) with little idea of how the negotiations would proceed; when the draft declaration would be released; how controversial issues, such as the Singapore issues, would be dealt with; or even whether the Ministerial was to be a stock-taking exercise with a very short declaration or was to make key decisions on matters of detail.

In fact, the preparatory process for Cancun was even less transparent than those for Seattle and Doha – and, it seemed, deliberately so. This once again left the way open for the major powers' familiar tactics of divide and rule and arm-twisting – and the elaboration of draft texts which simply ignored developing countries' views.

Divide and rule – efforts to break developing country unity

Perhaps the most striking feature of Cancun was the strength and unity of developing country coalitions, particularly the emergence of the G20. The G20 played a central role in the negotiations – and the stronger it became, the greater the efforts of the USA and EC to divide and destabilize the group. Even before Cancun, the USA and EC had attacked the G20 repeatedly, seeking to intimidate actual and potential members. EC Agriculture Commissioner Franz Fischler delivered a particularly scathing attack: 'When considering the recent extreme proposal sponsored by countries such as Brazil, China, India and other countries, I can't help but think that we are in different orbits entirely. If they want to do business, they should put both feet on the ground. If they want to continue in their space orbit, they will not get the moon and the stars, but rather empty hands' (*WTO Conference Daily* 2003a).

Just before Cancun, the USA tried to split the Africans from the G20. On 6 September, Ugandan President Yoweri Museveni, whom President Bush had visited two months before Cancun, sent a letter to African ministers (reproduced in Appendix 1), advising them against 'reflexive solidarity with other developing countries' – that is, Asian and Latin American countries – since that might be 'detrimental to our own interests'. The letter's similarity in style and content to former assistant USTR Rosa Whitaker's (Box 9.1) is too striking to be coincidental.

When the letter surfaced in Cancun, the Ugandan media accused Museveni of being in bed with the Americans. Sheila Kawamara Mishambi from the East African Legislative Assembly, a member of the Ugandan government delegation, said:

Unlike the official delegations from Kenya and Senegal, our Head of State broke with the consensus that was building up in Cancun by purportedly circulating a letter that urged African countries to stay out of the G21. This prevented Uganda from joining the African countries in the forefront. However, it did not have much impact on the conference as it was so clearly out of step with the positions being taken by the Africa Group and the ACP/LDC alliance. (*Pambazuka News* 2003)

By pointing fingers at Asian countries on dumping, Kawamara alleged, the letter was trying to divert attention to 'toys and light bulbs' from Taiwan, when the real damage was done by the USA and others dumping food and depressing Africa's agriculturally-based core industries (Khana 2003).

In Cancun, accusations against the G20 flew fast and furious, as Washington lost its cool. In a bilateral meeting, the USA lambasted Brazil for leading 'a coalition of paralyzers', revitalizing the struggle of the 1970s, creating a North–South divide and formulating its trade positions on the principles of a 'welfare state'. In a press statement, US Senate Finance Committee chairman Chuck Grassley also attacked the G20, issuing a scarcely veiled threat:

> I'm disappointed by the position of many countries in the so-called G-21 ... What I find most disturbing is that some of the nations that have aligned themselves with the G-21 position, such as Colombia, El Salvador, Costa Rica, Morocco, Thailand, Egypt, Guatemala, and South Africa, are seeking to deepen their relationship with the United States through the negotiation of free trade agreements, but are resisting opening their own markets in agricultural trade. This makes me question their commitment to free trade and their interest in pursuing the strong market access commitments required to conclude free trade agreements with the United States. (Grassley 2003b)

Within the G20, there was a heated debate about how to respond. While Brazil and others wanted to make a joint statement openly denouncing bilateral pressures, those countries under attack refused to speak up publicly. In the end, Brazil put out its own statement, noting pointedly: 'It is even more important, at this stage, that we concentrate our efforts in trying to negotiate and not direct our energies at attacking countries or groups of countries' (Brazil 2003).

Despite the mounting pressures, however, the G20 remained

united, and even increased its membership, as Nigeria, Egypt and Indonesia joined (as did Turkey for a few hours, before pulling out), while only El Salvador succumbed to the pressure and pulled out during the Ministerial. Even many developing countries outside the group supported its leadership.

For the first time, the G20 allowed the developing countries to exert some degree of influence on the negotiations – if only by preventing another unfavourable outcome. This seems to have surprised even some of its members. One Colombian official commented: 'The G20 became a political force in Cancun. We had not expected that to happen.'

Arm-twisting and bullying

The arm-twisting began well before Cancun. Tanzania's Trade Minister, for example, received a letter from a developed country two months earlier, complaining about his ambassador in Geneva taking a line which it opposed. According to a Tanzanian government spokesperson: 'This country is one we have a bilateral programme with ... I wonder whether the international system can really accept and nurture a multilateral trading system which can be based on fair rules without arm-twisting tactics.' Zoellick also called Kenya's Trade Minister, 'offering' him a US$150 million loan he was already negotiating with the IMF – the unspoken implications were obvious.

With such pressures on their capitals, negotiators in Geneva became very careful not to be seen as overly strident in stating their positions, so as not to be branded as obstructive. Speaking as a coalition was critical. Uganda's WTO ambassador Nathan Irumba highlighted the irony: 'African countries were told before that they should take a more active role in WTO negotiations. But as you become effective, there is an attempt to tone your voice down, to divide the group and to weaken the group position.'[13]

As Cancun approached, the focus of the strong-arm tactics turned to breaking the solidarity of the developing countries, especially the G20. Just days before the Ministerial, President Bush was rumoured to have telephoned the leaders of the G20 – South Africa,

Brazil and India – in an unsuccessful bid to prevent them from taking a strong position on agriculture. On 3 September, in a further attempt to intimidate Brazil, Senator Chuck Grassley asked the US Department of Agriculture to launch an investigation into Brazilian farmers' alleged planting of genetically modified soybeans without paying licensing fees to US companies – allegations disputed by the Brazilian government (Grassley 2003a; *High Plains Journal* 2003).

US attempts to intimidate and pressurize countries out of the G20 in Cancun were recounted by Magdi Farahat, from Egypt's Mission to the WTO. While Egypt was not pressurized to leave the G20, he said, his minister was asked pointedly in a bilateral meeting with the US

> why Egypt was taking such a negative position to the US/EU position produced in Geneva. I know a lot of pressure was applied on the Latinos and some of them took their bags and went somewhere else [mostly after Cancun]. They [the USA] used the FTA [free trade agreement] negotiations to pressure them. Of course the pressure is couched in nice language: 'Listen, guys, why are you pushing this multilaterally. We could make something out if it between ourselves, there is no need to multilateralize these things' – obviously with the message that we [should] keep things smooth on the multilateral front.[14]

The bilateral pressures on individual countries were intense, particularly on those negotiating trade agreements with the USA, including El Salvador, Guatemala, Nicaragua, Costa Rica and Thailand. Calls were made from the White House to capitals, and threats to terminate trade benefits or ongoing FTA negotiations, and there were rumours that the USA had offered to increase quotas for exports from Costa Rica, El Salvador and Guatemala in exchange for their defection from the G20 (*WTO Conference Daily* 2003b). The EC appear to have focused on discouraging ACP countries, which enjoy preferential trade arrangements with them, from joining the group (ICTSD 2003a).

In a rare acknowledgement of the Secretariat's awareness of, and apparent acquiescence with, the arm-twisting process, Richard Eglin,

Director of the Trade and Finance Division, said at an NGO meeting: 'How do you get some kind of agreement that 146 countries can sign on to, given they all have different views? In that process, people will get their arms twisted. If you want more textiles in my market, I may twist your arm to get more investment. There are trade-offs, arm-twisting, bullying and all the rest of it going on.'[15]

Arm-twisting, it seems, also extended to institutions providing advice and technical support to developing countries, as a leaked letter from Elaine Drage, Director of Trade and Development in the UK's Department of Trade and Industry (DTI) to Robert Hole, Counsellor in the New Zealand High Commission in London, dated 27 August 2003, reveals (see Appendix 2).

In Doha, the letter alleged, the Commonwealth Secretariat's Deputy Director for International Trade, Roman Grynberg, 'had consistently gone around discouraging developing countries from agreeing to a new Round' and was 'preaching essentially protectionism and isolationism'. Drage said that the DTI and the UK's Department for International Development (DFID) would 'try and keep track on Roman's activities' in Cancun, and asked Hole to find out about procedures for filling posts at the Commonwealth Secretariat, so that Grynberg could be replaced. She also criticized Vinod Rege, another Commonwealth Secretariat staff member based in Geneva, whose contract was not to be renewed. The New Zealand government has since admitted its collusion in the Grynberg affair.[16]

The letter also revealed that, in Doha, 'Clare Short [then UK Secretary of State for Overseas Development] ... phoned Don McKinnon [Secretary General of the Commonwealth] and got him to insist Roman Grynberg ceased to play this role'. After Cancun, McKinnon accused UK Trade Minister Patricia Hewitt of having a 'neo-colonial mentality', adding: 'This is not the 19th century. We don't ... take instructions from Whitehall' (Pallister and Denny 2003).

The Drage letter also suggested that the DTI review the 'effectiveness' of the work of the Commonwealth Secretariat and other institutions that received UK funding, including the South Centre, the International Centre for Trade and Sustainable Development,

UNCTAD and the Advisory Centre on WTO Law. In the context, there is little doubt that 'effectiveness' is closely related to the pursuit of the UK's WTO agenda.

The IMF and World Bank also got into the act, formulating their technical assistance and loan packages to encourage developing countries to acquiesce to the demands of the major powers in the negotiations. On 20 August 2003, they submitted a letter to Supachai, saying:

> We strongly believe that a successful conclusion of the Doha round is essential for the world economy and will benefit all countries ... We are therefore working to package our support, building on what we are already doing in order to help countries to implement commitments they make as the Doha Development Agenda proceeds ... We are examining ways to use and tailor our lending authority to respond to the specific challenges posed by the Doha Development Agenda. Such lending could take place at the project, sector, and country levels. In the context of coherent country financing plans, we also aim to provide support in mobilizing donor resources. (IMF 2003)

The slippery Secretariat

As the hand behind negotiating texts, the WTO Secretariat wields tremendous influence over the negotiations. Its tendency to reflect developed countries' interests is therefore highly problematic. One Secretariat staff member characterized the 'top guys' in the institution as the 'mafia', and maintained that the staff's phones were bugged and their e-mails checked.

The slippery Secretariat did an outstanding job undermining the negotiating positions of the developing world before and in Cancun. When developing country unity on the Singapore issues was threatened by the mysterious appearance just before Cancun of a West African Economic and Monetary Union (WAEMU)[17] communication, the Secretariat was widely seen as responsible. Originally dated 26 June 2003, but repackaged as a new WTO document (WTO 2003g), the document summarized proposed WAEMU negotiating

positions for Cancun, including support for negotiations on investment and competition. However, this pre-dated the African Union
(AU) and LDC Ministerial meetings which firmly established these
groups' *opposition* to negotiations.

The sudden emergence of the WAEMU document angered many
African delegates and, for some hours on the opening day, appeared
to jeopardize the Africa Group's unity. But having confirmed the
WAEMU countries' support for the G90 stance, the AU submitted a
formal statement to Pierre Pettigrew, restating its original position
(African Union 2003b).

According to an African official in Geneva:

> This recrimination [that the Secretariat produced the paper de-
> liberately to destabilize the Africa Group] was widely shared and
> known by everybody in Cancun ... The Secretariat did this at the
> insistence of somebody. We've had some difficulty expressing this
> openly. When we returned from Cancun, there was still more
> pressure to adjust to the situation, and say, 'Let's forget about it
> and have a mutual understanding about how to proceed.'
>
> The Secretariat always said they had nothing to do with it.
> Even if we blame them, nothing has happened to them. It was
> no point talking to them again about it.

In the negotiations themselves, an African negotiator recounted
that the Kenyan Minister Mukhisa Kituyi, facilitator of the Development Working Group, was 'short-circuited by the Secretariat,
because they eventually presented him with a report [summar-
izing the results of his consultations], which he did not prepare.
He was even given some notes to read, which said that the report
was ready – but he had not seen it, although he was chairing that
particular group.'

While the African Group proposed alternative language for the
twenty-four SDT provisions, 'Even when this was brought to the
attention of the Kenyan Minister, the WTO Secretariat said that
they were only dealing with confessionals, and that was going to
be the basis of the Minister's reports.'

Supachai's role was also questionable. According to a South East

Asian official: '[Supachai] may not be so neutral in what he does, especially on TRIPs and Health. He played quite a role in getting developing countries on board to the US position. Towards the end, he played a key role when the decision was already on the table. He got together the relevant developing countries. He did help to close the deal.'

Supachai also angered African negotiators after Cancun by circulating a letter from the IMF and World Bank heads to WTO missions in Geneva. Dated 11 November 2003, the letter promised loans to countries willing to show flexibility to resuscitate the negotiations. Incensed, one African official remarked:

The World Bank and IMF were urging countries to get talks back on the table. If countries went back to negotiate, they would be given lending facilities to meet the adjustment costs. Obviously developing countries felt extremely offended by that. Why should I lose revenue that I now collect [e.g. by making commitments to reduce tariffs], and be given a loan? I would rather collect revenue, especially if my tariffs are much lower than others. There is no way we are going to take on deeper commitments in the WTO and get deeper into debt. It doesn't make sense. Also, what can we use to repay the loans if there is no revenue to collect? The DG sent us copies of this letter. This is very weird. I'm telling you, this organization is crazy.

After Cancun, Supachai also seems to have taken a less than positive view of the G20. According to one G20 delegate: 'the DG goes almost out of his way to play down the G20. Not in so many words, the DG has said that the G20 is a problem.'

The draft Ministerial declaration – on the chair's own irresponsibility

As in Doha, the process of producing a Ministerial declaration was little short of scandalous. Since Doha, the chairs of the committees on the various issues had been formulating their own negotiating texts after unrecorded and non-transparent consultations with members. As one negotiator observed: 'Members can say whatever they want, but ultimately, what is decided is what the *Chair* says the meeting has decided.' Most such texts, drafted by the WTO Secretariat, tended to reflect primarily the positions of the major players – particularly the USA and EC.

A former GATT and WTO delegate remarked on the chair's role:

> Chairpersons are supposed to facilitate negotiations between Members, not divine on negotiations and expound their own interpretation of a compromise position. We would never have dared to do such a thing before. We were much more prudent. We would never have dared to put *our* best interpretation of a compromise position when Members were still holding divergent positions.
>
> By virtue of the fact that Chairs are chosen because they are closer to the major players or have the ears of the major players, they would have certain viewpoints. Therefore, for Chairs to come up with their text invariably means that the positions they take would reflect more the interests of certain players rather than others.

A complete draft of the Cancun Declaration was not made available to members until barely two weeks before the Ministerial – in stark contrast with Seattle and Doha, when it arrived six to eight weeks before. This was clearly a deliberate effort to prevent discussion until the last minute, and to force upon members submission of a text which did not reflect divergent views 'on the Chair's own responsibility'.

When the draft did finally emerge, on the evening of Sunday 24 August, the anger and frustration were palpable, as the language blatantly favoured US and EC positions. Then General Council Chair, Uruguayan ambassador Perez del Castillo, further incensed delegates by declaring that the text would not be amended, despite strong developing country objections.

One official articulated developing country negotiators' deep frustration:

All that we fought for in the last eighteen months has been coolly set aside. They released [the draft] in the evening on Sunday, after we had met for the whole day. At the end of a whole day's discussion, they say, 'Here is the text!' They were wasting our time! Then they give us no time to assess the text because they convened an informal meeting on Monday afternoon. On Monday, *after* all the delegations had completed making their statements, the Chair announces that the formal General Council meeting will be held the next day, so please don't repeat yourself ... So they ensure that people let off their steam in the informal [off-the-record] meeting, so that in the formal [on-the-record] meeting there would be less opposition. This whole process is absurd. They have gone ahead and issued modalities [on the Singapore issues] which were put out by the EC and Japan, as if these had been discussed by members ...

And he [Perez del Castillo] has been calling meetings late into the night – at ten or twelve at night, as if everyone can be mentally alert. This is worse than the Doha process. This is a mid-term review and he is submitting a text, I would say on his own personal *ir*responsibility. What is the guarantee that in the future, when we are discussing decisions about trade agreements, that this type of practice won't prevail. It will be more dangerous then. This manner of operating is absolutely ridiculous.

In Cancun, delegates were again prevented from registering their disapproval of the draft – or commenting on procedures for the Ministerial – by the combination of the first business session with the formal opening ceremony.

On Day 2, however, as the stand-off between the developed and developing countries continued, the AU publicly denounced the anti-democratic process that had produced the draft:

The African Union is equally concerned that the current draft Ministerial text is not a consensual outcome of the Geneva preparatory process. This has both substantive and systemic implications ... For this reason, all proposals submitted by African and other developing countries should be accommodated at this conference

... It is our view that the conduct of these negotiations should be open and transparent. (African Union 2003a)

Zoellick clearly felt threatened by such attacks on a process which served the interests of the major powers so well, writing later: 'The tactics of confrontation included an assault on one of the few devices that the WTO can use to prod its 148 members towards consensus: presenting a chairperson's text for discussion and negotiation. Brazil, India and others refused even to work off an agricultural text drafted by the Uruguay WTO chairman' (Zoellick 2003a).

The 13 September Derbez text epitomized the abuse of power in producing drafts that did not capture the views of the majority. Despite the explicit written opposition of sixty-nine countries – nearly half the membership – the text endorsed negotiations for three of the *Singapore issues* and an accelerated process of discussions leading to negotiations on the fourth (competition). In *agriculture*, the text reproduced almost exactly the US/EC joint position – unambitious on cutting US and EC subsidies and providing an enhanced 'Blue Box' in which to hide increasing US farm supports, but extremely ambitious on developing country tariffs, adopting a formula most developing countries had already said they could not accept, especially with continued US and EC subsidies. The formula on cutting *industrial tariffs* was also overly ambitious, representing a sure road towards the destruction of developing countries' industries.

The passage on *cotton* simply ignored the West and Central African (WCA) countries' request, instead adopting the US position that the countries concerned should diversify their production. Even Lamy recognized this, saying 'Where [the draft] fell down badly was in failing to capture the middle ground on issues like cotton, where it took a strongly pro-US line.'

The Cancun 'whodunnit'

Back in Geneva, reconstructions of the final hours in Cancun resembled an Agatha Christie murder plot, as the blame heaped on developing countries made the question of 'whodunnit?' more important.

Some Geneva diplomats summarized the plot as follows. There were twelve people in the room, each with a motive to kill. When they turned on the light after the murder, poor Botswana, the last to enter the room, who had picked up the knife on the floor, was assumed to be the murderer. This was splashed all over the newspapers the following day. But who really killed Cancun?

Was it Derbez?

Derbez was widely criticized after Cancun for terminating the talks when he did. Many felt that, with no consensus in the 'green room' on the Singapore issues, he should have turned the discussion to agriculture, as a deal there might have made delegations more conciliatory elsewhere. Most found it curious that he did not do this, some putting this down to his inexperience as chair.

One Latin American diplomat suggested that it was not beyond the 'very mercurial' Derbez to walk out suddenly, and that he might just have had an impulse. He might have become nervous, or taken his cue from the Americans – or he might have done it for domestic reasons, as the Mexican public was vehemently against further agricultural liberalization. While the Mexican economy is integrally linked with the USA, US–Mexican relations were at an all-time low due to Mexico's refusal to support the USA in Iraq.

Defending himself, Derbez told the press: 'I don't think I made a rash decision, I think I made a rational decision … Consensus was not there and there was no way to build it' (Elliott and Denny 2003).

Was it the EC?

One developing country diplomat characterized the EC as either 'extremely smart' or 'extremely stupid' for their handling of the Singapore issues, depending on what outcome they wanted. Perhaps they wanted a collapse. They did not want to move further on agriculture, and, according to Agriculture Commissioner Franz Fischler, the Derbez draft 'crossed several red lines the European Union has clearly set out' (Thornton 2003).

According to this theory, the EC did not really care about making progress on the 'Singapore issues', but used them only as a 'stalking horse' (Raghavan 2004) to divert attention from agriculture. When developing countries refused to accept the dropping of two or three issues as a *quid pro quo* for accepting the EC position on agriculture, the EC might have decided not to move negotiations forward. The Commission, which had proposed the Singapore issues, was also wrong in assuming that the member-states would rally behind all four issues, and its legitimacy was severely strained when the UK and others vocally supported dropping investment and competition.

Certainly, the UK government and MPs publicly blamed Lamy for Cancun's collapse. Like many in Europe, a UK Department of Trade and Industry (DTI) post mortem accused Lamy of a 'tactical misjudgement' by making concessions too late (Elliott 2003). The UK's Parliamentary Select Committee on International Development also found that:

> The EU's offer to unbundle the Singapore Issues, and to withdraw its demands for a start to negotiations on Investment and Competition, came far too late. The European Commission's strategy of brinkmanship was destined to derail Cancun, particularly given the complications introduced by the emergence of new country-groups. The timing of the Commission's offer to unbundle the issues left countries with little time to consider their position, consult with their allies and respond constructively … The EU was the primary demandeur, and regarded developing countries' opposition as largely tactical. (International Development Committee 2003)

A USTR spokesperson at the Ministerial said that the EC had 'isolated themselves from the rest of the planet on these issues' (ICTSD 2003) – even the USA was unenthusiastic on investment and competition.

It is also possible that the Commission's interest in the Round had waned since its launch in 2001. Then, it was useful to force member-states to reform the Common Agriculture Policy (CAP); but once the reform was underway, the need for the Round might have slackened considerably.

Like Derbez, Lamy was quick to defend himself, countering accusations that he was too slow to move by asking: 'Compared to what or to whom, might I ask? Compared to the total immobilism of the other big players, not one of whom budged an inch?' (Lamy 2003b). Those close to the 'murder scene' were in any case convinced that the Europeans did not have the same influence over Derbez as the USA.

Was it the USA?

Lamy, deflecting the criticism from himself, pointed the finger at the Americans:

> The US too keeps a close eye on the tilt of the scales. My feeling is that the fading prospect of any additional access to markets for farm produce or manufactured goods in keeping with their initial hugely ambitious aims upset a precarious balance. What tipped the scales the wrong way was the prospect of separate negotiations on one politically neuralgic commodity, cotton. (Lamy 2003b)

A South East Asian negotiator, like others in Geneva, also suggested that the USA made the decision to end the conference due to the cotton issue: 'Some calls were made to Washington during the lunch break [of 14 September]. That is why the conference was stopped after lunch. The US was really firm. They did not want anything that led to the removal of subsidies [on cotton], but if the text could involve something of a comprehensive solution, that would be OK.'

The US position on agriculture is schizophrenic, with a strong lobby for agricultural liberalization (who were behind the original US agriculture proposal at the WTO), and a strong lobby for subsidies (who were behind the May 2002 Farm Bill). At present, the latter is predominant. Farm states were the backbone of President Bush's support in the 2000 election; and agribusiness, which profits from agricultural subsidies, has shifted its allegiance to Bush's Republican Party, which received 72 per cent of its $53 million of political contributions in 2002 (Becker 2003). As one senior US delegate said after Cancun: 'Bob Zoellick is a master at strategy and I think he had little room ... President Bush was not going to upset his farmers before his re-election' (ibid.).

William Greider highlighted this issue even before Cancun:

> The Administration rhetoric suggests these matters are ripe for serious negotiation. But Brazil's wish list makes clear why such reforms won't happen, given President Bush's priorities. Soybeans are Missouri, Iowa and Arkansas, among other Republican-voting states. Beef is Kansas, the Dakotas and the Solid South. Oranges are Florida. Open markets for oranges would allow Brazil's abundant and efficient citrus production to devastate Florida ... Whatever gets said by the US Trade Representative, whatever declarations are issued in Cancun, count on this: there will be no agriculture deal for developing nations, not one that is real, not one that can even be whispered about, at least until long after the 2004 elections. (Greider 2003)

Similarly, a Brazilian delegate commented: 'The US has lost interest in agriculture negotiations, as they have done in the past so many times.' Certainly, the US agricultural lobby did not seem unduly disappointed with the outcome. Robert Stallman, head of the American Farm Bureau Federation, said: 'He [Zoellick] did his best ... The Ambassador has done an excellent job.'

Was it the G90?

The G90, co-ordinated by Botswana, was asked to concede both on drastic agricultural and industrial tariff reductions and on trade facilitation, in exchange for the EC dropping the other three Singapore issues. As one African LDC ambassador commented:

> The EC wanted us to show flexibility. I asked: 'Flexibility for what? What are we getting? Why should we pay a price in exchange for getting nothing? We are not *demandeurs*.' We have said that the clarification process should continue. They said that if we don't accept [negotiatons on trade facilitation], the conference will break up and we shall be blamed. That was a kind of ultimatum. But we had not got anything on development issues. We were given

nothing on cotton, nothing on S&D [Special and Differential Treatment]. And now you drop three Singapore issues. Should I be happy? The Ministers did not buy that.

Most of the G90 countries were backing the four West African cotton countries. They mainly faced a trade problem – US and EC subsidies driving down world prices – but were told that the IMF and the World Bank would step in to devise 'development programmes'. How would that help them resolve a systemic trade problem?

The G90 might also have wanted the negotiations to stall because trade liberalization would erode their trade preferences especially in the EC market. According to South Africa's Alec Erwin: 'The agricultural protectionists [the EC] lost no time in mobilizing this vulnerability. Africa was chaired by Mauritius – a more preference dependent economy is hard to find – and the result was rather chaotic' (Erwin 2003).

In the final analysis, however, the G90 has the strongest defence of all – that it represents the majority of the membership in a one-member-one-vote organization.

Was it the G20?

Since Cancun, Lamy has characterized the G20, not inaccurately, as having an agricultural mother and a geopolitical father, observing that: 'The G20 … is self-consciously positioning itself as a counterweight to the G8 in terms of global economic governance' (Lamy 2003b). In Cancun, these agendas dovetailed. Breaking with the Cairns Group tradition, Latin American G20 members pushed not only for reduced US and EC supports, but also for a less ambitious tariff reduction formula so as to protect domestic markets from dumped imports. In doing so, they carried many developing countries with them.

Zoellick clearly saw the G20 as the prime suspect. As well as his 'can do/won't do' jibes, he said:

Even after Singapore's tireless minister had worked non-stop with all parties to prepare a new agricultural draft reflecting a balanced compromise [*sic*], Brazil and its colleagues presented a massive list of required changes. If they were serious about negotiating a compromise for 148 countries, they overplayed their hand by failing to signal that intention. They returned home without any cuts in subsidies and tariffs. (Zoellick 2003a)

Frank Vargo, vice president for international economic affairs for the (US) National Association of Manufacturers, also placed the blame squarely on the G20, whom he thought had made a 'major miscalculation': 'What the G21 has done in Cancun is to covert the Doha Development Agenda into the Doha Stagnation Agenda, and that's a shame' (*International Trade Daily* 2003a). They 'were not willing to negotiate, they were just making demands' (*International Trade Daily* 2003b).

It is also possible that Amorin remained intransigent in the hope that a collapse in Cancun would give Brazil greater leverage in the Free Trade Area of the Americas (FTAA) negotiations two months later in Miami. The FTAA was more worrying for Brazil than the WTO negotiations, and Amorin had little hope that the USA would move on that front either. In Miami, he expressed the view that to expect the USA to reduce agricultural subsidies in the near term was like 'believing in fairly tales' (Esterl 2003).

In any event, the ministers leading the G20 responded robustly to the harsh recriminations, asserting their right to represent their own interests in the negotiations.

To attack Brazil, who should be congratulated for their wonderful capacity, patience and hard work, as some kind of naïve ringleader of dreamers is merely to be looking for the sunset when a new dawn begins to touch the cattle horns ... Far from being political and polemic the developing countries – be they in the G22 formation or the numerically large Africa, ACP and LDC group – were right. The balance of the agenda that the developed countries had engineered was wrong ... These are political processes and as the system of colonialism was wrong so is the imbalance in the world trade system. (Erwin 2003)

The question here is not whether a modest outcome would have been better than the absence of result. The real dilemma that many of us had to face was whether it was sensible to accept an agreement that would essentially consolidate the policies of the two subsidizing superpowers – with very modest gains and even some steps backward ... The G22 and other developing countries will not be reduced to the role of supporting actors in discussions that affect their development prospects. Consensus cannot be imposed through pre-cooked deals that disregard previous commitments and ignore the legitimate aspirations of the majority of the world's population. Trade must be a tool not only to create wealth but also to distribute it in a more equitable way. (Amorin 2003)

Retorting to USTR Robert Zoellick's 'can do'/'won't do' characterization, Indian Commerce Minister Arun Jaitley said: 'I think the simpler assessment was that the participating countries on agriculture comprised of those who subsidize and those who cannot subsidize. That is the more obvious distinction amongst the participating countries' (Jaitley 2003). However, since the negotiations ended before agriculture was even discussed in the 'green room', it is unlikely that Brazil or the G20 played a major role in pulling the plug.

Was it Korea and/or Japan?

Lamy's offer to drop two or three of the Singapore issues took Japan and Korea completely by surprise. For them, as for the EC, these issues were a 'stalking horse' to limit movement on agriculture. The Koreans also had an explosive domestic situation on their hands following the suicide of Korean farmer Lee Kyung-Hae in Cancun on 10 September, in protest against further agricultural liberalization.

Who killed Cancún?

The prevailing theory is that Cancun collapsed because the USA and EC were not ready to move on agriculture or, in the US case, cotton. According to former World Bank employee Michael Finger, neither had gone to Cancun with a positive agenda, the US objective being 'not to offend any country that might be some help to the United States in Afghanistan or Iraq', and the EC's to prevent any discussion of agriculture (Raghavan 2004). Of the two, the critical importance of US–Mexican relations makes the USA the prime suspect. As one developing country ambassador who was in the 'green room' said: 'I find it difficult to believe that Derbez would have done it without having first consulted with the Americans.'

Some believe the decision might have been planned before the release of the 13 September draft. One Asian negotiator characterized the draft as being 'really calculated to provoke developing countries', particularly on cotton and the Singapore issues, speculating that the USA and EC were not comfortable with the text on agriculture. While very close to the US/EC joint text, the draft contained two watered-down clauses from the G20 paper. One called for caps on trade distorting support to specific products which the USA and EC were not prepared to accept; the other for annual reductions to the Blue Box.

The USA and EC might therefore have told Derbez to start negotiations in the 'green room' on the Singapore issues to give them a safe exit. When it became clear that the G90 would not move on the Singapore issues, Lamy made the gesture of offering to drop two or three of them to look 'flexible' and divert blame to the developing countries.

Another theory is that the USA was responsible for the decision, due to its concerns about agriculture and cotton, and that the EC offered to drop investment and competition, not to pander to the developing countries, as has been widely assumed, but in an unsuccessful attempt to keep the USA at the negotiating table. Zoellick pulled a fast one on the EC by breaking the US/EC 'alliance' and ensuring that the Ministerial collapsed over the Singapore issues rather than cotton or agriculture, so as to deflect blame from the USA (Raghavan 2003b).

However, more important than US and EC concerns about agriculture and cotton was the threat posed to them by the unity and strength of the G20 and the G90. The major powers might have stopped Cancun to give themselves more time to wear down and disempower these coalitions before resuming negotiations. Certainly, the USA missed no opportunity after Cancun to kill the G20, although without success.

As one South East Asian observed:

> The more time is given to US and EC, the more they can bring developing countries round to their thinking. Time is on their side – it is never on developing countries' side. I've been sitting here for long enough to realize that. The more time is given, the more the US and EC can work on developing countries and exert their unilateral pressures ...
>
> You see it from even the selection of the DG [Director General] four years ago. If they had made the decision there and then [when the deadline for selection was reached], we would have selected Supachai. But because they had more time, the US had more time to lobby capitals ... Similarly even on the TRIPs and Health issue. The first draft came out in August 2002. Developing countries did not adopt it. But on hindsight, that was more favourable. The 16 December text eroded somewhat the scope given to developing countries, and now the Chair statement is even worse.
>
> Somehow fatigue sets in. People are more amenable to closing the deal when the pressure to do so becomes more intense. You give in more than what you had done in the beginning. Each time a text is on the table, we say no. But after going several rounds, and for months, who has the longest staying power? The pressures get to you eventually. It gets to the negotiators and to the capitals. Many capitals may hold a certain position, but can it be sustained for so long, over months and years? To me, eventually conditions change and then you may need to be more flexible than you initially thought.

The collapse of the talks, however, had its genesis long before Cancun. India's Commerce Minister Arun Jaitley wisely reasoned:

Why was India isolated in its position on the refusal to commence negotiations in the Singapore issues in Doha, but had the [verbal] support of over a hundred countries in Cancun?

One of the obvious effects was that if you offer trade preferences [as the EC had done in Doha], if you offer other agreements, you may temporarily win over, but that is not how a long-term dialogue can go on ... [By the end of the Ministerial] 69 countries ... had officially given in writing saying that we do not agree. (Jaitley 2003)

Post-Cancun: impact of the blame game

Immediately after Cancun, Malaysia's then Prime Minister Mahathir Mohammed had predicted that 'Some countries will be threatened after this with sanctions or with deprivation of aid, or forced to pay back loans ... I'm quite sure tremendous pressure will be brought to bear on the group of developing countries which have made a stand ... Life is going to be made difficult for them, in order to prevent them from coming together' (*Dow Jones* 2003).

Soon after, the major powers indeed embarked on a vicious blaming exercise to deflect blame from themselves and, as the mudslinging continued in the world's press, Zoellick, Lamy and Supachai all visited capitals, preaching 'flexibility'. The USA also called a meeting of Washington-based developing country negotiators soon after the Ministerial, complaining about the unreasonable positions of their Geneva counterparts, leading the Nigerian ambassador to the USA to write to President Obasanjo, questioning the position his counterpart in Geneva was taking.

Together with a barrage of threats, this had a significant impact in toning down the objections of the developing world to the developed countries' unbalanced agenda, as developing countries were made to feel that they would be punished if they remained 'inflexible'. Two months after Cancun, signs of 'flexibility' were emerging: acceptance of the Derbez text as the basis of negotiations, and fairly widespread endorsement of a new agreement in trade facilitation (strongly opposed by the G90 in Cancun). An African LDC negotiator lamented a month after Cancun: 'My Minister played a major role in Cancun. Now he is being called by everybody including the US, to ask how he proposes to move the talks forward.'

Post-Cancun: attempts to destroy the G20

The main instrument used against the G20 members was bilateral trade deals. Senator Chuck Grassley, chairman of the Committee on Finance, made the threat explicit:

> Let me be clear. I'll use my position as chairman of the Senate Finance Committee, which has jurisdiction over international trade policy in the U.S. Senate, to carefully scrutinize the positions taken by many WTO members during this ministerial. The United States evaluates potential partners for free trade agreements on an ongoing basis. I'll take note of those nations that played a constructive role in Cancun, and those nations that didn't. (Grassley 2003c)

And USTR's Richard Mills told the press: 'Part of being a "can do" country and part of the criteria [for FTA negotiations] ... is that they share our vision of opening markets through the WTO ... We've reminded countries that these [agreements] have to be approved by Congress' (Sparshott 2003).

The onslaught on G20 members began immediately after the Ministerial. The countries which were then concluding the US–Central America Free Trade Agreement (CAFTA), including El Salvador, Guatemala, Honduras, Nicaragua, Costa Rica and the Dominican Republic, were particularly vulnerable. The USA made it clear to these countries that free trade agreements were conditional on their co-operation at all levels.

Honduras and the *Dominican Republic* – prominent champions of developing countries' interests in Doha – have taken a low profile in the WTO since their involvement in the CAFTA negotiations, and stayed out of the G20, while *El Salvador* was intimidated into leaving the G20 in Cancun.

Costa Rica and *Guatemala* were told by Zoellick that they would be excluded from CAFTA if they remained in the G20: 'I told them that the emergence of the G-21 might pose a big problem to this agreement since our Congress resents the fact that members of CAFTA are also in the G-21. If we want to construct a common future with them, resistance and protest do not constitute an effective strategy. I sense that they are drawing the right conclusions' (Bello 2003).

On 25 September, Costa Rican Trade Minister Alberto Trejos responded with a statement declaring that the country had joined the G20 'with a view to engaging constructively towards progress in the [agriculture] negotiations', and 'did not support any efforts to use this group as a political platform, nor to extend its scope of action to other topics in the WTO' (*Inside US Trade* 2003).

On 1 October, Zoellick, in Costa Rica for the CAFTA negotiations, announced a $6.75 million grant for CAFTA partners to support improved labour conditions (USTR 2003b). A week later, Costa Rica withdrew from the G20 – according to one Central American official, feeling 'that the Cairns Group is a more appropriate venue to pursue its agricultural liberalisation goals'. Trejos believed the 'rhetoric' of some G20 members was 'not convenient', indicating in a letter to Brazilian Foreign Minister Celso Amorin on 7 October that Costa Rica no longer believed all members in the G21 shared its desire for 'a high level of ambition' in the negotiations – clearly implicating India, which preferred a more gradual tariff reduction formula (*Inside US Trade* 2003). Guatemala, too, yielded to the pressure, and duly withdrew from the G20 – and both were duly included in CAFTA when negotiations concluded in January 2004. At a March 2004 US Senate hearing, Zoellick characterized CAFTA as 'useful economically and politically' (Farrington 2004).

Colombia, Peru, Ecuador and Bolivia feared mainly for their access to the US market under the Andean Trade Promotion and Drug Eradication Act (ATPDEA). *Colombia* was particularly vulnerable, having set its sights on beginning bilateral trade negotiations with the USA. Another concern was US funding for military programmes – particularly as Washington had, in July, suspended military aid to some thirty-five countries which did not agree with giving US soldiers immunity in the UN International War Crimes Tribunal. Of $575 million in military assistance originally earmarked for Colombia in 2004, some $112 million was at stake (Associated Press Online 2003).

Visiting Colombia after Cancun, US Senator Norm Coleman warned President Alvaro Uribe that 'remaining in [the G20] will not lead to good relations between Colombia and the United States', and told the press that the President had assured him the country would leave the group (Bello 2003). By the end of September, Colombia had indeed announced its withdrawal from the G20. A Colombian government spokesperson explained:

> You know, the US supports us in a lot of other areas, not just in trade, due to our internal conflict. The Minister of Trade therefore decided to leave the G20 when we arrived in Geneva [after Cancun] … Our first market in the world is the US. We export almost 50 per cent of goods to US. We know what our market is, and what is our priority.

Colombia was duly rewarded: in March 2004, USTR announced the beginning of negotiations on a US–Colombian FTA.

Peru and *Ecuador* also dropped out of the G20, Peru's Commerce Minister, Raul Diez Conseco, saying that Peru would not continue to participate in 'a group that adopts positions that hinder the progress of Doha Round negotiations' (Alden et al. 2003). Both countries were rewarded on 18 November 2003, when Zoellick indicated his intention to negotiate a US–Andean FTA 'with countries that have demonstrated their readiness to begin' – including Peru and Ecuador (USTR 2004). *Bolivia*, however, which exports least under the ATPDEA ($37 million in 2002) has remained in the G20.

Other Latin American countries also distanced themselves from the G20, at least publicly. *Mexico*'s WTO ambassador Eduardo Perez Motta implied that his country could pull out of the G20 any time, while *Paraguay* made it clear that 'we are allied with the G22 only with respect to the liberalisation of trade in farm products with the developed countries' (Cevallos 2003).

Already under US pressure, *Thailand* released a statement after Cancun stressing its role as a moderating influence within the G20. However, this was still insufficient for the USA, who again brought the FTA carrot into play. Negotiations on a US–Thailand FTA were announced at an Asia Pacific Economic Co-operation (APEC) meeting hosted by Thailand in mid-October – subject to approval by the US Senate. On 16 October, the eve of the APEC meeting, Senate Finance Committee chair Chuck Grassley had written to President Bush urging him to make the US–Thailand FTA conditional on Thailand's withdrawal from the group:

> Before initiating negotiations with Thailand, I would urge you to obtain a firm commitment from the Government of Thailand that it will provide meaningful and timely market access for U.S. agricultural exports and remove other unjustified impediments to U.S. products. Repudiation by the Government of Thailand of the unbalanced approach displayed in Cancun by the G-21 would be a good first step. (Grassley 2003d)

At the time of writing, Thailand remains in the G20 but, according to a Ministry of Commerce official, is 'not active at all'.

A still greater victory for US pressure at the APEC meeting was the acceptance by APEC Heads of State of the Derbez draft text – described by Lamy as 'dead and buried', so vehemently was it rejected by the developing world in Cancun just a month earlier – as the starting point for negotiations. Thailand played an important role in this, as Zoellick acknowledged when he wrote to the Speaker of the House of Representatives in February 2004, informing him of his intention of commencing FTA negotiations with the country (Zoellick 2004).

The USA lost no time in taking revenge on *China* for its role in Cancun. On 15 September, the day after the Cancun collapse, Commerce Secretary Donald Evans announced the creation of a new Unfair Trade Practices Team in the Bush administration to look into allegations of dumping and intellectual property 'theft', mainly by China. The following day, a US Chamber of Commerce report called China's compliance record with WTO rules 'uneven and incomplete'. 'Unless this picture improves,' the report threatened, 'there will be an increasing crescendo of complaints' (Hiebert and Murphy 2003).

The next day, the US National Association of Manufacturers and other trade groups complained about China's fixed exchange rate under Section 301,[18] arguing that the Chinese currency was undervalued by 40 per cent (*Dow Jones Newswires* 2003), and that this undercut American producers, causing a trade deficit with China of $125 billion in 2003, and the loss of 2.7 million industrial jobs in the previous three years. USTR was asked to investigate and consider bringing a case at the WTO. Senators even suggested a 27.5 per cent tariff on Chinese exports to the USA unless Beijing devalued; and on 20 September, the G7 (the USA, the UK, France, Germany, Italy, Japan and Canada) also called for exchange rate flexibility. Ironically, during the Asian financial crisis of the late 1990s, many in the USA had praised China for *maintaining* its fixed exchange rate in the face of sliding Asian currencies, despite China's loss of export competitiveness.

On 18 November, Washington imposed quotas on imports of Chinese bras, bathrobes and knitwear, and a week later slapped provisional duties of 28–46 per cent on Chinese televisions for alleged dumping (Kynge and Harney 2003). The Chinese retaliated by cancelling a mission to the USA to sign orders for agricultural products (Hutzler 2003).

Exacerbated by pre-election protectionist fervour, Zoellick promised the Senate Finance Committee aggressive measures, saying: 'If we're going to remain open to [China and India], it's got to be a two-way street' (*International Trade Daily* 2004). When the USA filed a case against China's allegedly discriminatory tax rebate policy for integrated circuits on 18 March, Frank Vargo of the National Association of Manufacturers warned: 'This case looks like it is only the first. Now that the door has been opened, there will be more' (Bloomberg 2004).

US hostility extended beyond the trade arena, as it announced on 23 March 2004 that it would sponsor a UN resolution criticizing China's human rights record. It had not done so in 2003, but now alleged 'backsliding' (Dinmore and Dickie 2004).

After Cancun, the USA vilified *India* as inflexible and difficult, and trade relations, already flat, were further deflated. The problem was compounded by India's refusal, despite persistent requests, to send troops to Iraq, and its dissension from APEC's endorsement of the Derbez draft as the basis of negotiations. Indian Commerce Minister Arun Jaitley said that the text 'cannot be the starting point of any discussion … It completely failed to gauge the mood at Cancun and in fact was contrary to the mood prevalent there.' USTR responded that 'India's apparent refusal to even negotiate from [the Derbez] text is very unfortunate. It highlights the paralysis within the Brazil–India group that will stall the process' (Palmer 2003).

India's punishment came in January when the US Senate executed a 180-degree turn from the USTR's pre-Cancun position by banning federal government outsourcing of services. Despite assuring Jaitley of Washington's strong opposition to US states curbing business process outsourcing in June 2003 (Haniffa 2003), Zoellick made it clear in February 2004 that Washington would use legislation preventing outsourcing by government departments as leverage in the WTO negotiations. He added: 'Since India has not signed the [plurilateral – i.e. voluntary] agreement on government procurement, there is no point in complaining' (*Financial Express* 2004).

Zoellick's February 2004 trip to Delhi was quickly followed by visits from Secretary of State Colin Powell and Under Secretary of State Alan Larson. All portrayed India as a 'closed economy' and underscored the *quid pro quo* for lifting the outsourcing bans: more effective policing of intellectual property rights; further liberalization of financial services; market access for US legal professionals and chartered accountants; and market access for US agricultural products (i.e. relinquishing the G20 position on agriculture) (Subramaniam 2004).

These visits did little to thaw relations. At a Finance Committee Senate hearing on 9 March, Zoellick characterized India as 'one of the more difficult players' in the current round of negotiations (*International Trade Daily* 2004), warning that the USA might restrict imports if Delhi refused to open its market, and saying, 'We have to send the message that they need to step up to the plate' (Farrington 2004).

As a prominent African player in the WTO, *Kenya* has long been a favourite target for co-option by the major powers; and rumours abounded, in Cancun and before, that Kenya was under pressure from the EC not to join the G20. If so, the pressure worked: despite holding similar positions, Kenya did not join.

Soon after Cancun, Kenya watered down its previous position of rejecting all four new issues when Trade Minister Mukhisa Kituyi indicated the possibility of accepting negotiations on trade facilitation. As this 'flexibility' was shown, the IMF announced on 8 October that it would resume lending to Kenya after a three-year suspension, promising loans of up to US$300 million (Reuters 2003a).

Kenya's exports to the USA under the Africa Growth and Opportunities Act (AGOA), which trebled from $45 million in 2001 to $150 million in 2003, also became a political tool. Under AGOA II, Kenya's ability to import fabric and yarn from countries other than the USA was to expire in September 2004, after which Kenya would be required to use yarn produced locally, or imported from the USA or another AGOA country. But none of these options is viable. Kenya's own cotton-growing industry collapsed in the 1980s under the weight of falling world prices – largely due to US and EC subsidies; imports from the USA would make exports too expensive; and regional yarn does not meet US standards.

Kenya helped to move the WTO process forwards, accepting the Derbez text as the basis of negotiations, and hosting a meeting between Lamy, Zoellick and about twelve African countries in Mombasa on 18 February – and in March, Washington promised to extend Kenya's 'third country fabric provision' for another four years (Akumu 2004). While Minister Kituyi and his negotiators have done an outstanding job in pushing a development line in the negotiations, the interest the USA has taken in Kenya as a leader in the Africa Group inevitably sets real political limits to their positions.

Washington also used AGOA as a political lever to dissuade other African countries from joining the G20. In December 2003, at a US–Sub-Saharan Africa Trade and Economic Co-operation Forum in Washington, Zoellick promised an extension of AGOA from 2008 to 2015; FTA negotiations with the five SACU (Southern African

Customs Union) countries; and money for capacity building. In return, he sought 'Practical solutions to the differences that are preventing progress on the Doha Agenda' (Zoellick 2003b).

The emphasis was again on dividing the African countries from other developing countries:

> The real opportunities for sub-Saharan African countries in the future lie in some of the large market developing countries such as Brazil and India, where tariffs remain very, very high. Given this dynamic, we were puzzled that African countries did not urge mid-level developing countries to open their agricultural markets, too. Many of these mid-level developing countries offer African countries the most to gain in terms of market access, because their barriers are high, their populations are large, and their growth prospects offer opportunities to all. (Zoellick 2003b: 4)

Zoellick portrayed India as selfishly working against the interests of African countries at the WTO, citing a case filed by India against the EC's preference programme, which India won on the basis that the programme violated the most-favoured-nation principle:

> I think this is an extremely unfortunate precedent, and we ought to think closely about what it could do to AGOA. So, this is a classic example of how some developed nations, the United States, the EU, African countries have some common interests. Because if this precedent takes hold, it could put AGOA at risk. And it's not us who's doing it, it's a fellow developing country. (ibid., pp. 4–5)

In fact, India had blocked the waiver only because the EC had refused even to negotiate on the compensation to which the country was entitled.

Like-Minded Group[19] member *Sri Lanka* was conspicuously absent from the G20. A possible US–Sri Lankan FTA was announced in March 2004.

The US threats had some success: a month after Cancun, five countries (Colombia, Costa Rica, Guatemala, Peru and Ecuador) had withdrawn from the G20. But six months on, the G20 remains alive and well. Zimbabwe and Tanzania joined after Cancun – although without US and EC pressure more would no doubt have done so. Members now include Argentina, Bolivia, Brazil, Chile, China, Cuba, Egypt, India, Indonesia, Mexico, Nigeria, Pakistan, Paraguay, Philippines, South Africa, Tanzania, Thailand, Venezuela and Zimbabwe.

Conclusions

After Cancun, the USA and EC were in shock at the power shift that had taken place and the failure of their efforts to break the resolve of the developing country blocs. For Zoellick and Lamy, this was also a personal setback – aggravated in Zoellick's case by his failure to move the Free Trade Area of the Americas (FTAA) negotiations forward. Lamy, heavily criticized by his constituency, retreated for a couple of months, bruised and in deep reflection.

Did they learn anything from Cancun? Their speeches and positions – particularly on agriculture and institutional reform – suggest not, as does the now overt arm-twisting.

The neo-colonial attitude highlighted in the concluding chapter of this book persists – a sense that the developed world knows what is best for the developing countries, and has the right to impose it. Jamaica's WTO ambassador Ransford Smith alluded to this at an UNCTAD session:

> We find curious the line of analysis by some commentators which almost seems to suggest that developing countries have a responsibility to be flexible and to keep the negotiations on track and on schedule since, according to this view, developing countries, and particularly the poorest among them, are likely to be major beneficiaries of the Round's outcome. The somewhat patronizing suggestion is in fact that developing country negotiators acted against their own best interests at Cancun. (Permanent Mission of Jamaica 2003)

Worse still is the mind-set among Northern governments and corporations that the developing world, its resources, markets and people, are there merely for their use. The repeated message, 'We want to open markets in this Round', ignoring the appalling results of the Uruguay Round's forced market liberalization, speaks for itself.

After Cancun, to EC officials' surprise, developing countries wanted to move negotiations on the substantive issues rather than looking at institutional reform – a reflection of the developed countries' systematic subversion of their attempts at democratizing the WTO after Seattle and Doha. The Like-Minded Group proposal on internal transparency (see Appendix to Chapter 5, p. 143), according to one of its sponsors, is 'in the deep freeze', so thoroughly has it been shunned by the developed countries.

Lamy's own proposals to reform the 'medieval' WTO, if followed through, would throw it into the stone age. His vision of an executive council run by a privileged few, and greater powers for a Secretariat which already receives its orders from the major powers, are not about democratization, but ensuring that the most powerful will continue to win the day. Seasoned developing country negotiators realize that such proposals would only worsen their position still further.

The current negotiating agenda would close off development options by forcing developing countries' markets open before their producers are remotely able to compete. The major economies have the financial, legal, technical and political means to protect their interests in the negotiations. Most developing countries do not. And US bullying has reached such a level that, according to former Dominican Republic ambassador Federico Cuello, there is 'no freedom of speech or association' in the WTO.[20] The G20 members have discovered as much, as did the African group when they came under US pressure to distance themselves from the middle-income countries.

However, Chinese analyst Xu Weizhong is optimistic that the traditional balance of power has been destabilized:

In the short term, although the developing nations shall not be able to change the dominant position of the developed nations, in the WTO negotiations, however, for the developed nations, it has

Box In.2 Trade and trickery in agriculture

The USA and EC are ramming through the market access they want by negotiating on *formulae* without *numbers*, so that negotiations take place in the dark. The numbers will be inserted only after the 'framework' has been accepted. This 'blended approach' will apply 'equally' to the developed and developing countries – but difference in tariff structures means the same formula will have up to triple the market opening effect on the developing world, ripping open their markets. And because there are no numbers, developing countries will not know how much US and EC subsidies will be cut.

There is much resistance to this approach among developing countries, led primarily by India. But US 'persuasion' during the Bangkok APEC Ministerial (in October 2003), combined with the post-Cancun 'blame game', has led to a tacit endorsement of the Derbez text – including the 'blended approach' – as the basis of negotiations. Civil society must urgently lobby against this if developed country pressure is to be countered.

The EC has been nothing if not creative in massaging its interests through in the agriculture negotiations. 'Multifunctionality' and the preservation of rural landscapes have been succeeded by 'collective preferences' as a justification for subsidies and dumping. Europe, says Lamy, has never promoted entirely free trade but 'rationalized' free trade, taking account of other concerns or 'preferences' such as environmental protection, food safety, cultural rights and health. Europeans have 'defended themselves' on these principles 'for fifty years, and launched the construction of Europe' on this basis – and, by implication, will continue to do so (Lamy 2004).

But subsidies justified by protecting European 'collective preferences' lead to widespread unemployment and poverty in the developing world. At the end of the day, whose 'collective preference' is preserved is really a result of who has the power to institutionalize their 'collective preference' in the multilateral trading system. The 'collective preferences', and more critically the rights, of those without voice or bargaining power are ignored.

The king of all the US/EC trickery is 'decoupling'. Supports that are not linked to production, such as fixed annual payments to producers, they argue, have 'no, or at most minimal, trade distorting effects' (WTO 1995: Annex 2, p. 56). Thus the CAP 'reform' left subsidies undiminished, instead of simply redefining them as non-trade distorting, so that they could be placed in the 'Green Box', where subsidies are unlimited. The bulk of American subsidies also fall into this category. Herein lies the heart of the inequity of agricultural trade. The assumption that these subsidies are non-trade distorting must be debunked and the effects on dumping highlighted, or the injustice in the trade system will become ever more entrenched.

become increasingly clear that after today, they will increasingly face difficulties in the WTO negotiating process and that the voices and interests of the developing countries will increasingly reflect on future WTO negotiations. The spirit of unity demonstrated by the developing countries during the WTO talks will impact on the entirety of development of North–South relations. (quoted in Chandrasekhar 2003)

These sentiments have been echoed by Brazilian WTO ambassador Luiz de Seixas Correa:

There is the belief or understanding that everything can be solved when the two majors get together and carve out a deal that represents their convergence of interests. And that the rest of the world, being so disunited or being so fragmented or having so many different perspectives, ends up one by one being co-opted into an agreement – for lack of an organisational framework.

This has not changed in terms of the mentality or perceptions of people because the majors insist on acting and behaving in the same way they did in the old GATT days. I believe that what happened in these negotiations and the fact that we were able to work out together an innovative coalition shows that this model no longer stands. (de Seixas Correa 2003)

But this change depends on developing countries' ability to maintain their solidarity under intense bilateral pressure. The developing country coalitions – the G20 and the G90 – must hang together and be strengthened. This will require intensified capacity building and education on economic and trade policy matters for governments and civil society; and increased civil society pressures on governments, as a counterweight to developed country pressure. North–South civil society alliances are critical: by cross-examining their governments, and exposing their unjust trade and foreign policies, Northern NGOs can open up political space for Southern governments.

As recent history demonstrates, the economic dependence of most developing countries on the major powers makes maintaining solidarity far from easy. This applies particularly to the LDCs, Africans and Caribbeans. But their strength in numbers, and their moral authority as those at greatest risk, should be harnessed as leverage in the negotiations. As in Cancun, the involvement of parliamentarians and civil society delegates can help keep governments faithful to their positions. More capacity building and advocacy at the national level would go a long way, as would exposing the many downsides to 'carrots' such as AGOA and other trade arrangements.

The real test of the major powers' responsiveness to developing countries' concerns is in *agriculture* – and the signs are bleak. The question is not even whether developing countries should receive special treatment, but whether the developed world will forgo the special treatment they have institutionalized for themselves in the current agreement. Even the UK's opposition Conservative spokesman on overseas development, John Bercow, describes the present trade injustice as 'the knowing, deliberate and calculated policy of governments of the most powerful nations on earth. It is shameless and shameful' (Conservative Party 2004). Yet the *status quo* continues.

Agriculture is the litmus test for the WTO's future. This is where the power struggles between the G20 and the USA and EC will be played out, and the WTO's impact on the lives of the world's poor will be determined. Upon the outcome of these negotiations hinges the WTO's very legitimacy. But the USA and EC continue to hide behind technical details to ensure that further unfair rules are couched in acceptable language and logic (see Box In.2), thus leaving behind or persuading their domestic constituencies who monitor these games. They still show no interest in giving up their privileged status in distorting agricultural markets, and no sense of responsibility for the havoc their policies have wrought, creating unemployment and poverty in the South.

The G20 position on agriculture is still very dangerous for struggling small farmers in developing countries, endorsing yet another round of market opening, while maintaining special treatment for developed countries' subsidies and potentially increasing dumping[21] in the developing world. The domestic market must be protected from dumped imports in order to safeguard the livelihood of small farmers. Civil society in G20 countries should therefore strengthen and improve the group's position by holding their governments' feet to the fire. This is particularly important in India, which is the main force holding the coalition to a less ambitious tariff reduction formula in agriculture. Pressure is needed to stop the government giving in, especially over outsourcing.

In Brazil, too, pressure is needed to keep the Lula administration true to its promises to the rural poor, whose interests lie mostly in land reform and access to *domestic* markets, as Agriculture Minister Roberto Rodrigues now seems to be on the side of corporate agriculture (Taylor 2003), which benefits from the market opening agenda. The same applies to other G20 countries (particularly in Latin America, but also, for example, Thailand) which have tended to support corporate agriculture.

The public campaign on agriculture should be amplified, with

Northern NGO support, with two clear messages: that the negotiations on tariff reductions cannot continue until dumping is halted; and that the Derbez text does not provide a basis for negotiations, as it would legitimize dumping rather than curbing it. Subsidies can certainly be provided, but not for products which are exported. This would mean remodelling the US and EC subsidy systems, and reforming the current industrial agricultural production model. As long as the current system continues, the lives of millions in the South are daily put at risk.

Cotton should be kept on a separate track, given the stalemate in agriculture and the likelihood that the *status quo* in US/EC dumping will be endorsed. This is a systemic problem requiring a systemic solution, including a financial compensation mechanism in the WTO, funded by those who distort world markets by dumping. While the EC and USA are fearful of setting such a precedent, they must take responsibility for the poverty and destruction they create. World Bank loans to the WCA countries, to be repaid later, would be a slap in the face for the poor.

On the *Singapore issues*, since there was no explicit consensus to launch negotiations at Cancun, as required by the Doha Declaration, the Doha mandate is now over. These issues should not be revived even as plurilateral agreements (as Lamy has proposed), as developing countries would then be arm-twisted and dragged on board later. European NGOs, which played a major role in splitting the EC, particularly on investment, need to maintain their pressure until these issues are dropped completely.

Urgent support is also needed for developing countries' resistance to drastic liberalization of their industrial sectors under *Non-Agricultural Market Access* (NAMA). Otherwise, future efforts to use industrial policy to promote development will be blocked. More studies are needed of the impact of liberalization and deindustrialization on the South.

At the heart of the problem lies the WTO's free trade ideology, widely preached but never followed by any successful economy. This has to be thrown out. What is needed is a fundamental rethink of the whole system and its underlying ideology. Until this happens, continuing 'busines as usual' would only do further long-term harm to the developing countries. And it seems clear that such a rethink will require another inconclusive Ministerial. The immediate project is therefore to ensure that the WTO talks do not move forwards, particularly in agriculture. But the stakes for the major powers will be much higher at the next Ministerial, magnifying the pressures on the developing world.

Since Cancun, many have bemoaned the possible demise of multilateralism, represented by the WTO; its replacement with bilateral negotiations has been held over the developing countries as a dire threat. This is a false choice. For the USA and EC, bilateral agreements and the WTO are not alternatives but two parts of the same strategy. What cannot be attained in one arena is pursued in the other, and 'progress' in one strengthens the other.

In any case, the USA and EC are not about to abandon the WTO. Both need it to discipline each other and to exploit the bigger developing countries – especially India and China. More critically, the WTO has never been about true multilateralism or international co-operation. For the major powers, the sole aim is access to markets, no matter what the devastation or protests in developing countries. Intransigence across the board – even on issues that are blatantly iniquitous, as on cotton, given the plight of poor African farmers – is not co-operation.

The WTO is an agent, not of multilateralism but of the USA and EC's economic imperialist tendencies towards the developing world. In its current form, as a vehicle for corporate interests, its disempowerment would be a victory, not a loss, for the world's poor. It needs to be downsized considerably and get back to basics – making trade a means towards employment, the fulfilment of people's rights and ecological sustainability, with trading arrange-ments built upon greater co-operation between developing countries and between vibrant domestic economic blocs. Only then might we get a taste of real multilateralism.

Appendix I

Uganda's President Museveni's Letter to African Heads of States and Ministers

6 September 2003
Re: Guidelines for the WTO meeting

Below is my guidance to your delegation to the World Trade Organization (WTO) round of negotiations in Cancun. I am also writing to their Excellencies, the Presidents of the AU countries so that Africa fights for her trade interests. You should inform your colleague African Ministers that trade is the only serious and sustainable stimulus to development. The last 40 years have shown that aid cannot develop Africa. Here below are some of the unresolved issues on which you should insist:

We need to keep our eyes firmly on the prize at next week's WTO ministerial meeting in Cancun.

The prize is an international trading system based on rules that promote African development by stimulating trade and investment and by reducing Africa's often-crippling dependence on foreign aid.

In pursuit of this prize, our governments need to form a range of alliances, depending on the specific issues under negotiation, and be clear-eyed about the agendas of potential allies.

African countries form the single largest bloc in the WTO and should pick and choose with whom they partner. Reflexive solidarity with other developing countries is not only unnecessary, but may even be detrimental to our own interests.

By firmly standing up for our interests, we rescued last weekend's agreement to prevent patents becoming a barrier to poor countries obtaining badly needed medicines.

We did this by refusing to go along with Asian and Latin American countries, which claimed to have our best interests at heart but which. in truth, had their own commercial agendas.

As important as it is to prevail on rich countries to stop dumping heavily subsidized agriculture on world markets, shutting out

African producers, we must equally press for access to other heavily protected markets in advanced developing countries.

We also need to ensure that the preferential market access we now have with the US and EU is not eroded, in which context all calls to accelerate the phase-out of apparel and textile quotas should be resisted.

Equally, it will not be in Africa's interest for more advanced developing countries to prevail in their bid to receive the same levels of 'special and differential' treatment, which accords concessions (more lenient rules) to African and other poor countries.

Below is a summary of the areas of unresolved divergence between Sub-Saharan African (SSA) and the more advanced developing countries elsewhere in the world.

Agreement on Textile and Clothing: The WTO Agreement on Textile and Clothing (ATC) mandates the elimination of global textile and apparel quotas by the end of December 2004. The more advanced developing countries in Asia and Latin America generally support an accelerated phase-out of these quotas. The elimination of such quotas is not in SSA's interest as most of these nations already enjoy quota-free access to major western markets through trade preference schemes, such as AGOA and the Cotonou Accord. An accelerated phase-out of quotas would reduce the SSA's current margin of preferences and prematurely expose these countries to strong competition from the more advanced apparel producing nations, such as China. SSA will need more time effectively compete against the Asian apparel producers who occupy a domineering presence in western markets. For example Bangladesh alone exports more textile and apparel to the US than the 48 sub-Saharan African nations combined.

Access to advanced developing country markets: In addition to eliminating agricultural export subsidies, African countries need to press for lower tariffs in advanced developing country markets. The US and EU have substantially lowered tariffs for African agricultural exports and yet the average world agricultural tariffs is 62 percent. Lowering tariffs in other developing markets would expand demand for

African products ... Indeed, South–South agricultural trade grew faster than world trade during the 1990s and now accounts for more than one-third of all developing country exports. Forty-five percent of developing country trade in non-agriculture goods is with other developing countries. Liberalizing trade in agriculture is a priority for only a few of the more advanced developing countries; it is, however, the most important issue in the WTO for Africa.

Anti-dumping rules: Asian countries, the EU and South Africa are trying to focus more of the WTO's attention on changing the WTO's anti-dumping rules (measures under which countries can protect their domestic industries against unfairly traded imports). The focus has primarily been on US anti-dumping laws. However, African countries are not dumping products into the US and the US is not dumping products into African markets. Africa's biggest dumping challenge is from Asian products that are being dumped into fledgling African markets – killing domestic industries. The WTO requires member nations to have WTO consistent anti-dumping regulations in place before it can bring a dumping case to the WTO. Most African nations do not have such procedures in place and have therefore been unable to address Asian dumping practices in the WTO. It would be in our own interest, therefore, to press for WTO capacity building and technical assistance to help it develop national WTO consistent anti-dumping procedures. We should not join Asia in an exclusive focus on US anti-dumping laws, but should equally focus on the dumping practices of Asian nations in our markets.

Trade capacity building: The WTO has devoted more resources to providing technical assistance to build WTO negotiating skills and trade capacity in Africa. This is much more important for us than for the more advanced developing countries. Trade capacity building should therefore remain at the core of an African WTO agenda.

In conclusion, Sub-Saharan Africa, the poorest region of the world, not Asia or Latin America should define the development agenda in the WTO, according to its own priorities and interests. The agreements being negotiated in the Doha Round must be concluded as a 'single undertaking'. Which means that nothing is adopted until everything is adopted. Therefore, African countries must have a clear understanding of their priorities and of the various alliances that will be needed to achieve them. In the WTO, Sub-Saharan Africa should have neither permanent friends nor permanent enemies – just permanent interests.

Yoweri Kaguta Museveni
PRESIDENT

Appendix 2

Leaked letter from UK DTI's Dr Elaine Drage to NZ Counsellor Robert Hole Esq, regarding muzzling the Commonwealth's Deputy Director for International Trade in Cancun

27 August 2003
Dear Robert,
COMMONWEALTH SECRETARIAT AND TRADE
It was good to have the opportunity to talk to you in some depth yesterday about how we might work together to make the Commonwealth Secretariat's input in London and Geneva more constructive and effective. We agreed to work together as far as we could on this, knowing the Australians and less focusedly, the Canadians have similar concerns.

2. As to Roman Grynberg, you will try to find out when his current three-year contract expires. We both believe he is already into his second and therefore (ought to be) final three-year contract. Also you will discover what the normal procedures are for filling posts at the Commonwealth Secretariat. I will speak on similar lines to Asif Ahmad at the FCO (who lead in the UK on Commonwealth matters), but not till after Cancun.

3. We both knew that Roman was going to be at Cancun, probably as a member of the Fijian government delegation which will give him a considerable degree of access. I recounted the details of his participation at Doha (possibly as a member of the Solomon Islands' delegation) when he had consistently gone around discour-

aging developing countries (the Pacific and smaller Commonwealth particularly) from agreeing to a new Round. My colleague Charlotte Seymour-Smith (DFID) and I had been so concerned we raised this with Clare Short who had phoned Don McKinnon and got him to insist Roman Grynberg ceased to play this role. Although the Commonwealth does not have a formal policy on trade, the Durban CHOGM Declaration makes it clear there is Commonwealth support for the processes that help integrate all Members into the wider world trading system. So preaching essentially protectionism and isolationism does not accord with this and is inappropriate for a member of the Commonwealth Secretariat's trade staff. I am copying my DFID counterpart – Dianna Melrose – in on this since a task she, her colleagues and I will share at Cancun will be to try and keep track on Roman's activities. It may be an issue we should ask our (new) Minister to raise with Don McKinnon when he pays an introductory call this Autumn.

4. You also mentioned the advance information you were getting from the Australian academic who is on the panel writing the Commonwealth's 'Development and Democracy' paper for the December CHOGM. The trade section was said to be very protectionist in tone. We recognized the dangers if the document, which is likely to be nodded through at CHOGM because of the bulk of its content, contains a protectionist trade policy section. You thought some recent revisions might have modified this tenor, but would let me have the latest draft if you could get it. We need to work to ensure a text consistent with the Durban Declaration, if possible before it comes to the COW on 11–12 November.

5. We also discussed the ongoing problems with the Commonwealth Secretariat's Vinod Rege in Geneva. You have had considerable concerns about the effectiveness of his management of TIAF, which DFID here also fund. Don McKinnon has agreed to the re-advertising of Vinod Rege's post after Cancun and you expect the selection panel to include a developed country representative (possibly Canada). We need to do what we can to ensure any successor works within a more clearly defined and monitored management structure.

6. It might also be useful to try and look more systematically across the various systems in place in Geneva to provide support to developing country negotiators. From the UK's part I am conscious of work we find not only via Commonwealth, but also through the South Centre, ICTSD, UNCTAD, ACWL and there may be more. You no doubt do similarly. I will discuss with my DFID colleagues whether a small project to assess what assistance is in place, how it fits together, its effectiveness and whether there are any gaps would be a useful contribution to more effective TRCB.

7. My colleague Eleanor Fuller at our Mission in Geneva, who leaves in a few months' time, has much experience in this area so her views and input would be valuable to us. As I agreed I will consult various colleagues and we should aim to speak again after Cancun.

8. I am copying this letter to Asif Ahmad (FCO), Dianna Melrose and Lisa Phillips (DFID), Eleanor Fuller (UKMTS, Geneva) and to Edmund Hosker, Claire Williamson and Ramil Burden here.

Dr Elaine Drage
Director, Trade & Development

Notes

1. The membership changed slightly during and after Cancun, and the group was accordingly referred to as the G21 or G22.

2. 'Green room' meetings are unofficial, informal, off-the-record meetings of a select group of members, usually chosen by the major players, held with the support of the WTO Secretariat. Those not invited are generally not informed of the meetings.

3. Quotations in this Introduction for which no sources are cited are taken from interviews conducted by Aileen Kwa and Fatoumata Jawara between May 2003 and March 2004. The names and countries of the delegates interviewed have mostly been withheld to protect their positions.

4. Marc Maes, informal communication, 'What Happened in Cancun', 15 September 2003.

5. Richard Eglin, meeting with NGOs, Geneva, 21 March 2003.

6. Letter to Minister Pierre Pettigrew, Minister for International Trade of Canada, and facilitator for the Singapore issues at the Cancun Ministerial Conference, Cancun, 12 September 2003, from Rafidah Aziz,

Minister of International Trade and Industry, Malaysia, and Arun Jaitley, Minister for Commerce and Industry, India, on behalf of Antigua and Barbuda, Bangladesh (on behalf of the LDCs), Barbados, Belize, Botswana, China, Cuba, Dominica, Egypt, Grenada, Guyana, Haiti, India, Indonesia, Jamaica, Kenya, Malaysia, Nigeria, Philippines, St Kitts and Nevis, St Lucia, St Vincent and the Grenadines, Surinam, Tanzania, Trinidad and Tobago, Uganda, Venezuela, Zambia and Zimbabwe.

7. Under the blended formula, a proportion of tariff lines would be cut by a fixed percentage (the Uruguay Round formula), the bulk by a Swiss formula (cutting higher tariffs more than lower tariffs), and some to zero or near zero.

8. Payments for production limiting farm programmes, currently used by the EC but not the USA.

9. USTR press conference, 12 September 2003, 9.30 a.m., Cancun, Mexico.

10. Document of the Netherlands delegation at the OECD.

11. It is even possible that Washington anticipated that the Ministerial might collapse due to their unwillingness to move on the cotton issue, and that they therefore needed a decision on TRIPs to avoid the public relations disaster of Cancun failing because of US intransigence on both cotton *and* TRIPs.

12. Nelson Ndirangu, press conference launching *Behind the Scenes at the WTO*, UN, Geneva, 2 September 2003.

13. Nathan Irumba, press conference launching *Behind the Scenes at the WTO*, UN, Geneva, 2 September 2003.

14. Magdi Farahat, interview with Aileen Kwa, 23 October 2003.

15. Richard Eglin, meeting with NGOs, Geneva, 21 March 2003.

16. New Zealand Parliamentary Question No. 01469 (lodged 25/2/2004) from Rod Donald to Foreign Affairs and Trade Minister Phil Goff. Response published on 8 March 2004.

17. The WAEMU members are Benin, Burkina-Faso, Côte d'Ivoire, Guinea-Bissau, Mali, Niger, Togo and Senegal.

18. Section 301 of the Trade Act 1974 authorizes the US government to take trade sanctions (including suspending benefits under trade agreements, and duties and other restrictions on imports) against countries it deems to be engaging in unfair trade practices.

19. The Like-Minded Group is an informal coalition of about fifteen developing countries. While cohesive and effective at the time of the Seattle and Doha Ministerials, it has since been weakened by US pressure on individual countries and the removal of key ambassadors.

20. Federico Cuello, press conference launching *Behind the Scenes at the WTO*, London, 2 September 2003.

21. Dumping refers to the sale of goods below their cost of production.

References

African Union (2003a) 'Press Statement by the African Union on the Ongoing Negotiations', Cancun, Mexico, 11 September.

— (2003b) 'Submission by the African Union to the WTO Facilitator on the Position of the Negotiations on the Singapore Issues', Cancun, Mexico, 11 September.

Akumu, W. (2004) 'AGOA Trade Bills May Now Be Harmonised', *The Nation*, Nairobi, 2 March.

Alden, E., A. Thomson and T. Buck (2003) 'Defectors Peel Away from G21 Doha Round Challengers', *Financial Times*, 10 October.

Amorin, C. (2003) 'The Real Cancun', *Wall Street Journal*, 25 September.

Associated Press (2003) 'WTO Reeling from Trade Defeat in Cancun', 15 September.

Associated Press Online (2003) 'US Cuts Off Aid Over Tribunal Dispute', 2 July.

Baker, B. (2003) 'Trade: WTO Decision on Medicines Eviscerates Doha Declaration', *South–North Development Monitor (SUNS)*, Third World Network, 5411, 4 September.

Becker, E. (2003) 'Coming U.S. Vote Figures in Walkout at Trade Talks', *New York Times*, 16 September.

Bello, W. (2003) 'Washington Pursues Post-Cancun Vendetta Against Group of 21', *Inside Costa Rica*.

Bloomberg (2004) 'U.S. Files WTO Complaint Against China on Chip Tax', 18 March.

Brazil (2003) Press statement, Cancun, Mexico, 12 September.

Cevallos, D. (2003) 'Cancun: Can the G22 Survive Success?', Inter Press Service, 24 September.

Chandrasekhar, K. (2003) 'Issues Drive Coalitions, not Ideologies or North–South Divide', *South Bulletin*, 68, South Centre, Geneva, 15 November.

Congress Daily (2003) 'WTO Ag Negotiators Making Little Progress on Trade Plan', National Journal Group, 2 July.

Conservative Party (2004) 'World Trade Policy is "Shameless and Shameful"', Press release, 26 February. <http://www.conservatives.com/news/article.cfm?obj_id=90236>

Correa, C. (2004) 'Access to Drugs Under TRIPs: A Not So Expeditious

Solution', *BRIDGES*, 1, International Centre for Trade and Sustainable Development, Geneva, January.

de Seixas Correa, L. F. (2003) 'G-20: A Powerful Tool for Convergence in Negotiations', *South Bulletin*, 68, South Centre, Geneva, 15 November.

Dinmore, G. and M. Dickie (2004) 'US to Sponsor Resolution Criticising China', *Financial Times*, 23 March.

Dow Jones (2003) 'Malaysia PM Expects Retaliation vs Poor Countries on WTO', 16 September.

Dow Jones Newswires (2003) 'US Commerce Secretary Says China Must Open Market', 24 October.

Elliott, L. (2003) 'DTI Leak Blames Lamy for Cancun Failure: Report Says Tactical Error Left WTO Talks without a Deal', *Guardian*, 22 October.

Elliott, L. and C. Denny (2003), 'Breakdown Means No End in Sight to Doha Round', *Guardian*, 16 September.

Elliott L., C. Denny and D. Munk (2003) 'Blow to World Economy as Trade Talks Collapse', *Guardian*, 15 September.

Erwin, A. (2003) 'Report to the South African Parliament on the Cancun Meeting', 26 September.

Esterl, M. (2003) 'Commerce Secy Evans: US Flexible on Agriculture Tariffs', *Dow Jones*, Miami, 20 November.

Farrington, M. (2004) 'USTR Robert Zoellick Testimony, US Senate Hearing', *Public Citizen*, Washington DC, 9 March.

Financial Express (2004) 'Zoellick, Jaitley in BPO Spat: India Has No Right to Protest, Says USTR', 17 February.

Fischler, F. (2003) 'State of Play of Agriculture Negotiations', Press conference, Cancun, Mexico, 12 September.

Grassley, C. (2003a) 'Grassley Seeks More Answers on Brazil Soybean Production', Press release, Cancun, Mexico, 3 September.

— (2003b) 'Comment on Trade Talks in Cancun', Press release, Cancun, Mexico, 11 September.

— (2003c) 'Collapse of Trade Negotiations in Cancun', Press release, Cancun, Mexico, 14 September.

— (2003d) 'Grassley Urges President to Consider Ag Concerns Before U.S.–Thailand Trade Agreement', Cancun, Mexico, Press release, 17 October.

Greider, W. (2003) 'Why the WTO is Going Nowhere', *The Nation*, 22 September.

Haniffa, A. (2003) 'US Strongly Opposed to Ban on Outsourcing', rediff. com, 13 June.

Hiebert, M. and D. Murphy (2003) 'The One-Two Punch', *Far Eastern Economic Review*, 2 October.

High Plains Journal (2003) 'Grassley Calling for Soybean Probe', 4 September.

Hutzler, C. (2003) 'China Hits Back at U.S., Delaying Trade Mission', *Wall Street Journal*, 20 November.

ICTSD (2003a) *BRIDGES Daily Update on the Fifth Ministerial Conference*, no. 2, International Centre for Trade and Sustainable Development, Geneva, 11 September.

— (2003b) *BRIDGES Daily Update on the Fifth Ministerial Conference*, no. 4, International Centre for Trade and Sustainable Development, Geneva, 13 September.

IMF (2003) 'IMF and World Bank Announce Plans to Support Developing Countries with Trade-Related Adjustment Needs in WTO Round', Press release 03/140, 21 August.

India (2003) Statement by India at the Heads of Delegation Meeting, Cancun, Mexico, 13 September.

Inside US Trade (2003) 'Costa Rica, Colombia, Peru Drop Out of Shrinking G-21', 10 October.

International Development Committee (2003) 'Trade and Development at the WTO: Learning the Lessons of Cancun to Revive a Genuine Development Round', First Report of Session 2003–04, Vol. 1, House of Commons, 4 December.

International Trade Daily (2003a) 'WTO Talks Crashed when Developing Nations Balked at Taking Up Some "Singapore Issues"', 16 September.

— (2003b) 'Support for WTO in Congress, Private Sector Wanes After Collapse of Cancun Trade Talks', 16 September.

— (2004) 'USTR Says India Has "No Right" to Criticise U.S. for Seeking to Halt Outsourcing of Jobs', 10 March.

Jaitley, A. (2003) 'Consensus Based on Fairnes Workable', *South Bulletin*, 67 (p. 12), South Centre, Geneva, 30 October.

Khana, T. (2003) '"Museveni Letter" Threatens Third World Unity at Mexico's WTO Talks', *The East African*, 15 September.

Khor, M. (2003a) 'Singapore Issues: No Negotiations, Say 70 Developing Countries', Cancun News Update, 3, Third World Network, Penang, 12 September.

— (2003b) 'Fate of Ministerial Hangs on a Thread Today – as Developing Countries Express Frustration with Text', Third World Network, Penang, 14 September.

King, N. and S. Miller (2003) 'Developing World "Victory" May be a Long-term Loss', *Wall Street Journal*, 16 September.

Kwa, A. (2003) 'EU's CAP "Reform": Let Us Not Be Fooled', *South Bulletin*, 60 (p. 26), South Centre, Geneva, 30 June.

Kynge, J. and A. Harney (2003) 'Big US Duties on Televisions Shock Chinese', *Financial Times*, 26 November.

Lamy, P. (2003a) Press conference closing the World Trade Organization Fifth Ministerial Conference, Cancun, Mexico, 14 September.

— (2003b) Statement at the European Parliament, 24 September.

— (2003c) 'The EU, Cancun and the Future of the Doha Development Agenda', Speech at the *Journal for Common Market Studies*, London, 28 October.

— (2004) 'Co-existence between Public Policy and Free Trade: Can We Achieve "Good protectionism"?' Presentation at Green/EFA Conference 'Remaking the Global Trading System', European Parliament, Brussels, 5 March.

Lannin, P. and R. Waddington (2003) 'Cancun Trade Talks Collapse; Poor Blame Rich', *Reuters*, 14 September.

Love, J. (2003) 'CP Tech Statement on WTO Deal on Exports of Medicines', Consumer Project on Technology, Washington DC, 30 August.

Oxfam (2003) 'Cultivating Poverty: The Impact of US Cotton Subsidies on Africa', Briefing paper.

Pallister, D. and C. Denny (2003a) 'Commonwealth Fury at Whitehall "Meddling"', *Guardian*, 31 October.

Palmer, D. (2003) 'US Says India Hampering Efforts to Revive WTO Talks', *Reuters*, 24 October.

Pambazuka News (2003) '"No Longer Dinner": African Activists Speak on Cancun', Weekly Electronic Newsletter for Social Justice in Africa, 126, 2 October.

Permanent Mission of Jamaica (2003) 'Review of Developments and Issues in the Post-Doha Work Programme of Particular Concern to Developing Countries: The Outcome of the Fifth WTO Ministerial Conference', Statement at Fifth Session of the UNCTAD Trade and Development Board, 8 October.

Raghavan C. (2003a) 'Trade: Implementation Issues, S&D Treatment Get Short Shrift', *South–North Development Monitor (SUNS)*, Third World Network, 5404, 26 August.

— (2003b) 'Trade: EU–US Trade War Over Steel Safeguards or Only Game of Bluff', *South–North Development Monitor (SUNS)*, Third World Network, 5460, 12 November.

— (2004) 'Trade: Can Life Be Breathed Back into the Doha Round at WTO?', *South–North Development Monitor (SUNS)*, Third World Network, 5509, 11 February.

Reuters (2003a) 'IMF, Kenya Agree on Program for Economic Recovery', 10 October.

— (2003b) 'US, EU Seek Sign Others Serious About WTO Talks', 4 November.

South Centre (2003) 'Chronology of Events in the Cancun WTO Ministerial Conference, 10–14 September', 22 September.

Sparshott, J. (2003) 'Zoellick Starts Tour to Negotiate CAFTA', *Washington Times*, 2 October.

Subramaniam, G. (2004) 'US Gets BPO Key to Indian Market', *Economic Times*, 23 March.

Taylor, E. (2003) 'Brazil Struggling to Hold G-21 Coalition Together, Says Peru Undecided on Stance', *WTO Reporter*, Bureau of National Affairs, Washington DC, 9 October.

Thornton, P. (2003) 'Trade War Looms as African Nations Storm Out: Huge Gulf Between Rich and Poor on Farm Subsidies', *Independent*, 15 September.

USTR (2003a) 'US Trade Representative Robert Zoellick Evening Press Conference, Cancun, Mexico', Press release, 14 September.

— (2003b) 'United States Provides $6.75 Million Grant to Support Good Labour Conditions in Central American FTA Partners', Press release, 1 October.

— (2004) 'U.S. and Colombia to Begin FTA Negotiations on May 18', Press release, 23 March.

Waddington, R. (2003) 'Failed Cancun Talks Throw up New Trade Power', *Reuters*, 15 September.

Watkins, K. (2003) 'Cultivating Poverty: US Cotton Subsidies and Africa', Presentation at WTO Public Symposium: 'Challenges Ahead on the Road to Cancun', Geneva, 16–18 June.

WTO (1995) 'The Results of the Uruguay Round of Multilateral Trade Negotiations: The Legal Texts, Agreement on Agriculture', WTO, Geneva.

— (2001a) Declaration on the TRIPs Agreement and Public Health, adopted on 14 November 2001, Document No. WT/MIN(01)/DEC/2, 20 November.

— (2003a) 'WTO Negotiations on Agriculture. Poverty Reduction: Sectoral Initiative in Favour of Cotton', Joint Proposal by Benin, Burkina Faso, Chad and Mali, Document No. TN/AG/GEN/4, 16 May.

— (2003b) Statement by Malaysia addressed to Minister Luis Derbez,

Chairman of the Fifth WTO Ministerial Conference, Cancun, Mexico, 13 September, Document No. BPA(P)WTO/MC/6, 13 September.

— (2003c) 'Decision Removes Final Patent Obstacle to Cheap Drug Imports', Press release, Press/350/Rev.1, 30 August.

— (2003d) 'Paragraphs 13, 14, 15 & 16, Dealing with Singapore Issues of the Draft Cancun Ministerial Text Contained in Document Job (03)/150/Rev.1 – Communication from Bangladesh (on behalf of the LDC Group), Botswana, China, Cuba, Egypt, India, Indonesia, Kenya, Malaysia, Nigeria, Philippines, Tanzania, Uganda, Venezuela, Zambia and Zimbabwe', Document No. WT/MIN(03)/W/4, 4 September.

— (2003e) 'Cancun 5th Ministerial, 2003: Summary of 10 September'. <www.wto.org>

— (2003f) ' Cancun 5th Ministerial, 2003, Summary of 11 September'. <www.wto.org>

— (2003g) 'Memorandum on the Common Negotiating Positions of the Member States of the West African Economic and Monetary Union (WAEMU) on the Occasion of the Fifth WTO Ministerial Conference in Cancun', Document No. WT/L/539, 29 August.

WTO Conference Daily (2003a), 'Intransigent Developing Countries May End up with Empty Hands – Fischler', *El Economista*, 10 September.

— (2003b) 'US Pushes Alliance with Central America: Special Trade Privileges Offered for Support', *El Economista*, 13 September.

— (2003c) 'Developing Nations Stand Firm on Subsidy Cuts', *El Economista*, 14 September.

Zedillo, E. (2004) 'Can the WTO Ultimately Deliever the Goods?', Presentation at World Economic Forum, Davos, 24 January.

Zoellick, R. (2003a) 'America Will Not Wait for the Won't-do Countries', *Financial Times*, 22 September.

— (2003b) 'U.S. Trade Representative Robert B. Zoellick Remarks' at US Sub-Saharan Africa Trade and Economic Co-operation Forum, Private Sector Session, Washington, 8 December.

— (2004) Letter to the Speaker of the US House of Representatives, J. Dennis Hastert, 12 February.

ONE
The devil you know – an introduction to the WTO

Until 1999, relatively few people outside the ranks of economists, diplomats and political analysts and commentators had heard of the WTO, or even knew that the initials stood for the World Trade Organization. That changed dramatically in November 1999, with the Third Ministerial Conference in Seattle – not because of the conference itself, but because of what went on outside it. While the ministerial failed completely to achieve its objective – agreement on a new round of multilateral trade negotiations – thousands of people took to the streets to demonstrate against the conference, calling for a more democratic WTO more favourable to the interests of developing countries, or for the abolition of the organization altogether. As the ill-prepared police over-reacted, media and public attention focused on the protesters outside. Suddenly, the WTO was in the limelight; the burgeoning anti-globalization movement has kept it there ever since.

What the public could not ascertain clearly at the time of Seattle was what the root causes of this furore were. This book aims to expose exactly that, showing to a wide and diverse public how the political and decision-making processes of the WTO really work in terms of what happens behind the scenes, and what its members really think about the institution. It examines how the diverse members of the WTO work with each other to reach agreements, and how the WTO Secretariat functions in the process of negotiations.[1] The primary focus is on the period before, during and immediately after the Fourth Ministerial Conference in Doha, Qatar, in November 2001.

The book is based primarily on research and semi-structured interviews with thirty-three Geneva-based missions to the WTO right across the spectrum of its membership, and with ten WTO

Secretariat staff members, conducted between February and August 2002. Interviewees were informed of the purpose of the interviews and given the option of anonymity. Wherever possible, delegates are quoted directly or indirectly, and their views reflected as closely as possible. Interviewees are named wherever feasible, but in many cases preferred to remain anonymous – a symptom of the level of pressure on delegates not to rock the boat. (Some of the reasons for this preference for anonymity become apparent in Chapter 6.)

This chapter provides a brief introduction to the WTO. A short discussion of the significance of the WTO is followed by a historical overview of the international trading system in the period after World War II, culminating with the establishment of the WTO itself in 1995, and an outline of the structure of the WTO. This part of the chapter is based mainly on WTO publications (WTO 1999c, 2001d) and materials on the WTO website (www.wto.org). The chapter concludes with an overview of democracy in WTO decision-making, highlighting the differences in the size of country missions and pressures on them, and the role of regional and other groupings. This is followed, in Chapter 2, with an introduction to the key issues at the Doha Ministerial.

The book continues, in Chapters 3 to 5, with an extensive discussion of how the WTO works in practice, focusing on the process before and during the 2001 Doha Ministerial Conference. Chapter 6 highlights the process of 'arm-twisting', by which the major powers pressurize developing countries into agreeing to their proposals. Chapter 7 looks more closely at the role of the WTO Secretariat. Chapters 8 and 9 review developments over the year following Doha, on the substantive issues and decision-making processes, in preparation for the Fifth Ministerial Conference in Cancun, Mexico, in September 2003. Conclusions and recommendations to democratize the functioning of the WTO are presented in Chapter 10.

Why the WTO matters

The WTO, based in Geneva, Switzerland, is made up of 146 member countries, four-fifths of which are developing countries. It was founded at the beginning of 1995 as a successor to the General

Agreement on Tariffs and Trade (GATT), as a result of the Uruguay Round of multilateral trade negotiations, which took place under the auspices of the GATT between 1986 and 1994.

The WTO is often viewed as an esoteric institution negotiating trade rules incomprehensible to the ordinary person on the street. The general state of ignorance about the WTO, and the GATT before it, however, belies its importance. The WTO establishes the rules governing the international trading system, which have a major effect on people's livelihoods. These rules often require that member countries change their intellectual property legislation, industrial and agricultural policies, basic service provision and sometimes even their constitutions. They affect employment, incomes and the prices people pay for imports and locally produced goods that compete with imports.

With the completion of the Uruguay Round of trade negotiations in 1994, and the foundation of the WTO at the beginning of 1995, these rules extended into a number of areas that had been outside the GATT system – notably agriculture, textiles, trade in services and intellectual property rights (essentially patents and copyrights). This greatly increased the potential effect of WTO decisions on people's everyday lives, particularly in developing countries, not only by extending the scope of the effects on employment, incomes and prices, but also by introducing measures affecting trade in services that affect the provision and regulation of public services such as health amenities, education, water and sanitation.

The WTO has been characterized as having a 'mercantilist ethic' (Finger and Schuler 2000), and its agreements, forced through by political and economic pressure from the major developed countries, institutionalize corporate access to the markets and resources of the developing world. The interests of the developing countries are routinely ignored:

> Our analysis indicates that the WTO obligations reflect little awareness of development problems, and little appreciation for the capacities of least developed countries to carry out the functions that SPS [Sanitary and Phytosanitary Measures], customs valua-

tion, intellectual property, etc. regulations address. The content of these obligations can be characterized as the advanced countries saying to the others, *Do it my way!*

From their [developing countries'] perspective, the implementation exercise [of Uruguay Round commitments] has been imposed in an imperial way, with little concern for what it will cost, how it will be done, or if it will support their development efforts.

To least developed country negotiators, the reforms [from the Uruguay Round] were imposed by the major trading countries. The government agencies that must implement the rules blame the large countries and their own negotiators. To them, the rules were imposed by the major trading countries over the weakness of their own negotiators. (ibid., original emphasis)

The WTO is unique among international bodies in including mechanisms to enforce its agreements with *sanctions* – although in practice these sanctions are largely ineffective in the hands of most developing countries (see Box 1.1). This means, in effect, that compliance with the WTO rules is likely to be given precedence over other international agreements and commitments, for example on the environment and human rights, which have no effective sanctions attached to them.

Moreover, the WTO Secretariat interprets its remit as being the *progressive liberalization* of international trade in the areas in which it operates. Many developing countries had already lowered their trade barriers further than required by the WTO before the Uruguay Round agreements, under structural adjustment programmes supported by the International Monetary Fund (IMF) and the World Bank; the Uruguay Round affected them none the less, by limiting their ability to raise the barriers again if their circumstances required.

Another important issue is the *accession* process countries must go through in order to join the WTO. The process is vigorous and time-consuming – it took China no less than fifteen years to accede, from its application to join the GATT in 1986. No least developed country has acceded since the inception of the WTO, prompting one developing country delegate interviewed to ask: 'Are we really welcome? Those countries that did not join at the time of GATT are really finding it tough to get in.'

Moreover, any existing member has the right to veto accession by any new member; the more powerful (developed) countries use this right not only to keep out countries they feel should not be part of the grouping (Iran's request for accession has been vetoed by the USA since 1996, for example), but also to make demands on them that go beyond the commitments required of existing members or the scope of existing WTO agreements on the routine trade and economic requirements for accession. A staff member of the WTO Secretariat interviewed for this book wondered aloud why a small island like Vanuatu was going through such a vigorous accession process – including being asked to sign an agreement on civil aviation when it did not have any aeroplanes.

In short, the WTO is a key part of the globalization process, which affects everyone's lives. It brings increasing limitations on the ability of governments to enact policies in the interests of their own populations – even, in some cases, policies that affect trade only indirectly – and effectively gives precedence to trade and international commercial interests over people and international commitments and agreements directed at their benefit. This would be a matter of serious concern even if the WTO's decision-making processes were a model of democracy, transparency and account-ability. If, as this book argues, WTO decisions are taken in a way favouring the interests of the few over the many, and commercial interests over ordinary people's livelihoods, the cause for concern is even greater.

The multilateral trading system before the WTO

While the WTO came into being only in 1995, the trading system over which it presides is nearly half a century older. Since 1948, the rules for the system had been provided by the 1947 General Agreement on Tariffs and Trade (GATT). While the original idea of creating an international trade organization alongside the Bretton Woods institutions (the International Monetary Fund and

Box 1.1 The dispute settlement mechanism

The Dispute Settlement Body of the WTO is presented by proponents of the WTO system as enhancing democracy and assisting small countries in trade disputes against other members (particularly the more powerful ones) with reference to the rules of the organization. The WTO dispute mechanism, introduced in 1994, is indeed a great improvement on the previous (GATT) system. In practice, however, it is much less beneficial to most developing countries than the theory suggests.

A major problem of the dispute settlement mechanism is that the enforcement of its decisions is through the sanctioning of retaliatory trade restrictions. This creates a serious asymmetry. Trade restrictions by the USA or the European Communities (EC)[2] against any other country would have a real impact on its economy; but the effect of trade restrictions by any but the very largest developing countries would have no effect at all. There is therefore little incentive for most developing countries to incur the considerable cost and inconvenience of using the dispute settlement mechanism, even if they have a rock-solid case, when there is no effective mechanism to enforce its findings. This applies particularly to disputes with the major developed countries, when there may also be a considerable political price to pay for incurring their displeasure.

In addition, there are serious obstacles to developing countries using the mechanism effectively. The South Centre (1999) highlights three key areas in which such obstacles arise:

- the cost of, and access to, the dispute settlement process;
- problems in the implementation of decisions and compensation arising from the process; and
- the implementation of provisions regarding Special and Differential Treatment in favour of developing countries.

A developing county delegate interviewed for this book illustrated some of the problems.

> My country has not yet been involved in a dispute, because it is a very long and expensive system to get engaged in. Although we do now have the independent Advisory Centre on WTO Law[3] to assist us, it is still much more practical for us to settle out of court. The European Communities, for instance, banned all fish exports coming from my country into their markets some years ago, saying the fish was infected with the cholera bacteria as a result of an outbreak of cholera we encountered. The WTO formally objected to this notion because there was no scientific proof that our fish were infected. Yet we could not afford to go through the dispute settlement process with the EC for various reasons. We eventually settled the matter bilaterally with the EC after suffering huge losses in fish exports. Really, the power of enforcement of the rulings coming out of the dispute settlement system is based on your capacity to retaliate against a country that has bent the rules. As a small country, however, the impact of retaliating against a big country is virtually nil, though some developing countries have been able to do this with some amount of success.

the World Bank) was aborted, an unofficial *de facto* international organization, also known informally as the GATT, emerged to preside over the system.

According to the WTO Secretariat (WTO 2001d), the multilateral trading system is based on a number of core principles, namely that national rules affecting trade:

- should not discriminate between a country's trading partners, but grant all equally *'most favoured nation' (MFN)* status;

- should not discriminate between the country's own products and imports, but accord foreign suppliers *'national treatment'*;
- should become *progressively freer*, lowering trade barriers over time through negotiations;
- should be *predictable*, so that foreign companies, investors and governments can be confident that trade barriers will not be raised arbitrarily;
- should *discourage 'unfair' practices* such as export subsidies and dumping products at prices below their cost of production to gain market share; and
- should be *more beneficial for less developed countries*, giving them more time to adjust, greater flexibility and special privileges.

The GATT presided over a succession of rounds of multilateral trade negotiations. The first five rounds (the Geneva Round of 1947, the Annecy Round of 1949, the Torquay Round of 1951, the Geneva Round of 1956 and the Dillon Round of 1960–61) focused on the reform of import tariffs and quotas. Participation was limited, just twenty-five countries taking part on average, and sensitive areas of trade such as agriculture and textiles were excluded from the negotiations.

Subsequent rounds also covered tariffs and quotas, but progressively broadened the scope of negotiations. The Kennedy Round (1964–67) also covered anti-dumping codes, while the Tokyo Round (1975–79) covered a much wider range of issues, including non-tariff measures such as subsidies and countervailing measures, technical barriers to trade, import licensing, customs valuation, government procurement, and trade in civil aircraft. Because not all members formally subscribed to these agreements, however, they were informally known as 'codes'.

The Uruguay Round (1986–94) went much further. This was the first 'comprehensive' round of multilateral trade negotiations, not only creating the WTO, but also including agreements covering:

- tariffs;
- non-tariff barriers;
- textiles and clothing;

- agriculture;
- trade in services;
- Trade-Related Aspects of Intellectual Property Rights (TRIPs);
- Trade-Related Investment Measures (TRIMs);
- the GATT system;
- GATT articles;
- subsidies;
- dispute settlement;
- anti-dumping; and
- the Tokyo Round codes.

The Marrakesh Agreement – the birth of the WTO

Ministers from the 124 governments who were members of the GATT at the time met in Marrakesh, Morocco, between 12 and 15 April 1994 to sign the agreements that embodied the results of the Uruguay Round. Prominent among these was the Marrakesh Agreement Establishing the WTO, under which the WTO was formally established on 1 January 1995.

The main function of the WTO, like the GATT before it, is to ensure that member governments keep their trade policies within agreed limits, and its members sign agreements to this effect every so often, following a long process of negotiation. Once signed, the agreements provide the legal ground rules for international trade within a multilateral framework – they are essentially binding contracts to which governments are expected to adhere.

The preamble of the Marrakesh Agreement clearly establishes the principle that trade liberalization is not an end in itself, but a means towards the larger objective of improving living standards in WTO member countries. It begins:

The Parties to this Agreement,

Recognising that their relations in the field of trade and economic endeavour should be conducted with a view to raising standards of living, ensuring full employment and a large and steadily growing volume of real income and effective demand, and expanding the production of and trade in goods and services,

Table 1.1 WTO members and observers

High-income countries		Upper-middle-income countries
Australia	Slovenia	Antigua and Barbuda
Austria	Spain	Argentina
Barbados	Sweden	Bahrain
Belgium	Switzerland	Botswana
Brunei	Taiwan	Brazil
Canada	United Arab	Chile
Cyprus	Emirates	Costa Rica
Darussalam	United	Croatia
Denmark	Kingdom	Czech Republic
European	United States	Dominica
Communities	of America	Estonia
Finland		Gabon
France		Grenada
Germany		Hungary
Greece		Korea
Hong Kong		Malaysia
Iceland		Mauritius
Ireland		Mexico
Israel		Oman
Italy		Panama
Japan		Poland
Kuwait		St Kitts & Nevis
Liechtenstein		St Lucia
Luxembourg		Slovak Republic
Macao		South Africa
Malta		Trinidad & Tobago
Netherlands		Turkey
New Zealand		Uruguay
Norway		Venezuela
Portugal		
Qatar		
Singapore		

Observer governments: Algeria, Andorra, Azerbaijan, Bahamas, Belarus, Bhutan, Bosnia and Herzegovina, Cambodia, Cape Verde, Ethiopia, Former Yugoslav Republic of Macedonia, Holy See (Vatican), Kazakhstan, Lao People's Democratic Republic, Lebanon, Nepal, Russian Federation, Samoa, Sao Tome & Principe, Saudi Arabia, Seychelles, Sudan, Tajikistan, Tonga, Ukraine, Uzbekistan, Vanuatu, Vietnam, Yemen, Federal Republic of Yugoslavia.

Lower-middle-income countries		Low-income countries	
Albania	Suriname	*Angola	Mongolia
Belize	Swaziland	Armenia	*Mozambique
Bolivia	Thailand	*Bangladesh	*Myanmar
Bulgaria	Tunisia	*Benin	Nicaragua
China		*Burkina Faso	*Niger
Colombia		*Burundi	Nigeria
Cuba		Cameroon	Pakistan
*Djibouti		*Central African	*Rwanda
Dominican		Republic	*Senegal
Republic		*Chad	*Sierra Leone
Ecuador		Congo	*Solomon
Egypt		Côte d'Ivoire	Islands
El Salvador		*Democratic	*Tanzania
Fiji		Republic	*Togo
Guatemala		of Congo	*Uganda
Guyana		*The Gambia	*Zambia
Honduras		Georgia	Zimbabwe
Jamaica		Ghana	
Jordan		*Guinea	
Latvia		*Guinea Bissau	
Lithuania		*Haiti	
*Maldives		India	
Morocco		Indonesia	
Namibia		Kenya	
Papua New Guinea		Kyrgyz Republic	
Paraguay		*Lesotho	
Peru		*Madagascar	
Philippines		*Malawi	
Romania		*Mali	
St Vincent and the Grenadines		*Mauritania	
Sri Lanka		Moldova	

International organisations observers to the General Council: United Nations (UN), United Nations Conference on Trade and Development (UNCTAD), International Monetary Fund (IMF), World Bank, Food & Agricultural Organization (FAO), World Intellectual Property Organization (WIPO), Organisation of Economic Co-operation and Development (OECD).

Source: www.wto.org.
Note: * = least developed country

while allowing for the optimal use of the world's resources in accordance with the objective of sustainable development, seeking both to protect and preserve the environment and to enhance the means of doing so in a manner consistent with their respective needs and concerns at different levels of economic development … (WTO 1999c: 4)

As of May 2003, the WTO was made up of 146 member countries, while a further twenty-eight countries had observer status (see Table 1.1). With the exception of the Holy See, observers must start negotiations for accession to the WTO within five years of becoming observers.

Developing countries (including least developed countries) make up about four-fifths of the membership and have special provisions within the rules that are meant to deal with their special needs. The General Agreement on Tariffs and Trade has a special section (part 4) on trade and development, which includes:

- provisions on *non-reciprocity* in trade negotiations between developed and developing countries, so that when developed countries make trade concessions for developing countries, they should not expect the developing countries to match the offers in return; and
- the key provision known as *Special and Differential Treatment* (SDT), which states that countries can grant special concessions to developing countries without having to do so for the entire membership. To date, however, these SDT provisions have been in 'best endeavour' language, and have not been implemented.

Other provisions allow developing countries extra time to fulfil their WTO commitments. *Least developed countries* (LDCs), in particular, are granted extra attention in the trade rules. Ministers issued a decision in Marrakesh that LDCs that are net food importers would be eligible for aid to adjust to agriculture subsidy reduction commitments by developed countries. As subsidy reduction could raise world market prices of basic commodities imported by LDCs, the International Monetary Fund and World Bank were tasked with providing financial assistance to cushion them from the effects while they adjusted. In practice, however, the Marrakesh decision has not been implemented at all. A plan of action was drawn up at the first WTO conference in Singapore in 1996. This formed the basis of the 1997 Integrated Framework for Technical Assistance to LDCs. However, only a relatively small number of LDCs have received technical assistance under the Framework, and such assistance has been widely used as a 'carrot' in negotiations (see Chapter 6).

WTO bodies and decision-making

The decision-making structure of the WTO is summarized in Figure 1.1. All WTO members can participate in all bodies except the appellate body, dispute settlement panels and plurilateral committees (see below). On decision-making, Article IX of the Marrakesh Agreement says: 'The WTO shall continue the practice of decision-making by consensus followed under GATT 1947. Except as otherwise provided, where a decision cannot be arrived at by consensus, the matter at issue shall be decided by voting. At a meeting of the Ministerial Conference and the General Council, each Member of the WTO shall have one vote' (WTO 1999c: 8).

Trade ministers make up the highest and most directly authoritative body at the WTO, making all major decisions, primarily through *ministerial conferences* such as those held in Seattle in 1999 and Doha in 2001. Article IV of the Marrakesh Agreement requires a ministerial to be held at least once every two years, to take decisions on all matters under any of the multilateral agreements. The Doha Ministerial is discussed in Chapters 4 and 5.

A practice has recently emerged of influential members holding *mini-ministerial meetings* during the months before ministerials. These are unofficial meetings hosted by a member country, to which selected countries are invited, to move matters along before the ministerial itself. While they do not form part of the WTO's formal decision-making processes, and are not governed by its rules, they play a critical role in determining the outcome of negotiations. They have been roundly condemned as illegitimate by civil society groups, as they allow a small, self-appointed group of powerful

Ministerial Conference

General Council

General Council meeting as Trade Policy Review Body

General Council meeting as Dispute Settlement Body

Appellate Body; Dispute Settlement Panels

Supervisory role: Trade Negotiations Committee Chaired by WTO DG (*ex officio*)

Negotiating groups (special sessions): Agriculture; Trade and Environment; Trade in Services; TRIPs; Dispute Settlement; and Trade and Development

Negotiating groups: Rules (Anti-dumping, Subsidies and Regional Trade Agreements); and Non-Agricultural Market Access

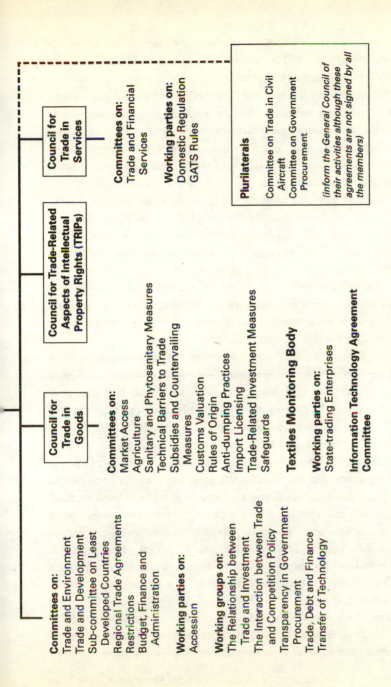

Council for Trade in Goods

Committees on:
Market Access
Agriculture
Sanitary and Phytosanitary Measures
Technical Barriers to Trade
Subsidies and Countervailing
  Measures
Customs Valuation
Rules of Origin
Anti-dumping Practices
Import Licensing
Trade-Related Investment Measures
Safeguards

Textiles Monitoring Body

Working parties on:
State-trading Enterprises

**Information Technology Agreement
Committee**

Council for Trade-Related Aspects of Intellectual Property Rights (TRIPs)

Committees on:
Trade and Environment
Trade and Development
Sub-committee on Least
  Developed Countries
Regional Trade Agreements
Restrictions
Budget, Finance and
  Administration

Working parties on:
Accession

Working groups on:
The Relationship between
  Trade and Investment
The Interaction between Trade
  and Competition Policy
Transparency in Government
  Procurement
Trade, Debt and Finance
Transfer of Technology

Council for Trade in Services

Committees on:
Trade and Financial
  Services

Working parties on:
Domestic Regulation
GATS Rules

Plurilaterals

Committee on Trade in Civil
  Aircraft
Committee on Government
  Procurement

*(inform the General Council of
their activities although these
agreements are not signed by all
the members)*

Figure 1.1 The WTO structure (February 2002)

members to act, in effect, as an executive council (Focus on the Global South 2002). The major mini-ministerials that preceded Doha are discussed in Chapter 3.

The day-to-day work of the WTO is carried out by government officials of each member country working in trade missions in Geneva. The second most important body after the ministerial meetings is the *General Council*, which is composed of representatives of all the members (most of them Geneva-based, although some twenty least developed countries are not represented in Geneva). It is mandated to meet as appropriate in the intervals between ministerial conferences to perform functions assigned to it by the agreements signed by ministers. It carries out the day-to-day business of the organization in Geneva between ministerial meetings, and reports to the ministers on the progress and status of negotiations.

As with most WTO bodies, a new chair is selected every year from among the trade missions in Geneva. Since the council's inception, the chairmanship has alternated between representatives of developed and developing countries.

The General Council also sits as the Dispute Settlement Body and the Trade Policy Review Body (see below), but under different terms of reference and different chairs. The *Dispute Settlement Body* (DSB) governs the process of settling trade disputes. It has the sole authority to establish panels of experts to consider a trade dispute between members, and to accept or reject each panel's findings or results. This DSB also monitors the implementation of rulings and recommendations, and has the power to authorize one side to retaliate against the other when rulings have not been implemented. Either side can appeal against a panel's ruling, the appeal being heard by three members of a permanent seven-member *appellate body* (each member serving a four-year term) set up by the DSB, and broadly representing the WTO membership. Since the process can be lengthy and expensive, in practice the majority of cases are settled 'out of court'.

The *Trade Policy Review Body* focuses on individual members' own trade policies and practices. 'Peer' reviews by other members are documented, where relevant taking into account the country's developmental needs within the trade and economic environment in which it operates. The reviews are designed to provide feedback to the country concerned on its performance, and to provide information to outsiders (mainly the business community) about its trade policies and circumstances. The four biggest traders (the EC, the USA, Japan and Canada, known as the 'Quad' or Quadrilateral Group) are reviewed every two years, the next sixteen biggest trading nations every four years, and the remainder every six or more years.

The *Trade Negotiations Committee* (TNC) is an offspring of the 2001 Doha Ministerial. Consisting of all WTO members, it was set up on 3 February 2002, charged with overseeing the negotiations mandated by the ministerial. It will not necessarily be a permanent structure of the WTO, but will remain operational until 1 January 2005, when a new trade round is supposed to be completed. The TNC reports directly to the General Council, and is chaired, *ex officio*, by the WTO director general to push negotiations along. It will hold special sessions in the six areas identified in Doha, namely agriculture, intellectual property rights (TRIPs), the environment, dispute settlement, trade in services, and trade and development. Two new negotiating groups were also set up after Doha, namely the rules and non-agricultural market access groups. The process by which the TNC was established and its chairmanship decided is discussed in Chapter 8.

Also reporting to the General Council are three other councils, each responsible for day-to-day activities in a broad area of trade (Trade in Goods, Trade in Services and Trade-Related Intellectual Property Rights); and six committees, covering issues such as trade and development, the environment, etc., whose functions are less broad. Working groups were set up at the 1996 Singapore Ministerial Conference to look at investment, competition policy, transparency in government procurement and trade facilitation; and two additional working groups, on trade, debt and finance, and on transfer of technology, were set up following the Doha Conference in 2001.

Of critical significance, though not part of the WTO's formal structure, are *informal or 'green room' meetings*,[4] at which a select group of members meet in an unofficial atmosphere to discuss trade negotiations and possible agreements in areas of contention. Minutes are not taken during these gatherings. Such meetings were established during the Uruguay Round negotiations and have remained a key part of the WTO landscape – there were some 500 informal meetings at the WTO in 2001. Following the Seattle Conference, members agreed to hold open-ended informal meetings to ensure greater participation in the process. 'Green room' meetings also occur at ministerial meetings.

'Green room' meetings are extremely problematic, as they are totally non-transparent. Attendance is 'by invitation' only, invitations being issued either by the director general or by the chair of the negotiating group. Most members who are uninvited are left in ignorance about what consultations are taking place, between which members, on which issues.

Most of the real deals at the WTO, especially the all-important bilateral trade deals, are discussed at still more informal meetings (sometimes within the WTO) and cocktail parties (outside the WTO). Selected delegates, led by the powerful countries, meet at the Japanese mission, for instance, and discuss important trade negotiations and deals informally over sushi.

Democracy in the WTO

In September 2001, two months before the Doha Ministerial, an article appeared in *The Economist* (2001) which began: 'The WTO is no would-be tyrant. It is democratic to a fault and has few powers of its own.' It emphasized that the rules of the organization are devised and altered solely by its members through consensus – that is, they require unanimity. Far from being anti-democratic, as its critics say, the article argued that this made the WTO hyper-democratic. It went on to suggest that, because the WTO uniquely had in place an independent Dispute Settlement Body, member countries could always resolve trade disputes in a just and fair manner.

Delegates representing member countries in Geneva take a different view, particularly those from developing countries. Even

Ian Wilkinson of the EC,[5] asked whether the institution was democratic, was taken aback, and had to ask what democracy really meant! He went on to say

> I don't believe [the WTO] is undemocratic, in that members come from democratically elected governments ... Well, in the case of the USA, the needs of big business are a huge part of the process – and to a lesser extent the EC – in which case it is a bit of a mix ... There is going to be power play. People are paid to defend and promote the interests of their countries ...
>
> I think you can make a plausible case that it is democratic. It is an intergovernmental organization that is opening up more to NGOs and parliaments ... The WTO is sometimes feared, sometimes maligned. I think it is still a very new institution that is going through a transition from being the GATT to being the WTO ... It is member-driven – though I think that is a bit of a stalemate. If we were drivers, I think we would have our licences revoked! ... It is not democratic in the sense that people can just come in and say what they think ...The organization itself has no policy or mind of its own.

The Malaysian ambassador to the WTO, M. Supperamaniam,[6] representing a middle-income country, had this to say.

> Well, [the WTO] is *supposed* to be democratic – it is member-driven, and every member has a vote, so it has all the elements of a democratic institution, on paper at least ... In practice, there have been complaints that the agenda is dictated by very few powerful countries. Changes have, however, taken place. Developing countries make up two-thirds of the membership,[7] and are participating more actively in discussions. There is greater inclusiveness and transparency. I am not claiming everything is rosy, but there have been changes for the better.

As the following extracts from interviews with delegates from two other developing countries demonstrate, however, some take an altogether less optimistic view. 'There is no democracy at the WTO. Power reigns. In theory, consensus is supposed to protect

Table 1.2 Professional staff in Geneva missions (April 2001)

Quad members

Canada	12	Luxembourg	2
European Communities	18	Sweden*	6
Japan	23	USA*	14

Other high-income countries

Barbados	5	Norway	8
Hong Kong*	7	Qatar	1
Korea	16	Singapore	7
Liechtenstein	1	Switzerland*	5
Mexico*	8	United Arab Emirates	2
New Zealand	5		

Upper-middle-income countries

Antigua and Barbuda	0	Hungary	4
Argentina	7	Malaysia*	4
Botswana	2	Oman	2
Brazil	12	Panama*	3
Chile*	7	Poland	3
Costa Rica*	2	St Lucia	0
Croatia	1	Slovakia	2
Estonia	5	South Africa	5
Gabon	4	Venezuela	8
Grenada	0		

Lower-middle-income countries

Albania	3	Latvia	2
Bulgaria	2	Morocco	5
Cuba	6	Namibia	0
Dominican Republic	6	Philippines	7
Egypt	10	Romania	5
El Salvador*	3	Sri Lanka	2
Honduras*	3	Thailand*	13
Jamaica	4	Tunisia	3
Jordan	2		

Low-income countries (excluding LDCs)

Congo	3	Kenya	7
Georgia	2	Nigeria	10
Ghana	3	Pakistan	5
India*	7	Zimbabwe	5
Indonesia	8		

Least developed countries (LDCs)

Bangladesh	4	Mauritania	4
Burkina Faso	0	Mozambique	0
Central African Republic	1	Senegal	5
Congo DR	2	Solomon Islands	0
Guyana	0	Tanzania	5
Lesotho	2	Uganda	4
Malawi	0	Zambia	6
Mali	0		

Note : * signifies a mission devoted exclusively to the WTO. Others also cover other Geneva-based international organizations

the weaker countries. In practice, the strength of numbers does not hamper the will of the rich countries.'

> In my opinion, it is not democratic. You are not allowed to gain anything as a small developing country fighting for your legitimate interests unless you manage to get the powerful countries on your side. It does not matter how much effort you put into producing credible position papers, you will get nowhere without the rich countries' backing. You generally have two options if you try to take on this system: you are either excluded, or you are diminished as a person and a country.

The size of WTO missions

A major obstacle faced by developing countries in the WTO is the discrepancy between the human resources available to them and those available to the developed countries. Among the members of the Quad Group, the US mission in Geneva has fourteen professional staff devoted exclusively to the WTO, the EC eighteen (also covering other Geneva-based international organizations) in addition to the missions of its fifteen member countries, Japan twenty-three and Canada twelve. While a handful of developing countries have between eight and thirteen professional staff, most have between two and five (see Table 1.2). The great majority have to represent their countries in more than twenty other international agencies based in Geneva as well as the WTO. Twenty least developed country

(LDC) and developing country members, as well as eleven observer countries and those in the process of accession, have no permanent missions in Geneva at all (WWF et al. 2001).

Predictably, those developing countries with the largest missions, such as Brazil, Thailand and India, are among the most active in WTO negotiations. Staffing levels are critical, because of the need to participate in numerous meetings, which often take place simultaneously, putting considerable pressure on mission staff. A statement on 13 February 2002 by WTO deputy director general Miguel Rodriguez Mendoza illustrates this perfectly. He described no fewer than sixty-seven WTO bodies, including thirty-four standing bodies open to all members, twenty-eight accession working parties and five plurilateral bodies (in which agreements are not signed by all WTO members). In addition, there is the Trade Negotiations Committee (TNC) set up after the Fourth Ministerial Conference in Doha (November 2001), and two new negotiating groups.

The WTO has a thousand meetings a year in total, many of them running parallel to each other. Ministerial meetings, as mentioned above, take place at least once every two years, and are preceded by a number of mini-ministerials attended by only some members. In addition, according to WTO Conference Office statistics, on the basis of half-day units (so that a meeting lasting a full day is calculated as two meetings), there were nearly 400 formal meetings of WTO bodies in 2001, more than 500 informal meetings and ninety assorted symposia, workshops and seminars under the auspices of WTO bodies.

A former Central American envoy with only one extra staff member in his mission for nearly all his term as ambassador was amazed when South Korean mission officials complained about being over-stretched and overloaded with WTO work – despite having a total of thirty staff!

Key regional groups and alliances within the WTO

As well as the organization-wide bodies and meetings, a number of country groupings, based on geographical regions (often regional trade blocs) or common interests, also play an important role in the

WTO. The extent of their collaboration varies, from negotiating as a single entity (in the case of the EC) to informal discussions of issues being negotiated. Some countries are members of more than one grouping, while others are in none.

The Quad (Quadrilateral Group), comprising the USA, the EC, Japan and Canada, forms the most formidable alliance within the WTO. Breakthroughs in difficult negotiations are often a result of the Quad coming to an agreement on how to proceed. The role of the Quad is discussed further in Chapter 3.

The European Communities (EC) is composed of the fifteen member countries of the European Union. The individual member nations coordinate their positions, and the European Commission alone speaks on behalf of all members at key WTO meetings, representing a common position of all the EU members.

The LDC (Least Developed Country) Group consists of the thirty WTO members, mostly low-income countries, defined by the UN as having a particularly low level of economic development. (Another nineteen LDCs are not in the WTO.) The LDCs are becoming increasingly strong and coherent as a group, and had a coordinator at the Doha Ministerial, as well as producing a joint declaration (the Zanzibar Declaration) beforehand.

The ACP (Africa, Caribbean and Pacific) Group is made up of the fifty-six developing country WTO members in these regions which benefit from EC trade preferences under the EC–ACP Partnership Agreements. (Another twenty-two ACP countries are not in the WTO.) The group sometimes presents joint statements on trade matters, and had a coordinator at the Doha Ministerial.

The Africa Group comprises all the African countries at the WTO, and often produces joint statements and declarations. It took the lead in threatening to walk out of the Seattle Ministerial if its members continued to be marginalized in the talks, and has since been instrumental in calling for fundamental changes in the TRIPs Agreement.

The Like-Minded Group (LMG) has a diverse membership that includes Cuba, the Dominican Republic, Egypt, Honduras, India, Indonesia, Jamaica, Kenya, Malaysia, Mauritius, Pakistan, Sri Lanka,

Tanzania, Uganda and Zimbabwe. The group meets informally at the WTO, and has attained the reputation of being the grouping that most frequently voices pro-development positions at the WTO. It has played a major role in raising implementation issues, and, after Doha, in putting procedural issues on the agenda.

The Cairns Group was set up just before the Uruguay Round began in 1986 to argue for agricultural trade liberalization. The members are diverse but generally share a common objective in agriculture negotiations as major exporters of agricultural products. The Cairns Group has seventeen members from four continents, mostly high- and middle-income countries[8] (Argentina, Australia, Brazil, Canada, Chile, Colombia, Costa Rica, Guatemala, Hungary, Indonesia, Malaysia, New Zealand, Paraguay, the Philippines, South Africa, Thailand and Uruguay).

Notes

1. While the focus of this book is on process rather than substantive issues, a simple explanation of some key issues will be provided where necessary.

2. Within the WTO, the European Union (EU) is formally referred to as the European Communities (EC). To avoid confusion, the latter term is used throughout the book.

3. The Advisory Centre on WTO Law is an independent body, launched at the 1999 Seattle Ministerial, most of the financial and technical support coming from developed countries (including the Netherlands, Canada and Norway) and a few middle-income countries. It provides legal assistance in WTO matters to developing country members, free of charge in the case of least developed countries.

4. The name was coined because such meetings were originally held in the office of the director general of the GATT, which was green in colour.

5. Interview with Ian Wilkinson, deputy permanent representative of the EC delegation to the international organizations in Geneva, 14 March 2002.

6. Interview with M. Supperamaniam, Malaysian ambassador to the WTO, 7 March 2002.

7. This excludes high-income countries which are generally regarded as developing countries.

8. Indonesia is the only low-income country in the Cairns Group.

TWO

The battleground – the key issues in Doha

This chapter provides a brief introduction to the major issues at the Doha Ministerial Conference – industrial tariffs and market access for non-agricultural goods; agriculture; trade in services; Trade-Related Aspects of Intellectual Property Rights (TRIPs); the 'new issues' (competition, investment, transparency in government procurement and trade facilitation); implementation issues; and Special and Differential Treatment. In each case, it outlines the history of the issue within the GATT and WTO, major developments leading up to the preparations for Doha, and the implications of the issues for developing countries. Chapter 3 continues with the major pre-Doha mini-ministerial meetings.

Industrial tariffs and market access for non-agricultural products

Liberalization and tariff reductions for non-agricultural products are the traditional remit of the GATT/WTO. Unlike agriculture and services, however (see below), they were not part of the 'built-in agenda' specified in the Uruguay Round Agreements, on which negotiations were to proceed regardless of whether or not there was a new round. Many developing countries therefore opposed the launch of yet another round of industrial tariff reduction before Doha. Kenya, Mozambique, Nigeria, Tanzania, Uganda, Zimbabwe and Zambia submitted a joint paper explaining why they did not want negotiations to take place. Instead, they called for a study process, taking into account the impacts of previous liberalization on domestic firms, employment and government revenue, and tariff peaks and tariff escalation[1] in developed countries. Egypt, India and Brazil supported this position.

The African paper pointed out that many developing countries had already liberalized their imports of industrial products as a result of structural adjustment, and that this had led to serious problems, such as local industries losing market share and closing down, causing unemployment and loss of government revenue. They provided many examples, from Senegal, Côte d'Ivoire, Nigeria, Sierra Leone, Zambia, Zaire, Uganda, Tanzania, Sudan, Kenya, Ghana, Zimbabwe, Mozambique, Cameroon and Malawi. The experience of Latin American countries such as Peru, Nicaragua, Ecuador and Brazil was also mentioned.

Though unwilling, however, developing countries found it difficult to oppose strongly a subject area at the core of the WTO's agenda.

Agriculture

While agriculture was in principle covered by the 1947 GATT Agreement, in practice it was outside GATT disciplines until the Uruguay Round. In the 1950s, the USA had sought a waiver from Article XI of the GATT (which prohibited quantitative restrictions on imports), and threatened to leave GATT unless it was allowed to maintain protective mechanisms for agricultural commodities. Washington was given a 'non-time-limited waiver' on agricultural products, and the GATT did not enforce Article XI on other agricultural producers for fear of being accused of double standards.

By the 1980s, however, the USA was embroiled in a subsidy war in agriculture with the EC. Both sides were giving huge subsidies to their farmers, creating large surpluses that needed to be exported, and the USA was fast losing its markets to the EC. Washington responded by pushing hard to bring agriculture back under GATT/WTO disciplines. The final details of the Agreement on Agriculture were in fact decided bilaterally between the USA and the EC in the now infamous Blair House Accord in 1992. Other WTO members were given little choice but to go along with the terms of the accord.

The Agreement on Agriculture (AoA) is widely seen as one of the most iniquitous agreements in the WTO, in effect providing special and differential treatment to developed rather than developing countries. Developing countries accepted the Uruguay Round

Agreements as a whole largely because they believed that they would benefit from agricultural liberalization and subsidy reduction in the OECD countries under the AoA. These promises were not fulfilled, however. Loopholes, such as the 'Green Box' permitting supposedly 'non-trade distorting subsidies', were created by the developed countries in the negotiations and used in implementation; and the terms of the agreement were carefully designed to minimize the actual changes required. As a result, OECD countries' agricultural subsidies and dumping (the sale of products below the real cost of production) have been legitimized rather than illegalized, and have increased rather than decreased, since the Uruguay Round.

The USA dumps staple crops in developing countries in large amounts, exporting corn at prices 20 per cent below production cost, and wheat at 46 per cent below cost. The EC spends more than €40 billion (US$40 billion) per year – half of its total budget – on agricultural subsidies.

While the EC boasts of having made trade fairer by reducing its export subsidies, much of this supposed reduction is fictitious, subsidies merely being shifted into other agricultural subsidy programmes that ultimately have the same effect. The EC claims, for instance, that it has reduced its cereals dumping by 60 per cent, and its export funding from Ecus 2.2 billion in 1992 to €883 million in 1999. Adding the €2.1 billion of direct payments on cereals exported in 1999 to the €883 million in export subsidies, however, total export subsidies have actually increased by 36 per cent (Berthelot 2002).

Einarsson explains: 'When the gap between the protected internal price level and world market price is reduced, the need for export subsidies is thus reduced. But for the importing country, there is no difference. Whether the export price is artificially lowered by export subsidies or by direct payments, the dumping effect is the same' (Einarsson 2002: 18).

EC and US agricultural subsidies and dumping have had a devastating effect on developing countries' agricultural sectors. Subsidies lead to over-production that is dumped on the world market, depressing world prices; and these subsidized imports enter developing

Box 2.1 Thai rice farmers: hunger amidst plenty

Thailand is well known for its bounteous food production, particularly the export of Jasmine rice. It is, in fact, Asia's only net food exporter, and accounts for at least 35 per cent of the world's rice exports, also exporting rubber, sugar, cassava and chicken meat.

The majority of Thai farmers, however, endure very low living standards, some 40 per cent of the rural population living below the poverty line. Of 5.7 million farming families, 4.7 million have no land or inadequate land to sustain them. Food insecurity is a reality even for the rice farmers: the FAO estimates that 25–30 per cent of the population is chronically undernourished. The rural crisis has been going on for several decades, set in motion by the commercialization of agriculture and its subordination to industrial development. It has worsened in recent years, however, as a result of further liberalization and the 1997 financial crisis.

Farm-gate prices have fallen to historically low levels. The price of palm oil fell from Baht 4.00 per kg in 1997–98 to Baht 0.75 in 1999, when the Thai market was opened to Malaysian exports. Similarly, the price of rice fell from Baht 8–10,000 per ton before the 1997 economic crisis to Baht 4,000 in 2000. Rice was also one of the items Thailand had to liberalize under the AoA, lifting the prohibition on rice imports (except by the government), lowering the tariff by 0.2 per cent every year until 2003, and increasing annual imports to 250,000 tons by 2004. The price of milk was also greatly depressed when Thailand opened its market to subsidized EC milk powder. At the same time, the cost of farm inputs – fertilizers, pesticides and herbicides – has increased by some 40 per cent in the last five years.

Many farmers are finding it impossible to make ends meet. Once all the bills are paid, there is not enough left to buy food or look after their families' needs, and they find themselves in a chronic cycle of debt. The Ministry of Finance estimates total farm debt at Baht 15 billion (US$405 million), with 4.77 million families owing money to banks. Official figures suggest that a further 2 million farmers owe some Baht 5 billion (US$135m) to loan sharks, at interest rates as high as 25 per cent. NGO estimates are much higher.

The story of a sixty-two-year-old farmer, who hanged himself outside the government house in Bangkok in 1998, is typical. He had borrowed Baht 200,000 (or $5,405) and pledged to pay back the loan at Baht 270,000; but because he was unable to pay off the loan on time, it increased to Baht 370,000. He borrowed the Baht 370,000 from a relative to repay the loan, and lost his land to the relative. Most small farmers are in a similar debt trap where one loan is taken to pay off the previous loan.

Sources: Bello et al. (1999); FAO (forthcoming); *Bangkok Post* (1998a, 1998b, 1999a, 1999b); Interview with Phitthaya Wongkul, Chair of the Thai Development Support Committee (TDSC), February 2000

countries' markets with lower tariffs as a result of the AoA and IMF and World Bank conditionalities. Farmers in developing countries cannot compete and go out of business, destroying local agricultural production, sometimes completely, as imports of 'cheap' subsidized food replace local production.

Developing countries' small farmers have borne the brunt of this unfair trade, as dumped and subsidized products have flooded their domestic markets. Cheap European milk powder has displaced dairy farmers in India and Jamaica, and is threatening the livelihoods of Thai farmers. Corn farmers in Mindanao in the Philippines have been wiped out. It is not uncommon to see farmers there leaving their corn to rot in the fields as domestic corn prices have dropped to levels where they cannot compete. The same scenario has been repeated across Latin America, Africa and Asia, in crops that are vital to small farmers' livelihoods and food security. As a result, more and more farmers have been squeezed out of farming or lost their land.

The Food and Agriculture Organization (FAO 2000) conducted fourteen country case studies across Asia, Latin America and Africa on the effects of liberalization (under structural adjustment as well as WTO commitments) since 1995, when the AoA was implemented. Their findings are disturbing.

- There was a 'general trend towards the consolidation of farms as competitive pressures began to build up following trade liberalisation'.
- This 'led to the displacement and marginalisation of farm labourers, creating hardship that involved typically small farmers and food-insecure population groups, and this in a situation where there are few safety nets'.
- 'While both cultivated area and productivity have been increasing, many small farmers have been marginalised.'
- 'Tariff reductions resulted in a surge of imports of products which were previously locally produced.' In all fourteen countries, food imports in 1995–98 exceeded the 1990–94 level.
- The flood of imports (usually dumped or subsidized crops) 'put pressure on some domestic sectors, affecting rural employment'.
- Key sectors critical to food security and rural employment (e.g. wheat, rice, cotton, onions and potatoes) shrank due to competitive pressures.
- This created problems, because in some cases 'the possibility of diversification away from these crops … is limited'.

Import surges in various sectors led to 'import-competing industries facing consequential difficulties … The fear was expressed that without adequate market protection, accompanied by development programmes, many more domestic products would be displaced, or undermined sharply, leading to a transformation of domestic diets and to increased dependence on imported foods' (ibid.).

For the majority of countries, while food exports are increasing, food imports are rising much faster. Developing countries' share in world food exports has increased from 30 per cent in 1970 to 34 per cent in 1997. But their agri-food imports have increased much more, from 28 per cent to 37 per cent over the same period. Many countries are thus turning from net food exporters into net food importers.

For least developed countries (LDCs) and net-food-importing developing countries, 'cereal import bills are now on a much higher plateau than prior to 1995'. Developing countries experienced a net food deficit of US$13 billion in 1997, and the LDCs' food deficit increased by 60 per cent between 1994 ($1.6 billion) and 1998 ($2.6 billion).

In summary, while a small minority of bigger farmers in the developing world may have benefited from the AoA, it has worsened, not improved, the plight of the majority of resource-poor small farmers (Box 2.1).

The General Agreement on Trade in Services (GATS)

Trade in services was also brought into the GATT for the first time in the Uruguay Round, despite many misgivings among developing countries. Unable to block the GATS, they finally agreed as a compromise that it would have a 'bottom-up' approach rather than the usual across-the-board liberalization approach, so that each member would have the right to decide which sectors, if any, they would open, the pace and extent of the market opening, and the limitations to liberalizing in each sector.

Because of this 'bottom-up' approach, the GATS has been presented by Northern governments as development-friendly. In reality, its very inclusion in the WTO was a huge concession to the developed countries from which developing countries reaped little or no benefit, because of the tremendously unequal competitive positions of service suppliers from the North and South. Developing countries are now being put under enormous pressure to liberalize in many sectors, where they cannot compete. This could destroy existing local services industries, jeopardizing social and development objectives.

Moreover, the agreement acts as a 'ratchet': once a country makes a commitment in a particular sector it can neither breach the commitment nor change it in a way that makes it less favourable to exporters without 'compensating' potential exporters with trade concessions in other areas, or facing trade sanctions if it fails to do so. This applies equally in basic services such as health, education, water and sanitation.

The GATS is all about allowing big business to seize a far greater market share than before, by granting it access to those parts of the economy now controlled by the state, and harmonizing regulatory standards worldwide. Since international trade in services is dominated by a few large MNCs from developed countries, Northern governments are eager to encourage this corporate expansion. Developed countries account for 70 per cent of world exports of services, but only 20 per cent of WTO membership (WTO 2002c). The USA has the largest service exports by a large margin – $263 billion in 2001, compared with $108 billion for its closest competitor, the UK – with a surplus in services trade of $76 billion. The EC accounts for 42 per cent of world trade in services, and service exports account for 7.3 per cent of its GDP (WTO 2002c). Trade Commissioner Pascal Lamy (2000) has publicly announced that the EC has 'offensive export interests' in services.

The massive financial strength, worldwide networks, access to technology and sophisticated IT infrastructure of the major MNCs make it difficult, if not impossible, for developing country providers (mostly small and medium enterprises) to catch up – or in some sectors even to compete with them in their domestic markets. Liberalization has thus aggravated the alarming divide in supply capacity between developed and developing countries.

Since the GATS, developing countries' service imports have surged by 15 per cent (WTO 1999a). Even an upper-middle-income developing country such as Malaysia, despite exporting services, has a deficit in services trade. The Malaysian authorities' own assessment 'had not found that developing countries had benefited from services trade' (WTO 2000a: 7; see also WTO 1999b). Developing countries with less developed services sectors have fared still worse.

Egypt's service imports, for example, increased by 52 per cent between 1996 and 1997 (WTO 1999a).

Developing countries made substantial commitments under GATS with respect to many service industries, often permanently committing themselves to adopting legislation and future policies without having had much experience in their implementation (UNCTAD 1999). A greater proportion of their commitments also included allowing foreign suppliers to establish a commercial presence. They have not, however, received concessions of any meaningful economic value in the main area of interest to them – the movement of people to supply services in other countries. When concessions were made, they were offset by non-transparent barriers, such as economic needs tests, which limit new entrants into a market by reference to existing local capacity, and unspecified immigration rules. Such obstacles have minimized the extent of their commitments. As a result, most developing countries have a deficit in trade in services, except in tourism and travel and workers' remittances. Even an OECD assessment of the GATS, submitted to the Council for Trade in Services by Slovenia, Bulgaria, the Czech Republic, Poland and the Slovak Republic (WTO 2000c: 12), concluded that 'Liberalisation of trade in services within the GATS has not brought about specific tangible results for transition economies.'

Many people in both developed and developing countries are extremely apprehensive about the prospect of further GATS negotiations. Developing countries, in particular, have already had in-depth liberalization experiences as a result of World Bank, IMF and Regional Development Bank conditionalities, often with negative consequences.

- In low-income countries, low domestic savings and weak capital markets prevent local companies from competing with MNCs to take over from government providers. This has increased reliance on foreign investment, and often created a monopolistic environment.
- Governments often find it difficult to sell run-down and indebted enterprises; and when MNCs do take them over, the terms and

conditions are often weighted against the government. When a US company was awarded a contract to develop a power plant in Uganda, for example, the contract required the government to buy all the power produced at a price fixed in foreign exchange, so that the price would rise dramatically in the event of a devaluation (Bayliss 2000).

- Limited institutional capacity to regulate means that regulations are often copied from developed countries, which may not be appropriate for smaller and more monopolistic markets. MNCs' market power also allows them to exert unhealthy influence on regulators – sometimes backed by pressure from their home governments. In Argentina, for example, when the foreign investor involved in railway privatization sought changes in the regulatory framework before the end of its five-year term, its monopolistic position greatly weakened the government's bargaining power. With such power imbalances, regulatory processes may have very little effect (Wells 1999).

- While it is often assumed that the private sector (appropriately regulated) is substitutable for the state as a service provider, private companies typically prefer to provide services only in areas where they are profitable, and to charge all consumers at commercial rates. Cross-subsidization, often practised by governments, is less likely, especially in an environment of deregulation and where services are unbundled,[2] leaving rural areas and low-income households without access to basic services.

Before Doha, many developing country delegates were eager to see various issues dealt with before market access negotiations began – not least the assessment of the effects of trade in services, required by the GATS itself before a new round of negotiations could begin. Article XIX.3 of the Agreement states that 'For each round, negotiating guidelines and procedures shall be established. For the purposes of establishing such guidelines, the Council for Trade in Services shall carry out an assessment of trade in services in overall terms and on a sectoral basis with reference to the objectives of this Agreement, including those set out in paragraph 1 of Article IV.'

Developing country delegates have repeatedly raised the importance of such an assessment in GATS talks in Geneva for several years, and continued before and after Doha. Their efforts, however, have been blocked by key developed countries. As WTO analyst and former Indian Ambassador B. L. Das observes,

> There is no specific recognition of the fact that the liberalisation process undertaken so far has clearly been one-sided in the sense that the benefits have mainly accrued to the major developed countries, because of their having enormous supply capacity in the services area. A quantitative assessment would have helped to know the benefits of liberalisation. Qualitatively, however, one can easily say that [developing countries] have not got any significant gains so far because of their weak supply capacity. (Das 2002)

Developing countries also wanted an emergency safeguard mechanism (ESM) to be put in place, to provide an exit strategy if liberalization had adverse effects. While this is also mandated in the GATS Agreement, there has been no political will on the part of the major powers, and the original 1998 deadline has been repeatedly rescheduled. The current timeline is that an ESM should be agreed by 15 March 2004.

The third issue developing countries made submissions on before Doha was credit for autonomous liberalization. Since the GATS Agreement, many developing countries have been forced to liberalize trade in services under World Bank and IMF structural adjustment programmes; and they wanted this 'autonomous liberalization' to be usable as a bargaining chip in negotiations. The major powers, clearly unwilling to move on this matter, threw several spanners in the works, asking for developing countries to 'bind' their liberalization under the GATS in order to receive this credit, and asking for such a 'credit' scheme also to apply to developed countries. It was finally agreed that binding would not be required, but that it would be taken into account in determining the extent of a country's credit. This largely defeated the purpose of the exercise, leaving developing countries dependent on bilateral negotiations.

Trade-Related Aspects of Intellectual Property Rights (TRIPs)

The TRIPs Agreement has generated heated controversy, contributing significantly to the WTO's negative reputation. Like trade in services, intellectual property rights (IPR) were brought into the GATT/WTO framework for the first time in the Uruguay Round, at the behest of MNCs in the pharmaceutical and information technology industries, particularly in the USA, which claimed they were suffering huge losses from inadequate protection of their intellectual property abroad. These MNCs drafted the basic language for the negotiations.

The developing countries fought against the TRIPs Agreement, arguing that it would benefit MNCs while preventing their own companies from copying technologies in order to develop, as had been done historically in the industrialized countries. The USA, Germany, Japan and Korea, for example, all industrialized largely by copying existing product and/or process technologies; and this also provided much of the impetus for China's recent spectacular growth in its early stages. But the late industrializer's 'technological diffusion' is the industrial leader's piracy. As Walden Bello observes, 'TRIPs enables the technological leader, the US, to greatly influence the pace of technological and industrial development in rival industrialised countries, the newly industrialised countries, and the third world' (Bello 2000).

The developing countries' resistance was overcome, however, by a powerful US-led campaign, and the TRIPs Agreement came into effect in 1995. It sets high standards of protection for patents, copyrights, trademarks, and industrial design and licences, allowing patents to be granted on products and processes for twenty years, including on seeds, pharmaceuticals, genes and diagnostic tests, and minor innovations which are more 'discoveries' than 'inventions'.

The TRIPs Agreement has been justified on the grounds that it balances the interests of rights-holders and consumers, and encourages investment in research and development (R&D). In practice, however, its effects on R&D are at best unproven and ambiguous (for example, it discourages collaboration and information-sharing in research); and it arguably tilts the balance in favour of rights-holders, rather than the public.

Several analysts have recommended the removal of TRIPs from the WTO on the grounds that, unlike other WTO Agreements, it does not promote free trade. Rather, by granting strong patent rights to those who produce patentable ideas (primarily MNCs), it gives them a monopoly against potential competitors. Even free-trade advocate Jagdish Bhagwati has described the WTO's intellectual property protection as a 'tax' that most poor countries pay on their use of knowledge, 'constituting an unrequited transfer to the rich, producing countries' (Sexton 2001: 10). Moreover, while the WTO is based on the principle of reciprocal obligations and benefits, the TRIPs has proven to be one-sided, benefiting only the industrialized countries with technological capacity, while developing countries bear the costs (Khor 2002).

The issue of patenting of life forms under the TRIPs Agreement (Article 27.3b) has received widespread criticism. As well as raising fundamental ethical issues, such as the patenting of the human genome, this has facilitated 'biopiracy' – the patenting of life forms, including plants and their medicinal functions, which had previously been available for public use.

Biotechnology MNCs such as Monsanto may alter very slightly seeds that have been bred by farmers for hundreds of years, and patent them for twenty years. These patented seeds are then sold to farmers worldwide, who are not allowed to follow the conventional practice of using seeds from one year's harvest for their next year's planting. As the industrial form of agricultural production spreads, and farmers purchase 'high-yielding' seeds[3] from agri-business corporations, MNCs gain increasing control and monopoly power over the world's genetic resources, increasing the prices charged to farmers.

A review of Article 27.3b has been under way since 1999, but has not been completed because the industrialized countries do not want any loosening of the TRIPs rules. In the review, the Africa Group, for example, has taken a strong position that patents on all life forms and genetic resources should be prohibited, and called for a moratorium on implementing the TRIPs Agreement until the completion of the review.

The most controversial issue relating to the TRIPs Agreement, however, has been its implications for access to medicines and public health. By extending patent protection for pharmaceuticals internationally and blocking imports of low-cost generic copies of patented drugs, it increases drug prices considerably, pushing them beyond the reach of most people in developing countries. This was a key issue at the Doha Ministerial.

The profile of this issue was raised dramatically by the crisis caused by the HIV epidemic, and the inability of people with HIV in developing countries to afford the cocktail of antiretrovirals (ARVs) they needed. In Sub-Saharan Africa alone, 29.4 million people are living with HIV/AIDS, with infection rates of 30–40 per cent in several countries; and the epidemic is fast taking hold in other regions, including Eastern Europe, Central Asia, China and India. Only a tiny fraction of the tens of millions of people in need of ARVs are receiving them, however, largely as a result of unaffordable prices. (The US price was around $10,000 per patient per year in 2001.)

In principle, the TRIPs Agreement allows governments to issue a compulsory licence to produce generic copies of patented drugs locally, predominantly for the domestic market, if a voluntary licence on reasonable commercial terms has been rejected, or in other specific circumstances[4] – although 'adequate remuneration must still be paid to the patent holder, taking into account the economic value of the authorization' (WHO/WTO 2002: para. 61). Apart from these restrictions, however, a number of limitations remain. The requirement that production is predominantly for the local market prevents developing countries without a local pharmaceutical industry, or without an adequate local market to make production viable, from benefiting.

While proponents of access to drugs have been very active, they face a formidable opponent. The pharmaceutical MNCs see the better-off (about the top 5 per cent of the population) in developing countries as an important growth market, and are therefore anxious to retain their monopoly on medicines for conditions which affect higher-income groups as well as the poor, such as diabetes, asthma, hypertension, etc. (Baker 2002). The last thing they want is for generic producers to supply this market with cheap drugs.

The largest US drug companies made a profit of $37 billion in 2001, about $7 billion of which came from sales in developing countries, representing an annual rate of return of 39 per cent – the highest of any industry. They guard this position jealously, through well-resourced industrial associations that lobby actively at the national and international levels. According to analyst Brook Baker, 'the US government in general and the US Trade Representative in particular act as proxies for the US pharmaceutical industry – the largest lobby group, the most profitable industry and the most generous campaign contributor in the world' (ibid.).

Both the USA and the pharmaceutical industry have been pro-active in promoting still stronger patent protection for pharmaceuticals. The pharmaceutical MNCs took the South African government to court in 2001 to prevent it from introducing a law that allowed compulsory licensing. And the USA has taken advantage of the need for developing countries to introduce new patent laws to implement their obligations under the TRIPs Agreement to pressurize them to implement legislation that goes far beyond what the TRIPs Agreement requires ('TRIPs-Plus').

The new issues

As noted earlier, successive rounds of multilateral trade negotiations since the 1960s have progressively extended the scope of the GATT/WTO system. At the First WTO Ministerial in Singapore in 1996, the EC pushed aggressively to extend the scope further by introducing new agreements in investment, competition and government procurement. Together with trade facilitation, these are referred to as the 'Singapore issues' or 'new issues'. These issues are essentially about removing any domestic legislation in developing countries that favours local companies over foreign companies. The developed countries want these agreements situated in the WTO because of the principle of national treatment and the most favoured nation (MFN) principle.[5]

Despite the opposition of the developing country majority, the EC secured 'agreement' on launching working groups to study these issues (though not to negotiate on them) through a process of informal 'green room' meetings, excluding most delegations, before and during the Singapore Ministerial. Since then, pressure to launch negotiations in these areas has increased continuously, particularly before each ministerial. While the USA strongly supports negotiations on government procurement and trade facilitation, it has been more reticent about investment and competition. Nevertheless, realizing the potential for US/EC differences to break the negotiations, it has supported the EC on the whole 'new issues' package.

The 'new issues' were a key battlegound in Doha, where it was agreed (again despite developing country opposition) that negotiations would take place on the 'new issues' after the Fifth Ministerial in Mexico in 2003, based on explicit consensus on the modalities of negotiations (see Chapters 4–5).

Investment and competition

Before the Singapore Ministerial, work on investment and competition policy within the WTO had largely taken the form of specific responses to specific trade policy issues. Some (mainly developed) member countries, however, want to harmonize rules in these areas within the framework of the multilateral trading system, so as to reduce anti-competitive practices and to improve investment opportunities and rules as they relate to international trade.

The EC, the leading proponent of agreements on these issues, sees them as working in tandem: while an investment agreement would ensure investors' rights in a host country, a competition agreement would oblige host countries to institute domestic competition legislation requiring changes to laws that directly or indirectly disadvantaged foreign companies. The EC wants to house competition rules in the WTO because of the national treatment and MFN principles, and justifies this by arguing that 'private barriers' which engender uncompetitive practices can offset the benefits of trade liberalization.

In a 1999 submission to the WTO working group on trade

and competition policy, the EC stated that there should not be either *de jure* or *de facto*[6] discrimination between local and foreign companies. The EC cited the GATS definition of national treatment, that 'formally identical or formally different treatment shall be considered to be less favourable if it modifies the conditions in favour of services or service suppliers of the Member compared to like services or service suppliers of any other Members'.[7] They also want domestic competition laws to treat hard-core cartels (groups of powerful MNCs which keep their prices artificially high by working together through bid-rigging, price-fixing, etc.) as a serious breach of competition law.

The USA is unenthusiastic about a competition agreement, which could curtail its current use and abuse of anti-dumping rules and put its anti-trust laws into question. While it is also less than keen on an investment agreement, it wants any such agreement to include portfolio investment as well as foreign direct investment (FDI),[8] and ultimately investor-state dispute settlement (as in NAFTA). These are very controversial issues.

The majority of developing countries in the WTO oppose agreements on investment and competition. World Bank studies indicate that favourable policies towards FDI are less important in determining inflows than other factors such as strong domestic markets and macroeconomic and political stability (Bachmann and Kwaku 1994; Bergsman and Shen 1995). It is not surprising, therefore, that FDI in African countries that have fully liberalized is much less than that to Asian economies that retain stricter regulations. Moreover, unless FDI is carefully regulated and fits well into a host country's development programme, technology transfer and other economic benefits may not take place, and the effect may merely be to 'crowd out' local investment. Foreign investment also arguably played an important role in the Asian financial crisis of the late 1990s (Woodward 2001).

On competition, as the Dutch delegation to the WTO has observed: 'A big problem is that a large number of developing countries do not have competition laws nor authorities in place at present' (Permanent Mission of the Netherlands in Geneva 2001). As many as sixty developing country members are in this situation.

Even where competition authorities do exist, there is huge diversity in terms of their understanding, capability and ability to implement vital functions. Even some upper-middle-income countries such as Malaysia have only recently put in place fair practices legislation. Malaysia has yet to establish a competition commission, while Thailand's new commission is still grappling with its 'rather unfamiliar mandate' (WTO 2002d).

Transparency in government procurement

Government procurement covers all purchasing activities of governmental authorities, for everything from pencils and paper clips to computer systems, telecommunications equipment and consulting services. Typically, this accounts for between 10 and 15 per cent of GDP for developed countries, and up to 20 per cent of GDP for some developing countries. While the WTO already has an Agreement on Government Procurement, this is only a *plurilateral* agreement – that is, only some members (the EC and about a dozen others) have so far signed it. The main area of work for the working group set up in Singapore is the study of government procurement practices, taking into account national preferential procurement policies. The second area of work is to develop elements for inclusion in a possible agreement.

In talks in Geneva, developing countries have made clear the need to protect government procurement, as this is now one of the few policy tools still available for developing countries to pursue their socio-economic and development objectives. Precisely because of the significant markets involved, however, the EC and USA would like to see the plurilateral agreement become a multilateral agreement applying to all WTO members, as this would increase market opportunities for their own firms. So far, they have couched their arguments in terms of a 'transparency' agreement, with no consequences for market access. Internal EC documents produced by the European Commission after the Singapore Ministerial, however, leave no doubt that the EC sees this as a first step towards an agreement covering market access (Raghavan 2002d).

An agreement on transparency in government procurement is

thus a first step towards ensuring that all goods and services purchased by governments are subject to international bidding. Once it was expanded to include 'market access', national governments would no longer be able to use government procurement to support local companies or as an instrument of regional policy or affirmative action for disadvantaged minorities.

Trade facilitation

The 1996 Singapore Ministerial also instructed the WTO Goods Council to start exploratory and analytical work on trade facilitation. This refers to simplification, harmonization and automation of import and export procedures, reduced documentation, and increased transparency. The EC argues that a WTO Agreement on Trade Facilitation is needed because inefficient and unnecessary procedures impede trade flows. 'Everyone would benefit from a push to simplify trade procedures, cutting out unnecessary bureaucracy via modern methods ... Traders both big and small would enjoy reduced costs and fewer delays, which means more competitive terms of trade' (DG Trade 2001).

According to the WTO (2001b), the average customs transaction involves between twenty and thirty different parties, forty documents, 200 data elements (thirty of which are repeated at least thirty times) and the rekeying of 60–70 per cent of all data at least once. With the lowering of tariffs across the globe, the cost of complying with customs formalities has been reported in many instances to exceed the cost of duties. The WTO also argues that red tape at borders limits the ability of small and medium-sized enterprises to participate in international trade, and impedes fast and predictable delivery of goods, essential in the modern business environment.

The EC wants an agreement encompassing:

- application of key WTO principles – MFN, national treatment and transparency;
- harmonization and simplification of documents and data, so as to reduce delays and costs to traders and assist in the introduction of automated procedures;
- modern customs and management techniques, e.g. pertaining

to pre-arrival processing, post-release payment, time limits for release, etc.;

• automation and convergence of official controls – commitments to introduce automation over time, replacing paper procedures, so as to speed up transactions, and allow for seamless integrated transactions between exporting and importing administrations; and

• coordinated capacity-building to strengthen human and physical infrastructure and improve import and export management in developing countries.

Behind these rather beguiling objectives of facilitating trade, however, lies a different agenda: to limit the ability of customs authorities to question the transaction value declared by Northern MNCs, to prevent unfair transfer pricing.[9] This issue has been on the table since the Tokyo Round, when the Quad tried to push through 'rules' that would virtually disarm the customs administrations of developing countries and force them to accept the invoices of MNCs and their agents unquestioningly as 'transaction values'. This was rejected by a coalition of developing countries, and a customs valuation code was adopted, allowing developing countries a certain amount of autonomy in demanding proof of the transaction value claimed. The ability of importing countries to challenge transaction values, however, was further curtailed by the Uruguay Round agreements on customs valuation and preshipment inspection (Raghavan 2002e).

Implementation issues – addressing the imbalances of the Uruguay Round

A key priority for developing countries is the implementation of the Uruguay Round agreements, many of which contain provisions that discriminate against their interests while favouring developed countries, or whose provisions have not been implemented by the developed countries. 'Implementation issues' include:

• correcting imbalances in individual agreements that have in-stitutionalized existing trade imbalances;

- ensuring that developed countries implement their commitments to developing countries in good faith;
- a standstill and rollback of various WTO agreements, for example the Trade-Related Investment Measures (TRIMs) Agreement, where developing countries want the continued use of local content requirements[10] to be permitted; and
- operationalization of Special and Differential Treatment provisions for developing countries (see below).

In fact, implementation issues have been on the agenda since as far back as 1982.[11] Even then, developing countries were asking for their interests to be reflected in the GATT agreements, particularly in textiles and clothing, tropical products, subsidies, anti-dumping, and Special and Differential Treatment. When pressure from the major powers mounted to launch the Uruguay Round, the developing countries demanded that these implementation issues should be addressed before taking on new issues. As now, they were told that their concerns would be taken on board only in the context of a full round. Twenty years later, the same concerns remain on the table – together with new implementation issues resulting from the imbalances in the Uruguay Round agreements, e.g. on agriculture, services, TRIPs and TRIMs.

Despite their promises of liberalization, the developed countries have, for example, increased the level of protection and subsidization in agriculture (see above), while the Agreement on Textiles and Clothing allows them to hold on to most of their quantitative restrictions on textiles (banned for other goods) until 2005. According to Finger and Schuler (2000), 'What the industrialized countries promised in agriculture and in textiles and clothing is still more a promise than a reality.'

Similarly, the Sanitary and Phytosanitary (SPS) Agreement requires agricultural exports to meet the standards laid down by standard-setting bodies such as the Codex Alimentarius (the joint WHO/FAO body responsible for setting food safety standards), which are dominated by developed country experts, many from the corporate sector. Before Seattle, India sought a decision that only standards developed by relevant international bodies *with the involvement of developing countries* would be treated as international standards for the purposes of the SPS and Technical Barriers to Trade (TBT) agreements. This was refused by the major powers.

As a result, the standards put in place are more or less those of the developed countries, and difficult for developing countries to implement because of their limited technical capacity and the high financial cost. The SPS Agreement has thus become a tool by which developed country governments and their corporations restrict exports from the South, and such 'trade harassment' places a heavy burden on developing countries (FAO 2000).[12]

Developing countries have raised the 'implementation issues' at every WTO ministerial since Singapore in 1996. Before Seattle, the Like-Minded Group compiled a list of about 100 items of implementation concern. These were supposed to be dealt with as part of the post-Seattle 'confidence-building package', and the General Council undertook on 3 May 2000 to 'take decisions for appropriate action not later than the Fourth Session of the Ministerial Conference' (the Doha Ministerial). At the end of 2000, after a year of 'confidence-building', the developed countries struggled to come up with agreements on five items, all of which were fairly insignificant in trade terms. Such mean results were seen more as an insult than as a confidence-building measure in the developing world.

Special and Differential Treatment – a public relations exercise?

The concept of 'Special and Differential Treatment' (SDT) in international economic relations emerged in the period after World War II, when developing countries (mainly in Latin America) challenged the assumption that trade liberalization on a most favoured nation basis would automatically lead to their growth and development. This position gathered support in Asia and Africa as more developing countries gained their independence. Developing countries argued that special treatment was needed to allow them to improve their terms of trade, reduce their dependence on exports of primary commodities, and industrialize through infant industry protection (Gibbs 1998).

As a result, under the GATT before the Uruguay Round, developing country members were given flexibility in their tariff structures; the right to use quantitative restrictions to deal with balance of payments problems; the right to maintain tariffs to protect 'infant industries'; and the right to offer government support to their domestic industries using various industrial and trade policy measures.

The USA has generally been unsympathetic to SDT provisions, however, seeing them as introducing an inappropriate two-track approach to WTO agreements. It prefers instead to integrate all members completely – apparently forgetting that agriculture and textiles agreements have been a derogation of the GATT for fifty-five years because of their and other developed countries' interests.

Accordingly, SDT was considerably watered down in the Uruguay Round, provisions being included *ad hoc* in each agreement, with no overall coherence or real integration of development concerns into the agreements. SDT measures were limited to:

- allowing longer timeframes for developing countries to implement WTO commitments, mostly expiring by 2005;
- limiting developing countries' obligations to two-thirds of those undertaken by developed countries in certain agreements; and
- 'best endeavour' language, calling on, but not requiring, developed countries to consider developing countries' development interests before taking any actions that might impede their trade.

The majority of these 'best endeavour' provisions have not been implemented,[13] and in practice seem to serve a public relations purpose rather than being of any real value.

Moreover, the developed countries are trying to 'roll back' SDT, even attacking weak SDT provisions such as longer implementation periods. Since 1997, the USA has taken the position that *no* transition period should extend beyond 2005 (USTR 1997) – although they relented somewhat on LDCs' obligations under the TRIPs Agreement following the public relations fiasco of the TRIPs and public health issue in Doha (see Chapter 4).

Notes

1. Tariff peaks are tariffs well above the average level in a country, often imposed by developed countries on 'sensitive' products, particularly where developing countries have a comparative advantage. Tariff escalation refers to the imposition of higher tariffs on a product in a processed form than in an unprocessed form (e.g. low tariffs on coffee beans but high tariffs on ground coffee), which is a serious obstacle to the development of processing industries in developing countries and diversification into higher value-added production.

2. Unbundling refers to the division of a service sector into component parts, each provided by a different provider. This often happens when privatization takes place.

3. These seeds are in fact 'high-yielding' only because they require high chemical inputs.

4. These circumstances are 'national emergencies', 'other cases of extreme urgency', 'public non-commercial use' and anti-competitive practices. None of these terms is defined.

5. National treatment means that foreign goods and services should be given at least as favourable treatment as that given to equivalent locally produced goods and services. The most favoured nation (MFN) principle means that a concession given to one WTO member should be extended to all members.

6. *De jure* discrimination refers to rules that *explicitly* discriminate between local and foreign companies. *De facto* discrimination means that rules are discriminatory *in their effects*.

7. However, in 2002 the EC made it clear that they wanted all countries to incorporate *de jure* national treatment into their domestic competition laws, but that they would not seek *de facto* national treatment.

8. FDI is investment by foreign companies or individuals in productive capacity, either by buying existing companies or facilities or by building new facilities. Portfolio investment is investment in financial instruments such as shares accounting for less that 10 per cent of the value of a company.

9. Transfer pricing refers to the manipulation by MNCs of prices on sales between different parts of the same company in different countries, as a means of transferring profits invisibly between countries. This is usually motivated by a desire to escape taxation and/or exchange controls.

10. Local content requirements require a foreign investor to use a certain percentage of locally produced material in assembling the final

product, to help local industry, provide employment and build domestic manufacturing capacity. Such requirements are now prohibited under the TRIMs Agreement.

11. A joint statement was issued by India on behalf of an informal group of developing countries in November 1984, stressing the need for implementation of prior commitments by developed countries (Yu 2002b).

12. The use of SPS standards to block exports from developing countries is a regular complaint. According to a Chilean negotiator, when the EC changes its standards, Chilean producers scramble to meet the new standards, only for them to be changed again.

13. Examples include Article X.1 of the SPS Agreement, Article XV of the Anti-Dumping Agreement and Article XXI of the Dispute Settlement Understanding.

THREE
Setting the stage – the pre-Doha mini-ministerial meetings

In theory, major WTO decisions are made at ministerial meetings, such as those in Seattle and Doha, and they are made by consensus. Nothing is agreed unless and until everyone agrees on it.

The reality, of course, is very different. The conflicting agendas and interests of the countries involved, the dynamics of negotiations between 145 ministers, and the limited time available at ministerial meetings, create a boiler room atmosphere at the conferences.

Thus if the WTO is ever to agree on anything, much of the discussion has to take place before the ministerial. However, pre-ministerial negotiations take the form of political manoeuvring by pairs and small groups of countries in private and semi-private meetings, often behind closed doors. This sets the scene for the ministerial itself, and in many ways is as important to the final outcome as what happens at the ministerial.

The WTO is supposed to operate on the principle of 'one country one vote', and the big players – the USA and the EC – represent a small minority of the membership. As the story of the pre-Doha process shows, a central theme of the negotiation process is how the USA and the EC contrive to get what they want, despite their lack of votes. The process develops into a game for high stakes, between unequally matched teams, where much of the game is played with few rules and no referee.

This chapter outlines the process leading up to the WTO's Fourth Ministerial Conference in Doha, Qatar (9–14 November 2001). It begins with a historical parallel to the pre-Doha process – a brief summary of the process leading up to the negotiations to establish the International Monetary Fund and the World Bank in 1944. It moves on to an overview of the agendas of the different players in the process, and the approach taken to WTO negotiations by

the major players – the USA and the EC. It then goes step by step
through the process towards Doha: from the mini-ministerials in
Mexico and Singapore to the production of the final draft ministerial
declaration for the Doha conference. It concludes with an assessment of the outcome from various perspectives.

The prelude to Bretton Woods

The story of the build-up to Doha bears striking parallels with
the process leading up to the negotiations on the establishment
of the International Monetary Fund (IMF) and the World Bank at
Bretton Woods, New Hampshire in July 1944. For all the political
and economic changes of the last sixty years – particularly the end
of colonialism and the development of international institutions – it
appears that the process of international negotiations on economic
issues has changed little. The summary of the pre-Bretton Woods
negotiations below, based on Robert Skidelsky's eloquent account
in *John Maynard Keynes – Fighting for Britain, 1937 to 1946* (Skidelsky
2000: Ch. 10), may therefore provide a useful backdrop to the discussion of the pre-Doha process that follows.

By April 1944, the USA and the UK had finalized the principles
on which an International Monetary Fund would be formed in a
'Joint Statement by Experts'. The US government was committed
to it, the British government not quite, although the hurdles were
generally minor. The International Bank for Reconstruction and
Development (the World Bank), on the other hand, remained more
of a US Treasury proposal at this stage.

For the Fund to be established, however, other countries would
need to accept the proposal. To this end, the US Secretary of State
at the time, Cordell Hull, invited forty-four nations to participate in
negotiations at Bretton Woods. The key players in the negotiation
process were Harry Dexter White (Director of Monetary Research
to the US Treasury, considered in all but name the Assistant Secretary to the Treasury) and John Maynard Keynes, a highly acclaimed
British intellectual and an unofficial, but hugely influential, adviser
to the British Chancellor of the Exchequer (Finance Minister).

In June 1944, John Maynard Keynes boarded a boat headed for

the United Sates with a team of negotiators and experts from the UK and allied countries – the Netherlands, Belgium, Greece, Norway, Czechoslovakia, India and China – most of whom were on a smaller drafting committee that was to meet in Atlantic City, New Jersey before the main conference at Bretton Woods commenced. By the time they arrived in Atlantic City, this team had produced two 'boat drafts', on the Fund and the Bank.

The British wanted to have Greece and India on the committee, but White thought 'the Greeks were nothing but stooges for the British', and made it clear he would accept Indian delegates only as members of the British team. (India was at the time under British colonial rule.) The rather snooty letter from Sir John Anderson, the British Chancellor of the Exchequer, to US Treasury Secretary Henry Morgenthau, which brought these exchanges to a close, prompted White to exclaim: 'God how they must treat their colonies!' Conversely, Keynes thought it outrageous that White selected Cuba to be on the smaller committee while leaving the Netherlands out. White's brutal response was that the role of Cuba on this smaller committee was merely to provide cigars.

In Atlantic City, Keynes presented the 'boat drafts' to White at a private meeting. White had divided seventy-five experts from seventeen countries into four specialist groups that would go through all the suggested amendments to the joint statement, reporting back once a day to a general meeting of all participants. In parallel with this process, the British and Americans met bilaterally, to resolve the key disagreements between themselves before they proceeded to the 'monkey house' (the general meeting) at Bretton Woods. They would present the alternatives to the 'monkey house', having already agreed which alternatives they would drop or press. White realized that nothing on the Fund or the Bank would get through without British support, so he tried – as far as his abrasive nature would allow – to charm Keynes, and soon they began to click as human beings.

Time constraints prevented the production of a streamlined Anglo-American document at Atlantic City. According to one of Keynes's team members, however, the main achievement at Atlantic City had been to consolidate 'the friendly understanding between ourselves and the American technical experts', with most of the issues of principle resolved.

Agendas: who wanted what in Doha?

The EC's agenda, according to a pre-Seattle press release, is to 'sharpen' and 'refocus' its trade policy, 'making it more effective at opening foreign markets which European companies consider most vital to their exports'. This strategy involved identification of 'the most stubborn obstacles in specific countries that are hindering trade and investment', and employing 'the most effective trade instrument' to ensure 'swifter, more coherent and more coordinated action to remove those barriers' (European Commission 1996). While the EC continued to assert this agenda aggressively after Seattle, it couched it in such a way as to make it appear beneficial for developing countries.

The EC has always been keen on the launch of a comprehensive new round that includes negotiations on all the 'new issues' (competition, investment, trade facilitation and transparency in government procurement). The scrapping of export subsidies in agriculture was never a favourite subject; but due to a strong environmental lobby, they wanted greater ambition on the links between trade and the environment. The EC supported lowering of industrial tariffs by developing countries and strengthening labour standards within the global trading arena, stressing that the WTO should work closely on the latter with the International Labour Organization (ILO), the UN body responsible for labour issues.

The USA, on the other hand, favoured a round that focused mainly on further liberalization in the established areas of agriculture, services and industrial tariffs. The scrapping of export subsidies in agriculture was a key US aim. Among the 'new issues', they were especially keen advocates of transparency in government procurement and trade facilitation, as US-based multinational corporations (MNCs) were very eager to ensure the existence of rules in these two areas, but they could do without competition and investment policy. Linking trade and environment has never been a US priority, and the USA had backed down on labour standards after President

Clinton met stiff opposition from developing countries when he tried to push the topic at the 1999 Seattle Ministerial. It has also not been a priority for the Bush administration.

Most developing countries rejected the idea of launching a new round of negotiations, particularly on the 'new issues', instead wanting a greater focus on implementation issues stemming from the Uruguay Round. Singapore, Mexico, Korea, Morocco and South Africa, however, supported the new issues; and some Latin American countries, such as Argentina, Brazil, Paraguay, Uruguay, Bolivia and Chile, while not active promoters of a comprehensive trade round, were willing to accept it provided the agenda included an end to all farm subsidies (WSJ 2001). Many developing countries reject negotiations on environment and labour standards in the WTO, seeing them as a form of back-door protectionism.

organizations and non-governmental organizations have an important role to play in improving the situation.'

MNCs also play an important role in lobbying developing country delegates and the chairs of committees whose deliberations affect their commercial interests. A developing country delegate highlighted one instance. 'The Zimbabwe mission experienced lobbying from multinationals first hand. The ambassador was the Chairman of the TRIPs Council pre-Doha [when the interpretation of the TRIPs Agreement in relation to pharmaceuticals was a key issue of discussion] … He received many invitations for lunch and supper from pharmaceutical company officials. I don't think in this case their lobbying was effective because we [developing countries] got the preferred language we wanted on TRIPs and public health at the Doha Conference.'

In this case, their efforts may have been frustrated in part by the high level of public awareness of and concern about the TRIPs and pharmaceutical issue. On other, lower-profile issues, their lobbying may have been more successful.

Developing countries generally emphasized the need for greater market access for agricultural products in the North, and in particular phasing out by developed countries of tariff peaks, tariff escalation and export subsidies, particularly on agricultural produce (see Chapter 2). They wanted to limit the major developed countries' abuse of anti-dumping procedures[1] (tariffs imposed on imports which the recipient country considers to be 'dumped' at prices below the cost of production, permissible under WTO rules) to keep out developing country exports; and they complained that the gradual replacement of textile quotas with tariffs, agreed in the Uruguay Round, had generally excluded products they supplied, rendering the agreement useless, and wanted this reversed.[2] They also sought greater commitment to the principle of Special and Differential Treatment, and measures to address their supply-side constraints. A major concern of developing countries is that the 'benefits' of trade liberalization – market access – have not been reaped in real terms. Even when markets are opened to them, developing countries, particularly lower-income countries, are hampered by supply-side constraints. Technical and food standards have also often been used opportunistically by developed countries to block exports, nullifying the market opening.

On the high-profile issue of TRIPs and public health, they sought wider application of the options in the existing TRIPs Agreement to allow them to override patent rights of large pharmaceutical companies and produce or import generic versions of essential drugs. In the GATS negotiations on trade in services, their main area of interest was 'movement of natural persons' (Mode IV), where they had requested greater liberalization from developed countries, so that skilled workers from the South could move more freely to offer their services in the North.

As well as the agendas of WTO members, those of big business leaders, and particularly multinational companies, are also of great significance. Clearly companies in different sectors have specific interests in different areas of the WTO's work. Common themes, however, are further liberalization of trade in goods and services and the removal of barriers to foreign direct investment. MNCs in general were keen supporters of a new round, but generally suspicious of the inclusion of labour standards or the environment in negotiations.

The prelude to Doha – widening the circle

As noted at the beginning of this chapter, the major players – primarily the USA and the EC – face a major challenge in WTO negotiations. They are a small minority in a one-member-one-vote organization where most other members have very different agendas and objectives. Their strategy to deal with this situation revolves around winning over successive groups of countries, starting with the most powerful and those with whom they have the most common ground (see Figure 3.1). As they enlarge the support base for their agenda, so it becomes more difficult for others, especially the

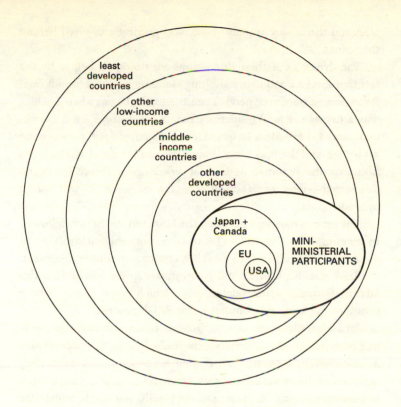

Figure 3.1 Circles of power

less influential, to resist their advance, even if they have strength in numbers.

As at Bretton Woods, much of the pre-ministerial negotiation takes place bilaterally between the two leading players (then the USA and the UK, now the USA and the EC), to resolve major differences before others have a say. US Trade Representative (USTR) Robert Zoellick spent much time in face-to-face and telephone meetings with EC Trade Commissioner Pascal Lamy in preparation for the mini-ministerial meetings. 'That has been a vital part of our strategy related to a WTO round because if the EC and the United States are at loggerheads they are not likely to be successful' (Zoellick 2001). The differences in positions that do emerge between the

USA and the EC are usually slight, and generally resolved behind the scenes.

The dynamics of these discussions are no doubt helped by the fact that Zoellick and Lamy are long-standing personal friends (and fellow long-distance runners). Their friendship began when Zoellick was a negotiator for Presidents Reagan and George Bush Senior, and Lamy EC President Jacques Delors' Chief of Staff, between the mid-1980s and the mid-1990s. Lamy spent a weekend at Zoellick's home on the Potomac River near Washington before Doha, no doubt exchanging marathon-running tips between the discussions of trade issues.

The private meetings between the USA and the EC are followed by meetings with Canada and Japan, often with the full involvement of the WTO Secretariat, to establish common positions. Together, the USA, the EC, Canada and Japan make up the 'Quad' (Quadrilateral) Group – a formidable bloc, which often shares similar positions publicly, and dominates the WTO process.

An added advantage for the Quad is that those countries seeking accession to the EC follow the EC's line in the negotiations almost entirely, knowing that, if their accession is successful, they will have the same trade policies as the EC – and, perhaps more importantly, fearing that failing to toe the EC line might jeopardize their prospects of joining the EC at all.

The Quad meetings represent a stepping-stone between the US–EC bilaterals and the 'mini-ministerial' meetings. Two mini-ministerials took place before the WTO Doha Ministerial Conference, in Mexico at the end of August 2001, and in Singapore on 13–14 October 2001. The key players, as ever, were the USA and the EC, and the theatrics and the power politics were almost identical to the process leading to Bretton Woods – although developing countries are now involved in the WTO process in their own right, rather than remaining largely dormant and merely supporting one or other of the key players.

Mini-ministerials represent an opportunity to extend the common ground beyond the inner circle of the Quad. Participation is by invitation only, but invitations are extended to a slightly wider circle of countries, usually including some developing countries – primarily those dubbed 'friendlies', such as South Africa, and those such as India and Brazil who, though more 'difficult', are too large to be safely ignored. Who issues the invitations, as discussed below, is not always clear.

A developing country WTO delegate interviewed for this book recalled that mini-meetings had been organized in Frankfurt and Geneva not long before the Mexico meeting. These did not achieve the results the major developed countries wanted, however, because some Geneva-based delegates were sent to represent invited ministers. The choice of more distant locations such as Singapore and Mexico for mini-ministerials was the start of a concerted effort by the Quad and the top Secretariat staff to involve ministers rather than ambassadors from key developing countries in the pre-Doha negotiations. Some developing country ambassadors believe this was because most of their ministers are less familiar with the details of the issues than negotiators who deal with them every day, and they are more susceptible to short-term political pressures, and therefore more easily manipulated.

This strategy by the Quad and the Secretariat had some success. As the same delegate observed, 'Things started to go the way of those in favour of the "new issues" after the Mexico mini-meeting … People started to see things differently.'

The Mexico mini-ministerial

The mini-ministerial in Mexico was attended by thirty-one out of 142 WTO members at the time (counting the EC as fifteen). The participants were the USA, the EC, Canada, Japan, Argentina, Egypt, Jamaica, South Africa, Tanzania, India, Hong Kong, Singapore, Switzerland, Uruguay, Mexico, Brazil and Australia.

Key Secretariat staff members also attended, as did the chair of the General Council at the time, Stuart Harbinson (Hong Kong ambassador for seven years until September 2002, and a former UK colonial administrator). Harbinson later emphasized, however, that he had attended only as a representative of Hong Kong, sitting behind his minister during discussions, as he 'did not feel it appropriate' to attend in his capacity as General Council chair.[3]

Participation in the Mexico meeting was strongly skewed towards the developed countries (Table 3.1). All the Quad members were present, together with three of the twelve other OECD countries, and two out of twelve other high-income countries. At the other end of the scale, Tanzania was the only one of the thirty least developed countries to be invited, together with just two of the sixteen other low-income countries. Cuba, of course, was not invited to any of the mini-ministerial meetings and thus missed out on 'providing cigars', in the words of Harry White.

Those WTO members who were not invited were unable to ascertain who had actually organized the meeting. The WTO Secretariat flatly denied organizing it, claiming that they were merely invited to attend by the host country. One of the deputy director generals at the WTO, Andrew Stoler (a US national), made it clear that countries that felt left out should blame the government of Mexico. He also pointed out that the Secretariat had attended many pre-Doha meetings held by different groups of countries, for example in Gabon and Zanzibar, at the invitation of the host country.[4] Some mini-ministerial meetings are clearly weightier than others, however, and the level of involvement of the Secretariat staff varies accordingly. The meetings in Mexico and Singapore were clearly the important ones to attend.

Stuart Harbinson[5] acknowledged that, while any member is entitled to invite a group of other members for a meeting, 'there was a lot of feeling the hosts could have been more inclusive. Some members were left out, which was not the case in previous years, and I got this from both developed and developing countries.' While the Secretariat denied hosting the meeting, however, so too did the Mexican government – a US favourite at the time – claiming a facilitative role instead (Sharma 2001). Several delegates confirmed that Mike Moore was in contact with the host country to facilitate the organization of the meeting in Mexico, and that some countries who asked if they could attend were turned down by the 'hosts' *through* the Secretariat and General Council chair. As one delegate observed, 'This tactic of "playing dumb" employed by both the

Table 3.1 Participation in the Mexico and Singapore mini-ministerials

	Countries attending mini-ministerials in		% of WTO members in each category attending		
	Mexico	Singapore	Mexico	Singapore	both
The Quad	USA EC Japan Canada	USA EC Japan Canada	100	100	100
other OECD	Australia Switzerland Mexico	Australia Switzerland Mexico Korea	25	33	25
other high-income countries	Hong Kong Singapore	Hong Kong Singapore Qatar	17	25	17
upper-middle-income countries	South Africa Brazil Argentina Uruguay	South Africa Gabon	17	8	4
lower-middle-income countries	Jamaica Egypt	Jamaica Colombia	7	7	3
low-income countries	India Indonesia	India	12	6	6
least developed countries	Tanzania	Tanzania	3	3	3

Secretariat and the "hosts" worked well, in that it left delegates wanting to attend [but not invited] bemused, with nowhere to present their case'. When asked why so many developing countries were left out of the Mexico and Singapore mini-ministerials, a middle-income country delegate whose trade minister was present at both meetings replied: 'Frankly, there are only a handful of countries doing business at the WTO. Some West African countries don't even know what they have signed up to. Even the Nigerians don't have much of a clue about the technicalities and complexities of negotiations. The mini-ministerial meetings are really "limited edition" meetings for ministers who are considered influential.' This point of view exposes two things: first, that there are still remnants of the old GATT approach, where the strong trading countries, developed and developing, got together, made deals and tried to impose them on the other nations; and second, the different levels of development that exist among developing country members. It also raises the question of why so many developing countries are still members of the WTO if they are indeed so clueless about its rules and obligations.

The atmosphere at the mini-ministerial in Mexico was described by one delegate as 'relaxed', presenting an opportunity for ministers to discuss issues in a way that they would not be able to at a full ministerial meeting. 'It is impossible to negotiate with over 140 ministers in a room. These people have big egos and poor listening skills, so you will have a situation where a large number of ministers are talking and no one is listening.' During one such discussion, Pascal Lamy had said to the delegate's trade minister, 'If you want agriculture [reduction of export subsidies by the EC] you must give me what I want on the environment.' His trade minister replied, 'If you give me everything I want on agriculture I will give you everything you want on the environment.'

Zoellick described the Mexico mini-ministerial as a very useful meeting at which 'a first-rate group of people' sought to integrate the economic and political elements of the negotiations, which would feed into the Geneva process. He was there, he said, to 'listen and learn' (US Department of State 2001).

From Mexico to Singapore

The September 11th terrorist attacks on New York and Washington were a key influence on the process leading up to Doha, and on the ministerial itself. The USA adopted a new tactic: an all-out campaign to link terrorism and trade, presenting a new round of trade negotiations as essential to promote world peace, economic growth and political stability.

The US campaign began on 20 September 2001, with an article by Zoellick in the *Washington Post* entitled 'Countering Terror with Trade', in which he used the September 11th attacks to urge Congress

> to enact US trade promotion authority so America can negotiate agreements that advance the causes of openness, development and growth ... Now we must thrust forward our values against our adversary: openness, peaceful exchange, democracy, the rule of law, compassion and tolerance ... Open markets are vital for developing nations, many of them fragile democracies that rely on the international economy to overcome poverty and create opportunity.

The frequent speeches and public statements on the 'War Against Terrorism' by President Bush and members of his administration had as a recurrent theme: 'those who are not with us are against us'. Coupled with the campaign to link the new WTO round with terrorism, many delegates felt during the months that followed that this view was implicitly applied to trade – and to them – as well.

On 26 September, Stuart Harbinson, as chair of the WTO General Council, released the first draft of the Doha Ministerial Declaration and an implementation report (on how the Uruguay Round agreements had been implemented). Many developing countries were surprised and disappointed by the lack of ambition on implementation issues. Egypt, Indonesia, Jamaica, Malaysia, Cuba, Honduras, Pakistan, Kenya and the LDCs (represented by Bangladesh) made statements to this effect at an informal General Council meeting on 1 October.

There was equal disappointment on the draft declaration. For months before, Harbinson had held one-to-one consultation meetings ('confessionals') with delegates representing most of the members of the WTO, to seek their views on the draft. The day after the first draft was released, however, the thirty LDCs, plus India,

Indonesia, Jamaica, Malaysia and Pakistan, released statements detailing their frustration and dismay at the streamlined and carefully crafted draft he had produced. A particular concern was that the text failed completely to identify the differences between major groups of countries, for example on the 'new issues'. This was a huge contrast to the thirty-page Seattle text in 1999, which was loaded with 'brackets' highlighting all the different views in the different areas of negotiations.

The majority of developing countries did not support negotiations on the 'new issues', because they did not think that these agreements would benefit them, and felt that there were still too many outstanding implementation issues that needed attention. Yet in the section entitled 'Future Work Programme' the text mentioned the possibility of negotiations and the launching of a new round of trade talks. This section clearly favoured the positions of the EC in particular, and other supporters of 'new issues' such as Singapore, Korea, Mexico, Morocco and South Africa (Sharma 2001).

A high-ranking developed country negotiator praised the way Harbinson and top Secretariat staff had ensured that the draft text was scrupulously kept under wraps until its release, unlike the Seattle text. 'The WTO Secretariat often comes under pressure to reveal the document early so that some countries can demand changes before it goes out.' One need not be a rocket scientist to work out which countries the negotiator was referring to. In fact, a Secretariat staff member confirmed that there have been instances where representatives of certain countries have actually stolen documents from WTO staff offices.

Singapore

A second major mini-ministerial meeting (dubbed the 'final travelling green room meeting') was held in Singapore on 13–14 October 2001, as a follow-up to Mexico. It was attended by thirty-five members (again counting the EC as fifteen), mainly at ministerial level. These were the EC, the USA, Canada, Japan, Singapore, Australia, Colombia, Gabon, Hong Kong, India, Indonesia, Jamaica, Korea, Mexico, Qatar, South Africa, Switzerland, Tanzania, Egypt and Brazil. The trade minister of Malaysia was invited but did not see the purpose of attending.

Participation at Singapore was even more tilted towards richer countries than it had been in Mexico. Once again, all the Quad members were there, together with the same OECD countries (plus Korea) and the same other high-income countries (plus Qatar). Participation by upper-middle-income countries was halved, only partly because of Malaysia's non-attendance; Tanzania remained the solitary, token LDC; and there was only one other low-income country. For the Quad, other OECD and other high-income groups, participation was between 25 per cent and 100 per cent. For each of the four developing country categories, it was between 3 and 8 per cent. There was no country from North Africa, the Middle East, Eastern Europe or the former Soviet Union at either of the mini-ministerials, perhaps partly reflecting the EC accession factor. For countries awaiting accession to the EC, there was no need for the Quad either to listen or to persuade (see 'The Prelude to Doha – Widening the Circle', above).

For the USA and the EC, the Singapore meeting represented a dramatic switch from listening mode in Mexico to tough negotiating (TRIG 2001). As the Fourth Ministerial grew closer, the gloves of the powerful countries were coming off.

The mainstream press reported that consensus was building, with India standing out as the lone opponent. (This was to become a familiar theme, as discussed in Chapter 5.) This interpretation of events has been firmly denied by India, as countries such as Jamaica and Tanzania (on behalf of the thirty LDCs) also held similar views, particularly on the 'new issues'.

A Geneva-based ambassador who attended the meeting confirmed that the broad agenda for the Doha Ministerial was thrashed out in Singapore. The USA also took the opportunity to garner support for its war against terrorism following September 11th.

The location for the Fourth Ministerial

Robert Zoellick, along with delegates from the rest of the Quad and South Africa, also used the Singapore meeting to try to change the venue of the Fourth WTO Ministerial Conference from Qatar to Singapore, following a month of rumours about some delegates' concerns regarding the venue's safety.

The Qatari delegation rejected this move outright, pointing out that their government had spent a huge amount on the preparations for the meeting and on security measures, particularly after September 11th, and had been assured by Secretariat staff and the General Council chair, after several visits to Qatar, that the security measures taken were adequate. A reliable source put the message across simply by stating that in all fairness 'any decision to change the venue would have had to come from the State of Qatar itself'.

Qatar had fought hard at the 1999 Seattle Ministerial Conference to get the WTO and the Quad, especially the USA, to accept their bid to host the conference. After Seattle, the USA had tried to convince Chile to host it, even offering them funding to cover expenses. According to informed sources, Chile turned down the proposal on the grounds that the meeting would coincide with elections in the country, clearing the way for Qatar's unwelcome (to the USA) bid.

Ian Wilkinson, the deputy permanent representative of the EC delegation in Geneva, admitted that 'nobody wanted to go to Qatar after September 11th, especially since the country is the host of Al-Jazeera [the media network that had access to and broadcast pre-recorded speeches by Usama Bin Laden]. However the organization of the meeting turned out to be far better than the Seattle Ministerial.'[6]

On a visit to the White House after September 11th, the Emir of Qatar condemned terrorism but defended Al-Jazeera's position, reminding journalists that freedom of speech and expression as preached by the West was a key objective in the 'War Against Terrorism'.

Two weeks before the ministerial meeting, the WTO Secretariat confirmed Doha as the venue of the Fourth WTO Ministerial, as originally planned.

From Singapore to Doha

The transition from the mini-ministerial in Singapore to the ministerial meeting in Doha appears to have been a smooth one. Although the Singapore mini-ministerial was not an official WTO meeting, the Singaporean delegate gave a briefing on its outcome at the WTO in Geneva. The issues identified as important in Singapore – the 'new issues', the environment, TRIPs, subsidies and countervailing duties, and agriculture – were given priority in the negotiating groups in Doha (see Chapter 4), while other matters such as institutional reform and matters of concern to LDCs were given little priority because of 'time constraints'. And the facilitators and chairpersons of the various discussion groups at Doha remained largely unchanged from Singapore. The chair of the Doha meeting, Qatari Trade Minister Youssef Hussain Kamal, had been invited to the Singapore meeting primarily to meet potential 'friends of the chair' (facilitators) – according to one delegate 'because really Kamal did not know anybody'.

At Singapore, according to Egypt's WTO representative in Geneva, Dr Magdi Farahat, 'developing country delegates ... made it clear to the Quad that, although some agreements were reached [in Singapore], consultations with the majority of delegates absent would have to take place before anything was finalized'.[7] While Doha was not entirely a 'pick up where we left off' scenario, however, it is difficult to avoid the conclusion that the privileged few who were invited to Singapore had largely set the agenda and secured most of the influential positions at the ministerial itself before it even started. Most developing countries – especially the least developed – just had to swallow this state of affairs like a bitter pill.

After Singapore

The key issue after the Singapore mini-ministerial was the preparation of the final draft ministerial declaration for the ministerial itself. Before Mexico, members had been consulted on what the declaration should say, through Stuart Harbinson's 'confessionals'. Between Mexico and Singapore, they had received a first draft; and

Box 3.2 TRIPs and public health

In parallel with the mini-ministerial process, developing countries sought to attain a clarification or amendment of the TRIPs Agreement to define more clearly their rights in relation to public health. The Africa Group tabled its concerns at the WTO in mid-2001, but every step of the road was laden with obstacles by the developed countries and their pharmaceutical industries, and months of wrangling over the agreement's legal jargon followed. Developing country delegates complained informally that they were being outmanoeuvred by the greater legal prowess of developed countries, with their teams of intellectual property lawyers.

Eventually, it was agreed that a political declaration should be signed in Doha. Media coverage of the high-profile public campaign by NGOs such as Médecins Sans Frontières, Oxfam, Consumer Project on Technology and Third World Network had made the issue too politically sensitive for the developed countries to escape delivering *something*. They were also mindful of the fiasco at the previous ministerial in Seattle, which collapsed without a declaration after developing countries revolted, and feared that refusal to grant a declaration could lead to developing countries walking away from the negotiating table.

Even then, however, the *title* was heatedly disputed to the last, the USA insisting on 'TRIPs and Access to Medicines', while developing countries insisted on (and finally secured) the broader title 'TRIPs and Public Health'.

many, if not most, developing countries had objected strongly to it as failing to reflect their views. On 23 October, the 'Group of 77' (representing 133 developing nations, not all in the WTO) added their voice, issuing a declaration expressing disappointment at the lack of progress on implementation issues arising from the Uruguay

Round agreements; seeking more binding rules on Special and Differential Treatment; and calling for negotiations on the 'new issues' to be dependent on their impact on the developmental objectives of the G77 members, and to be based on consensus.

Now it was for Stuart Harbinson, working with WTO director general Mike Moore, to produce a revised draft, reflecting the views of the membership. At midnight on 27 October, the second and final draft appeared, together with draft decisions on implementation issues, and on TRIPs and public health (Box 3.2).

The new draft was discussed at a meeting of the General Council on 31 October. With limited time available, representatives of developing countries made formal statements raising their concerns. As at the General Council meeting on the previous draft, on 2 October, ambassador after ambassador objected to the complete failure of the draft to reflect their views (see Box 3.3).

Harbinson listened attentively – and then proceeded to transmit the text unchanged to ministers a few days later. A covering letter accompanying the draft text stated that the final draft declaration was not a fully accepted one as there were differences; but there were no brackets to indicate what they were. According to one LDC delegate, 'Harbinson was not specific enough about the differences, and thus gave an impression that there was a possible agreed language.'

While they had lost the battle over the draft declaration, developing countries maintained their positions. As a final act of reaffirmation, just days before Doha, ministers of the Africa, Caribbean and Pacific (ACP) Group of countries meeting in Brussels on 5–6 November 2001 – with Mike Moore and Pascal Lamy in attendance – issued a declaration stressing, among other issues, the need to make Special and Differential Treatment for developing countries more meaningful, and to address all outstanding implementation issues; and calling for the various WTO working groups to continue work on the Singapore issues until such time as an explicit consensus had been reached to begin negotiations on them.

Box 3.3 Statements to the General Council on the Second Draft Ministerial Declaration, 31 October 2001

Tanzania, on behalf of the LDCs: 'This text that you will present to the Ministers is deceptively simple since it has no brackets but we all know it hides major differences in some areas ... What caused the failure in Seattle was not the mere presence of the brackets, but it was the lack of political will to resolve the differences for reasons that we all know ... As there is not consensus, there cannot be negotiations, if the spirit and letter of the Singapore Ministerial decision is to be adhered to. Therefore, we propose that the option of continuing the study process for all the four Singapore Issues be included in a new draft to be transmitted to Doha and this is in line with the LDC Ministers' decision in Zanzibar [the Zanzibar Declaration of July 2001] ... '

Nigeria: 'Mr Chairman, my delegation requested you at the General Council meeting of 19 October 2001 to reflect the different views/proposals of various delegations in square brackets for clear reading and understanding by Ministers, and in order to show that consensus has not been reached on those issues. This was not done. The Revised Draft you now present to the General Council gives the impression that the whole membership agreed to it. Mr Chairman, you know we have not agreed on this Draft. Our views and positions have not been reflected. During the General Council meeting of 19 October my delegation requested that you presented a square bracket where consensus had not been reached. Perhaps I had angered the Chairman by this request because even the small square brackets that existed in the first Draft Declaration were completely removed in the present Revised Draft ... This Draft supports only the views of one side of the table ... Under this circumstance, the Draft is not acceptable to my delegation and we urge you to please reflect our views either in brackets, as an annex or in an explanatory letter to enable Ministers to see their way clearly in Doha.'

India: 'Sometimes we acquiesce when a Chairman comes out with a text after wide-ranging consultations. Today we are dealing with a momentous issue, which will have tremendous impact on the commercial, economic and social life of billions of people. This is therefore not an ordinary issue ... It is impossible for me to acquiesce in a situation where a Draft Ministerial Declaration is transmitted to Ministers without reflecting concerns and objections from a large number of countries including mine.'

Malaysia: 'We appreciate that the Chair has forwarded a two-step approach [on the Singapore Issues] that was what we had envisaged as a way out of the *impasse*. However the Chair's approach and ours differ in its outcome. Malaysia's two-step approach would allow Ministers to decide based on the focused study whether negotiations would be undertaken. On the other hand the thrust of the Chair's proposed approach automatically leads to negotiations.'

Zimbabwe, on behalf of the Africa Group: 'We take note of the Draft Declaration on Intellectual Property [and Public Health] as a basis for advancing work in this area. Clearly, there are some elements in this Draft, which had not been fully discussed in the General Council, which raise a number of complex technical and political issues, which still need to be resolved.'

Barbados: 'It should be recalled that many developing countries have repeatedly called for the completion of a study process aimed at analysing the effects of previous and future [industrial] tariff reductions on developing country economies prior to the launch of new Market Access negotiations. We have difficulty with the fact that this call, which we fully support, has been ignored.'

Indonesia: 'My delegation is deeply concerned to see that the revised Draft fully retains paragraphs 38 to 45, without brackets. We reiterate our position, that we consider the provisions of the Organisation and Management of Work Programme, which signify the launching of a new round in the WTO, as still being controversial.'

Source: These short extracts are taken from the longer extracts in TWN (2001). Readers are strongly encouraged to read the latter for a fuller picture of the extent and strength of developing countries' disagreement with the draft.

A rules-based organization?

Never have the wishes of so many been ignored by so few, over key areas of contention, in a supposedly rules-based and consensus-driven organization. As one developing country delegate put it, 'the position of the chair was to produce a a 'members" text reflecting members' positions. Instead, the language was reflective of the views of the major powers. We went to negotiate a document that was already skewed against us.' This raised serious issues, not only politically, but also legally:

The WTO membership is faced with an unprecedented situation … Can the name of the General Council appear on any document that has not been prepared either by it or under its authority? … Can the document prepared by the Chairperson and the WTO Director General be transmitted to Ministers, without the approval of the General Council?

The answer to these questions is NO and is supported by WTO law and practice. (South Centre 2001)

Article IX of the Marrakesh Agreement establishing the WTO

states very clearly that 'The WTO shall continue the practice of decision-making by consensus followed under GATT 1947. Except as otherwise provided, where a decision cannot be arrived at by consensus, the matter at issue shall be decided by voting.' The WTO Rules of Procedure for Ministerial and General Council Meetings (WTO 1996) reaffirm this practice, stating that decisions within the General Council must be taken either by consensus or by voting. The General Council (as a body made up of all the members) may decide at any time, by consensus, to revise these rules or any part of them. No such decision, however, had been taken.

When asked at a press conference to cite the particular rule of the 'rules-based' WTO that provided such an authority, the WTO's chief spokesman, Keith Rockwell, found himself unable to do so. Instead he said, 'Whilst accepting that the Secretariat's research showed that there was "a degree of inconsistency" in the procedures about the right of chair and the DG to act in this way, it was anticipated that "flexibility" would be the watchword' (Raghavan 2002j).

'A balance of unhappiness'?

Unsurprisingly, most developed countries thought Harbinson had done the best he could in the circumstances, given the pressure he was under from all sides, and saw the draft as a balanced one. A typical Northern delegate's view was that 'the draft text did not really fully reflect *anyone's* views ... Besides, if you look at it closely you will see that it takes into consideration issues of importance to developing and least developed countries in nearly every paragraph.' Mike Moore took a similar view, describing the text as 'a balance of unhappiness'.

The USA viewed the draft positively. Zoellick said the revised draft 'makes additional progress towards a successful launch of negotiations at Doha, although we still have more work to do'. He reminded developing countries that, as much as they needed development assistance and debt relief, the way forward as far as sustainable economic growth was concerned was full participation in the multilateral trading system: 'Doha is an opportunity neither we nor the developing world can afford to miss.' He went on to reiterate the much publicized US threat that 'if the WTO falters, the US would revert to regional and bilateral negotiations' (ICTSD 2001a, 2001b).

The EC on the whole emphasized the differences between the draft and their objectives, expressing disappointment at the lack of ambition on 'new issues' and on trade and the environment in the draft text. The EC ambassador in Geneva, Carlo Trojan, felt that the needs of developing countries were comprehensively addressed in the text, but voiced disappointment that the environment approach fell short of what the EC was expecting; that investment and competition did not go far enough; and that agriculture went too far on subsidy reduction (ibid.). Neil McMillan, minister and deputy permanent representative of the UK mission in Geneva, reinforced this view: 'We went to Doha with not one of the four issues we wanted on the environment mentioned'.[8]

All in all, though, the developed countries could live with the somewhat ambiguous text, relying on their negotiating strengths and capacities and behind-the-scenes 'activities' to get what they wanted. The Quad members were looking forward to 'a controlled bedlam' (as envisaged by Harry Dexter White at Bretton Woods) at the ministerial meeting, in which they could manipulate other participants to achieve their objectives; and the Doha draft gave them just what they needed to do so.

On the Secretariat side, one of the WTO deputy director generals at the time of Doha, Ablassé Ouedraogo (a Burkina Faso national), hailed the Doha draft, and subsequently the final text, as 'potentially' very exciting for developing countries. 'Just over two years ago, when we started our terms in office, the word "development" was not well received at the WTO. They said trade was the priority. However, 80 per cent of the membership is composed of developing countries. Finally development is being accepted.'[9]

Many developing country delegates, however, were hugely disappointed with the process as well as the outcome. Most of them had until that point regarded Harbinson as an able General Council chairperson who possessed a great deal of patience coupled with impressive listening skills, and a reputation for transparency and inclusiveness. He was seen as further consolidating the work of the previous General Council chair, Norwegian ambassador Kare Bryn, in terms of opening up the process and taking into consideration the views of a range of members.

Some saw this process as having been reversed in the preparations for Doha. According to Zimbabwean ambassador Boniface Chidyausiku, 'Seattle was actually much more democratic in terms of the process of producing a draft text. At least all opposing views were presented [in brackets] in the draft declaration that went to Seattle. This enabled ministers to carefully assess the different options and positions. Of course the Doha process was different. The draft text and working document was smoothly packaged.'[10]

The developing countries had not expected all their proposals to be accepted – but they had hoped that the rationale behind their reservations on some of the key issues, which they had expressed at every opportunity, would be reflected.

Stuart Harbinson: the case for the defence

Harbinson defended his handling of matters during an interview with the authors in March 2002:[11]

The WTO has changed a lot over the last seven years. There is a higher level of activity by a broader range of members. You now need to involve ninety to a hundred delegations when consulting. This makes it a very complex task because of the diversity of the membership, but it is not impossible to handle, as the success at Doha has proven. I got a strong message from every delegation that Seattle did not work, therefore something had to be done differently this time.[12]

The Seattle document was over thirty pages long and contained all the different positions on all the different issues, providing a very complex situation. We only had six weeks of discussions in Geneva. In the end, no agreements were reached. As a result, the chairperson at the time, Tanzania's Ali Mchumo, had to forward the text as it was to ministers. In the case of Doha, a first draft text was out by 26 September, which no one objected to [sic]. We put in an option on investment [one of the four 'new issues'] in the first draft but then we had a delegate suggesting that an option on agriculture should also be considered. For these reasons, we decided to have a virtually clean final draft – although there were complaints that the option on investment should not have been removed.

When asked who suggested his method of producing a text without brackets he replied only: 'It was a technique that was adopted.'

On some of the problems faced during the process of producing a draft declaration text, Harbinson said:

> Because we started seriously preparing for Doha six months before the meeting, other very important issues that needed our attention, such as the guidelines for the selection of the director general and observership matters, were paralysed. I also did not expect the degree to which the chairperson was approached by everyone and told what results they were expecting. In agriculture, for example, delegation after delegation came forward with different positions making it impossible to find a compromise. The only thing I could do was come up with a neutral best shot. In the end, the final draft was not that different to the ministerial declaration. There were some differences in trade facilitation and transparency in government procurement. In the case of the Singapore issues, 50 per cent were in favour of launching negotiations in Doha and 50 per cent were against it. As a result we had to go for a compromise of beginning negotiations after the Fifth Ministerial Meeting in 2003.

The 'new issues'

The comment that 50 per cent were in favour of the 'new issues' and 50 per cent were not is made frequently by their supporters. Developing country delegates interviewed were convinced that, while convenient, this figure was grossly inaccurate. Such differences of perception are perpetuated by the non-transparency of the process. As one delegate remarked:

> There must be more transparency in the consultations. Maybe the chair needs to construct a table indicating the number of coun-

tries consulted on a matter and what their positions are. At the moment you just have to believe what the chairperson says. It is obvious why a vote on the Singapore issues was not encouraged. WTO rules suggest a vote on divisive issues, but that would not have gone down well with the powerful countries. Instead you are told that 'consensus is building'.

Another said these consultations (before the first draft was produced) were 'like you were just talking to the wall'. The chair listened to their views and proceeded to read out already prepared conclusions. Another delegate echoed these sentiments, adding: 'Despite the fact that the membership and structures are changing in the WTO, the way in which decisions are made is largely unchanged. The countries with the biggest trade weight run the show.'

A number of delegates remained silent on the 'new issues' because they were threatened by the USA. This is a regular occurrence, but beyond the control of the General Council chair. A Latin American delegate confirmed, for example, that the Costa Rican ambassador[13] before Doha 'will stop some of us Latin Americans and ask whether or not we were going to support negotiations on transparency in government procurement. If the answer happened to be no, your name would be written on a list and sent directly to the US mission in Geneva.' He explained that the USA would threaten to withdraw from bilateral preferential trade agreements with a country in response to an unfavourable negotiating position. In some cases personal threats were made. In the end, negotiators had little choice but to toe the line. The 'arm-twisting' process is discussed in greater detail in Chapter 6.

In view of the statements and declarations by developing countries, and the threats against them by some Quad members, you would have to live in cloud cuckoo land to believe that members were genuinely split down the middle on the 'new issues'.

Conclusion

The WTO proclaims itself as a transparent, democratic and rules-based institution with a one-country-one-vote system, which makes decisions by consensus among all its members. The reality is starkly different. Meetings are held between small groups of members, hand-picked by the most powerful. Developing country members may be consulted over major documents, but their views are ignored when they differ from those of the major powers. They object vociferously, using all the means open to them, but their objections are overridden – apparently in blatant contravention of the rules of the organization. The whole process leading up to Doha was carefully orchestrated by the USA, the EC and the Secretariat, to ensure that there would be a new round of negotiations, including the 'new issues', irrespective of the views of the Southern majority of the organization's membership.

Developing countries may now participate in international negotiations in their own right, rather than merely as supporters of one or other of the major players; but in terms of their ability to have their voices heard, and to influence the outcome, little has changed since the colonial era.

Notes

1. There have been many cases where anti-dumping action has been sought by the USA and the EC against a developing country, but investigations have found that dumping did not in fact take place. The very initiation of an anti-dumping case, however, can damage the exporting industry concerned, as importers switch to other 'more reliable' sources of supply.

2. The agreement to phase out the Multi-Fibre Arrangement required countries to remove quotas for a certain number of product categories each year, rather than for products representing a certain volume of consumption or inputs. This allowed them to start with insignificant categories, leaving those that represent the bulk of the market until the end of the ten-year process.

3. Interview with Stuart Harbinson, then Hong Kong ambassador to the WTO, 18 March 2002.

4. Interview with Andrew Stoler, then WTO deputy director general, 5 March 2002.

5. Interview with Stuart Harbinson, 18 March 2002.

6. Interview with Ian Wilkinson, deputy permanent representative of the EC delegation to the international organizations in Geneva, 14 March 2002.

7. Interview with Dr Magdi Farahat, Egyptian minister plenipotentiary in charge of WTO affairs, 21 March 2002.

8. Interview with Neil McMillan, minister, deputy permanent representative of the UK mission to the WTO and UN, 27 February 2002.

9. Interview with Ablassé Ouedraogo, then deputy director general of the WTO, 7 May 2002.

10. Interview with Boniface Chidyausiku, then Zimbabwean ambassador to the WTO and UN, 22 February 2002.

11. All quotations in this section are from this interview.

12. As Chakravarthi Raghavan, a seasoned Geneva-based journalist, has observed, 'Everyone said they did not want a repeat of Seattle, [but] it was not always clear what they meant – street demonstrations, civil society protests, green room processes of decision-making – or exactly what did they not want?' (Raghavan 2001a).

13. The Costa Rican ambassador, Ronald Soborio Soto, is regarded as a firm US and Secretariat 'friendly', and has been chair of the working group on transparency in government procurement for the past four years.

FOUR
A controlled bedlam – the Doha Ministerial 2001

After months of preparations, delegates began to descend on Doha for the Fourth WTO Ministerial Conference on Thursday 8 November. The conference was to be opened formally the following day, and negotiations would last just four days, from 10 to 13 November. This was the decisive time: by the thirteenth, either there would be an agreed ministerial declaration, or there would not – and if there was not, after the previous failure at Seattle, there would be a real question-mark over the future of the WTO. The participants – not least delegates from the Quad countries and members of the Secretariat – knew this all too well.

Like the last chapter, this chapter begins with a summary of the 1944 Bretton Woods Conference, based on Skidelsky (2000), to draw out the historical parallels. After introducing the two key players at Doha – US Trade Representative Robert Zoellick and EC Trade Commissioner Pascal Lamy – it goes on to describe the events at Doha, day by day.

The Bretton Woods Conference

Skidelsky's account of the Bretton Woods process goes on to tell how, from Atlantic City, the drafting committee (a sort of 1944 inter-state 'travelling green room') moved on to Bretton Woods, New Hampshire, USA for the grand final meeting. Some 750 delegates and clerical staff descended on the Mount Washington Hotel and nearby lodgings respectively. Henry Morgenthau, the US Treasury Secretary, was the conference president, with Harry Dexter White, his assistant, as chairman.

Although the key issues had been resolved in principle in Atlantic City, seventy suggested amendments to the text were submitted to the Bretton Woods Conference itself because of time constraints. The main unfinished business was the allocation of IMF quotas, which would determine voting and borrowing rights. White had cleverly reserved this issue for the conference itself, rightly anticipating this would be the only matter of interest to most delegates. One thing the delegates fully understood was that there was a stash of American dollars available, of which they wanted as much as possible.

White set up two main commissions. Commission I, on the Fund (which he chaired), was to work on the draft from Atlantic City, while Commission II, on the Bank (of which Keynes was in charge), was to knock the constitution into shape. Commission III was a 'residual rag-bag' entitled 'Other Means of International Cooperation'.

White was determined to maintain control of the outcome while at the same time creating the illusion that there was genuine participation in the process, to make the imposition of the *fait accompli* easier. A commission chairman, he explained to Morgenthau, must be someone 'who knows the complete matter', who would 'prevent a vote' on anything he did not want voted on, and who would 'arrange the discussion' so as to prevent agreement 'on something we don't want'.

White's own commission (on the Fund) was made up of four committees plus a few *ad hoc* sub-committees, whose primary function was to keep most delegates aimlessly active. While the chairmen of these committees were non-Americans, they had American rapporteurs and secretaries, appointed and briefed by White. Unresolved issues were discussed by a Special Committee on Unsettled Problems, chaired by Morgenthau. Once firm decisions were reached, they were turned into 'Articles of Agreement' by lawyers on a Drafting Committee headed by Canadian Treasury official Louis Rasminsky.

The golden rule during the conference was to 'let anybody talk as long as he pleases provided he doesn't say anything'. This proved not to be difficult, as most delegates were assertive but not necessarily very competent. The conference language was English, which many did not speak or understand, and the legalistic language added to the difficulty. 'The great many varieties of unintelligible tongues

… the Russians for instance struggling between the firing squad … and the English language' made it easy for the Americans, backed up by the British and the Canadians, to control the agenda. As the conference progressed, the text became incredibly complex.

The conference was mainly orchestrated by White. He arranged for a daily conference journal to be produced to keep everyone informed of the main decisions and also participated in daily press briefings, which gave him an opportunity to display an 'efficient charm'. While White and his small group of technical experts were in complete control of the text of the articles to be included in the agreement, 'the powerhouse of the conference was in Morgenthau's office'.

As expected, the allocation of quotas became a contentious issue as the conference progressed. Raymond Mikesell, who served under White in the US Treasury, worked out a complicated formula, partly based on national income data, to produce the results White wanted. The formula itself remained secret, and the uncertainty of the figures it used (e.g. for national income) enabled the US Treasury to adjust quota allocations in a manner that supported its political agenda. Predictably, when the quotas themselves became known, the major players vied for position, seeking increases in their own quotas and those of their allies relative to others.

White responded to this flurry of demands by setting up a Quota Committee headed by Judge Frederick Vinson, the vice-chairman of the US delegation. Professor Mosse, a member of the French delegation, recalled later that the quotas were established 'more or less arbitrarily by the USA in a series of deals'. When the Russian negotiator was told that Soviet national income statistics did not justify a quota of $1.2 billion, he replied cheerfully that he would provide new statistics.

A member of the British team stressed that 'utmost vigilance was needed to ensure that the differences between ourselves and the USA do not once more become active'. The Americans and the British were at loggerheads over where the institutions should be located, and on the issue of monetary sovereignty. Britain wanted greater flexibility on the latter, and even suggested that the executive directors of the Fund should work only part-time. Where differences arose between the USA and another country, decisions were made bilaterally, behind closed doors. The Americans got their way on most of the issues of contention.

The Americans saw fit to include private sector representatives in their negotiating team. In fact, Keynes saw Edward Eagle Brown, President of the First National Bank of Chicago, as their star performer. 'He is an enormous man of twenty stone who lives exclusively on beef ... but his mental grasp and force of character are altogether unusual ... It is a long time since I met a more competent or distinguished banker.'

After a few extensions of the end date, the conference finally ended with a grand banquet on 22 July 1944. *The Commercial and Financial Chronicle*, however, reported that 'the delegates did not reach agreement, they merely signed a paper which *looked* like an agreement'.

Thursday 8 November

Delegates began to arrive in Doha. The American delegation, led by Zoellick, arrived, accompanied by a large contingent of US marines to ensure their security. Delegates were whisked around in high-speed motorcades, while sniffer dogs checked for bombs and journalists were searched one by one before every American press briefing. One American journalist brought his own food with him from the States for fear of being poisoned. According to Walden Bello of Focus on the Global South, 'super paranoia is the only way to describe the state of mind of the US security force in Doha' (Bello 2001).

The Peninsula, a Doha newspaper, reported that the number of delegates remained broadly the same as in Seattle. However, following September 11th, many participants cancelled plans to attend, reducing attendance from the 4,500 originally announced by the organizers to 3,800. NGO, business and media attendance, however, was some 70 per cent lower, only 388 NGO and business representatives attending compared with 1,300 in Seattle, and 808 media representatives compared with 2,700.

Box 4.1 The key players – Zoellick and Lamy

Robert Zoellick was appointed USTR by President George W. Bush Junior in 2001, his career having previously meandered between academia and government. He had served in a senior position under James Baker when the latter was Secretary of State during the administration of George Bush Senior. In this capacity, he played a key role as a behind-the-scenes tactician, helping to broker German reunification and the North American Free Trade Agreement (NAFTA). He also campaigned vigorously for George Bush Junior in the key state of Florida during his successful presidential campaign in 2000.

Zoellick is a highly cerebral workaholic who has been described as having a temper. As USTR, however, he has done his best to project an image of mutual respect and 'constructive engagement' with his counterparts, and believes that the secret of negotiation is 'knowing when to cajole and when to harangue' (Khan 2001). For the most powerful nation in the world, this tactic has a good chance of working.

Zoellick came to Doha extremely well prepared, having dissected what went wrong in Seattle in minute detail and studied a RAND Corporation[1] report on how negotiating styles varied across cultures. He had worked relentlessly to court ministers and presidents on different continents and attempted to mend bridges with 'difficult' countries such as Malaysia, Indonesia, India and several African countries. As an African official recalled, Zoellick 'made calls to people who had not heard from an American cabinet secretary in decades … He impressed the Kenyan trade minister by speaking to him in his local language, Swahili … and badgered Japan to play a more cooperative role by bluntly asking Japanese officials to practise "respectful followership".'

Africans felt that George W. Bush and his administration seemed to continue the focus on Africa by the previous Clinton administration when he became the first president in more than twenty years to visit the continent. The USA also improved relations with Brazil, which had long viewed it with suspicion in the rivalry for influence in the western hemisphere (de Jonquières 2001c).

Pascal Lamy was appointed EC Trade Commissioner in 1999, just before the Seattle Ministerial. Between 1994 and 1999 he had had a taste of the corporate world when he was appointed director general responsible for the restructuring of the French bank Crédit Lyonnais. Prior to this, he had a high-profile post at the European Commission, following some years as a civil servant in his native France.

Lamy might be described as a French socialist who happens to be a promoter of free trade in a 'sustainable' manner, and has praised the American sense of enterprise. He believes that developing countries need to be on board if negotiations in the WTO are to be successful, and travelled extensively to developing countries after Seattle to establish dialogue. He has a fierce intellect, works non-stop, and is known to detest parties. Zoellick has described him as someone who has 'an astute sense of how to operationalize a vision' (quoted in Stokes 2000).

A developing country WTO delegate described him as someone who 'quietly does his homework surprisingly thoroughly and is very practical', adding that 'the American negotiators are more overtly arrogant and use the stick more than the carrot compared to those of the EC'.

One high-profile developed country delegate observed that 'there are always far too many people attending these ministerial meetings. You get a whole lot of people walking in one direction and five minutes later you see them walking in the opposite direction, looking very important, yet 90 per cent of them have nothing to do.' One might wonder how he had the time to make these observations – perhaps having dozens of negotiators at one's disposal helps.

The size of the delegations varied enormously. The EC had a presence of 508 (including fifty delegates of the European Commission), Japan had 159 delegates, Canada had sixty-two, Indonesia sixty, the United States fifty-one, and India forty-eight. At the other end of the scale, some smaller developing countries such as Maldives had two representatives, St Vincent had one, and Haiti, the poorest nation in the western hemisphere, had none (WDM 2001). Twenty-eight countries with observer status at the WTO and forty-eight international organizations were also represented.

After months of talks, the two trade supremos, Zoellick and Lamy (see Box 4.1), had forged a unified front to promote the launching of a new round including the 'new issues'. A 'carefully pre-scripted co-operation' was evident between the two (de Jonquières 2001c) – as before Bretton Woods. A breakdown of communication between the two big players – one of the main reasons Seattle failed – was being avoided at all costs.

On the first day of Doha, Lamy and Zoellick were beginning to position themselves for the negotiations to come. Lamy announced that he had offered some developing countries a total of €50 million (US$50 million) in aid to meet their WTO commitments, and indicated that the EC member states were ready to open up their markets to more textile imports. Zoellick met the Group of Latin American and Caribbean Countries (GRULAC) to seek their support for a new round, suggesting that the details of negotiations on the various parts of the work programme would be thrashed out later. ('Work programme' was subtly substituted for 'new round' by developed countries and the Secretariat in view of the controversy generated by the latter.) Was this the Bretton Woods-style *fait accompli* rearing its ugly head?

An African negotiator described what went on at the bilateral level: 'Zoellick would invite you to his hotel suite in Doha. He would say: "Minister, I have just spoken to your President." [When he says this he is serious.] "He said he is with us and will cooperate. We have told him that this is very important for AGOA" [the US African Growth and Opportunity Act].' AGOA was a key element in US pressure on African countries in the negotiations (see

Chapter 6). Zoellick's efforts to woo developing countries on the basis of the USA's generosity in trade matters, however, received a setback when it become known that Congress had voted against negotiating on anti-dumping rules and increasing textile quotas for developing countries.

The developing countries too were setting out their positions. Meeting on 8 November, the LDCs reiterated their complete opposition to accepting negotiations on the 'new issues', and decried the lack of provisions for LDCs in the draft text. India remained adamant that it would rather not accept such a biased draft. Other developing countries, including Fiji, Sri Lanka, Bolivia, Dominican Republic and Honduras, also opposed the introduction of the 'new issues'.

Meanwhile, the *Financial Times* published the results of a poll of 521 business leaders and 'economic experts' in seventy-two countries, carried out by a German research institute, indicating their overwhelming support for a new trade round in the expectation that it would increase consumers' prosperity and demand, and improve market access for rich and poor countries. The poll found concern that the public did not fully recognize the benefits of trade; that WTO agreements had yet to be translated into everyday business practice; and that anti-globalization protesters and the political influence of NGOs slowed the process of liberalization (de Jonquières 2001b).

Advocates claimed that a success at Doha would lead to the creation of $400 billion of new wealth, of which $150 billion would flow into developing countries. A cynical LDC delegate, however, laughed at these projections, recalling the highly exaggerated projections put forward by supporters of the Uruguay Round: 'The advantages we were supposed to gain from the Uruguay Round have not materialized, to put it mildly. For example, there has not been an increase in the flow of trade for Africa. Today our share of world trade is 2 per cent [a decline from 8 per cent since the Uruguay Round] – and this includes South Africa.' The LDCs' share of world exports of goods and services is less than 0.6 per cent, compared with 62 per cent for the Quad (WTO 2002c).

Friday 9 November

Plenary sessions at the 'monkey house' began. For two days, ministers took turns to give set-piece speeches, in parallel with all the other group and bilateral meetings. A negotiator from a middle-income developing country described these sessions as 'dull', going on, 'Who wants to listen to all the bullshit those ministers have to say? They were literally talking to empty rooms ... People wanted to be in the bilateral and small group meetings where the real action was.'

An African negotiator observed that, since many developing country ministers had complained of having nothing to do at the Seattle Ministerial, the plenary was designed to keep them busy while the other more important meetings were taking place. 'Mike Moore hand-picked those who attended the small informal meetings once the conference commenced.' As at Bretton Woods, the formal sessions kept the rest of the ministers talking 'provided they did not say anything'.

In the early evening, the opening ceremony took place, in the Al Dafna Hall of the Sheraton Hotel. The Emir of Qatar formally inaugurated the meeting, effectively launching the new round. This was followed by speeches from, among others, WTO director general Mike Moore; Rubens Ricupero of the United Nations Conference on Trade and Development (UNCTAD), on behalf of UN Secretary General Kofi Annan; and Stuart Harbinson, as chair of the General Council.

Mike Moore made it clear to delegates that the global recession and the threat of protectionism demanded a commitment to launch broad-based negotiations. He warned that the proliferation of regional trade agreements could render the WTO defunct if the multilateral system were not strengthened. Despite deep disagreements on some key issues, however, he was confident that the level of preparedness for negotiations was more advanced this time round than in Seattle.

Moore's speech echoed the views of the EC, the USA, the heads of the IMF and World Bank and the Western media in general that a new round was needed to fight the global recession. An African negotiator commented: 'Africa has been in a recession for about ten to twenty years. Do you think the current so-called recession affects us? The IMF and World Bank structural adjustment policies have already put us under tremendous strains, and so this new round is not our answer to our recession.'

The decisive moment of the opening, however, came in Harbinson's speech. He took advantage of the mêlée of the Emir taking leave of his guests to present the draft declaration (unexpectedly) as the working document for the conference. By doing so in a ceremonial session, he effectively prevented delegates from objecting to it, as they undoubtedly would have done in a working session.

A reliable source detailed how Mike Moore and Stuart Harbinson approached the conference chairman and Qatari trade minister Kamal behind the scenes, asking him to consider handing over the running of the conference to more 'experienced' hands, in view of the enormity of the task ahead. They also discussed the selection of conference facilitators (also known as 'friends of the chair') to chair discussions on the main negotiating topics. Kamal refused to take a back seat during the proceedings and made it clear that he was going to chair the conference, as was customary, and that, as chair, he would like to select at least some of the 'friends of the chair'. Eventually a compromise was reached: conference facilitators would be chosen by Moore, Harbinson *and* Kamal, and Kamal would be allowed to take a relatively central role in the process. This private agreement made Kamal look less of a stooge for the powerful nations and the Secretariat.

Harbinson later insisted he had no role at the conference except to 'whisper in the ear' of Minister Kamal during conference sessions, and that if anyone wanted to know how the facilitators were chosen they should ask Moore and Kamal.[2]

Some delegates were shocked by the way the facilitators appeared as if by magic. Ian Wilkinson of the EC, however, believed the early selection of facilitators in Doha was a good idea. 'In Seattle we went three days into the meeting without facilitators because some ministers refused to take on the task.' He laid the blame squarely on Charlene Barshefsky, the USTR at the time and chair of the Seattle Ministerial, whom he described as someone 'with a brittle personality, who did not have the moral authority or the technical capacity to pull the whole thing off', adding that 'the relationship between the EC and the USA was at a low point'. Kamal on the other hand 'did not speak English that well, nor did he have the technical know-how on the issues – but he had a great personality and a natural charm, and was able to tell ministers to shut up'.[3]

Saturday 10 November

The process of negotiations began in earnest, with the heads of delegation meeting at the opening session to outline the work schedule for the conference. Minister Kamal opened the session by announcing that, as agreed by all the delegates at the opening ceremony, the Harbinson text would be the basic document for discussion at the conference!

Six issues had been identified as needing intensive discussion if a consensus were to be reached, and six 'friends of the chair' had been chosen to address these issues:

- George Yeo, Trade and Industry Minister of Singapore (agriculture);
- Pierre Pettigrew, Canadian Minister of International Trade ('new issues');
- Pascal Couchepin, Swiss Economic Affairs Minister (implementation issues);
- Heraldo Munoz Valenzuela, Chilean Under-Secretary of Foreign Affairs (environment);
- Luis Ernesto Derbez Bautista, Mexican Secretary of Finance (TRIPs and health); and
- Alec Erwin, South African Minister of Trade and Industry (rule-making).

While none of the main conference facilitators was from the USA or the EC (as at Bretton Woods), all represented countries sympathetic towards EC and/or US positions. Their task was to hold consultations with members and make amendments to the text according to what members decided. It was totally unclear, however, whom they were consulting with, when and where; and as brackets and additional texts on the different issues crept in and out of the working document during the conference, a majority of members remained unsure who exactly was making the 'adjustments', which did not reflect their views and suggestions. Most developing country delegates came to view the facilitators as the reincarnation of the green room process, leading NGOs to dub them 'the green men' (Hormeku 2001).

Other facilitators for small group meetings were identified as the conference progressed. Egypt's trade minister eventually became a facilitator overseeing one of the small group discussions during the conference, but he was at pains to keep this under wraps because of the anger some of his colleagues expressed over the way facilitators appeared out of the woodwork. 'Normally he loves to be in the thick of things, but many of his colleagues felt slighted by the process. As a result, he tried to maintain a low profile,' said a developing country delegate.

While the facilitators played the key public role, behind the scenes it was the Secretariat staff, headed by Andrew Stoler, who were running the show, taking charge of the administration and the drafting process under the watchful eye of the Quad.

At the first Committee of the Whole (COW) meeting, each of the six topics was discussed. Each delegate wanting to speak or make a presentation was given three minutes to do so. Some developing countries pointed out that this was another gathering where ministers' views were barely taken into account – it was a semi 'monkey house'.

During this meeting, Kamal, as chair, suggested an immediate move to begin discussions on the first topic, agriculture.[4] At this point the Indian Minister of Commerce, Murasoli Maran, raised his flag to speak. Mike Moore, sitting beside Kamal, alerted him that India and others wanted to raise procedural questions, to which Kamal replied: 'In that case we don't give them the time.' His utterance reverberated throughout the hall – he had not realized that his microphone was switched on. Many delegates burst into laughter. Harbinson referred to this incident as an illustration of the more relaxed atmosphere in Doha than in Seattle: 'Everyone laughed. This would not have been the case in Seattle.'[5] But some of the laughter was rather derisive.

Left with little choice following his gaffe, Kamal allowed procedural points to be raised. Speaking first, Minister Maran suggested that delegates should be able to analyse facilitators' reports before meetings, and that no attempt should be made to present a consensus text when in fact there was no consensus. Ambassador Ransford Smith of Jamaica requested that the chairman inform the floor when issues of contention outside the six areas identified would be discussed. The Bangladeshi minister asked when LDC issues would be discussed. The Ugandan trade minister demanded to know how the facilitators were chosen. Pakistan and a few others also raised questions, and there were other flags raised.

The chair concluded the session, replying that the facilitators did not represent any group and would thus act in their personal capacities; that the facilitators had taken note on the issue of transparency; and that the time for meetings on other issues would be announced later. He assured delegates that the COW would remain central to the negotiating process, despite the numerous smaller sessions in the form of small-group, bilateral and plurilateral meetings that were scheduled to take place.

The scheduled session on TRIPs did not take place due to time constraints. The various meetings that day ended late, with many feeling quite exhausted – and this was just the first day. Overall the divisions over the issues that existed in Geneva were still intact.

Outside the conference

Qatar was never a protester's dream venue, and September 11th exacerbated the lack of enthusiasm of anti-globalization movements to descend on the Arab state. Nevertheless, though rather thin on the ground, protesters managed to do their bit. About sixty gathered outside a US press briefing chanting, 'What goes on behind closed doors? Arm-twisting, arm-twisting … No more arm-twisting!' and 'Zoellick go home!' (Blustein 2001). A press briefing given by Pascal

Lamy was picketed, and later that evening, a protest theatre staged by Northern and Southern NGOs, ironically entitled 'Why the Developing Countries Love the EC and US', drew massive media coverage.

Thousands of miles away in New York, the Indian Prime Minister, Shri Atal Bihari Vajpayee – a democratically elected leader from a country of more than 800 million people – made an impassioned speech at the Fifty-sixth Session of the UN General Assembly. After the obligatory condemnation of terrorism, he reminded world leaders that the Uruguay Round had done very little for economic growth in developing countries, as poverty levels and income gaps continue to rise. He warned that implementation issues must be resolved before the WTO launched a new round: 'Our public is unwilling to accept another post-dated cheque, when an earlier one has bounced' (UN 2001).

Zoellick had visited India in August 2001 to try to convince the government to back down on its refusal to support the launching of a new round of trade talks, announcing on his arrival in Delhi that the USA would cut $540 million worth of duties on imports from India.[6] India had apparently refused to make deals, however, and Trade Minister Maran reiterated their position in Geneva.[7] This resistance may have been one of the reasons for the deliberate attempt to isolate India in Doha.

Sunday 11 November

China finally gained entry into the WTO after fifteen years as an observer. Developing countries welcomed the decision wholeheartedly. 'It will increase our negotiating power,' said one delegate.

At a Committee of the Whole meeting chaired by Canada's Pierre Pettigrew (also the facilitator on the 'new issues') at 11 a.m., delegates were informed that bilateral talks were taking place on the 'new issues', and would continue, but there was no indication as to who was being consulted. India, Zimbabwe (chair of the Africa Group in Geneva), Nigeria (chair of the Africa Group in Doha), Kenya (chair of the ACP Group), Senegal, Malaysia, Indonesia, Thailand, Egypt, Jamaica, Cuba, St Lucia, St Vincent and Belize all reiterated their opposition to negotiations on the 'new issues', and requested that the working groups continue their work on these issues in Geneva.

Colombia, Uruguay and Peru were in favour of the inclusion of the 'new issues', but wanted certain conditions (in agriculture) to be met, while Morocco was frustrated that the working groups had gone on for so long in Geneva and wanted negotiations to begin, and South Africa suggested that capacity-building provisions for developing countries on the 'new issues' might move things along. The Philippines responded that those who rejected these issues did so for fundamental reasons, not because they lacked the capacity to negotiate.

The EC, Japan, the USA, Australia and Switzerland, predictably, requested that negotiations on the 'new issues' commence sooner rather than later.

To the astonishment of many delegates, George Yeo (Singapore), the agriculture facilitator, began his session by calmly informing delegates that the EC could not make any more concessions on the agriculture text, and asking them to try to accommodate them by being less ambitious on phasing out export subsidies. Developing country delegates were flabbergasted by his audacity and reminded him that it was their job to make these decisions, not his.

Other business not covered by the facilitators was also brought to the COW, including discussions of labour standards (raised by the EC); improving the dispute settlement procedures prior to trade retaliation measures (Japan); increasing the external transparency of the WTO (EC, USA and Canada); establishing a study group on the relationship between trade, debt and finance (Malaysia, Pakistan, Malawi and others); the need for a feasibility study before further negotiations on high industrial tariffs (Mauritius and other African countries); and a renewed request for the ACP Cotonou Agreement waiver, which had been stuck in the WTO's Trade in Goods Council for over a year (various African countries). No conclusions were reached on any of these topics.

According to one delegate, Mike Moore told some ministers privately that it was inappropriate for ambassadors to make statements at heads of delegation meetings, stressing that, as this was a ministerial meeting, it was preferable for ambassadors to take a back seat. Pakistani Commerce and Industries Minister Abdul Razak Dawood was given a particularly stern warning, as his Geneva-based ambassador Munil Akram was widely known for taking the Quad and certain Secretariat officials to task. As a result, at the request of his minister, Ambassador Akram remained quiet for the remainder of the proceedings at Doha.

WTO deputy director general, Andrew Stoler,[8] denied that ambassadors were silenced in Doha. He explained that only Akram was asked by his minister not to speak in public for the rest of the Doha meeting, because 'the minister discovered Akram was keeping him [the minister] away from meetings ... Akram thought he was smarter than his boss ... This is not a way to treat your boss ... When the minister found out, he asked Akram to shut up.' A senior negotiator at the Pakistani mission strongly denied this 'twisted' version of events, saying 'Mr Akram will never undermine his minister. He is a man of integrity.'

As at the mini-ministerials (Chapter 3), the shift from ambassadors to ministers was significant. As then Dominican Republic ambassador, Dr Federico Cuello Camilo, observed, while ACP ministers had taken strong positions at their meeting in Brussels, they slowly began to change their minds when they got to Doha. 'We [ambassadors] were totally ignored and left out of the process ... I think developing country ministers should be more cognisant of their national interests and pay less attention to political posturing. This is the only way we can take on the Quad. Some ministers were so in awe of being in the company of Zoellick and Lamy they were oblivious of their obligations.'[9] He suggested that ambassadors should make sure in future that their concerns were adequately dealt with in Geneva before going to ministerials.

After two extended ACP meetings, the Kenyan minister and one of his colleagues attempted to persuade the other ministers to soften their positions on the 'new issues', but without success. The Kenyan minister had stunned NGOs at a press conference the day before by claiming that there were no green rooms in Doha, and that the process was very transparent. In contrast, Uganda's minister expressed concern that the way in which the informal consultations were constituted discriminated against LDC concerns.

India, Nicaragua, Bangladesh, Jamaica, Zimbabwe, Pakistan, Bolivia and Tanzania also raised process issues. Some said it was not clear where meetings were being held (a recurrent complaint throughout the conference), who was being consulted, or on what basis, and that there were simply too many of them.

During the course of the day, there were rumours of a rift between the EC and the USA, who were said not to be talking to each other because of the deadlock on agriculture. Press conferences went on, though, as the powerful countries tried to prove publicly that everything was going reasonably well, and as far as possible to control what the press reported. Like Harry Dexter White at Bretton Woods, the Quad and the WTO Secretariat were falling over themselves to display an 'efficient charm' towards the media. The USA went a step further by providing free alcoholic drinks for journalists – no doubt greatly appreciated in a Muslim state where alcohol is difficult to obtain freely. By contrast, the developing countries generally made much less effective use of the press. A developing country delegate interviewed by the authors shared the view of many NGO observers that this was regrettable.

In the evening, WTO chief spokesman Keith Rockwell informed the media that the members were still deeply divided on the 'new issues', on agriculture, on the environment, on rules and on TRIPs and public health. Only two days remained before the scheduled close of the conference.

At a late meeting of some twenty or thirty ministers, ending at 2 a.m. on Monday, Zoellick and Lamy once again attempted to display an air of unity, compromise and flexibility. However, developing country ministers appeared unimpressed, especially after briefing colleagues who did not attend, as the EC had refused to make any concessions on export subsidies in agriculture while continuing to press for more on the environment. While Sweden and the Netherlands were willing to compromise on agriculture, the French and the Irish, who faced an election year, were not. In the case of France, neither President Chirac nor his prime minister wished to displease the powerful agricultural sector.

Monday 12 November

As the EC and the USA warned developing country delegates that they would close their markets to their goods if the *impasse* over 'new issues' continued, some of the world's poorest nations started to complain that they were being browbeaten. Clare Short, Britain's International Development Secretary and head of the developed countries' Technical Cooperation Ministers' Group at Doha, denied that the powerful countries were issuing threats to developing countries, but repeated the now familiar warning that the WTO and the fragile world economy could not afford another Seattle.

India continued to be criticized in the Western media, which presented it as the only stumbling-block to the launch of a new round of talks – although WTO spokesman Keith Rockwell confirmed to members of the Indian press corps that India was not alone in its opposition to 'new issues'. He ruled out, however, the possibility of voting on the issue – just as Harry Dexter White would have done.

In response to complaints from LDCs about the failure of the six core facilitators to cover all of their concerns, the COW appointed Botswana's Trade Minister, Tebelelo Seretse, as a main facilitator on 'other issues'. With only a day and a half before the end of the conference, she was asked to cover labour standards, TRIPs, biodiversity, WTO internal transparency, dispute settlement reform and the need for working groups on trade, debt and finance, and on technology transfer. As with Commission III on 'Other Means of International Cooperation' at Bretton Woods, a 'residual rag-bag' was created for those topics of no interest to the major players. As a Geneva-based LDC delegate pointed out, lumping all these issues together and handing them over to the minister so late in the process made any serious discussion impossible. As a result, 'she was unable to answer questions and adequately report back on the proceedings on these matters during the final marathon [green room] meeting in Doha'.

Non-English-speaking delegates, particularly from Francophone

Africa, and Latin America, were becoming increasingly frustrated by the lack of simultaneous interpretation in the other officially recognized WTO languages (French and Spanish) during discussions held by the facilitators. A delegate from Senegal, Iba Mar Oulare, confirmed that interpretation facilities were confined to the big conference rooms only. Federico Cuello Camilo of the Dominican Republic recalled that 'ministers from non-English-speaking countries who did not have good English were unable to communicate well and articulate their concerns at Doha'.

When asked why this was still the case at WTO ministerial meetings, Andrew Stoler nonchalantly replied: 'We do have a big problem with working mainly in English and then later translating the texts or what was said. This is the norm at present.' Receiving translated texts only later, however, prevents non-English-speaking delegations from participating effectively in the discussions. Iba Mar Oulare's interpretation was that 'it was expected that countries provide their own interpreters during the small informal group discussions'.[10] Most developing countries, however, already short on negotiators, would have been unable to afford to bring in more delegates for interpretation purposes. As a result, as at Bretton Woods, some delegates were 'caught between the firing squad and the English language'.

At this point, India was still standing by its position, and refusing to have bilateral talks with the USA and the EC. Minister Maran's firm stance was due partly to widespread pressure being exerted on his government at home. According to the Indian press, 25,000 protesters had marched through the streets of New Delhi to oppose WTO negotiations the previous week. Although Minister Maran is well known as a supporter of liberalization policies, he had to be seen to be fighting on behalf of Indian public opinion.

India circulated a statement directed at the ACP, LDC and Africa Groups, denying Kenyan suggestions that they had backed down on the 'new issues'. 'Kenya was playing tricks,' said one developing country negotiator. Kenyan delegates later insisted, however, that 'less than honest people' within the WTO Secretariat had wrongly informed their minister that India was changing its position, and even announced that Kenya was going to call a press conference in support of the 'new issues', in view of the fact that India had backed down. 'It was pure disinformation. Kenya had no plans to hold a press conference on the matter.' At an NGO briefing by the ACP later that afternoon, Kenya's trade minister, as ACP Group chair, emphasized that they were only willing to reach a compromise on the 'new issues' if they could win the ACP waiver (a waiver of the WTO rule that any deal granted to one member must be extended to all, to accommodate the EC–ACP Partnership Agreement), along with provisions for capacity-building and greater transparency at the WTO.

The Latin American banana-producing countries opposed the ACP waiver, as, to some extent, did Thailand and the Philippines, who wanted greater access to the EC market for their tuna exports. The Thai ambassador commented that, on this particular issue, the EC 'was taking from the poor and giving to the poor ... The ACP waiver issue was brought up at the conference without any prior consultations. Though we were not totally opposed to the idea, we were ignored, despite the fact that we were in talks with the EC regarding our waiver requests for tuna before Doha.'[11]

TRIPs and public health

A key issue in Doha was the text on the flexibility within the TRIPs Agreement for countries to adopt patent policies that would allow greater and cheaper access to medicines, particularly in the context of the HIV/AIDS pandemic. The choice was broadly between two alternative texts, Option One (supported by most developing countries) allowing greater flexibility, and Option Two (supported by the major pharmaceutical MNCs and the USA), which was more restrictive.

On 8 November, before the conference had been formally opened, Zoellick tried to persuade African ministers to support Option Two, presenting Option One as merely a ploy by India and Brazil to advance the interests of their generic pharmaceutical industries. 'The idea was to drive a wedge between the African countries and India and Brazil' (Khan 2001).

There were reports that some African countries, particularly Kenya, were warming to Option Two, following an AGOA meeting between the United States trade representative and African ministers in the USA on 29 October. According to a developed country delegate who supported Option One, however, 'the NGOs and some delegates from developing and developed countries successfully managed to reorient the Kenyan minister [Nicholas Kipyator Biwott, chair of the ACP Group in Doha] on the matter. They suggested to him that Option One in the draft text on TRIPs and public health was the viable option for African countries.'

Brazil played a key role, representing the interests of the developing countries. A Brazilian negotiator described the process.

> At the end of the day, a deal was brokered between the USA and Brazil ... The USA fought it, but they realized there would be no round if they refused to budge, so they gave in ... The EC tried to act as a mediator between us and the US, and claimed they were on our side. We, however, realized they were creating more obstacles than helping us, so we bypassed them and went face-to-face with the USA ... The breakthrough was the first one at Doha and it sent a very good sign to developing country delegates.

A major public campaign in developed and developing countries, which had started well before Doha, was a key factor. As a developed country negotiator who supported Option One observed,

> Public pressure was huge on the TRIPs and public health issue because of the following: the HIV/AIDS pandemic; South Africa and Brazil successfully challenging US pharmaceuticals to gain the right to produce cheap generic drugs for AIDS patients; and the fact that the USA found itself in a position where it had to override its patent laws to seek cheap Cipro drugs when it had to tackle the Anthrax scare following the September 11th terrorist attacks. These issues strengthened the arguments for developing countries.

Late on 12 November, Option One was accepted as the language for the final text. While the USA had succeeded in blocking any legal changes to the original TRIPs Declaration, developing countries got the political language they wanted, recognizing the need for countries to override patent laws for public health purposes. This move immediately brought countries like Brazil and Thailand closer to Quad positions.

A representative of an American NGO recalled that employees of pharmaceutical MNCs broke down in tears in an elevator they happened to be sharing when the news broke. 'They feared they would lose their jobs after the conference.'

Tuesday 13 November

The latest offspring of the Harbinson text was released by Minister Kamal as conference chair at noon.

- As in the Harbinson draft, negotiations on two of the 'new issues' pushed by the USA in particular, transparency in government procurement and trade facilitation, were to begin immediately after Doha.
- The Harbinson text's reference to a decision on *modalities* of negotiations on investment and competition policy being taken up at the next ministerial (as pushed by the EC) was watered down: instead, a decision would be taken on *whether* to negotiate.
- The EC achieved the inclusion of new areas on the environment, in brackets, and the phrase that 'the ILO was the appropriate forum for a substantive dialogue' on labour standards was removed, implying that the issue could be brought up in the WTO in the future.
- On market access for non-agricultural products (including textiles), fully-fledged negotiations aimed at reducing tariff peaks and tariff escalation (in developed countries) were brushed aside following objections by the USA.
- Negotiations on the reduction of high industrial tariffs in developing countries were also excluded – a move that pleased developing countries, until they were put back in the final draft.
- Phasing out of all export subsidies in agriculture was put in brackets, and elimination of high agricultural tariffs was not mentioned.

- The USA had succeeded in watering down the language on new negotiations on anti-dumping significantly, but had agreed to negotiate after intense pressure from Japan in particular. The US Congress's opposition to tougher anti-dumping legislation left Zoellick with very little room for manoeuvre.

One developing country delegate said: 'If the LDCs and African Group had not fought so hard, the Harbinson text would have been strengthened. However, because they did, the draft which emerged on the thirteenth was in fact downgraded. The environment text had been scaled up, but investment and competition could not be argued to be part of the single undertaking.'

At 2 p.m., the Committee of the Whole (COW) met to discuss the latest draft. The USA and Australia accepted the text as it was, while the EC found the changes made on investment and competition unacceptable, wanting greater ambition on this. Japan and Korea wanted negotiations to start immediately in all areas; but Nigeria (on behalf of the Africa Group), India, Zimbabwe, Tanzania (chair of the LDC Group), Cuba and Barbados all rejected negotiations on the 'new issues'.

Kenya appealed to the chair that the ACP Group must get its waiver in order that its preferential arrangements on certain products with the EC could be resumed, and the EC pleaded with members to help them move the waiver forwards; but Latin American countries opposed this following their victory against the EC preferential arrangements with the ACP during what became known as 'the banana dispute'.

No agreement was reached, and the COW was recessed until 11 p.m., as small group consultations continued.

The Western press now started to target France as well as India, claiming that it had isolated itself on agriculture and that French negotiators were being criticized by other members. This fuelled reports that British Prime Minister Tony Blair and German Chancellor Gerhard Schroeder were preparing to telephone President Chirac of France to urge him to take a softer line (de Jonquières 2001a). Lamy reportedly kept asking his negotiating team to stand firm, believing a crisis was needed if the talks were to get anywhere.

A developed country delegate and Cairns Group member described how the issue of agriculture was eventually solved later that afternoon.

> We were all under a lot of pressure as members of the Cairns Group. After agreeing to the phasing out of all forms of agricultural export subsidies, the EC insisted on adding those words 'without prejudging the outcome of the negotiations'. We were faced with the option of walking out of the conference, but we decided not to, in view of Seattle. The EC made it clear that if they did not obtain a 'get-out' clause in agriculture they were going to walk out and there would be no deal, so we had to accept the clause, although there was some very tough exchanges of words at this stage.

According to informed sources, France was bought off by the 'get-out' clause, giving Lamy room to step up his demands on the 'new issues'.

As this day was meant to mark the end of the conference, those delegates with scheduled flights had begun to leave during the afternoon, although negotiations were still continuing. Only the previous day, Canada had categorically stated that the ministerial meeting would end by midnight on Tuesday, as planned, while a Middle Eastern negotiator recalls that 'Minister Kamal made it very clear towards the final days of the conference that the Qatari government was going to host the meeting for five days maximum'. As at Bretton Woods, delegates were informed that they would be sent home the next day, whether or not they had reached agreement. As the scheduled end of the Conference loomed with no agreement in sight, however, it was extended into Wednesday. Significantly, this decision was not put to the membership for discussion, nor a decision taken by consensus. This was a very serious procedural omission (raised by the LMG post-Doha) since a significant number of ministers and delegates were unable to reschedule their flights and had to leave Qatar late on Tuesday. Some who left did so totally convinced that the entrenched divisions could not be resolved, so that their absence would not influence the outcome. As a result, the most crucial decisions were made in the absence of a significant number of developing country ministers.

A group of twenty to thirty participants – including ministers, their ambassadors and top Secretariat staff – returned to the 'green room' process, beginning what was to be a marathon all-night meeting at 7 p.m. As a result, the COW meeting which had been recessed until 11 p.m. was rescheduled every few hours, in the event resuming only the following day. A meeting on the ACP waiver, between ACP, EC, Central American and South East Asian ministers and negotiators, ran in parallel. An African delegate summed up the gruelling and seemingly endless sessions:

> It was as though the other side were on steroids. They stagger their countless negotiators and they seemed to be more awake as the night went by. This was the second all-night meeting. In contrast, because our delegations were small, we were not able to stagger our negotiators. After forty hours of continuous talks, our ministers gave in to things out of sheer exhaustion. This is a critical part of the developed countries' strategy.

The green room meeting – 13–14 November

The 'green room' meeting, which began at 7 p.m. on the final scheduled day of the conference, continued for twelve hours, finally finishing at about seven o'clock the following morning. Participants included the USA, the EC, Canada, Japan, Switzerland, South Korea, Singapore, Hong Kong, Egypt, Tanzania, Nigeria, Kenya, South Africa, Botswana, Chile, Mexico, Uruguay, Australia, Jamaica, Brazil, Malaysia, India, Pakistan, Zimbabwe and Georgia. As at the Mexico and Singapore mini-ministerials (see Chapter 3), all the Quad members were present. There was also a striking overlap among the other participants: of the twenty-one other green room participants, all but seven had been invited to Mexico and / or Singapore. All thirteen WTO members who attended both mini-ministerials were again present in the green room.

Even among those who were allowed to attend, some were

more equal than others. According to one participant, while most developing country delegates were allowed two advisers in the green room, the USA had five. Ambassadors were asked not to speak but only to observe, even though some represented ministers who had already left the conference. Some ministers in the room, for example the Zimbabwean, were not allowed advisers at all. In fact, the Zimbabwean minister spent the entire night sitting on the floor, according to informed sources, because he had not been invited but had managed to enter the room together with the other 'invited' African ministers.

Once uninvited delegates who had not managed to gatecrash the green room meeting discovered that it was in progress, many kept vigil in the hotel corridors, waiting for the final outcome. As one delegate complained, 'You are representing a country, and it's humiliating and ridiculous to be hanging around the corridor ... Who gave legitimacy to this meeting? ... It was not discussed at the Committee of the Whole.'

The green room – the final hours

On the *environment*, the EC said they needed something to take away from Doha – and they got it. As a developing country delegate recalled,

> Countries went silent in the night of the final green room, so that in the end it was the EC's position that prevailed. When the EC saw that countries such as Nigeria, which had previously been strong opponents, were quiet, they kept raising their ambitions through the night, and developing countries were unable to stop them. The text on environment was further strengthened.

According to a member of the Cairns Group,

> We said, along with developing countries, that this part of the negotiations was just another form of protectionism. The precautionary principle, labelling, etc. was just clothing for protectionism. Lamy said 'You have to give me something – we don't have anything on labour or investment and competition. We can't leave with nothing.' Zoellick came to the rescue and said, 'Okay,

we will have something on the environment.' The problem was that not many ministers in that room were briefed enough or knowledgeable enough to reject what Lamy was after – even those from developed countries.

According to a developed country delegate, 'The EC and USA made a deal on the environment and anti-dumping. The environment text was essentially written by the US delegation and inserted in the declaration at the last minute – and, of course, the anti-dumping issue was emasculated by the USA.'

On *textiles*, an Asian negotiator recalled that

> when India and Pakistan wanted to push for a greater quota share on textiles, the Canadian minister, Pettigrew, was almost screaming … 'We have given you almost everything!' he said. Mike Moore and Zoellick supported Canada's comments, saying the EC had given a lot … Lamy sat quietly letting others do the persuading for him. The small gain that India had on textiles in the text was eventually removed, with the issue being referred to the WTO's Council for Trade in Goods, as a punishment for Minister Maran's 'obstinacy'.

On the *'new issues'*, it was eventually agreed that a decision would be taken on whether to begin negotiations at the Fifth Ministerial. At about 5 a.m., however, Japan changed the wording to read that *modalities* of negotiations would be decided at the Fifth Ministerial, effectively pre-empting the decision.

As the meeting drew towards a close, confusion reigned. A developed country negotiator reports that

> at about 6 or 7 a.m. on the fourteenth, the meeting was still on and we had to pull it all together. We asked if we had gotten a deal or not, and the Africans in the room said they felt they had nothing to say to their colleagues outside the room, because they could not ascertain what was agreed. They said something like 'You guys have pulled one on us again'. That was when there were pretty tough exchanges. The South Africa Trade Minister, Alec Erwin, intervened and made an impassioned speech to his fellow

> Africans saying it was in the overwhelming interest of Africa to
> support the final offer Lamy and Zoellick made ...

A developing country delegate in the room echoed this view of increasing confusion among developing country delegates.

> Members of the Secretariat were drafting bits of the document
> in the green room alongside the major players in the final hours.
> Andrew Stoler, the US deputy director general, was in charge of
> the drafting process. It was difficult to keep up with the changes
> that were going on and especially difficult to maintain discussions
> with those outside as the night progressed.

Liaison with those not invited to the meeting was a critical factor. In the words of an African negotiator,

> the ministers in the green room meeting had documents given
> to them by the members who were outside the room, which
> they consulted. They had to come out to brief those outside ...
> During the final hours there were disagreements between some
> developing country members over the 'new issues'. Crucially,
> many delegates inside the green room began to change their
> positions in favour of the developed country ones.

The liaison was appreciated by those outside the meeting. An uninvited delegate from an African LDC said that 'Minister Iddi Simba of Tanzania did very well in the room, though we [Africans] should have been putting more pressure on them. At some stage, however, they looked exhausted and did not have the stomach to take it any further.'

An African negotiator who was at the meeting said: 'I will say that the ministers were expressing the views of the members they represented – though many African ministers gradually softened their positions.'

Despite all the difficulties and the pressures they faced, however, the African delegates had some small influence on the green room process. A middle-income country negotiator emphasized:

> Thanks to the Africans in the room, mainly Kenya and Tanzania,

what would have been agreed was slightly toned down. They were as tough as nails ... There were no undiplomatic exchanges or abuse in the room, but you could hear some really tough arm-twisting going on. The system is totally opaque, but it gets things done. Even in mini-ministerial meetings there was some pressure, but when we came to plenary we still said no on some issues.

Wednesday 14 November – the morning after

After many hours of discussions, the waiver request was finally granted to the ACP countries. Ecuador, the world's most efficient banana producer, which had objected to the special arrangements on bananas between the EC and ACP countries, announced that its objections had been dealt with. The Central American countries had also given in (Clover 2001). The Thai ambassador recalled that both Thailand and the Philippines 'managed to get the procedural arrangement we required to get a waiver on tuna', adding: 'We really had to stand up for our rights.'

On the afternoon of 14 November, a final meeting of the Committee of the Whole was held to approve the draft declaration that emerged from the green room process. India still had trouble accepting the draft, but, as a developing country delegate observed, 'those who supported the text were given the floor to speak first ... It was arranged in this way to literally set the consensus ... People cheered and clapped after every endorsement of the text ...This made those who wanted more clarifications feel like they were the bad guys ...This is a common tactic, to make a certain viewpoint appear dominant.'

The EC said the document was a good compromise and that the 'Doha Development Agenda' (DDA) was good for the environment and development. South Africa urged everyone to support the DDA, suggesting that it would be unwise not to reach an agreement. Kenya proclaimed Doha a success, while Tanzania said they had a great sense of happiness, and thanked the EC for the ACP waiver. Several Latin American countries (Chile, Mexico, Bolivia, Venezuela, Ecuador, Colombia, Paraguay, Costa Rica and Brazil) also accepted the text, as did Nigeria, Botswana and Senegal.

A number of Asian countries accepted the text more grudgingly, or only with reservations. Pakistan said it had mixed feelings, as it felt there was more give than take on the part of the developing countries, but that they would work towards achieving a development round. The Philippines said they could live with the text despite the fact that some of their expectations were not fulfilled. Indonesia had concerns about labour, the environment and the 'new issues', Malaysia about 'new issues', and Korea about the commitment to improve WTO disciplines on fisheries subsidies.

Other countries were more strongly critical. When India was finally allowed to take the floor, Maran, with a certain lack of enthusiasm, supported the TRIPs and implementation texts (especially negotiations on market access for textiles), but insisted that some changes had to be made on the 'new issues' text. Bangladesh expressed disappointment at the weakness of the textiles agreement, saying that, as a result, they were leaving the conference empty-handed.

Barbados was also very concerned about the paragraphs on the 'new issues', seeking clarification regarding whether negotiations would actually take place after the Fifth Ministerial or if a decision was to be made at the Fifth Ministerial on whether or not to negotiate, supporting the latter interpretation. This request was supported by Malaysia.

Jamaica went further, dismissing the wording on the 'new issues' as ambiguous, and proposed that the reference to deciding on 'modalities of negotiations' at the next ministerial meeting in 2003 be deleted from the text. Zimbabwe, Zambia, Gambia, Uganda and Grenada supported this suggestion, as did Kenya (who had initially supported the draft).

Cuba made it clear that it shared the concerns of India and Barbados on the 'new issues', and explicitly challenged the view that consensus had been reached on the matter. The delegate also criticized the extension of the conference after many delegates had left as unjust and unfair.

Once again, despite the number of other countries raising similar concerns, the Western press was mobilized to paint India as the villain at Doha. Qatari officials also started to apply pressure on India, because naturally they wanted a successful outcome in Doha.

The final hours

Zoellick spent the final day (14 November) 'helping' the EC to get something on the 'new issues', because it was felt that Europe had made some compromises on the farm subsidies issue, despite the 'get-out' clause they had managed to get in the text. According to an American trade official, 'there was a sense that our issues were settled'. Zoellick's 'help' mainly took the form of haranguing India.

India remained adamant, however. A negotiator from the Middle East described what followed.

The American trade representative had called the Indian prime minister in order to get India to back down. I think there was an element of politics involved. India wanted a bit of attention because the West – especially the USA – seemed very focused on their rival Pakistan after September 11th, although I think India and Pakistan are very cooperative on the issues here in Geneva, and also at the Doha Ministerial meeting. I also believe that India does resist certain positions on behalf of all developing countries.

At 3 p.m., a small group of trade ministers, including Minister Biwott of Kenya and Robert Zoellick, called Minister Maran of India into a private room for discussions. Mike Moore was also said to be present for some of the meeting, pressurizing India to be reasonable and to accept the document. According to one negotiator, Moore 'firmly retorted back to any doubts and objections Maran had ... The minister was protecting the interests of his country, the director general had no business saying all this.'

The Kenyan minister attacked Maran for throwing the landmark deal on TRIPs and public health into jeopardy. Zoellick suggested Maran have a telephone call with US President George W. Bush to discuss his concerns. Instead, Maran 'went out to the corridor and called New Delhi on his cellular phone' (Cooper and Winestock 2001b).

At about 7 p.m., after hours of hectic behind-the-scenes talks,

India finally accepted the conference document amid cheers by delegates at the conference centre. The text on all the 'new issues' was amended to read 'we agree that negotiations will take place after the Fifth Session of the Ministerial Conference on the basis of a decision to be taken, *by explicit consensus*, at that session on modalities of negotiations'. The text seemed even more ambiguous and confusing than the previous versions. As a developing country delegate remarked, 'some really bad English was used in the final Doha Declaration'.

Many developing countries were deeply unhappy with the implications of the text, and continued to show their reluctance, but no country took the step to break the consensus and walk out.

As part of the 'deal', Minister Kamal released a statement (drafted by then DDG Andrew Stoler) at the final plenary, before the document was adopted, which appeared to clarify matters.

> I would like to note that some delegations have requested clarification concerning paragraphs 20, 23, 26 and 27 of the draft declaration [on the 'new issues']. Let me say that with respect to the reference to an 'explicit consensus' being needed, in these paragraphs, for a decision to be taken at the Fifth Session of the Ministerial Conference, my understanding is that, at that session, a decision would indeed need to be taken, by explicit consensus, before negotiations on trade and investment and trade and competition policy, transparency in government procurement and trade facilitation can proceed. In my view, this would give each member the right to take a position on modalities that would prevent negotiations from proceeding after the Fifth Session of the Ministerial Conference until that member is prepared to join in an explicit consensus.

In hindsight, however, this 'clarification' proved almost worthless, and has since been ignored by the major developed countries, who have pressed ahead with preparations for negotiations regardless.

Conclusion

Some 3,800 delegates from 142 countries spent a week in Doha, attending meetings which continued into the early hours of the morning, and even overnight, to agree on a ministerial declaration. This represents more than seventy person-years of time – equivalent to nearly two entire working lives – quite apart from the multi-million-dollar cost of travel, accommodation, security, conference administration, interpretation and translation, etc., and all the time devoted to preparations for the conference, in Geneva and Doha. For all this time and effort, as Harbinson observed, the contentious text he had drafted, which had been roundly condemned by many delegates in Geneva for reflecting the agenda of the major developed countries to the virtual exclusion of developing country concerns, 'remained virtually unchanged', and a substantial proportion of the countries attending still had serious reservations about it.

In the end, despite the principle of consensus, and the reservations of many developing country members, the text was pushed through. This had more to do with the process of the meetings, and behind-the-scenes pressure on the more reluctant members, than with honest persuasion or democracy. They offered the crumbs of the TRIPs and public health Option One and the ACP waiver to buy the support of developing countries, then they simply wore down the opposition. According to an Asian delegate, 'Lamy and Zoellick, the marathon runners, are physically fit and knew our minds were not working [due to exhaustion], so they put out a draft after an all night meeting and got it through ... It was a psychological thing.' And, of course, it is easier to continue after an all-night meeting with dozens of negotiators than with a mere handful.

Even then, and even manipulating the final Conference of the Whole meeting, they faced substantial opposition. They used blatant political pressure, backed by manipulation of the media, to neutralize India, and simply ignored the other objectors. In the end, the Quad prevailed, and they got what they wanted – a new round, including a major advantage in the decision to be taken on 'new issues' at the Fifth Ministerial, with minimal concessions to the developing countries.

Notes

1. The RAND Corporation is a US non-profit 'think tank' specializing in research and analysis on international, social and military issues.

2. Interview with Stuart Harbinson, then Hong Kong ambassador to the WTO, 18 March 2002.

3. Interview with Ian Wilkinson, deputy permanent representative of the EC delegation to the international organizations in Geneva, 14 March 2002.

4. The description of the heads of delegation meeting is based mainly on Khor (2001) and ICTSD (2001c).

5. Interview with Stuart Harbinson, then Hong Kong ambassador to the WTO, 18 March 2002.

6. *Financial Times*, 9 August 2001, as summarized in the World Bank's 'Development News' press review.

7. India's position emphasizes the need to deal with the 'asymmetries and imbalances' in the 1995 Uruguay Round trade agreements before a new round is launched, including accelerating the timetable for lifting US and EC quotas on developing country textile exports; allowing a more flexible interpretation of intellectual property rights in the developing world; and restricting the use of anti-dumping provisions by the USA, notably on steel imports.

8. Interview with Andrew Stoler, then WTO deputy director general, 5 March 2002.

9. Interview with Dr Federico Cuello Camilo, then Dominican Republic ambassador to the WTO and UN, 4 March 2002. He was removed from his Geneva posting in August 2002. According to Geneva trade diplomats, his removal was due to US pressure.

10. Interview with Iba Mar Oulare, second counsellor in charge of WTO and UN issues at the Senegalese mission in Geneva, 19 March 2002.

11. Interview with Apiradi Tantraporn, then Thai ambassador to the WTO, 9 April 2002.

FIVE
Look back in anger – post-Doha reflections

As with most historical events, it was only with hindsight that the implications of the Doha Ministerial could be assessed – and only after the personal and political traumas it represented that the delegates had the chance to reflect on what had happened. This chapter takes an initial look back at the process through the eyes of some of the delegates, beginning, once again, with a brief look at the historical precedent of the Bretton Woods Conference, based on Skidelsky's (2000) account. It goes on to present some general views on the outcome of the negotiations, and the effect of September 11th on the proceedings. A brief summary of who gained, and who lost, is followed by assessments by developing countries of the outcome and the process by which it was reached.

After Bretton Woods

Skidelsky (2000) recounts how, in the end, Bretton Woods produced some kind of an 'agreement'. This is attributed to the greater ease of agreeing on finance than on trade; the main work having already been done in bilateral Anglo-American negotiations; the careful management of the conference itself by White and the US Treasury; and the desperation of both Morgenthau and Keynes, for different reasons, to sign a document – Morgenthau to deliver a re-election present to Roosevelt, Keynes to lock the United States into a rules-based post-war financial order.

However, the 'agreement' was possible only because the agreed text contained ambiguities, which countries with opposing views could interpret according to their own preferences, and left some key points implicit. Some such points were quickly exposed. For example, a little-noticed amendment to Article IV (Section 1) laid down that the par values of currencies should be expressed in terms of gold or US dollars. This made the dollar the only gold-convertible currency, and thus the key currency of the new system. While every other currency could devalue against the dollar, the dollar could be devalued only against gold.

The Americans needed this type of monetary strength if they were to control the Latin Americans; but it led Henry Clay, a British economist at the World Bank, to describe Bretton Woods later as 'the greatest blow to Britain next to the war', as the convertibility of sterling into gold and dollars would remove the incentive for sterling area countries to buy British goods and hold balances in London.

If there was one underlying agenda behind the whole process, it was Morgenthau's determination to concentrate financial power in the USA. Britain wanted the IMF to be based in London, but they had to concede to the USA, which was contributing two or three times more money than anyone else. Morgenthau thus succeeded in establishing the headquarters of both the Fund and the Bank in Washington. In effect, Bretton Woods meant the end of London's pre-eminent position as the financial centre of the world.

Keynes himself had not had time to read the complete text of the ninety-six-page document covering the Fund and the Bank before he signed it. He had hardly been able to attend the plenary sessions because of ill health, and his dual role as head of delegation and chairman of the Bank Commission took its toll. White was aware of this and aimed to neutralize him, knowing that, as a result of his failing stamina, Keynes would only be able to focus on Bank matters, and would have little time or energy left to deal with Fund matters. This strategy worked well. 'Our only excuse,' Keynes later explained, 'is that our hosts had made final arrangements to throw us out of the hotel, unhoused, disappointed, unanealed, within a few hours.'

After Doha

Doha has been described in different ways by its many participants. A widely expressed view among Northern delegates is that Doha represented a bit of gain and a bit of loss for everybody, allowing all governments to claim some degree of victory. Guy de Jonquières of the *Financial Times* concluded that 'the Doha Conference will not directly affect the wealth of nations or prices paid by consumers' (de Jonquières 2001c).

A more candid delegate from an EC member state, however, saw the conference and the possibility of negotiating on the 'new issues' as potentially detrimental for developing countries: 'On competition, for example, if your economy is on its knees [as in many developing countries], then as a government you would need to regulate it. If, however, you have multinational corporations on the scene, you are unable to do so because the competition rules will not allow it.' C. Rammanohar Reddy, deputy editor of *The Hindu*, a leading independent daily newspaper in India, took a cynical view of the Northern 'something-for-everyone' line: 'At Doha the major powers scripted an agreement that created a mirage of a triumph for an equitable global trading system. They did so by weaving an illusion that all countries, rich and poor, gained something' (Reddy 2001).

The USA gave the impression that it went to Doha with limited objectives compared with the EC, and was seen as having given up a lot more, on TRIPs and public health and on anti-dumping (de Jonquières 2001c). The latter issue was seen as a huge sacrifice, because Zoellick overrode the decision of 400 US congressmen and -women to support negotiations, while the former was seen as dealing a blow to US-based pharmaceutical companies, whose role in setting negotiating agendas for the US government, especially on patent issues, is well known.[1] In fact, 'US diplomacy was so effective that it trumped, at least temporarily, [the EC's] claims to be the developing countries' friend. Frustrated European officials were left protesting lamely that the [EC] bought far more from poor countries than the US' (ibid.).

The Western media presented India as the villain of the piece, while pouring praise on Zoellick – and this adulation extended well beyond the media. Such was Zoellick's newfound friendship with African ministers that nearly all of them clamoured to sing his praises after the deal in Doha was brokered. 'Mr Zoellick put this whole thing together,' said Tanzania's Trade Minister, Iddi Mohamed Simba. Morocco's ambassador at the time, Nacer Benjelloun-Touimi, added, 'This is what leadership is about. He

[Zoellick] has been brokering the deal between the Europeans and the African countries' (quoted in Cooper and Winestock 2001b).

Zoellick further strengthened his friendship with African leaders by visiting Kenya in February 2002 to build on the cordial relations between the two countries – and perhaps to reward the Kenyan government for the helpful role it had played at Doha. According to the *Financial Times* (Alden 2002a), this was the first ever visit to Sub-Saharan Africa by a United States trade representative.

In the final analysis, however, for all the cost, the time and the toll on participants, these were negotiations about whether to hold negotiations and how they should be structured; and the declaration that came out at the end differed very little from the draft which had gone in, with all its imperfections. This was the *fait accompli*.

The shadow of September 11th

As the Bretton Woods Agreement was delivered for reasons beyond the obvious, so too was the so-called 'Doha Development Agenda' – and one of the reasons was the drive to launch a new round just to keep the WTO alive after September 11th. The powerful Northern countries, especially the USA, needed to boost their sagging economies. They also wanted (more than the South) to maintain the multilateral system intact, in order to keep an eye on potential 'troublemakers' – the so-called 'rogue states' *outside* the system were enough of a headache.

WTO deputy director general Andrew Stoler[2] said he did not think September 11th had had much of an impact on the Doha process. 'We needed success at Doha regardless – although the [post-September 11th] situation made things a bit more dramatic.' Others, however, saw a hardening in the US line and tactics. An EC delegate said he had hoped that the Americans' behaviour would improve after September 11th 'but it is actually getting worse'.

A Latin American delegate echoed this view: 'The battle was lost to level the playing field at the WTO after the September 11th terrorist attacks against the USA. Although they gave a few carrots, they became even more aggressive than usual when faced with any kind of opposition to their positions behind the scenes.'

The USA saw particular advantage in China's accession to the WTO at this crucial stage in the war against terrorism. Mexico had reportedly been trying to block China coming on board at the last minute because of certain trade concerns. However, according to one delegate, 'The USA by this time was satisfied China could join, so Mexico was convinced to change its mind, bearing in mind the close relationship between the current Presidents of Mexico [Vicente Fox] and the USA [George W. Bush Jr].'

Winners and losers: who got what?

In assessing who gained and who lost at the Doha Ministerial itself, it is important to remember what went before. Thanks to the mini-ministerial conferences (see Chapter 3), the starting-point for Doha was a draft text the content of which broadly coincided with what the Quad – and particularly the USA and EC – wanted, while largely ignoring the concerns of the developing countries. Even without making any further progress at Doha, the Quad would secure most of their objectives, just so long as they were not forced to make concessions.

They were broadly successful in this endeavour. The *International Trade Daily* reported: 'In the end it was the developed world, led by the United States and the EU, that appeared to come away with what it wanted. The developing countries achieved a victory in only one area – albeit relatively significant – dealing with intellectual property rights and public health' (*International Trade Daily* 2001).

Even on TRIPs, it became apparent after Doha that the developing countries had gained less than they originally believed, as further discussions were stalled in Geneva (see Chapter 9). As a delegate from a middle-income country observed, the developed countries were given all they wanted 'on a silver platter'.

According to WTO analyst and former Indian ambassador to the GATT, Bhagirath Lal Das (2002), developing countries had been drawing attention for several years before Doha to the need to eliminate the imbalances in the WTO agreements, giving special treatment to the areas of interest of developed countries, while ignoring or undermining the interests of developing countries.

He decried the Doha Work Programme as having 'enhanced the imbalance in the WTO system significantly', because it was 'not the result of any serious negotiation among the members of the WTO. The major developed countries have not engaged in any negotiation of give-and-take; they just put up their proposals and asked the developing countries to accept them.' He went on to cite the pressure put on countries that made them relent, warning that 'if the developing countries do not guard against it, and defend themselves, they will be losing further ground'. He concluded:

> The Work Programme is a gain for the major developed countries, but the developed countries have given nothing in return to the developing countries. This is totally contrary to the GATT/WTO process where reciprocity is expected to be the main guiding principle in negotiations … Ironically, the Work Programme has been sometimes termed as a 'development agenda' which is quite erroneous …The agenda of the Work Programme has been totally set by the major developed countries guided by their own economic interests. (ibid.)

The USA ensured it remained in the driving seat at Doha. The Americans went to Doha focusing on opening markets for agriculture, industrial goods and services, and succeeded in doing so. They managed to obtain a 'get-out' clause on the environment; negotiations starting in 2003 on the two areas of the 'new issues' they really wanted (transparency in government procurement and trade facilitation); and negotiations on greater market access for industrial goods. In return, they offered carrots on the TRIPs political statement; a rather loose commitment to renegotiate anti-dumping rules; and the inclusion of investment and competition.

For the EC, President of the European Commission Romano Prodi commented to journalists after the conference that the Doha agreement was a sign that 'it would not be one world against another but a shared agreement', while EC Agriculture Commissioner Franz Fischler claimed Doha was a 'magnificent success' (Mann 2001).

They wanted to begin negotiations on investment, competition and government procurement, and environment, while limiting damage to their agricultural interests. The final text – on the environment and negotiations on all the 'new issues' in 2003 – represented a major coup for the EC, achieved with the support of the USA. They also obtained a 'get-out' clause on the phasing out of subsidies in agriculture, and the ACP waiver. In this context, Lamy's statement to reporters that the EC was the 'orphan of the conference' because they came away with nothing (quoted in de Jonquières 2001c) seemed more than a little disingenuous.

Developing countries got very little, since most of their apparent gains were in language rather than in substance; and they lost out on several of the key issues. As the Dutch delegation commented in a guide to the draft declaration, 'The LDCs get a lot of text instead of substance' (Permanent Mission of the Netherlands in Geneva 2001). Much the same could be said of the final declaration.

The developing countries got a political statement on TRIPs and public health; the ACP waiver for the relevant developing countries, which was blatantly used as a bargaining chip in the negotiations; a delay until 2003 for negotiations on the 'new issues', with a vague clause leaving it ambiguous whether or not they will actually commence then (see below); a commitment to capacity-building and technical assistance on the 'new issues' (though without any firm commitment on improving supply-side constraints); new working groups to discuss trade, debt and finance, and technology transfer; and a commitment that provisions on Special and Differential Treatment 'shall be reviewed with a view to strengthening them', which past experience suggests may not in the event bring tangible benefits. Even their apparent victories were limited (see below).

On the negative side, the text on revisiting anti-dumping rules was emasculated; the wording on export subsidies and domestic supports in agriculture was watered down, allowing a 'get-out' clause for the EC; greater market access for industrial goods, opposed by developing countries, was brought into negotiations; and wording on the environment, which they wanted totally out of the negotiations within the WTO and instead left with expert UN agencies, was strengthened, with a 'get-out' clause for the USA.

According to WTO analyst and former Indian ambassador to the WTO Bhagirath Lal Das (2002), the Doha Work Programme will also involve an even heavier workload for developing countries than the Uruguay Round. As the Kenyan delegation observed in commenting on the draft declaration at the General Council meeting of 31 October 2001:

> Developing and least developed countries with small missions have consistently said that even with the current work programme, they are unable to follow all deliberations in the WTO. Small missions like ours will be disadvantaged by the creation of additional bodies to handle future work programme ... The more issues on the agenda the more meetings will be required and this will be very difficult for the small delegations to effectively engage in the process. Hence pursuing what is being touted as a broad and balanced agenda risks continuing marginalization of poor developing countries. (TWN 2001)

One disheartened LDC delegate said after Doha that developing countries should have demanded the removal of all references to the development interests of LDCs. This would have made no practical difference, but would have prevented the major powers from cynically using the ministerial declaration to trumpet their supposed commitment to development to the public and to trade ministers unfamiliar with WTO technicalities and politics.

As regards the WTO Secretariat, Mike Moore personally encouraged key staff to push for a new round, not just to get rid of what Zoellick called the 'stain of Seattle', but also for his own personal sense of achievement. According to a Southern delegate, 'The Secretariat was playing the EC role, and openly championing a new round ... Certain people who wanted to advance their careers had to be pushing a certain line ... Of course, you had to take the cue from the director general.' The role of the Secretariat is discussed in greater detail in Chapter 7.

Above all, Moore and his deputies – and, indeed, the Secretariat in general – wanted to avoid reaching the end of the DG's three-year term having presided over two failed ministerial meetings. Moore got what he wanted. A Geneva-based ambassador from an Asian country observed:

> The Secretariat staff as a whole warmed up to Moore a bit after Doha, because he is now seen as being a bit more competent. They feel he proved himself as a result of the 'success' at the Fourth Ministerial ... bearing in mind that after the failure at Seattle the Secretariat was under attack, things came to a standstill, morale was extremely low, and Mike Moore shouldered much of the blame.

A year on, however, the WTO Secretariat staff seem to have had second thoughts about the 'success' in Doha. In November 2002, they went on strike, complaining of work overload and asking for a pay increase of 8 per cent and the employment of twelve more new staff, primarily in the agriculture and services divisions, where negotiations were under way. According to WTO staff, the number of formal and informal meetings had increased by 35 per cent between 1999 and 2002, and the amount of written material produced (judged by the number of words translated) by 29 per cent (Sharma 2002c).

What happened on the 'old' issues?

Much of the discussion so far has focused on the 'new issues'. While these were a key area of contention, however, a number of other issues were also important. The highest-profile issue was the Declaration on TRIPs and Public Health. Politically, this was a small success for developing countries, although its wording – 'We agree that the TRIPs Agreement *does not and should not* prevent members from taking measures to protect public health' (paragraph 4) – was significantly weaker than '*shall not* prevent', which the developing countries wanted. The declaration had serious limitations in its practical effect, however, and the developed countries extracted a considerable price in terms of concessions on other issues (see Chapter 6).

The success was limited because there were no changes made to the legal text of the TRIPs Agreement. It was a political declaration that would carry some weight in a dispute, but still left developing countries vulnerable to counter-interpretations by the developed countries and their pharmaceutical corporations of the actual measures developing countries could take to protect public health interests.

For instance, the exact mechanism of how developing countries without manufacturing capacity could have access to generic drugs remained unresolved. Many of the developing countries in greatest need do not have the capacity to produce generic drugs. While the TRIPs Agreement allows a government to issue a licence to a local generic manufacturer, enabling the manufacturer to produce a copy of a patented drug, Article 31(f) requires it to be sold 'predominantly' on the local market. Thus countries without manufacturing capacity cannot use this option to produce cheaper drugs; and those with capacity would be largely limited to their domestic markets, limiting the potential for economies of scale and thus increasing production costs.

Paragraph 6 of the TRIPs and Health Declaration therefore states: 'We recognize that WTO Members with insufficient or no manufacturing capacities in the pharmaceutical sector could face difficulties in making effective use of compulsory licensing under the TRIPs Agreement. We instruct the Council for TRIPs to find an expeditious solution to this problem and to report to the General Council before the end of 2002.'

For the next year, developing countries were alarmed by the vicious attempts by the major powers to water down severely even the fragile political gain they had attained. The USA, the EC and Japan used these discussions to limit the scope of concessions as far as possible, and beyond the terms of the declaration itself, and the end-2002 deadline was missed (see Chapter 8).

The developed countries' foot-dragging on the patenting of biological materials (Article 27.3b of the TRIPs Agreement) continued in Doha. The declaration side-steps any commitment to deal squarely with this issue, and gives no commitment in terms of a time-line for completion of the review begun in 1999. Even the Dutch delegation, commenting on the language of the declaration, said:

There is no commitment to negotiate, only to continue a work programme in the TRIPs Council, not even a deadline to report to the Fifth Ministerial Conference as is done for trade and environment ... Ministers do not really address the widespread criticism on TRIPs-rules in these areas. This will be a disappointment for many developing countries ... [The] reason is the resistance from the US and a few other OECD countries. (Permanent Mission of the Netherlands in Geneva 2001)

Since Doha, the TRIPs Council has neither done any work to further the review of Article 27.3b nor seriously undertaken the review of the overall agreement mandated in Article 71.1.

The Declaration also failed to deal substantively with other TRIPs-related problems, such as the prevention of technology transfer and diffusion.

In preparing for Doha, the EC once again made it clear that it was willing to address implementation issues only as part of a comprehensive round including 'new issues'. The USA and Japan echoed this position, arguing that some of the implementation issues involved changes to the rules, and that such changes could be made only as part of a new round.

Clearly, developed countries had to appear to deliver something in Doha, but there was simply no political willingness to provide anything concrete. Consequently, while decisions were made on forty-eight implementation items, in a document running to eleven pages, only about three decisions were of any value. The remainder were limited to 'best endeavour' language, merely 'urging' developed countries without making action mandatory, or only requesting WTO bodies to 'examine' an issue, thus postponing any real decision. The remaining issues – those of greater importance to developing countries – were to be taken up as a priority in the relevant WTO bodies, which in turn would report to the Trade Negotiations Committee by the end of 2002 for appropriate action. It was also agreed that decisions on providing larger quotas on textiles would be taken by 31 July 2002. Once again, these deadlines were missed (see Chapter 8).

In their desperate efforts to get a new round off the ground while portraying the work programme as 'development-oriented', developed countries agreed in Doha that 'all special and differential treatment provisions shall be reviewed with a view to strengthening them and making them more precise, effective and operational'. The declaration called on the Committee on Trade and Development to come up with recommendations for decisions by July 2002. Like implementation issues, SDT provisions were put on the 'fast track', although they remained part of the 'single undertaking' (i.e. nothing is agreed to until everything is agreed to).[3] The July deadline was subsequently extended to December; and by December no progress had been made due to the developed countries' intransigence (see Chapter 8).

The developing countries' opposition to negotiations on industrial tariffs and market access for non-agricultural products was further undermined by the draft declaration produced by Stuart Harbinson, which said that there was agreement on beginning negotiations. The final Doha text stated that negotiations should reduce or eliminate tariff peaks, high tariffs and tariff escalation, as well as non-tariff barriers; and that negotiations should take fully into account the special needs and interests of developing countries and LDCs, 'including through less than full reciprocity in reduction commitments'. Despite this apparently reassuring language, however, it also stated that 'product coverage shall be comprehensive and without *a priori* exclusions'. That is, even products that are important for local employment will have to be liberalized.

An understanding that further negotiations on agriculture would commence by 1999 was built into the 1995 Agreement on Agriculture. The Doha Declaration did not launch new negotiations in this area, but specified deadlines for the completion of negotiations on modalities[4] (31 March 2003) and the submission of draft schedules – how the general rules and modalities would be applied to specific agricultural products (by the Fifth Ministerial, in September 2003).

Most disappointing for developing countries was that developed countries wriggled out of agreeing to end export subsidies – legalized dumping, which has long been banned for industrial products.

The words 'without prejudging the outcome of the negotiations' were slipped into the agriculture paragraph of the declaration after France blocked language suggesting that subsidies would be eliminated, indicating that there is no guarantee of an end to export subsidies or a substantial reduction in domestic support.

Further negotiations on trade in services were also mandated in the GATS and would have taken place with or without the launching of a new round in Doha. The Doha Ministerial fast-forwarded the negotiations, however, the declaration setting dates for the start of the requests phase of negotiations (30 June 2002) and the offers phase (31 March 2003).[5] The repeated requests of developing countries for the assessment required by the GATS Agreement before new negotiations continued to be ignored.

On trade and the environment, the final declaration agreed to negotiations on the relationship between existing WTO rules and specific trade obligations set out in Multilateral Environmental Agreements (MEAs);[6] on criteria for granting MEA secretariats observer status at the WTO; and on the reduction or elimination of tariff and non-tariff barriers for environmental goods and services.

Developing countries are concerned about this outcome for a number of reasons. First, it expands the mandate of the WTO to include trade and the environment as a new issue for rule-making. While the issues for negotiations are limited at present, proponents, particularly the EC, are likely to put pressure on countries to expand this mandate further in the course of the current round and in future rounds (Khor 2002).

Second, many developing countries fear that the negotiations endorsed in Doha will make the WTO rules subservient to the MEAs. In principle, at least, WTO rules and MEAs are international agreements of equal status, each with their own rights, obligations and mechanisms for implementation and dispute settlement, providing some checks and balances. At present, Article XX of GATT 1994 allows countries to impose trade restrictions on environmental grounds, but also allows such restrictions to be challenged by another member.

The concern is that the present talks may eventually mean MEAs automatically taking precedence over WTO rules. While this could be beneficial in some cases, experience suggests that it could be used opportunistically by developed countries to protect their markets against developing country exports (Khor 2002; Das 2002), as in the case of food safety standards (see Chapter 2). Moreover, developing countries have fewer resources to challenge such trade restrictions, and their sanctions against developed countries are limited, so that they often end up simply having to accept the injury to local industries caused by the disruption of trade (see Chapter 1, Box 1.1).

The declaration also specifies that 'The negotiations shall be limited in scope to the applicability of such existing WTO rules as among parties to the MEA in question' – that is, the provisions of the MEA would apply only to its signatories. This provides an escape clause for the USA, for example, which is not a party to most MEAs. The USA would not, for instance, want to abide by the Biosafety Protocol, which could limit their exports of genetically modified agricultural produce. Thus, US exports would remain unrestrained, while those countries that are signatories would be bound by their MEA obligations, subject to the WTO dispute settlement mechanism, which is tougher than those of MEAs. This would both create an imbalance in the obligations taken on by the USA, for example, and MEA signatory developing countries, and could deter countries from signing MEAs.

Delegates' reactions to the Doha process and outcome

The views of developing country delegates on the process and outcome of Doha are as varied as the developing countries themselves – within country groupings as well as between them. This section is drawn from interviews with some of these delegates, conducted during the first half of 2002. Delegates are identified by numbers rather than by name or country, to preserve their anonymity.

Least developed country delegates

One LDC delegate took a positive view of the coordination between developing countries, at least in the Africa Group. *Delegate 1*:

I think up to the last day at Doha the Africa Group was very well organized. We had a good deal of NGO support too. If your share of world trade is near zero you can't give in so easily! We were very unpopular in Doha for opposing the 'new issues'.

Others, however, felt that the strength of coordination had faded as the conference proceeded. *Delegate 2*:

We [developing countries] do really well when the basketball game begins. We work well as a team, score consistently, have a healthy lead ... Just as the game starts to heat up and really get exciting ... we collapse.

Another delegate took a more critical view. *Delegate 3*:

There was a sense of deception – not by what some of the African ministers who were representing the rest of us were saying, but by what they were *not* saying.

Another felt that the collaborative efforts of developing countries were doomed from their start, long before Doha, for reasons beyond their control. *Delegate 4*:

Developing countries have been highly engaged in producing very firm positions on substantive issues. We did so at the LDC-III conference in Brussels in May 2001; in Zanzibar in July 2001, LDC trade ministers produced the Zanzibar Declaration; in Abuja, Nigeria, at the Conference of Ministers of Trade of the Organization of African Unity [OAU] in October 2001, firm positions were outlined on what we had to achieve in Doha to redress the imbalances in the world trading system – not to mention the strong positions the ACP group took in Brussels just before Doha. However it is clear that at the end of all this hard work, the chairman of the General Council and the WTO director general will come up with statements and declarations that do not reflect most of our [developing countries'] views on the issues.

Part of the reason for the failure was the dynamics of the negotiation process – and the relative strengths of the opposing sides. *Delegate 5*:

We thought ministers would correct the problem ambassadors experienced in Geneva with the text when we got to Doha, but they were instead preoccupied with trying to avoid another Seattle. Carrots were dangled at them so the issue of process went underground. Besides, those who were in the green room were up against some highly skilled developed country negotiators. The big guys are a different breed altogether ... This is all part of learning and growing up.

Delegate 1:

I have observed a few problems that Africans have in the multilateral system. Firstly, we have never known how to apply our available human resources – the confidence to play the game is lacking; and secondly we have difficulty defining our positions and always allow disinformation [often spread by Northern countries] to undercut our positions.

For whatever reason, there was a sense of at least partial defeat. *Delegate 6*:

In Doha, the LDCs, the Africa Group and the ACP and some sympathizers were not for a new round. We all worked together at one stage to get our concerns heard. Eventually we backed down on 'new issues' because we got the [ACP] waiver and were promised technical assistance and capacity-building. So, we'll see what happens. We did not want to, but we had to back down in the end. When we came back we had a lot of retrospective meetings to ascertain what went wrong. The ACP Group, the LDCs, the Commonwealth, etc. met. Eventually, we decided that we had to put the past behind us. We did get something in Doha – sometimes you have to compromise.

Nevertheless, there was some degree of guarded optimism about the outcome among some delegates – although scepticism about the prospects of the carrots which were offered materializing was widespread. *Delegate 7*:

The developed countries now have to deliver on their promises and recognize the real needs of the LDCs. Supply-side constraints need to be addressed. I think, as a road map to where we want to get to, the declaration was not bad. It is a start.

Delegate 1:

There appears to be a genuine appreciation that capacity-building for LDCs is needed – whether the assistance will be channelled meaningfully remains to be seen. We need capacity-building, not as a tool for blackmail, but rather as a genuine gesture to help LDCs.

Middle-income country delegates

The views of delegates from middle-income countries were at least as varied, as the three examples below demonstrate. One delegate was positively enthusiastic – although this may in part reflect the behind the scenes bilateral trade agreements secured with the Quad. *Delegate 1:*

Officially, I would say we had a work programme that is balanced, although a lot of ambition was not satisfied. Unofficially, I would say we came out great! It could have been a lot worse – the fact that we got a document in the end was crucial.

Others took a more nuanced view. *Delegate 2:*

I think the group as a whole would have liked more on agriculture, and transfer of technology, and GATS Mode 4 [temporary migration of professionals] issues, and less on the environment and the 'new issues'. On textiles, some of us have special arrangements with the big countries that cater to our needs.

A third delegate, well known among colleagues for standing up to the negotiators from the developed countries in trade meetings, was seen by others breaking down in tears in the corridors on the final night at Doha. He could hardly contain his frustration. *Delegate 3:*

I felt so much pain in my heart. They sold out, our ministers. We burn our days and nights working to protect the interests of our countries, and it is all a waste of effort. Our ministers went in and gave everything away, on a silver platter, especially to the EU, in the new issues and on environment. Now we have to deal with controlling the damage. We fight so hard in Geneva and all of this goes to waste. Instead, we should devote more time to our families.

The role of India

India warrants special treatment in any discussion of the Doha Conference. It played a unique role, as a leader, and often lone spokesperson, of the developing world – and as the main scapegoat of the supporters of a new round. According to S. Narayanan, recently retired as Indian ambassador in Geneva, however, their opposition was not to a new round but rather to the 'new issues'. He added: 'What mattered was the agenda ... India's concerns are based on its experience with the Uruguay Round, during which an open-ended process was in operation whereby subjects got added on and the mandates got changed as the negotiations proceeded' (FICCI 2001: 15).

India paid the price for its stand, both in terms of its international position, and in the frustration of its delegates. Guy de Jonquières of the *Financial Times* saw India as the one clear victim of Doha – not because of the outcome of the talks, but because of the damage to its international image. 'The only real loser in Doha was India. It achieved no obvious gains, except for the dubious pleasure of delaying the close of the meeting. Its relentlessly negative and obstructive approach left it isolated and exasperated other poor countries, weakening its claim to lead them in a North–South struggle in the WTO' (de Jonquières 2001c).

Certainly, the EC and US delegations were not pleased with Maran for holding up the talks. After all, said an EC delegate, 'India has a small share of world trade compared to developed countries'. Once again, the full weight of condemnation was heaped on India, the one country with the political weight and courage necessary to allow it to voice its concerns, and the support it received from other developing countries was ignored.

As the conference progressed, however, the leaders of the various Southern regional and interest groups caved in, one by one, to EC and US pressure. India remained steadfastly fighting – but it became an ever more lonely struggle.

In the end, India had little choice but to concede, receiving only Kamal's assurance, as conference chair, that member countries would have the opportunity to block negotiations on the 'new issues' at the Fifth Ministerial if they so chose (see Chapter 4). Although those developing countries still resisting the 'new issues' were promised that this interpretation would be respected, however, the EC, the USA and other developed countries reneged as soon as the Doha Declaration was accepted. They have since ignored the chairman's statement, insisting that negotiations will indeed be launched.

The only crumb of comfort is that negotiations on the 'new issues' will not formally begin until after the Cancun Ministerial in September 2003 – and that the developing countries can, in principle, block agreement on the modalities, and thus the launch of the 'new issues'. S. P. Shukla, formerly India's ambassador to GATT and secretary in the commerce and finance ministries, however, questions even this:

[The notion that the] Indian Delegation has 'succeeded' in postponing the launch of the New Round or, at the minimum, the negotiations on the New Issues by two years is as naïve as it is false … The change of nomenclature [from New Round to Work Programme] does not alter the pith and substance of the process. The past 'Rounds' have followed a pattern: the Ministerial Declaration lays down a broad negotiating mandate for every subject on the agenda; a time frame is indicated; a Trade Negotiations Committee (TNC) is set up to supervise and direct the negotiations. The concept of treating the negotiations as a 'single undertaking' was invented in the Uruguay Round. All these elements are unmistakably present in the Doha Ministerial Declaration … In the negotiations on the New Issues more often than not it is the developing countries that would be 'paying' in the sense of accepting new obligations and paring down their autonomy in economic decision making. (Shukla 2002)

The resurfacing of the green room

Unsurprisingly, views on the final green room meeting reflect a wide range of opinions. Harbinson, as ever, was quick to defend the process.

> How the hell do you manage such a process without some small meetings? The facilitators were open to people asking questions and consulting with them – this did occur. They also had very good reporting-back sessions. When it comes to two or three critical issues, you need to be practical. You can't have 144 ministers in one room trying to come to a conclusion. Agriculture was solved by this stage. It was the 'new issues' and the environment that were outstanding.[7]

Developed country representatives also generally took a positive view. According to an EC negotiator, 'Mike Moore was in charge of the composition of the green room [and] he got a lot of African ministers in who were articulate', while a Cairns Group member from a developed country argued that 'if you consider their share of world trade, there were a lot more Africans in the room compared to Seattle … The whole of the Nordic countries weren't there,[8] and the Latin American and ASEAN countries were under-represented.'

Considering the number of members or votes, of course, gives a rather different perspective. Half of the high-income and upper-middle-income countries were represented in the green room, but less than one-eighth of the low- and lower-middle-income countries – even including those like Zimbabwe who managed to attend un-invited.

Others were somewhat more guarded in their defence of the process, seeing it more as a necessary evil. According to a delegate from the EC:

> We learnt lessons after Seattle, but green rooms surfaced again during Doha. Green rooms are terrible but it is a devil you can-

not avoid when you want to advance things. There have been great improvements on them since Seattle, but when it comes to ministerial meetings we appear to reinvent things. There is a pressure cooker atmosphere at these meetings.

A negotiator for an Eastern European country anticipating accession to the EC also took a positive view, though suggesting that this was not universal among countries in this position:

We [Eastern European countries] weren't invited to be physically in the meeting, but we were regularly informed about what was going on. We had access to the facilitators. Some of us who sat in the corridors also got information from the EC negotiators. I understand some were very upset in the green room about the way the negotiations were going and as a result had to be lobbied to change their positions. Time was very limited in Doha, so countries like us that did not have problems with the document were not invited in the final negotiations. A number of my colleagues were angry that they weren't invited. I asked, 'Do you have a major problem with the negotiations?' – because as far as I knew we all took the EC positions. They said 'No.' I said: 'So?'

The ambassador for Georgia, who attended the green room meeting to represent the countries which had newly acceded to the WTO, also took a fairly positive view: 'We were very modest in our demands [mainly on further negotiations on geographical indications in the TRIPs Agreement and capacity-building]. We did not behave like India, for instance. They applied last-minute pressure. The Quad recognized that our demands were modest which was why we got 90 per cent of what we asked for'.[9]

Unsurprisingly, the views of other developing countries, and especially of the LDCs, were generally less favourable. One delegate from an African LDC conceded: 'We cannot complain that we weren't represented, because the chairpersons of the Africa Group, the Africa, Caribbean and Pacific and the least developed countries were there.'

According to another LDC negotiator, however,

the psychological and political pressure was huge in the green room. There was the impression that if Doha failed then those responsible would be accused of obstructing world economic recovery. The links to September 11th and the recession created a huge pressure. Additionally, we repeatedly heard that us developing countries needed the WTO more than the developed countries did, so that if Doha failed we would be the worse for it. These views were in the air and in the press and reflected the attitude in the room.

Perhaps the strongest condemnation of the green room process in Doha, however, came in a post-Doha speech by Indian Commerce Minister Murasoli Maran at an economic summit in India. Only a handful of WTO members were requested to participate.

Even during discussions on the entire night of 13/14 November, the non-stop session lasting for thirty-eight hours, texts were appearing by the hour for discussions without giving sufficient time to get them examined by the respective delegations. Who prepared the avalanche of draft after draft? Why? We do not know. In the eleventh hour – probably after thirty-seven hours forty-five minutes – they produced a draft – like a magician producing a rabbit out of his hat – and said that it was the final draft.

The tactics seemed to be to produce a draft in the wee hours and force others to accept that or come nearer to that. Has it happened in any [other] international conference? Definitely not. Therefore with pain and anguish, I would say that any system which in the last minute forces many developing countries to accept texts in areas of crucial importance to them cannot be a fair system. I would strongly suggest that the WTO membership should have serious introspection about the fairness of the preparatory process for ministerial conferences. (Maran 2001)

The 'Like-Minded Group' proposals

A more formal reaction to the process issues arising from Doha came from the Like-Minded Group (LMG). This is an influential group of fifteen very diverse developing country members of the

WTO (India, Mauritius, Pakistan, Malaysia, Cuba, Zimbabwe, Dominican Republic, Kenya, Egypt, Tanzania, Indonesia, Sri Lanka, Uganda, Honduras and Jamaica).

In January 2002, the LMG circulated a draft proposal, focusing on how the process leading up to and at ministerial meetings could be improved, through the introduction of checks and balances. On 14 May 2002, after the proposal had been agreed among the LMG members and approved by ministers, Indian Ambassador K. M. Chandrasekhar presented it to the WTO General Council, chaired by Canadian ambassador Sergio Marchi. While Chandrasekhar acknowledged that the Doha process was in some ways 'marked by transparency and inclusiveness', he noted that there were 'aspects with which developing countries were not comfortable'.

The LMG proposals (see Appendix to this chapter, p. 143) make alarming reading – not because of their radicalism, but because they are so basic. That so many Doha participants should find it necessary to make proposals that seem so essential to any open, transparent and democratic process is, in itself, a searing indictment of what happened at and before Doha. What is still more extra-ordinary is that these same proposals were *opposed* by a number of leading WTO members.

General Council chair Sergio Marchi described the proposal as a very helpful contribution on the whole issue of internal transparency at the WTO, and said that it would be listed in the agenda for the next General Council in July 2002, after which he would decide whether to hold consultations on the matter.

Several developed and (richer) developing countries opposed the LMG proposal. Chile, Costa Rica and Singapore politely rejected it, arguing that 'flexibility' should be maintained at ministerial meetings. Hong Kong's Stuart Harbinson also stressed the need for flexibility, and defended the process leading up to Doha, particularly the transmission of the draft text. The EC agreed with the need for transparency, but argued that the procedures followed at Doha were satisfactory and could be built upon with flexibility and room for manoeuvre. Korea felt the guidelines were too detailed, and New Zealand, while agreeing that there was a need for inclusiveness in the process, also more or less rejected the proposal. Colombia and Venezuela saw the merits of meetings being held outside of Geneva. While the former agreed with the idea of guidelines, they thought some points in the paper went too far.

The USA expressed appreciation for the efforts behind the paper and suggested the codification of best practices for ministerial conferences. They emphasized, however, that different conferences had different objectives, so that a 'one-size-fits-all' set of procedures would not do – there was a need for flexibility, and the success at Doha would not have been possible without it.

There was also a strong core of support for the proposals, however, mainly among developing countries. The Philippines shared the objectives of the paper, saying that 'flexibility' should not be a licence to bring up sensitive issues at a midnight meeting not attended by all members. Brazil and Norway praised the proposal, calling for consultations on the matter. China, also supporting the LMG paper, stressed the need for neutrality and impartiality on the part of the Secretariat and the DG. Malaysia said guidelines were needed to avoid last-minute surprises at ministerial meetings. Japan agreed on the need to develop guidelines for transparency and inclusiveness. Pakistan expressed disagreement with those who viewed the process leading up to and at Doha positively, and stressed the need to rid ministerial meetings of non-conventional negotiating tactics.

WTO director general Mike Moore ended the discussion. He said he saw the discussions as healthy, but stressed that no one who wished to speak at Doha was denied that right. He said he would present his own ideas on process in the light of Doha in due course.

Following the discussion, some delegates and NGOs highlighted the irony of the rejection of a 'one-size-fits-all' set of procedures for ministerial conferences by the USA and others. Chakravarthi Raghavan sums up this view: 'The major trading entities and a few of their followers who have benefited most from the "one-size-fits-all" set of *rules* and *obligations* [but not rights] of the rules-based multilateral trading system appear to be rejecting a more uniform set of *procedures* for Ministerial Conferences' (Raghavan 2002a).

A Southern delegate commented that, while the WTO rules are largely rigid, the procedures at ministerial conferences, where the rules are endorsed, are questionably flexible. The delegate was of the opinion that the current system was not beneficial for smaller countries as flexibility in this instance would lead to uncertainty and defeat the larger objectives (ibid.).

The final twist[10]

When the Bretton Woods Agreement was put into effect, it produced dramatic changes to the world economic and financial order, which helped to propel the USA into superpower status, while Britain watched helplessly from the sidelines. The immediate aftermath of Doha was rather different. Having largely secured the terms it wanted at Doha, through a show of unity with the other members of the Quad, the USA proceeded over the following months to ignore major elements of its obligations under the WTO agreements, creating a rift between itself and the EC, Japan, Canada – and indeed the rest of the WTO membership. While perhaps not as dramatic as the effects of Bretton Woods, these tensions may prove difficult to resolve before the next ministerial conference in Mexico in September 2003.

In March 2002, that great advocate of free trade and a rules-based international trading system, President George W. Bush, slapped 'safeguard' tariffs of up to 30 per cent on imports of foreign steel, in America's most protectionist single action in two decades. It was alleged that the USA imposed the tariffs to protect the steel industry in some politically sensitive states for George Bush's Republican Party, and members of Bush's own cabinet acknowledged that the president's decision was essentially political.

The EC and others initiated legal action against the tariffs through the WTO Dispute Settlement Body. The process is slow, however, and the effects of tariffs serious and immediate, leading the EC, Japan and China, among others, to take interim measures – often accompanied by strong criticism of the US action. The rhetoric from top EC officials was particularly stinging against the USA, as they introduced their own tariffs on steel imports, to stop the European steel market being flooded by exports diverted from the USA. The EC also demanded compensation from the USA for the cost of steel tariffs, and threatened to slap tariffs on up to $336 million worth of a range of American products if they did not receive compensation by 18 June 2002[11] (*The Economist* 2002b). In view of the political nature of the American tariffs, the EC announced that goods subject to tariffs would include orange juice from Florida and textiles from North Carolina – also politically sensitive states for Bush's Republican Party.

The US administration claimed to be incensed by these threats, as both sides insisted – with no apparent sense of irony – that their own actions were consistent with global rules, and that their own tariffs (but not the other side's) were, in fact, being imposed in order to steer free trade in the right direction (ibid.).

On 8 May 2002, the US Senate added insult to injury – this time to a wider group of countries – by passing a Farm Subsidy Bill, endorsed by President Bush. This promised US farmers at least US$190 billion over the following ten years, increasing subsidies to farmers by more than 63 per cent, making loans and direct payments available immediately. Payments were to rise if world commodity prices continued to fall, providing a safety net for US farmers, but depressing world prices still further, and thus reducing incomes for farmers elsewhere around the world. The bill focused mainly on cotton, wheat, corn, soya, rice, barley, oats and sorghum, most of which are important crops, closely linked with food security and rural employment in developing countries.

While Washington argues that the subsidies to farmers are non-trade-distorting, since they are supposedly delinked from production, even the OECD (2000) disagrees, because of the large sums provided and the impact on farm incomes, which enables farmers to invest more in production. Above all, the bill makes it clear that the USA, far from reducing agricultural subsidies, has every intention of using the money at its disposal to increase its markets abroad. Introducing the bill, George W. Bush said: 'Let me put it as plainly as I can: we want to be selling our beef and our corn and our beans to people around the world who need to eat.'

Some US officials argue that steel tariffs and the Farm Bill were parts of deals the Bush administration had to make with Congress and the Senate in return for passing 'fast-track' trade authority, which the administration needed to assure its trading partners that Congress would not renege on trade deals. After much resistance, Congress approved fast-track authority by a single vote, and the Senate followed suit a couple of months later, giving their approval by two votes on 27 July 2002, also amid much resistance (*The Economist* 2002c).

Supporters of the bill said it would restore stability to beleaguered US farmers. Senior Republican Senator Charles Grassley, however, said that he could not think of a more 'effective way to undermine everything we hope to accomplish at the negotiating table during the next three years, than to pass a Farm Bill that we know might break our WTO obligations'.

A barrage of international criticism followed. Members of the Cairns Group of major agricultural exporters, led by Australia, also roundly condemned the bill, as did Latin American countries, saying the massive increase in US agricultural subsidies would hurt export sectors vital to their economies, and vowing to fight it tooth and nail at the WTO. South African ministers said the bill would imperil Africa's ability to grow out of poverty. Their Trade Minister Alec Erwin warned against 'a spate of protectionism in the US'. It was only a matter of months, however, before the Cairns Group was welcoming an ambitious (and, in the light of its domestic subsidy programmes, rather hypocritical) US proposal on agriculture (USDA 2002). Moses Ikiara, policy analyst at the Institute of Public Policy Research and Analysis, a Kenyan think-tank, remarked: 'This is a complete contrast to what everybody has been expecting. It will be very difficult now to convince African countries about liberalization.'

Belgian Prime Minister Guy Verhofstadt took a similar view, commenting at an OECD gathering that it was 'hypocritical to talk about market liberalization and not go along with it'. On 23 May 2002, Canadian WTO ambassador Sergio Marchi said 'there is no delegation in Geneva that is not looking at these issues with concern and greater attention, and they can very well interfere with the Geneva process and negotiations'.

In an unprecedented display of disapproval, the heads of the three main multilateral economic institutions, Mike Moore (WTO), James Wolfensohn (World Bank) and Horst Koehler (IMF) released a statement on 16 May condemning a rise in protectionism – though of course without naming the culprits directly. IMF managing director Horst Koehler also criticized the Farm Bill separately for distorting the global market in agricultural produce and damaging the incomes of poor farmers. World Bank vice-president for Europe, Jean-François Richard, however, spread his criticism more widely, pointing out that 'Europe is not beyond reproach either. Its agricultural subsidies are among the highest in the world.'

In October 2002, German Chancellor Gerhard Schroeder and French President Jacques Chirac proved his point, striking a landmark deal on agricultural subsidies which made it clear that EC dumping would continue until at least 2013. They agreed that there would be no decrease in EC agricultural subsidies, and that direct farm aid would be phased in from 2004 for the ten countries to accede to the EC by that year. From 2007 to 2013, spending will be frozen at the 2006 levels. EC farm subsidies will therefore increase to accommodate the acceding members in real terms, although they may fall relative to production. This is bad news for the developing countries. Far from being apologetic, EC Trade Commissioner Pascal Lamy arrogantly stonewalled criticism of EC farm subsidies, reportedly telling critics during a visit to Africa that 'what the European Union did with its money was its business'! (Khan 2002).

Notes

1. For countless examples of the political influence of the US pharmaceutical industry, particularly on TRIPs-related issues, see www.cptech.org/ip/health/politics.

2. Interview with Andrew Stoler, then WTO deputy director general, 5 March 2002.

3. The fact that implementation issues and Special and Differential Treatment issues are part of the single undertaking suggests that developing countries could, in principle, hold up the other parts of the round until they receive what they have been promised in these areas.

4. Modalities basically refers to the new commitments countries will have to undertake in agriculture, and the specific formulae of how these commitments will be reached, e.g. 36 per cent reduction in bound tariff rates on all products, etc.

5. The request and offer phase of negotiations is bilateral. In the request phase, any WTO member can approach any other member with a request to liberalize particular sectors and modes of supply. The member receiving the request is not obliged to comply. In the offer phase, members make offers to other members to open up services in a particular sector. When these bilateral negotiations are completed, the offers are then multilateralized, that is opened to all other WTO members, unless the member concerned has already notified an exception to the most favoured nation (MFN) principle.

6. MEAs include, for example, the 1985 Vienna Convention for the Protection of the Ozone Layer, the 1987 Montreal Protocol on Substances that Deplete the Ozone Layer, the UN Convention on Biological Diversity (the Biodiversity Convention) and the UN Framework Convention on Climate Change.

7. Interview with Stuart Harbinson, then Hong Kong ambassador to the WTO, 18 March 2002.

8. It should be noted, however, that all the Scandinavian countries except Norway were represented by the EC.

9. Interview with Amiran Kavadze, Georgian ambassador to the WTO and UN agencies, 25 March 2002.

10. This section is based mainly on contemporaneous press reports, as summarized by the World Bank's Development News Press Reviews (DevNews) in May 2002, available from www.worldbank.org.

11. In the event, the 18 June deadline came and went without the EC implementing retaliatory tariffs. Instead US–EC discussions led the USA to revise its steel tariffs.

APPENDIX
The Like-Minded Group proposal

Preparatory process in Geneva and negotiating procedure at the Ministerial Conferences

Since the WTO was established in January 1995, four Ministerial Conferences have been held so far. The procedures adopted, both in the preparatory process in Geneva and at the Ministerial Conference itself, have been different. This uncertainty in the process makes it difficult for many Members to prepare themselves for the conferences. Some basic principles and procedures for this Member-driven organisation need to be agreed upon, so that both the preparatory process and the conduct of the Ministerial Conference are transparent, inclusive and predictable.

The Geneva preparatory process

The aim of the process should be to finalise the agenda for the Ministerial Conference and a broad work programme flowing from the agenda, to be proposed for consideration at the Ministerial Conference. The Geneva process should aim to finalise a draft Ministerial declaration, which reflects the priorities and interests of the entire membership. The following elements should guide the preparatory process:

1. All consultations should be transparent and open-ended. The preparatory process should be conducted under the close supervision of the General Council and chaired by the Chairman of the General Council. Any consultations or meetings held outside this process are not part of the formal preparatory process. Any negotiating procedure to be adopted should be approved by Members by consensus at formal meetings.
2. The draft agenda should be drawn up only after Members have been given an opportunity to express their view. Once the agenda

and its parameters are agreed upon, changes should be permitted only if so decided by the entire membership.

3. There should be frequent formal meetings of the General Council to take stock of the progress in the preparatory work and minutes should be drawn up of such meetings. This would help Members who do not have delegations in Geneva and will give an indication of the status of work to capital based officials. In view of the difficulty that non-Geneva based delegates have in sending representatives for such meetings, a formal meeting of the General Council should be scheduled just before or just after the Geneva Week, for such delegations.

4. There should be sufficient time for delegates to consider documents to facilitate proper consideration by and consultation with the capital.

5. Language of draft Ministerial declaration should be clear and unambiguous. The draft Ministerial declaration should be based on consensus. Where this is not possible, such differences should be fully and appropriately reflected in the draft Ministerial declaration. This could be done either through listing various options suggested by Members or by the chairperson reflecting different positions on issues. If the majority of the membership has strong opposition to the inclusion of any issue in the draft Ministerial declaration then such an issue should not be included in the draft declaration.

6. The work on the declaration should be completed in Geneva to the maximum extent possible. Only those issues, which are reflected either as options or where the chairperson has reflected different positions should be left for the Ministers to deliberate and decide at the Ministerial Conference.

7. A draft Ministerial declaration can only be forwarded to the Ministerial Conference by the General Council upon consensus to do so.

8. In the preparatory process for the Ministerial Conference the Director General and the Secretariat of the WTO should remain impartial on the specific issues being considered in the Ministerial declaration.

9. Sectoral work by working groups is an effective way for expediting resolution of pending issues. The number, structure and chairpersons/facilitators for such working groups should be decided in the General Council in Geneva, in advance of the Ministerial Conference through consultations among Members.

Process at Ministerial Conferences

1. The agenda for the conference should not be adopted at the ceremonial opening session, but at the first formal plenary session immediately thereafter.
2. A Committee of the Whole should be established at all Ministerial Conferences. This Committee should be the main forum for decision-making. All meetings of the Committee of the Whole should be formal.
3. The chairpersons, including facilitators, who would conduct consultations and meetings on specific subjects at the Ministerial Conference, should be identified by consensus at the preparatory process in Geneva, through consultations among all Members. Such persons should be persons from Members that do not have a direct interest in the subject assigned for consultations.
4. Consultations by chairperson/facilitator should be open-ended meetings only. The chairperson/facilitator should convene meetings for proponents and opponents on the subject assigned and any other interested Member should be free to join such meetings. For this to be achieved, the schedule for each meeting shall be announced at least a few hours before the meeting.
5. Consultations should be transparent, inclusive and all Members should be given equal opportunities to express their views. Chairpersons/facilitators should report to the Committee of the Whole periodically and in a substantive way.
6. All negotiating texts and draft decisions should be introduced only in open-ended meetings.
7. Late night meetings and marathon negotiating sessions should be avoided.
8. Language of declaration should be clear and unambiguous. All

drafts should be completed and finalised in a drafting committee to be appointed for that purpose by all Members and membership of which should be open to all Members.

9. The Secretariat and Director-General of the WTO as well as all the chairpersons/facilitators should assume a neutral/impartial and objective role. They shall not express views explicitly or otherwise on the specific issues being discussed in the Ministerial Conference. Specific rules to conduct the work of the Chairs and Vice-Chairs of the Ministerial Conference should be elaborated.

10. Discussions at the Ministerial Conference on the draft Ministerial declaration should focus on issues not agreed upon in the Geneva process and the various alternate texts developed at Geneva.

11. Any new draft on specific issues should be circulated to all Members well in advance so that Members have sufficient time to consider them. To ensure transparency in the negotiating process a draft text on specific issues should clearly indicate the Member(s) suggesting the draft.

12. The duration of the Ministerial Conference should be in accordance with the schedule agreed upon in Geneva, as many delegations make their travel and accommodation arrangements accordingly. If an extension is required, it shall be formally approved through consensus.

13. In various meetings, formal as well as informal, during the Ministerial Conference arrangements should be made for the Ministers to be accompanied by at least two officers. It is the right of any Member to designate its representative and in this connection the Head of Delegation has the discretion to mandate his/her officials to speak on his/her behalf.

Venue of Ministerial Conferences

This issue has been discussed during the Uruguay Round, when it was felt that the Conferences should be held in the WTO itself. Apart from convenience this would also result in savings in costs and efforts. Many developing countries find it prohibitively expensive to participate in the Conferences. There could be a case for having all the future Ministerial Conferences after Mexico in Geneva itself.

Recognising that the Ministerial Conferences are to be held at least once every two years, and recalling paragraph 1 of Article IV of the Marrakesh Agreement Establishing the WTO, it is strongly recommended that Members review the evolving tendency of holding Ministerial Conferences that are primarily focused on the launching or review of negotiations.

Source: WTO (2001e)

SIX
The gentle art of persuasion – arm-twisting and pay-offs

'There can be no greater error than to expect or calculate upon real favours from nation to nation.' George Washington

This chapter goes a little further behind the scenes than the previous chapters in an attempt to unveil the arm-twisting that went on before and during the Doha Ministerial Conference, and events after the conference that have a bearing on these activities. As a former delegate observed – and as this chapter makes clear – 'At the end of the day, the complexity of the game and the desire to protect your country's interests can lead to all sorts of situations.'

The chapter begins by outlining the hierarchy of bullying within the WTO and the key arm-twisting tools used by the powerful countries to achieve their objectives. A heated exchange of letters before Doha between a Southern delegate and USTR Robert Zoellick is used to illustrate the process. Finally, a selection of countries are profiled, detailing their different roles on the giving and receiving end of the arm-twisting process, and their changing positions before and at the Doha Ministerial.

In view of the obvious sensitivity of much of the information in this chapter, direct quotes are avoided and sources remain anonymous. Such is the climate of intimidation surrounding WTO issues that the authors were requested by the authorities to remove one of the most telling case studies in this chapter in its entirety, for fear of the repercussions in terms of their bilateral relations with the USA. In order to avoid jeopardizing the country's position, the authors complied with this request.

While the information on which the country profiles are based does not necessarily come from representatives of the countries in question, the sources are well-informed, reliable sources inside the WTO system; most observed the events they described at first hand; and their accounts have been independently corroborated wherever possible.

The bullying hierarchy

While both developed and developing countries participate in the sophisticated political games played by different blocs to try to get what they want at the WTO, the Quad and other developed countries, being the most powerful players by far, are firmly entrenched at the top of the bullying hierarchy. Their much greater political and economic muscle means they are better placed to call the shots, and to issue threats and promises where necessary to further their interests. As well as their bilateral political influence, they have it in their power to provide or withhold (and very largely to ensure that international agencies provide or withhold) technical assistance, financial aid, bilateral and multilateral debt relief and preferential trade agreements. They can thus force developing countries into walking a thin line between safeguarding such short-term 'benefits' and protecting their long-term interests at the WTO.

Next in the bullying hierarchy are the upper- (and a handful of lower-) middle-income countries. Their influence is primarily on a bilateral political level, and their game is more complex. While their alliances with other developing countries, especially the least developed, are strategically important to them, they face a strong temptation to dance with the devil (the major players) and succumb to their divide-and-rule tactics; and reaping the potential benefits of doing so is generally uppermost on their agendas. One of the main bargaining chips they can offer in this process is the influence they can exert on other developing countries, particularly through regional and other groupings.

As some of the country profiles later in this chapter illustrate, the Quad members often exploit this weakness for bilateral benefits to get such countries to lobby other developing countries on their behalf. Thus certain middle-income countries that had been openly apprehensive about US and EC positions before Doha could be found secretly lobbying their less affluent counterparts to adopt these very positions at the ministerial itself, or simply remaining (in some cases uncharacteristically) silent when they were discussed. Offers of bilateral trade and other agreements played a key role in such changes of heart.

Some middle-income countries go beyond stabbing other developing countries in the back when necessary to be ahead of the game, and use their relatively influential positions to pit one big country against the other. As a delegate from a middle-income country said, 'The only way we can effect change in the system is to get on the back of one of the big players to fight the other big players.' Some of the stronger middle-income countries can achieve this on occasions because they have a great deal more to offer the Quad in terms of trade deals than their low-income counterparts. Taking on the developed countries *as a whole*, however, is not generally an option. Here, strength of argument is the only instrument available.

LDCs and other low-income countries are at the bottom of the ladder as the archetypal 'beggars can't be choosers' living on handouts – except that there is no 'free meal' at the WTO. In exchange for a few crumbs on their plates from the powerful countries, LDCs are expected to align their negotiating positions accordingly.

Tools of the arm-twisting trade

When developing countries (especially LDCs) decide to take strong positions against the wishes of their powerful masters, as before Doha, a variety of tactics may be deployed against them. These may include some combination of inducements in the form of a few more crumbs to negotiators and their governments; putting the country on a blacklist of unfriendly countries who deserve to have their preferential trade agreements suspended; putting pressure on capitals, often backed by disinformation and/or threats, to relieve negotiators (including ambassadors) of their jobs, making their positions untenable; and, in classic divide-and-rule style, the deployment of middle-income countries to convince low-income countries to change their positions.

Threats against ambassadors

Threats against ambassadors were rife before, during and after Doha. Faced with a determined ambassador, the major players would go over his or her head to the government of the country and apply direct political pressure for his or her removal, often on the basis of disinformation. The USA, in particular, is known to have a blacklist of ambassadors they would like to see removed. As an LDC delegate observed:

If you go against the majors, they go to the capital and twist things around saying things like you are anti this and that. There is always a good deal of disinformation deliberately being spread at the capitals. This is why it is essential to have a good rapport with the capital and it is also important that you refrain from reacting too quickly when you feel or suspect that you might be under threat.

One Geneva-based ambassador was sacked soon after Doha, following complaints from the USA that the delegation (though following instructions from the capital) had not toed the precise line of US positions, and had complicated matters for the USA by holding firm to positions contrary to US interests. At least four other ambassadors unpopular with the USA were also removed from their Geneva missions following the conference and promoted to less controversial posts elsewhere. To the authors' knowledge, at least two more Geneva-based representatives remained on the US blacklist at the time of writing (early 2003).

One deposed ambassador told the authors:

I was not the only one removed due to pressure by the USA on my capital authorities. Immediately after Doha, Ambassador [A] did not even have the time to empty luggage ... Ambassador [B] did not even make it to Doha, and about a month afterwards was left without a job ... Ambassador [C] had to travel to Doha with the company of his substitute ... Ambassador [D] was removed and sent back to his native continent ... Ambassador [E] was almost fired in Doha itself ... By a sheer miracle, he was able to survive for a few more months in Geneva ...

I survived just till [date] ... My head was presented on a tray to the US authorities during an official visit by my president to the USA. Until this was done, my authorities were not able to put any other bilateral issue on the table ... After that, the modest contributions made by my country's diplomats in Geneva and in [negotiations with the USA] were put in the dustbin. Within three months, a ministerial delegation ... had aligned my country with the USA on agriculture, government procurement, intellectual property and distribution services.

Worst of all has been the explicit policy decision taken: to be silent, even complacent with the US delegations in all fora, in order to consolidate a 'change of perception'. All this, without getting anything in return, while the USA gets our support in key areas of their interest where we had been putting pressure, with the expectation of eventually increasing our leverage in the areas of our interest.

Ambassadors' names and countries and other information which could reveal their identities have been removed for their protection. Another source questioned whether the removal of two – but only two – of those named had in fact been a result of US pressure.

Preferential trade deals

Another important weapon in the developed countries' arsenal is the offering, or threats of withholding or withdrawal, of preferential trade agreements under the Generalized System of Preferences (GSP).

The GSP is a programme under which developed countries can grant reduced or zero tariffs to selected imports from developing countries without having to extend the same concessions to other members, and without the beneficiaries having to reciprocate, as WTO rules would otherwise require. It was proposed by Raul Prebisch, then Secretary General of UNCTAD, at the UNCTAD I Conference in 1964. Its objectives, as defined at the UNCTAD II Conference in 1968, were 'to increase [developing countries'] export earnings; to promote their industrialisation; and to accelerate their rates of economic growth' (WTO 2001a: 3). Examples of GSP programmes include the US African Growth and Opportunity Act (AGOA) and the EC's 'Everything but Arms' initiative, which in theory allows tax-free imports from the poorest countries, both introduced in 2000.

Despite the laudable objectives of the GSP, however, there are serious limitations to the economic benefits of GSP programmes (see Box 6.1); and their discretionary nature makes them an effective arm-twisting tool for the powerful countries. Threats to withhold or withdraw eligibility from certain developing countries if they refuse to toe the line, and offers to extend their benefits to countries if they 'behave' in negotiations, are commonplace.

AGOA provides a prime example. It is subject to a whole range of conditions that not only limit the number of countries that benefit, but also allow the USA to select *which* countries benefit and to withdraw eligibility from a country at any time (Amosu 2002). These conditions require countries to show commitment, not only to the rule of law, democracy, fighting corruption and reducing poverty, but also to lifting barriers to US trade and investment and protecting intellectual property rights. While some thirty-five of the forty-five countries in Sub-Saharan Africa are eligible, as of March 2002 only thirteen (Botswana, Ethiopia, Kenya, Lesotho, Madagascar, Malawi, Mauritius, Namibia, South Africa, Swaziland, Tanzania, Uganda and Zambia) had actually been given approval to export to the USA under the act. The possibility (without the assurance) of benefiting from AGOA was an important carrot for African countries in Doha.

Some also question the benefits for those countries which do qualify. When AGOA was presented to one African delegation in Doha, one of the delegates responded sceptically.

My question to my colleague was 'How is AGOA going to help us?' As far as I know, AGOA is mainly focused on textiles – we are going to be assisted to modernize our textile industries. First, we will get into debt making this transformation. Second, after all this investment, the Multi Fibre Agreement within the WTO,

Box 6.1 Limits to the economic benefits of GSP programmes

A WTO Secretariat report on the GSP (WTO 2001a), prepared at the request of the US delegation and issued shortly before Doha, highlighted some key concerns raised by members regarding the effectiveness of the scheme, exposing the flaws which limit its benefits to developing countries.

- Items of particular export interest for developing countries, such as agricultural produce, textiles and clothing, are often not eligible for GSP benefits, or only partially included in the schemes.
- Some GSP schemes in reality benefit only a few developing county exporters of the few products covered by the scheme, so that the benefits are highly skewed in terms of both beneficiaries and products.
- Developing country exports have been progressively excluded from a number of GSP schemes, as such exports have reached the competitiveness criteria defined by GSP-granting countries. The negative effects on the market position of certain developing county products have been magnified by the inclusion of competing countries.
- Specialization and development indices can lead to discrimination between developing countries competing for the same market. Such indices favour producers of raw materials and partially-processed goods, while penalizing more advanced suppliers.
- Sector and country graduation (whereby countries no longer benefit from a scheme once they reach a certain level of development) are contrary to the principles of non-discrimination and non-reciprocity that underpin the GSP, and therefore alien to the original intentions underlying the GSP concept.
- The withdrawal, or threat of withdrawal, of preferences is used as leverage to obtain non-trade objectives. As recipi-

> ent countries cannot rely on the preferences, they have
> become less useful, and the consequent uncertainty of
> access is a major concern to the countries affected.
>
> * Linking GSP benefits to non-trade issues, such as environmental and social (labour) standards as well as intellectual property rights and (especially in Latin America) the fight against drugs, curtails the benefits under the scheme and introduces elements of discrimination and reciprocity to the GSP scheme. These aspects go against the fundamental principles of the GSP.
>
> *Source*: WTO (2001a)

which makes room for preferential trade agreements in textiles, expires in 2005. Once the trade in textiles becomes truly competitive, how do we then recoup the funds invested, when faced with stiff competition with a giant like China for instance? No one analysed this.

As the country profiles later in this chapter show, the powerful countries also use other economic instruments at their disposal to pressure poorer countries to accept their agendas – notably bi-lateral aid (e.g. Pakistan) and multilateral and bilateral debt relief (e.g. Tanzania).

The ACP waiver

The ACP waiver was another key bargaining chip in the hands of the developed countries in Doha. While this might, in principle, be regarded as a legitimate part of the normal give and take of ne-gotiations, the fact that it had been blocked in the General Council for more than a year suggests that it may have been deliberately held back to provide additional leverage on the ACP countries. And at Doha itself – like the allocation of IMF quotas at Bretton Woods (Chapter 4) – it was left until the very end, as a 'carrot' for the ACP countries.

An African delegate described the waiver, not as a carrot, but rather as a 'crumb', which

> was dangled at the last minute by the powerful countries to get the desired results, from the Africans in particular. It shifted attention away from the main issues of contention in the draft declaration. The waiver was left lying in the Council for Trade in Goods for a year, and should have been settled before Doha. Instead it was successfully used as a bargaining chip.

Like GSP schemes, however, the benefits of the waiver to the ACP countries may be much less than they at first appear (Box 6.2); and by no means all of the beneficiaries were convinced that the price they paid for this 'crumb' in Doha was a good deal.

The ACP waiver provides an insight into the complexity of the arm-twisting process. On the surface, it was a carrot offered by the EC to the ACP countries to elicit their support (or at least their silence) on the 'new issues'. In order to offer this carrot, however, the EC needed to secure the compliance of those countries that opposed it – principally the smaller Latin American countries. Bolivia, for example, was threatened that the EC's Andean Preferences, which are negotiated every year and fraught with conditionality, would not be carried forward for the country if it did not support the waiver. According to a former delegate, the Bolivian government and its trade officials succumbed because they were 'very careful and afraid at that level … It really is a jungle out there … They feared a backlash from the EC.'

Not all the opponents, however, were sufficiently vulnerable to EC pressure to secure the waiver. To get enough countries on board, US support was needed. While the USA had initially supported the Latin American producers in opposing the waiver (and promoted the interests of US-based MNCs in the region), when it came to Doha they actively supported it, presumably in the interests of EC–US solidarity and the broader Quad agenda. According to a Central American delegate, 'The USA forced us to agree to the waiver by threatening to cut off preferential agreements it has with us if we did not toe the line. The USA, though initially on our side

Box 6.2 Views on the benefits of the ACP waiver

A negotiator for an African ACP country felt that: 'In retrospect we made a mistake by linking success at Doha to the waiver, which expires in 2008. This is actually not a very long time, yet we could not resist accepting the waiver in exchange for endorsing the launch of the New Issues.'

A delegate from an EC member state explained that 'The [EC and US] banana distributors are the ones who benefit from the trade, not the ACP farmer ... I have difficulty seeing why countries like the Ivory Coast, Ghana and Cameroon were given preferences [banana quotas] in Doha. The waiver is not favourable for the Caribbean countries, after all ... Chiquita [a US MNC based in Latin America] is also not interested in free market policies. They need the quota system, which I suspect will be corrupted. The whole thing is very difficult to defend – it does not make economic sense.'

A delegate from another EC member state believed that 'preferential agreements can have negative effects, because of the conditionality attached ... Bananas don't really do well in the Caribbean climate anyway – their natural environment is in parts of Latin America. In ten years, the preferences just negotiated will be gone and ACP countries that had depended on bananas will then resort to growing marijuana.'

Andrew Stoler,[1] however, argued that the waiver was important because 'the EC needed to protect the ACP farmers from sudden shock, not because it would favour them'.

when the dispute began years ago, backed out to support the EC because they wanted to launch a new round.' To get some of the Asian countries on board, even the 'politically neutral' Secretariat got into the act (see Chapter 7).

Technical assistance

Technical assistance programmes on trade-related matters, mainly provided by the WTO Secretariat and funded by the Quad, have historically been used to put pressure on developing countries to sign on the dotted line on agreements. Moreover, the major powers have used their position as funders to increase the role of the WTO in technical assistance, while systematically weakening other international organizations such as UNCTAD.

In a rare act of 'generosity', on 11 March 2002, Northern donors pledged $18 million – twice the amount the WTO had requested – to the Doha Development Global Trust Fund for capacity-building and technical assistance for developing countries. The support was to focus primarily on the 'new issues', and to be controlled by the WTO Secretariat. UNCTAD was to be provided with funds to organize joint training programmes with the WTO on investment and competition issues.

An African delegate noted:

> It is evident that [UNCTAD] are losing their edge as far as pro-viding useful training for developing country officials. Northern donors did not approve of the type of assistance UNCTAD, for instance, have provided us over the years. They have therefore threatened such organizations, and have subsequently cut their funding support in selected areas ... Attention has now shifted to the WTO's Global Trust Fund.

During the Doha Conference, developing countries were promised funding for technical assistance and capacity-building that would better enable them to understand negotiations on the 'new issues'. Developing countries refusing to begin negotiations on the 'new issues' because they felt they were too complex and preferred to focus on improving existing agreements were made offers of technical assistance they felt they could not refuse, as a means of neutralizing their arguments.

Like other 'carrots' offered to developing countries, there is some scepticism about the benefits of technical assistance. An African delegate, for example, questioned the value of the technical assistance supported by the Global Trust Fund to developing country delegates, pointing out that seminars alone would not help them to negotiate. Rather, they needed impact assessment studies on the effects of subsidy and industrial tariff reductions, for example. Civil society organizations are also concerned about how effective the training programme will be in terms of producing meaningful results.

As Professor Yash Tandon has observed,

Capacity building was conceived narrowly in terms of compliance. The objective of technical assistance was to assist the developing countries to comply with the obligations they had undertaken on signing the Uruguay Round Agreements ... In the early years, most of the technical assistance took the form of short courses either in Geneva or in the capitals of developing countries ... However these workshops had severe limitations as they did not, for example, analyse for the participants how the Uruguay Round Agreements, as negotiated, prejudiced their countries, and how they might negotiate a better deal for themselves at subsequent rounds of negotiations... [Importantly,] whilst they helped to increase the individual knowledge of participants they did very little to help build the infrastructural capacity of the countries, nor to develop their supply capacity, nor to overcome the very many hurdles the developed countries erected against imports from developing countries. (Tandon 2002: 5–7)

A 'diplomatic' exchange between two 'friendly' nations

An exchange of letters between a Southern envoy and USTR Robert Zoellick immediately before Doha provides clear evidence of the extent to which developing countries are bullied into taking up the preferred positions of the world's superpower. Following a meeting with USTR officials, the ambassador of the country concerned wrote to Zoellick, complaining that

During the course of our meeting, [a senior USTR official] made several comments on our position in Geneva with regards to WTO issues, such as Export Subsidies, Textiles and Clothing, and Access to Medicines under TRIPs, all these within the context of the preparations for the Doha Trade Ministerial, to be held in Qatar between the 9th and the 14th of November 2001.

Even though we consider that the expressions and references made on my country's position are not reflective of the type of dialogue normally held between two friendly nations, we expressed that it is our belief that all differences can be resolved through dialogue and close consultations ...

At one point during the conversation, [the same official] expressed that the USTR was in the process of defining a list of those countries that were friends of the United States and those that were not, and that our country at this point was most certainly not on the list of friendly countries. It was also made emphatically clear to us that any USTR support in other areas of mutual interest would be subject to our support in Geneva.

I wish to express to you that these types of threats are unacceptable between two friendly nations that maintain a continuous and open dialogue on all issues of bilateral interest. In order to launch a successful round, confidence building should be the basis for moving forward, and not the issuance of threats.

In between diplomatic niceties, Zoellick replied:

We are committed to a productive, positive trade relationship with your country ... My deputy in Geneva, Ambassador Linnet Deily, is working hard to lead successful talks. We have been discouraged that your country has so consistently, and so vocally, adopted positions counter to those of the United States. We would very much appreciate the cooperation of your team there in helping move forward issues of common interest.

Country profiles
The United States

Gross national income per capita[2] *$34,870 (high-income country)* The USA played a tough game in the months leading up to Doha. As the above letters show, there were no holds barred when it came to pushing their agenda through and ensuring 'success' at the Doha

Conference. A country that was a friend of the USA had no right, it seems, to 'consistently, and ... vocally, adopt positions counter to' – or even at variance with – 'those of the United States'. For a developing country to adopt a position in its *own* interest in the negotiations rather than toeing the US line was deemed inappropriate.

This type of behaviour is consistent with the US approach in other multilateral institutions, particularly at the United Nations, where top international civil servants judged to be out of step with Washington in the war against terrorism and its insistence that the USA have the last word in all global governance issues have been removed from their positions. Internationally respected civil servants such as Mary Robinson (former UN High Commissioner for Human Rights) and Jose Mauricio Bustani (the former head of the Organization for the Prohibition of Chemical Weapons), among others, were targeted and removed from their jobs (Williams 2002).

As noted above, preferential trade agreements were a key weapon in the US armoury. In Doha and before, Zoellick regularly reminded African ministers how difficult it had been for the Clinton administration to get congressional approval for the Africa Growth and Opportunities Act (AGOA), and the gratitude they should feel for this. The act had been passed by Congress in the final months of the Clinton administration in 2000, after several years of debate. He and his colleagues also regularly suggested to African trade ministers, ambassadors, delegates and advisers – and at least one president – that an unfavourable position in the WTO negotiations might influence their prospects of benefiting from AGOA.

Zoellick also promised greater trade concessions to LDCs, in discussions with them in Doha, if they supported US positions during the conference. To his embarrassment, however, humanitarian bodies present at the meeting reminded Zoellick that he had no power to make such offers without congressional approval, and that the US Congress had not agreed to these concessions.

Possible free trade arrangements also regularly cropped up in discussions with Asian and Latin American countries; and countries' aspirations for such agreements were used to put pressure on countries to dismiss 'uncooperative' ambassadors and to leave the Like-Minded Group.

Such threats were a complement to, rather than a substitute for, subtler forms of diplomacy. For example, US embassies in African countries circulated leaflets setting out and supporting the US position, giving relevant government ministries an insight into what was at stake. And these gentler methods also had their effect. As a trusted source said of the leaflet campaign, 'These activities did make a difference in-country ... It was a very subtle exercise that made developing country ministers aware of what developed countries wanted.'

The European Communities

Members' GNI per capita between $10,670 and $41,770 (high-income countries) The EC approached the issue of arm-twisting in a more subtle manner than the USA in the run-up to Doha. Pascal Lamy and his trade team held intense bilateral negotiations with countries opposed to negotiations on the 'new issues', which were a key EC objective.

Developing countries detected a subtle carrot and stick approach in the countdown to Doha, to make sure that negotiators were aware of the EC's expectations on the 'new issues' in Doha, and on the ACP waiver, which they used to elicit support from the ACP countries. EC Trade Commissioner Pascal Lamy's endless trips to developing countries after the Seattle Ministerial were in essence an attempt at constructive engagement with his Southern counterparts on the need for launching a new round including the 'new issues'.

The Least Developed Countries III conference in Brussels in May 2001 provided an opportunity for Lamy to hold bilateral discussions with African delegates on the EC positions, according to informed sources. He also 'gently reminded' some trade ministers of the importance of the various preferential economic and trade arrangements their countries enjoyed with the EC. Delegates reported that EC trade officials had sent communiqués to their capitals before Doha clearly stating EC positions, though stopping short of demanding explicitly that Southern trade ministries align their positions accordingly.

The EC was not always so gentle in its approach, however, as the case of Bolivia and the ACP waiver (see above) demonstrates. Neither did they show any more concern for the interests of developing country members than the USA. According to a Central American delegate, 'Franz Fischler, EC Agriculture Commissioner, said directly to us Central American negotiators that they [the EC] would get what they wanted – i.e. the [ACP] waiver – and that he did not care about our rights. Even Mike Moore, who was present when he lashed out at us, was a bit taken aback by his comments.'

Mexico

GNI per capita $5,540 (upper-middle-income country) Mexico, noted as a US and Mike Moore 'friendly', was one of the middle-income countries that aligned themselves most closely with the positions of the powerful countries. Mexico is not only a member of the North American Free Trade Agreement (NAFTA) with the USA and Canada, but was also the first Latin American country to negotiate a free trade agreement with the EC. Mike Moore visited Mexico after Doha, and was awarded a medal of honour by the government. Mexico's main concern in Doha was to ensure that its support for the USA and EC would be rewarded with bilateral agreements and more favourable anti-dumping and agriculture rules within the WTO. It is not surprising, therefore, that Latin American countries opposed to the 'new issues' failed to elicit Mexico's support.

Mexico's ability to influence other Latin American countries will be strengthened when a proposed free trade agreement with Uruguay, Paraguay, Brazil and Argentina becomes a reality. This process was initiated by Mexico, partly because the economic impact of the slowdown of the US economy has forced the government to look for other potential markets in the region. In the meantime, this may also increase Mexico's vulnerability to US pressure further, as it is using its preferential access to the US market under NAFTA as a key selling-point for such an agreement, which it presents as a springboard for the other countries' exports to the USA (ICTSD 2002b).

Chile

GNI per capita $4,350 (upper-middle-income country) Chile is another favourite of the big countries and top Secretariat staff. Following a provisional trade agreement with the USA, the country became the second in Latin America (after Mexico) to sign a bilateral trade agreement with the EC in May 2002. Although four-fifths of Chile's exports to the EC ($4.6 billion in 2001) already enter tariff-free, the agreement provides a guarantee of permanent market access, and the government estimates that it could boost exports to the EC by 15 per cent, partly at the expense of its neighbours (*The Economist* 2002e).

The prospect of the EC agreement, on which negotiations were under way at the time of Doha, convinced Chilean trade officials in Geneva to persuade other Latin American countries to consider their positions on the 'new issues' before the conference.

Costa Rica

GNI per capita $3,950 (upper-middle-income country) Costa Rican trade officials in Geneva believe that trade liberalization and foreign direct investment are the only way forward economically. The country abolished its army to focus its resources on other areas of importance, not least trade with the USA; and American MNCs largely control the key agriculture, textiles and information technology sectors in the country. As a result, Costa Rica is sometimes viewed as a US 'clone' within the WTO.

As mentioned in Chapter 3, the Costa Rican ambassador to Geneva sent a list of Latin American countries opposed to negotiations on government procurement to the US mission in Geneva before Doha. These 'hostile' countries were subsequently put on a USTR blacklist.

Malaysia

GNI per capita $3,640 (upper-middle-income country) Malaysia, a member of the Like-Minded Group (LMG) within the WTO, has traditionally been a strong leader of developing countries, actively opposing Quad positions counter to their interests. One informant stated categorically that no country or Secretariat staff member would dare to make threats against Malaysia. The current Malaysian Trade Minister, Rafida Aziz, has a reputation as a formidable, no-nonsense character.

In Doha, however, delegates report that the Malaysians were uncharacteristically quiet throughout the conference. Apart from a few public comments against the immediate launching of negotiations on the 'new issues', they toned down their opposition to the agenda of the powerful countries considerably. A developed country negotiator even noted that, in the final green room meeting, 'Minister Rafida Aziz of Malaysia was very much on the side of developed countries and even implored the Africans to go along with the deal. She decided that we could not afford another failed ministerial. This was an unusually conciliatory stance from Malaysia.'

In Geneva, too, the attitude of the Malaysian mission towards the big players has switched from cynicism to constructive criticism and dialogue. Although still a member of the Like-Minded Group (LMG), its approach has become altogether more conciliatory. This new-found moderation led a high-ranking EC negotiator in Geneva to question why Malaysia felt the need to be a member of the LMG, commenting that 'Malaysia has nothing in common with a fellow member such as Cuba'. These remarks appear to be part of a wider behind-the-scenes effort to split up the threatening LMG.

While Malaysia was one of the countries Robert Zoellick attempted to woo before the Doha Ministerial, the country's sudden change of tone was primarily a result of the events of September 11th and their aftermath. US–Malaysian relations had for years been marked by antagonism, partly connected with Malaysia's independent style and what is viewed by the USA as strong anti-Israel – and sometimes anti-US – rhetoric; and partly as a result of the arrest and incarceration in 1999 of Deputy Prime Minister Anwar Ibrahim, seen as a champion of political and economic reform, allegedly on evidence fabricated by the government.

After September 11th, Western governments' previous fierce condemnation of Ibrahim's plight was abruptly silenced, and the USA engaged Malaysia in discussions aimed at curbing terrorism in the South East Asian region in return for more 'cordial' relations. After Doha, bilateral relations went from strength to strength. In May 2002, for the first time in years, Prime Minister Mahathir was invited to the White House, holding talks with President Bush on 14 May and addressing representatives of corporate America later that day (*The Economist* 2002a). His defence minister had met with US officials in the first week of May. In July, the US ambassador to Malaysia, Marie T. Huhtala, embarked on an information-gathering mission on the condition of American businesses in Malaysia, to enable her to tell US investors why they should invest in Malaysia. Mahathir used meetings of the Organization of the Islamic Conference and the Association of South East Asian Nations (ASEAN) in 2002 to launch anti-terrorism and international trade promotion pacts with the USA.

This rekindled relationship suited Dr Mahathir just fine. The war against terrorism enabled him to spread concern about Islamic militancy, to frighten voters away from the PAS, an Islamic opposition party, and to jail political opponents categorized as suspected terrorists without trial (*The Economist* 2002d). On the economic front, while Malaysia recovered from the 1997 Asian financial crisis more successfully than some of its neighbours (largely because of its independent stance and refusal to follow IMF-backed recovery policies), it was left searching for yet more foreign direct investment to get fully back on track.[3] Closer economic ties with the USA were an important means to this end, made more urgent after September 11th by the threat of a global recession, particularly affecting middle-income countries such as Malaysia.

While keen to avoid openly bowing to the wishes of the USA, Mahathir has made concrete steps towards healing past rifts with the American government under the anti-terrorism banner. The launch of a successful round at Doha (as defined by the powerful countries) was an important prerequisite for this improvement in relations.

Panama

GNI per capita $3,290 (upper-middle-income country) The Panamanian mission in Geneva was on a USTR blacklist before Doha.

Though not opposed to the launching of a new round of trade negotiations, Panama wanted to proceed with caution on the 'new issues', and had called for negotiations to address some issues important for the country. These included more balanced agreements on subsidies and agriculture, reform of the dispute settlement system, liberalization of the maritime sector under GATS, and other issues of interest to developing countries more generally.

Panama also challenged the USA over its maritime laws. The USA claims that its maritime legislation is exempt from WTO disciplines under paragraph III of the WTO Agreement, suggesting that the most favoured nation (MFN) principle is therefore not applicable in this instance. Panama's position, following instructions from the capital, was that no decision had ever been taken on whether or not the US legislation met the requirements of paragraph III. Panama was convinced that this was not the case – under paragraph III, the mere notification of legislation does not automatically confer exemption.

As a result of these credible challenges, the USA called Panamanian government officials asking what its ambassador was up to, giving them an opening to disavow that the ambassador was acting under instructions. The USA had previously punished the country under the GSP scheme, with hints of more to come, for choosing not to include the Canal Authority in the entities list in the country's offer under the Government Procurement Agreement.

While the government of Panama chose to protect its ambassador, Dr Alfredo Suescum, at the time, he no longer represents his country at the WTO. His tour of duty was not renewed when it ended in December 2001, a month after the Doha Conference.

Brazil

GNI per capita $3,060 (upper-middle-income country) Brazil has always been a critic of US dominance in the multilateral trading system, and has often posed a challenge to the major developed countries because of its size, its substantial economic ties with them, and its relatively strong regional influence.

While Brazil remained neutral on the issue of whether the 'new issues' should be launched in (or soon after) Doha, they had an interest in pushing the powerful countries to reduce their export subsidies in agriculture; to see the USA, in particular, relax its strict anti-dumping rules on goods entering the country; and, of paramount importance, to have acceptable language on TRIPs and public health.

The USA had been issuing threats to developing countries, through their intellectual property departments, to support Option Two in the draft text on TRIPs and public health prepared by Stuart Harbinson. Brazil, however, launched a counter-offensive directed at developing country foreign and health ministries, to garner support for the more flexible Option One; and such was the influence of the Brazilian trade team that their intense bilateral lobbying of other developing countries had a significant effect on the outcome (see Chapter 5).

South Africa

GNI per capita $2,900 (upper-middle-income country) South Africa supported a new round of WTO negotiations including the 'new issues' even before the 1999 Seattle Ministerial, deciding to define its own positions irrespective of those of other African governments. After Seattle, the EC and the USA decided to delegate part of the responsibility for aligning African positions with theirs to South Africa. According to Dot Keet, 'In the succeeding months, taking their cues from a string of visiting European government representatives, the [South African] media reported, for example, that both the [South African] and French Ministers of Trade and Industry agreed that another WTO round was necessary sometime next year' (Keet 2002: 15).

As relative newcomers (South Africa having joined the WTO only in 1994), the country's trade officials relished the onus placed on them as major players in the WTO and as newly appointed referees of the rest of Africa, despite the much greater experience of some of their African counterparts in how the game is played.

South Africa's negotiating stance was to trade off the 'new issues' against implementation issues, and technical and other assistance. They stayed out of the Like-Minded Group, instead joining the

Cairns Group, which is dominated by Australia, New Zealand and Canada among others, and forging alliances with India and Brazil (particularly on the TRIPs and health issue), Nigeria and Egypt.

In the pre-Doha period, South Africa made no secret of its advocacy for the launch of negotiations on the 'new issues', particularly during the various meetings held by African countries. Trade officials started their campaign by 'persuading' their less affluent neighbour, Lesotho, to support their position, which Lesotho duly did. They also used the country's dominance within the Southern African Development Community (SADC) and the Africa and ACP Groups within WTO to push the idea of a new round that included the 'new issues'. This agenda met stiff opposition, however, not only within the Africa and LDC Groups, but also, significantly, from India.

South Africa's support before and during the Doha Conference (particularly in the final green room meeting) helped the powerful countries to achieve their 'success' in Doha; and their trade officials believed they had made some gains in return. Within the negotiations, South Africa benefited from the ACP waiver. Bilaterally, South Africa was one of the first, and largest, beneficiaries of the African Growth and Opportunity Act (AGOA). South Africa's duty-free exports to the USA under AGOA were $923 million (21 per cent of total exports), the third largest after oil exporters Nigeria and Gabon (USTR 2002b). Zoellick also promised South Africa $9 million in technical assistance to train customs officers to check for counterfeit goods entering the market, together with $8.7 million in trade capacity building for the SADC members and $500,000 technical assistance for the Common Market for Eastern and Southern Africa (COMESA), both under AGOA, and a $300,000 grant to support COMESA's court of justice, which adjudicates disputes within their common market (NEABC 2002).

Another crucial reason for South Africa's reluctance to rub the powerful countries the wrong way in the WTO was the urgent need for Western financial support for the highly ambitious New Partnership for Africa's Development (NEPAD) initiative,[4] of which President Thabo Mbeki is a leading architect. (More than $60 billion per year is needed to fund the initiative.) Here, the pay-off was not forthcoming. While NEPAD was put on the agenda of the G8 Summit in Canada, in June 2002, what emerged was a 'no-action plan' for Africa, offering words of advice but little in the way of new cash. Half of the $12 billion in aid already earmarked for developing countries following the March 2002 Monterrey Summit on Financing for Development would go to Africa, plus an additional $1 billion for debt relief.[5]

Zoellick included South Africa in his historic visit to Africa in February 2002, to explore the possibility of establishing a free trade agreement with South Africa and other members of the Southern African Development Community (SADC), while also discussing advancing the 'objectives' of the WTO (ibid.). He also convinced the South African government (and those of Kenya and Botswana) to support the USA in a possible suit against the EC in the WTO for blocking imports of genetically modified seeds from the USA.[6]

In a critique of her country's strategy, Dot Keet observes, 'South Africa threw away considerable bargaining leverage by committing itself beforehand, and publicly to a new round ... The government missed the strategic importance of adopting an initial advanced bargaining position in order to try to alter the terms of the debate and the balance of power before accepting formal negotiations, even if that is what is ultimately expected' (Keet 2002: 17).

The lukewarm support for NEPAD, and the US steel quotas and farm subsidy increases announced after Doha (see Chapter 5), should provide a strong lesson to the South African government – that when it comes to back-stabbing and double standards, the powerful countries are the masters.

Egypt

GNI per capita $1,530 (lower-middle-income country) As a member of the LMG, Egypt was once a formidable force within the WTO – but as one of the three biggest recipients of US aid since it signed the Camp David peace accord with Israel in 1978, it knows where its priorities lie when faced with stiff opposition from the big players. Since the late 1990s, there has been a significant softening of Egypt's position.

There remains a struggle within the government, however, about how far to go in terms of toeing the line of the big players. Egypt is one of a handful of developing countries within the WTO that has an ambassador in Geneva appointed by the Ministry of Foreign Affairs and a trade mission, located in different premises in Geneva, whose staff are appointed by the Ministry of Trade and headed by a minister plenipotentiary. The two ministries, and the two missions, have different views on trade: the Ministry of Foreign Affairs and its former ambassador to Geneva, Fayza Aboulnaga, were altogether less zealous about further liberalization of industrial tariffs by developing countries and a speedy launching of the 'new issues'. This created tensions between the two ministries and missions – and, more importantly, between the USA and Egypt. As a result, according to trusted sources, the former ambassador 'was quietly relieved of her duties at the request of the USA during the Doha Ministerial, and promoted when she returned to Egypt'.

After September 11th, Egypt needed more than ever to be seen to be in the US camp, particularly after it was reported that Mohammed Atta, an Egyptian, was one of the hijackers who crashed airliners into the World Trade Center and the Pentagon. Moreover, the economic after-shock of September 11th exacerbated the recession the country was already suffering: the number of Western tourists plummeted, causing a $2 billion shortfall in earnings, and thousands of lay-offs in the tourism sector; Egypt's other main sources of foreign currency earnings – revenues from the Suez Canal, oil and workers' remittances – fell victim to the uncertainty gripping the world economy; and foreign direct investment, viewed as essential for Egypt to modernize its ancient industrial infrastructure, fell from $902 million in the first half of 2000 to just $334 million in the second half of 2001 (*Financial Times* 2002).

Against this background, it is hardly surprising that, after September 11th, the Egyptian trade minister became particularly keen on launching negotiations on the 'new issues'. Before Doha, certain delegates in the Egyptian trade mission in Geneva made no secret of stirring the Africa Group to reconsider their opposition to the issues. An African delegate confirmed that a handful of those opposed to the 'new issues' had had to move around, trying to make sure that Egypt and other proponents of the 'new issues' did not change the African position. Whilst the Geneva-based negotiators stood firm, however, 'when we reached the ministerial, ministers were more flexible than diplomats'.

The Swiss government is believed to have offered to initiate a bilateral free trade agreement with Egypt if it supported the EC position on the environment before Doha. Egypt rejected this, according to informed sources, because of the conditions attached. In the final green room meeting in Doha, however, Egypt declined to join other developing countries in defending their position on trade and the environment against the EC's push for greater ambition.

In February 2002, Western donors announced $10.3 billion in support for Egypt over the following three years (ibid.); and in March Egyptian President Hosni Mubarak visited Washington to start substantive talks on a free trade agreement with the USA. On 9 June, USTR Robert Zoellick reciprocated, confirming during his trip that further economic reform in Egypt would lead to a free trade agreement with the USA.

Indonesia

GNI per capita $680 (low-income country) Indonesia, a member of the LMG, was one of the countries to oppose the launch of a new round of trade talks before Doha. At a WTO General Council meeting in Geneva, just days before the Doha Conference, Indonesian delegates expressed disappointment with the Harbinson text, regarding the launch of a new round as 'still being controversial'.

As the world's most populous Muslim nation, the events of September 11th were of particular importance to Indonesia. Just after the attacks, Indonesian President Megawati Sukarnoputri held talks with President Bush and Robert Zoellick on various issues, including, of course, trade and the war against terrorism. On 19 September, Zoellick announced that the USA would expand Indonesia's benefits under the Generalized System of Preferences to cover additional products, including lumber, minerals and fish, estimating that these new trade benefits would cover exports worth some $100 million. They also discussed the WTO negotiations (USTR 2001).

Despite these high-level talks, Indonesia remained openly sceptical about talks on the 'new issues' in Doha. According to Geneva-based sources, however, Japan then stepped up the pressure, making a bilateral agreement with Indonesia the week before Doha, offering Japanese investment – on condition that the government endorsed the start of negotiations on trade and investment, one of the topics covered in the 'new issues'.

At the final Committee of the Whole meeting in Doha (see Chapter 4), Indonesia stated that it had concerns about labour standards, the environment and the 'new issues', but eventually went along with the final deal.

Following the Doha 'success', Zoellick visited Indonesia in April 2002 to cement relations between the two countries, announcing that the USA would endeavour to include Indonesia in some aspects of its free trade agreement with Singapore. He expressed strong support for the president and her government 'with efforts that they are making on many fronts in terms of economic reform, establishing democracy in Indonesia, and also obviously with the very difficult security questions' (USTR 2002c).[7] In August 2002, US Secretary of State Colin Powell also visited Indonesia during a trip to the region, to discuss restoring military-to-military ties with the country, pledging $50 million in aid over three years to assist the country in its anti-terrorism struggle (Gedda 2002).

Indonesia too, it appears, succumbed to promises of bilateral trade deals and funds to fight terror at the expense of its multilateral trade goals.

Indonesia appointed a new ambassador in Geneva in July 2002.

Senegal

GNI per capita $480 (low-income country – LDC) Before Doha, Senegal, a member of the ACP and Africa Groups, supported the strong positions taken by the Africans against the launching of a new round. At the ministerial itself, however, Senegal began to move rapidly away from its original positions. The ACP waiver and the fact that President Abdoulaye Wade, like South African President Thabo

Mbeki, is one of the leading architects of the New Programme for Africa's Development (NEPAD) played a role.

Five months after Doha, on 24 April 2002, the USTR announced that it had signed a Trade and Investment Framework Agreement (TIFA) with Senegal and seven other West African countries (Benin, Burkina Faso, Côte d'Ivoire, Guinea-Bissau, Mali, Niger and Togo), which make up the West African Economic and Monetary Union (WAEMU). The agreement was to promote trade with these countries and to 'help fulfil the promise of AGOA', from which WAEMU members had not previously benefited. A delegation from the USA was to visit Senegal in July 2002 to present a seminar 'to help regional entrepreneurs and trade officials take full advantage of AGOA benefits' (USTR 2002a).

Intellectual property and other issues were also to be discussed within the TIFA 'where appropriate', raising concerns among some non-governmental organizations (NGOs) that the USA would use it to try to impose their preferred interpretation of the TRIPs Agreement ('TRIPs-plus'), notwithstanding the Doha Declaration on TRIPs and public health.

It is perhaps significant that Zoellick took the opportunity of the TIFA signing to praise the role the WAEMU countries had played in helping to launch the new WTO negotiations successfully, and went on to say that 'the US looks forward to working with them [the WAEMU members] through this agreement to strengthen cooperation in the WTO and pursue common objectives in the Doha Development Agenda' (ibid.).

Pakistan

GNI per capita $420 (low-income country) Before September 11th, Pakistan was a vocal and articulate member of the LMG, but has since become more reticent and compliant towards the major powers. In Doha, the Pakistani delegation largely fell silent and accepted the final document, as a barrage of threats from all quarters kept the ambassador at the time, Munil Akram, quiet for most of the conference (see Chapter 4). A trusted source noted, 'Pakistan was constantly being asked to "behave". They were receiving messages from the highest level in the capital. Any objections made were seen as unhelpful as regards their alliance with the USA on the war against terrorism. The Pakistani minister was eventually very accommodating. This was very unusual.'

Meanwhile, the rest of the Pakistani delegates, led by their trade minister, were holding bilateral discussions with Zoellick. They reportedly made repeated requests that America import more clothes from Pakistan to make up for reductions in Pakistani exports as a result of the war on terrorism. While Zoellick resisted this request, on 10 November 2001, President Bush promised Pakistani President Pervez Musharraf, who was visiting the USA, $600 million in US aid and $500 million in debt relief.

Pakistani envoys in Doha were disappointed when they heard this news, as they had hoped that their eventual caving-in to Quad positions would bring more substantial rewards. They estimated Pakistan's loss of export revenues as a result of the military campaign against Afghanistan at around $2 billion a year. Munir Akram said of the deal: 'We don't like it … but it's a question of whether we'll have to swallow it' (Cooper and Winestock 2001a).

Bridges Weekly Trade News Digest (ICTSD 2002a) reported that Pakistan did eventually get its quota concessions on textiles from the USA, to the tune of $476 million over three years (far short of the $1.4 billion requested) as a result of the final deals made at Doha. Delegates at the Pakistani mission, however, were quick to denigrate this offer, saying that the statement was misleading.

If you have a closer look at these concessions, you will see that Pakistan can only fulfil a few categories in the package we were offered. In total, we might have concessions worth only about $146 million per year for three years, which is nothing really … They [the Quad] don't want to see anybody take on the system. Instead they promise you deals that never materialize or are over inflated … Washington inflated the figures to impress the Pakistan people. The Pakistan minister has publicly announced that he was extremely disappointed over the outcome of the package.

The former ambassador of Pakistan to Geneva, Munir Akram,

was given two months' notice to leave his post in February 2002, for a United Nations post in New York. As a Southern delegate put it: 'If you become too outspoken you disappear, simple as that.'

Kenya

GNI per capita $340 (low-income country) As members of the LMG and the Africa Group, Kenyan delegates have gained a great deal of confidence within the WTO, and, together with other developing country delegates, devised positions against negotiations on the 'new issues'. They also did a lot of work on TRIPs and public health, supporting the more flexible Option One of the draft declaration.

After a strategically timed AGOA meeting between African ministers and the US trade representative in the USA on 29 October 2001, however, Kenyan Trade Minister Nicholas Biwott began to warm to the idea of supporting Option Two in the draft text. A developed country delegate who supported Option One said that 'the African ministers were brainwashed at this meeting in Washington'. Another source confirmed that ministers were promised innovative methods of treating HIV/AIDS patients by the US government if they supported Option Two.

According to reliable observers, Biwott quickly established a rapport with Zoellick and was enthralled by the attention he received. One delegate suggested that Biwott's political ambitions may have given him a particular interest in developing good relations with senior figures in the Quad countries. He was finally convinced by supporters of Option One in Doha, however, that this was the more beneficial option for developing countries in the long run (see Chapter 4).

As chair of the ACP Group in Doha, the ACP waiver dangled before him by the EC, in return for supporting the Quad positions, was a major preoccupation for Biwott. When the waiver was granted, he saw this as a huge victory, and consolidated his support for the powerful countries' positions in other areas such as the 'new issues'.

After the Doha Conference, Kenya received technical assistance to establish training programmes on international trade at the University of Nairobi in collaboration with the WTO Secretariat.

Both Mike Moore and Robert Zoellick visited Kenya, to build on the cordial relations with Biwott and the Kenyan government. According to delegates, Moore was awarded a medal of honour by the Kenyan government during his trip.

Nigeria

GNI per capita $290 (low-income country) Before Doha, the Nigerian delegation in Geneva strongly criticized and condemned the tactics of Stuart Harbinson, then WTO General Council chair and Hong Kong ambassador, in transmitting the draft declaration to ministers. At the ministerial itself, however, as chair of the Africa Group, the Nigerians remained relatively quiet. A negotiator from a middle-income country observed that, in the final green room meeting, 'Nigeria was very quiet and sweet – they did not really seem to be aware of what was going on.' The Nigerian trade minister was to be seen moving around with Cheadu Osakwe,[8] a former Nigerian negotiator and a close associate of Mike Moore within the Secretariat, who had assisted Moore in his campaign to launch a new round.

After collaborating closely with South Africa on NEPAD and other areas of mutual interest, the Nigerian minister eventually took his cue from the South Africans and, despite a few public displays of resistance, went along with the deal.

Apart from benefits arising from the ACP waiver and pledges of technical assistance, it remains unclear exactly what Nigeria got in return in terms of specific bilateral deals. Nigeria is by far the largest beneficiary of AGOA, however, with duty-free exports under the scheme of $3.2 billion in 2001 – 64 per cent of total Nigerian exports to the USA, and around 70 per cent of all exports under AGOA (USTR 2002b).

In March 2002, in a dramatic twist of fate, Nigerian parliamentarians demanded that the country should pull out of the WTO,[9] as the skewed trade rules negotiated by members (under the watchful eyes of the Northern-dominated Secretariat) were harmful to small and medium-sized enterprises and to the overall development goals of the country.

A Nigerian Labour Congress leader, Adams Oshiomhole, declared that Nigeria's membership of the WTO was harmful to its economy, saying in a speech to the thirty-fourth Annual General Meeting of the Ikeja branch of the Manufacturers Association of Nigeria, entitled 'Human Capital and Industrial Development', that 'the country's membership of the WTO would turn the nation into a dumping ground for all manner of imports which would lead to retrenchment of workers ... Nigeria's challenge is how to fight poverty which would not be realised if workers were being retrenched' (Ibharuneafe 2001).

In March and April 2002, as such views began to catch on among politicians in the country, the WTO Secretariat deployed its technical assistance team – led by none other than Cheadu Osakwe – to hold discussions and training sessions for government officials and parliamentarians. The exercise was aimed at reminding politicians and civil servants of the virtues of the multilateral trading system. As an additional 'sweetener', two Nigerian delegates in Geneva were asked by the Secretariat to chair committees within the WTO. As most, if not all, of the key committee chairs had been selected in February 2002, however, the delegates concerned had to make do with chairing near-defunct bodies such as the State Trading Enterprises Working Group.

At the time of writing, Nigeria remains a member of the WTO.

Uganda

GNI per capita $280 (low-income country – LDC) Uganda has played a leading role in advancing LDC interests in the WTO. Under the leadership of ambassador Nathan Irumba, Ugandan delegates helped to formulate strong LDC positions before the Fourth Ministerial Conference, putting them under great pressure before, during and after Doha. The delegates opposed the launching of the 'new issues' in the near future, producing strong declarations endorsed by their ministers in Zanzibar and campaigning widely to justify their positions.

During parliamentary discussions on WTO issues before Doha,

Geneva-based delegates were asked why they proposed an indefinite delay on negotiations on the 'new issues' pending the report of the study groups, when Uganda was already committed to similar measures at the country level through structural adjustment programmes (SAPs) formulated by the IMF and the World Bank. The trade delegates successfully argued that, unlike SAPs, WTO rules are binding and as a result have far greater long-term implications – they are like a written constitution rather than a piece of legislation.

After these briefings, but five months before Doha, US Assistant Trade Representative for Africa Rosa Whitaker visited Uganda and had talks with Ugandan President Yoweri Museveni. Whitaker announced that AGOA was worth $8 billion in exports and $1 billion in investment for Africa, and the president was persuaded that AGOA would be very important for Uganda, and must not be jeopardized.

Armed with the president's assurances and enthusiasm for free trade, Whitaker proceeded to Cairo, to attend a conference of the Southern African Development Community (SADC) and the Common Market for Eastern and Southern Africa (COMESA). There, she assured African delegates, in typical divide-and-rule style, that the Ugandan president was in full support of a new round of trade negotiations, contradicting the LDC position. Ambassador Irumba, however, clarified that he had received no such directive from the capital, and continued to pursue the position adopted by LDC ministers. Whitaker was reportedly taken aback, amazed that a mere African civil servant could with poise respond firmly to defend his position (*The Monitor* 2002).

In Doha, Irumba continued to push hard for the LDC positions to be incorporated in the ministerial declarations, and soon earned himself a distinguished place on the USTR blacklist. *The Monitor* (ibid.) subsequently reported that Zoellick had called President Museveni informing him that his ambassador was not being 'co-operative'. Irumba's opposition to negotiations on the 'new issues' was misrepresented as signifying opposition to the USA and AGOA, and rumours began that he was going to be moved from Geneva, also appearing in the international media.

A member of a Southern-based non-governmental organization (NGO), who also was a member of the Ugandan delegation, confirmed that he too was warned in Doha that he had to watch what he said, because AGOA could be jeopardized.

When friends and supporters of Irumba contacted Ugandan officials in the capital to ask about his situation after Doha, they were told that ambassadors were rotated every so often, and that he was one of six ambassadors who might be involved in a reshuffle. At the time of writing, however, Irumba remains in Geneva as the Ugandan ambassador and chairman of the Group of Commonwealth Developing Countries in WTO – as well as one of the key players in the LDC, African and LMG groups.

Tanzania

GNI per capita $270 (low-income country – LDC) Like the Ugandans, the Tanzanian delegation worked extremely hard in the process leading up to Doha to develop firm LDC positions signed by their ministers, and chaired the LDC group in Geneva.

Although Tanzanian officials fought admirably in Doha as representatives of the LDC group, like others they eventually caved in under the pressure and succumbed to the offer of a few 'crumbs'. Like all ACP countries, Tanzania stands to benefit from the ACP waiver; but most of the crumbs were of a bilateral nature.

In the few months after Doha, Tanzania finally benefited from key concessions in the international economic arena, which it had been awaiting for a year or more. Just a week later, on 27 November 2001, the IMF and World Bank suddenly announced that Tanzania would receive external debt relief of $3 billion over time, under the Heavily-Indebted Poor Countries (HIPC) initiative. Ironically, during the year it had been awaiting the announcement, Tanzania suffered a catastrophic fall in the price of its main export commodities, particularly coffee and cotton, pushing it still further into debt (Jubilee Plus 2002). In February 2002, Canada announced the cancellation of a further $80 million in bilateral debt for Tanzania under the Canada Debt Initiative (AllAfrica.com 2002). And in the same month, coinciding with Zoellick's visit to the region, Tanzania was finally accredited to AGOA, after eighteen months of anxious waiting by the business community as the country struggled to meet the AGOA requirements.

Conclusion

Arm-twisting, through a combination of threats and inducements to countries and ambassadors, was a key feature of the process leading to the 'agreement' in Doha. Without it, there can be little doubt that no agreement would have been possible. This is not merely the give-and-take one would expect in a negotiation process. With the exception of the ACP waiver and the TRIPs and public health issue, all of the threats and inducements were directed at countries' own individual interests – and in some cases even at ambassadors as individuals – rather than at concessions in the negotiations themselves.

This is widely recognized by delegates, and even seen as normal. According to an Asian delegate:

> Bilateral deals are what most developing countries look out for. At the end of the day, it is your own economic interest you have to watch. It is, of course, always preferable to get multilateral agreements – but if this is not possible in the final stage of a ministerial meeting, people resort to bilateral deals to jettison the sinking ship. This is normal and is part of the game.

The effect, however, is to shift the decision-making process away from the formal process, in which all countries are at least *notionally* equal, into the realm of bilateral horse-trading. Here, only the rich have any real leverage, while most developing countries are so desperate for trade opportunities, aid, debt reduction, etc., that they have little choice but to succumb. The irony is that, by skewing the international trade rules still further towards the interests of the developed countries, this process, and the 'agreements' that emerge from it, will make their need still more desperate, and their ability to resist still weaker, in future negotiations.

Countries from both developed and developing countries lined up *en masse* before and after Doha to sign free trade agreements with the USA, as it voraciously pursued a dual strategy to ensure that it remained in control at the multilateral and bilateral levels. Zoellick has been quoted as saying that 'there's no shortage of customers out there ... we would like to move forward with negotiations and we'll move forward one way or another' (Alden 2002b).

The preparation strategies for the Doha Conference were arguably the best the majority of developing countries had mounted since the inception of the WTO. Developed countries knew exactly where the cracks were, however, and systematically, through webs of coercion, shattered their opponents. They got away with these tactics in part because the often fragmented and disunited front presented by developing countries provided an all too easy target. If developing countries are to reap any substantial benefits from the multilateral trading system, they need to be more serious about their efforts to right the many wrongs it currently embodies, and to resist the temptation to sell their souls to the big players for short-term bilateral promises and deals – most of which in any case either never materialize, or, when they do, amount to no more than 'crumbs' that mostly benefit a small minority of local elites. This requires a much greater show of unity among developing countries, despite their different levels of development – and, indeed, between trade ministries and their representatives in Geneva.

Developed country negotiators always seem eager to point out that most developing countries have a very small share of world trade and therefore cannot be allowed to control the process totally. Yet the strong-arm politics carried out by the major powers today sabotages any serious attempts by developing countries to unite and fight for more equitable trade agreements that might improve their economies and/or trading positions. The developing countries thus find themselves locked in a vicious cycle of political impotence, unfair trading rules and weakening trade performance. This has left many critics of the WTO sceptical that the institution can ever be reformed to be of any real benefit to developing countries.

Notes

1. Interview with Andrew Stoler, then WTO deputy director general, 5 March 2002.

2. Gross National Income (GNI) per capita figures are World Bank figures for 2001. A country with GNI per capita of $755 or less is considered low-income; between $756 and $2,995 lower-middle-income; between $2,996 and $9,265 upper-middle-income; and $9,266 and above high-income.

3. Malaysia has a particularly large and rapidly growing stock of inward foreign investment, requiring ever increasing amounts of new investment to offset the outflow of profits (Woodward 2001).

4. African civil society organizations have criticised NEPAD as elitist, as lacking a clear vision for Africa's development, as based on the neoliberal model that has already failed most ordinary Africans, and as increasing dependency on aid and foreign investment (Ong'wen 2002).

5. *International Herald Tribune* (29 June 2002) and Reuters reports, as reported in the World Bank's DevNews press review, 1 July 2002.

6. *Wall Street Journal* and *Wall Street Journal Europe*, as reported in the World Bank's DevNews press review, 21 February 2002.

7. The Al-Qaida network, allegedly responsible for the September 11th terrorist attacks in the USA, reportedly has a base in Indonesia. The country's security problems were highlighted in November 2002, when two terrorist bombs killed more than 300 people, locals and Western tourists, in Bali.

8. Osakwe, a former Nigerian delegate in Geneva before joining the WTO Secretariat in 1999, was promoted to the post of Director of the Technical Assistance Division within the WTO Secretariat after Doha (see Chapter 7).

9. On 15 March 2002, Philippines Trade Secretary Manuel Roxas announced that his country too was considering pulling out of the WTO over claims that the organization was biased towards developed countries. A key reason for the announcement was the continued failure to address the tuna issue between the EC and Thailand and the Philippines, despite its resolution in principle in Doha (see Chapter 4) in return for Thai and Philippine support for the ACP waiver (ICTSD 2002d).

SEVEN
Mike Moore and the WTO Secretariat – wolves in sheep's clothing

The 1994 Marrakesh Agreement establishing the WTO provided for a Secretariat to support the organization's work. The Secretariat is based in Geneva, and has around 550 regular staff, headed by a director general (DG). The staff are divided between twenty-three divisions, each headed by a director, under the supervision of four deputy director generals (DDGs). (See Figure 7.1.)

Both the staff and the budget – 140 million Swiss Francs (US$95 million) in 2002 – are surprisingly small for an international organization of such influence. By way of comparison, the International Monetary Fund (IMF) had 2,633 staff plus 343 contractual employees at the end of 2001, with an administrative budget of $736.9 million (IMF 2002). Like the IMF, the WTO Secretariat's budget is mainly funded by individual members' contributions, and it is calculated on the basis of their shares in total trade.

In principle, the WTO Secretariat has no decision-making powers, and trade decisions are made only by the members. Beyond this, however, the Marrakesh Agreement did not define the Secretariat's role, or provide rules on its functioning, which thus remain ambiguous. Successive DGs have thus assumed different roles, as each has deemed appropriate. The Secretariat's current responsibilities are described as (WTO 2001d):

- administrative and technical support for WTO delegate bodies (councils, committees, working parties and negotiating groups) for negotiations and the implementation of agreements;
- technical support for developing countries, especially LDCs;
- analysis of trade performance and trade policy;
- legal assistance in the resolution of trade disputes involving the interpretation of trade rules and precedents; and

Figure 7.1 The structure of the WTO Secretariat (July 2002)

- dealing with accession negotiations for new members and providing advice to governments considering membership.

In principle, then, the Secretariat's role is largely administrative
– and Secretariat staff present themselves as neutral, faceless bureaucrats who merely carry out administrative duties and provide
support and advice to the members. They claim that members
are particular about maintaining the member-driven nature of the
WTO, and therefore they simply carry out orders. A regular mantra
is: 'if we lose our neutrality, we lose everything'.

The reality, as this chapter shows, is rather different. The chapter focuses on how the interaction of the WTO Secretariat with
the members has evolved since its inception, up to and including
Doha, and particularly during Mike Moore's term of office as
director general (DG). It begins with a discussion of the process
by which Mike Moore and Supachai Panitchpakdi were selected as
DGs, and how Moore was seen by delegates and staff after Doha.
A discussion of the role of the deputy directors general (DDGs)
is followed by an overview of the evolving mood and role of the
Secretariat from Seattle to the post-Doha period. The chapter then
considers the geographical composition of the Secretariat staff and
the issue of favouritism in recruitment, before going on to consider
the political neutrality of the Secretariat, which is illustrated by a
telling pre-Doha episode.

The selection of Moore and Supachai as directors general

According to WTO delegates, one of the reasons for the failure
of the WTO's Third Ministerial Conference in Seattle was that there
was insufficient preparatory work due to so much time being spent
sorting out the acrimonious battle over the post of director general
after Renato Ruggiero[1] completed his term.

Four candidates stood for the post: Supachai Panitchpakdi of
Thailand, Mike Moore of New Zealand, Abu Yaoub of Morocco
and John McLaren of Canada. There was a prior understanding
that the next DG should be from the developing world, and support quickly gathered for Thai Commerce Minister Supachai, who

'appeared to be leading in all quarters among the then 135 WTO members' (Pitsuwan 2002). A consensus, however, was prevented by conflicting interests and expectations among WTO members – primarily between the South, who generally relied on Supachai's goodwill and sympathy to help them attain a fairer trade regime; and the North, who generally preferred Moore. The Moroccan and Canadian candidates withdrew in late 1998, leaving Supachai and Moore to go head to head.

Among the developed countries, Japan and Australia reiterated their support for Supachai, while the USA and the majority of the EC actively supported Moore. Moore's ties with the USA dated back to the Uruguay Round, when he was New Zealand's trade minister, and New Zealand, as an enthusiastic advocate of agricultural liberalization, was regarded by US trade negotiators as 'one of America's best allies' (Choudry 2001).

Faced with a large majority against them, Moore's supporters among the major Western powers launched a war of attrition against Supachai. While stating that they would not stand against a consensus, they worked behind the scenes to chip away at his support, and ensure that no consensus emerged behind him. While his support held steady in Asia and other developing regions, his initial overwhelming lead was progressively undermined.

Thus, the General Council toiled over the issue day in and day out for several months in Geneva, in what had become a North–South issue, threatening to divide the world trading system still further – and perhaps the most contentious and acrimonious selection process in the history of international organizations.

Supachai's then cabinet colleague Surin Pitsuwan recalls:

The Thai Campaign Managing Team was forced to change tactics – from putting our resources to win more support to holding the ground that was left beneath Dr Supachai. The strategy was to send signals to the Moore Camp that if our candidate did not get it, neither would theirs. News from Geneva was a daily diet of hope and despair for the Thai public. The sentiment was building fast against some of the major allies in the West for their tricks and

Box 7.1 How the deal was made

The following is the then Thai foreign minister's own account of the telephone conversation in which the 'compromise' deal was reached to resolve the contest between Supachai and Moore.

In mid-June 1999 the then US Secretary of State, Madeleine Albright, telephoned her Thai counterpart [Surin Pitsuwan]. The message she conveyed was rather disturbing. 'The president was rather concerned about the long-drawn WTO campaign,' she began, adding that she was calling from a plane shuttling between Paris and Helsinki, trying to negotiate the Kosovo crisis.

She asked if it would be possible for Dr Supachai to consider accepting a new post to be created for him – the chief liaison to establish policy cohesion among the WTO, the World Bank and the IMF. 'Only Supachai has the qualities to do it,' she said ...

The answer from the Thai foreign minister was that it would be inappropriate for Thailand and Dr Supachai to accept any other position, let alone a position that did not even exist yet.

... A soft but determined voice came through with an even more alarming statement. 'Then both of them, Moore and Supachai, would go down the drain; we are ready for a third candidate,' she said plainly.

A measured voice went back from the Bangkok end of the line: 'Madam Secretary, are you sure about that? I do not think it would solve any problem for any party. That third candidate of yours would not be able to do anything useful as long as he or she sits in that position in Geneva.'

'Why not?' she shot back from halfway around the globe.

'Because as long as he or she sits in the WTO, he or she would be the symbol of divisiveness of WTO and the failure of the selection process. He or she would not accomplish anything. Are you sure that would be good for anyone?' the Thai foreign minister replied.

There was a long pause again. Finally, the US Secretary of State responded in a more conciliatory tone: 'Then what are we going to do, Surin?'

Her Thai counterpart seized the moment and made a bold suggestion. 'Instead of one director-general for four years, why don't we think about six years divided between both of them?'

'That sounds interesting!' she said ...

That was how Dr Supachai's position was secured – at the highest diplomatic level between Bangkok and Washington. Not at the WTO General Council in Geneva, as many had come to believe.

Source: Pitsuwan (2002)

---

less-than-fair and transparent games in the WTO General Council meeting. Emotions and negative reactions were beginning to spill over into Bangkok streets. Noisy demonstrations and strong verbal attacks were fast appearing in front of embassies and in newspaper columns. Some ugly behaviour and strong words not seen or heard for years were reappearing. (Pitsuwan 2002)

Finally, the stalemate was broken by a compromise solution – that in place of the usual four-year term, Moore and Supachai would each hold office in turn, for three years each. This was not agreed at the WTO itself, however, but in a telephone conversation between then US Secretary of State Madeleine Albright and then Thai Foreign Minister Surin Pitsuwan, in which Albright offered to create another post for Supachai elsewhere and threatened to block his WTO candidacy in favour of a third candidate if he did not stand down (Box 7.1).

The following day, the USA and Thailand agreed on the compromise, and on leaving the decision on whether Supachai or Moore should serve first to the General Council. They also agreed, however, that it was important for the whole membership to *feel* that they were included in the process, and that the proposal should be announced by a third party – the Australian deputy prime minister and minister of trade at the time, Tim Fischer. He made the proposal public in late June 1999, not at the WTO, but in the corridors of the APEC Trade Ministers Meeting in Auckland, New Zealand.

Gradually, the so-called 'Australian Formula' gathered support and was ultimately adopted; and Mike Moore became the first non-European to head either the WTO or the GATT on 1 September 1999. Moreover, he came into office, not only as a long-time US ally, but, in the view of many, as the 'poodle' of the USA, which had secured his appointment (*The Economist* 1999).

In an interview with the authors, Dr Federico Cuello Camilo,[2] ambassador of the Dominican Republic in Geneva at the time, was critical of the process: 'Members were not allowed to vote [between Supachai and Moore], as I believe Supachai had greater support. After some relentless campaigning – and when it was felt that Mike Moore had a small majority – he was declared the winner.'

Hong Kong ambassador Stuart Harbinson,[3] who supported Supachai during the race, confirmed that there were some questionable goings-on during the campaign: 'Ali Mchumo [the Tanzanian ambassador], the chair of the General Council at the time of the Seattle Conference, suspected that there were people supporting both Supachai Panitchpakdi and Mike Moore. This meant that the number of those who supported Moore and those of us who supported Supachai surpassed the total number of representatives.'

In short, faced with the opposition of a large majority of the WTO members, the major developed countries stalled a decision, while they actively wore down Supachai's support. Once it had been eroded sufficiently, the USA sought to buy off their opponent by offering him a non-position where they thought he would be less obstructive to their agenda, while making it clear that his candidacy would be blocked if he did not accept it. While this offer was refused, their threat carried sufficient weight to force a 'compromise', which they launched through a third party, to conceal its origins.

The result was, despite the support of a large majority of WTO members for Supachai rather than Moore to be DG, to delay Supachai's term of office by three years; to shorten it by one year; to install Moore, a long-time US ally who was opposed by the great majority of the members, as DG in the interim, to preside over the launching of the new round of negotiations; and to put him into office knowing that he owed his position almost entirely to the intervention of the USA.

Delegates and Secretariat staff on Moore

Mike Moore was a controversial figure long before his appointment as DG. Although often known as a former prime minister of New Zealand, he was in fact prime minister for only eight weeks before his Labour Party lost resoundingly to the National Party in 1990. The New Zealand media had long dubbed him 'Mad Mike', one journalist describing him as having ten ideas a minute, but not being sure which was the good one (Choudry 2001).

During a series of post-Doha interviews, the authors sought the opinions of WTO delegates and Secretariat staff about Mike Moore's performance as DG and his role during the Doha process. The main criticism from all sides was that he was very much a politician, with limited patience when it came to adhering to rules and procedures. The Anglo-Saxon 'old-guard' within the Secretariat generally gave him credit for lifting the institution off its knees after Seattle, but continued to regard him as an 'outsider' who lacked the finesse to run the institution in the 'subtle' managerial style to which they had become accustomed over the decades.

Moore's personal style was particularly controversial. He has never been known for being diplomatic, and this reputation long preceded his time at the WTO. He railed at critics of free trade in New Zealand in 1996 as 'primitives who if they had their way would plunge our nation and the region into chaos and depression' and 'grumpy geriatric communists ... a mutant strain of the left ... who tuck their shirts into their underpants'. In Seattle, just months after taking office, he said of protesters: 'The people that stand outside and say they work in the interests of the poorest people ... They make me want to vomit. Because the poorest people in our planet, they are the ones that need us the most' (ibid.). This characteristic did not go unremarked in Geneva. A Canadian Secretariat member was blunt on the subject. 'Mike comes from New Zealand and has no class. He never went through a formal education system and rose up the ranks from very humble beginnings ... His predecessor, Renato Ruggiero, for instance, was very tough and rough when he had to be – I mean *really* rough – but he also handled things with a certain class ... Mike is very rough around the edges.'

According to a Secretariat staff member from another developed country: 'Moore can be very protective of some of his staff, but he is very impatient and unpredictable. Typically he does not like it when you suggest anything contrary to what he wants to do. He would say, "Why don't you do as I say?"' Neither was Moore's abrasiveness reserved for Secretariat staff, as an Asian ambassador made clear: 'The director general became very rude and hostile towards me in Doha, and said he would speak to my minister about my behaviour.' A Central American delegate provided a more specific illustration of Moore's undiplomatic style: 'Mike Moore came up to me during the ministerial meeting in Doha, while I was with my vice-minister, and asked if I wanted to be "consulted or *terminated*" during the negotiations. I said I wanted to be consulted. He was quite aggressive, and generally has a habit of yelling at people who are obstructing his agenda.' An African staff member, however, provided a more positive perspective: 'As far as I know, Moore is fun to be around at parties, for instance. He has a great sense of humour, but sometimes it is hard to know whether or not he is speaking English because of his accent. You really feel he needs a translator – especially in the early days of his term.'

The reference to Moore being 'very protective of *some* of his staff' is perhaps telling – there were some concerns about his favouritism within the Secretariat, as discussed later in this chapter. This does not appear to have created divisions among the staff, however. According to the same Canadian staff member, 'Mike has a few "favourite sons" – that is common knowledge – and he does distance himself from most of the Secretariat [although he works closely with his cabinet]. But we are not a divided Secretariat. We are not jealous, for instance, that he has favourite sons, or when someone he favours gets a promotion.' His African colleague also did not see this as a problem: 'I am not aware that there are factions within the Secretariat at the higher levels – that is, those who support Moore and those who don't. I can confirm, though, that even at my level there are factions, in that there are ideological differences and opposing views on our role during negotiations – that is very common.'

Nevertheless, it seems Mike Moore's passing may not have been entirely unwelcome among the Secretariat. One staff member said: 'He has been sending threatening e-mails to the staff saying he is going to restructure the Secretariat, which made us weary. This has not happened yet, however. Most of us around here keep reminding ourselves – *"only four months to go!"'* A delegate from an EC member state also seemed less than devastated at the prospect of Moore's departure, saying, 'Anyway, I don't think Supachai could possibly be worse than Mike Moore!'

Some, however, were more appreciative of Moore's performance as DG. The Canadian staff member again:

> After the Seattle débâcle, to give him some credit, the DG did work to set up a strong programme for developing countries that focused on LDCs, technical assistance, implementation issues, etc. He did clean up the mess. Pre-Seattle, the powerful had bullied the small countries, which backfired on the big countries. However, I think the DG should be pressuring *all* sides to reach agreements. This should be his job. But I am not sure where Mike Moore's priorities are – there is probably too much emphasis on technical assistance.

A colleague from another developed country echoed this last concern.

> His focus on technical assistance is questionable. At the moment,

there is so much money for technical assistance that we need to recruit more temporary staff to cover the training. I don't think we will use up all the money we raised through the Global Trust Fund.[4] Meanwhile, there are other important areas that are severely under-funded, such as the travel budget for staff to relevant international conferences where we can meet with CSOs and NGOs to frankly discuss important issues.

Views of Mike Moore among developing country delegates varied widely, at least partly along regional lines; and here, it seems, his support for technical assistance won him some friends. A delegate from a newly-acceded Eastern European country took a very positive view.

Mike is very active and helpful. It was through his efforts that we had some amount of success at Doha ... We always remind him not to forget small countries ... He will be speaking at a big meeting in Tbilisi, Georgia, in May 2002, to discuss capacity-building for the region. It was his idea, and it is expected that representatives from Russia, Afghanistan and so on will attend.

A Middle Eastern delegate was critical of Moore's early performance, but felt there had been some improvement more recently.

Mike Moore is okay, but he is a politician. During the Seattle conference he was openly in the camp of the EC and USA, but I think after the failure of that ministerial meeting he is making efforts to reach out to the developing countries. He can be easy to work with, but sometimes we have difficulties ... because of differing views. However, I believe he is trying to improve the lack of capacity of Arab countries that are WTO members. He recently hired the former Moroccan ambassador, Mr Nacer Benjelloun-Touimi, as his special adviser on technical cooperation and relations with international bodies. I think the former ambassador will also advise him on how to improve Arab representation within the WTO and improve technical assistance.

A Secretariat staff member also saw Moore as having distanced himself somewhat from the USA following Seattle: 'Moore realized that he was not protected by one of his staunch supporters during his campaign – the USA. As a result, he decided to take a slightly more independent role as director general in the aftermath of the Seattle Ministerial Meeting.'

The increased attention to the needs of Arab countries, however, is a more recent phenomenon, at least partly as a result of pressure from the USA after September 11th. The appointment of Benjelloun-Touimi, a US and Secretariat 'friendly' who resigned as ambassador to take the Secretariat job, is a reflection of this.

Other developing countries took an altogether more negative view of Moore's performance, well summarized by an Asian delegate.

> When we came back from Doha, one ambassador said: 'This guy Mike Moore will go down in history as the enemy of the developing countries.' He pretends he is for the developing countries, emphasizing capacity-building and technical assistance. He canvassed around, played it nicely, got the round started and tagged it a 'development agenda' … Some ambassadors are very angry at the way he has pulled this through.

A particular source of antagonism for some developing country representatives is the spreading of disinformation on delegates to their capitals when it suits Quad interests. An African ambassador complained: 'Certain members of the Secretariat went to my capital with complaints about me, and suggested that I was making decisions without consulting my bosses back home. Mike Moore definitely talks to the ministers!' The rifts he created between ministers in capitals and their Geneva officials were clearly not appreciated.

Even if Moore took 'a slightly more independent role' after Seattle, he remained far from neutral on the issues discussed by the WTO. After Doha, he made a number of public statements supporting the 'new issues', and shocked delegates by writing an article in the *Financial Times* on 18 February (Moore 2002) urging developing countries to support proposals for WTO rules on competition and investment, as it was in their own economic interest. As de Jonquières (2002) observed in the same edition, 'It is unusual for a WTO director-general to take a public position on such politically contentious questions.' This attracted more than a little criticism – and not only among the developing country delegations. A delegate from an EC member state told the author: 'I had a word with Mike Moore, because I did not think he should be making public statements on the "new issues" after the Doha Conference. But this is typically Moore!' Even his deputy director general Andrew Stoler[5] was critical on this subject:

> When it comes to the dispute settlement process or a debate between two members of the WTO on issues such as labour standards or the environment, and the 'new issues', then we are neutral ... I would say the director general [Mike Moore] has slipped a bit on this. I won't say how much, but I think he should not have made these statements. However, I think he is working very hard in trying to open up markets for developing countries ... I also do not believe that he should have come out with a position on the accession of Russia to the WTO. We should not be saying whether or not we think Russia should be giving up all its subsidies.

The deputy directors general

The deputy directors general (DDGs) play a key role in the WTO; and their countries of origin play a key role in their selection. Andrew Stoler[6] (one of the DDGs at the time of the Doha Ministerial) gave a historical account:

> Traditionally, there has always been one American and one Indian deputy director general during the GATT era. When Peter Sutherland[7] became DG, he created a third DDG position to give something to the Latin Americans. Renato Ruggiero created a fourth DDG position when he came into office. When Mike Moore came in he appointed one American, one European,[8] one Latin American and [for the first time] one African.
>
> Supachai will decide what geographical representation he wants, because nothing is written down as regards what the combination should be – although the EC and the USA might make a

noise if they don't get anything. The USA does contribute 17 per cent of the WTO budget, although it is unlikely that a US citizen will ever be director general. The EC contributes 50 per cent of the budget, so must have someone at least at DDG level.

The insistence that the USA and the EC should necessarily be represented at the DDG level would seem to cast some doubt on the principle of political neutrality. If Secretariat staff were genuinely neutral, it would make no difference where DDGs came from, except that they would have greater familiarity with the circumstances of countries similar to their own. It would therefore make more sense to ensure geographical balance, for example by requiring one DDG from each of four roughly equal regions, than to insist that one country always has a DDG, and another single negotiating bloc of fifteen members should have another, leaving just two to be shared among the remaining 129 members.

Concern about political impartiality is heightened by the fact that Stoler worked for USTR for more than fifteen years, and Paul-Henri Ravier (the DDG from the EC under Moore) for the French trade ministry for twenty years, including active roles in GATT/WTO negotiations on their respective countries' behalf. The same is true of their successors, Rufus H. Yerxa of the USA and Roderick Abbott of the UK, appointed in September 2002 during Supachai Pinitchpakdi's term.

Some observers confirm that the role of the US and EC DDGs is, at least partly, to represent their respective interests within the Secretariat. An old-time Secretariat official said that Stoler took care of America's interests while Ravier attended to French and then the EC's interests, suggesting that they and Mike Moore had, in the process, further delegitimized the WTO as an institution (Raghavan 2001b).

Otto Genee,[9] a Dutch delegate in Geneva, saw this as a factor contributing to the politicization of the Secretariat.

I won't say the Secretariat is neutral, because various factions within manage it … The USA has always had a deputy director general who is in charge of personnel, finance and dispute settlement at the Secretariat. In my opinion the EC have not been clever in the way they have allowed things to evolve ... Personally I think there are too many DDGs, which politicizes the organization. I think one or two DDGs should suffice.

The Secretariat from Seattle to Doha

The Seattle Ministerial in November 2001 became a disaster just as Mike Moore took office, as the WTO members failed to reach an agreement on how to steer the multilateral trading system forward. While views on the reasons for the failure of the Seattle Ministerial Conference vary, there is a general feeling that the Quad could not reach an agreement on issues such as subsidies in agriculture, while crucially the developing country members felt left out of the negotiation process, much of which took place in green room meetings.

A staff member reflected on the aftermath of the failed ministerial:

> Staff morale was distressing after Seattle – we had put in a lot of work. But there had been other failures. For example, the 1990 mid-term review, which was meant to close the Uruguay Round, did not in fact end the round. Not reaching your goal is frustrating. It is not the end of the world, though – I mean the staff members were not crying about it. And besides, staff morale has picked up since, as the Doha Conference two years later has proved to be a success.

After the failure in Seattle, Moore and his deputies were determined to ensure, not only that Doha was a success, but also that it was a success according to the terms of the Quad. Before Doha, he and his key staff went on tours to promote the new round, particularly in the Latin American region. Tensions were high to get the WTO back on track, and of course September 11th created an even greater need for success. The extent of the concern among senior WTO staff to ensure the success of Doha is illustrated by the leaked e-mail on the WHO/WTO Guide to the WTO Agreements and public health, as discussed later in this chapter.

At the Doha Ministerial itself, as noted in Chapters 3 and 4, key Secretariat staff, and especially Mike Moore, were heavily involved in choosing the facilitators for the conference. They also played an active role in the final green room meeting, harassing developing country delegates to accept the draft declaration, while senior Secretariat staff, including Andrew Stoler, took charge of redrafting texts alongside US and EC delegates.

A particularly disturbing incident occurred when the Philippines and Thailand expressed concern that the EC/ACP waiver was being considered, while their efforts to negotiate a preferential agreement with the EC on tuna had been to no avail. The Secretariat began spreading rumours that the two countries were opposed to the EC/ACP waiver, driving a wedge between them and the ACP.

Stoler went further when he informed the Philippine delegation that the EC would like to talk to them about the tuna issue. Since they were working closely with Thailand on the matter, the Philippine delegates said they would meet the EC only together with their Thai counterparts. Stoler said that the Thai minister was nowhere to be found, so that the Philippines delegation would have to go it alone. In fact, the Thai minister was at the time in another room talking to another EC delegation, having been told that the *Philippine* head of delegation was nowhere to be found.

Eventually, the two delegations found out what was going on, lashed out at Stoler for his behaviour, and continued to fight together for their cause. They ultimately agreed to the deal when a procedural arrangement was made that they too would have preferential arrangements on tuna.

Having helped to bring Doha to a 'successful' conclusion, Moore went on a media rampage, labelling the 'work programme' emanating from the Doha Conference as the 'Doha development agenda'. He continued to campaign for a comprehensive round, including the 'new issues', at the next ministerial conference, in Mexico in 2003. Moore commented publicly at the World Economic Forum in New York that launching a new round would lift 360 million people out of poverty over a period of ten years. In response to this example of the DG's habit of using spurious figures in his press meetings, a Secretariat staff member said, 'Well, I will be very careful about throwing about figures ... Who knows, really?!'

Geographical diversity in the Secretariat staff

The geographical diversity (or rather lack of diversity) of the WTO Secretariat staff is a key issue. As one developing country delegate interviewed for this book said, 'The best-kept secret of the Secretariat is its geographical composition,' especially in the higher echelons of the institution.

While four-fifths of WTO members are developing countries, four-fifths of the staff is from *developed* countries. In 2001, of the 512.5 posts within the organization (with an additional 39.5 posts vacant or under recruitment), 410 were filled by people from developed countries, and only 94 by people from developing countries. The composition of staff is heavily biased in favour of Western European countries: there are 129 French staff, 71 British, 31.5 Swiss, 26 Canadians and 23.5 Americans. The entire African continent, on the other hand, is represented by just 10 staff.[10]

When asked about the geographical diversity of the Secretariat, Andrew Stoler,[11] the DDG responsible for personnel and recruitment, gave this response:

> We have a lot of staff that have been around for years and years, basically since GATT. It will be costly to retire them forcibly so they are going to be around until they retire. We are trying to work on this and are presenting a paper to the Budget, Finance and Administration Committee on this issue ... One has to bear in mind that we advertise about ten to twelve jobs a year so the rate of intake of new staff is quite low ...
>
> We already do have sixty-three different nationalities working at the Secretariat. We do not have an affirmative action policy, we simply aim to hire the best person for the job. However, where we have two good candidates we will choose a woman over a man and a developing country candidate over a developed country one ... We do not have a quota system as such – our recruitment is based on budget contributions. Should we have a quota system based

on the share of world trade, then I would say Japan and Asia and South East Asia generally are under-represented. Candidates from this region do not find WTO posts attractive for many reasons. It could be the distance they would have to move, the language difficulties they might face, the salary may not be as attractive, etc. I think we should reject people who only speak one language. We should expect staff to speak at least two languages.

Stoler's comments offer limited prospects for improvement in the North–South balance of WTO staff. Basing recruitment on budget contributions will do little to help, as the EC and the USA between them provide around two-thirds of the budget. And it is by no means clear, when Stoler talks about expecting staff to speak more than one language, that he is thinking of Urdu or Swahili!

Moreover, an Asian delegate saw the practical obstacles highlighted by Stoler as a poor excuse for Mike Moore reneging on a key promise in his campaign to become DG. '[Moore] keeps saying he does not have the money to make some of the old staff redundant and hire a new breed of staff. He claims pensions for the outgoing staff would be very expensive. Yet getting a new more diverse breed of staff in the Secretariat was one of his campaign slogans.'

The historical legacy of the GATT is a key issue. For most of its history, the GATT was made up mostly of developed countries, and its staffing reflected this. As a result, irrespective of more recent recruitment policies, the great majority of the longest-serving – and therefore the most senior – Secretariat staff are from developed countries, with a particularly strong Anglo-Saxon presence.

While there has been some change in the staff composition since the GATT era, many developing countries view the changes as too slow. An analysis by Sabrina Varma of the South Centre[12] shows that 'There has been very little improvement in the breakdown [in 2001] compared to one in 1997 which says a lot about the pace of the WTO's response to changing realities. The list of countries has by and large remained the same, as has the bias in recruitment from the same group of developed countries.'[13]

The Anglo-Saxon 'old guard', some of whom have been working

in the GATT/WTO system for twenty years or more, have a shared ideological and socio-cultural background with the USA, the EC and Canada, for example, making it easy for them to lean subconsciously towards the views of these members. Among this 'old guard', there exists a general air of arrogance, and a desire to control the direction of the organization as a whole, albeit very subtly, behind the scenes. They instinctively know how to manipulate weaker chairpersons to ensure that negotiations go a certain way, often, perhaps coincidentally, the way of the powerful developed country members. This creates a feeling among developing country delegates that it is difficult to tell in some instances where the Secretariat ends and the powerful Northern countries begin.

More generally, as a developing country delegate observed, 'the big countries ... have a high number of their own people in the Secretariat, which can only help them further their goals with ease'. Stoler,[14] of course, disagreed – although his argument seems less than convincing: 'I do not agree with the notion that the strength in numbers of Northern staff has any bearing on the power structures within the WTO. There are many Secretariat staff from Britain, yet they do not have the greatest power as members.' The UK, of course, forms part of the EC bloc within the WTO, and it seems difficult to argue that they are not among the most influential members.

There are some indications that the problem may run deeper than the practicalities of recruitment. An Asian ambassador recalled:

When I raised the issue of the composition of the Secretariat with a couple of Quad members during an informal discussion, one member of the Quad agreed that this is a problem. Another commented later, when they thought I was out of sight, that he can't imagine what the Secretariat would be like if it were filled with black and brown faces. This is a serious case of institutional discrimination.

Recruitment – an overview of favouritism in the hiring process

Apart from the question of geographical composition, a Southern delegate suggested that there was a substantial degree of favouritism in appointments in the WTO Secretariat during the time of Moore.

> Although the perception is that the recruitment for permanent staff is a rigorous process, there is also evidence of political favouritism going on at the Secretariat. Mike Moore appoints friends as special advisers. The ex-president of Mexico is part of a special advisory committee and the ex-Morocco ambassador is a special adviser. The latter was a very unpredictable and ambiguous ambassador – when it came to giving in to the Quad on crucial issues, he was always the first to do so. He was given the post after the Doha Ministerial Meeting.

Another former developing country delegate who then moved into a senior Secretariat position is Cheadu Osakwe, until recently director of the Technical Assistance Division. Osakwe used to work for the Nigerian mission in Geneva, where he is said to have played a role in Mike Moore's campaign for the WTO directorship. He is described by most delegates and staff members as charismatic, brilliant – and one of Moore's 'favourite sons'. As one delegate commented: 'If Osakwe happens to be batting for you then you are in luck. If, however, he is on the other side then you had better have a powerful batsman.' Moore allegedly created the post of LDC coordinator, within the DG's office, especially for Osakwe.

Osakwe was promoted to his current post after Doha, following the early retirement of a few long-serving Secretariat staff. One delegate's interpretation was: 'The reshuffle that followed provided Mike with the opportunity to promote [Osakwe] as reward for his loyalty.' This perceived favouritism, and the close friendship between Osakwe and Moore, generated some resentment among the other staff.

At least two other developing country delegates are widely believed to have been hired at the Secretariat because of their support for Mike Moore during his campaign to become director general.

Another delegate revealed an alternative route into the Secretariat for staff from developing country missions, recounting how the former Indian ambassador (who retired after Doha) had told him of a telephone call from Mike Moore asking if he could recommend someone at the Indian embassy he could hire at the Secretariat. This was seen as a gesture that might keep the challenging ambassador quiet on WTO matters. The ambassador replied that he had no one in mind, and reminded Mike Moore of the importance of accountability and transparency in the recruitment of WTO Secretariat staff.

A delegate from another Asian country suggested that this call was not exceptional – but that such conversations did not always lead to actual appointments: 'Mike Moore will ask developing country ambassadors to recommend someone for a WTO post only when he wants something in return, and often he does not necessarily hire that person anyway – especially after he gets what he wants.'

The 'neutrality' of the Secretariat

As noted in the introduction to this chapter, the Secretariat is in principle a neutral body performing an essentially administrative function and providing impartial advice to the members. This is a sensitive issue among the staff, who are emphatic about their neutrality. As a Northern Secretariat staff member said:

> We have to be neutral. My value is my neutrality. If I lose that, I lose everything – no one will come to me again for advice … By our very nature we carry out orders. We consider that we are the best Secretariat in Geneva – we are very small and very tight. Take the World Health Organization and International Labour Organization, for instance. They provide background papers and set agendas for meetings and conferences – not us. At the WTO, when members adopt negotiations in a particular area it is their baby, not ours. We generally only put out statistics.

As Vinod Rege, a retired senior officer of the GATT Secretariat, now a consultant to the Commonwealth Secretariat, observes:

WTO officials take pride in saying that they are only international bureaucrats who remain true to the oath to remain neutral which all persons joining the international civil service have to take. They express no views and take no sides. They only prepare factual papers that provide the basis for discussions and reports reflecting the main points made in the discussions. The responsibility for taking views lies entirely with the Member States acting jointly in the meetings of either the council or the committees.

This, of course, is a fiction; it is promoted because it suits the interests of both the Secretariat and the Member States. In practice, because of it being a Secretariat of a negotiating body as well as a body responsible for settlement of disputes, the officials tend to be more cautious and circumspect in expressing opinions and weigh carefully the possible reactions of Member States on subjects on which differences of views exist among Member States. (Rege 1998)

The real problem, however, is that some members carry much more weight than others. According to a Secretariat staff member from the South: 'Members dictate what we do. I love travelling with the US and EC WTO negotiators to meetings, because when developing country negotiators and ministers attack me, I simply refer them to the USA and EC.' A British Secretariat staff member acknowledged: 'Nobody is neutral. You have to take into account the power politics that goes on, especially by the USA, the EC, etc.' Vinod Rege makes the point more explicitly: 'The US and the EU exercise, at present, overall hegemony over the activities in all these three organizations [the WTO, the IMF and the World Bank]' (ibid.).

Rege further observes:

The high management would generally discourage publications by the Secretariat of any papers that express views that go against the negotiating positions of the major players. The officials themselves may be reluctant to do so, because they fear that this may affect their long-term career prospects. Further, the experience has shown, that if any official persists in pursuing approaches, that in their view are in the interests of countries with weaker bargaining positions, but not favoured by the major players, the latter build up pressures through complaints to the higher management and require them to shift to other assignments. (Rege 2000)

In between their proclamations of neutrality, top-level staff and representatives of Northern member states regularly assert – apparently without seeing any inconsistency – that the fundamental role of the Secretariat is to promote trade liberalization, within a multilateral framework, to the best of their abilities. The principle that 'relations in the field of trade and economic endeavour should be conducted with a view to raising standards of living' (WTO 1999c: 4) – one of the founding principles of the WTO as set out in the preamble to the Marrakesh Agreement – is never mentioned.

The lack of neutrality with respect to liberalization was openly acknowledged by then DDG Andrew Stoler.[15] 'We make an effort to ensure that the Secretariat is neutral. When you say neutral, you need to ask on what? We are not neutral when it comes to liberalism versus protectionism. We do not believe in the introduction of new subsidies, for example, which is against the principles of free trade on which this organization is based.' Similarly, Secretariat staff member Cheadu Osakwe (a Nigerian national)[16] said: 'The Secretariat is always neutral. If we lose it [our neutrality] we lose everything – we take it very seriously. We always think about the institutional mandate of the WTO, which is a permanent forum for the elimination of trade barriers and the promotion of trade liberalization.' This fundamental contradiction – between the Secretariat as impartial servants of the WTO members, and as active promoters of trade liberalization – is critical. In practice, the Secretariat promotes further trade liberalization in the WTO negotiations irrespective of, and at times at the expense of, the development needs and goals of developing country members.

There is some recognition of this tension among developed country delegates. Ian Wilkinson,[17] EC deputy trade representative in Geneva, for example, said: 'The objective of the organization is to promote and expand trade and liberalization, so the Secretariat will work to further these objectives ... However, liberalization has not been contested in the way it is now in many years, so if liberalization is not fashionable then you could say they are not neutral.'

Views are understandably stronger among developing countries. According to an African delegate, 'The Secretariat has very strong views on liberalization, and they do aggressively pursue that way of thinking. The transition from the old GATT Secretariat is ongoing, but it is slow. I think that they are professionals, but they have a very similar ideology with the Quad.' Moreover, the ideological issue goes beyond liberalization to some more specific issues. A Secretariat staff member from a developing country, for example, expressed concern about the Secretariat's position on trade and the environment.

> The ideology of the Secretariat has always been an issue for me. I think it should be improved. You get questions like 'Why don't developing countries want to talk about environment?' ... This emphasis on environmental issues could be a means of intro-ducing back-door protectionist policies by developed countries, and thus have a negative effect on developing country trade. Besides, it is a hypocritical view, because one of the conditions for China's accession to the WTO was that it had to purchase $6 billion worth of vehicles from the big countries, which is hardly an environmentally-friendly conditionality. The counter-argument was that the vehicles were environmentally friendly and therefore would pollute less ... There is always a well thought-out rebuttal to every argument at the WTO Secretariat.

As well as its bias towards liberalization, developing country delegates interviewed for this book suggested that the lack of defini-tion of the Secretariat's role and functioning at times compromises its neutrality *between WTO members* – particularly towards the Quad (the USA, the EC, Japan and Canada), who also happen to be the largest contributors to the Secretariat budget, at the expense of developing countries. Despite its general predisposition towards liberalization, the Secretariat is thus seen as standing idly by as the developed countries erect trade barriers that impact directly on developing countries.

Perhaps not surprisingly, representatives of developed countries and their allies do not see a great problem here. While acknowledging that power politics affects the way the WTO is run, most believe that the Secretariat is, by and large, a neutral body. According to Neil McMillan,[18] a UK delegate, for example, 'The Secretariat is neutral. They really only provide desks and chairs for meetings. It is studiously neutral compared to some other international organizations – although members do obviously insert a strong political flavour into many aspects of the WTO process.'

Developing country delegates, on the other hand, are altogether less convinced of the Secretariat's neutrality, seeing the staff as professional, but having a different orientation to the majority of the WTO membership. A Southern African delegate linked this strongly to the historical legacy of the GATT in the Secretariat's staffing.

> Most of the Secretariat staff has been around since GATT. The majority of them, in my opinion, still have a GATT mentality, which was generally an organization led by developed countries, with developing countries leaning more towards the United Nations Conference on Trade and Development [UNCTAD] … Developed country governments seconded their government officials to work in the higher echelons of the Secretariat staff during the GATT era – they now work at the WTO Secretariat. This makes it difficult for the staff to be neutral.

A former Southern delegate did not seem confident that the staff were really on his side: 'You get assistance with general administrative issues, etc., but I never felt the staff worked in my favour. I do not believe the staff are dishonest. I am aware, however, that there is a difference in ideology between the majority of the staff and the majority of developing country delegates.' A Southern African delegate provided a specific instance of a lapse in the Secretariat's neutrality in its support to delegates, over the sensitive TRIPs and public health issue: 'The Secretariat staff, for example, had a lot of information on TRIPs, which they refused to share with the developing country members who requested to see the documents, pre-Doha. The information was required by the members to assist them to shape their negotiating positions.'

If the role of the Secretariat was indeed a purely administrative one – if they merely provided the chairs for meetings and produced statistics, as some interviewees suggested – their lack of neutrality would have little impact. Some Secretariat staff deny both that the Secretariat is biased between members and that they go beyond their administrative functions. According to one developed country national on the staff:

> The top guys of the Secretariat will not bow to the wishes of the USA or EC. They would simply spend a lot of time convincing them to participate and to ensure they are on board, because if they aren't then you do have a problem. The USA alone has a 20 per cent share of world trade. There is an element of power politics – not everyone is created equal … I, however, do not believe that the USA will pull out of the WTO if things don't go their way – those are just empty threats … India, Brazil and Hong Kong have a lot of say in the WTO, for example, because of trade share and the skilled negotiators they have … When we hold meetings on textiles, we cannot exclude a country like Bangladesh, for instance, because they are an important player … When a country like Kenya or Egypt addresses the floor on issues, say in agriculture, for example, everybody pays attention. These countries are becoming key players.
>
> There is no behind-the-scenes agenda-setting by the Secretariat. I have been around for eighteen years, and I know that some chairpersons are stronger than others. They talk to the Secretariat one day, and talk to a wide range of members the next day. We as the Secretariat do prepare speaking notes that reflect what the chair needs *vis-à-vis* the members he consulted with … For example, yesterday the chairperson's notes in a certain committee were greatly frowned upon by representatives who said his comments did not reflect their positions. The chair had to withdraw those notes because of the strong opposition he faced. As far as

I know, these members said one thing during consultations and then changed their mind, so the whole thing was scrapped … We do not direct meetings, rather we give the chairperson [representing a member country] the options – we say go this way or that way, and that if you go this way so-and-so will not be happy. It will then be up to the chair to decide which groups to talk to in order to move the issue along.

Once again, however, the view from Southern delegates is very different. An Asian delegate detailed the influential role of the Secretariat:

Being chair of a committee at the WTO gave me the opportunity to see how the Secretariat functions, and how some group of countries would subtly get what they want into draft documents. It is done in a very clever, sophisticated and subtle manner … If, for example, the majority of delegates don't agree with a negotiating text produced by a chairperson and thus demand changes, the chair could turn to the Secretariat for help, especially if he or she is not technically competent. The clever lawyers of the Secretariat will then redraft the text in such a way that it would lean towards what the Quad want, and, importantly, it would also seem that consensus was reached. The chair would then be placed with the responsibility of presenting this skewed document to the membership without further consultations … A strong and competent chair would reject this approach and insist on further consultations …

There is a crafty way of drafting things. If you are not up to speed, things will be interpreted a certain way … If you are technically sound as chair, then you control the Secretariat. If not, things will go the other way because you would depend on them.

An East African delegate strongly supported this view.

They [the Secretariat] are neutral in theory, but not in practice … For example, if I was chair of a committee, my opening remarks would be prepared by the Secretariat. The work programme, the scheduled meetings, the back-to-back informal meetings would all be the usual Secretariat garbage, which I would just be regurgitating. This is normal practice throughout ... If the chair can't answer a question, he would lean over to the Secretariat staff for a response ... When the chair receives proposals, it is the Secretariat that would sit down and try to capture the arguments. This was the case in Seattle regarding the Mchumo text. You will see it had all the views in it [in brackets]. That was the work of the Secretariat ... In Doha there were no such brackets – Mike Moore and Stuart Harbinson submitted the document they wanted.

The WTO is amorphous. The Secretariat is running the show, but behind certain chairpersons. You are left negotiating with the chairman, only to realize that the chair is powerless. Somehow, we need to look at containing the Secretariat – the hidden power of the Secretariat ... We all know that the show is going to be run by the Secretariat, not Supachai the *person*, when he starts in September 2002. We all respect Supachai as a person, but it is the Secretariat who will prepare all the notes. It is the Secretariat who will be gauging the mood and advising him accordingly ...

There is a third party in negotiations, which is the Secretariat. How do we keep them out? They should be strictly confined to administrative duties. The moment you bring them in, you will have the same results as the Uruguay Round, where Arthur Dunkel[19] came up with his own text, and you need a consensus to change it ...

This last concern was echoed by a former Central American delegate: 'The Secretariat has biased positions, which has helped create another layer on to the WTO negotiating structure. Mission officials from developing countries not only have to negotiate with their counterparts, they also have to negotiate with a so-called "neutral" Secretariat.'

A case study of 'neutrality' – the WHO/WTO Guide[20]

Shortly before Doha, a leaked e-mail between senior WTO staff members gave a rare insight into how the 'neutral' WTO Secretariat operates in practice.

In early 2000, the World Health Organization (WHO) had decided to produce a guide to the possible implications of the WTO agreements for public health (WHO/WTO 2002). The guide was to be aimed primarily at public health professionals in developing countries, to increase their awareness and improve their understanding of the WTO agreements and their implications for health, in part to inform deliberations ahead of the Doha Conference. The WHO staff involved in developing the guide had consulted their WTO counterparts extensively throughout its preparation, and were careful to ensure that the trade view as well as the health view was presented. Some senior WTO staff, however, appear to have become apprehensive about its contents in the pre-Doha period, particularly in view of the sensitivity of the TRIPs and public health issue.

After the project had been under way for eighteen months, and a complete draft of the Guide had been submitted for external review, senior WTO staff requested that it should be a joint publication, and that the text should be agreed between the two organizations. They said they were generally happy with the text, and wanted only two changes. Despite serious misgivings on the part of the WHO staff involved, and of the external scientific review group of the WHO department involved, the collaboration was agreed at a senior level.

Once the collaboration was agreed, the WTO proceeded to submit to the WHO completely rewritten versions of every chapter of the guide – except for the final chapter, looking forward to issues in future negotiations, which they insisted should be removed entirely. There followed a long and at times acrimonious 'collaboration', in the course of which the principal author of the guide, frustrated at being constantly overruled in disagreements with the WTO on the text, refused to continue working on it, and another WHO staff member who expressed his disagreement with the WTO over their proposed text simply ceased to be shown drafts or informed of meetings.

The task of coordinating the WTO's input to the project was given to Miguel Rodriguez Mendoza (a Venezuelan national), then DDG in charge of the rules division. As the profile and sensitivity of the TRIPs and public health issue increased still further, Adrian

Otten, director of the WTO's intellectual property divison, became more and more involved – and, it would seem, more worried.

In September 2001, Otten drafted an e-mail to the DDGs at the time, Andrew Stoler (of the USA) and Paul-Henri Ravier (of the EC), which was leaked and widely circulated before it could be sent.[21] The following are extracts from his message (emphasis added).

Mr. Rodriguez may well believe that my aim is to kill his project. This is not the case ... However, *I do feel very strongly*, for reasons indicated below, *that we should not send it* [WTO's input to the guide] *to WHO prior to Doha*. I have two major concerns on the TRIPs side.

The first and most important is that I think it unnecessarily risky for the WTO Secretariat to share texts on TRIPs Agreement's provisions on pharmaceuticals with the WHO at this stage ... It is true that we cannot live without risk and *I would not have any problems with proceeding after Doha* to share the text with WHO after some more work has been done on it ... I think it is only wise to keep our focus on the need for not doing anything that could put in jeopardy the process of developing language on the issue of access to drugs prior to Doha.

My second concern about TRIPs is that [the guide] does not as yet contain *a section which discusses the positive impact of the TRIPs Agreement on public health,* namely *through promoting research and development into new drugs.* The totality of the section on the TRIPs Agreement so far is on the implications for access to existing drugs. We are working on such a section but it will involve several days work ... To finalise this text would require a significant diversion of effort from the Doha preparatory process.

The main general concern I have about this guide is that the basic approach is *to address the extent to which trade liberalisation may stand in the way of health measures.* This is an important aspect and needs to be treated in some detail, *so as to reassure people that the GATT* [the General Agreement on Tariffs and Trade] *and GATS* [the General Agreement on Trade in Services] *do not have this effect* where measures are necessary for health purposes.

However it seems to me that *at least on an equal footing should be a general discussion on the relationship between an open trading system, economic growth and standards of health*. What is the evidence in this connection. Do countries which have a more liberal trading system tend to have higher standards of health? Is trade liberalisation correlated with the movements towards higher health standards? ... We have made the same arguments in the area of environment, namely that higher living standards bring with them higher environmental standards and that, from an environmental point of view, it is foolish to stand in the way of trade liberalisation that would bring higher living standards.[22]

The main messages that we want to give are: (a) that open trade and the movement towards open trade brings with it higher standards of health; and (b) concerns that the WTO rules will stand in the way of legitimate health measures are unfounded. At the moment only (b) seems to be addressed in any degree of detail.

The message reveals two objectives in relation to the Guide. First, whereas the original purpose of the Guide was in part to promote more informed discussions on issues relevant to health at the Doha Ministerial, its appearance had to be delayed until after Doha, to ensure that it did *not* influence the negotiations ('the process of developing language'), particularly on TRIPs and public health. This objective was fulfilled admirably: while the WHO had submitted a complete draft for external review eight months before Doha, the WTO's involvement meant that it did not appear until August 2002, nine months after Doha.

Second, the Guide had to be turned from a balanced and objective assessment of the implications of the WTO agreements from a health perspective into an instrument of WTO propaganda. It should aim to convince people that the TRIPs Agreement promoted the development of new drugs (an assertion for which there is little or no evidence, particularly in terms of drugs of public health priority); that the agreements themselves did not limit governments' ability to take measures to improve health; and that trade liberalization promoted health through faster economic growth.

In this regard, too, the WTO was largely successful. Despite a rearguard battle by some WHO departments, once they were finally consulted, to regain some of the ground which had been lost in the WTO collaboration, a marked pro-trade and pro-liberalization 'spin' was evident throughout the final version, which duly included a section entitled 'Patent Protection Provides Incentives for R&D [Research and Development] into New Drugs'. Otten did not, however, get his wish of equal emphasis for the effects of trade liberalization on economic growth as for the direct implications of WTO agreements for health policies – perhaps in recognition that this would be of rather less interest to the intended audience (public health professionals).

Conclusion

After seven years of existence, the WTO Secretariat has not changed much from the old GATT days, when it clearly catered to the needs of the developed countries and was dubbed the 'rich man's club'. During his time as director general, Mike Moore showed no signs of reorienting the organization towards the needs of developing countries. Rather, it was politicized still further, to the point where certain staff members became disillusioned about their role and purpose as international servants.

Representatives of developing country members became increasingly agitated by the blatant lack of neutrality exhibited by Mike Moore and his cronies, particularly during the Doha process; and Moore's habit of bypassing Geneva-based ambassadors and going over their heads to their capitals to voice his opinions and concerns reached unprecedented levels, leaving delegates reeling with anger.

Clearly, it is difficult for the WTO to satisfy 146 diverse members. Nevertheless, there is growing concern among developing countries that the Secretariat's highly ambiguous role within the WTO makes it, in effect, an additional layer in the negotiating structure.

Notes

1. WTO director general between 1995 and 1999 (Italian national).

2. Interview with Dr Federico Cuello Camilo, then Dominican Republic ambassador to the WTO and UN, 4 March 2002.

3. Interview with Stuart Harbinson, then Hong Kong ambassador to the WTO, 18 March 2002.

4. Northern donors pledged $18 million towards the Doha Development Global Trust Fund on 11 March 2002 (twice the amount the WTO Secretariat had requested). The fund, controlled by the WTO Secretariat, will support capacity-building and technical assistance for developing countries, primarily on the 'new issues'. UNCTAD will be provided with funds to organize joint training programmes with the WTO for developing countries on investment and competition issues.

5. Interview with Andrew Stoler, then WTO deputy director general, 5 March 2002.

6. Ibid.

7. Peter Sutherland (Irish national) was director general of GATT between 1993 and 1994 and WTO director general for a year in 1995.

8. The absence of Europeans from the ranks of the DDGs until Mike Moore's appearance is less surprising when one recalls that until then the DG had always been from Europe.

9. Interview with Otto Genee, then Netherlands deputy permanent representative to the WTO, 8 March 2002.

10. It should be noted that this breakdown does not capture the types of positions held by staff from the different continents. In particular, WTO's location in Geneva and local recruitment of support staff mean that a large proportion of the Swiss and French staff are likely to be in administrative, secretarial and junior professional positions rather than more influential technical and managerial posts.

11. Interview with Andrew Stoler, then WTO deputy director general, 5 March 2002.

12. The South Centre is a Geneva-based intergovernmental organization of developing countries, which prepares, publishes and distributes information on international economic, social and political matters of concern to the South.

13. Sabrina Varma, South Centre, electronic communication, March 2002.

14. Interview with Andrew Stoler, then WTO deputy director general, 5 March 2002.

15. Ibid.

16. Interview with Cheadu Osakwe, then director of the Technical Assistance Division, WTO, 13 March 2002.

17. Interview with Ian Wilkinson, deputy permanent representative

of the EC delegation to the international organizations in Geneva, 14 March 2002.

18. Interview with Neil McMillan, minister, deputy permanent representative of the UK mission to the WTO and UN, 27 February 2002.

19. Director general of GATT between 1980 and 1993 (Swiss national).

20. The account of the WHO/WTO collaboration in the early part of this section has been corroborated by a former WHO staff member involved in the process.

21. The draft message was inadvertently leaked in print form by the intellectual property division, when it was accidentally included in a submission to the TRIPs council by the Australian delegation. While it was recalled almost immediately, some recipients discovered the error and copied the e-mail before it could be reclaimed. The full text is available at http://lists.essential.org/pipermail/ip-health/2001-September/001892.html.

22. This is presumably a reference to Nordström and Vaughan (1999). It is rumoured that a similar process occurred between the WTO and the United Nations Environment Programme (UNEP) to that between the WTO and the WHO on the Guide. While the study was initiated by UNEP and the WTO, the UNEP staff member responsible (Scott Vaughan) subsequently moved to the WTO. The report was published as a WTO-only product.

EIGHT
After Doha – business as usual

Of course, the WTO process did not stop after the Doha Ministerial. Discussions continued on the key issues, institutional and
procedural changes were made, committee chairs were appointed
– and the WTO's first ever DG from a developing country took
office. Despite the change of leadership, however, subsequent developments in Geneva served only to reinforce the 'flexible' interpretation of WTO rules and the ignoring of developing countries'
views that characterized the Doha Ministerial and the process that
led up to it.

This chapter discusses major developments on process issues
in the year after Doha, focusing particularly on two specific issues
of particular relevance to the current round of negotiations: the
modalities and chairmanship of the Trade Negotiations Committee
(TNC); and Stuart Harbinson's appointment as chair of the Agriculture Committee. After a general discussion of mini-ministerials
and green room meetings, the chapter concludes with a review of
Supachai's role and performance in the early months of his term
of office as DG.

The Trade Negotiations Committee[1]

The establishment of the Trade Negotiations Committee (TNC)
was a critical paragraph of the Doha Ministerial Declaration, because it would shape the manner and therefore contribute significantly to the outcome of the subsequent negotiations. Prior to
Doha, most developing countries opposed the idea of establishing
a TNC, and made it clear that there was no consensus on the
issue. While a similar body had been established during the GATT
Uruguay Round, the Marrakesh Agreement establishing the WTO
(Articles IV and IX) gives the authority to make decisions on negotiations between ministerials to the General Council. Having a TNC

therefore seemed an unnecessary waste of precious meeting time and personnel of under-staffed delegations.

Like many of the paragraphs that were disputed in the run-up to Doha, however, the paragraphs on the TNC were included in the draft ministerial declaration as a clean text; and, having been included among the thirty-nine paragraphs presented to the minister from Botswana to deal with in the last one and a half days of the conference (see Chapter 4), they changed very little as a result of the discussions in Doha.

Establishment and procedural issues

After Doha, it became clear to most developing countries that a basic set of rules and procedures was necessary to give effect to transparency, inclusiveness and the effective participation of all member states in negotiations. Given the experience of Doha and previous ministerials, many wished to build in accountability in the selection of chairs, their roles and responsibilities, and the general conduct of negotiations.

On 21 December 2001, a group of nine developing countries[2] submitted a communication to the General Council (WTO 2001c), addressing the systemic problems of transparency and inclusiveness that plague the WTO. The paper echoed some of the concerns expressed by other members of the Like-Minded Group, the LDCs and the Africa group. It stressed that the TNC should be subordinate and accountable to the General Council, where the 145 members are formally represented; and that chairs must be selected in a formal setting on the basis of 'explicit consensus'. It outlined general procedures for a balanced composition of TNC chairs, with chairs and vice-chairs rotating annually between developed and developing countries. By proposing Geneva-based ambassadors as chairs, it also stressed the need for neutrality as a central feature of the chairmanship, and indirectly indicated that the DG was not an appropriate choice as TNC chair (see below).

Finally, the paper addressed some core concerns regarding transparency and accountability, in view of past misreporting of meetings and misrepresentation of draft negotiating texts. It insisted on having accurate and objective minutes within ten days of a TNC meeting, and proposed that all drafting be done in open meetings, and that negotiating texts be made available in the three official WTO languages (English, French and Spanish) at least two weeks in advance, in order to enable delegations to receive feedback from their capitals on their positions. Most importantly, it insisted that all disagreements must be reflected either in bracketed texts or by listing various options as suggested by members. This was a direct reaction to the clean text forwarded to Doha by General Council chair Stuart Harbinson (Chapter 3). In sum, they called for basic rules for the TNC and the ministerial process that were unambiguous and appropriate for a rules-based international organization.

There was considerable opposition by the major powers, however, to the creation of detailed procedures and a code of conduct for the TNC. This would make negotiations slower, but more predictable and systematic than previously in terms of process. Countries like the USA said that this would bog down the negotiations, and that they did not want to put the process in a 'straitjacket'.

Among the procedures the developed country delegations considered cumbersome was the writing of minutes of WTO meetings. In the December General Council meeting, Australia said, 'The necessary progress [on the Doha Mandate] would be impossible if, for example, there were procedural requirements that minutes had to be prepared before another meeting could be held, or that no groups could meet simultaneously. Australia appealed to all delegations to think seriously about their ability to deliver what Ministers wanted, if they were bogged down in procedure' (WTO 2002a: 26). This question of 'what Ministers wanted' is, of course, ambiguous, as different ministers clearly have different interests and want different outcomes.

The TNC chairmanship

While the nine countries which submitted the TNC paper, together with the LDCs and the majority of the Africa Group, among others, supported the appointment of a Geneva-based ambassador as chair of the TNC, it was equally clear from public statements by EC Commissioner Pascal Lamy and others that the Quad supported the then DG, Mike Moore, for the position. Harbinson, as chair of the General Council, was again asked to consult with the members so that a decision could be made by the first TNC meeting, scheduled for 28 January 2002.

In the run-up to Doha, many delegations and even Secretariat staff had expressed concern about the DG's lack of neutrality ahead of the Doha Ministerial. In visit after visit to capitals, and in one media article after another, Moore had unequivocally supported the launch of a new round of talks while members were in complete disagreement on the issue (see Chapter 6). In view of this, many delegates did not view Moore personally as an appropriate choice for a neutral chair in the upcoming negotiations. They also felt, on an institutional level, that the head of the Secretariat could not perform a dual function as TNC chair.

In view of concerns about Moore's personal suitability as TNC chair, the idea was floated, supported by the Association of South East Asian Nations (ASEAN), that the DG should serve as TNC chair *ex officio* – that is, that whoever was DG would automatically also chair the TNC. This would enable the next DG, Supachai Panitchpakdi of Thailand (an ASEAN member country), to take over the TNC chairmanship from September 2002 until the mandated negotiations were completed in January 2005.

In the last General Council meeting of 2001, the LDCs opposed the idea of the DG as *ex officio* chair of the TNC, on the grounds that it gave rise to a conflict of interest and would force them to negotiate with the Secretariat – as during the Uruguay Round, when the DG of the GATT, Arthur Dunkel, chaired the TNC. Tanzania spoke on behalf of the LDCs, saying

> It would be extremely disappointing if the choice of TNC Chair, whose decisions and influence would have a long-lasting impact on Members' trade activities and development, were to be imposed. The LDCs had participated in launching these negotiations and wished to see their concerns taken on board. The Chair should be impartial throughout the process, unbiased and strong enough to

ensure that LDCs' interests and concerns were not marginalized, as they had been in the past. The imbalances and asymmetries of the Uruguay Round were well known, had undermined the multilateral trading system, and had also created numerous implementation problems for developing countries, especially the LDCs ... LDCs were convinced that the Chair should hold his post for only one year to allow for rotation among regions ... Regarding other negotiating bodies, their Chairs and Vice-Chairs should also be Geneva-based representatives in order to exercise membership control and to uphold the Member-driven principle. The Secretariat should provide support services and should not be involved in the negotiations. (ibid.: 25)

In an interview with the authors, an East African delegate raised another widespread developing country concern: 'My fear about the arrangement whereby the director general is chair of the Trade Negotiations Committee in an *ex officio* capacity, is that these negotiations [stemming from the Doha Ministerial] will not be completed by 2005 as indicated. After Supachai, the guy who comes might be worse than Dunkel. That guy will come from the Quad.'

'Consultations' and 'consensus' on the TNC

According to one delegate, the process of consensus-building at the WTO through consultations is like a 'black box', in that the chair's actual consultations are not recorded, and what he presents as middle ground is left entirely to his discretion. He or she produces a compromise 'Chairman's text' to the best of his judgement; but there is no paper trail to indicate how he or she arrived at the position proposed. While countries can, in principle, oppose or reject a chairman's text, weaker countries find it hard if not impossible politically to exert their opposition in the face of 'consensus' decisions.

This was also the situation in the case of the TNC statement and decision on the chair, which once again did not reflect the concerns of the majority of developing countries. The LDCs had not only made their formal statement at the December 2001 General Council meetings, but had reiterated that position several times during the Harbinson consultations in January 2002. The Africa Group had also submitted their position to Harbinson in writing on 16 January, and other developing countries had submitted two formal papers on the subject by the time of the first TNC meeting.

As in Doha, however, the political pressure exerted by the most influential WTO countries was so strong that many countries had to change their position or remain silent in order to avoid being seen as obstructionist. As in the case of Doha, certain country delegates received calls from their capitals asking them not to block 'consensus'.

Some of the developing countries' concerns were voiced at a General Council meeting on 23 January. The central complaints included the failure of consultations to reflect the concerns of all the members, and the need for rules of procedure for negotiations. Two days later, on Friday 25 January, a small group of delegates participated in an informal closed session to 'air views' about the chairmanship of the TNC, and to discuss the formal meeting of the General Council scheduled for Monday 28th, where developed country members hoped to launch the TNC. By this time, China was also opposed to moving forward on negotiations without a clear declaration that differences in positions must be clearly marked in negotiating texts.

Around twenty-five countries were represented at the meeting,[3] including Brazil and Canada (as co-chairs), the EC, the USA, Japan, Switzerland, Australia, Hungary, Uruguay, Costa Rica, Chile, Argentina, Egypt, South Africa, Uganda, Kenya, Jamaica, Korea, Singapore, India and Pakistan. Participation was strikingly similar to the Mexico and Singapore mini-ministerials: three-quarters of those present were also at the mini-ministerials – and, as always, all the Quad members were there. Bizarrely, the meeting also included a presentation by Mike Moore himself on technical assistance.

At the informal meeting, developing country delegations repeated their position that the role of the TNC must be established, that the negotiating process must be clarified, and that the role of the TNC chair must be clearly delineated before negotiations began.

According to one delegate, however, many of the countries which strongly opposed the selection of the DG as chair at the informal meeting on the Friday were quiet at the General Council meeting on the Monday, following several rounds of phone calls to capitals. One ambassador told the Like-Minded Group that he/she could not openly oppose the DG chairmanship at the meeting. He/she was clearly frustrated that officials in his capital did not know WTO politics well enough to see the importance of keeping the Secretariat out of the negotiations. Another delegate was instructed by his capital not to oppose Moore because Moore was about to visit his country, and officials were keen to remain in line.

The developed countries continued to insist that the negotiation process should not be put in a straitjacket, and that 'flexibility' should be allowed. In response to the need for ground rules, the developed countries proposed a 'chairman's statement' of principles for negotiations – to the dismay of many of the developing countries, who saw this as sidestepping the responsibility to establish clear and binding rules of procedure.

On 29 January, as the heated controversy continued, a group of twelve developing countries (the original nine, minus Egypt, plus India, Indonesia, Jamaica and Malaysia) submitted an official proposal to the TNC on its role, the negotiation process, and the role of the chair of the TNC and its negotiating bodies (WTO 2002j).

The outcome – slim majority/substantial minority

Despite widespread opposition, the DG was selected as *ex officio* chair at the TNC meeting, as 'an exceptional arrangement'. Once again, agreement was reached by a 'slim majority' after Geneva-based delegations were bypassed and pressure put on capitals to support a clearly non-consensual decision.

In its final statement at the TNC meeting, Tanzania, on behalf of the LDCs, spoke out strongly against the decision. The LDCs

believed it was institutionally wrong and even harmful to have the Director General of the WTO to chair the TNC, which was a body of an intergovernmental institution ... This was like arguing that the best guarantee for objective decision-making in the organization would be to surrender the Chairmanships of the various bodies to the DDGs [Deputy Director Generals] and other members of the Secretariat. (WTO 2002b: 7)

On process issues, developing countries failed to get any binding commitments on due process of negotiations. All they got were vague 'principles and practices' for the negotiations, stressing 'transparency and inclusiveness in decision-making and consultative processes'. The nature and status of these 'principles and practices' are indicated by the extraordinary way in which they were introduced by chairman Stuart Harbinson: 'It may assist delegations if I set out my understanding, derived from the extensive consultations I have held, of some basic principles and practices which I believe it is widely felt we should keep in mind as the TNC carries out its work under its Ministerial Mandate' (ibid.: 2).

Harbinson's emphasis on this being *his own* understanding of his consultations (not of the General Council discussion) has strong echoes of Minister Kamal's 'clarification' on the 'new issues' at the end of the Doha Ministerial (see Chapters 4–5), which the USA and the EC flagrantly ignored as soon as the ministerial was over. This would seem to leave the status of the 'principles and practices' ambiguous.

On internal transparency, members were merely asked to 'build on the best practices established over the past two years'. Many developing countries have openly discounted these 'best practices' as ineffective and non-operational. The Bulgarian delegate was particularly critical: 'Such practices had never been established and his delegation could not agree to an institutionalization of something which had never been agreed upon through the back door ... The problem of transparency in the negotiations needed to be dealt with in a much more specific way through the adoption of clear and explicit rules' (ibid.: 12).

Various developing countries put forward a number of overlapping proposals (as discussed above) to concretize the 'best practices' concept in terms of transparency, inclusiveness and the role of chairpersons. Proposals included: an end to green room meetings; requiring transcripts or accurate minutes to be made available no later than two weeks after each meeting; protecting the limited and neutral role of the DG and the Secretariat; and establishing clear rules to govern ministerial conferences. None of these proposals was reflected in the 'principles and practices'.

Even the critical issue of producing accurate negotiating texts that reflect differences in members' positions was left ambiguous. What developing countries wanted was explicit language forbidding chairs from submitting texts in their 'personal capacity', and requiring differences in members' positions to be reflected in negotiating texts – and China threatened to stall the process if this issue was not addressed appropriately. In the end, the wording was: 'In their regular reporting to overseeing bodies, Chairpersons should reflect consensus, or where this is not possible, different positions on issues.' Since draft negotiating texts do not constitute part of 'regular reporting to overseeing bodies', however, this left open the possibility of such drafts *not* reflecting different positions.

The Jamaican ambassador summed up the progress made on the TNC process most articulately, pointing out that ministers had agreed, in paragraph 49 of the Doha Ministerial Declaration, to negotiations in a transparent manner, and continuing:

> In making this affirmation ministers had made a clear link between process and substantive outcome. Developing guidelines and procedures would ensure the fullest possible adherence to the Doha Declaration from the outset. Although some delegations had expressed concern over what was perceived as either procedural quibbling or the imposition of too many procedures, Jamaica remained convinced that clear rules and transparent guidelines would contribute to efficiency through clarity and predictability. Too much flexibility and too much vagueness would be counterproductive.

Moore made an inauspicious start to his tenure as TNC chair. One of the 'principles and practices' adopted by the General Council was that 'Chairpersons [of the TNC and Negotiating Bodies] should be impartial and objective, and discharge their duties in accordance with the mandate conferred on the TNC by Ministers' (WTO 2002k: 2). But less than three weeks after his appointment as TNC chair, Moore wrote an article in the *Financial Times* urging developing countries to support negotiations on competition and investment, in their own economic interest (see Chapter 7). Soon afterwards, in the face of open opposition from developing countries, he exceeded his mandate by inviting the chairs of the investment and competition working groups to a meeting with the TNC chair, although neither issue falls under the purview of the TNC.

Another 'exception' – the Agricultural Committee chairmanship[4]

Soon after the Secretariat had bulldozed its way into members' territory in the TNC, seasoned observers at the WTO were treated to a reprise of this rule-breaking in the agriculture negotiations.

Stuart Harbinson, WTO ambassador of Hong Kong, and chair of the General Council in 2001, whose 'magical' clean text for Doha had omitted the objections of many developing countries, was appointed chair of the agricultural negotiations, the most politically sensitive issue at the WTO, in February 2002. He was the preferred candidate of the major powers for the position – and their task in securing his appointment was made all the easier by the fact that it was Harbinson himself, in the last days of his General Council chairmanship, who was responsible for consulting members on the appointment of committee chairs, including for agriculture.

In June 2002, however, it was announced that Dr Supachai, who was to take office as DG on 1 September, had appointed Harbinson as his *chef de cabinet*. Harbinson took leave from his government position and assumed his new post in the Secretariat from 10 September – but without relinquishing his position as chair of agriculture. In national terms, this is the equivalent of an MP stepping down from his or her parliamentary seat to join the civil service, but continuing to serve as chair of a key parliamentary committee. In the WTO, Article VI.4 of the Marrakesh Agreement says that 'the staff of the Secretariat shall be exclusively international in character' – that is, that they should not be involved in the politics of chairing negotiating bodies.

The appointment of DG Mike Moore as chair of the TNC was 'an exceptional arrangement' – and yet this 'exceptional arrangement' was repeated within months.

Countries such as the Quad, other developed countries and members of the Cairns Group, who wanted to see the agricultural talks moved along and concluded (in their favour), or who simply trusted Harbinson's abilities, were all for Harbinson staying on as chair. One of the reasons they cited was that he was, after all, 'neutral'. Therefore, even if he was a member of the Secretariat staff, this could be excused because his 'neutrality' would not create a conflict of interest. They were also concerned that changing the chair would significantly set back the timetable of the intensive talks in the Agriculture Committee planned for the ensuing six months.

Harbinson has described his own style of compromise as follows: 'The whole thing is to construct a balance of interests in which everybody gives something and everybody gets something' (*South China Morning Post* 2002). Many developing countries, however, were uneasy with this situation. They had given a lot and got very little, and they did not want to see a repetition of Doha, where their opposition to the 'new issues' was ignored in the Harbinson negotiating text. For them, the appointment also set a dangerous precedent for involving Secretariat staff directly in negotiations.

Several delegations raised their concerns privately with Supachai as DG. At least one country also wrote a formal letter to the chair of the General Council, stating its displeasure at the arrangement. Several members of the Africa Group believed that it had also taken a decision to write a formal letter to the General Council. No follow-up materialised, however, after key members of the group were approached by the powerful WTO members. As one African diplomat explained privately, 'Some countries whom we thought were our friends are no longer with us on this. They have come under bilateral pressure.'

Another delegate, explaining why the issue remained under

wraps more generally, said: 'I get the impression that no one is willing to be the spoiler. The major powers see such a high stake in this. Many developing countries are still feeling the post-September 11th threat that "you are with us or you are against us".' An African ambassador said more explicitly that members saw the issue as highly problematic but remained quiet out of fear that they could be punished by the influential countries if they stepped 'out of line'.

When he took office as DG, Supachai's position was that he would remove Harbinson as agriculture chair if the membership so indicated. He appears, however, to have done nothing on this critical process issue – and many developing countries, well aware of the hard battle they had to fight three years ago to get him into the position, had no desire to embarrass him by pressing the issue. They preferred to keep things at an informal level, speaking to Supachai about it on the quiet, in order to maintain a good working relationship with him.

Whatever the reason (see the section on Supachai's term as DG below), Supachai does not appear unduly concerned about the Secretariat bulldozing its way into members' territory, or the need for a clear division of powers. When questioned about the matter at a meeting with NGOs, he showed a surprising nonchalance about the flouting of clear rules:

> You seem to have a view that the staff is not neutral. You seem to have said that he [Harbinson] would be less of an impartial person than he used to be if he joined the Secretariat and chairs agriculture. I don't think he would like to do this job. I think it is mainly in the interest of the whole membership. The rules do not forbid anyone from chairing a negotiating Committee if Members agree to it. (Supachai Panitchpakdi, quoted in Kwa 2002a)

Countries are already wondering if their positions in agriculture (predicted to be a key sticking point in the forthcoming Fifth Ministerial in Cancun) will be reflected in the agriculture modalities paper that Harbinson will be releasing and revising between December 2002 and March 2003 – particularly in view of the ambiguity of the 'principles and practices' relating to the conduct of committee chairs in this respect, as discussed above. And at the end of 2002, many developing countries already found themselves spending their time lobbying Harbinson, as chair, to reflect their proposals in his agriculture negotiating texts, rather than lobbying the developed countries to change their positions.

Anticipating a repetition of his pre-Doha antics, some countries, such as India, warned Supachai that they would not accept a repeat of the Doha text. Politically weaker countries, however, are not so confident that they will be able to stand up against the tide.

Mini-ministerials and green room meetings

The process of mini-ministerial meetings – at which selected countries discuss key WTO issues at ministerial level with no written records, to set the agenda and build the process of railroading the remainder of the membership – continued unchanged after Doha. A mini-ministerial in Sydney in November 2002 was attended by twenty-five WTO members, including (as always) all of the Quad members, plus Brazil, China, Colombia, Egypt, Hong Kong, India, Indonesia, Kenya, Korea, Lesotho, Malaysia, Mexico, New Zealand, Nigeria, Senegal, Singapore, South Africa, Switzerland, Thailand and one representative from the Caribbean. Most (with the notable exception of China, as a new member of WTO) are among the regular invitees for such meetings.

A similar meeting was held in Tokyo on 14–16 February 2003, to be followed by a meeting at vice-ministerial level in Paris in April; and at the time of writing Egypt is planning to hold another mini-ministerial between then and the Cancun Ministerial in September 2003. All these meetings are, of course, attended by the EC's Pascal Lamy and USTR Robert Zoellick (or, no doubt, their deputies in the case of Paris).

Bilateral deals continue to be made at these meetings, and efforts are made to soften up the leaders of developing country coalitions (particularly the Africa Group, the LDCs and the Caribbean countries) and the more influential developing countries (particularly India and now, no doubt, China), and thus to isolate the other 100 or so politically weaker developing countries. This is critical to the process of manufacturing a 'consensus' behind the major powers' positions, and eliminating the possibility of other countries standing up to oppose the final package they put together (see Chapter 2).

'Green room' meetings – similarly selective, unrepresentative, informal and unofficial meetings between the DG or chair of a negotiating committee and negotiators in Geneva – also remain an important part of the landscape. On 19–20 December 2002, just days after assuring civil society groups that 'everyone would be involved' in the post-Doha negotiations (see the next section), Supachai himself was organizing green room meetings, to try to resolve the stalemate on TRIPs and public health. It quickly became apparent at these meetings that their purpose was to gather support behind the narrow US 'interpretation' of the Doha mandate on TRIPs with as few concessions as possible to the health concerns of the developing countries – and Supachai himself played a key role in this process.

The noted Geneva-based journalist on WTO issues, Chakravarthi Raghavan, reported:

> the few developing nations called in were being pressured to agree to a virtual rewrite of the Doha Ministerial mandate in order to 'give comfort and accommodate' the United States and the PhRMA [the pharmaceutical industry]. They were asked to agree to a restrictive meaning to the scope of public health problems and diseases enabling countries to act against patent monopolies and rules of the TRIPs ...
>
> Dr Supachai ... in the first green room, had suggested a footnote to qualify the references in the decision to para one of the Doha [TRIPs and Public Health] declaration: by mentioning – besides HIV/AIDS, TB and malaria – some 11 or 12 diseases most prevalent in Africa ... This was rejected by developing nations ... (Raghavan 2002i)

Raghavan also observed: 'The repeated "green room" meetings were held contrary to the normal practice, and only a few (and not all those who had participated actively and expressed some views on the Chairman's texts at the TRIPs Council meetings) were invited' (ibid.).

Dr Supachai Panitchpakdi: WTO's first developing country director general

Supachai finally became DG in September 2002 – the first ever DG of the GATT or WTO from a developing country. A very smooth and experienced politician, he has a personal style quite different from Moore's. He comes across as patient, soft-spoken, a good listener, versatile in the complex trade issues, and with all the trappings of a first-rate diplomat. Keenly aware that it was primarily the developing countries who brought him into office, he put some effort into prioritizing their concerns, for example on Special and Differential Treatment and TRIPs and public health.

Unsurprisingly, however, in view of the highly politicized selection process (see Chapter 7), Supachai found himself walking a political tightrope. Even before he took office, the major powers had declared their displeasure at some of the comments he had made about the WTO. In his first months as DG, he tried to find a balance between *appearing* to push the developed countries in areas where they did not want to give ground, and avoiding 'losing his credibility' with them. In a meeting with NGOs in Geneva on 2 December 2002, he said, 'I have been around long enough to know how much developing countries will have to give in order to get. I am trying to balance as much as I can without losing my credibility. I can't go out and say, "Just stop negotiating." On all fronts, I would like to see movement' (Supachai Panitchpakdi, quoted in Kwa 2002a).

He gave the example of an unrealistic US proposal on industrial tariffs, criticized by developing countries. Rather than joining the criticism, he had emphasized that he felt challenged by ambitious proposals, and called for tariff peaks and escalation (high tariffs on sensitive products and processed goods, imposed mostly by developed countries) to be tackled (ibid.).

Supachai is also determined to keep to the timeframe specified in Doha, to conclude the new round in 2005, despite the difficulties. He has commented:

> If the Round is going to stretch six, seven, eight years, I don't think it will serve anyone, including the developing countries, since there may be some new means to block market access

for developing countries. This is a round in which developing countries certainly will have their say. I keep urging them to be actively involved and to be united. If they are united, they will carry more weight. (ibid.)

Despite the Robin Hood role he is portraying to the developing world, however, Supachai has endorsed the anti-democratic decision-making practices that undermine their position at the WTO, including organizing green room meetings himself (see above) – to the extent that undesirable practices such as mini-ministerial meetings (see Chapter 2) are in danger of being not only legitimized but also institutionalized. When questioned by civil society groups, Supachai stoutly defended mini-ministerials:

> I am there to listen to them [the ministers] and they can listen to me so that they can take stock of what is happening and give their analysis and input. This process is to eliminate surprises [at the ministerial]. They do not all have this opportunity to meet. If they can be briefed about what is taking place, there is a good chance that we will have a good meeting [in Cancun]. It is a chance for ministers to fully prepare themselves ... These meetings give us momentum [for talks in Geneva], but we do not intend them to bypass the Geneva process. (ibid.)

When challenged further, that these are actually 'decision-making' meetings, and the excluded majority, presented with the final package as a *fait accompli*, risk high political and economic costs if they stand in the way of their outcomes, Supachai replied rather lamely: 'How do we then deal with the process of reaching consensus? Do you have another way to achieve it? Normally no one is excluded. It is just that the meeting can only accommodate so many' (ibid.). He went on to say that, while final decisions would have to be taken in the plenary session, the WTO could not always have full meetings of 145 members.

> We need to have a process where we can achieve the outcome. It is not like the Uruguay Round anymore. It is not like Blair House.[5] I would agree with you the process is exclusive if we say that this

is the agreement and you take it or leave it. This is not going to happen. From what we know we should not under-estimate developing countries. They fully know what their rights are. You are under-estimating the developing countries. (ibid.)

Supachai seems to be ignoring the feeling of many developing countries that the Doha outcome did not reflect what they really wanted, but that the exclusive green room meetings, the chair's one-sided drafts and the bilateral pressures had prevented them from rejecting the final package. Discounting this reality, he said,

Everyone will have to be fully involved, otherwise, you will not have a round. In all these meetings, and in Sydney, more than half of those invited were from developing countries[6] ... Sydney was not really about decision-making. It is really about stocktaking and trying to alert ministers. They got to know each other better. You cannot avoid them discussing these issues amongst themselves. It would be worse if they discussed these matters on the phone, and only amongst the Quad. They do it all the time. (ibid.)

Within a few months of Supachai's taking office, however, there were rumblings of discontent among developing country delegations.

As ambassadors of key countries were coming down from the 'green room' meetings [on TRIPs and public health, on 19 December], and walking across the road to the Kenya permanent mission opposite to hold their own consultations and returning, they were getting exasperated with the WTO head, and in non-attributable comments made this clear.

A few merely spoke of it as part of the 'usual WTO tactics of wearing us down and testing our nerves'; but a few others, from countries that had campaigned for Dr. Supachai, remarked in anger that within four months of his unmoaned departure from the job, Mike Moore ... was looking better in retrospect – something for Dr. Supachai to ponder over. (Raghavan 2002i)

It is far from clear that Supachai's tightrope act is succeeding.

Conclusion

By early 2003, as might be expected, the process leading up to the Fifth Ministerial in Cancun in September 2003 already resembled the process leading to Doha. As the unwieldy post-Doha agenda teetered on the edge (see Chapter 9), the major powers clearly continued to control the process, hoping to repeat their success in ramming through their agenda at Doha. They loaded up the agenda relentlessly with their own issues, and used their political muscle to secure the negotiating framework and the committee chairs they wanted, irrespective of the WTO's rules – and to stifle opposition and criticism from other members.

For the first time in its fifty-five-year history, the multilateral trade system has a developing country national at its head. However, despite his efforts to present himself as the developing countries' friend, Supachai is so constrained by political pressure from the major powers, and so afraid of 'losing his credibility' by stepping too far out of line with them, that he appears unable to uphold the WTO's supposedly democratic principles. This is likely only to disenfranchize the developing world still further, and is a major obstacle to overcoming – let alone correcting – the institutional-ized bias against the interests of developing countries in the WTO during his tenure.

Supachai's endorsement of undemocratic processes such as mini-ministerials and green room meetings, and his willingness to ignore the WTO rules on committee chairmanships when it suits the interests of the major powers, suggests that the position of de-veloping countries may in practice be little better during his tenure as DG than under Mike Moore, and could well worsen should a fully-fledged round of trade negotiations be launched in Cancun. And with the negotiating text 'magician' Stuart Harbinson as *chef de cabinet* as well as chair of agriculture, the Secretariat is unlikely to be significantly more impartial, and could become more 'flexible' and ruleless than ever.

The scene has been set for Cancun – and the script looks omi-nously like what happened in Doha.

Notes

1. The authors are very grateful to Shefali Sharma of the Institute for Agriculture and Trade Policy, whose work forms the basis for this section.

2. Cuba, Dominican Republic, Egypt, Honduras, Kenya, Pakistan, Tanzania, Uganda and Zimbabwe.

3. Around forty, counting the EC as fifteen countries.

4. This section is based on Kwa (2002b). The authors are grateful to Focus on the Global South for their permission to use it.

5. This is a reference to the bilateral meeting between the USA and EC in the Uruguay Round, which finally broke the stalemate in the highly controversial agriculture negotiations. The package they agreed was then presented to the rest of the GATT signatories as a *fait accompli*.

6. This, of course, depends on counting the EC as one member, whereas in fact it represents fifteen.

NINE

The Doha development agenda – 'everything but development'

The outcome of the Fourth Ministerial Conference was trumpeted by the WTO and the developed countries alike as 'the Doha development agenda', and the ministerial declaration referred repeatedly to the need to take into account the development needs and interests of developing countries and LDCs. Meanwhile, the developed countries made use of the media to create an image of Doha as the ministerial at which developing countries 'came of age' and pulled their weight in the negotiations. This was good public relations at a time when the WTO was under attack as harming the interests of the developing countries.

Scratching beneath the surface of this seemingly favourable language, however, quickly reveals that there is nothing concrete underlying it. The outcome of the ministerial meant developing countries giving in in many areas, and getting next to nothing in return beyond sympathetic wording and further discussions in Geneva; and these discussions offer no real prospect of improvement of the situation of the developing countries within the WTO itself or within the international trading system.

This chapter reviews the progress – or rather the quite remarkable *lack* of progress – in the discussions on the major substantive issues until the end of 2002, taking each of the major issues in turn.

The 'new issues'

As discussed in Chapter 4, the Doha Ministerial ended with a ministerial declaration stating that negotiations on each of the 'new issues' '*will take place* after the Fifth Session of the Ministerial Conference on the basis of a decision to be taken, by explicit consensus, at that session on modalities of negotiations'; and an apparently contradictory statement by the chairman that a decision would be taken at the next ministerial on *whether or not* negotiations would commence on each of the issues. Predictably, the major powers – particularly the USA and the EC – ignored the chairman's clarification completely after Doha, instead insisting on the declaration language, that negotiations would be launched, and only their *'modalities'* would be decided in Cancun.

In the same vein, disagreement remained as to whether the 'new issues' were part of the 'single undertaking' defined in paragraph 47 of the Doha Declaration, or outside it. This paragraph states that, 'With the exception of the improvements and clarifications of the Dispute Settlement Understanding, the conduct, conclusion and entry into force of the outcome of the negotiations shall be treated as parts of a single undertaking.' This means that all members have to abide by all the multilateral agreements in the WTO.

The single undertaking concept appeared for the first time in GATT negotiations in the Punta del Este Declaration that launched the Uruguay Round, and was deeply disputed until the round was completed. The concept appeared in the section on goods, to mean that the various agreements relating to trade in goods should be treated as one package, with no understanding that countries would be bound by the results of the negotiations on services. In the course of the Uruguay Round, however, the major powers bullied developing countries into accepting their 'global' interpretation of the single undertaking to mean that goods, services and intellectual property negotiations would be treated as one package, and must therefore be accepted in their entirety by all members. The concept fundamentally changed the level of obligations developing countries were subjected to in the WTO, as compared to the GATT – previously, each contracting party had the freedom to choose which agreements to sign on to, and which to opt out of.

After Doha, the EC and the USA operated on the assumption that the 'new issues' negotiations would be part of the single undertaking, while developing countries assumed that members would decide whether or not this was the case in Cancun, as chairman Kamal's clarification implied. When the Indian representative at the Sydney mini-ministerial in November 2002 disputed that negotiations on the 'new issues' were part of the single undertaking, a developing country delegate reported, EC Trade Commissioner Pascal Lamy 'bit his head off' (Sharma 2002a). Japan has also stated that it is not willing to move on agriculture until the 'new issues' are accepted by developing countries.

Investment

After Doha, the proponents and opponents of an investment agreement talked as if they existed on different planets. The proponents were led by the EC, and included Japan, Canada, Korea, Switzerland, Taiwan and Norway. They wanted high standards of investor protection and strong disciplines against restrictions on the free flow of foreign direct investment (FDI) among WTO members, including the abolition of all performance requirements (conditions on employing local workers and transferring technology, environmental regulations, local content requirements, requirements limiting imports to the value of exports, etc.).

The EC mentioned the possibility of a bottom-up approach to investment, as in the GATS, allowing members to decide which provisions they wanted to be bound by. Opponents of an agreement, however, feared that they would increase their ambitions in the course of negotiations, or indeed, as in the GATS, extract what they wanted despite a bottom-up approach.

The USA continued to push for including portfolio investment (investment in shares, bonds and other financial instruments) in an agreement, arguing that the distinction between FDI and portfolio investment had become rather grey, with the growth of derivatives and hedge funds, and that not all FDI went into immovable assets; and for allowing investors to borrow and to export capital. The EC also indicated that it wanted a 'broad' definition of FDI, although European NGOs participating in 'dialogues' with Trade Commissioner Lamy reported that he was non-committal about whether he supported including portfolio investment. Taiwan also called for a dispute settlement system covering disputes between investors and governments, as in NAFTA. The USA and Taiwan may well realize that their demands are likely to be rejected by developing countries, and may be putting forward their maximum position as a negotiating strategy, in the hope that, once an agreement is in place, it can be made more ambitious in subsequent rounds.

Most developing countries continued to oppose an investment agreement in the WTO, seeing an agreement protecting investors' rights as potentially seriously damaging to their economies. Given the ambiguity in the Doha Declaration, they put forward their maximum position to widen the gap between themselves and the USA and the EC, in the hope of preventing agreement on modalities at the Fifth Ministerial.

India, China, Cuba, Pakistan and Zimbabwe, for example, proposed that future discussion of the issue should cover:

- barring investors from interfering in host countries' internal affairs and their determination of economic and other priorities;
- dealing with restrictive business practices (e.g. price fixing, collusive tendering, and market or customer allocation arrangements), abuse of market power, predatory behaviour, etc.;
- requiring technology transfer;
- ensuring that MNC activities do not aggravate host countries' balance of payments, requiring adherence to host governments' policies to safeguard the balance of payments, and barring transfer price manipulation to cover up the remittance of funds;[1]
- requiring compliance with consumer and environmental protection;
- requiring disclosure of financial and non-financial information, including transparency in speculative financial market transactions; and
- requiring legislation by home governments to prohibit corrupt practices of their corporations abroad and to protect consumers and the environment.

India also argued that there was no need for a WTO agreement on investment, which was better left to bilateral agreements, arguing that 'money is neither a good nor a service', and therefore should not be covered by the WTO or its dispute settlement process.

Predictably, the developed countries strongly opposed the emphasis on investors' obligations. Japan responded that there were serious legal questions on extra-territoriality, and that they would not be in a position to monitor and control the activities of their corporations abroad. The USA fundamentally disagreed with the investors' obligations approach, arguing that it would make private companies tools of industrial policy, which would 'chill' investments, and that its proponents overstated the power of MNCs. While developing countries used the Enron and Worldcom examples to highlight the need for strong domestic laws, the USA failed to address the issue of corrupt corporations, the vast funds they give to Congress and the White House to fund elections, and their ability to get laws written in their favour (Raghavan 2002c).

Competition

In the talks after Doha, many developing countries argued that a 'one-size-fits-all' approach did not work, and that each country should be free to choose a competition regime that reflected its own economic situation and development priorities. They also pointed out that a competition culture does not exist in most developing countries. These countries would therefore be less likely to assert their rights even if there were a multilateral agreement. The lack of institutional capacity was also seen as a serious problem (see Chapter 2).

The main reason for opposition, however, was that many developing countries, knowing that their local companies would not be able to compete with the foreign giants, were not in favour of providing national treatment to foreign corporations operating in their countries as well as to imported goods and services. Together with an investment agreement, a competition agreement would eliminate the remaining policy space available to developing country governments to build up their local industries.

The focus on 'hard-core cartels' was also viewed somewhat sceptically by some negotiators familiar with WTO political games. While it looks attractive superficially, they view this as merely a hook to lure developing countries into an agreement that will require them to eliminate regulations favouring local companies.

Transparency in government procurement

As for the other 'new issues', the ministerial declaration indicated that modalities for further negotiations on transparency in government procurement would be decided by explicit consensus at the Fifth Ministerial. According to Raghavan (2002d), however, if negotiations were to be agreed, the EC would seek 'as happened in the Uruguay Round (and at Doha), to change the mandate and scope of negotiations as they went along'. When developing countries raised concerns and questions about the need to limit discussions to transparency issues, the EC, the USA and Switzerland responded that these concerns could be addressed in the course of negotiations (Raghavan 2002d; ICTSD 2002c).

The EC was also at pains to suggest that it was agreeable to providing 'flexibility' and Special and Differential Treatment (SDT) in the obligations developing countries might undertake under 'transparency'. SDT provisions at the WTO, however, have been ineffective (see Chapter 2), and promises at Doha to agree on ways to strengthen and operationalize SDT provisions in general have been stalemated by the majors, including the EC (see below).

Other differences between the EC and developing countries include whether an agreement should include all levels of government or only central government. Malaysia and Indonesia, for example, stated that sub-central agencies and services should be excluded. India and others noted that including all levels of governments would be too burdensome, as governing entities in many large countries range from village and district levels to state and federal levels. Some developing countries also took the position that any agreement should carry no obligations to change domestic laws and regulations. Again, this point has been disputed by the major powers.

According to Chakravarthi Raghavan (2002d), the objective of the EC and the USA was to enlist WTO member governments to work to provide information for the benefit of their MNCs, to help them tender for projects. Why developing country governments should use their scarce financial and human resources to cut MNCs' costs is an important question.

Trade facilitation

On trade facilitation, the EC proposed:

- that Article X of the GATT (on publication and administration of trade regulations) should be converted into an agreement on trade facilitation;
- that members should 'take administrative actions, decisions or rulings affecting importers or exporters only where a legal basis to do so is established' (WTO 2002f: 2) – that is, that members' ability to take action at the border should be limited to what is allowed by a WTO trade facilitation agreement;
- that a 'regular consultative mechanism' with private sector bodies should be established, with provision for consultation between interested parties – both governments and the private sector – on proposed new legislation and regulations before they were implemented, in order to ensure 'sensible regulation'; and
- that notice should be given of proposed regulations, and comments invited, accompanied by publication of the reasoned motivations, as well as whether or not there are less trade restrictive measures available.

As developing countries become more integrated into the world economy, and transfer pricing increases in North–South trade, governments in the South need greater flexibility to investigate and prevent unfair transfer pricing practices. If adopted, however, these proposals would be likely to remove developing countries' autonomy in controlling transfer price manipulation. Developing countries were also indignant about being asked to take on such burdensome reforms – all in order to help suppliers from the developed countries. Malaysia made it clear that no amount of rule-making could build customs infrastructure in developing countries. India also pointed out that the situation of developing countries was very different from that of developed countries. Imposing the concepts, rules and formulae of the industrialized countries in this area was therefore not useful for developing countries (Raghavan 2002e).

Another major area not seriously addressed by the developed

countries was the cost to developing countries of implementing the proposed rules, and whether these should be a priority, in cash-strapped countries with a myriad of other more immediate concerns.

Trade and the environment

The EC has been the main proponent of beginning negotiations on trade and the environment, while developing countries have been vehemently opposed. Before Doha, they were joined in their opposition by Australia, who anticipated that environmental conditions would be used to block imports, and believed that agricultural exporters would ultimately pay the highest price.

While talks proceeded after Doha, positions remained just as far apart, and no agreement had been reached on the time-line for discussions by the end of 2002. Even the status of the talks was disputed: Australia and developing countries said the discussions should be considered to be pre-preparatory (that is, they should not even be considered as part of the preparatory phase of the negotiations); the EC suggested that the preparatory phase should end in Cancun, arguing that a study phase was no longer needed, as the environment has been on the WTO agenda (though not a negotiating subject) for the previous fourteen years.

There were also major differences on how to approach the MEA–WTO negotiations. The EC wanted to institute some broad overarching principles and parameters, while Australia suggested first identifying specific MEA obligations related to trade, and assessing whether countries had experienced problems in implementing them *vis-à-vis* their WTO obligations. The removal of EC and US agricultural subsidies was repeatedly brought up in the discussions, many countries citing references to the removal of these subsidies at the World Summit on Sustainable Development (Yu 2002a).

The Doha Declaration also emphasized the elimination of tariff and non-tariff barriers to environmental goods and services, and the EC proposed that obstacles to trade in 'environmental services' such as waste management and water supply should be removed as part of the GATS negotiations. Many environmental groups have criticized this and other EC goals as in fact thwarting 'environmental' goals. If the EC had its way in the course of negotiations, measures such as restricting the amount of groundwater extracted from particular areas could contravene binding WTO rules (Cronin 2001). It is small wonder, therefore, that developing country governments are somewhat sceptical about the 'greenness' of the environmental agenda proposed by the developed countries.

Industrial tariffs and market access for non-agricultural products

After Doha, it was agreed that the draft modalities of the negotiations would be ready by 31 March 2003, and agreed by 30 April. Issues were expected to include:

- the approach to be followed in negotiations on the restructuring of tariff lines (a 'request-and-offer' approach, or a formula approach based on reducing all tariff lines by an agreed percentage);
- coverage, and whether or not there should be exclusions;
- the definitions of tariff peaks, high tariffs, tariff escalation and non-tariff barriers, and how to address these; and
- how to deal with nuisance tariffs (tariffs at very low rates, whose nuisance effect is greater than their financial impact).

In discussions, the USA created some waves by tabling a proposal calling for zero tariffs on non-agricultural products by 2015. Developing countries rejected this proposal as 'ambitious but not realistic', and questioned why such tariffs would apply only to industrial products and not agricultural products.

India's ambassador K. M. Chandrasekhar told the meeting at which the USA proposal was launched that calling on developing countries to bind their tariffs at zero was 'clearly unfair', and ignored the concept of 'less than full reciprocity' in the relevant paragraph of the declaration. He also observed that the US proposal did not address the issue of tariff peaks, and reminded members of the importance of tariffs as a source of government revenue in many developing countries – as much as 30–40 per cent in some cases, compared with 1 per cent in the USA. To remove such an important source of revenue would be financially destabilizing and aggravate already serious government spending constraints.

Trade analysts also questioned the US proposal, noting that it was extremely unlikely that the USA itself would be able to implement it. There are more than 500 sensitive products where the US Trade Promotion Authority has limited authority to negotiate. If the USTR decided to negotiate on these products under the Trade Promotion Authority, he would first have to inform, and hold consultations with, five different congressional bodies – the House and Senate agricultural committees, the House Ways and Means Committee, the Senate Finance Committee and the Trade Supervisory Body. The International Trade Commission would also be required to conduct a special study on each product, assessing the impact of any tariff reduction on the market for the product and on the US economy as a whole. Only after this process could he go back to the five bodies for further consultations (Raghavan 2002b, citing UNCTAD Secretary General Rubens Ricupero).

It has also been suggested that non-tariff barriers imposed by the USA on developing country exports, such as safeguard abuses, rules of origin and technical barriers to trade, should be raised as an issue. The US textile industry, for example, has already filed for special safeguards, long before textile quotas are scheduled to be dismantled in 2005 (ibid.).

TRIPs and public health

Ironically, while the TRIPs and public health issue earned developed countries much credit for appearing compassionate and presenting the WTO with a human face, in fact it epitomizes their bad faith in WTO negotiations – despite their initial promises in Doha, and in the face of a humanitarian catastrophe suffered by the developing world.

The TRIPs Council spent the entire year following Doha working on paragraph 6 of the TRIPs Declaration (on compulsory licensing). The developing countries wanted to maximize the coverage of TRIPs provisions to allow access to medicines at low cost, but were prepared, reluctantly, to accept the attachment of several cumbersome and costly conditionalities to compulsory licensing. The USA, however, was much more intransigent in its efforts to limit the scope of such provisions, and thus the cost to the pharmaceutical industry.

The EC, pandering to its domestic civil society critics, supported the possibility of generic drug exports to countries in need,[2] and, as at Doha (see Chapter 4), portrayed itself as a bridge-builder between the USA and the developing countries. Beneath this veneer, however, it too sought to protect its corporate interests. (Glaxo SmithKline, for instance, warned the UK government that it would shift its base from the UK to the USA if the EC took a position contrary to its interests.)

With billions of dollars at stake, the chief executives of the major pharmaceutical companies made several calls to senior officials in the USA and the EC.[3] While George W. Bush was forced to hurt US pharmaceutical MNCs in order to get votes in the mid-term elections, once the elections were over, they demanded that USTR deliver on limiting the scope of TRIPs concessions (Love 2002).

During 2002, the USA pursued an aggressive campaign to limit the coverage of the Doha Declaration to HIV/AIDS, tuberculosis and malaria. (While the Doha Declaration named these diseases, it also refers to 'other epidemics' and to 'public health' in general.) They also attempted to prevent diagnostic equipment from being included in the declaration, although diagnostic tests and medical equipment (also patented by the pharmaceutical industry) are an important element of the high cost of AIDS treatment.

Japan also attempted to limit the declaration by excluding vaccines, on the grounds that they are not strictly 'pharmaceutical products' (Baker 2002). According to Brook Baker,

It's long been true that PhRMA [Pharmaceutical Research and Manufacturers of America, the organization of the major US pharmaceutical MNCs] would rather invest in antiretroviral drugs which people have to take day-after-day thereby generating daily mega profits rather than invest in research and development of vaccines and microbicides which might forestall the transmission of HIV. As a result, it is primarily governments and charities that are funding basic research into AIDS vaccines. Nonetheless, PhRMA expects that it will be the eventual recipient of rights to market vaccines, and it would like to do so at respectable profits. Therefore, it has insisted, behind the scenes, that its future profits in successful vaccines be protected. (ibid.)

On 25 October, assistant USTR Rosa Whitaker sent a letter to sub-Saharan African trade ministers (Box 9.1), attempting to pressure them into accepting the US position linking the issue with market access in textiles under the African Growth and Opportunity Act (AGOA). On both issues, supporting the US position would have brought African countries into direct conflict with other developing countries – and in the case of TRIPs, it would also have limited the flexibility of the agreement rather than increasing it, with negative implications for their own populations.

Adopting their usual strategy (see Chapter 3), the USA also worked closely with the EC, Japan and Australia to get agreement among twenty-five or so powerful members, in the hope that other members would feel unable to refuse it, for fear of the political and economic consequences. The EC convened a meeting of senior officials from twenty-five countries plus the DG in Annecy, near Geneva, on 5–6 November 2002; and Australia convened a mini-ministerial of twenty-five members in Sydney on 14–15 November. One African ambassador who played a leading role on the issue but was not invited to the Sydney meeting observed that positions moved slightly closer to the US position directly after it.

The developed countries also pushed for a 'categorization' of developing countries between those with manufacturing capacity (which would not be allowed to import generics), those with no capacity at all, and those with limited capacity (which they sought to limit to importing active ingredients produced under compulsory licence rather than drugs themselves). This would limit drugs imports mainly to LDCs. The ambassador of one small low-income country with limited capacity commented that, under such a scheme, his country would still not have access to affordable medicines, as the small domestic market would make it too expensive to produce the drugs locally from the active ingredients.

Access to generic drugs could be greatly simplified by clarifying (or if necesary amending) Article 30 of the TRIPs Agreement, on exceptions to patent rights. This states that: 'Members may provide limited exceptions to the exclusive rights conferred by a patent, provided that such exceptions do not unreasonably conflict with a normal exploitation of the patent and do not unreasonably prejudice the legitimate interests of the patent owner, taking account of the legitimate interests of third parties.' This article could allow generic exports to meet a public health need with only a one-time change in the exporting country's legislation, without requiring authorization from the patent holder, compensation or licences. This much simpler procedure would provide WTO members with the widest choice of suppliers.

Twelve countries (India, Brazil, China, the Philippines, Indonesia, Argentina, Sri Lanka, Pakistan, Cuba, Thailand, Malaysia and Peru) requested such an amendment; and the general approach has been supported by the World Health Organization, the UK Commission on Intellectual Property Rights, the Belgian parliament and the French presidency. The EC, however, blocked this solution – ironically, at around the same time that the European parliament approved Amendment 196 to the EC Directive on Medicines Act, allowing the EC to export to a country in need without a compulsory licence.

Unfortunately, the developing countries' position on this issue was weakened by a split on the best mechanism to seek. The Africa Group, persuaded that barring other developing countries from exporting would strengthen their own pharmaceutical industries, instead advocated an amendment to the procedurally much more complicated Article 31(f) compulsory licensing mechanism.

Article 31(f) was also the EC's preferred option. Rather than trying to make it easier for countries to import generic drugs, however, their aim seemed to be to establish as many procedural, legal and other hurdles as possible to generic exports, so that even if a

Box 9.1 Letter from assistant USTR Rosa Whitaker to sub-Saharan African trade ministers

October 25, 2002

Dear Minister

   I want to urgently bring to your attention two time-sensitive matters currently under review at the WTO in Geneva. Both issues – TRIPs/Access to Medicines and the phase-out of global quotas on textiles and apparel – are critically important to Africa, and merit your immediate attention.

TRIPs/access to medicine

   The WTO Council on Trade Related Aspects of Intellectual Property Rights (TRIPs) has been charged with coming up with a practical solution before the end of the year to problems that African countries and others face in making effective use of compulsory licensing of pharmaceuticals. Compulsory licensing permits the production of drugs without the authorisation of the patent holder in circumstances where countries need to address a serious public health problem, such as HIV/AIDS, malaria, tuberculosis and other epidemics.

   With the year-end deadline fast approaching, much work remains to be done to reach consensus. African countries have a particular interest in helping to craft a practical solution given the devastating toll of HIV/AIDS and other epidemics in the region. The Chair of the TRIPs Council has circulated a paper that outlines a possible solution. We urge your government to respond favourably to the Chair's paper and to support a solution that addresses Africa's interests and particular circumstances. The U.S. approach and the Chair's paper were drafted in response to calls from many African leaders for a solution that focuses on the serious health problems confronting Africa. Sadly, while HIV/AIDS has taken its greatest toll in sub-Saharan Africa, most of the region's representatives to Geneva are not attending meetings related to this issue or engaging in the debate.

The attached papers summarise the main elements of this issue and the U.S. proposal. I urge you to instruct your officials in Geneva to work with the U.S. and other African countries to ensure that the solution the TRIPs Council develops benefits African countries and responds to the region's needs.

Elimination of global clothing quotas

The WTO Council on Trade in Goods has had before it a plan to eliminate textile and clothing quotas well before the planned phase-out of these restrictions in January 2005. Contrary to positions conveyed by the African Union and many African Trade Ministers, the African Group has also submitted a proposal supporting the early elimination of quotas.

These proposals would effectively erode the margin of preference African countries now enjoy under the African Growth and Opportunity Act (AGOA) and other developed countries' Preference programs. Under these arrangements, African countries already have quota-free access to U.S. and other major markets for apparel and textiles. Proposals under consideration in Geneva inadvertently help China, India and other countries with significant apparel capacity and markets abroad to further expand their exports, putting significant competitive pressure on poorer, African countries that are just beginning to see success in the U.S. and other developed country markets.

I am also attaching a paper further outlining my concerns on the quota issue, and I hope that you will immediately instruct your representatives in Geneva to act to protect the region from these simultaneous assaults on Africa's interests.

Like you, I strongly believe that sub-Saharan African countries should approach negotiations in Geneva based on their own interests – and not be party to developing country group positions that run counter to regional development goals. You know best where the interests of your country lie. However, I hope you give your attention to these critically important issues. I am confident that you too will recognise the convergence of interests between the U.S. and sub-Saharan Africa's interests on issues related to TRIPs and textile-apparel quotas.

Please feel free to call me at 202-395-9514 if you have any questions about the U.S. approach to these issues.

Please accept my best wishes and highest regards.

Sincerely,

Rosa Whitaker

Assistant United States Trade Representative for Africa

---

country issued a compulsory licence, the obstacles and high costs involved could lead to no supplier taking up the offer to export. At one point during the talks, the EC and its allies insisted that the TRIPs Council should be notified of and approve every individual compulsory licence for the export of generic drugs before exports could take place. Developing countries rejected the need to seek approval, but apparently agreed to notification.

Other conditions proposed by the EC and its allies would severely limit the possibility of generic drug producers attaining economies of scale. Specifically, they suggested:

- that an exporting country should be required to notify the TRIPs Council of the granting of the licence, the conditions attached to it, the products, quantities and countries involved, and its duration, and to place all this information on a website;
- that the exporting country should be required to prove that the generic drugs would not be sold to any developed country. Developed countries also attempted to persuade better-off developing countries to accept being included in the list of proscribed countries;

- that the packaging for the exported drugs should be distinctive; and
- that a country should be disqualified from importing if it was 'established' that its capacity to manufacture had become sufficient to meet its needs (although how such a decision should be made, and by whom, was unclear and potentially very problematic).

Brook Baker described the effect of the compulsory licensing obstacles.

> For example, even assuming that India would be willing (and had national legislation permitting production for export under a compulsory license) to issue a compulsory license to export a newly patented AIDS medicine to Zimbabwe, it would have to issue a companion license to each and every other African country trying to import that particular medicine. Since one medicine would not be enough for the AIDS cocktail, other antiretrovirals would have to be licensed, product-by-product country-by-country. Each license application would be predicated on: prior negotiations with the patent holder, preparation of expensive legal documents, and prosecution by legal experts. In other words, each license would be costly and time-consuming. (Baker 2002)

The disqualification issue also does not bode well for developing countries. The aim of the major pharmaceutical MNCs is to prohibit any country with any level of economic development from importing generics – not only India, Brazil, Korea and Thailand, but also, for example, Nigeria, Ghana and South Africa. Again, the issue is one of economies of scale: generic producers would not be able to access any of the significant developed or developing country markets, making generic drugs more costly, and largely defeating the purpose of the negotiations.

The need to notify the TRIPs Council also further enlarges the WTO's mandate, allowing it to oversee the issuing of compulsory licences, down to the detail of every individual licence. Such detailed notification is clearly designed to allow the pharmaceutical

Box 9.2 Making the point

In late November 2002, several civil society representatives publicly ridiculed the developed countries' efforts to limit the TRIPs Declaration in the following skit, performed at the entrance to the WTO in Geneva.[4]

A woman is laid out on a stretcher, about to be carried into an ambulance. The woman is dying from pneumonia. Attached to her is a drip. A representative from a pharmaceutical company is standing over her, scissors in hand, wanting to cut off her drip supply.

Pharmaceutical representative: What are you suffering from, lady?

Dying lady: Pneumonia.

Pharmaceutical representative: Sorry, lady. We cannot help you. Come back when you have AIDS. Pneumonia isn't serious enough.

Dying lady: Please, I really need the medicine.

Pharmaceutical representative: Which country are you from?

Dying lady: Bolivia.

Pharmaceutical representative: Sorry, lady. You've got to be poorer than that. We can only help least developed countries.

The pharmaceutical representative cuts off her drip supply and the lady dies on the stretcher.

industry and developed country governments to put pressure on individual governments and manufacturers on each licence if they are not satisfied with the conditions.

NGOs[5] have charged that the USA, the EC, Canada, Switzerland and Japan have escalated their efforts to make the solution 'more restrictive, more burdensome, and more problematic ... and have demonstrated bad faith' in addressing the TRIPs and public health problem.

How can any WTO member justify the exclusion of a particular disease from the solution? Either every country has effective and practical methods to protect the public health and in particular to promote access to medicines for all, or the WTO is a place where crude compromises on public health are hammered out disease by disease, product by product, country by country and patient by patient. (Statement by Consumer Technology Project, Médecins Sans Frontières, Oxfam, Third World Network and other NGOs, quoted in Raghavan 2002f)

The NGOs are not alone in their criticism. Professor John Barton, chair of the UK Independent Commission on Intellectual Property Rights, has also noted the limitations of the negotiations:

A legal solution of the kind now being negotiated at the WTO on compulsory licensing is unlikely to resolve the economic problems that the world will face after 2005. At that point India, in particular, is required to apply patent protection to new medicines and its new laws will inevitably reduce the ability of its generic suppliers to provide products in competition with those on patent. Even with 'liberalised' compulsory licensing rules, potential generic suppliers will then find it much more difficult to offer to produce medicines at low cost. This will reduce the value of compulsory licensing as a bargaining tool for governments negotiating with suppliers of medicines and will leave prices higher than they otherwise would be. Dealing with this coming situation may require alternative production arrangements; it will certainly require much more than a change in compulsory licensing rules. (John Barton, quoted in Raghavan 2002g)

The chair of the TRIPs Council, ambassador Eduardo Peter Motta of Mexico, adopted a similar strategy in drafting the negotiating text to that used by Stuart Harbinson as chair of the General Council before Doha (see Chapter 3). The negotiating texts that Motta produced, rather than fairly representing the various views on the table, tended to reflect the positions of the developed countries – and in some cases used language taken verbatim from a letter sent by PhRMA to the US Congress. Motta's texts were highly responsive to the US and Japanese suggestions on limiting the scope of diseases, but not to the developing countries' position on putting more emphasis on Article 30 (exceptions to patent rights) (Love 2002).

Just three weeks before the deadline for a decision, the developing countries, led by the Africa Group, walked out of the negotiations in frustration. The USA responded by intensifying pressure on developing country capitals, to side-step the Geneva negotiators who were stronger on the technical issues and less susceptible to direct political pressure. Trade ministers were duly convinced of the need to toe the US line, and duly called their Geneva negotiators (ibid.).

The USA was trying to cut a deal: in return for Africans accepting the application of the Doha Declaration to a limited number of diseases, the USA would recognize sub-Saharan Africa as a regional market (Raghavan 2002h). This would reduce the procedural nightmare of issuing compulsory licences, as they could then apply to the region as a whole rather than being required country-by-country. At the end of 2002, the Africa Group was still standing firm and refusing the US offer, with support from other developing countries.

On 19 December, the day before the close of negotiations for the year, Supachai himself intervened, holding a series of green room meetings on the issue of coverage, on which the USA was still holding out (see Chapter 8). In these meetings, developing countries were pressured to allow the USA, in effect, to rewrite the TRIPs Declaration, to limit its scope to a specific set of diseases. Supachai, in support of the US position, suggested including a list of diseases in a footnote, which was emphatically rejected by developing countries; the EC proposed that the TRIPs Council chair should instead take note of a US statement of its understanding of the coverage issue, and express the hope that implementation would take place within this framework.[6] Korea joined the major developed countries in putting pressure on the developing countries to support the selective approach, and put forward a list of fifteen diseases,[7] reportedly after the USA eased off the pressure to exclude Korea from countries eligible to import under the proposals. As economic diplomats discussed which diseases in which developing countries constituted a public health problem, the representative of the World Health Organization (which has observer status in the TRIPs Council)[8] was not permitted to offer advice, or even to attend the meetings (Raghavan 2002i).

The efforts to limit the scope of the TRIPs Declaration were consistently rejected by developing countries. No universally acceptable solution was found, and the end-2002 deadline for an 'expeditious solution' was missed. In the early hours of Saturday 21 December, the chair of the General Council, ambassador Sergio Marchi, acknowledged the failure to come to any decision, and hoped that some compromises could be found by early 2003.

The situation was best summed up by India's ambassador K. M. Chandrasekhar in that final General Council meeting of the year:

> We sometimes wondered whether the Council was discussing how to facilitate access to drugs at affordable prices to poor people or how to restrict the scope and ambit of the intended solution. Commercial interests appeared to have become predominant ...
>
> It will be difficult to justify why this organization could not rise to the occasion and satisfactorily respond to the crises being faced in several parts of the world on account of public health problems of the kind described in the Doha Declaration. At stake are the hopes of millions of people to get access to medicines at affordable prices. Let us not fail them. (K.M. Chandrasekhar, quoted in ibid.)

Agriculture

Despite the clear signals that developed countries intended to continue their subsidies (see Chapter 5), there was a general presumption that tariffs would be cut across the board in the post-Doha negotiations, the extensive discussions focusing rather on the depth of these cuts and the exact mathematical formulae on which reductions should be based. Meanwhile, the major powers tried to pay the least possible attention to the developing countries' insistence that how far they went in tariff cuts would depend on the extent of subsidy reductions.

The post-Doha talks on subsidies were disappointing for the developing countries, as even the Cairns Group appeared to have gone soft on the issue.[9] While the Cairns Group generally argues for the removal of agricultural subsidies, in the post-Doha negotiations they called for major cuts in 'trade distorting' but not 'non-trade distorting' subsidies. As a result, the green box loopholes in the AoA continued to be tolerated, including direct payments to OECD producers, which mainly benefit agri-business corporations. While permitted on the grounds that they are 'non-trade distorting', such subsidies in fact represent a major market distortion (OECD 2000). The one-sidedness of the 'liberalization' exercise, and the perpetuation of the loopholes and inequitable trade that resulted from the AoA, are making a mockery of the organization.

Developing countries will have to be wary that they are not swindled a second time into agreeing to tariff reductions while allowing developed country subsidies to be maintained or even increased. During the discussions, they suggested various instruments to protect their agricultural sectors from increasing dumping, including:

- exclusion of almost all products from tariff cuts and AoA commitments for food security and livelihood reasons, so that only products exported in large amounts would be liberalized; or exclusion of a set of crops important for food security and livelihood concerns from further liberalization;
- a temporary safeguard measure allowing countries to increase tariffs or put in place quantitative restrictions in the event of import surges or sudden price falls;
- a rebalancing/countervailing mechanism enabling countries to increase tariffs on products which have been subsidized by the developed countries, the higher tariffs corresponding with the level of subsidies provided; and
- a cap on the overall subsidies provided by the developed coun-

tries. Currently, there is no limit on the amount of support countries can provide under the green box.

It will be difficult, however, for developing countries to ensure that their proposals are not watered down completely. On the issue of crop exclusions, for example, some delegates saw the narrower second option as insufficient, given the enormity of the problem. They succumbed to pressure to retract from the more ambitious first proposal in late 2002, however, anticipating that that it would simply be ignored by the chair (Stuart Harbinson). The major players – the USA, the EC and the major Cairns Group countries – have shown little sympathy even for the diluted proposal. As major exporters, particularly of staple crops, opening developing country markets to these exports is prominent among their objectives in the negotiations.

It was also suggested that countries should be allowed to use any safeguard mechanism only for those products for which they have undertaken a further round of deep tariff cuts, pushing developing countries further in a direction more likely to exacerbate than to resolve their food security problems. The capping of subsidies and the rebalancing mechanism – instruments that would have brought some balance to an agreement – have been completely sidelined in the negotiations.

Stuart Harbinson's chairmanship of the Agriculture Committee (see Chapter 8) does not bode well, given his pre-Doha approach of excluding developing countries' positions from negotiating texts (see Chapter 3). In December 2002, for example, their delegates found themselves having to lobby Harbinson, as chair, to reflect their positions in his negotiating drafts, rather than lobbying other members on the substantive issues, as might be expected in negotiations.

The developing countries' fears were confirmed. Harbinson's first draft modalities paper (WTO 2003b), released ahead of the Tokyo mini-ministerial, was tabled 'on his own responsibility'. It was largely without brackets, the different positions of members on critical issues were not reflected, and the text unfairly reflected the positions of the major powers, particularly the USA and the EC.

Services

The main activity on trade in services after Doha was the request and offer process, in which members offer to make GATS commitments in different service sectors and request other countries to make such commitments. This proceeded despite the absence of the assessment of the effects of the GATS Agreement required by the agreement itself. As Bhagirath Lal Das (2002) observed, 'If [developing countries] go on making commitments without having an assessment of the current results, they will be put to further loss in the negotiations.'

Unsurprisingly, most of the requests came from the developed countries. The USA, for example, submitted requests to 141 of the other 144 members, and the EC to 109 of the other 130 (*International Trade Daily* 2002a). Some developed country negotiators expressed concern privately about the lack of requests by developing countries, and even encouraged developing countries to submit requests to them, to ensure some scope for bilateral trade-offs.

Since most developing countries are not significant exporters of services, however, it is extremely difficult (and largely irrelevant) for them to identify their export interests and the barriers preventing their access. Where export interests do exist, these are often only at the regional level, rather than in relation to the developed countries. The developed countries' requests, by contrast, show that their suppliers have already identified potential markets and the regulatory and other barriers they want removed, on a global scale.

According to a leaked document from Brussels, the EC requested unlimited access in a vast number of sectors (see Box 9.3 for an illustration). US requests were no less exhaustive and penetrated even deeper, not only covering market access, but also seeking changes in regulation, for example requesting trading partners to commit fully to the reference paper on regulatory principles in the telecommunications sector.

The US and EC requests included:

- liberalization of basic services, such as water supply, electricity distribution and postal delivery, across a wide range of countries;

Box 9.3 Service sectors covered by the EC's GATS request to Nigeria

Professional services
- legal services
- accounting, auditing and bookkeeping services
- engineering services
- integrated engineering serivces

Business services (other than professional)
- computer and related services
- other business services, including advertising; market research; management consulting services; services related to management consulting; technical testing and analysis services; related scientific and technical consulting services; maintenance and repair of equipment (not including transport equipment)

Telecommunications services
- Voice telephone services; packet-switched data transmission services, circuit-switched data transmission services, etc.

Construction and related engineering services
- general construction work for buildings
- general construction work for civil engineering
- installation and assembly work
- building completion and finishing work
- other

Distribution services
- wholesale trade services
- retailing services

Environmental services
- water for human use and wastewater management
- solid/hazardous waste management, including refuse disposal services; sanitation and similar services
- protection of ambient air and climate, including services to reduce gases and other emissions and improve air quality

- remediation and clean-up of soil and water
- protection of biodiversity and landscape
- other environmental and ancillary services

Financial services
- general
- insurance
- banking and other financial services

News agency services

Transport services
- maritime transport
- air transport, including maintenance and repair of aircraft and parts thereof; selling and marketing; computer reservation systems; groundhandling services; airport management services
- road transport, including freight transportation; maintenance and repair of road transport equipment
- services auxiliary to all modes of transport, including storage and warehouse services; freight transport agency / freight forwarding services and pre-shipment inspection

Energy services
- services related to exploration and production including services incidental to mining; related scientific and technical consulting services; construction and related engineering services
- services related to the construction of energy facilities, including construction work for civil engineering; long-distance pipelines, communication and power lines; local pipelines and cables; ancillary works; constructions for mining and manufacturing; installation and assembly work
- services related to networks, including operation of transportation/transmission and distribution facilities; services incidental to energy distribution, including operation of transmission/distribution of electricity; transportation of petroleum and natural gas

- storage services, including bulk storage services of liquids or gases
- services for the supply of energy, including wholesale, of energy products; retail sale of energy products (fuel oil, bottled gas, coal and wood); trading of energy products; brokering of energy products
- services for the final use including energy audit (production management and consulting services); energy management (production management consulting services)
- services related to decommissioning

Source: European Commission (2002).

- unlimited access for US- and EC-based MNCs to service sectors, from retailing to tourism; and
- the removal of specific regulatory restrictions that countries had placed in their GATS commitments during previous negotiations, to promote domestic development and limit the activity of MNCs, including limits on land ownership rights for foreign enterprises, laws subjecting foreign corporate takeovers to government approval, and laws requiring MNCs to form joint ventures when they enter the market.

It is clear from these requests that MNCs want to increase their economies of scale in order to sustain their growth. The market access and deregulation they are seeking are intended to standardize the conditions in which they work, so as to ease their entry into global markets. Unfortunately, this is likely to decimate the small and medium-sized domestic suppliers.

While developing country negotiators knew that they had nothing to gain from the GATS, some – particularly the Latin American countries in the Cairns Group – were prepared to make concessions in services in the hope of receiving concessions in agriculture. Unfortunately, given the present attachment to agricultural subsidies in the USA and the EC, any concessions developing countries may give seem unlikely to be reciprocated.

Implementation issues

Although the promise to review implementation issues was critical to developing countries' reluctant acquiescence to the Doha package, the deadlines for resolving the issues were missed, as the intransigent developed countries refused to engage in serious discussions. The USA, the EC, Japan and Canada, for example, flatly rejected the developing countries' request to be allowed to continue implementing local content requirements for development reasons. By the end of 2002, there had been no progress, nor even any sign of willingness to make progress. Some developed countries such as Canada even suggested that implementation issues should fall off the agenda, because no consensus has emerged, leaving developing country delegates with the impression that their interests were being sidelined.

While DG Supachai was sufficiently concerned about the *impasse* to undertake consultations on the way forward himself in the months before the Fifth Ministerial (Sharma 2002b), the developed countries seemed unlikely to yield. As a Quad negotiator told a developing country counterpart informally, 'Asking for implementation issues to be resolved is like asking a second-hand car salesman to take back the car after the deal has been closed.'[10]

At the time of writing (early 2003), it remains to be seen if developing countries will be able to put their foot down and hold up negotiations in the round on the basis that the promises on which their acquiescence was based have not been delivered.

Special and Differential Treatment

The undertaking to operationalize SDT provisions was one of the supposed 'victories' for the developing world in Doha, and in the twelve months after Doha, eighty-five SDT items were tabled for consideration, mostly by the Africa Group. A year of negotiations, however, produced no results. The July 2002 deadline for recommended decisions on SDT provisions lapsed and was carried forward to December 2002, which also passed without any decision.

In the course of the year, the EC attempted to sidetrack the talks by repeatedly bringing up the issue of 'graduation' – that developing countries that have attained a certain level of development should 'graduate' from SDT provisions. This was rejected by developing countries, as it would split them, and reduce their negotiating strength, still further. The developed countries also insisted that SDT negotiations could not lead to changes in the legal texts, trying to convince developing countries that the Doha mandate on SDT was about assessment and review rather than negotiation.

Many developing country delegates were extremely frustrated at the lack of results, seeing the time and effort they had devoted to this issue as having been wasted. In the final meeting of 2002, the Africa Group suggested that if decisions in critical areas were not reached by February 2003, the Cancun Ministerial should take a decision on the SDT package of proposals as it stood.

The lack of results on SDT is not surprising. India's former ambassador to the WTO, S. Narayanan, argued, just months after Seattle:

> The S&D provisions as they stand in various agreements are not proving any benefit or relief or value to the developing countries. If it were the intention that these provisions should have no value to the developing countries, I would suggest that these be deleted. By simply having these provisions without any operational significance or legal enforceability, we are creating an impression as though some benefit is being derived by developing countries … In future, we should not incorporate non-binding S&D provisions in agreements. In that situation developing countries will be made to evaluate their commitments without a false sense of complacency promoted by S&D provisions of the type we are having now. (Narayanan 2002)

While insisting on the promise to operationalize SDT provisions may be a better strategy in the post-Doha situation, Narayanan's key point – the need to avoid accepting empty promises in negotiations – remains extremely pertinent today.

Conclusion

Like gestures to 'democratize' the WTO process, it appears that supposed efforts to 'developmentalize' the substance of its negotiations and agreements are no more than a skilful and elaborate public relations exercise by the developed countries and the Secretariat. The 'Doha development agenda' emerging from the Fourth Ministerial Conference was another victory for the corporate-led globalization agenda, and another step in the wrong direction for developing countries. A year later, the promises made to developing countries – on TRIPs and public health, Special and Differential Treatment, and implementation issues – had all come to nothing. On TRIPs and health, developed countries made strenuous efforts to water down the declaration, seriously diminishing its value, and appear set on tightening the TRIPs Agreement rather than reinforcing its potential flexibility. On implementation issues and SDT, having limited the outcome of Doha to mandating WTO bodies to look at the issues, they then ensured that no progress could be made within these bodies.

One frustrated developing country ambassador lamented that 'the Doha development agenda is fast losing its development component', while civil society groups dubbed the post-Doha work programme scathingly as an 'everything but development' agenda.[11] Even UNCTAD secretary general Rubens Ricupero said that he avoided calling the negotiations launched in Doha a 'development round': 'I myself have refrained from using that description, because I don't see in any sense that it will be conducive to this result' (quoted in Raghavan 2002c).

As the unwieldy post-Doha agenda teetered on the edge, Supachai was apprehensive, clearly concerned about the overloaded agenda, the missed deadlines, and the inability of countries to come to agreement. 'With a number of deadlines now before us, we must be aware of the danger involved in putting too much off for later. We cannot risk overloading the agenda for ministers at Cancun. If that Ministerial Conference is not a success, then I fear the whole round could be put into jeopardy. I cannot stress enough how important it is to have a good result from that meeting' (Supachai 2002).

Given the experiences outlined in this and previous chapters, developing country governments could be forgiven for thinking that putting the whole round in jeopardy might not be a wholly unfavourable prospect. Rather than allowing themselves to go on being swindled time and time again, they would serve their people better by finally standing up to the bullying of the major powers.

Notes

1. These countries allege that MNCs have in some cases used their home governments to apply pressure on host governments to allow the remittance of funds even when host countries have been in extreme balance of payment difficulties.

2. Under the TRIPs Agreement, compulsory licences may be issued only if production is predominantly for the domestic market.

3. James Love, Consumer Project on Technology, informal communication, 25 November 2002.

4. Celine Charveriat, Oxfam International, informal communication, 9 December 2002.

5. The NGOs include Consumer Project on Technology, Médecins Sans Frontières, Oxfam and Third World Network.

6. Two weeks later, Pascal Lamy sent a letter to ministers (dated 7 January 2003) of the WTO members providing a list of twenty-two diseases that are to be included, with the caveat that the World Health Organization would be entrusted with the task of assessing the occurrence, or the likelihood of occurrence, of other public health problems in an importing member. The EC list includes: HIV/AIDS, malaria, tuberculosis, yellow fever, plague, cholera, meningococcal disease, African trypanosomiasis, dengue, influenza, leishmaniasis, hepatitis, leptospirosis, pertussis, poliomyelitis, schistosomiasis, typhoid fever, typhus, measles, shigellosis, haemorrhagic fevers and arboviruses (WTO 2003a).

7. The diseases include yellow fever, plague, cholera, meningococcal diseases, African trypanosomiasis, dengue, HIV/AIDS, leishmaniasis, hepatitis, leptospirosis, pertussis, poliomyelitis, schistosomiasis, typhoid fever, typhus, measles, shigellosis, haemorrhagic fevers, and arboviruses (Raghavan 2002i). See also Shefali Sharma, informal communication, 20 December 2002.

8. WHO does not, however, have observer status in the Council on Trade in Services, whose deliberations affect cross-border trade in health services.

9. This is not surprising, since Australia and New Zealand, the leaders of the group, are keen to be in the good books of the USA.

10. Informal communication by a Caribbean trade delegate, recounting a conversation with a negotiator from a Quad country.

11. This phrase was coined by Martin Khor of Third World Network.

TEN
Conclusion

Developed countries are benefiting from the WTO, as are a handful of (mostly upper-) middle-income countries. The rest, including the great majority of developing countries, are not. It is as simple as that. The benefits of the WTO go to a few powerful nations, under the guise of 'democracy', 'openness' and a 'neutral' Secretariat.

Even many supporters of globalization in developing countries do not see the WTO, as it currently operates, as benefiting them. In the words of a developing country delegate,

> I believe the policies emerging from the organization are loaded against developing countries. I think that if you let globalization do its work it will benefit the poor ...There is no real liberalization in the areas of textiles and agriculture, areas where developing countries will really benefit the most ... In GATS [the General Agreement on Trade in Services], we see liberalization in many service areas – except the movement of natural persons (Mode 4), which again would benefit workers from developing countries the most.

What happens in the WTO is part of a broader pattern of neocolonialism in the global economy. This has two strands. The first is the self-interest of the major powers; their close ties with multinational companies (through the financing of political parties and electoral campaigns, 'revolving doors' between industry and government, etc.); and their willingness to use their political and economic strength to achieve their ends, whatever the effects on other countries – or in some cases, where powerful commercial interests are involved, even their own populations.

The second strand is a combination of ideology, paternalism and missionary zeal. The true believers in globalization and liberalization feel sure that they know best – that markets work and globalization benefits all – but that the poor benighted heathens of the South have yet to realize this. The Enlightened Ones, armed with the Gospel According to Adam Smith, therefore have a duty to spread the Word – and to do whatever it takes to bring the unbelievers to the Promised Land of the globalized economy for their own good, even if they don't realize they want to be there.

This second strand is epitomized by Robert Cooper, an official in the British Foreign and Commonwealth Office (FCO), and a key adviser to British Prime Minister Tony Blair: 'When dealing with the more old-fashioned kinds of state outside the postmodern continent of Europe, we need to revert to the rougher methods of an earlier era – force, pre-emptive attack, deception ... The opportunities, perhaps even the need, for colonisation is as great as it ever was in the 19th century ...What is needed then is a new kind of imperialism' (Cooper 2002, as quoted in the *Guardian* 2002).

While this quote is unusual in its frankness, the mentality that underlies it is all too apparent in the functioning of the WTO and other international economic institutions. As the earlier chapters show, the 'rougher methods ... pre-emptive attack and deception' that Cooper recommends are already widely used by the major powers in the WTO.

Moreover, it seems inevitable that the powerful countries will stick to these tactics, which have served them so well, as long as they still have the opportunities and tools to do so. The questions, then, are whether it is possible to prevent these countries from abusing their political, diplomatic, economic and commercial strength to subvert an ostensibly democratic system to serve their own interests, and to impose their model of globalization on a generally unwilling world; and if so, how this can be done.

This chapter begins with an overview of the problems highlighted in the previous chapters, both institutionally and in terms of political dynamics, before going on to discuss possible changes at three levels, as identified by a member of an African delegation in Doha.

There are three layers of reality within the multilateral trading system: you have the *official* [above board], the *subterranean* [behind the scenes] and the *ideological*. There is a need to attack all these levels ... At the official level, everyone agrees to decisions that were based on 'consensus' ... The subterranean level is where you have the arm-twisting ... The deeper reality is the ideological level – the 'rationalization' of the system – the economic argument and the developmental aspects [the view that liberalization promotes growth and poverty reduction].

The problems

In theory, the WTO is a democratic organization, based on the principles of consensus and one member one vote, supported by a neutral Secretariat; and its purpose is to promote trade policies at the country level which help to raise standards of living for the population of its member countries. In practice, as the processes at and before the Doha Ministerial and over the subsequent year in Geneva clearly demonstrate, it is not. Much of the outcome of Doha was not wanted by at least a large minority, and quite possibly a majority, of the membership; and the living standards of the populations of the member countries were at best a minor consideration in the processes which led to this outcome.

There are a number of reasons for this disparity between the theory and the practice of WTO decision-making.

General pressures on delegates

From the beginning of the process leading up to Doha, the shadow of Seattle hung over the negotiations. Seattle had been a spectacular 'failure' for the WTO, which had drawn global attention. There was a widespread fear, among Secretariat staff and delegates alike – including some developing country delegates – that a second successive 'failure' would seriously undermine the WTO and the multilateral trading system itself, and could even lead to the organization's demise. The major powers did not want this, and, in their anxiety to put the WTO train back on its tracks, exerted a huge amount of pressure on developing countries to reach some kind of agreement.

While many developing country delegates regarded this apocalyptic view as mere rhetoric, bandied around to increase the pressure on ministers, it raised the stakes, and made ministers still more cautious about the risk of being singled out for blame by the powerful countries and the Western media as the villain jeopardizing the multilateral trading system by blocking an agreement.

The DG (whose reputation would have been seriously damaged by a second failure) and the Secretariat (whose jobs were at stake) were also under enormous pressure to set the principle of neutrality aside and do whatever was necessary to promote a new round.

A second shadow appeared part-way through the preparatory process for Doha, following the September 11th terrorist attacks in the USA. The resulting fears of a global recession put additional pressure on delegates to accept a new round, including the 'new issues', which was presented as an important element in stimulating a global recovery; and the explicit linking of trade issues with the 'War against Terror' by the US administration, and the repeated assertion that 'those who are not with us are against us', intensified the political pressure on developing countries to follow the US lead. For some (particularly Muslim) countries, there was an urgent political need to be seen by a suddenly belligerent US administration as being on their side. This was an important factor in neutralizing previously influential and independent voices such as Malaysia and Pakistan.

Political dynamics

A key factor was the political strategies of the Quad, particularly the USA and the EC, to overcome their lack of voting power, and their ability to manipulate the pre-Doha process through the Singapore and Mexico mini-ministerials to put this strategy into effect. Their strategy of progressively building support behind their positions and using strong countries within other WTO groupings (e.g. South Africa within the Africa Group) to garner wider support was a remarkably effective one. Coupled with divide-and-rule tactics, strategic use of bargaining chips, and a veritable arsenal of tools for arm-twisting, particularly of the smaller developing countries (see below), this made a major contribution to their ultimate victory.

The Quad's divide-and-rule tactics were facilitated by the divisions among developing countries, both within and between the established regional and other groupings. The greater the number of developing countries, the more disparate the nature of their interests even within groups (and still more across them) and the absence of collective decision-making processes at the political level (in contrast to the EC, for example) seriously impeded the development of common negotiating positions. These problems were compounded by their dependence on the patronage of the Quad members, particularly in the case of the smaller and poorer countries, making solidarity almost impossible in the face of concerted efforts at arm-twisting; and deliberate efforts to undermine the cohesion of influential coalitions such as the Like-Minded Group.

Peer pressure was a key element in forging the agreement in Doha. The anxiety to reach some kind of agreement post-Seattle coupled with the protracted last-minute discussions created a real pressure on the last remaining countries who maintained their positions against the draft. As ministers in the green room buckled under the pressure, those still holding out were made to feel that they were being extraordinarily unreasonable. The pressure on India, as the strongest country opposing a new round, was intensified by the Western media's inaccurate representation of the negotiations, portraying India as standing alone against a consensus, and stigmatizing the country accordingly.

The developing countries' position is further weakened by the perception that the importance of a country's voice is proportional to its share of world trade – in flat contradiction to the principle of one member one vote and the founding principle that the purpose of trade liberalization is the promotion of improved living standards. As discussed in earlier chapters, the number of African countries participating in the final green room meeting at Doha was judged by some relative to their (minimal) share of world trade, while India's alleged obstructionism was condemned on the basis of their small trade share relative to the developed countries. If the purpose of the negotiations was indeed to improve living standards, the fact that the Indian delegation was representing a fifth of the world's population – and a much greater share of those in greatest need of better living standards – would suggest a strong mandate to block an agreement even if they had not had widespread support among other developing countries.

Another key factor is the difference in human resources available to different countries, both in Geneva and at the ministerial. The fact that many meetings occur simultaneously makes effective participation for countries with only one, two or even three delegates very difficult, if not impossible. More generally, having more people means a greater capacity to keep up to date with events, to prepare for meetings and to liaise with potential allies, as well as more scope for delegates to specialize in particular topics and develop the expertise required for effective negotiation.

Besides the political dynamics among the member countries, the abandonment of the principle of neutrality by the DG and a number of senior Secretariat staff adds another dimension. Under Mike Moore's leadership, certain staff members actively promoted a new round including the 'new issues' – as did Moore himself – and played a significant role in facilitating the Quad's strategy in the negotiations. They also denied important information to developing country delegates, notably on TRIPs and public health. While the pressure arising from the Seattle fiasco was an important contributing factor, the key roles of DDGs with close ties to Quad members (notably Andrew Stoler) were also an important factor.

The current director general, Supachai Panitchpakdi, has been equally zealous in his efforts to complete the round on schedule, and has been instrumental in institutionalizing the non-transparent, anti-democratic 'green room'-style negotiations, both in Geneva and at ministerial and vice-ministerial levels. And the DG's chairmanship of the Trade Negotiations Committee, and Stuart Harbinson's continued chairmanship of the negotiations on agriculture, have brought the Secretariat into the negotiation process in a way not envisaged in the Marrakesh Agreement.

Bargaining chips in negotiations

As well as a range of threats and promises at the bilateral level, the Quad used two major bargaining chips within the negotiations: the declaration on TRIPs and public health and the Cotonou (ACP) waiver. While some give and take is to be expected in negotiations, these bargaining chips were artificially created to be used in this way. The TRIPs declaration did not offer any additional benefits to developing countries, but merely confirmed that parts of the agreement meant what the developing countries had understood them to mean when they had signed it; and the Cotonou waiver issue could and should have been resolved long before Doha, but appears to have been held up to provide an additional instrument of pressure in the hands of the Quad. Technical assistance was also widely used as a bargaining chip.

Arm-twisting and pay-offs

The Quad members – especially the USA – deployed a wide range of bilateral threats and promises against the developing countries, as detailed in Chapter 6. Favourite instruments were the promise of benefits under the African Growth and Opportunity Act (by the USA towards African countries), limited concessions on trade restrictions directed towards individual countries (notably on textiles), debt reduction (e.g. the sudden completion of Tanzania's long-overdue debt reduction under the HIPC initiative soon after Doha) and aid (offered to Pakistan, for example). Many of the promises were fulfilled; others either were quietly forgotten or turned out to be worthless.

As well as such activities at the country level, threats were made against individual ambassadors who were seen as uncooperative. The USA had (and no doubt still has) a blacklist of ambassadors in Geneva who stood up for their countries in negotiations with the USA, and systematically pressurized their capitals into removing them from their positions through a combination of diplomatic pressure and disinformation. The more outspoken ambassadors from countries in the Like-Minded Group, which has attempted to tackle issues critical to developing countries, as well as process issues, appear to have been particularly targeted. Some of these ambassadors have since disappeared from the WTO scene; others – for the moment at least – remain. Some countries have been rewarded for more compliant approaches with offers (some fulfilled, some not) to appoint their nationals to chair committees; ambassadors have been singled out to recommend individuals for positions in the Secretariat; and at least one former ambassador who was particularly compliant to the Quad's position has been appointed to a senior position in the Secretariat.

Process issues

The most powerful members of the WTO guard the 'flexibility' of its decision-making processes jealously. It is unquestionably true, as was observed in the discussion of the Like-Minded Group's proposals on WTO processes, that without this 'flexibility' there would have been no agreement in Doha. Unfortunately 'flexibility', in this context, is merely a euphemism for a system of governance where the most basic principles of democracy, transparency and accountability are blatantly flouted at every turn. This 'flexibility' was essential in Doha because a democratic, transparent and accountable process would not have produced an agreement acceptable to the Quad; and the Quad, unlike the developing countries, have the political muscle to block any deal which is not favourable to their interests. It brought an agreement by allowing all of the factors described above to drive the process to a 'successful' conclusion – by further empowering a rich and powerful minority to overcome the interests and opposition of a weaker minority.

Crucial meetings are held behind closed doors, excluding participants with critical interests at stake, with no formal record of the discussion. When delegates are, in principle, entitled to attend meetings, they are not informed when or where they are to be held. Meetings are held without translation into the languages of many participants, to discuss documents which are available only in English, and which have been issued only hours before, or even at the meeting itself. Those most familiar with issues (ambassadors) are sometimes discouraged or prevented from speaking in discussions about them at ministerial meetings. 'Consultations' with members on key decisions are held one to one, in private, with no written record, and the interpretation left to an individual who may have a stake in the outcome. Protestations that inconvenient views have been ignored in this process fall on deaf ears. Chairs of committees and facilitators are selected by a small clique, and often have an interest in the issues for which the committee is responsible. The established principle of decision-making by consensus is routinely overridden, and the views of decision-makers are 'interpreted' rather than a formal vote being taken, even in such key decisions as the selection of Mike Moore as DG and the chairmanship of the Trade Negotiations Committee. Rules are ignored when they are inconvenient, and a blind eye is turned to blackmail and inducements. The list is endless.

Any country whose political system operated as the WTO did before, during and after the Doha Ministerial – where procedures were interpreted with such 'flexibility', rules were routinely ignored, and people or interested groups routinely used bribery and blackmail to achieve their political ends – would not only be rightly condemned by the international community as undemocratic and corrupt, it would also face a real and constant threat of revolution. No developed country would contemplate running its government in this way; and yet they are happy both to exploit the system and to defend it against pressure for democratic reform at the international level. Australia, Canada, Hong Kong, Korea, Mexico, New Zealand, Singapore and Switzerland said in a proposal in June 2002, 'Processes need to be kept flexible. We need to avoid rigidities ... Prescriptive and detailed approaches to the preparatory processes are inappropriate and will not create the best circumstances for consensus to emerge in the Cancun meeting ... Restraint and flexibility will be essential' (WTO 2002g: 3–4). The Western media, which would be the first to condemn such processes and practices at the country level, do not raise so much as a murmur.

The official level – tinkering with the wiring and its limitations

This section presents some ideas on how the WTO should function, partly on the basis of suggestions from the delegates interviewed for this book. They are, however, presented subject to three important caveats:

- First, post-Seattle and post-Doha experiences suggest that the likelihood of such proposals being implemented in full – let alone in the full spirit of democracy, rather than as a mere show of it – is almost zero. They are offered essentially as a view of how negotiations clearly should be, but equally clearly are not, conducted.
- Second, even if they were implemented in full, while they might help to *limit* the major developed countries' abuse of their political and economic power, they would fall far short of *preventing* it.
- Third, the proposals do little more than 'tinker' with the current system, which is emphatically not an alternative to the more fundamental reorientation and restructuring the multilateral trading system clearly requires. This issue is taken up later.

After the revolt by developing countries in Seattle, even then US trade representative Charlene Barshefsky appeared to acknowledge the need for change: 'The process ... was a rather exclusionary one. All meetings were held among between twenty and thirty key countries ... and that meant 100 countries, 100, were never in the room. As you know, for many countries this led to an extraordinarily bad feeling that they were left out of the process ... ' (US Trade Representative Charlene Barshefsky, Press Briefing, Seattle, 2 December 1999).

When the ministerial finally collapsed, Barshefsky, in the closing plenary session, said, 'The WTO has outgrown the processes appropriate to an earlier time. An increasing and necessary view, generally shared among the members, was that we needed a process which had a degree of internal transparency and inclusion to accommodate a larger and more diverse membership' ('Remarks of

Ambassador Charlene Barshefsky', 3 December 1999, Closing Plenary www.ustr.gov/speech-test/barshefsky/barshefsky_57.html).

Her pronouncement proved, however, to be a false dawn, as the promises even to make the institution transparent to its own members came to nought. After Seattle, the then chair of the General Council, Ambassador Kare Bryn of Norway, conducted hundreds of hours of consultations with members on procedural issues. The process did not produce any binding rules but only four non-binding 'guidelines' (WTO 2000b):

- that members should be advised of the intention to hold informal consultations;
- that those members with an interest in the specific issue under consideration should be given the opportunity to make their views known;
- that no assumption should be made that one member represents any other members, except where the members concerned have agreed on such an arrangement; and
- that the outcome of such consultations should be reported back to the full membership expeditiously for consideration.

As the Doha experience clearly demonstrates, these few 'guidelines' have made little difference. They were either so deliberately vague, or interpreted so 'flexibly', as to have a minimal effect on the actual conduct of negotiations, or else they were simply ignored. As discussed in Chapter 8, post-Doha efforts by developing countries to secure real improvements in WTO procedures have also been systematically blocked. The stakes are high for the major developed countries, who make every effort to ensure that the process remains tightly in their control – and as one delegate remarked in an interview for this book, 'Power is best exercised in a situation of uncertainty and unpredictability, and that is why process issues are so vague at the WTO'.

The rhetoric may have improved, but real democratic decision-making remains elusive. More 'consultations' take place with more delegations – but their views are still ignored, as chairs give their own 'interpretation', and present non-consensual texts without brackets 'on their own responsibility'.

Mini-ministerial meetings

As noted in Chapter 3, while mini-ministerials have no formal status within the WTO, they seem to have become institutionalized. They set the parameters for ministerials themselves, and are a key part of the Quad countries' strategy to impose their agendas.

Mini-ministerial meetings should not take place. They are closed, non-transparent meetings between unrepresentative groups of members, generally hand-picked by the major powers to promote their agendas; and by shifting the discussion from the ambassadorial to the ministerial level, they take it out of the hands of those closest to the issues, politicizing the process and opening the way to arm-twisting and pay-offs in fields unrelated to trade. A core group of about twenty to twenty-five members attend all the most critical meetings, in effect instituting a *de facto* executive council, to which members have not agreed, by the back door. It is for this reason that such meetings are widely viewed as illegitimate.

The rationale for the exclusion of the majority, that these are private meetings hosted by individual countries, is little more than a convenient fiction, since the outcomes of the meetings affect all members. A final package is crafted between a selected minority of members and presented to the majority as a *fait accompli*. As one developing country ambassador commented: 'The informality of the process means that, in fact, it is a process of consultation and discussion behind closed doors. This means that those with clout will carry the most weight. There are few countries that would challenge a decision that has been put forward as a done deal.' Negotiations in preparation for ministerial conferences should instead remain at the Geneva level, where delegates are best positioned to deal with the technical issues.

Ministerial conferences[1]

The Like-Minded Group proposal (see Chapter 5, Appendix) should be implemented in full. The process and rules of procedure for ministerials should be established and agreed upon in advance. All consultations and meetings organized by chairs should be announced to all members well ahead of time, and all members, not only those perceived to have an interest in that area, should be allowed to attend. Ambassadors should be allowed to speak on behalf of their ministers at the request of the latter, or in their absence.

No green room meetings should be held, and negotiations should not take place throughout the night, as this does not allow for full and effective participation. Negotiations that go on continuously for 30 or 40 hours place smaller delegations at a serious disadvantage. There should be an agreed time set for negotiations to stop each day, and an agreed time for the conference as a whole to end, and the agenda should be set in accordance with the time available for discussion. If there is no agreement at the scheduled end of the conference, negotiations should be brought back to Geneva.

There should also be transcripts of the negotiations. This would facilitate the information flow, particularly for delegations that are too small to cover all the important meetings, as well as improving internal transparency. There should also be simultaneous translation of discussions at the very minimum in French and Spanish – the other official languages of the WTO – during all meetings at ministerial conferences. This is a common concern for Francophone African countries as well as Latin American countries. The director general and the Secretariat should remain strictly impartial both between members and on the substantive issues under discussion, and their primary role should be to provide logistical support, to produce and disseminate transcripts and translations, and to facilitate the information flow.

Green room meetings and informal consultations

Green room meetings – informal meetings of typically twenty to twenty-five WTO members, with no written records – were the main fora for negotiations during the Uruguay Round and in the early days of the WTO. The closed nature of the meetings and the absence of records make it difficult for members who do not attend to assess what transpired, and impossible even for those who do attend to refer to discussions. A delegate provided an illustration of the problem:

> Clearly, of thirty of us who discussed a certain issue at an informal before Doha, some twenty to twenty-five disagreed on the matter, but it was completely ignored. There are no records, though, so nobody knows who said what. You can have an innumerable number of meetings, but what does it reflect? Either informal meetings should be immediately followed by formal meetings, or what is discussed in informal meetings ought to be recorded.

Another delegate offered this perspective:

> The WTO has become an institution, but has not developed the institutional modes of behaviour and institutional structures. These were not in place before. They have to start thinking outside the box. They are still thinking inside the old GATT box when there was no Secretariat, and it was only an interim body, not an organization ...
>
> Yes, we are consulted, but I fully understand that what I say is hardly likely to weigh as much as what another country says. It requires superhuman conviction of one of the members to oppose what the major countries want, and you may not have it if you are not a major player ...
>
> We have formal meetings where we convene formally. In the informal meetings, I will say whatever my position is, but all of that is not recorded. I don't repeat what I had said in the informal meeting [at the formal meeting] because we have already spoken. The real difficulties are addressed informally without records and the formal meetings are mere rubber stamps. So it is difficult to find records that cover an issue and give a sense of history of the issue and the real substantive differences that members may have had, because all of that has happened in informal mode. When our successors come in ten years from now, they will have no idea about the history of an issue. All they will have are little minutes of the formal meetings ... There is good reason for informal

meetings, in that they put a lid on problematic issues, and help reduce tensions – but one has to have records. The WTO has a preponderance of informal meetings, a *huge* number.

After the bad publicity they received at the First Ministerial Conference in Singapore in 1996,[2] the then DG, Renato Ruggiero, announced that he would make every effort to avoid green room meetings in the future. They gave way, in part, to 'informal consultations', where the chair conducts consultations with individual members or groups of members which he or she chooses. These are effectively green room meetings in another form, and still less transparent. Not only are no records kept of the meetings, but there is no single negotiating process that can be tracked, making it difficult for members who are not part of the 'inner circle' to ascertain what consultations are taking place and with whom. Before and during Doha, and even more so with the current Director General Supachai Panitchpakdi, green room meetings are being held. At the same time, small group 'informal' consultations continue.

No consultations by the chair should be held without adequate advance notice being given to the entire membership, and all members should be informed of, and entitled to attend, all such meetings. These meetings should be publicized on the WTO website and on the WTO meeting notice board, similar to the way formal meetings are announced. Since these meetings and consultations conducted by the chair are at the crux of the decision-making process, they should be transcribed. This would help to ensure that chairs' 'interpretations' of positions reflect the reality of the discussions. While one developing country delegate interviewed feared that this could prompt the Quad and others to drive the process underground, a number of others felt it could improve transparency.

Conduct of chairpersons

Since Stuart Harbinson's pre-Doha stunt with the largely 'bracketless' draft declaration (see Chapter 3), other chairs at the WTO are now adopting a similar approach, producing non-consensual but bracketless texts at their own discretion, usually reflecting the skewed balance of power rather than the formal equality between members. This further marginalizes the LDCs and other developing countries, and sets the stage for arm-twisting against their ministers and officials, by creating a presumption that all support the text unless they explicitly speak out against it. The practice is now becoming so commonplace that developing country delegations are either becoming resigned to it, or are too fatigued to resist it at every turn.

This serious deviation from conventional international negotiating practice should not be permitted. While the developed countries, together with a few developing country allies, support 'flexibility' in the role of chairs, democracy demands that negotiating texts should accurately reflect the various positions on an issue, and that brackets should be removed from draft negotiating texts only when a consensus is reached. Chairs who fail to reflect differences between members in negotiating texts should be disqualified from chairing committees.

Voting on contentious process issues

Consideration should be given to formal votes on certain process issues in the WTO. Matters such as choosing committee chairs, the broad agenda for ministerial conferences and the transmission of draft texts to ministers, for example, should be voted on, especially where there are major disagreements. One delegate explains his reasons for such a suggestion: 'Formally, one can vote. But in the absence of a one country one vote, and in the presence of a decision-making structure that is based on consensus and an informal decision-making process, I will be ignored if I raise my flag. You will be ignored unless you are a major trading country.' The convention of taking decisions by 'consensus' rather than by voting removes the locus of decision-making from a formal process in which all members are (at least formally) equal to an informal system in which the law of the jungle prevails. The process of informal, one-to-one consultations behind closed doors after which an individual committee chair decides whether there is consensus does not add to the democracy or transparency of the process.

A useful first step would be to establish the practice of voting on major procedural issues, such as the TNC chairmanship (see Chapter 8). In this context, one ambassador said:

> It is not good to hear that Africa supports a certain position on the issue of the TNC chair [opposition to the DG chairing the TNC] and this is also the same position taken by the ACP and LDCs ... [while] some Asians say yes and some say no – but the conclusion of the chair is that the majority of opinion supports the DG. That doesn't build confidence. Some of these procedural issues can be resolved by ticking a little box. We need to bring greater certainty ... while being cognisant that some decisions by simple majority would be counter-productive ...
>
> For example, if we are going to take a legally binding substantive decision on reducing export subsidies, and a poor developing country says they expect a reduction of 90 per cent, but the EC says no, it can only offer a 15 per cent reduction, having a vote on the issue would be pointless because what will the developing country do if the EC refuses to comply? Are they going to coerce the EC? ... If we take decisions that are not implemented, we lose that legitimacy. It is easier that everyone agrees in some substantive areas through consensus ...
>
> We do, however, need to change the decision-making culture in process issues. I believe this could lead to a desire to change the process in substantive areas. The current situation is in itself untenable.

External transparency

The majority of delegates interviewed for this book were in favour of greater external transparency at the WTO – although they interpreted the concept in different ways.

Currently, Secretariat-produced papers and minutes of formal meetings are released to the public on the WTO website. The WTO prides itself for being an organization where a large number of its documents are publicly available. This perception, however, is rather misleading. The main reason for external transparency is to allow

A great majority of the delegates interviewed for this book (from both developed and developing countries) acknowledged the importance of involving NGOs and CSOs in the WTO's work. A number of developing country delegates, however, felt that correcting *internal* transparency issues in the WTO needed greater attention than improving external transparency.

An African delegate took the view that: 'If we can achieve *internal* transparency, then *external* transparency can follow ... I have no problems working with NGOs generally, only when some of them insist on being treated like governments ... In my country we have a national committee on WTO issues. It is multi-disciplinary and inputs from NGOs are always welcome ... Once a position has been formed by the committee, it is sent to me, and I in turn use it as my ammunition ... When we go to ministerial meetings, NGOs based in-country form part of our official delegation ...

'I don't object to NGOs being observers at General Council meetings, either ... However there are some sensitive areas, which I think NGOs should be cautious about. For example, if my country had a dispute with the USA on environmental

the public to express their views on issues to their representatives, so that the latter can take them into account in their deliberations and negotiating positions. The most pertinent documents, however, are usually not made publicly available while the negotiations are under way. These include documents on proposals which the chair is still getting a 'feel' of (which are not even circulated to all delegates), draft negotiating texts, and submissions from members which the member(s) concerned have chosen to restrict.

Chairmen's drafts on key substantive issues – for example on the heated TRIPs paragraph 6 negotiations, which affect people's matters, it will be unhelpful to have an NGO acting as a third party in the dispute. I think they should provide information to either my country or the USA, which would add value rather than stifle the process ... Intergovernmental relations must be maintained within the WTO, but we must also work with NGOs.'

A former Latin American delegate took an altogether less favourable view: 'I don't see why the WTO should talk to anybody outside the system, and certainly not to NGOs, whom I believe have no legitimacy. People interested in what goes on at the WTO should contact their home governments for information.'

A Secretariat staff member offered the following explanation for the limits to WTO's external transparency. 'As decisions are based on consensus, we cannot override the wishes of some of our members who do not want their capitals to know what they are saying when they come here.[3] Though I do not wish to make this a North versus South issue, those who do not want WTO matters made public are mainly from developing countries ... [But] I think the Dispute Settlement Body, for example, should be more open. The secrecy is not all that necessary.'

access to medicines – are not publicly available. Other general documents, such as minutes of General Council meetings, are not usually available until forty-five days after they have been produced (WTO 2002i); and the most critical meetings take place in 'informal' mode, so that records are not even kept.

As a result,

At present, virtually all of the documents that are important to the making and enforcing of WTO rules are generally not made available to the public until after the issues that they relate to have already been settled by the Members. This must change if the citizens of Member countries and NGOs are going to be able to affect the rules that are established and how these rules are applied. (Van Dyke and Weiner 1997)

In fact, deliberate efforts have been made by the Secretariat, clearly working with the relevant chairs, to ensure that certain texts are not even circulated beyond a certain group of members, even on issues fundamental to the working of the organization such as the voting system for the director general (see Chapter 8).

This external transparency issue has also become quite heated in the context of the post-Doha GATS negotiations. Many civil society groups are concerned that public services and global commons, such as water, are being privatized in currently secret negotiations, and have demanded that countries' requests and offers should be made public. At present, it is left to individual countries to decide whether or not to release the requests and offers they submit, and this call for transparency has not been taken up by the governments.

Developing countries have been reluctant to allow for minutes of meetings to be released more quickly than the current forty-five-day lapse after they have been produced. The reason they give is that they need first to check these documents before their public release to ensure that the Secretariat had accurately portrayed their viewpoints. This caution is in part due to their distrust of the Secretariat, as a result of past experience of inaccurate minutes produced. Delegates from Latin America also stressed the need to ensure that documents (especially minutes of General Council meetings) are translated into Spanish and French before their release, to avoid misinterpretations[4] and to ensure that they can be read by officials in capitals.

Delegates' views on whether non-governmental actors should become observers in the negotiations (as in the United Nations) are mixed (see Box 10.1). This has been opposed by some developing country governments, keenly aware that it could allow the corporate sector to become formally involved in the process, which would put the South at a disadvantage, and that Southern civil society groups are not as well resourced as those of the North.

In the authors' view, non-governmental and civil society organizations representing the public interest should, at the very least, be invited to observe the negotiations at General Council level, as well as meetings of the negotiating committees, while those representing corporate interests (e.g. PhRMA) should be strictly excluded (reflecting the primacy of the public interest over corporate profits). It is only with this type of opening that the public can hold their governments accountable, and ensure that positions formed with popular participation at the national level are not reneged upon in the secretive process of deal-making.

The Secretariat

1. The process of selecting a director general requires binding guidelines, and a transparent one-member-one-vote system, in accordance with the provisions of the Marrakesh Agreement. Since there is no provision in the agreement to override the one-member-one-vote rule, there should be no question of deciding on voting procedures each time a new DG is appointed. The situation in which Geneva delegates are induced to support a candidate in return for a cushy post at the Secretariat must also be avoided. This diminishes the integrity of mission officials, wholly compromises their objectivity, and creates a *quid pro quo* culture between the director general and the delegates.

2. The appointment of deputy directors general (DDGs) who have served powerful governments in key roles, particularly in trade negotiations, does not create an atmosphere of neutrality. These appointments are overtly political; the deputy directors from the USA and EC carry enormous weight; and, as a long-serving member of the Secretariat staff observed (see Chapter 7), they appear to have been appointed to further the interests of their respective governments during the Doha process. The criteria for selecting DDGs must be reviewed so that only international candidates with little or no affiliation with individual governments are selected; and geographical considerations should be limited to ensuring a balance between roughly equal geographical regions.

3. The WTO is very different from its predecessor, the GATT,

but its recruitment and staffing have not adapted to this changing context. The composition of its membership has shifted markedly from primarily a 'rich man's club', as more and more developing countries have joined, so that they now make up four-fifths of the membership; and the potential implications of the negotiations and agreements for development have increased considerably as issues such as agriculture, trade in services and intellectual property rights have been added to its remit. Only one-fifth of the WTO staff, however, are from developing countries, and most of the developed country nationals have little or no experience of the reality of developing countries.

One Secretariat staff member interviewed for this book also argued that increasing the numbers of developing country staff could also improve governance issues. For example, when a proposal has come from a Quad country through the chairperson of the General Council for translation into French and Spanish, some developing country staff have insisted that a proposal on the same issue but from a developing country group should also be translated and released at the same time, so that both sides of the argument are released together.

In theory, the staff are neutral. However, the composition and background of the Secretariat staff do make a significant difference in the advice and research they provide; and they are currently strongly dominated by developed country nationals, and those with neoliberal views. Efforts should be made to achieve a more proportionate balance between staff, both between developed and developing countries, reflecting the reality of the membership, and in terms of ideological leanings on economic issues. Much greater account should also be taken in selection of candidates' experience of development issues and the reality of developing countries.

4. There should be much clearer, binding rules on the mandate of the director general and the Secretariat staff, to ensure their neutrality. These should include a clear definition of their role, core principles for their advisory function, and a process for addressing situations of improper conduct. Secretariat staff should not be chairing negotiating bodies. Neither should they take upon

themselves the role of promoting trade liberalization. Rather, the fundamental principle, for the Secretariat and the organization as a whole, should be the conduct of trade relations *'with a view to raising standards of living'*, in accordance with the preamble of the Marrakesh Agreement. The role of the DG and the Secretariat during the preparation for, and at, ministerial conferences should be administrative in nature. The proposals of the Like-Minded Group (Chapter 5, Appendix), emphasizing the need for the Secretariat to maintain its impartiality and not to express views on specific issues being negotiated, should also be implemented.

5. The Secretariat has to change the way it operates; and this requires an improvement in monitoring and oversight. There should be internal performance evaluations on the director general, the *chef de cabinet* and senior staff, particularly on the issue of neutrality and appropriate conduct, taking equal account of feedback from all members. Where staff members overstep their mandate, this should be dealt with seriously. At present, many developing country delegates feel that the Secretariat staff not infrequently give advice that is in the interests of the powerful countries.[5]

While Mike Moore established a resource and performance analysis function attached to his cabinet office, to monitor and evaluate the activities of the Secretariat, it is defunct in all but name. A Secretariat staff member confirmed that a few consultants were hired to run the unit, but that there had been little progress because 'we don't have the right structure to get this operationalized ... The Secretariat is too small, and thus such a unit would be pointless. Besides, we are constantly being evaluated by the members, and we give honest advice 99 per cent of the time.'

6. The Secretariat should not be complicit in the 'carrotization' of technical assistance and capacity building by the powerful members to get their way with developing countries. As professionals they should advise members to the best of their ability what is in their interests within the WTO. Technical assistance and capacity-building are used to make palatable and acceptable something developing countries may not have accepted in the first place. But this is not what it should be for. Technical assistance and capacity building

should be devised in a way that empowers developing countries to achieve their objectives.

A common concern is that the technical assistance provided by the Secretariat – such as seminars on the WTO – is limited to basic information about the agreements, their commitments, and the implementation of their commitments, and does not equip delegates with a useful analysis of the possible national-level implications of negotiations and agreements – particularly the possible negative impacts. Any assistance provided should be administered in such a way as to prevent its use as a tool for influencing countries' positions in negotiations.

The dispute settlement mechanism and the accession process

While it has not been discussed in detail in this book, the dispute settlement mechanism is an important factor in the power of the WTO, the prevalence of its agreements over countries' other international commitments, and the asymmetry between developed and developing countries in their implementation (see Chapter 1). Readers are referred to the South Centre's (1999) proposals, relating to deterrence against misuse of the process; operationalization of all provisions regarding Special and Differential Treatment for developing countries; equal access to the dispute settlement mechanism; and provision of compensation pending resolution of disputes.

The accession process has been systematically abused by the powerful members to wring trade policy concessions out of developing country applicants that go far beyond what they would have been required to do had they been WTO members. There should be strict guidelines to ensure that countries seeking WTO accession are not required to take on commitments which go beyond those of their counterparts already in the WTO.

These tinkering-with-the-wiring measures are suggestions on how the organization should function pending more fundamental changes to the global economic system and hence the trade system. The suggestions are useful in terms of highlighting the contrasts and contradictions to the current reality. It would be misleading, however, to imply that these suggestions can in fact be implemented in the current WTO as we know it. The present experience tells us that too many political forces come into play to enable positive change to take root.

The subterranean level – arm-twisting and threats

In addition to the formal and informal decision-making processes, careful consideration needs to be given to how developing countries can best function within the framework of the WTO as it currently operates to protect their own interests in negotiations. Some suggestions are offered below.

The pace of negotiations, the scope of the WTO, and resource constraints on developing countries

The scope and pace of negotiations in the WTO are largely set by the developed countries, as they seek to rush through their globalization agenda. This creates confusion for the desperately under-resourced missions and trade ministries of many developing countries; and, if this is not a conscious objective of the developed countries, it is at least advantageous to them, and certainly not considered a constraint.

The scope and pace of negotiations must be brought in line with the capacity of all the members to participate *effectively* in all the negotiations. Developing countries have already requested limits on the number of meetings, but with no response, and the number of meetings has increased still further since. Limiting the WTO's mandate more strictly to trade issues, leaving 'beyond-the-border' issues such as intellectual property, investment, competition and procurement to the discretion of sovereign governments, would go a long way to addressing developing countries' resource constraints, as well as being intrinsically desirable. The policy frameworks imposed by WTO rules on such issues are often alien to the cultures of developing countries, and many developing countries do not have the institutional capacity or resources even to implement existing agreements.

Developing countries' problems in dealing with broad-ranging trade negotiations within an artificially limited timeframe are largely a result of the serious financial and human resource constraints they face, coupled with the greater priority quite reasonably attached to more immediate concerns of health, education and domestic economic policy in many developing country capitals. Increasing their capacity would require substantial additional resources which at present are largely not available, or if provided by developed countries, could have conditions attached (at least in the present scenario).

Where at all possible, developing countries' resources for WTO negotiations should be increased. For most countries, the number of professionals currently working on WTO issues, in the capital as well as in Geneva, is low compared with the potential impact of WTO agreements on policies and development prospects.

The more familiar delegates are with the issues at stake in negotiations, and the better prepared their positions are, on the basis of quality background information, the more confidence they will project, the more effective they will be in negotiations, and the less vulnerable they will be to threats. This would be helped by larger missions, but the appointment of staff based on relevant skills, rather than unqualified political appointees, is also important. Quality representatives who can tackle the substantive issues as well as the process issues would boost the position of developing countries.

Assessment of WTO agreements, clear trade objectives and strategies

Countries should ensure that WTO negotiations are a *means* to their development objectives, and not an *obstacle* to their attainment. The knowledge of the linkages between all the different aspects of policy potentially affected by WTO negotiations on the one hand, however, and the different aspects of development and social well-being on the other, is usually insufficient. As a first step towards filling this gap, impact assessments of the Uruguay Round agreements should be carried out before further negotiations. There should also be on-the-ground research on trade policy and its impacts on all groups within a country. Databases should be established within countries to give trade officials information on patterns of trade, growth and poverty; and studies should be conducted to establish the likely short- and long-term economic costs and benefits of proposed WTO rules for the country as a whole, the poor (especially farmers), the local business community and other groups, as well as what costs the country would incur, and what adjustments it would need to make, to implement the rules.

Clearly resource constraints are again a major obstacle. Since such information is a prerequisite for informed decision-making, however, independently provided financial and technical support could usefully be channelled to support independent and objective analysis in these areas. South–South technical support could be one such option.

Preferential agreements and aid

It is also important for each developing country to coordinate its policies in the WTO and other fora, to ensure that conditionality in agreements such as Generalized System of Preferences (GSP) schemes and bilateral and multilateral aid does not undermine their negotiating position at the WTO.

It would be ideal if conditionality could be abolished in such agreements as the GSP and aid, thus enabling countries to better negotiate at the WTO without fear of a backlash behind-the-scenes by developed countries ... Generally, there should be an acute awareness that powerful nations apply 'ratchet diplomacy' – i.e. if they make concessions for a developing country in one forum they nullify it in another forum. For example, as some Latin American countries were apprehensive about signing the Government Procurement Agreement within the WTO, they are being bullied by the USA to sign a similar agreement under the proposed FTAA [Free Trade Agreement of the Americas] with the USA ... Countries and their missions should draw up a matrix of all their preferential trade agreements, which would enable them to be aware of possible 'ratchet diplomacy' tactics and seek ways to prevent them.

Countries providing GSP programmes should also not be permitted to withdraw preferences arbitrarily, depending on the 'good conduct' of recipient countries. Once provided, they should be made to bind these preferences in their WTO schedules of commitments.

Coordination between developing country missions and their capitals

Regular contact and policy coordination between Geneva-based missions and capitals is essential for developing countries to avoid the type of tactics developed countries used during the Doha process to split ambassadors from their ministries.

> We have just over twenty diplomats in our embassy in Washington, in total. The USA, on the other hand, have nearly 3,000 American diplomats in our capital. The USAID alone has about 2,000 staff ... So they have inside information about everything we do, and regularly contact their capitals and relevant missions on any issue ... Developing countries therefore need to establish better and more regular communication channels, despite our low human resources capacities, in order that we can establish a degree of uniformity in our positions and objectives.

Involvement of developing country trade ministers in the WTO process

One of the key problems which resulted in the outcome at Doha was that ministers were in the dark about how the institution actually functions. As a result, they were more vulnerable to the public relations strategies and sweet talk that abound, such as empty promises in negotiating texts.

One ambassador outlined the problem thus:

> You never fail to be astonished at how much developing countries can absorb. We need to familiarize developing country leaders about this organization. Right now, you can never be sure how things will turn out at the critical moment. The division between Geneva and capitals has been exacerbated [by the Quad and its

allies]. They recognize that these issues are too complex and with too many nuances ... so they have found it effective to bypass the Geneva negotiators and go for decision-makers at other levels who won't see the complexities and nuances. It is not that easy to convince a minister as to why you object to Mike Moore as chair of the TNC. To grasp why, there are so many elements you have to intimate your minister with, and your minister will be disadvantaged if they get a call from the Lamys or the Zoellicks. We learnt that at Doha. The final position the groups took was not at all like the positions of the LDC and African Group meetings. That is why I believe there has to be more involvement of ministers with the day-to-day running of the organization. We need ministerial involvement, oversight and governance, which I don't see occurring in the WTO at all.

Before developing the idea further, he outlined the problems this could pose: 'But again, members don't want to see some limited ministerial body that meets. I do believe it [a small group of ministers meeting frequently] establishes a hierarchy beyond the hierarchy – that one group has an unequal influence over the organization by having more knowledge and intimacy of the organization, and a larger group that has no knowledge.'

His solution was that it could be beneficial for all ministers to be more involved, on a rotating basis.

I'm not satisfied with trade ministers being involved every two years. I think that, apart from the Lamys and Zoellicks, there is no real engagement with the WTO by ministers except every two years. Some developing countries see that as advantageous. However this is tantamount to being parachuted into a process every two years. Under these conditions, how do you exercise your ministerial oversight in a judicious way? ... Ministers don't even know how the Secretariat is structured, or what the budget is ... There needs to be some structural involvement of ministers, on a rotating basis ...

If you have a group that meets periodically, not only to launch a round, but to assess day-to-day issues, then there will be greater intimacy, therefore you will have a group that knows how the organization actually works … Some forty ministers should be in a position to review the operations of the WTO over the past six months, construct a table on the critical issues, discuss internal and external transparency issues, funding for capacity, exchange views, provide recommendations, improve the representation of the Secretariat – and assess why this is not happening – discuss gender and poverty issues, etc.

This may be one effective way in which ministers can become more aware of activities in Geneva, and therefore provide them with more robust support. Such a rotating committee would also be in a position to assess what rules governing the Secretariat should be made more binding in order to improve transparency, accountability and neutrality. However, the idea requires further fine-tuning to ensure that no one group of ministers has greater influence than any other on the outcome of negotiations, for example by being involved in the process at a particularly sensitive time in the negotiations. The risk of such a group becoming another *de facto* executive council to replace mini-ministerials should be avoided at all costs.

Personal threats and job (in)security of delegates

Delegates should be well aware of threats, and keep in constant contact with their capitals to diffuse any possibility of disinformation spread by developed countries. NGOs and journalists could also be involved, investigating such cases carefully (with the consent of the victims) and making them public knowledge.

From a political point of view, it is very difficult for ambassadors to openly protect each other because every country has its own pressures, and we have to focus on the interests of our countries. The only protection ambassadors have at present is their own legitimacy and integrity. I feel I would have been moved if I had not had a great deal of support from my government – they have shown that they have a great deal of trust in my work … I think, however, that our trade ministers should meet to decide how they would like to move on these types of issues. Ministers need to devise ways of collectively blocking political pressures from developed countries and thereby protecting ambassadors.

Opening up the negotiations to observers would go quite a long way in dispelling the disinformation that is often propagated by some of the powerful countries about developing country delegates, as would publishing minutes or transcripts of discussions and consultations. This would give ambassadors the opportunity to disprove charges of 'unreasonable behaviour' levelled against them by the major powers.

Coalition building and solidarity

Developing countries need to build and maintain strong coalitions if they are to resist pressures from the Quad. The Like-Minded Group (LMG) demonstrates the potential strength of such groups – but also the danger of deliberate efforts by the Quad to derail them. Since Doha, key ambassadors active in the LMG have been removed, and some countries have been pressured to withdraw from the group.[6] It is important that the members of the LMG and other developing country groups maintain their solidarity, and resist the efforts of developed countries to undermine their unity. 'You feel you are safe [in a group], but can be let down finally by other [developing] countries. So you must be very careful about what could happen finally. Up to Doha, there was a good coalition. At Doha, it broke.'

There is also a need to develop and sustain a more general sense of solidarity among developing country members. As long as green room and mini-ministerial meetings prevail, for example, the countries present must not see this merely as an opportunity to get bilateral deals for themselves. Such actions do not encourage trust.

Political developments outside the trade field, such as the aftermath of September 11th, can pose a particular threat to developing country solidarity, as the experience of Doha demonstrates. It is therefore particularly important (though also particularly difficult) not to allow the process at the WTO to be hijacked by such extraneous developments. 'The WTO is a useful body if it was not immersed in all the politics that goes on. I think we should focus on trade and try to implement the agreements we reach.'

Negotiations should not be carried out in 'rounds'

The WTO is a permanent negotiating body, unlike its predecessor, the GATT. It therefore makes little sense for countries to be pressurized into round upon round of negotiations, when the structure for permanent negotiations is already in place. This merely puts more pressure on developing countries' resources, as well as marginalizing the majority of countries from the outset because of their inability to participate effectively.

As one delegate observed,

The problem may be how we approach the question of negotiating rounds. If we are going to be negotiating legally binding agreements in ten or twelve agreements, it is impossible. If we are negotiating the Kyoto Protocol, 144 members can negotiate over a long period. In the WTO, we negotiate agriculture, rules, market access, services, TRIPs, and we are doing all of these simultaneously. That itself makes it impossible to have an inclusive structure. I am told we do the negotiations like this to have trade-offs. But having all the negotiations all at the same time poses a Herculean task. It is impossible for anybody [to be effective] except the EC or the USA, and impossible to have an inclusive process where each country can attend all meetings. So the very structure of the programme – the round – marginalizes you instantly if you are not a major player.

Quad and a few other countries can decide on almost anything and get away with it. Part of the solution is not to have these huge negotiating rounds. I would have liked us to work on small things in a concerted way ... small chunks of things. That would change the complexion of participation, decision-making and potential for inclusiveness. We have to remove the myth that there has to be round upon round, and structure an agenda where countries can participate effectively, even small countries, not only the USA or EC with hundreds of technocrats.

The ideological level – trade, growth and poverty

The idea promoted by the Secretariat and the major powers, that trade liberalization promotes growth and therefore reduces poverty, improves health and the environment, is a deceptively simple one. The Secretariat should be careful about making such statements and arguments without proper knowledge and understanding of how developing country economies really work. A long-serving member of the Secretariat staff from a developed country observed: 'It is essential to have a closer look at the various pieces of the jigsaw, and figure out how they fit in. The IMF/World Bank/WTO do not often see the bigger picture and the repercussions of the various liberalization policies … Constructive engagement is required.'

The belief that free trade increases incomes is one of the oldest and best-known principles of economics, originating with the concept of 'comparative advantage', developed by the classical economist David Ricardo (1772–1823). This states that countries prosper by taking advantage of their assets in order to concentrate on what they can produce most efficiently relative to other countries, and trading these products for those which *other* countries produce most efficiently.

The world, however, has changed a great deal in the intervening two centuries. In the early nineteenth century, it was entirely realistic for Ricardo to assume that capital could not move between countries. In the contemporary world of globalized financial markets, this clearly no longer holds. Economic theory has also moved on, and recent developments even in mainstream economics, such as 'endogenous growth theory', imply that trade restrictions can, in some circumstances, promote faster economic growth.

Moreover, although the theory that liberalizing trade promotes economic growth has been a mainstay of economics for nearly 200 years, a multitude of efforts to prove it have come to nothing. While there have been a number of cross-country statistical studies purporting to demonstrate that economic openness contributes to economic growth, recent analysis has shown them to be fundamentally and systematically flawed (Rodriguez and Rodrik 2000). Moreover, the 'globalization' era of widespread trade liberalization (at least among developing countries) has in fact corresponded with a marked slowdown in global economic growth, coupled with an increase in inequality both between and within countries (Cornia et al., forthcoming), suggesting a still greater slowdown in poverty reduction.

In short, after nearly 200 years, the idea that trade liberalization promotes faster economic growth remains no more than an unproven economic theory, which appears inconsistent with the experience of the contemporary world, and is by no means uncontested even within the economic mainstream. This provides no basis on which to design an international trading system.

Do we need the WTO?

This prompts the question of whether the world needs a World Trade Organization, and if it does, what it should look like. The WTO's supporters regularly respond to its critics that such an organization is needed, because the institutional framework provided by a 'rules-based' international institution at least puts the developing countries in a stronger position to challenge the developed countries than the anarchy of a ruleless system.

In *theory*, this is plausible. The existence of the WTO *should* put some constraint on the ruthless pursuit of self-interest by the most powerful countries in the field of trade. In *practice*, however, the defence mechanisms that exist are largely inaccessible to, and ineffective in the hands of, most developing countries; and many aspects of the WTO merely provide the developed countries with new instruments to put pressure on developing countries in pursuit of their own commercial agendas.

- The WTO's *dispute settlement system* is supposed to protect the rights of the weak. In reality, the high resource and monetary costs of litigation are so prohibitive that only some developing countries use the system; and the only means of enforcing a finding – trade retaliation – is of little or no use to a developing country in dispute with a bigger country.

- The *veto on the accession process* allows developed countries to put intense pressure on developing countries wishing to join the WTO to liberalize all aspects of their trade (and some non-trade) policies, far beyond what is actually necessary for membership.
- The *TRIPs Agreement* has provided a basis to force many developing countries into adopting patent and copyright legislation in the interests of the major developed countries and the MNCs – and for intense political and economic pressure to adopt legislation that goes far beyond the requirements of the agreement itself ("TRIPs-plus").
- The *General Agreement on Trade in Services (GATS)* offers a means to make liberalization in service sectors almost irreversible, even by future governments, giving developed countries a new tool in prising open developing country markets.
- The *Agreement on Agriculture (AoA)* ties the hands of developing countries to protect themselves against dumping by the OECD countries. Without the agreement, countries would be able to put up their tariffs to defend themselves against the highly subsidized imports flooding their markets. With the AoA, their only defence mechanism – use of defensive tariffs – is curtailed.[7] The on-going negotiations call for yet another round of tariff cuts by developing countries, yet fail to address the problems of subsidized agricultural imports flooding their markets.

These are only some examples. A strong case can be made that these effects more than offset the benefits of the protection the WTO in theory provides.

In short, appealing as the idea that some kind of multilateral trade system might be in principle, it seems clear that the WTO as it currently operates does not constitute such a system. Far from setting fair trade rules to protect the interests of the weak, the WTO has been complicit in reinforcing the interests of the strong. Anarchy – the threat (real or supposed) used to justify the

WTO – may be bad for the weak, but the tyranny of the strong may be worse.

The global economic system today is extremely problematic and in the long run untenable because it subordinates the economies of developing countries, putting them in the position largely as providers of primary commodities. The terms of trade are tightly controlled and stacked against the South. Developing countries' leaders are promised the eventual fruits of economic integration by keeping markets open. For most, however, this process of 'integration' has resulted in the exploitation of their resources for the purpose of profits for Northern corporations – labour as well as natural resources – and market opening has and continues to destroy the industrial and agricultural production base in many countries. In short, this kind of integration, supported by the WTO today, has been a form of neo-colonialism with devastating consequences.

Conclusion

Power remains deeply entrenched in the WTO, and there is a real question mark over the ability of the WTO, as it currently operates, to reform itself from within, given the magnitude of the problems and the skewed power structure and vested interests involved. It is extremely unlikely that the WTO will radically change its current anti-democratic processes, or reorient itself to prioritize social objectives over corporate profits. Developed countries watch like hawks for any attempts to loosen their control over the decision-making process, as well as attempts at changing agreements in such a way that their access to developing country markets may be limited or their commercial interests otherwise damaged (as on TRIPs and public health, implementation issues and Special and Differential Treatment). The developed country governments have been intransigent in their opposition to such efforts, and use all the considerable means available to them, inside and outside the system, to frustrate or subvert them.

Some specific suggestions have been provided on how to democratize the WTO in the short term. In the longer term, much more fundamental changes are needed in the global economic system.

Attempts to reform the WTO in recent years – particularly evident from post-Seattle and post-Doha experiences – have run aground. The underlying structural problem, developing countries' economic dependency on the North, renders them extremely vulnerable to the power politics of the North; and the roots of this dependency lie very largely in the global economic system itself. The solution to this problem lies in part in allowing countries to determine the extent and terms of their integration or *non*-integration with the world economy, so that they can develop at their own pace and rhythm, and in their own direction.

In the present system, developing countries have one weapon at their disposal. They constitute 80 per cent of the membership in a (supposedly) one-member-one-vote organization; and, as Seattle demonstrated, if they stand together they can sometimes prevail.

The best place to start is in Cancun. Developing countries should block the launch of the 'new issues', as well as the deeper 'liberalization' of critical sectors such as agriculture, services and industrial products, since their ill-prepared markets will be prised open, and their domestic production capacity further eroded.

Clearly, sustaining the necessary unity among developing countries in the face of the pressures exerted on them would be far from easy. One former ambassador, however, offered a small ray of hope. In early 2003, reflecting on what he described as 'the real impact of the tactics implemented' by the Quad, he wrote to the authors:

> The Quad and their allies may have thought that by removing the troublemakers [certain developing country ambassadors] from Geneva they would have been able to push their part of the agenda without having anybody else pushing our issues ... But ... the real implications have been the gridlock of the multilateral trading system, because the battles around our issues continue in spite of the backtracking and the sabotage on [TRIPs] and health and on agriculture.
>
> The clear lesson for all to learn is this: after the Uruguay Round, the South has awakened, and no matter the pressure put on their ambassadors in Geneva; no matter the procedural sabotage; no

matter the mini-ministerials ... our issues will continue to be on the table, because they reflect our real concerns with respect to a multilateral trading system that in theory promotes free trade but that in practice preserves the protectionist measures and policies implemented by the developed countries to the detriment of our products and sectors of interest.

Failure to stop the new round, for example by blocking negotiations on the 'new issues', in Cancun or beyond, will lead only to the creation of more highly inequitable trade rules, which will be hatched behind closed doors and only among a small minority, and the majority will be 'persuaded' (in a variety of ways) to accept. The results of these anti-democratic processes will be a wider repertoire of devices used to subordinate developing countries' economies. When implemented, this will increase the contradictions within the WTO, as well as erode – quite possibly beyond repair – its legitimacy. As the number of people disenfranchized by this crudely unequal globalization project increases, global civil society resistance can only be expected to increase, and move on to a larger stage.

Notes

1. Many thanks to Sabrina Varma for her suggestions.
2. At this first ministerial, the working groups on investment, competition and government procurement were established only because the main negotiations were conducted in green room meetings, and the majority were excluded. The final package emerging out of the green room was than presented to the wider membership as a *fait accompli*.
3. Inside sources suggest that Mexico and India are among the countries opposed to greater external transparency in the WTO.
4. Delegates have complained that Secretariat staff misinterpreted their arguments during General Council Sessions in the minutes.
5. One example is a country which made some serious mistakes in its schedule of commitments under the GATS, and sought the Secretariat's advice on whether it was possible to modify the schedule during the present round of negotiations. While this is legally possible, the Secretariat told him that it was not, because GATS is about 'progressive liberalization'.
6. One ambassador related that his minister was asked by one of the Quad countries why they were in a grouping in which Cuba was a

member. Also, in an interview with the authors, a developed country negotiator said, 'What do countries like Malaysia have in common with Uganda?' (both being LMG members).

7. Many developing countries have accepted World Bank or IMF conditionalities that keep their tariff levels down. While these conditionalities are usually severe, unlike the WTO, they are not permanent.

Bibliography

Alden, E. (2002a) 'Zoellick Takes Trade Path to Africa', *Financial Times*, 13 February.

— (2002b) 'Countries Line Up to Sign US Trade Deals', *Financial Times*, 1 November.

AllAfrica.com (2002) 'Canada Cancels Over US$80 Million in Debt', 19 February. www.allafrica.com

Amosu, A. (2002) 'The AGOA Bargain is Unequal Says Oxfam', *SEATINI Bulletin*, Southern and Eastern African Trade, Information and Negotiations Institute, Vol. 5, No. 12, 30 June.

Bachmann, H. and K. Kwaku (1994) 'MIGA Roundtable on Foreign Direct Investment Policies in Africa: Proceedings and Lessons', Washington, DC: World Bank.

Baker, B. (2002) 'Pharma's Relentless Drive for Profits Explains US Trade Negotiations', Global Policy Forum, 10 December, www.globalpolicy.org.

Bangkok Post (1998a) 'Shattering the Rice Bowl: Thailand's Farmers are Suffering, will the "Nobility" Ever Pause to Care?', 25 June.

— (1998b) 'Northeastern Farmers' Groups Muster 2,000 for City Rally', 25 June.

— (1999a) 'Jobless Farmers Issue Dire Threat: Plan to Seize Forest Land to Make a Living', 25 January.

— (1999b) 'BAAC Has Extended B7.4 bn to Almost 124,000 Farmers', 8 February.

Bayliss, K. (2000) 'The World Bank and Privatisation: A Flawed Development Tool', Public Services International Research Unit, University of Greenwich, November.

Bello, W. (2000) *Why Reform of the WTO is the Wrong Agenda: Four Essays on Four Institutions – WTO, UNCTAD, the IMF and the World Bank*, Bangkok: Focus on the Global South, www.focusweb.org

— (2001) *Snapshots from Doha*, Bangkok: Focus on the Global South, 8 November, www.focusweb.org

Bello, W., S. Cunningham and Li Kheng Po (1999) *A Siamese Tragedy: Development and Disintegration in Modern Thailand*, London: Zed Books.

Bergsman, J. and X. Shen (1995) 'Foreign Direct Investment in Developing Countries: Progress and Problems', *Finance and Development*, Vol. 32, No. 4, pp. 6–8.

Berthelot, J. (2002) 'Domestic Agricultural Supports and Dumping: The Legal Fragility of Exemptions Provided for by the Agreement on Agriculture', The Doha Development Agenda and Beyond, WTO Symposium, 29 April to 1 May, http://www.solidarite.asso.fr/actualites/domestic.html

Blustein, P. (2001) 'Protest Group Softens Tone at WTO Talks', *Washington Post*, 11 November.

Choudry, A. (2001) 'Mike's Masquerades', *ZNet Commentary*, 25 August, www.jca.apc.org/asia-apec/msg01340.html

Clover, C. (2001) 'EU Farm Threat to Trade Talks', *Daily Telegraph*, 14 November.

Cooper, H. and G. Winestock (2001a) 'WTO Reaches Agreement on New Round of Talks but Years of Tortuous Wrangling Lie Ahead', *Wall Street Journal (Europe)*, 15 November.

— (2001b) 'WTO Deal in Doha Shows New Climate in the Trade World', *Asian Wall Street Journal*, 16 November.

Cooper, R. (2002) 'Reordering the World', Foreign Policy Centre, March.

Cornia, G. A., F. Zagonari, D. Woodward and N. Drager (forthcoming) 'Income Inequality in the Globalisation Era: Counting the Cost for Health', mimeo, Strategy Unit, WHO, Geneva.

Cronin, D. (2001) 'Trade Plans May Thwart "Green" Effort', *European Voice*, Vol. 7, No. 28, 12 July.

Das, B. L. (2002) 'The New WTO Work Programme', Third World Network, 8 April, www.twnside.org.sg/title/das.doc

de Jonquières, G. (2001a) 'Trade Talks Falter as France Blocks Farm Subsidy Deal', *Financial Times*, 13 November.

— (2001b) 'Poll Backs Need for Trade Round', *Financial Times*, 8 November.

— (2001c) 'All-Night Haggling in Doha Ends in Agreement', *Financial Times*, 15 November.

— (2002) 'Moore Speaks Out on WTO Rules', *Financial Times*, 18 February.

DG Trade (2001) 'Trade Facilitation: Towards Better Procedures', European Commission, September, http://europa.eu.int/comm/trade/miti/tradefac/index_en.htm

Economist, The (1999) 'The Human Face of Globalisation', 28 August.

— (2001) 'Who Elected the WTO?' Survey: Globalisation, 27 September.

— (2002a) 'Malaysia – Silencing the Critics', 27 April.

— (2002b) 'Trade Disputes'. Special Report, 11 May.

— (2002c) 'Promoting the Noble Cause of Commerce', 3 August.

— (2002d) 'Terror in South-East Asia – the Elusive Enemy', 3 August.

— (2002e) 'Distant Friends', 18 May.

Einarsson, P. (2002) 'Agricultural Trade Policy as if Food Security and Ecological Sustainability Mattered: Review and Analysis of Alternative Proposals for the Renegotiation of the WTO Agreement on Agriculture', Globala Studier-NR5, Forum Syd, Sweden, November.

European Commission (1996) 'EC Calls for Sharper European Trade Policy', Press Release No. 9/96, 14 February.

— (2002) 'GATS 2000: Request from the EC and Its Member States to Nigeria', D(2002) 700829, 30 June.

FAO (2000) 'Agriculture, Trade and Food Security: Issues and Options in the WTO Negotiations from the Perspective of Developing Countries, Vol. II: Country Case Studies', Rome: Food and Agriculture Organization.

— (forthcoming) 'Implementation of the Agreement on Agriculture in Thailand', Rome: Food and Agriculture Organization.

FICCI (2001) 'Special Address on "Doha and India: Looking Back and Ahead" by Prof. Jagdish Bhagwati', Federation of Indian Chambers of Commerce and Industry, New Delhi.

Financial Times (2002) 'Egypt Survey', 26 June.

Finger, M. and P. Schuler (2000) 'Implementation of Uruguay Round Commitments: The Development Challenge', *World Economy*, Vol. 23, No. 4.

Focus on the Global South (2002) '150 NGOs Challenge Democracy Deficit at the WTO and Call for an End to Exclusive Meetings', press release, 14 November.

Gedda, G. (2002) 'Powell: Progress with Indonesia', Associated Press Asia, 3 August.

Gibbs, M. (1998) 'Special and Differential Treatment in the Context of Globalization', note presented to the G15 Symposium on Special and Differential Treatment in the WTO Agreements, New Delhi: UNCTAD, 10 December.

Guardian, the (2002) 'Imperial Delusions', editorial, 29 March.

Hormeku, T. (2001) 'Invasion of WTO by "Green Men"', Third World Network, 10 November.

Ibharuneafe, S. (2001) 'Labour Leader, Adams Oshiomhole, Says Nigeria's Membership of World Trade Organisation Would Affect Its Economy', *Newswatch* (Nigeria), Vol. 34, No. 8, 27 August.

ICTSD (2001a) *Bridges Weekly Trade Digest*, Vol. 5, No. 37A, International Centre for Trade and Sustainable Development, Geneva, 1 November.

— (2001b) *Bridges Weekly Trade Digest*, Vol. 5, No. 38, International Centre for Trade and Sustainable Development, Geneva, 6 November.

— (2001c) *Bridges Daily Update*, Vol. 1, No. 2, International Centre for Trade and Sustainable Development, Geneva, 11 November.

— (2002a) *Bridges Weekly Trade Digest*, Vol. 6, No. 6, International Centre for Trade and Sustainable Development, Geneva, 21 February.

— (2002b) *Bridges Weekly Trade Digest*, Vol. 6, No. 27, International Centre for Trade and Sustainable Development, Geneva, 17 July.

— (2002c) *Bridges Weekly Trade Digest*, Vol. 6, No. 21, International Centre for Trade and Sustainable Development, Geneva, 4 June.

— (2002d) *Bridges Weekly Trade Digest*, Vol. 6, No.10, International Centre for Trade and Sustainable Development, Geneva, 19 March.

IMF (2002) *Annual Report, 2002*, Washington DC: International Monetary Fund.

International Trade Daily (2001) 'Developing Countries Settle for Less', 15 November.

— (2002a) 'WTO Requests for Services Liberalisation Begin: U.S. Targets 127 Member Countries', 5 July.

— (2002b) 'Supachai Cites "Mixed" Results, Expresses Concerns for Cancun Meeting', 5 December.

Jubilee Plus (2002) 'Tanzania Reaches Completion Point – but Her Debt Remains Unsustainable', www.jubileeplus.org, 31 May.

Keet, D. (2001) 'South Africa's Official Position and Role in Promoting the World Trade Organisation and a New Round of Multilateral Trade Negotiations', Alternative Information and Development Center, Cape Town, South Africa, May.

Khan, F. (2002) 'EU Upbeat at the WTO Deal to Ease Access to Cheap Drugs for Poor', Inter Press Service, 2 December, www.aegis.com/news/ips/2002/IP021205.html

Khan, J. (2001) 'Trade Talks Hinge on Finesse of the US', *New York Times*, 10 November.

Khor, M. (2001) *Doha Meet Kicks off to a 'Democratic' Start*, Third World Network, 10 November.

— (2002) 'The WTO, the Post-Doha Agenda and the Future of the Trade System: A Development Perspective', Penang: Third World Network.

Kwa, A. (2002a) 'Supachai and Harbinson Endorse Exclusive WTO Meetings', Third World Network, 2 December, http://www.twnside.org.sg/title/5250b.htm

— (2002b) *Power Politics in the WTO*, Bangkok: Focus on the Global South.

Lamy, P. (2000) *Speech at the European Services Forum International Conference on GATS 2000 Negotiations*, Brussels, 27 November.

Love, J. (2002) 'Why the TRIPS and Public Health Talks at WTO Broke Down', *South–North Development Monitor (SUNS)*, Third World Network, No. 5246, 29 November.

Mann, M. (2001) 'Fischler Hails Doha Meeting as "a Magnificent Success"', *Financial Times*, 16 November.

Maran, M. (2001) 'WTO: A New Beginning after Doha', Speech at the India Economic Summit, 4 December.

Monitor, The (2002) 'Is US taking Museveni for a Ride with AGOA?', Editorial (Kampala), 28 April, http://allafrica.com/stories/200204 280037.html

Moore, M. (2002) 'Development Needs More than Trade', Personal View, *Financial Times*, 18 February.

Narayanan, S. (2000) 'Statement by Ambassador Narayanan of India at the 4th Session of the Seminar on Special and Differential Treatment for Developing Countries, Organised Under the Auspices of WTO Committee on Trade and Development at Geneva, on 7 March 2000, Geneva', WTO.

NEABC (2002) 'US Trade Representative Visit to Africa (Kenya, South Africa, and Botswana)', New England–Africa Business Conference, Worcester, Massachusetts, 21 May.

Nordström, H. and S. Vaughan (1999) 'Trade and Environment', Special Studies, No. 4, WTO.

OECD (2000) *OECD Agricultural Outlook 2000–05*, Paris: Organization for Economic Cooperation and Development.

Ong'wen, O. (2002) 'Nepad: Planting Sterile Seeds', www.econewsafrica. org, 24 June.

Oxfam International (2002) *Rigged Rules and Double Standards: Trade, Globalisation and the Fight Against Poverty*, Oxfam International, March.

Permanent Mission of the Netherlands in Geneva (2001) '1001 Nights in Doha: A Guided Tour Through the Draft Ministerial Declarations of the Fourth Ministerial Conference of the WTO', 5 November.

Pitsuwan, S. (2002) 'Dr Supachai's Long and Winding Road to Geneva', *Bangkok Post*, 25 August.

Raghavan, C. (2001a) 'Anger, Frustration, Marginalization, Helplessness and Alienation', *South–North Development Monitor (SUNS)*, Third World Network, No. 5006, 8 November.

— (2001b) 'Building New Trade Architecture (on Doha's Desert Sands?)', *South–North Development Monitor (SUNS)*, Third World Network, No. 5012, 19 November.

— (2002a) 'One-Size-Fits-All System Needs Flexible Procedures for Itself', *South–North Development Monitor (SUNS)*, Third World Network, No. 5119, 16 May.

— (2002b) 'Ricupero, Two LDC Ministers Debunk US Zero Tariff Proposals', *South–North Development Monitor (SUNS)*, Third World Network, No. 5248, 4 December.

— (2002c) 'Investment Rules Need Investors and Home Government Obligations', *South–North Development Monitor (SUNS)*, Third World Network, No. 5250, 9 December.

— (2002d) 'Trade: Behind the Talks on Transparency in Government Procurement', *South–North Development Monitor (SUNS)*, Third World Network, No. 5130, 3 June.

— (2002e) 'WTO Goods Council Discuss Trade Facilitation', *Third World Economics*, Third World Network, No. 281, May.

— (2002f) 'Trade: Differences Unresolved on Implementing TRIPS and Public Health', *South–North Development Monitor (SUNS)*, Third World Network, No. 5243, 27 November.

— (2002g) 'Trade: TRIPS Talks on Implementing Doha Run into More Problems', *South–North Development Monitor (SUNS)*, Third World Network, No. 5240, 22 November.

— (2002h) 'Trade: Armenia's Accession Cleared, TRIPS and CTD Consultations Continue', *South–North Development Monitor (SUNS)*, Third World Network, No. 5253, 12 December.

— (2002i) 'Trade: Scrooge's Gift for the Third World at WTO', *South–North Development Monitor (SUNS)*, Third World Network, No. 5260, 23 December.

— (2002j) 'Like Minded Group Calls for Principles and Procedures for Ministerial Conferences', *South–North Development Monitor (SUNS)*, Third World Network, No. 5117, 14 May.

Reddy, C. R. (2001) 'Trading Illusions', *The Hindu* (India), 24 November.

Rege, V. (1998) 'Developing Countries and Negotiations in the WTO', *Third World Economics*, No. 191, 16–31 August.

— (2000) 'WTO Procedures for Decision Making: Experience of Their Operation and Suggestions for Improvement', Background Paper, Commonwealth Secretariat, 21 January.

Rodriguez, F. and D. Rodrik (2001) 'Trade Policy and Economic Growth: A Skeptic's Guide to the Cross-National Evidence', in Ben Bernanke and Kenneth S. Rogoff (eds), *Macroeconomics Annual 2000*, Cambridge, MA: MIT Press/NBER.

Sexton, S. (2001) 'Trading Health Care Away? GATS, Public Services and Privatisation', *South Bulletin*, No. 15, South Centre, July.

Sharma, S. (2001) 'Mockery of the Multilateral Trading System: Who is Accountable?', Institute for Agriculture and Trade Policy, Geneva, 29 October.

— (2002a) *Geneva Update*, No. 9, IATP, Geneva, December.

— (2002b) 'Towards an Empty Development Round', *Geneva Update*, No. 10, IATP, Geneva, 21 December.

— (2002c), 'Update on the Industrial Action at the WTO: The Staff Revolts!', IATP, Geneva, 6 December.

Shukla, S. P. (2002) 'The Doha Debacle'. In CSGSTD: *WTO Doha Ministerial Conference: Implications for India*, New Delhi: Centre for Study of Global Trade System and Development, January.

Skidelsky, R. (2000) *John Maynard Keynes – Fighting for Britain, 1937 to 1946*, New York: Penguin USA.

South Centre (1999) 'Issues Regarding the Review of the WTO Dispute Settlement Mechanism', Trade-Related Agenda, Development and Equity Working Paper No. 1, South Centre, February.

— (2001) *Transmission of Recommendations by the General Council to the Ministerial Conference: South Centre Analysis*, South Centre, November.

South China Morning Post (2002) 'Freedom's Quiet Advocate', 29 April.

Stokes, B. (2000) 'Now Here's a Hot Seat', *National Journal*, Washington, Vol. 32, No. 10, 4 March.

Tandon, Y. (2002) 'A Brief History of Capacity Building Attempts within the WTO 1994 to 2001', *SEATINI Bulletin*, Southern and Eastern African Trade, Information and Negotiations Institute,Vol. 5, No. 12, 30 June.

TRIG (2001) 'WTO Ministers Close Ranks on New "Development" Round', *Washington Trade Daily*, Trade Reports International Group, Vol. 10, No. 206, 15 October.

TWN (2001) 'Comments by Developing Countries at the WTO General Council Meeting (31 Oct.–1 Nov.) on the Revised Draft WTO Ministerial Declaration (which will be Discussed at Doha)', Third World Network, Penang, Malaysia.

UN (2001) 'General Assembly Fifty-Sixth Session, 44th Plenary Meeting, Saturday 10 November 2001, 9 a.m., New York', Official Records, A/56/PV.44, United Nations, New York.

UNCTAD (1999) 'Assessment of Services of Developing Countries: Summary of Findings', UNCTAD/ITCD/TSB/7, 26 August.

USDA (2002) 'U.S. Proposal for Global Agricultural Trade Reform', US Department of Agriculture, 25 July.

US Department of State (2001) 'USTR Zoellick at WTO Mini-Ministerial in Mexico City', *Washington File*, 7 September.

USTR (1997) 'USTR Strategic Plan, FY1997–FY2002', Office of the United States Trade Representative, 30 September.

— (1999a) 'Press Briefing: U.S. Trade Representative Charlene Barshefsky; Secretary of Agriculture Dan Glickman; Acting Chair, Council on Environmental Quality George Frampton; National Economic Council Adviser Gene Sperling – World Trade Organization Conference, Seattle, Washington', Office of the United States Trade Representative, 2 December.

— (1999b) 'Closing Remarks of Charlene Barshefsky, Closing Plenary', Office of the United States Trade Representative, 3 December.

— (2001) 'USTR Robert B. Zoellick meets with President Megawati to Discuss Strengthening US–Indonesian Ties', Press Release, Office of the United States Trade Representative, 19 September.

— (2002a) 'US and West African Nations Sign an Agreement Promoting Trade', Press Release, Office of the United States Trade Representative, 24 April.

— (2002b) *2002 Comprehensive Report on U.S. Trade and Investment Policy Toward Sub-Saharan Africa and Implementation of the African Growth and Opportunities Act*, Office of the United States Trade Representative, May.

— (2002c) 'Ambassador Robert B. Zoellick, Press Statement, Residence of President Megawati Sukarnoputri', Press Release, Office of the United States Trade Representative, 7 April.

Van Dyke, B. and J. B. Weiner (1997) *A Handbook for Obtaining Documents from the World Trade Organization*, Centre for International Environmental Law, Geneva.

WDM (2001) 'Doha Number-Crunching Reveals Heavyweights EU and US Overwhelm Poorest Countries', Press Release, World Development Movement, 11 November, www.wdm.org.uk/presrel/current/number.htm.

— (2002) 'New WTO Chief Plans Rules to Limit Corporate Influence on Trade Negotiations', *SEATINI Bulletin*, Southern and Eastern African Trade, Information and Negotiations Institute, Vol. 5, No. 12, 30 June.

Wells, L. (1999) 'Private Foreign Investment in Infrastructure: Managing Non-Commercial Risk', Paper for Conference, Private Infrastructure for Development: Confronting Political and Regulatory Risks, Rome, 8–10 September.

WHO/WTO (2002) *WTO Agreements and Public Health: A Joint Guide by the WHO and the WTO Secretariat*, Geneva: WHO and WTO.

Williams, I. (2002) 'The US Hit List at the United Nations', Global Affairs Commentary, *Foreign Policy in Focus*, 30 April.

Woodward, D. (2001) *The Next Crisis? Direct and Equity Investment in Developing Countries*, London: Zed Books.

WSJ (2001) 'WTO Members Stall on Conditions for Trade Talks: Poor States Set Tough Stance Despite Warnings to Act Fast', *Wall Street Journal (Europe)*, 31 July.

WTO (1996) 'WTO Rules of Procedure for Ministerial and General Council Meetings', Document No.WT/L/161, 25 July.

— (1999a) 'Recent Developments in Services Trade: Overview and Assessment', Background Note by the Secretariat, Council for Trade in Services, Document No. S/C/W/94, 9 February.

— (1999b) 'Council for Trade in Services, Report of the Meeting Held on 21 September 1999, Note by the Secretariat', Document No. S/C/M/39, 15 October.

— (1999c) *The Legal Texts: the Results of the Uruguay Round of Multilateral Trade Negotiations*, Cambridge: Cambridge University Press.

— (2000a) 'Council for Trade in Services in Special Session – Report of the Meeting Held on 26 May 2000', Note by the Secretariat, Document No. S/CSS/M/3, 26 June.

— (2000b) 'General Council: Minutes of Meetings Held in the Centre William Rappard on 17 and 19 July', Document No. WT/GC/M/57, 14 September.

— (2000c) 'Communication from Slovenia, Bulgaria, Czech Republic, Poland and Slovak Republic: Note on Assessment on Trade in Services in Certain Transition Economies', Trade in Services Council Special Session, Document No. S/CSS/W/18, 5 December.

— (2001a) 'The Generalised System of Preferences: A Preliminary Analysis of the GSP Schemes in the Quad', Note by the Secretariat, Document No. WT/COMTD/W/93, 5 October.

— (2001b) 'Trade Facilitation: Cutting Red Tape at the Border', Doha WTO Ministerial 2001 Briefing Note, WTO, http://www.wto.org/english/thewto_e/minist_e/min01_e/brief_e/brief15_e.htm

— (2001c) 'Establishment of the Trade Negotiations Committee (TNC) and Related Issues – Communication from Cuba, Dominican Republic, Egypt, Honduras, Kenya, Pakistan, Tanzania, Uganda and Zimbabwe', Document No. WT/GC/58, 21 December.

— (2001d) *Trading into the Future*, Geneva: WTO (2nd edn, March).

— (2001e) 'Preparatory Process in Geneva and Negotiating Procedure at the Ministerial Conferences: Communication from Cuba, Dominican

Republic, Egypt, Honduras, India, Indonesia, Jamaica, Kenya, Malaysia, Mauritius, Pakistan, Sri Lanka, Tanzania, Uganda, and Zimbabwe', Document No. WT/GC/W/471, 24 April.

— (2002a) 'General Council – Minutes of 9–20 December 2001', Document No. WT/G/M/72, 6 February.

— (2002b) 'Trade Negotiations Committee – Minutes of Meeting Held in the Centre William Rappard on 28 January and 1 February, 2002', Document No. TN/C/M/1, 14 February.

— (2002c) *International Trade Statistics, 2002*, Geneva: WTO.

— (2002d) 'Working Group on the Interaction Between Trade and Competition Policy – Report on Meeting of 23–24 April 2002', Document No. WT/WGTCP/M/17, 26 June.

— (2002e) 'Preparatory Process in Geneva and Negotiating Procedure at the Ministerial Conferences', Document No. WT/GC/471, 24 April.

— (2002f) 'Trade Facilitation: Article X of GATT on the Publication and Administration of Trade Regulations – Communication from the European Communities', Document No. G/C/W/363, 12 April.

— (2002g) 'Preparatory Process in Geneva and Negotiating Process at Ministerial Conferences: Communication from Australia; Canada; Hong Kong, China; Korea; Mexico; New Zealand; Singapore; Switzerland', Document No. WT/GC/W/447, 28 June.

— (2002h) 'Procedures for the Appointment of Directors-General Communication from the Chairman – Revision', Document No. WT/GC/W/482/Rev. 1, 6 December.

— (2002i) 'Procedures for the Circulation and Derestriction of WTO Documents: Decision of 14 May 2002', Document No. WT/L/452, 16 May.

— (2002j) 'Organisation of Negotiations Envisaged in the Doha Ministerial Declaration: Communication from Cuba, Dominican Republic, Honduras, India, Indonesia, Jamaica, Kenya, Malaysia, Pakistan, Sri Lanka, Tanzania, Uganda and Zimbabwe', Document No. TN/C/W/2, 29 January.

— (2002k) 'Statement by the Chairman of the General Council', Document No. TN/C/1, 4 February.

— (2003a) 'Paragraph 6 of the Doha Declaration on the TRIPs Agreement and Public Health: Communication from the European Communities and Their Member States', Document No. JOB(03)/9, 24 January.

— (2003b) 'Negotiations on Agriculture: First Draft of Modalities for the Further Commitments', Committee on Agriculture, Special Session, Document No. JOB(03)/23, 12 February.

WWF, CIEL, IATP, ActionAid, FoE International and Oxfam International (2001) *Open Letter on Institutional Reforms in the WTO*, joint open letter, October.

Yu, V. (2002a) 'WTO Agenda: Moving Forward?', *Geneva Update*, IATP, Geneva, No. 8.

— (2002b) 'Background Note on Implementation-Related Issues: History, Implementation and Negotiating Strategy for Developing Countries', South Centre, 14 November.

Zoellick, R. (2001) 'Countering Terror with Trade', *Washington Post*, 20 September.

Index

167–8, 169, 209, 223, 230, 249, 253

Bretton Woods negotiations, 57, 74, 80–3, 88, 114–15, 138, 155; prelude to, 51–3

Brown, Edward Eagle, 83

Bryn, Kare, 75, 279

Bulgaria, 33

bullying, within WTO, 148–9

Burkina Faso, 174

Bush, George, Snr, 58, 84

Bush, George W., 54, 63, 84–5, 110, 118, 138, 139, 166, 172, 175, 247

Bustani, Jose Mauricio, 161

Cairns Group, 24, 103, 105, 140, 169, 228, 258, 259, 263

Cameroon, 26, 157

Camilo, Federico Cuello, 95, 98, 190

Canada, 17, 21, 23, 24, 58, 59, 64, 82, 86, 90, 103, 104, 138, 169, 180, 202, 223, 239, 254, 264, 277

Canada Debt Initiative, 180

Cancun ministerial meeting, 76, 109, 111, 112, 124, 125, 132, 229, 230, 233, 235, 237, 240, 242, 244, 264, 265, 305, 306

capacity-building, 291–2

Chandrasekhar, K.M., 136, 245, 257

Chidyausiku, Boniface, 75

Chile, 24, 54, 66, 90, 104, 108, 136, 223; country profile of, 164; exports to EC, 164

China, 36, 52, 155, 223, 226, 230, 240, 249, 251; accession to WTO, 4, 93, 118, 207

Chiquita, 157

Chirac, Jacques, 97, 102, 141

circles of power, 57

Clay, Henry, 115

Clinton, Bill, 54, 84, 161

coalition building, 299–300

Codex Alimentarius, 45

Colombia, 24, 64, 94, 108, 137, 230

Commission on Intellectual Property Rights (UK), 249, 255

Committee of the Whole (COW), 91, 92, 94, 97, 102, 104, 105

Committee on Trade and Development (WTO), 125

Common Market for Eastern and Southern Africa (COMESA), 169, 179

competition, 40–2, 241; rules governing, 40, 41

conditionalities, 29

consensus, on Trade Negotiations Committee, 222–4

consultations, on Trade Negotiations Committee, 222–4

Consumer Project Technology, 68

continuous negotiations, avoidance of, 281

Cooper, Robert, 270

copyright, 3

corruption, 153

Costa Rica, 24, 108, 136, 223; country profile of, 164

Côte d'Ivoire, 26, 174

Cotonou Agreement *see* ACP waiver

Couchepin, Pascal, 90

Council for Trade in Goods (WTO), 17, 43, 94, 106, 156

Council for Trade in Services (WTO), 17, 34, 251

Crédit Lyonnais, 85

Cuba, 23, 52, 60, 63, 93, 102, 109, 136, 165, 240, 249

customs transactions, 43, 44

Czech Republic, 33

Czechoslovakia, 52

Das, Bhagirath Lal, 35, 118, 121, 260

About the authors

Fatoumata Jawara is a freelance international trade and development analyst, currently working on the political dynamics of the World Trade Organization and pursuing a masters' degree at Cornell University. Prior to this, she was International Economics and Poverty Officer at the Catholic Institute for International Relations (CIIR), and adviser to the Manicaland Development Association in Zimbabwe (1997 to 1999). From 1992 to 1994 she was Assistant Project Co-ordinator for the Women in Development Horticultural Programme sponsored by UNDP and the Ministry of Agriculture in The Gambia. She was a nominated member of the Gambia Women's Council.

Aileen Kwa is a trade analyst with Focus on the Global South, a policy research and activist organization. She is currently based in Geneva, tracks WTO issues pertaining to developing countries and sends out analyses to civil society groups on the problems developing countries are experiencing in the negotiating process, as well as the implications of issues being negotiated. She is an expert in the area of agriculture and the WTO and has provided Geneva-based developing country delegates to the WTO with research and technical support in this area. She is the author of 'Power Politics in the WTO' and numerous articles on trade negotiations. Prior to her work at Focus, she worked for the Centre for Environment, Gender and Development, an Asian regional women's NGO.

INFORMATION TECHNOLOGY FOR THE SOCIAL SCIENTIST

SOCIAL RESEARCH TODAY

Series editor
Martin Bulmer

Additional titles to include:

Information technology for the social scientist

Edited by

Raymond M. Lee
Royal Holloway, University of London

UCL
PRESS

Throughout this book, product names are trade marks of their respective owners.

First published in 1995 by UCL Press
UCL Press Limited
University College London
Gower Street
London WC1E 6BT

The name of University College London (UCL) is a registered
trade mark used by UCL Press with the consent of the owner.

Isbns: 1-85728-280-9 HB
        1-85728-281-7 PB

British Library Cataloguing-in-Publication Data
A CIP catalogue record for this book is available from the British Library.

Library of Congress Cataloging-in-Publication Data

Information technology for the social scientist / edited by Raymond M.
   Lee.
      p.   cm. — (Social research today series : No. 7)
      Includes bibliographical references and index.
      ISBN 1-85728-280-9 (hb) : $65.00. — ISBN 1-85728-281-7 (pb) :
   $27.50
      1. Social sciences—Statistical methods—computer programs.
   2. Social sciences—Research—Statistical methods. 3. Information
   technology.   I. Lee, Raymond M., 1946–   . II. Series.
   HA32.I53 1994 1995
   300'285—dc20   94-39456
                                                        CIP

Typeset in Palatino.
Printed and bound by
Biddles Ltd., Guildford and King's Lynn, England.

Contents

CONTENTS

Notes on contributors

Angela Dale is Director of the Census Microdata Unit at the university of Manchester and Professor of Quantitative Social Research. She has held posts at the University of Surrey and City University and has written extensively about issues surrounding the secondary analysis of survey data.

Michael Fischer is Director of the Centre for Social Anthropology and Computing at the University of Kent at Canterbury. Since 1981 he has used computers in nine ethnographic projects in Pakistan and the Cook Islands. Future research will focus on documenting the links between the ethnographic past and present.

Mike Fisher is Senior Lecturer in the School of Applied Social Studies, University of Bristol. His interest in computers and social science arose out of an instinct for survival during data collection and analysis on five major research projects in social welfare. He is currently directing an ESRC-funded project on computer-assisted qualitative data analysis, and researching community care.

David Gilbert is Lecturer in Geography at Royal Holloway University of London and is the author of *Class, community and collective action* (Clarendon, 1992), a social history of community organization in British mining. He has written extensively both on the history and sociology of mining, and on the development of geographical computing. He has worked as a commercial database programmer, and designed the customized cartographic and information system for use with the Local Labour Markets Database at Queen Mary and Westfield, University of London.

Nigel Gilbert is Professor of Sociology at the University of Surrey. His research interests are broadly in the areas of interaction between sociology and computer science, and he has written on sociological approaches to human-computer interaction, expert systems and speech understanding systems. He is co-editor with Jim Doran of *Simulating societies: the computer simulation of social phenomena* (UCL Press, 1993) and has written and edited nine other books on various aspects of social research methods, statistics and human–computer interaction.

Anders Hansen is a lecturer in mass communication at the Centre for Mass Communication Research, University of Leicester. His main research interests include science communication, journalistic practices and media roles in relation to science and environmental issues. He has a long-standing interest in methods for the analysis of media content, including the application of information technology to traditional techniques such as "content-analysis". His work in these areas has been supported by the Economic and Social Research Council and the European Commission. Publications arising from his work on media, science and environmental issues include the book *The mass media and environmental issues* (Leicester University Press, 1993).

Noel Heather is Lecturer in Arts Computing, Royal Holloway University of London. His research interest lie in the areas of literary and linguistic computing, cybernetics and text, and in Renaissance studies. He has been a consultant on information technology to a number of government agencies in the United Kingdom.

Raymond M. Lee is Reader in Social Research Methods in the Department of Social Policy and Social Science, Royal Holloway University of London. His research interests are in research methodology, the sociology of labour markets and the sociology of religion. His most recent work has been concerned with the methodological problems and issues associated with research on "sensitive" topics and with the impact of new technologies on research methods in the social sciences. He is the author of *Doing research on sensitive topics,* and edited *Researching sensitive topics* (with

Claire Renzetti) and *Using computers in qualitative research*, (with Nigel Fielding).

Wilma Mangabeira has a PhD in Sociology from the London School of Economics. She is a Lecturer in the Centre for Research in Innovation, Culture and Technology at Brunel University. She specializes in the sociology of labour and research methodology. She has recently published a major study of union politics and democracy in Brazil.

Tony Manners is a Principal Social Survey Officer at the Social Survey Division of the Office of Population Censuses and Surveys. He led Britain's first implementation of CAPI and CATI for a national household survey, the Labour Force Survey. In 1991 he was the European member of a software panel advising the US Bureau of the Census on computer assisted interviewing issues. Since 1992 he has managed the Family Expenditure Survey, which moves to CAPI in April 1994. He is technical co-ordinator for CAI matters at OPCS, and co-ordinator of the International Blaise Users' Group.

Jean Martin is an Assistant Director of the Social Survey Division of the Office of Population Censuses and Surveys which she joined in 1972. She has been responsible for designing and carrying out several major government surveys. From 1988 to 1991 she was seconded to the Joint Centre for Survey Methods where she carried out research on survey methods, including studies of computer assisted interviewing. Currently she has responsibility for several financial surveys, for survey methodology and sampling, and for co-ordinating the move of all OPCS surveys to computer assisted interviewing.

Nicholas Rossiter is Lecturer in Computing Science at Newcastle University. His research interests include the handling of legal and other texts in databases and knowledge-based systems, and the development of textbases with a sound formal basis. Prior to 1989, he was programming advisor in the Computing Laboratory at Newcastle University with special responsibility for advising users on the implementation of database projects. From 1987–89 he was chair of the Inter-University Software Committee group for database software and a member of their group for information retrieval.

Ray Thomas is Senior Lecturer in Economics in the Faculty of Social Sciences at the Open University. He is a member of course production teams on information technology and social research methods.

Clare Ward is a Research Fellow in the Social Statistics Research Unit at City University. She is currently working on a project funded by the Joseph Rowntree Foundation to analyze women's economic dependence using the longitudinal National Child Development Study.

CHAPTER 1

Information technology for the social scientist: an introduction

Raymond M. Lee

The work of social scientists is being transformed by the increasing use of new technologies. For thirty years, the computer in the social sciences was traditionally a tool for analyzing quantitative data. Now, however, massive increases in computing power at declining cost put onto the desks of users ways of dealing with topics and problems thought traditionally to lie beyond the scope of computers (Brent 1993, Blank 1991). Indeed, few areas of research, teaching or scholarship now remain untouched by developments in information technology. This book seeks to examine some of these new developments, to bring them to a wider audience, including potential new users, and to assess their possible impact, good or bad, on how social scientists go about their work.

Transformative technologies of social research refer to new means of representing and manipulating information, in particular the use of computer technology to provide (a) improved tools for the acquisition, storage and management of data, (b) means for representing conventional media forms – numbers, text, audio, video, pictures – into a single (digital) medium, and (c) computer networks which facilitate communication with other individuals and within teams, and which also permit access to information resources that can be widely dispersed. Such technologies would include, in no particular order: computer assisted data collection, computer analysis of text and of visual materials, large scale database systems, new developments in statistical analysis, modelling and simulation, artificial intelligence techniques, large scale computer networks, data archives, hypertext, multimedia and visualization techniques (see, e.g., Blank 1991, Fischer 1994).

Each chapter of this book contains a state-of-the-art review of a recent and interesting development in the application of information technology to the work of social scientists. The attempt has been made to present this information in a way which is both comprehensive and comprehensible. Although it is impossible to eradicate technical language completely, contributors have tried as far as possible to keep their contributions free of jargon and "technospeak". Hopefully, therefore, the book will appeal to those who are relative computer novices as well as those who wish to widen their knowledge of current and possible future developments. It may also be useful on undergraduate and postgraduate courses on information technology taken by students in the social sciences. Increasingly such students are expected to have a basic familiarity with information technology and to be familiar with the basic computer tools in their discipline. To date, however, there has been a dearth of suitable texts which look broadly at computing developments in the social sciences.

The chapter by Mike Fisher of the University of Bristol is designed to provide an overview of desktop tools for the social scientist. In particular, he identifies a number of key areas where computers are useful: research management, maintaining contact with research participants, writing, and in the presentation of material both in print and before an audience. For each, Fisher describes appropriate software tools and some of the pitfalls in their use. Extending the craftwork metaphor with which he starts the chapter, Fisher closes, very appropriately, with a section on how computer tools may best be used wisely, safely and productively. Fisher's chapter has much in it which will be of use to social scientists whatever their level of computer literacy. Those who are new to computing or perhaps a little intimidated by it will also find a reassuring introduction to the possibility of harnessing computer technology to enhance individual productivity.

A number of contributors to this book make reference to the usefulness of electronic mail and to the ability to access by electronic means information held at remote sites. Indeed, this book itself provides one example of the use of such technologies. A good deal of its initiation, organization and preparation was carried out electronically. A number of contributors responded to a request for papers put out on an electronic bulletin board and much of the editorial work of negotiating deadlines, reviewing the manuscripts and maintaining contact with authors was done by electronic mail. To take another example, students on a course run by Noel

Heather (co-author of the chapter on expert systems in this volume) analyze a text by Emile Durkheim as an exercise, the machine-readable version of which was originally retrieved by ftp (file transfer protocol) from a site in Canada.

Many social scientists appear intrigued and puzzled in equal measure by such developments, especially since the "information super-highway" has become a buzz term for media pundits and politicians alike. In this context the chapter by Ray Thomas is a useful one. Thomas looks at the kinds of information available to researchers through on-line databases and on CD-ROM, and examines the ways in which computers increasingly mediate communication between social scientists. After briefly recounting the development of computer based methods of information retrieval, Thomas reviews a major use of such technologies, the retrieval of bibliographical and text based material and the increasing access to library resources through worldwide computer networks. He then looks at the availability of statistical and administrative data in electronic form. (See also David Gilbert's chapter on geographical information systems.) Thomas concludes his chapter with a discussion of how electronic mail, electronic bulletin boards and list servers are used by social scientists to communicate and exchange information with one another. Given the rapid pace of change such a chapter can only be indicative of the range of material available through forms of electronic dissemination and communication. For those unfamiliar with such developments, however, Thomas provides a basis for exploring the possibilities opened up by on-line retrieval and computer mediated communication.

In his chapter on desktop tools Mike Fisher gives an instance of how he used a database to track participants in a research study over a period of time. Databases have many uses in social research. They are best-adapted to situations where the researcher needs to store, order, update, retrieve and display information for a relatively large number of structured records. Databases are often used, therefore, to deal with bibliographic references, contact records and the like where, on the one hand, the data are, for example, not amenable to detailed statistical analysis but are more ordered than unstructured text on the other. There are various approaches to the design of databases depending on how data are structured and manipulated within them. Nick Rossiter describes the various types of database currently available and evaluates the strengths and weaknesses of each approach. Although the details of Rossiter's account are sometimes intricate, he shows with examples from a social historical study and from political science research how databases can handle large amounts of disparate data to answer complex research questions.

The idea that a computer is predominantly a tool for the analysis of data dies hard. Increasingly, however, researchers are exploring ways in which the computer can be used to collect data, particularly in survey research. Jean Martin and Tony Manners have been at the forefront of these developments in Britain. In their chapter Martin & Manners explore the development of computer assisted personal interviewing (CAPI). Increasingly survey researchers no longer go out into the field armed with a clipboard. Instead they carry portable computers loaded with special software. This software allows them to enter directly responses to questions displayed on the computer's screen. The program also automatically manages question-skips and edit-checks, making the process of data collection less prone to error.

Martin & Manners begin their article with a brief recapitulation of existing work on CATI, computer assisted telephone interviewing. They note that CATI was first embraced in the United States by commercial survey organizations, encouraged no doubt by high levels of telephone coverage and the geographically dispersed nature of the population in the US. By contrast, CAPI systems were developed first in Europe and by national census offices. Martin & Manners describe the main features of CAPI systems and discuss in detail their advantages and disadvantages. Moving to CAPI involves balancing the advantages of time and cost savings and a marked improvement in data quality against the capital cost of the equipment required, various constraints imposed by available software and the need for technical support. Martin & Manners also remind us that computers are not neutral in terms of their social impact. As they put it, "From the start of CAPI development it was apparent that there would be major organizational implications." Based on their own extensive experience of implementing CAPI systems, Martin & Manners point up some of the organizational contexts and constraints which surround the introduction of new technologies into the data collection workplace. In a concluding section Martin & Manners look forward to improvements in hardware and software over the next few years and to the development of increasingly modular systems. They close their chapter, however, with a reminder that, despite the intervention of technology, the interview is still a social situation and, as such, remains dependent on the social skills of interviewers.

There are substantial academic and commercial markets for statistical software packages. Although there are clear market leaders, deciding on which particular package to use is not always an easy task. Moreover, the choice is becoming more difficult in some respects as packages spread across different hardware platforms, acquiring as they do subtle, and sometimes not so subtle, modifications in interface design. In their chapter devoted to statistical software, Ward and Dale provide a sure-footed guide to this treacherous terrain. For the purposes of their chapter they distinguish between packages mainly designed for the management of data and those primarily useful for data analysis. The latter they further distinguish into those designed for exploratory analysis and those for confirmatory analysis. In their final part they discuss a number of other aids to survey analysis in the form of spreadsheets and databases as well as a number of specialist programs. In each case they look at the major features of packages, their ease of use and the level of expertise required of the user.

Based on a long involvement with computer technology and his own extensive experience of anthropological fieldwork, Michael Fischer, of the Centre for Social Anthropology and Computing at the University of Kent, considers how computers can be used in ethnographic fieldwork. As he points out, although traditionally associated with research in anthropology, ethnographic, qualitative or field research is now common in many disciplines. Two particular aspects of this kind of research are relevant to computer use. The first has to do with the size, portability and reliability of hardware. If you are going to use a computer for this kind of research, you need to be able to take it with you and it has to be unobtrusive. Moreover, for some kinds of research there are also climatic and environmental considerations to be borne in mind. Fortunately, this is one area where commercial and academic imperatives for once align. If the executive flying in business class from Kuala Lumpur, say, to Copenhagen is not to be denied the benefits of portable computing, then they potentially also become available to the academic squashed into economy class on the same flight who is en route to or from a field site. The second aspect of using computers in ethnographic research is the use of information technology to handle and maintain ethnographic data. The stuff of ethnographic research is messy. Field research typically produces an assemblage of data which is multi-stranded, multi-sourced and takes a multiplicity of forms (Lee 1993). In other words, a complex set of themes and topics is woven through the research material, which itself may take many different forms depending on the nature of the study: fieldnotes, genealogies, maps, diagrams, audio-visual materials and so on. In a way, Fischer extends here some of the themes already developed by his near namesake Mike Fisher in the chapter on desktop tools, by discussing tools appropriate to handling the richness of ethnographic data. Those interested in the use of visual materials, particularly videotape, in ethnographic research will find his discussion particularly useful as it provides an introduction to relevant software and hardware for video-based research.

One area which has recently attracted a good deal of attention is the use of computers to analyze qualitative data. In this context the term qualitative data refers to unstructured data such as fieldnotes or transcriptions of depth interviews or focus groups. Developments in this field are discussed in the chapter by Wilma Mangabeira, a sociologist at the Federal University of Rio de Janeiro and someone who began early on to explore the implications of using computers to analyze qualitative data. Although clearly written, Mangabeira's chapter may be less accessible to readers new to computing than some of the other chapters in this collection. In a sense this reflects the field itself, which has developed rather rapidly within a relatively short period of time. It may be appropriate therefore to review, very briefly, developments to date. (Further information can be found in Pfaffenberger 1988, Tesch 1990, Fielding & Lee 1991, Huber 1992.)

The use of computer software to analyze textual data is not entirely new. Humanities researchers, especially biblical scholars and the like who have to deal with very large volumes of textual material, have long been interested in the use of computers for analyzing non-numeric data (Lee & Fielding 1991). Traditionally, in disciplines like sociology, qualitative researchers used manual methods to analyze data from field research, perhaps marking up fieldnotes or interview transcripts with coloured pens, or making multiple xerox copies of relevant segments of field material. Only in the 1980s did computer packages specifically designed to replace these cumbersome and tedious procedures begin to emerge. These early programs which were mainframe-based were replaced quite soon by microcomputer programs which allowed researchers to delineate and collate patterns or themes appearing in, say, an interview transcript through a process of attaching codes to segments of text. As Mangabeira points out, however, this mimicking of traditional "cut and paste" methods gave way to programs which aim to facilitate the development of sophisticated interrelated systems for categorizing data and, in some cases, for hypothesis testing. These "third generation" programs, as they have been called, form the subject of Mangabeira's chapter, which is made more valuable by being based on a close involvement, in the course of a Fullbright fellowship, with the developers of two of the more intriguing packages in the genre. Mangabeira explains the thinking behind third generation software and seeks to relate the underlying models to new substantive and methodological concerns.

There is a sense in which one can regard Mangabeira's contribution as a "third generation" paper. Just as the software has evolved, so has commentary upon it. Much of the early literature reported, with an air of faint amazement, that, yes, computers could be useful in qualitative research. Later, users and developers of the software began to speculate on the possible impact CAQDAS programs would have on the craft of qualitative research. Only now are we beginning to see papers like Mangabeira's which place computer assisted qualitative data analysis in context by going beyond speculation to material based on empirical analysis and/or explicit evaluation.

Hansen's chapter, along with a number of others in this collection, reflects a trend in which the computer is no longer seen as a device, quite literally, for computing, for handling numeric data, but one which handles many different forms of information, numeric, visual and textual. In effect what the computer allows is the translation of many media into one medium. Specifically, Hansen describes ways of harnessing information technology to the analysis of newspaper text. While newspapers are an extremely important source of data on social life, their analysis has traditionally been hampered by a number of factors. The dross rate for mass media data is high. In the case of newspapers, the physical characteristics of the data source in terms of size, bulk and, over time, friability additionally complicate the analyst's task. Hansen describes recent developments which make newspaper data available, at a price, in electronic form. He then shows how the computer can be used to address, manipulate and analyze the information so provided. He also points to the way in which the computer affects the analysis process, in this case in the ease with which it is now possible to counterpose a quantitative approach of the kind traditionally associated with content analysis with a more qualitative analysis based on themes, images, narrative and so on. How far it might be possible in the rather distant future to extend such methods to other forms of mass media remains to be seen.

As David Gilbert points out in his chapter on geographical computing, maps were important tools for the pioneers of empirical research in the social sciences. From Booth's attempts to show the distribution of poverty in nineteenth century London to the delineation of Chicago's ethnic ecology in the 1920s, maps served social researchers as a major means of data display. Social scientists who need to produce relatively simple, but usable, maps as an adjunct to their research will find in Gilbert's chapter information on the basic computer tools and techniques needed to produce them. (The topic is also briefly covered in Michael Fischer's chapter on the use of computers in ethnographic research.) The main focus of Gilbert's chapter is on geographical information systems (GIS), powerful computer systems for the handling of spatial data. Writing in a style accessible to social scientists in disciplines other than his own, Gilbert profiles the main features of GIS, indicating not only their strengths but also their weaknesses and limitations. Gilbert gives a variety of examples of how geographical information systems might be used in social research including, usefully, discussion of recent developments in the use of data from the 1991 census in the United Kingdom and an introduction to some of the statistical issues raised in the analysis of spatial data. Gilbert concludes by examining some of the criticisms advanced in relation to the use of GIS. He draws attention, for example, to issues relating to the availability of data and to some of the assumptions underlying the operation of such systems. He also suggests that for social and cultural geographers other forms of new technology – in particular the use of hypertext techniques and multimedia – open up exciting possibilities.

It was not long after the invention of computing that people began to muse about the similarities between the workings of a computer and the capabilities of the human mind. The idea was fostered in the media by the popular use of phrases such as "artificial brain". The term "computer memory" took its place in the technical vocabulary, becoming a permanent reminder of the supposed parallels between the make-up of humans and machines. Scientists talked of the potential for "artificial intelligence" (AI), and speculated on how long it would be before a computer would be able to field questions in a convincingly human way. Most, however, foresaw that the quest for genuine artificial intelligence would be a lengthy one, and such has proved to be the case. Over the years, the field of artificial intelligence has become increasingly fragmented into distinct research areas as scientists concentrated on reproducing or imitating separate aspects of human behaviour. Main areas of interest have included remote sensing, robotics and natural language processing, each of which, it is claimed, has shown slow but continual progress. One other area of AI has had an immediate and lasting success, having gained a niche in the real world because of its straightforward practical applications: expert systems. Heather & Lee describe the role of expert systems in the social sciences. The picture they reveal is of growing, if patchy, development. To date, expert systems have found most use as decision aids in areas of the research process such as sample design where researchers often need help in making intricate technical judgements. Heather and Lee also provide an assessment of the role expert systems have in teaching.

Artificial intelligence techniques are also relevant to the use of computers as tools for the simulation of social behaviour. As Nigel Gilbert points out in his chapter on the topic, computer simulation is not new. Renewed interest in the topic has emerged, however, both from technological developments which now make available the computer power needed for complex simulation models and from the increased availability of suitable data sources. Gilbert's concern is with the role of computer simulation to develop and test social theories in situations where the social phenomenon to be studied is inaccessible, hazardous or too large in scale to be studied by conventional means. In an extremely clear and succinct way Gilbert explores in particular two computer based simulation techniques, dynamic micro-simulation, which looks at the longer term macro consequences of individual behaviour, and distributed artificial intelligence where "intelligent" computer "agents" interact in complex ways to produce outcomes. Gilbert observes that to date these techniques have remained isolated from one another and proposes that a synthesis might be fruitful.

It should be clear that transformative technologies allow considerable scope for enhancing, sometimes in radical ways, problem formulation, research planning, theorizing, data collection, the representation and analysis of data and the dissemination of research results. Exploring the possibilities of information technology for the dissemination of research, Lyman (1989: 17) offers, for instance, the following scenario.

Using optical disk as a mass storage technology, ethnographers could store video images of the people they write about, allowing the readers to see and hear images of another culture for themselves, even as they read the sociologist's interpretation; statisticians could store the survey instruments and data sets, and the

9

SAS or SPSS runs upon which their analysis is based, allowing readers to turn directly to the structure of the research as they read.

Brent (1993) argues that what he sees as the computational revolution in the social sciences will undermine traditional polarities. In Brent's view such polarities, between quantitative and qualitative research, between micro- and macro-level analysis and between theory and method, are frequently devices for circumventing problems otherwise too unwieldy for successful resolution. Social scientists, he argues, can harness the power of new technologies to make those problems more tractable. Brent sees the likely consequences of the computational revolution in a largely positive light. New technology will encourage the advent of research projects wider in scope than at present, a trend towards more collaborative research, and greater cumulation of research findings than at present. But social scientists cannot, of course, feign innocence about the possible negative consequences of such developments. We cannot accept new technologies but pretend that they will have no unintended consequences or that they will not affect the social relations between researchers and research participants, researchers and colleagues, or researchers and their audiences.

While, clearly, contributors to this volume are enthusiastic about the possible uses of computers in the social sciences, they resist over-zealous endorsement or the advancement of utopian claims. In other words, to speak of transformative technologies is not necessarily to approve of the transformations wrought. There is, for example, more than a little substance to the charge that, while the advent of powerful and easy-to-use statistical packages in the 1960s increased levels of technical proficiency, this was not accompanied by greater theoretical acumen. Technology takes time to learn, time which could be used for research. The interposing of technology between researcher and research can encourage distance from data, use of research procedures because they are easy not because they are appropriate, and isolate researchers from the fundamentals of their methods to the point where these become poorly understood (Fischer 1994).

Innovations such as electronic mail or computerized library catalogues make information available at low cost and over great distances. But here too there are penalties. For example, the process of converting library card catalogues into electronic form is not error-free and on-line searches

easily produce large volumes of references which may be of only peripheral interest (Baker 1994). Electronic mail brings with it problems of information overload, while concerns have also begun to be raised about
the circulation of offensive or potentially harassing material. Issues also
surround the question of who owns and controls electronic information.
The provision of such information is big business. In the 1980s, for example, revenues from on-line databases in the United States increased by 30
per cent annually (Starr & Corson 1987). Some commentators see in this
the growth of a concomitant gap between the information rich who can
afford to buy what is on offer and the information poor who cannot.
There are countervailing tendencies, some of which are driven by technological developments or by factors such as increased competition within
the database industry itself. Nevertheless, the danger remains that, as
Starr & Corson put it, "The more the national information base passes
into the proprietary sphere, the more constrained will be our resources
for public life and social inquiry" (1987: 446).

The developments sketched in this volume are exciting and challenging. At the same time it is clear that the impact of new technology on social research has not been entirely uniform and, in some areas, has had a
hesitant and piecemeal character. This reflects in part the substantial barriers to software development which still exist in the academic environment. Oppenheimer & Winer (1988) enumerate some of the difficulties
involved in attempting to develop software for social scientists. There are
limited financial returns from developing products directed solely at the
academic market while software development has substantial personal
costs in terms of time, energy and financial investment. Software developers operate in a fast-changing technological environment which may
render current products obsolete as hardware and software standards
change and develop. Finally, not only is there a lack of institutional support for software development in academic institutions, according to
Oppenheimer & Winer, but social science software is difficult to market
because of resistance by academics to computer based methods.

It is probably a mistake to see this resistance, as Oppenheimer & Winer
tend to do, as a manifestation of mere technological conservatism, although that is undoubtedly present. Rather, as Blank emphasizes, it is
important to recognize that there is "an entrenched base of users with
heavy sunk costs in conventional procedures" (1991: 600). Blank argues
that software developers and others need to demonstrate to social scientists that new technologies can solve substantive research problems. As a

11

means of doing this he advocates the development of so-called "killer apps". The term "killer apps" is a piece of journalese for computer applications so useful that they cannot be ignored. The obvious example of such an application in the commercial environment is the development of desktop publishing software. Blank's prescription is more satisfactory as a call to innovative software development than as a rallying cry to revolutionary disciplinary change. It is likely that we only come to recognize particular software products as killer apps after the event rather than before. Furthermore, because social science provides a smaller and more fragmented market compared to the kind of areas transformed for example by desktop publishing, killer apps may not have such a dramatic impact as in commercial environments. Finally, a danger exists that developers will be tempted to make inflated claims for software in order to assume the mantle of the killer app, potentially generating cynicism among users as a result.

Like Oppenheimer & Winer, Blank also identifies institutional inertia as contributing to what he regards as the unsatisfactory pace of change in applying new technologies to social research. One difficulty here is that there are relatively few vehicles for the assessment of new developments and for disseminating information about them in a comprehensive but sober way. There are obvious training implications in introducing new technologies more widely. Again, most of the efforts here have been piecemeal, although there are indications that even modest outlays by funding bodies do seem to be effective in encouraging the diffusion of new methods and technologies (Fielding & Lee, forthcoming).

It is an article of faith in computing that new technology will not supply creativity, insight or wisdom where these are already lacking in the user. Computers do, however, lower barriers of detail, tedium and complexity in ways which allow the faculties we do have to go at least a little further. The developments sketched in this volume are exciting and challenging. Only time will tell how well we have fulfilled their promise.

Acknowledgements

I would like to thank Michael Fischer for a number of useful conversations about the notion of transformative technologies, Noel Heather for help and assistance at various points during the preparation of this book, and Sheila Sweet for secretarial assistance.

References

Baker, N. (June), 1994. Annals of scholarship: discards. *The New Yorker* 64–86.

Blank, G. 1991. Why sociological computing gets no respect. *Social Science Computer Review* 9, 593–611.

Brent, E. 1993. Computational sociology: reinventing sociology for the next millennium. *Social Science Computer Review* 11, 497–99.

Fielding, N. G. & R. M. Lee (eds) 1991. *Using computers in qualitative research*. London: Sage.

Fielding, N. G. & R. M. Lee forthcoming. Confronting CAQDAS: choice and contingency. In *Studies in qualitative methodology, volume 5: computers in qualitative research*, R. G. Burgess (ed.), New York: JAI Press.

Fischer, M. D. 1994. *Applications in computing for social anthropologists*. London: Routledge.

Huber, G. 1992. *Qualitative Analyse: Computereinsatz in der Sozialforschung*. Munich: Oldenburg.

Lee, R. M. 1993. *Doing research on sensitive topics*. London: Sage.

Lee, R. M. & N. G. Fielding 1991. Computing for qualitative research: options, problems and potential. In *Using computers in qualitative research*, N. G. Fielding & R. M. Lee (eds). London: Sage.

Lyman, P. 1989. The future of sociological literature in an age of computerized texts. In *New technology in sociology: practical applications in research and work*, G. Blank, J. L. McCartney, E. Brent (eds). New Brunswick, NJ: Transaction.

Oppenheimer, J. & M. Winer 1988. A simulation authoring system for cooperation and conflict situations. *Social Science Computer Review* 6, 12–26.

Pfaffenberger, B. 1988. *Microcomputer applications in qualitative research*. Beverley Hills, Calif.: Sage.

Starr, P. & R. Corson 1987. Who will have the numbers? The rise of the statistical services industry and the politics of public data. In *The politics of numbers*, W. Alonso & P. Starr (eds). New York: Russell Sage Foundation.

Tesch, R. 1990. *Qualitative analysis and software tools*. New York: Falmer Press.

CHAPTER 2

Desktop tools
for the social scientist

Mike Fisher

Introduction

People who work with hand tools (sculptors, carpenters) often remark that the best tools are those they hardly know they are using. This does not imply, however, that they disregard issues in choosing and maintaining their tools: on the contrary, selecting and sharpening tools, acquiring familiarity with the particular purpose of each, becomes an integral part of creative activity.

This chapter assumes that most social scientists want to use computer based desktop tools to achieve certain goals rather than because they are fascinated with the devices themselves. It assumes that readers are prepared to spend time selecting tools and becoming familiar with their use, but that most do not wish to specialize in technical aspects. Accordingly, this chapter is not a catalogue of all the computer programs available and their features. Instead, it focuses on the kinds of things social scientists typically need to achieve in their daily work and how computers may assist. Where technical details are given, the purpose is to enable readers to investigate whether the general category of software is of use to them, rather than whether any specific program will meet their needs precisely.

As the title implies, these tools are intended to be immediately and conveniently available to the social scientist. The chapter therefore focuses on the desktop computer in its own right, rather than as a link to a mainframe computer. An exception is the use of electronic mail to enhance communication with research colleagues (which is routed to and from desktop computers via a network controlled by central computing facilities).

14

This chapter concentrates on introductory information, rather than on assisting social scientists to become expert users. For example, the chapter assumes that the reader is primarily interested in simple databases to keep track of information, rather than in programmable databases which are used to create specialist, dedicated computer programs, such as a university library catalogue. Similarly, desktop publishing is mentioned to assist, for example, in the production of high quality papers rather than in setting up a publishing house, and statistics software is mentioned to assist the occasional user rather than to underpin specialist quantitative data analysis (for which see Ward & Dale, this volume). The chapter includes sufficient introductory detail to engage relative beginners, but extends the discussion into areas where experienced users might still gain additional knowledge.

The two principal types of personal computer available today are known as IBM (or IBM-compatible, hereafter called IBM) and Apple Macintosh computers (Macs). Until recently, manufacturers of IBM computers dominated the market, although some universities have always preferred Macs for their ease of use (e.g. the Open University). The difference between the two types of computer used to be considerable, but the advent of Windows software on IBM machines means that users can work with these computers in much the same way as with Macs. This chapter covers both types of computer. (A list of software is provided at the end of the chapter.)

Research management

Social scientists are under increasing pressure to increase their research activity, and computer software has much to offer. This section explores issues in managing research, while the next will focus on analysis. Readers may be concerned about relying on electronic records, and it may help to state some principles of using computer tools underpinning this approach. First, data are immensely valuable, and the costs of backing up are extremely small compared with the costs of losing vital information (see later section on the wise user). Secondly, although electronic data would ideally be constantly available through the use of portable computers such as IBM's ThinkPad or Apple's PowerBook, cost makes the use of these computers relatively rare in university research. Researchers need printed copies of much information, and database programs offer flexible ways of printing essential information. For those who absolutely must carry information in a Filofax, there is even a program which will produce printouts in the appropriate format (DynoDex). Thirdly, information should be keyed in just once: thereafter information which is required in a different format in a different program is exported. Databases typically offer several formats for data exchange, including formats to translate data from a database to a statistics program.

Contact management

Most projects involve creating and maintaining lists of people. Recording and maintaining such lists is the province of database software, which offers significant advantages over recording on paper. To illustrate this, consider a recent project monitoring the effects of introducing new practices in a social services setting. The project trained 15 workers in a new assessment approach and gathered basic demographic details from the workers. These details were transferred to a database, in this case FileMaker Pro (a program available on both IBM and Mac computers). Other programs include Panorama and Helix Express (on the Mac) and Paradox and Dbase (IBM). Like all databases, FileMaker Pro holds information in fields, and information can be extracted from these fields in an unlimited number of ways. For example, some work was undertaken by external trainers, who needed brief summary data on participants. Instead of photocopying several sheets of paper on each participant, the database software was used to generate specific information. One sheet contained names, addresses and contact numbers, in alphabetical order, while another summarized participants' previous training. Instead of sifting through paper sheets, researchers employed database software to access specific information arranged in the format which suited a particular purpose.

Holding records in electronic format also makes it easier to explore simple, initial questions. For example, although the project above was the fifth time the researchers had used this approach with small groups of workers, it was always necessary to adapt the basic format to each group. Data on age, sex, experience can easily be drawn from previous projects and used as a comparison for the current group. Similarly, each worker agreed to supply information on five pieces of work, but as the project progressed it appeared this target would not be reached: the database software was used to print a list of each worker with the number of assessments undertaken so that local managers could identify the shortfall.

Different software is required where a sample builds up over time. There is some similarity between salespeople contacting potential buyers and researchers contacting people in samples. If undertaking a survey, for example, researchers may make what salespeople refer to as cold calls to a large number of people to identify those who fit study criteria and are willing to participate. Going through contact lists is a fundamental research activity, and recording the contacts made and the outcome of each is important to understand the representativeness of the achieved sample. Software such as ACT!, CAT IV, Field Assistant or Contact Ease can assist by providing a standard format for recording details and by streamlining subsequent steps. For example, the initial details are recorded in a database, and a wordprocessing part of the software can construct a standard letter, with the recipient's address and name automatically inserted. If required, the software can generate a unique code for each addressee so that at a later stage the identifying details of respondents can be removed. The response can be logged in this database, and if further contact is warranted, the wordprocessing part can be requested to generate the next standard letter giving further details, again personalized for the recipient. When a standard response period has expired, the database part of the software can be requested to generate a list of all outstanding responses and, if required, construct a personalized follow-up letter to enhance the response rate. If a quota is required of a particular type of respondent, the database can construct a running total of people who fit particular criteria.

Colleague communication

Research is usually collaborative, in the broad sense of drawing on the collective research endeavour of the social scientific community, or in the immediate sense of working with colleagues in a current project. Computers offer several ways of enhancing this collaboration. The chapter by Thomas will address the use of electronic networks to keep abreast of research activity. The value of electronic mail is that it allows people to send information to each other with minimal delay and at almost no cost.

Email travels fast: a message to a colleague in Australia may arrive less than 24 hours after despatch. Unlike telephones, email does not require that the recipient is in: information is stored on the recipient's network and accessed when the mail is checked. Email offers one-to-many communication with little effort: a group of recipients interested in a particular topic can establish a forum with a single address, and each member can access the information. In short, email offers the opportunity to communicate with the social scientific community with almost instant response and minimal cost.

Collaboration on specific projects requires a more focused approach. Often projects use a single database of research contacts distributed to each member of the team. If portable computers are used in the field, some programs (e.g. Contact Ease) can update the reference copy held in the research base with new information. If no network connection is available, it is possible to use telephone lines to transfer files. The research team should standardize the basic software so that incompatibilities are minimized, and establish a secure method of file transfer. It may be wise to use a security program to prevent access to data sent via networks, and it is essential if telephone lines are used or if the file is copied to a floppy disk and put in the mail.

Analysis

Some initial aspects of analysis have already been touched on in the example of a research project evaluating social services innovation. This section will take this further by exploring basic statistical and qualitative data analysis.

Using computers for basic statistics

As a broad introduction, this section aims to alert the reader to the potential for using computers in basic statistical analysis. Readers seeking detail should examine Ward & Dale, this volume, the section on computer aided analysis of quantitative data in Hall & Marshall (Hall & Marshall 1992), or an introductory text on data analysis which features computer use (e.g. Bryman & Cramer 1990, Marsh 1988, Rose & Sullivan 1993). In the project involving 15 social services workers, it was necessary to compare the characteristics of this group with others. The information was stored in a FileMaker Pro database and some simple issues could be analyzed within this program. For example, FileMaker allows a summary field which summarizes data from other fields: by using this and adding a formula, a field was created which cumulatively averaged the age of participants, giving a crude comparative dimension. More complex work requires transferring the data to a statistics program. Systat, SPSS and MiniTab are programs available on both IBM and Mac computers, while Mac users might also wish to explore JMP, DataDesk or StatView.

Once in a statistics program, the data can be analyzed using a wide range of statistical facilities, showing in the example whether the differences in age profile between different groups of workers reaches statistical significance. The author uses StatView which, like other statistics software, allows data to be manipulated, so that for instance age could be recoded into five year increments. Statistical analyses in StatView are accomplished by selecting variables and requesting, via a menu, a particular type of analysis. The results are shown in a separate window, and graphical displays are available, both to explore the meaning of analyses and to offer a visual means of communicating results.

Basic qualitative data analysis

Researchers often have a large of amount of "soft" data, comprising field notes, records of meetings, press and informal reports and, most frequently, interviews. With certain caveats, computers can assist the analysis of this information. Again, the material here is intended to be introductory and the reader looking for more detailed information should see Mangabeira, this volume, and consult the literature (e.g. Fielding & Lee 1991, Pfaffenberger 1988, Tesch 1990). If information is not in the form of computer files, some important decisions must be made. Some software for qualitative data analysis, such as NUDIST, assists with the analysis of such information by working on the codes which the researcher allocates to significant text segments. It is the codes, rather than the text, which the computer is used to manipulate. If the researcher prefers not to use a program like NUDIST, then a painful decision awaits about whether to have written or printed information translated into electronic format. No researcher should do this unless adequately supplied with funds and gumption. Typing textual data into a word-processor is time-consuming and error-prone, assuming legible text. If a good printed copy is available, an alternative is to use optical character recognition (OCR), where a page of printed text is scanned as a digitized picture and software (such as OmniPage or TypeReader) is used to recognize shapes and translate them into letters. Apart from the expense of the software and the scanner, the software demands powerful computer processing to reach acceptable speeds (i.e. faster than the text could be typed). The process is not easy to automate, even using a sheet feeder for the scanner: someone must feed sheets into the scanner and save the resulting files, and much textual material is not available in the appropriate format.

OCR programs are prone to errors (e.g. an "e" recognized as a "c") and the time required to check the results can rapidly approach that required for retyping the text. Specialist spelling checkers, tuned to recognize OCR errors, are available, but they still require a substantial investment of time. OCR programs do offer a realistic approach where there is good quality copy and funds available to pay an operator to check the results, but users should not mistake them for cheap typists.

If the files are available in electronic form, a now wide range of analysis software exists. Some of it is oriented to text retrieval (e.g. Sonar), where the user identifies key phrases and the program selects them, together with a slice of surrounding text and details identifying the location. In effect, these programs replace the scissors and paste of generations of qualitative researchers. Other programs look for relationships between text segments the researcher has identified (e.g. HyperSoft, HyperQual, ATLAS/ti, NUDIST and The Ethnograph). In either case, it is important to bear two issues in mind. First, there is no single accepted method for qualitative data analysis and these programs are strongly imprinted with the methodological approaches and personal style of the people who wrote them (see Mangabeira, this volume). Secondly, these programs are there to assist researchers and not to replace them. Nothing will replace the human brain as a sensitive instrument to detect meaning, and nothing will reduce the need for researchers to know the stories their data contain. Software can speed up certain aspects of qualitative data analysis, and can add to its validity, but nothing in the programs themselves guarantees either.

Academic writing

The aim of this section is to show how computers can assist the writing process and to highlight some of the limitations of computer based writing. More detail may be found in Dorner (1992) and an overview of the field is provided by Williams & Holt (1989, 1991).

Reference management

Academics typically start writing by finding out what others have already said about the issue. The chapter by Thomas will assist the reader to discover more about the processes involved in finding references; the emphasis here is on ways of retaining relevant material. Electronic reference files have many advantages over card indexes and other paper based catalogues. A leading program on both Mac and IBM is EndNote Plus, and the following examples are based on this program (others include Pro-Cite and Papyrus). EndNote Plus is a specialized database, optimized for academic referencing. It holds a catalogue of references, organized alphabetically but capable of being re-ordered using other criteria (such as year or publisher). There are fields for all the usual referencing detail of volume and page numbers, but also a field for notes, and this is a key starting point for writing. Notes can be entered while reading material, and users typically enter a page number, their comments, and any direct quotes which may later be required. Although it is preferable to keep references in a single file (for cross referencing between academic fields), users may have any number of separate databases corresponding to their areas of interest. Within a single file, it is possible to use a Keywords or Label field to identify sub-areas. Having this information in electronic format means it can be quickly searched, using either simple find commands or more complex combinations of search criteria. For example, while writing this section the author recalled a quote by Ada Augusta to the effect that the strength of computers lies in reminding us of what we already know. A search on the word "Ada" showed that the quote actually reads that the computer can assist us "in making available what we are already acquainted with", and that this may be found on page 24 of Pfaffenberger's book (1988). Retrieving such detail from a paper index can be very time consuming, and would have required typing the quote: in this case the author copied the text directly

21

from EndNote Plus and inserted it in this paragraph. More complex searches simply build up criteria, such as that for a research proposal concerning the effects of migration on the mental health of Irish people living in Great Britain, where the words "mental health" and "Ireland" *or* "Irish" and "migration" were entered to find relevant literature.

A reference database can be invaluable in retaining and retrieving scholarly materials. However, its use is not restricted to acting as a database. In the above example, an EndNote Plus command was used to insert the reference to Pfaffenberger in a special format into this word-processed text. When the paper was finished, the author requested EndNote Plus to process it, replacing these special markers with the particular in-text reference format required by the publisher, and formatting the references at the end of the paper in the required style. EndNote Plus has numerous pre-formatted styles and writers may modify or create one to fit a particular publisher's requirement (that required for this book was, perhaps inevitably, unique). EndNote Plus is smart enough to annotate multiple publications by a single author in one year using 1994a, 1994b and so on, and if re-writing is required, EndNote can remove the formatting, allowing new references to be inserted, which when formatted will appear in correct alphabetical or numerical order. Apart from the sheer relief at not having to seek high and low for that missing page number, this approach has the bonus that, provided the initial information was correct, the reference will not need to be checked. And should a paper be rejected, the process of reformatting it to another publisher's requirements is reduced to selecting the appropriate reference style and requesting EndNote to re-process the paper.

The process of writing

The use of wordprocessors is now widespread. However, writers rarely use the software to maximum effect, and academic writers can benefit enormously from some simple techniques. Key wordprocessors are Microsoft Word and WordPerfect, although there is a host of less widely used programs such as MultiMate and Prof Write for the IBM, and MacWrite Pro and WriteNow for the Mac. Academics rarely have trained keyboard skills. It therefore becomes important to check for typographical errors and to minimize the labour of typing. Most wordprocessors include spell checking, but other methods are available to catch errors before they occur. In writing this chapter the author frequently fumbled the keys for "wordprocessor", so a unique abbreviation "wp" was used instead. The wordprocessor's search and replace command was used to ensure that the correct word replaced the abbreviation. This technique may be used for many difficult and tedious words: a colleague writing about President Carter's National Security Adviser much preferred to search and replace his initials (ZB) than to chance the spelling of his name (Zbigniew Brzezinski) every time. A similar technique uses the wordprocessor's glossary function. A glossary contains names of frequently used phrases: typing the name followed by a glossary command replaces the name with the text. This is cumbersome and useful only where a substantial amount of text will be entered (for example a standard acknowledgement to a research funding body). A simpler approach for shorter text is to use a memory-resident program (such as Thunder 7 on the Mac), which monitors the typing and replaces known abbreviations with glossary text as the typing progresses. This approach can also be used for the standard typographical mistakes that most amateur typists acquire: every time this author types "theoretcial" (which is to say quite often) the glossary automatically corrects it to "theoretical".

Using computers can also assist collaborative writing. Provided the authors are all using compatible programs, it becomes much easier and faster to send an electronic copy of the file to a colleague than to print it out, work from the hard copy and then re-enter modifications. Some wordprocessors offer the facility to annotate text. For example, Word allows the writer to insert text which will not print but which can be made visible by a command, and annotation where a marker is inserted which can be activated to show a separate "window" containing a co-author's comments. If the annotations or hidden text contain a suggested re-writing acceptable to the originator, it can be copied and inserted. If an intended publication consists of separate contributions, and a single reference list is envisaged, a single reference database may be compiled and distributed among all contributors so that correct house style is used throughout and accuracy is maintained. If there is the danger of variations among contributors in using abbreviations (e.g. academics writing on the history of North American defence policy referring to NORAD and N.O.R.A.D), a single glossary may be created and distributed to all authors.

Risks of academic writing on computer

Academic writing on computer is not without its drawbacks, however. First, some authors still think in terms of a notional page and paragraph length and arguments are constructed with this unit in mind. In contrast, few computer screens show a full page of text and many are limited to just 25 lines. Authors sometimes find themselves writing more briefly, or in an elliptical, coded manner, trying to cram into 25 lines what they previously wrote more expansively. Pending the mental transition to regarding the screen as a window on a scrolling piece of paper, the solution is to print out text in the page format of the intended publication. Secondly, wordprocessing allows text to be inserted time and again, and the temptation when returning to a topic about which the author has previously written is to re-use earlier text. Although this saves time, this almost always reduces the quality. The earlier text may be useful as template to guide the writing of a related section and to remind the author of key arguments, but essentially writing should remain writing, rather than the electronic assembly of related pieces of text. Thirdly, access to public electronic databases brings the possibility of copying substantial amounts of information and incorporating it into papers. For example, some on-line databases include brief overviews of academic fields, and most offer an abstract of articles. When summarizing a field or the contribution of a particular paper, the question arises whether to insert the copied text. Copyright law is unclear on this issue, but concepts of scholarship should prevent this: even if publicly available and not attributed to a specific author, such text represents the academic perspective of someone other than the author of the paper into which it is inserted, and if used it should be attributed to its source. As in the example in the previous paragraph, there is nothing to stop the author using the publicly available text as a guide to writing.

Presenting academic material

Translating material composed on the computer into a book, chapter, paper or presentation requires technical as well as academic ability. One of the advantages of computer based writing is that the processes of publication remain more in the control of the writer, and this section addresses briefly how computer tools can assist this process. Readers seeking greater detail should consult Taylor & Heale (1992). Finally the section will mention tools for presenting material to live audiences.

Preparing for publication

Although desktop publishing software and wordprocessors are the key programs, database software can be invaluable in preparing material from research for publication. Research reports often require the addition of appendices summarizing research data, and if this data has been recorded on a database, the program can be used to prepare it. In the example used earlier of social services innovation, brief case summaries were required to give the flavour of the work. These were originally typed into FileMaker Pro, and this program's layout abilities were used to create a summary of each case, containing a code for the person's name, brief demographic details and the details of the request for assessment. The resulting printed copy was then added as an appendix to the main report.

Publishers realize that the costs of publication can be reduced by accepting electronic files. The incentive for writers is that expensive time in checking rekeyed text can be substantially reduced. Publishers give detailed guidance on how text should be prepared, including how to insert style markers to show headings and subheadings. If you use a wordprocessor or desktop publishing program which uses "style sheets" (instructions on formatting sections of the document such as body text or headings), some publishers will either send authors a blank file containing in-house style sheets, or accept the author's and substitute in-house values prior to publication. Some will accept file transfer by modem, but most require a disk copy and accompanying printout.

Desktop publishing

For their own in-house materials and for informal papers, authors are increasingly turning to desktop publishing. Programs include PageMaker, Quark Express and Ventura, although wordprocessors such as Word, WordPerfect and MacWrite Pro include some desktop publishing capabilities (such as fitting text around a graphic, or running text in two or more columns). The key reason to use desktop publishing is to make materials attractive to the reader. Programs allow graphics to be used freely, and text to be flowed around them, typeface and type size to be selected to make impact and (usually) to improve readability, and, with appropriate printing facilities, the use of colour. For longer publications, programs allow text to be marked to build automatically into a contents list or index. Most academics have no training in design, and some desktop published documents are anything but attractive. However, some programs (PageMaker, for example) include templates for the design of common documents, and provided academics are not too ambitious, simple attractive materials can be easily produced.

Presenting to a live audience

Finally, software can assist social scientists in presenting materials to a live audience. Programs such as Cricket Presents, Aldus Persuasion and Astound offer the ability to produce the electronic equivalent of OHPs, but with substantially added impact. Use of these programs requires some initial decisions about technology. The programs may be used to produce slides for a projector, which involves sending an electronic file to a photographic shop equipped to translate it into slides. This produces high quality, but once on film it is expensive to correct mistakes or to make changes. The program may be used to print conventional acetate OHP slides, or used in conjunction with an LCD panel which connects to the computer and lies on an OHP projector: what is shown on the computer screen is transferred to the LCD panel and projected. LCD panels are available in monochrome and colour.

Presenting academic material is an art, and presenting it using computers and presentation software requires additional craft. The key is to present ideas rather than text, and this requires the ability to create brief, memorable phrases to represent ideas. If presenting a paper already written, social scientists may find they have already identified these phrases in the title, headings and subheadings of their work. The language may not be totally gripping, but it will at least provide a starting point. Most people find that each topic is best represented by a separate slide, with each of three or four major points in the supporting argument listed below. Rather than numbering points, which can come across as rigidly didactic, presenters usually highlight them with a symbol (so called "bullets"). Simple layouts with one or two typefaces work best, and most programs include preformatted templates which require the user simply to enter text in placeholders. If using colour, predesigned palettes are included to prevent visual incoherence. Rehearsal is essential if it is intended that the audience remember the message rather than the equipment. Although it may appear that the equipment draws attention to itself, the audience will forget this aspect during a well delivered presentation of interesting ideas. If using an LCD panel, rehearsal should include using it for the same length of time as the intended presentation, as panels can change colour balance over a lengthy presentation and may become unstable due to overheating. Presentation programs include the facility to reproduce the slides in a printed format to distribute to the audience (handouts), and to produce a version containing miniatures of the slides with the presenter's notes. This means that the presentation can progress on the basis that the presenter is addressing the audience (rather than trying to read the screen) and that the audience is listening to the presenter (rather than trying to copy the slides).

The wise use of tools

This chapter encourages social scientists to employ computers as tools in their work. Inevitably we come to rely on tools, and wise users will wish to consider the impact of intensive computer use on their work and to anticipate problems.

Safety

Using computers is like using any other sort of machinery – there are hazards which must be minimized. One hazard arises from the physical position adopted to use the computer. Desk height and monitor position are critical to ensure a safe working posture. There is not space to review computer ergonomics, but readers should be aware that prolonged computer use with poor ergonomic position can lead to serious strain injuries. Regulations ensuring the health and safety of computer users should be available from university computer centres and may assist in making the case for proper ergonomic conditions. With or without such improvements, users should ensure they take regular breaks during which they physically move away from the computer.

Computer monitors represent another hazard. All monitors (except LCD screens) emit magnetic radiation, the health effects of which constitute a highly politicized research area. This author's view is that the research satisfactorily demonstrates adverse health effects of prolonged exposure to low frequency magnetic radiation (Brodeur 1990). Manufacturers are reducing the magnetic radiation of their equipment, but some basic precautions are still required. The strength of radiation declines with distance from the monitor, so that at 28 inches it falls to levels which are barely measurable. Computer users should therefore ensure this distance between themselves and the screen (extending the arm so the fingers just touch the screen is about right). This radiation is emitted over a 360° radius, so users should not sit alongside or close to the back of another monitor.

Maintenance

Maintenance means ensuring that files are stored in the right places, that access is controlled, files are backed up and that virus programs have not entered the computer. Hard disks require periodic checking to ensure that files are properly recorded, and the periodic use of a formatting program to verify the disk is recommended. The original system software accompanying the computer will have an appropriate program. Social scientists often have extremely sensitive information, and access to it must be controlled. Physical access may be controlled by locking devices which prevent the computer from being started, but software to control electronic access is usually required in addition. This ranges from password protection of the start-up procedure, through password controlled access to directories or folders containing files, to encoding the entire disk so that its contents are meaningless unless translated by a decoding program. The university computing centre will usually offer advice and appropriate software.

Power failure, accidental file erasure and hard disk mechanical failure will all happen at some stage to intensive computer users. Wise users save their work often and make back-up copies. The system software always includes a copy command, and some programs include an option to copy their files automatically (e.g. Microsoft Word), although this has the disadvantage of storing copies on the same hard disk against whose failure the user is seeking to insure. Much better is to use back-up software, which can automate much of this procedure, and to back up to a second hard disk or to floppy disks. On the Macintosh, DiskFit Pro provides a simple option to copy only those files which have changed, and to restrict this to designated folders, while Retrospect offers more complex file selection and automation. On the IBM, similar options are available from Norton Backup and Central Point Backup. Consideration should be given to storing a set of copies in an alternative location to that of the computer, so that fire or theft cannot obliterate irreplaceable files.

Virus programs are designed to sabotage the computer. They may be hidden in software from manufacturers or in shareware, or they may be copied via floppy disk or arrive via a network. Even those intended to be harmless may be poorly written or untested in the innumerable configurations they will encounter and so damage the host computer files. Virus prevention programs are available which detect the presence of a virus on entry or when requested to check the hard disk. Commercial programs for IBM and the Mac include SAM, Virex, Central Point AntiVirus and Norton AntiVirus. University computer centres will also have shareware (i.e. free) programs, such as Disinfectant (Mac). All antivirus software requires regular updating to include detection of new viruses.

Transferring files between IBM and Macintosh computers

Transferring files between different types of computers can be tedious because of differences in file formats. Files may be sent from one machine to another via a network designed to allow computers of different types to communicate with each other, or a special, two-machine network may be established specifically to allow transfer (using MacLink Plus, a software package which comes with a cable to link the machines). Floppy disk transfer is possible if both machines are equipped with high density disk drives accepting 3.5" disks and the receiving machine is equipped with special software (MacDisk or Mac-in-DOS for the IBM and Macintosh PC Exchange, AccessPC or DosMounter Plus software for the Mac). However the file is physically copied, there remain problems of formatting, and the wise user will ensure that cross-platform programs are used (such as Word or PageMaker), so that a file recorded on one machine may be read by the same program on the other. A third and quite different solution is SoftPC, a Mac program which creates a software emulation of an IBM machine in a separate "window", in which it is possible to run IBM software and to read IBM disks.

Conclusion

In almost any area of academic activity, the use of computer programs can assist social scientists to achieve productivity and creativity. As with any tool, learning to use it requires some effort and discipline, and brings some risks as well as benefits. Readers should assume some learning will have to be repeated when a program proves unsuitable, and that they will encounter new problems as well as new solutions. Although this chapter describes a range of programs under each heading, the intention is not to encourage endless experiment: rather readers should find a tool which works for them and stick with it. The intention of this chapter has been to provide information which allows social scientists to reach that point faster than if they had not read it.

References

Brodeur, P. 1990. The magnetic-field menace. *MacWorld* (July), 136–45.

Bryman, A. & D. Cramer 1990. *Quantitative data analysis for social scientists*. London: Routledge.

Dorner, J. 1992. *Writing on disk*. Hatfield: John Taylor Book Ventures.

Fielding, N. & R. Lee (eds) 1991. *Using computers in qualitative research*. London: Sage.

Hall, L. & K. Marshall 1992. *Computing for social research: practical approaches*. London: International Thomson Publishing.

Marsh, C. 1988. *Exploring data*. Cambridge: Polity.

Pfaffenberger, B. 1988. *Microcomputer applications in qualitative research*. Sage University Paper Series on Qualitative Research Methods, vol. 14. Beverley Hills, Calif.: Sage.

Rose, D. & O. Sullivan 1993. *Introducing data analysis for social scientists*. Buckingham: Open University Press.

Taylor, J. & S. Heale 1992. *Editing for desktop publishing: a guide to writing and editing on the personal computer*. Hatfield: John Taylor Book Ventures.

Tesch, R. 1990. *Qualitative research: analysis types and software tools*. London: Falmer Press.

Williams, N. 1991. *The computer, the writer and the learner*. London: Springer-Verlag.

Williams, N. & P. Holt (eds) 1989. *Computers and writing: models and tools*. Oxford: Blackwell.

Software

Name	Type	Computer
AccessPC	PC translation	Mac
ACT!	contact management	IBM/Mac
Astound	presentation	Mac
ATLAS/ti	qualitative data analysis	IBM
CAT IV	contact management	IBM/Mac
Central Point AntiVirus	antivirus	IBM
Central Point Backup	back-up	IBM
Contact Ease	contact management	Mac
Cricket Presents	presentation	Mac
Data Desk	statistics	Mac
Dbase	database	IBM
Disinfectant	antivirus	Mac
DiskFit Pro	back-up	Mac
DosMounter Plus	PC translation	Mac
DynoDex	database	Mac
EndNote Plus	bibliographic	Mac
Field Assistant	contact management	Mac
FileMaker Pro	database	IBM/Mac
Helix Express	database	Mac
HyperQual	qualitative data analysis	Mac
HyperSoft	qualitative data analysis	Mac
JMP	statistical	Mac
Mac-in-DOS	PC translation	IBM
MacDisk	PC translation	IBM
Macintosh PC Exchange	PC translation	Mac
MacLink Plus	PC translation	Mac
MacWrite Pro	wordprocessing	Mac
MiniTab	statistics	IBM and Mac
MultiMate IV	wordprocessing	IBM
Nisus	wordprocessing	Mac
Norton AntiVirus	antivirus	IBM
Norton Backup	back-up	IBM
NUDIST	qualitative data analysis	IBM/Mac
OmniPage	OCR	Mac
PageMaker	desktop publishing	IBM/Mac
Panorama	database	Mac
Papyrus	bibliographic	IBM/Mac
Paradox	database	IBM
Persuasion	presentation	IBM/Mac
Pro-Cite	bibliographic	IBM/Mac
Prof Write	wordprocessor	IBM

(continued overleaf)

31

DESKTOP TOOLS FOR THE SOCIAL SCIENTIST

Name	Type	Computer
Quark Express	desktop publishing	Mac
Retrospect	back-up	Mac, MacLine
SAM	antivirus	Mac, MacLine
SoftPC Pro	PC emulation	Mac
Sonar	qualitative data analysis	IBM/Mac
SPSS	statistical	IBM and Mac
StatView	statistical	Mac
Systat	statistical	IBM/Mac
The Ethnograph	qualitative data analysis	IBM
Thunder 7	wordprocessor utility	Mac
TypeReader	OCR	Mac
Ventura	desktop publishing	IBM
Virex	antivirus	Mac
WordPerfect	wordprocessing	IBM/Mac
WriteNow	wordprocessing	Mac

CHAPTER 3

On-line services and CD-ROM

Ray Thomas

The aim of this chapter is to discuss the impact of electronic communication and storage technologies on the activities of social scientists. The major impact of these developments so far has been in the area of information retrieval, and most of this chapter is about information retrieval facilities. The new technology also provides facilities for information exchange and discussion among social scientists and for the dissemination of the work of social scientists through electronic publishing. It may be that the stimulus provided by what is usually called computer mediated communication (CMC) will have a greater influence on the work-style of most social scientists than those which are limited to retrieval. The chapter ends therefore with some reference to developments in CMC.

The chapter does not aim to give a comprehensive or up-to-date account of the facilities available. The range and variety of services and information sources of interest to social scientists is already too large, and is developing too rapidly, to make such coverage practicable. Nor does this chapter give detail about how to access these services or sources, or how to use CMC. For practical help on such matters the reader should use the latest editions of the guides cited in the references of this chapter, the new guides which will undoubtedly be published, or should turn to librarian/information specialists and computer systems administrators whose responsibilities involve these developments. This chapter focuses on the nature of the information technology developments which have made these services available, and aims to gives indications, by means of examples, of the range of information services and other facilities which have become available.

A basic point is that the information made available through these developments is not really new. The technology itself does not create data. The data were there before and are now made accessible so conveniently that the word revolutionary is not inappropriate. The new technology supports new methods of storing, accessing and communicating existing data; these facilities can be used to extract useful information from what would otherwise be unused or under-utilized and provide support for debate and exchange of ideas between people who never meet each other. But the technology itself does not create new data – nor new theory.

Underlying the developments described in this chapter is the representation of data and information in digital form. When data are digitally recorded there is scarcely any limit to the extent to which it can be processed, stored and communicated. A few keystrokes on a computer keyboard can produce useful information from data which would formerly have required the work of thousands of clerks to produce. A few strokes on a computer keyboard can transmit data between England and Australia and it arrives within seconds – instead of the days which would formerly have been necessary. A single CD-ROM disk can provide data or information which would otherwise occupy hundreds of thousands of punched cards or twenty feet of book storage space.

The computer can systematically search digital forms of processed, communicated and stored data in ways which would not be practicable for information recorded in other forms. The crucial ability of the computer is simply to decide whether one alphanumeric set of characters is less than, greater than or equal to another. This operation supports the matching of a string of alphabetical characters by the user in a search for occurrences in any kind of text database expressed in digital form.

The matching of characters supports the sorting of survey microdata in order to produce statistical tables in accordance with the design of the user. These operations used to be carried out by mechanized means using punched cards. But the cost of making multiple copies of the dataset and the relatively slow speed of punched card operations restricted the number of uses. Digital technology allows for easy duplication of the dataset. The computer achieves simple searching within seconds, and the searching and counting of large numbers of records within minutes.

The matching of characters supports packet switching of data on telephone and other networks. Packet switching makes more efficient use of national and international telephone networks, designed for voice transmission, than voice transmission itself, and supports the transmission of data and information from a computer in any one part of the world to a computer at any other location.

Access to many databases is not free, but, in the Western industrialized world at least, academics have free use of the data network – which also supports electronic mail and computer conferencing. The cost of national systems, such as JANET (Joint Academic NETwork) in Britain, and the cost of supporting international connections, mainly through Internet, is met by governmental bodies, not by individual users. This is a logical form of financial support because costs are attributable to the establishment and maintenance of the network, and do not depend in the short run upon the volume of traffic. But such support is not so easily given in countries without extensive and thriving telephone networks. Free use of the data network is not available to most academics in countries of the third world, to those in the former Soviet Union, or in the countries of Eastern Europe. The academic community in the West leads the world in making use of this international data network. Academics cannot expect to learn from others, such as those in commerce, about how the network might come to be used. But it is difficult not to be both optimistic and enthusiastic about the potential value of a worldwide communication system which, in terms of convenience and effectiveness, can often be superior to face-to-face meetings.

An overview of developments in information retrieval

In the 1960s information gathering activities were carried out by searching through catalogues, books and journals in libraries. In the 1970s bibliographical databases became accessible on-line, i.e. through the telephone network. In the 1980s the range of on-line services of interest to the social scientist expanded substantially. The number of databases increased – particularly with the availability of full text as well as bibliographical material. Network services improved allowing easy access to a variety of new types of information sources – such as library catalogues, electronic yellow pages and microdata from social surveys.

In the 1980s most of the databases available on-line which were used by social scientists also became available in CD-ROM form and so became accessible without the inconvenience of on-line connection. CD-ROM is a form of optical storage using the technology of the compact disk. A mass produced CD-ROM can be conceptualized as publication of reference material with special search facilities. A text-only CD-ROM can contain the equivalent of about 500 average sized books. Apart from compactness, the main value of publication of text in this form derives from the indexing and searching facilities which the computer can provide. Five hundred books is a small library for browsing. The same books on a CD-ROM are reference material which can be systematically scanned, searched and analyzed.

CD-ROM is expected to be one of the growth industries in the 1990s, and it seems likely that some of the new CD-ROMs will prove to be of value to social scientists, but it is not easy to make predictions. A wide ranging discussion of the prospects for CD-ROM was published by Microsoft (the world's dominant microcomputer software firm) in the mid 1980s (Lambert & Ropiequet 1986, Ropiequet et al. 1987). There have been many developments since that time, but the principles discussed in these volumes may have not changed.

At the time of writing in 1994 small scale production of CD-ROMs had already become economic. Where only a few copies are being made it may make sense to conceptualize CD-ROM as a form of data delivery rather than as a publication. The CD-ROM can be the means of distributing text or microdata tailored to the particular needs of an individual or a small group of people. Storage of data in this form exploits the wide availability of microcomputers and the low cost CD-ROM drives.

Bibliographical and text databases

So what types of information have become available, either on-line or on CD-ROM? Of widest interest are bibliographical and other text databases – library catalogues, abstracts of articles, full text databases, citations. Bradley & Hanson (1993) provide a general introduction. Brent & Anderson (1990) give an account geared to the needs of the social scientist.

The most common type of database in use is that for abstracts of academic journals. Since the early 1970s users have been able to conduct searches of social science materials on the Dialog database host in Palo Alto, California, using keywords to identify articles relevant to any topic. There have been parallel developments in Europe with the establishment of the Datastar host in Switzerland (now owned by Dialog) and the European Space Agency database at Frascati in Italy.

More recently many new databases have been created or made available in machine readable form, and many new database hosts have come into existence. At the time of writing it is estimated that there are worldwide more than 3,600 databases which are accessible on-line through the telephone network, or accessible through database hosts such as Dialog Information Service, ESA or more than 500 other database on-line hosts (see Convey 1992, Chapter 3).

Most of the major database hosts are commercial organizations dependent on revenue earned from news and financial data in the business world, and access is generally restricted to members or account holding customers. For academics the most common means of access are through the library of an institution which pays a subscription to the database host. But access is also possible through any connection which includes a billing facility – such as an existing commercial on-line service like Compuserve.

Text databases cover two kinds of material of special importance for research in the social sciences. One category comprises the abstracts of articles in academic journals and PhD dissertations. The databases cover most of the leading academic journals back to the 1970s or earlier. The other category comprises the full text of non academic journals such as the "heavy" newspapers, *The Economist*, and many specialist journals of interest to social scientists.

For both abstract and full text categories the search technique is similar. The researcher identifies key words or phrases covering the area of interest. The computer program identifies abstracts or articles which include those key words. The researcher can then read the article or abstract. Typically the researcher would use a combination of keywords of the form ("gender" OR "sex") AND ("pay" OR "earnings" OR "salaries") AND "teaching". Such a search query might be expected to identify articles which covered differences between men's and women's earning in teaching. The AND and OR in this context are called boolean operators. The boolean operator NOT is also sometimes used. (See Humphrey & Melloni 1986 for extensive discussion, Colvin 1986 for discussion of possible developments, and Hansen this volume.)

A major problem in using these on-line databases for most researchers is cost. Typically the cost is about £80 an hour. This may be small in relation to both the cost of maintaining the database and in relation to the

Table 3.1 Selected CD-ROM databases relevant to research in the social sciences

Title, approximate annual cost	Contents, updating
"Academic" bibliographical databases:	
Econlit £1,300	Corresponds to the *Journal of Economic Literature*. Covers journals, dissertations, chapters in books. Since 1969.
ERIC £460 upwards	Produced by Educational Resources Center of US Department of Education. Research reports. 750 journals. Quarterly updates.
PsychLIT £2,700	Compiled by the American Psychological Association. 1300 journals. Books and chapters. From 1974. Updated quarterly
Sociofile £1,500	1800 journals since 1974. Dissertations since 1986. Updated three times annually.
Other text databases:	
ASSIA PLUS (£1,100)	Applied Social Science Index and Abstracts. 550 journals from 1987. Updated quarterly.
ABI/Inform	Abstracts and indexes from 900 business journals. Back files to 1971.
CINHAL (Cumulative Index of Nursing and Allied Health) £950	Index of nursing journals. Articles from bio-medical journals. From 1983. Monthly updates.
Cross-cultural (£1,000 per area)	Full text files on life in 60 different societies. Areas covered: sex & marriage; family & social problems; old age & dying; childhood/education, etc.
Hansard (£1,900)	Full text of House of Commons debates, etc., updated three times a year. From 1988/9.
Statistical:	
British Social Attitudes Survey £29	Microdata from British Social Attitudes Survey 1983 to 1989. Produced by Data Archive at Essex University. NB: Future CD-ROMs on BSA or other surveys are likely to be produced to special order.
FAME (Financial Analysis Made Easy) £3,000	Company reports and accounts. 125,000 British companies. Financial ratios. Compiled by Jordan and Sons.
International Statistical Yearbook (£2,700)	500,000 time series from EC, IMF, OECD, and Deutsche Bundesbank.

value to the user of the information retrieved. But most users would consider £80 an hour as a large cost for learning a query language necessary to conduct a search. In the conduct of searches the researcher commonly works with a specialist librarian who is familiar with the query language.

Cost problems change with the advent of CD-ROM. From the point of view of the researcher the major advantage of CD-ROM is that a search can be conducted without any cost and, in particular, without pressure from the equivalent of a taxi meter ticking away while the search is being conducted.

From the point of the view of the library or other department responsible for providing information to researchers within an organization the cost of licensing a database in CD-ROM form has to be balanced against the costs of providing on-line service. The heavier the usage of on-line service the more economic it becomes to license the database in CD-ROM form. If expenditure on a particular on-line database is close to the cost of licensing the CD-ROM, then it makes sense to license because the cost of using the database is then no longer time related. The CD-ROM can also be used for self-learning by researchers independently of the library staff.

From the point of view of the database provider, revenue gained from licensing CD-ROMs to users has to be balanced against the potential loss of revenue from on-line users. Where all or part of a database is published in CD-ROM form the cost has to take into account data production costs, not just CD-ROM production costs. The licensing fee usually reflects "what-the-traffic-will-bear". Table 3.1 includes information on the cost of a number of CD-ROMs relevant to the social sciences.

A worldwide reference library

When the researcher has used an on-line bibliographical service or CD-ROM to identify relevant publications, the next task is usually to locate the actual material. The first source to be consulted is likely to be the library of the user's own institution, and the method of consultation will be the computerized catalogue. Nowadays almost all major libraries have computerized catalogues, and, if it computerized, it can be expected that it will also be networked. The library catalogue of the institution should be accessible from any networked computer on site.

In Britain the local network which links the library catalogue and most computers on the site to the institution is likely to be connected also to JANET (Joint Academic Network) which connects to other universities in Britain. JANET itself is linked to other national and regional networks through the Internet system which connects every major university in the rest of the Western world. Users need not limit their searches to the library of their own institution. Academics can through JANET examine the catalogue of almost any other university library in Britain, and through Internet can examine the catalogue of every major library in the world.

Library catalogues are just one example of the information sources which can be accessed through JANET and Internet. These networks also give access to many other kinds of computerized information: catalogues and lists, computer programs, electronic journals, bulletin boards, messages on electronic mailing lists, the full text of books, and in the US, at least, governmental documents of many kinds. Users of this worldwide library are not restricted to the electronic equivalent of reading material on the premises – as they would be in a reference library. Users can download material and print copies. And because this material is expressed in digital form, users can examine the material using the searching and other information processing facilities made available by the computer.

The availability of information sources accessible on-line will continue to grow. Computerization of the library catalogue and making the catalogue available on-line makes life easier for the librarian as well as the user. Users who do more for themselves are less likely to make lengthy enquiries of library staff. Similar considerations can be expected to apply to other information providers – and potential information providers. Giving on-line access, from the point of view of the information provider, can be both the equivalent of a free advertisement and a means of satisfying enquirers' needs without the use of staff resources. In the United States, which is committed to freedom of information, it appears to have become standard practice to "publish" all major governmental documents electronically at the same time as they are released to the press.

Searching the worldwide library and downloading documents is not as easy as finding books in a library and borrowing them. The major difference is that users have to carry out the searching and downloading processes by themselves – without being able to ask questions of the electronic equivalent of a librarian whenever they are uncertain of the next step. But a number of tools have been developed to make finding a way

40

around this worldwide library easier. The best first step for most users and potential users is to examine one of the many recently published books which describe the information available through Internet and the various tools which can be used to access the material. LaQuey & Ryer (1992) provide a good introduction. Kehoe (1992) is available on-line for free. Krol (1992) gives a comprehensive users' guide.

Statistical information

Statistical surveys typically involve centralizing a mass of information into a single dataset. For many decades these datasets comprised a mass of forms and punched cards. Restriction on access was inevitable because duplication of the dataset would have been costly. Central control was necessary in order to make checks on accuracy and to enable unanticipated enquiries of the dataset to be answered. The results of these surveys could only be made available as aggregate data, i.e. as statistical tables.

The advent of the computer changed the situation. When the dataset is expressed in electronic form it becomes more tractable in every way. The technology makes it easier to exercise central control. It can easily be anonymized so that individual records cannot be identified. Computer programs can facilitate checks on accuracy. Programs can usually deal with unanticipated queries.

The technology can also be used to duplicate and communicate. The dataset can be made available to anyone, anywhere, who has suitable computing and communications equipment. Anyone with suitable programs can make their own extractions and analysis of the data. Provided that the microdata are anonymized so that it is not possible for individuals to be identified, there is little necessity for central control. Centralisation in terms of the collection of statistical information can be part of a system which is quite decentralized in terms of the distribution of the results – see Thomas (1984) and Thomas (1990).

By the late 1960s a number of survey or data archive centres were developed in the leading industrial countries. These centres encouraged individuals and organizations responsible for conducting a survey to deposit a copy of the results of the survey data with the archive in the form of anonymized microdata so that the results could be made avail-

41

able to other researchers – for what is usually called secondary analysis. Microdata can be defined as datasets comprising anonymized individual records, and can be contrasted to aggregate data which is expressed in the form of statistical tables.

Access to the microdata means that, with the help of suitable computer programs, new kinds of analysis can be conducted. If a survey questionnaire comprises 100 questions, for example, nearly ten thousand (i.e. 100 times 99) different two-way tables can be constructed from the microdata. It is unlikely that any single report on the survey would include more than a small fraction of the combinations possible. The potential for the use of microdata has established the value of *secondary analysis* which has been defined as "any further analysis of an existing dataset which presents interpretations, conclusions, or knowledge additional to, or different from, those presented in the first report on the enquiry as a whole" (Hakim, 1982).

Already the term "secondary analysis" has become problematized by information technology developments. There is often no clearly identifiable "first report on the enquiry as a whole". Major surveys, such as those listed in Table 3.2 below, are increasingly being designed with a multiplicity of users in mind. The order in which reports on these surveys are made is related to the activities and interests of users and not to the production of general reports.

Table 3.2 indicates that in Britain there has been a gradual growth in the coverage of survey data in the 1980s and that this growth of coverage seems to be continuing. New areas covered by survey are the British Crime Surveys of 1982, 1984, 1988 and 1992, the National Study of Sexual Attitudes and Lifestyles in 1991 and the British Household Panel Survey from 1992. The European Labour Force Survey is now conducted quarterly. The British Social Attitudes Survey – with parallel surveys in many other countries – is now conducted annually. It can now be said that every major kind of human activity in Britain and, probably those in most other advanced industrial countries, is covered by a major survey, and that the raw data of these surveys is available to any interested researcher.

The access point for researchers in Britain is the Data Archive at the University of Essex. The researcher can log on to the BIRON service at the Data Archive and make a systematic search of surveys held by the Archive. The Archive holds copies of all the major surveys listed in Table 3.2. A search using BIRON would cover the thousands of smaller surveys

STATISTICAL INFORMATION

Table 3.2   Selected major survey datasets.

Name and year of origin	Sample size	Topics covered
Census of Population 1801 Decennial	100 per cent	Usual residence/visitors. Household composition, housing, occupation, workplace, migration, car ownership
National Food Survey, 1940. Annual	8,000 households	Quantity and value of food purchased
Family Expenditure Survey, 1953–4 Annual	12,000 households	Expenditure patterns. Household composition. Income from all sources
National Travel Survey, 1965	26,000 individuals	Travel by all means of transport including walking and cycling
General Household Survey, 1971 Annual	20,000 households; 10,000 individuals	Topics have included education, employment, fertility, health, housing, income, migration
Labour Force Survey, 1973. Quarterly.	96,000 households	Employment, unemployment, housing, nationality, ethnic groups
British Crime Survey, 1981, 1984, 1988, 1992	16,000 households	Crimes whether reported or not, attitudes to crimes and to police
British Social Attitudes Survey, 1983. Annual	3,000 households	Attitudes on enterprise, family, health, unions, welfare, etc.
Sample of Anonymized Records from Census, 1991	2 per cent of households, and 1 per cent of individuals	All census variables
Census Longitudinal Study, 1991 – with sample dating from 1971	1 per cent of individuals	All census variables plus births, deaths
Sexual Attitudes and Lifestyles, 1991	19,000	Attitudes to sex behaviour, sex education, sex experience.

carried out in Britain and would also cover major surveys conducted in other countries which are held by the Archive. (See the quarterly *ESCR Data Archive Bulletin* as the source for information on BIRON and other Archive matters discussed in these paragraphs.)

43

For data from small surveys it may be convenient for the researcher to take delivery directly from the Data Archive – which can supply on CD-ROM, and in a variety of magnetic formats. For large datasets it may be more convenient to use the services offered by Manchester University Computing Centre. MUCC have their own copies of all the major datasets – such as the Sample of Anonymized Records from the 1991 Census.

The advantages of using the MUCC include the use of the disk space, programs and advice. Many of the large datasets together with the programs necessary to analyze them need more disk space than is available on the typical microcomputer. The advice of the Centre may be important in order to handle the data. Most of the major government datasets originating from the Office of Population Censuses and Surveys, for example, are stored in SIR format. SIR is a programming language and database system suited to handling hierarchical data (e.g. covering households and individuals in the households). It is necessary to write a short program in SIR in order to create a dataset in a form which can be easily exported to a system using a more widely used program such as the Statistical Package for the Social Sciences (SPSS). (For more detail, see Ward & Dale, this volume.)

Other sources are available to the on-line researcher besides the Data Archive and MUCC. NOMIS (National Online Manpower Information Service) gives access to most surveys relating to the labour market – including the biennial Census of Employment (conducted through employers). SWURCC (South West Universities Regional Computing Centre) hosts a database of economic data. This gives longer runs than are available from other than a collection of printed volumes, and collection in digital form allows the data to be imported into another program such as a spreadsheet for further processing and integration with other datasets.

Administrative statistics and geographical information systems

An important aspect of research in the social sciences is the inductive synergy of the bringing together of information of different kinds to increase understanding. Such synergy is graphically illustrated by the use of geographical information systems – or GIS for short – as described in Chapter 11 in this volume by David Gilbert. Up to the time of writing the major developments in GIS have been in use for research into matters belonging to the physical world where existing information is used such as that from existing maps, and information which can be collected automatically is used, such as by aerial photographic survey. The only major set of data relating to human populations which has the 100 per cent coverage necessary for local area analysis has been that of the decennial Censuses of Population. But this situation may change substantially if administrative data become more widely available for local areas.

Administrative data is typically collected on a 100 per cent rather than a sample basis, and usually includes the address of the subject. Nowadays virtually every address in Britain is postcoded and lists are available which make it possible to attach a postcode to an address which is otherwise incomplete. This means that, for the first time, it has become administratively possible to code all addresses from a dataset according to geographical location. Such possibilities have potent implications for the development of geographical information systems relating to human activities (Shepherd 1993).

Central government holds many records which include address, income tax, national insurance details, child allowances, welfare payments, etc. Gas boards, electricity companies and mortgage companies likewise hold records which include the address of their customers. In principle these data could now be made available on the basis of postcode areas (or aggregates of postcode areas if there was danger of revealing information on individuals). The value of statistics of these kinds to local government, as well as to researchers, could be substantial. For the first time it would be possible for local government social services departments, for example, to monitor the level of central government welfare payments in their area.

Such data would also give enormous scope for analysis of many different kinds by social scientists. The ready availability of maps bringing together information such as income levels, unemployment, crime rates, educational achievements, etc., and the facility automatically to compute and display descriptive statistics of any kind on the basis of these data, could have a major impact on the way much social research is conducted.

To what extent will these administrative data become available for local areas? At the time of writing early in 1994, it appears that government has been slow to recognize the governmental advantages which could accrue from postcoded data. The only major example has been the postcoding of the statistics for the number of registered unemployed. Local authorities have been able to obtain monthly figures for the number of registered unemployed on a postcode basis through the Data Archive at Essex University since 1982. But there is little indication that other central government datasets will become available on a postcode basis. (See discussion in IMAC Research, forthcoming; D. Gilbert, this volume.)

Computer mediated communication and the production of social science

So far this chapter has looked at new technology mainly from the point of view of the use of information produced by others. But what is usually called computer mediated communication (CMC) also enables social scientists to exchange information and interact – and thereby to produce new information. The easiest and most widely used system is that for electronic mail. Email has the advantage over post of being faster, and is asynchronous, that is to say it has the advantage over voice telephone of not requiring both parties to be on-line at the same time. The convenience, and time and cost saving, of email are being exploited, for example, by a growing number of electronic journals. Email can be used to support co-operative working of many kinds. It makes the joint production of papers and books much easier. To give an example from my personal experience, use of email cuts something like six months off the time needed to organize an international conference (see also Fisher, this volume).

CMC includes a variety of facilities besides email LISTSERVs and other email lists. Bulletin boards and computer conferences support many-to-many communication and can create interactions which are qualitatively different from those produced by the use of email for one-to-one communication and paper based communication systems. LISTSERVs and other email lists provide the electronic equivalent of a kind of continuous newsletter. The distinguishing feature of a mailing list system is that messages from a user are automatically sent to the full list of all users. In 1992 the Economic and Social Research Council set up such a system on computers at Newcastle University which can be inspected through the NISS system.

Bulletin boards and conferences are in effect electronic notice boards. They support the posting of documents and the discussion of documents. In conferencing and bulletin board systems messages are stored on a host computer. Users log on to the host computer in order to read and post messages. Making effective use of lists and conferences depends in part upon being attuned to the culture of a particular system – as well as being familiar with the software features. Four modes of interaction seem typical of most systems, but the relative importance of these modes varies between systems.

One mode is straightforward information giving. Frederick (1993) describes, for example, how the international APC (Association for Progressive Communications, with British partner GreenNet) disseminated news from Moscow at the time of the attempted coup in August 1990, from the Middle East during the Gulf War in 1991, and from the United Nations Conference on Environment and Development in Rio de Janeiro in 1992. (See also Farwell et al. 1993 for detail of the range of topics covered by APC conferences.)

Another mode is information exchange. The type of message which is most likely to get a response on any system is a request for information. Exchange of information of this kind is typical of conferences whose subject matter is computer programs and equipment. But information exchange is not limited to such subject matter. The natural function of these systems, it is argued by Jones & Thomas (1992), is mutual support. The character of these exchanges is captured by the FAQ (Frequently Answered Questions) topic which is set up on many conferences. Many organizations exploit the information exchange features of this system as a means of giving information to their customers/clients/users, etc. The organization's own staff can answer questions, but it is likely that many will be answered by other customers or clients.

Another mode is serious and purposeful discussions. The achievement of such discussions is one of the principal goals of the use of computer conferencing for education, and such discussions are characteristic of topics devoted to assignments on the Open University's CoSy conferencing system (Chapters 9 and 11 of Mason & Kaye, 1989). Discussions on specialist email lists, and on internationally oriented conferencing systems such as the APC network, can involve the world's leading authorities in the subject matter. Discussion can be geared to political purposes – such as that on the WELL system, hosted but far from limited to California, which led to the creation of the Electronic Frontier Foundation (see Sterling 1992 and, for a general account of WELL, see Rheingold, 1993).

The fourth mode which is characteristic of nearly all systems is chat messages – that is light hearted greetings, banter and witticisms. On

some systems chat messages dominate and on most systems chat dominates some of the time. Systems which are moderated, i.e. messages are
subject to editorial control by an editor, can avoid chat messages. Moderated systems tends to be dominated by information giving and exchange
with little discussion.

There are no formal systems for exploring these lists and conferences
as there are for databases. Harasim (1993) gives an excellent overview of
the possibilities and problems for worldwide networks, but the guides to
the Internet, such as that by Krol already cited, are of more practical help
in finding systems which might be useful or stimulating. On many systems the messages are available only for a short period of time, and, of
course many messages and discussions have only ephemeral value. Perhaps the best method of using these systems is to become an active participant by contributing to a discussion and by asking questions on
whatever system seems accessible and most relevant. Such initiatives
might elicit the kind of responses that are needed or might lead to suggestions about other systems where the discussion or questioning might
be more appropriately pursued.

Conclusion

The impact of the developments described in this chapter on the work of
social scientists seems likely to take two forms – a major impact on a minority of social scientists and a slow but inexorable influence on the work
of all social scientists. A growth is already apparent in the number of social scientists who make use of on-line services, and of data provided on
CD-ROM, a substantial part of their work. This pattern is well developed,
for example, in the area of the secondary use of survey data. A number of
researchers make the analysis of surveys carried out by others a major
means of pursuing their own specialism. The reports of the British Social
Attitudes surveys, for example, and the corresponding international reports, comprise chapters written by specialists in the different subject areas (Jowell et al. 1992 and 1993). The individual authors draw upon their
expertise in interpreting the survey results and their expertise in turn
contributes to developments in the design of the survey. The computer
technology has enabled more people to be involved in these surveys than
would otherwise have been possible, has helped to bring more expertise

into the interpretation of the results and into the design of the question-naire, and has supported the more rapid production of reports.

There are parallel patterns in other areas. The availability of world-wide information services supported by Internet allows for social scientists to advance knowledge within their specialism by conducting research and writing reports which bring together information from different sources in different countries. Electronic mail, mailing lists and computer conferences support discussion and exchange of information between social scientists, support and encourage co-operative work involving social scientists in different parts of the world, and facilitate rapid production of reports on the work conducted. It seems likely that a growing proportion of advances in the social sciences will be based upon such on-line activities. These advances will depend upon bringing together information from a wider range and variety of sources than was previously possible, on bringing together knowledge and ideas in the minds of social scientists with diverse interests, and in making and reporting on these syntheses more rapidly than would have been possible without the use of the on-line technology.

Making advances in the social sciences in this kind of way is not typical of the work style of most social scientists. A division is apparent between a relatively small proportion of social scientists who give a high proportion of their time to exploiting the possibilities of on-line facilities and CD-ROM as described in this chapter and the large majority whose work style has not yet changed significantly in spite of these technological advances. This division seems likely to endure for some time. Advances in social science achieved through exploitation of network and data storage facilities do not lessen in any way the scope, possibilities or need for advances in the social sciences using traditional tools and methods.

On-line and storage technologies are likely to have a general impact on the work of most social scientists only slowly. Typically the first stage has been the computerization of the library catalogue and it seems likely that nearly all academics have got used to using a terminal rather than a card index or microfiche. At the time of writing it seems that only a minority of social scientists in Britain are electronic mail users, but nearly all could become users if they chose to do so. As well as offering email facilities, most universities are introducing a range of networked servers giving various information services – such as access to Internet and various Internet tools. It seems likely that as email and information services of all

ON-LINE SERVICES AND CD-ROM

kinds become more established that the quality of the alternative provisions made will decline – at least in relative terms. If so there will be steadily increased pressure for social scientists to become users of email and computerized information services.

The new technology may be more familiar to many entrants to the social sciences than to established social scientists, and the pressures on younger social scientists to use the technology may be greater than on established social scientists. It would not be surprising, for example, if university regulations began to require that PhD theses demonstrated ability to conduct a computer aided search of the relevant literature and other sources of information – including the identification and use of relevant microdata from surveys.

In these kinds of ways the technology is likely to change gradually the nature of the work of nearly all social scientists.

References

Bradley, P. & Hanson, T. 1993. *Going online and CD-ROM*. London: ASLIB.
Brent, E. E. & Anderson, R. E. 1990. *Computer applications in the social sciences*. Philadelphia: Temple University Press.
Colvin, G. 1986. The current state of text retrieval. In *CD-ROM – the new papyrus*, S. Lambert & S. Ropiequet (eds), 131–6. Redmond, Wash.: Microsoft Press.
Convey, J. 1992. *Online information retrieval – an introductory manual to principles and practice*. London: Library Association Publishing.
Economic and Social Research Council. Quarterly. *Data Archive Bulletin*, ESRC Data Archive, University of Essex.
Farwell, E. et. al. 1993. APC networks: global community activism. *Proceedings of International Conference on Information Technology and People*, Moscow, May 1993, vol. 1, 206–16.
Frederick, H. 1993. Computer networks and the emergence of global civil society. In *Global networks: computers and international communication*, L. Harasim (ed.), 283–95. Cambridge, Mass.: MIT Press.
Hakim, C. 1982. *Secondary analysis in social research: a guide to data sources and methods with examples*. London: George Allen & Unwin.
Harasim, L. (ed.) 1993. *Global networks: computers and international communication*. Cambridge, Mass.: MIT Press.
Humphrey, S. M. & B. J. Melloni 1986. *Databases – a primer for retrieving information by computer*. Englewood Cliffs, NJ: Prentice Hall.
IMAC Research, forthcoming. *Regional and local statistics: conference papers and discussion*. Statistics Users' Council Annual Conference, 16 November 1993. Esher: IMAC Research.

REFERENCES

Jones, A. Q. & R. Thomas, 1992. Group dynamic in computer mediated communication. In *Emerging trends in education,* Proceedings of a conference held in Moscow, April 1992. Moscow: International Centre for Scientific and Technical Information.

Jowell, R. et al. (eds) 1992, *British social attitudes – 9th report.* Aldershot: Gower.

Jowell, R. et al. (eds) 1993 *British social attitudes – 10th international report.* Aldershot: Gower.

Keyhoe, B. P. 1992. *Zen and the art of the Internet – a beginner's guide.* Obtainable from author: brendan@cs.widener.edu

Krol, E. 1992. *The whole Internet catalogue and user's guide.* Sebastopol, Calif.: O'Reilly & Associates.

Lambert S. & S. Ropiequet (eds) 1986. CD-ROM – *the new Papyrus.* Redmond, Wash.: Microsoft Press.

LaQuey, T. & J. C. Ryer. 1992. *The Internet companion – a beginner's guide to global networking.* Reading, Mass.: Addison-Wesley.

Mason, R. & A. Kaye (eds) 1989. *Mindweave: communication, computers and distance education.* Oxford: Pergamon.

Rheingold, H. 1992. *A slice of life in my virtual community.* In *Global networks: computers and international communication,* L. Harasim (ed.) 57–80. Cambridge, Mass.: MIT Press.

Ropiequet, S. et al. (eds) 1987. CD-ROM – *optical publishing.* Redmond, Wash.: Microsoft Press.

Shepherd, J. 1993. Getting more from postcoded data. In *Regional and local statistics: conference papers and discussion,* IMAC Research, 167–85, Statistics Users' Council Annual Conference, 16 November 1993. Esher: IMAC Research.

Sterling, B. 1992. *The hacker crackdown.* Harmondsworth: Penguin.

Thomas, R. 1984. Why have government statistics? (And how to cut their cost). *Journal of Public Policy* 4(2), 85–102.

Thomas, R. 1990. The case for the abolition of the government statistical service. *Radical Statistics* 46, Autumn, 7–12.

51

CHAPTER 4

Computer assisted personal interviewing in survey research

Jean Martin and Tony Manners

The term computer assisted personal interviewing (CAPI) describes the use of portable computers by interviewers in face-to-face interviews to record respondents' answers directly into a computer rather than onto a paper questionnaire. CAPI questionnaires are computer programs which usually run on notebook computers. The question text appears on the screen, with possible response categories or an indication of what sort of answer is required. The interviewer reads out the question, enters the response and the next appropriate question appears automatically. Instructions to interviewers and messages about errors also appear on the screen.

History of computer assisted interviewing (CAI)

Computers have been used for many years in survey research, first for data analysis but more recently for data collection. Although computer assisted interviewing for face-to-face interviews is one of the more recent developments, the history of CAI goes back to the early 1970s.

Early developments in North America were rather different from those in Europe (see, for example, Baker 1990, Martin & O'Muircheartaigh 1991, Weeks 1992). In the USA in particular, much survey work is carried out by telephone. Interviewers using networked PCs usually work in a central location, to facilitate control of work and centralized training and supervision. From controlling interviewers' work the next step was to use computers to control the interview – and computer assisted telephone interviewing (CATI) was born. In centralized CATI installations the computer software controls the sequence of questions in the interview and the flow of work to different interviewers. It may also sample and dial telephone numbers, provide up-to-date response information and enable supervisors to listen in to interviewers and monitor their performance. In the USA CATI was first implemented in market research, but during the 1970s it spread to academic social research (Freeman & Shanks 1983), and then to government research (Nicholls & Groves 1986).

CAI developed along a different route in Europe because telephone interviewing was much less widely used, particularly for social research. In Great Britain and in many other European countries there are serious limitations on the use of the telephone for surveys which are designed to be representative of the general population, partly because telephone ownership tends to be lower than in North America, but also because there are still major methodological obstacles to obtaining adequate probability samples for telephone surveys (Collins & Sykes 1987, Foreman & Collins 1991). Interviewers also find more difficulties in gaining public co-operation, and lower tolerance of long interviews, than on face-to-face surveys. Thus although telephone interviewing is becoming more common for market research surveys, it is rarely used for social research other than for following up an initial personal contact.

In Europe the main starting point for CAI development was not interviewing but data entry from paper documents. Organizations such as the Netherlands Central Bureau of Statistics (NCBS) recognized that savings could be made using interactive computer-assisted data input and editing (CADI) systems, and developed software to support this. The advent of light cheap portable microcomputers which could be used by interviewers in the field for face-to-face interviews led to the CADI software being developed further to support CAPI. Early initiatives were taken by the NCBS (van Bastelaer et al. 1987) and Statistics Sweden (Statistics Sweden 1989), each of which developed their own software system.

The use of CAPI for large scale household surveys was pioneered by NCBS for its Labour Force Survey (LFS) starting in January 1987, followed by the British Office of Population Censuses and Surveys (OPCS), which has used combined CAPI and CATI on the British LFS since 1990, and Statistics Sweden for the Swedish LFS the following year. In the US, however, despite extensive development work on a number of surveys, CAPI was not used for a complete major government household survey until January 1994 when the Current Population Survey (the US LFS) moved to a CAPI/CATI system. In Europe transition to CAPI has accelerated in recent years: most major British government surveys will have converted to CAI by the end of 1994 (Martin 1993), and CAPI is increasingly being used on other national surveys by most survey organizations which carry out face-to-face interviews. (See, for example, Nicholls & Matchett 1992, and numerous reports in NCBS 1992 and OPCS 1993.)

A further option which, unlike CAPI and CATI, avoids the need for an interviewer is computer assisted self-interviewing (CASI). CASI can be accomplished in a number of ways (Weeks 1992). For example, for business surveys a questionnaire on a floppy disk can be sent for organizations to complete on their own computers. CASI for household surveys is limited at present; it has been used on a multi-purpose panel survey where it has proved cost-effective to leave computers in households for a lengthy period for respondents to transmit information at regular intervals (Saris & de Pijper 1987). A further use of CASI is in the course of a CAPI interview when the interviewer turns the computer over to the respondent to enter his or her answers directly – generally because sensitive information is required. This method is being used on the British Crime Survey in 1994 to ask questions about drug use, sexual victimization (for women) and handling stolen goods. CASI may be augmented by providing the respondent with a headset and playing questions through it (audio CASI), avoiding literacy problems (O'Reilly et al. 1992).

This chapter concentrates on CAPI, but much of what is said applies equally to CATI. It describes the main features of a CAPI system compared with traditional paper based surveys, the likely impact on a survey organization of changing to this mode of interviewing, the advantages and disadvantages of CAPI, and finally looks at some of the possibilities for future developments in this field.

Main features of a CAPI system

The interview is just one part of the whole survey process. An integrated computer assisted survey system therefore goes beyond simple data entry. The aim is to integrate and automate as much of the survey process as possible. However, the questionnaire specification is even more important than in paper and pencil interviewing (PAPI) surveys since the resulting program provides the data description – the survey metadata – which is carried with the data throughout later stages of the survey process, including the analysis.

The questionnaire for a CAI survey is specified in a computer program generally using one of the specialized software packages designed for this purpose. Examples include Blaise, Cases, Ci2, Microtab (called Autoquest in North America) and Quancept. The program includes the question wording and response categories, as for a paper questionnaire. In addition it specifies the range of permissible answers for each question – the response codes or the range for numeric answers. It is also possible to indicate that the answer is to be in the form of free text. The program specifies the order in which questions are to be asked and routing instructions which determine which respondents are asked which questions. It allows question wording to be tailored in various ways – inserting respondent's names, conditional text like the appropriate gender, and relevant computed values like dates and totals.

Various types of check are carried out as the interview proceeds. Most CAPI software does not allow answers outside the specified range to be entered: if the interviewer tries to do so, an error message appears on the screen. In addition other checks can be included in the questionnaire program, for example to check consistency between different answers. Most CAI software distinguishes between hard and soft checks – the former have to be resolved before the interviewer can move on to the next question while the latter are generally warnings that an answer is unlikely but interviewers can over-ride such checks if they are sure that the answer given is valid.

Text answers may be entered for later clerical coding or may be dealt with using computer assisted coding. This can operate in a variety of ways. In the simplest form a list of possible codes appears on the screen and the interviewer (or coder) selects the appropriate code which is then added to the record. More sophisticated systems involve matching the text of the answer to text in a dictionary of responses; matches between the text entered and the dictionary responses are displayed on the screen for the interviewer or coder to choose from or confirm. Fully automated coding systems include algorithms to determine which is the best match, taking coding decisions out of human hands entirely. However, automated systems work best with simple data which are rarely found in social research. Thus at present a fully automated coding system is likely to

55

lead to inadequate matching for a significant proportion of the codes, and a switch to an assisted mode where the coder makes the final selection is necessary.

Ideally all checking of the validity of answers is carried out during the interview so that at the end of the interview no further editing is required. When the interview is complete interviewers can transmit the information collected back to the office via a modem. At the office completed interview data are received from all the interviewers working on a survey as soon as the interviews are finished. On simple surveys the data are then immediately available for analysis, although coding of text answers like occupation details will be necessary in some instances. This may be carried out by interviewers at home before they transmit completed interviews, as on the British LFS (Manners 1992), or by office based staff as a separate operation.

On complex surveys it may not be possible to carry out all the editing required during the interview. In Britain, the Family Resources Survey, which is a complex income survey, and the Family Expenditure Survey (FES), which collects detailed financial information about household income and expenditure using a combination of interviews and two week expenditure diaries, both require an office editing stage. There are several reasons for this. Respondents and interviewers together may be unable to decide precisely how some questions should be answered; for example, respondents generally know their total income from welfare benefits but may be unable to split it into amounts for different benefits. Interviewers make notes and an expert in the office translates the notes into survey codes. Other checks are too complex to operate during the interview and are carried out later. If an office editing stage is required, it is important that it is designed to integrate well with the fieldwork data collection stage (Manners et al. 1993).

The best CAI software is designed to ensure that different modes of data collection – CAPI, CATI and CADI from paper questionnaires – can readily be combined. A single questionnaire program creates both CAPI and CATI versions, so the data collected in one mode can be transferred to the other mode without being reorganized in any way. This level of integration makes survey processing faster and less error-prone than in systems which require special programs to transfer data between interviewing modes. Likewise, office editing should ideally be carried out in the same CAI software as the interview. In the best systems it is possible to switch the software from the CAPI mode in which the data were collected to CADI mode, which is more appropriate for editing. Here the screen displays many question fields at a time, like a page of listed items, with those in error flagged. An editor needs to have free movement around the questionnaire, to look at any answer relevant to a particular edit query. This is possible in CADI, whereas CAPI generally restricts movement to questions on the current route and does not allow forward movement until any edit query on the current question has been resolved. Since CADI software is principally designed for data entry after the interview, it permits data to be entered in any field and only applies range, routing and consistency checks when the editor chooses.

As noted earlier, the aim is to computerize and integrate other parts of the survey process with the interview. On surveys with preselected samples, sampling information is fed into the system so the interviewer has on his or her computer information about the addresses or people selected for the survey. Information about calls and progress can be entered for each case, providing office staff with the basis for monitoring progress of the fieldwork and response rates. Selection stages which take place in the field can be automated: for example, if the interviewer enters details of all adults in a household, the computer can be programmed to select one at random for the interviewer to approach when a sample of individuals is required. Brewster (1993) describes a system for quota sampling on a CAPI survey.

Interviewers' instructions, training materials and other documentation can also be provided in electronic form (although the extent to which this happens in practice varies). Case management information on the progress of the data through collection, return to the office and further processing can be monitored by automated systems instead of involving clerical work. Administrative information, such as that needed for interviewers' pay claims, may be provided directly from computer logs (Kindel 1991).

CAI software packages often include analysis and publication modules which can read the data from the data collection modules automatically. They also usually include facilities for converting the data into forms required for standard database and analysis packages, like Oracle, the xBase products, SIR, QUANTUM, SPSS and SAS. Data definitions are carried across so it is a simple matter to produce a file ready for analysis.

Comparison of CAPI and traditional paper based methods

Table 4.1 summarizes the main stages in traditional PAPI surveys compared with CAPI surveys. It illustrates the elimination of some of the stages required for PAPI surveys and the greater number of stages required before interviewing can start for CAPI surveys, compensated for by fewer stages after the fieldwork.

Clearly on CAPI surveys there is no need to type and print paper questionnaires. However, the edit checks are incorporated into the questionnaire program so they have to be specified and tested before the fieldwork can start. The integrated nature of CAPI means that data description is part of the questionnaire design. On a PAPI survey this is generally a separate stage when a program is written to allow the data to be input into a computer prior to editing. Coding of text answers is required in both modes, although computer assisted coding in conjunction with CAPI may make it easier for interviewers to code answers rather than having an office coding stage. Unlike PAPI surveys, CAPI surveys do not require interviewers to carry out checks on the completeness of questionnaires before they are returned to the office. On a PAPI survey completed questionnaires need to be keyed and an edit program written and tested; the data are then entered into the computer, and edited and corrected – often several cycles are required until the data are considered sufficiently "clean" to be ready for analysis; this stage contributes significantly to the time taken for complex PAPI surveys.

In a paper based system, the paper questionnaire itself is a vital document which customers, researchers and others interested in the survey use as a detailed record of what the survey covers, over and above the

Table 4.1 Main stages in PAPI and CAPI surveys.

PAPI	CAPI
Design questionnaire	Design questionnaire
Type and print questionnaire	Define data
Interviewing	Program edit checks
Define data	**Interviewing**
Program edit checks	Code text answers
Code text answers	Add derived variables
Key data	**Data ready for analysis**
Edit and correct	
Add derived variables	
Data ready for analysis	

sort of broad outline and objectives which are likely to be included in a formal survey proposal. On a CAPI survey some form of paper record of the questionnaire is required in addition to the electronic version to facilitate discussions between customers and researchers, and for reference at the analysis stage. CAI software varies in what sort of paper documentation can be produced. Some packages rely on the ease with which their program scripts, with suitable comments where necessary, can be understood by those not versed in the programming language; others produce an approximation to a conventional paper questionnaire. Program scripts have the advantage of usually showing the edit checks as well as questions whereas on paper based surveys a separate record of these is required.

Organizational impact of changing to CAPI

The transition from paper based to CAPI methods, with all that is implied for other parts of the survey process, is one of the most significant changes to affect survey organizations in fifty years. For almost everyone a lengthy period of learning and adaptation is involved. Much of the huge body of knowledge about traditional paper based methods which has accumulated over the years needs to be relearned or adapted. For example, most experienced survey researchers build up expertise in estimating how long particular tasks will take, what sort of staff are required to carry them out and how much they will cost. Designing, planning, costing and timetabling a CAPI survey means starting again, almost from scratch – a difficult process as the authors will testify.

From the start of CAPI development it was apparent that there would be major organizational implications (Brakenhoff et al. 1987). For all major British government surveys a business case has had to be made to show that the initial costs of development and equipment for CAPI would be recovered by savings in running the survey and earlier availability of results. Competition for survey work among all survey organizations means that CAPI can only be justified if there are tangible commercial advantages. The major cost savings arise from reductions in the number of staff required to carry out a survey, which affects the organization as a whole.

As well as some jobs such as data keying disappearing altogether, CAPI implies major changes to the jobs of staff involved in most parts of the survey process. For example, the process of designing a questionnaire is very different when it is in the form of a computer program rather than being laid out on paper. Different organizations take different approaches to CAPI questionnaire design, some expecting their research staff to do the major part of the programming while others expect the research staff to specify questions, response codes, routing and checks for computing specialists to write the CAPI program. Rather than receiving a paper document to look through, the field staff need to work through the questionnaire screens to judge whether they will be suitable for the interviewers.

As yet few survey organizations have completed the full transition to computer assisted methods and only a small number have published accounts of the process. The introduction of widespread automation at NCBS and its impact on the whole organization is well documented (de Heer 1991, Bethlehem & Keller 1991). Nicholls & Matchett (1992) and Jamieson et al. (1992) describe some of the issues facing the US Bureau of the Census and Statistics Canada respectively, while Martin (1993) describes the transition to CAPI at the Social Survey Division of the Office of Population Censuses and Surveys in Britain. These accounts are all of major government statistical organizations; commercial survey organizations do not seem to have published accounts of the process of organizational change they are undergoing – but perhaps it is too early to expect this as most are still in a state of transition.

Advantages and disadvantages of CAPI

The advantages of CAPI over traditional paper based methods are considerable; however, there are also some disadvantages (e.g. Baker 1990, Martin & O'Muircheartaigh 1991).

Advantages of CAPI

Acceptability to interviewers and respondents
At first the main concern was whether interviewers could adapt successfully to the new mode of interviewing and whether respondents would

accept their answers being entered directly into a computer. Early trials focused mainly on these two aspects of CAPI but it soon became apparent that there was little cause for concern. One study after another showed that respondents were largely indifferent to the change in mode of interview and most interviewers positively preferred CAPI to PAPI (Statistics Sweden 1989, Baker 1990). Moreover, no adverse effect of CAPI on response rates has been found (e.g. Bradburn et al. 1991, Sperry et al. 1991, Martin et al. 1993). In the most detailed studies to date, Wojcik & Baker (1992) and Couper & Burt (1993) have confirmed the very positive attitudes of interviewers to CAPI in general, despite some criticisms of aspects of particular hardware or software or particular agencies' procedures, and some general concerns about personal safety while using expensive equipment in public areas.

Reduction in time elapsed between fieldwork and the availability of data for analysis

At the end of the interview the data are in electronic form and, apart from any coding of text answers, are ready to be combined into a dataset for analysis. Since more tasks need to be carried out before fieldwork can start than on traditional paper based surveys the total time taken from the start of the survey to the analysis stage will not necessarily be shorter on CAPI than PAPI surveys but the experience of NCBS and OPCS indicates that this is the case for all but the most complex one-off surveys.

Improved data quality

A number of features of CAPI lead to improved data quality. First, since routes through the questionnaire are programmed and the next appropriate question appears automatically on the screen, there is no possibility of interviewers asking the wrong question or inadvertently omitting a question, both common types of error on PAPI surveys. The range of possible answers is defined in the program, so there is also no possibility of answers being entered outside the specified range. Finally, because checks are carried out during the interview as the data are entered, errors can be resolved between the interviewer and respondent rather than being left to office based editors who cannot ask further questions to clarify the situation. The net result is that CAPI leads to lower levels of item non-response, greater consistency of responses and little need for office editing after the interview.

The impact CAPI has on the data quality of a given survey will depend on its complexity and the type of answers required, but even on the simplest some improvement can be seen. Martin et al. (1993) found lower levels of item non-response in CAPI compared with PAPI interviews on a simple attitude survey with mainly precoded answers and very little routing. Much greater improvements have been detected on more complex surveys such as the British Family Expenditure Survey where trials showed much lower levels of office editing required than for the paper based FES to achieve the same levels of completeness and consistency in the data (Manners et al. 1993).

So-called "sensitive behaviour" is generally under-reported on surveys. The mounting evidence that respondents are more likely to admit to such behaviour in a CAPI than a PAPI interview can be taken as an indication of improved data quality (Bradburn et al. 1991, Baker & Bradburn 1991), although disadvantages are discussed below.

Savings in costs

Elimination of data keying and the elimination or reduction of office based editing and coding produce savings. Some savings also result from not having to handle paper documents – no printing or postage costs, no staff to handle and log returned questionnaires. Against this must be set additional set-up costs (see disadvantages below).

There has been some debate about whether CAPI results in cost savings on surveys overall, partly as a result of not separating clearly the costs to an organization of moving to CAPI and the costs of running a CAPI survey. Baker & Bradburn (1991) question whether CAPI results in cost savings in the short term, largely because of additional training and support costs, but expect costs to fall as organizations gain experience. The economics of CAPI work out differently on different surveys and for different organizations. As Bateson & Hunter (1991) point out, for large continuous surveys where the initial investment in CAPI development can be spread over several years, savings in moving to CAPI can be realized on one survey alone which is why the move to CAPI has been led by organizations carrying out large, continuous (and for the most part government) surveys. (See, for example, Manners (1991).)

Improved field and data management

If interviewers are provided with modems to transmit completed interviews back to the office, work is returned much more quickly than sending paper documents through the post. Case management systems which allow interviewers to send back details of progress as often as every day provide field managers with accurate up-to-date information on response and progress for all interviewers. When necessary cases can be reassigned quickly between interviewers, and electronic mail can facilitate communications between interviewers and the office. Large survey organizations have found it worthwhile to develop quite sophisticated case management systems which may include other facilities such as checking that cases are complete on the interviewers' computers before transmission – particularly important when several people in the same household need to be interviewed. Data handling systems receiving completed interviews need to separate out interviews belonging to different surveys and can also separate interviews assigned to different months or quarters of a continuous survey.

Ability to carry out more complex procedures

The most obvious advantage of CAPI compared with traditional paper questionnaires is that routing happens automatically whereas in PAPI interviewers have to follow the printed instructions to work out which question to ask next. This means that in CAPI it is as easy to route from a question asked ten pages earlier than from the previous question and routing which depends on several previous answers is as easy as routing from just one. On paper surveys interviewers are required to copy answers to earlier questions needed for complex routing – an error prone procedure which is unnecessary in a CAPI program. Calculations can be carried out much more easily and accurately by computer than by interviewers and can therefore be used for routing and checking during the interview. Of course care must be taken when writing the CAPI program to ensure the routing commands are correct as interviewers are much less likely to spot errors than with paper questionnaires.

There are a number of other procedures which can be automated in CAPI. For example, sampling procedures are easier to carry out in the field; response categories can be presented in random order. Because answer choices can depend on answers to previous questions stated preference techniques can be tailored to respondents' circumstances and answers from a previous interview can be fed forward to the current interview on a panel survey. For market research applications advertisements can be shown on the computer screen to elicit respondents' reactions. Since it is easy to provide more than one version of particular questions or a whole questionnaire, or have different interviewers asking questions in different orders, CAPI facilitates the introduction of methodological experiments.

Improved security and confidentiality of the data

Provided that simple procedures are followed systematically, electronic data can be backed up and encrypted while still in the field and during transmission to the office, as paper questionnaire data cannot. Initial fears that electronic data would be more accessible to unauthorized readers, with easy duplication, and more likely to be lost or corrupted through equipment and transmission failures, have proved unfounded.

Disadvantages of CAPI

Costs of moving to CAPI

It will be obvious from the above that although savings in running costs are a clear advantage of CAPI, there are considerable costs associated with the initial move to CAPI from paper based methods. New equipment and software is required, most obviously notebook computers (and modems if used) for each interviewer, plus extras for spares, development, training and support; additional file servers and other equipment may be needed, depending on the sophistication of the data handling and processing system required. There are costs associated with developing data handling systems and for training not only interviewers but many other staff in the new skills required to program and use CAPI. Most of these are transition costs which can be repaid by the lower running costs of CAPI over a few years for a survey organization.

Organizational change

A survey organization has to expend time and resources managing the change to CAPI – the loss of some jobs, the changes affecting almost everyone in the organization, the retraining required and the adjustment to new ways of thinking, as outlined above.

Possibility of mode effects

There has been concern that survey results will be affected by a change in the mode of interviewing from PAPI to CAPI. Early fears about effects on response were soon allayed as studies showed no difference between CAPI and PAPI response rates.

Attention then moved to the answers given in the interview. Here there is mounting evidence of some mode effects, mainly in response to what are generally called sensitive questions (see under improvements in data quality above), but also to some attitude questions (Martin et al. 1993) and apparently to some other questions, but unless well designed experiments are carried out it is easy to confound mode effects with effects due to changing other aspects of the survey during the transition to CAPI. The general problem is that even improvements in data quality have the disadvantage of disrupting time series.

Limits on entry of large amounts of text

In general the demands on interviewers' keyboard skills are not great since numbers, rather than text, are entered. However, interviewers employed by most survey organizations are unlikely to be competent typists so entering large amounts of text will tend to be slower than writing longhand. In qualitative research or on small less-structured surveys where typically the researcher carries out the interviewing, a good typist may well be able to key text answers directly into the computer avoiding the need to transcribe from tape recordings of the interview.

Possible limits on survey length and complexity

Almost all early CAPI software had limits of some sort, for example on the numbers of questions which could be included, the levels of hierarchies possible, the type of data and how it was handled. This meant that complex surveys could only be programmed in the most sophisticated CAPI software and even then some limitations were likely as each system had its strengths and weaknesses. Attempts have been made to specify the requirements of an ideal CAI package and to evaluate the different ones available (e.g. de Bie et al. 1989), but the evaluations dated rapidly. As with any software, the designers constantly improved their products, adding new features and removing limitations. There are now several products which can handle very long and complex surveys, and also have a wide range of other features which ease questionnaire design and other survey tasks.

Less flexibility in the interview

All questionnaire designers aim to have an error-free instrument which caters for all the situations which arise in the field. Experience shows this is rarely achieved. Professional interviewers, however, are adept at coping when problems do arise during an interview. With paper questionnaires they often spot routing errors and ask the appropriate questions anyway; they make notes about unusual circumstances which the designer did not foresee. But with CAPI questionnaires this is all more difficult. Since routing is automatic, interviewers are unlikely to realize that some questions have been bypassed in error. Good CAPI software provides a facility for making notes but it is still necessary for interviewers to enter a response which will lead them to the next appropriate question. On complex surveys programming errors are both more likely and more difficult to deal with when they occur, although sending a new version of a CAPI questionnaire via a modem is easier than issuing amendments or new versions of paper questionnaires. The only solution to the dangers of programming errors is very thorough testing and checking before a questionnaire goes into the field.

Although in general CAPI allows more complex procedures to be carried out in the interview, there is less flexibility for the interviewer to move around at will and ask questions in different orders. It has been possible to allow two people to be interviewed at the same time (concurrent interviewing) (Costigan et al. 1992), but with less flexibility than on a PAPI survey.

Difficult to interview standing up

Interviews on most large scale social surveys take place either in the home or in other surroundings where interviewer and respondent are sitting down, making it easy for the interviewer to use a computer either on the lap or on a table. But some surveys require a short screening interview to determine whether someone at the address meets the requirements for a full interview or to select one member of the household for interview. On PAPI surveys this stage normally takes place while the interviewer stands on the doorstep. It is less easy to manage the current notebook computers weighing around 3 kg with a keyboard to operate than it is to cope with a paper questionnaire on a clipboard. However, interviewers at several survey organizations have managed to carry out very short screening interviews while standing. Others surveys where interviewers normally interview standing up will be very difficult in CAPI until more suitable computers are developed.

Need for technical support

All computer systems need technical support and CAPI systems are no exception. When an organization starts using CAPI the support required can be quite considerable but some of the problems will turn out to be teething difficulties. Nevertheless, interviewers will sometimes have problems and need a readily accessible source of help. Many problems can be sorted out over the phone, although there will be occasional equipment failures which mean PCs or modems have to be returned to the office and replacements issued. For a large survey organization it may be helpful not only to have spare equipment for replacements but also for those answering interviewer queries over the phone so they can follow the same keystrokes as the interviewer to see what the problem is.

Possibilities for the future

CAPI concepts and systems, and the software and hardware which support them, are evolving very fast. Developers constantly add new facilities to meet demand which is forever pressing against current limitations and to take advantage of hardware and operating system improvements. We summarize selected current developments which may have major significance for CAPI in the next few years.

Hardware improvements

The price of basic notebook computers has remained roughly constant while their performance has improved dramatically. Those currently available, with 80486 processors and large RAM and fixed disks, may well provide more power than necessary for simple surveys, but may provide advantages for more complex surveys. Extra power may be used for going well beyond the possibilities of PAPI surveys, e.g. showing video extracts and graphical displays tailored according to previous answers. Notebooks with colour screens have been available for some time, and will soon be cheap enough for large scale survey work. Colour displays may improve data quality through making it easier for interviewers to read screen instructions and by providing more information to respondents who are interviewing themselves or sitting alongside an interviewer to discuss what is on screen. They may indeed encourage the trend away from the PAPI style of interview, which is literally face-to-face, to a CAPI style which may be characterized as side-by-side shared viewing of the screen.

Pen-based computing is developing fast. There are two particular potential advantages for CAPI. First, since the physical keyboard is no longer necessary, the computers can be much lighter. For this reason, survey organizations which make considerable use of doorstep interviewing have been particularly interested in pen-based computers. Secondly, adequate handwriting recognition may eventually offer a means to capture lengthy verbatim answers.

Portable computers are reducing in weight even where the keyboard is retained at a size suitable for fast typing, as fixed and floppy disk drives and batteries become lighter; such drives may be supplemented or replaced in the near future by card-like solid state storage devices.

Software improvements

CAI software is becoming available which imposes no limits, beyond those of machine capacity, on the length and complexity of questionnaires. A problem with complex surveys, even when simply specified, is the sheer length of the questionnaire program. Tools are beginning to be provided to describe and edit the structure of such programs. These will, among other benefits, make it easier to put into practice one of the early but largely unfulfilled promises of CAI: to build questionnaires from code libraries (see, for example, Pierzchala 1992).

One of the early concerns about CAI was that programs would not run fast enough to be acceptable to interviewers and respondents. In general, hardware and software development has just kept ahead of the demands from increasingly complex surveys. This tension is likely to be maintained, and from time to time existing CAI software packages may need to be restructured or replaced by more modern software. It will be important to maintain the currently acceptable levels of reliability and data integrity.

Modularity and integration

Experience has supported the choice of modular approaches to CAI system development (Nicholls & Matchett 1992). The importance of being able to move data seamlessly between the modules of CAI software and between that software and other packages is central to recent developments. The integration of new modules is likely to continue, and may draw in old processes. For example, at OPCS the booking-in system for

REFERENCES

paper documents has now been written in CAI software to form an integral part of the case management system.

Face-to-face interviewing itself is likely to become more closely controlled, both by the interviewer and by office staff, through better case management and telecommunications which will enable some of the monitoring capabilities of a centralized CATI unit to be reproduced in the CAPI context. Interviewers have been somewhat independent agents in PAPI systems while out in the field. They will come to see themselves much more as linked in a wide managerial and electronic network. It will be important not to lose their vital social skills in the course of the closer monitoring of their activities that will be available.

References

Baker, R. P. 1990. What we know about CAPI: its advantages and disadvantages. Presented at the Annual Conference of the American Association of Public Opinion Research, Lancaster, Pa.

Baker, R. P. & N. M. Bradburn 1991. CAPI: impacts on data quality and survey costs. Presented at the 1991 Public Health Conference on Records and Statistics, Washington DC.

van Bastelaer, A. M. L., F. A. M. Kerssemakers, D. Sikkel 1987. A test of the Netherlands continuous labour force survey with hand-held computers: interviewer behaviour and data quality. In *CBS select 4: automation in survey processing*, R. J. Mokken (ed.), 37–54. Netherlands: NCBS.

Bateson, N. & P. Hunter 1991. The use of CAPI for official British surveys. *Bulletin de méthodologie sociologique* 30, 16–26.

Bethlehem, J. G. & W. J. Keller 1991. The BLAISE system for integrated survey processing. *Survey methodology* 17(1), 43–56.

de Bie, S. E., I. A. L. Stoop, K. L. M. de Vries 1989. *CAI software: an evaluation of software for computer assisted interviewing*. Amsterdam: VOI Association of Social Research Institutes.

Bradburn, N. M., M. R. Frankel, R. P. Baker, M. R. Pergamit 1991. A comparison of computer-assisted personal interviews (CAPI) with paper-and-pencil (PAPI) interviews in the national longitudinal study of youth. Presented at American Association for Public Opinion Research Conference, Phoenix, Ariz.

Brakenhoff, W. J., P. W. M. Remmerswaal, D. Sikkel 1987. Integration of computer assisted survey research. In *CBS select 4: automation in survey processing*, R. J. Mokken (ed.), 13–26. Netherlands: NCBS.

Brewster, K. 1993. Using Blaise for a customer satisfaction system. In *Essays on Blaise 1993. Proceedings of the second international Blaise users conference 1993*, T. Manners & J. Gray (eds), 1–7. London: OPCS.

Collins, M. & W. Sykes 1987. The problems of non-coverage and unlisted telephone numbers in telephone surveys in Britain. *The Journal of the Royal Statistical Society A* **150**(3), 241–53.

Costigan, P., S. Sjödin, K. Thomson 1992. The development of the Family Resources Survey in Blaise for the Department of Social Security, GB. *Essays on Blaise. Proceedings of the first international Blaise users meeting 1992*, S. Vogelesang (ed.). Netherlands: NCBS.

Couper, M. P. & G. Burt 1993. Interviewer reactions to computer-assisted personal interviewing (CAPI). Presented at the Bureau of the Census 1993 Annual Research Conference, Washington DC.

Foreman, J. & M. Collins 1991. The viability of random digit dialling in the UK. *Journal of the Market Research Society* **33**(3), 219–27.

Freeman, H. E. & J. M. Shanks 1983. Special issue on the emergence of computer-assisted survey research. *Sociological Methods & Research* **12**(2), 115–18.

de Heer, W. F. 1991. The use of handheld computers in social surveys of the Netherlands Central Bureau of Statistics. *The Statistician* **40**, 125–38.

Jamieson, R., M. Coutts, B. Williams, A. Braslins 1992. The building of an integrated collection operation in Statistics Canada's regional offices: a time for change. Presented to Bureau of the Census 1992 Annual Research Conference, Arlington, Va.

Kindel, K. K. 1991. Design and development of computer assisted survey information collection at the US Census Bureau. Proceedings of the section on social statistics of the American Statistical Association, Atlanta, Ga.

Manners, T. 1991. The development and implementation of computer assisted interviewing for the British labour force survey. Proceedings of the section on social statistics of the American Statistical Association, Atlanta, Ga.

Manners, T. 1992. New developments in computer assisted survey methodology (CASM) for the British labour force survey and other OPCS surveys. Presented to Bureau of the Census 1992 Annual Research Conference, Arlington, Va.

Manners, T., S. Cheesbrough, A. Diamond 1993. Integrated field and office editing in Blaise: OPCS's experience of complex financial surveys. In *Essays on Blaise 1993. Proceedings of second international Blaise users conference 1993*, T. Manners & J. Gray (eds), 56–69. London: OPCS.

Martin, J. 1993. PAPI to CAPI: the OPCS experience. In *Essays on Blaise 1993. Proceedings of the second international Blaise users conference 1993*, T. Manners & J. Gray (eds), 96–117. London: OPCS.

Martin, J. & C. O'Muircheartaigh 1991. *Evaluation of computer assisted survey systems. Report 1: Introduction to computer assisted survey systems.* Joint Centre for Survey Methods Working Paper No. 4. London: JCSM.

Martin, J., C. O'Muircheartaigh, J. Curtice 1994. The use of CAPI for attitude surveys: an experimental comparison with traditional methods. *Journal of Official Statistics* **9**(3).

Netherlands Central Bureau of Statistics 1992. *Essays on Blaise. Proceedings of the first international Blaise users meeting 1992*, S. Vogelesang (ed.). Netherlands: NCBS.

Nicholls II, W. L. & R. M. Groves 1986. The status of computer-assisted telephone

REFERENCES

interviewing: part I – introduction and impact on cost and timeliness of survey data. *Journal of Official Statistics* 2(2), 93–115.

Nicholls II, W. L. & S. D. Matchett 1992. CASIC issues at the Census Bureau as seen by members of outside panels. Presented to Bureau of the Census 1992 Annual Research Conference, Arlington, Va.

Office of Population Censuses and Surveys 1993. *Essays on Blaise 1993. Proceedings of the second international Blaise users conference 1993*, T. Manners & J. Gray (eds). London: OPCS.

O'Reilly, J. M., M. Hubbard, J. Lessler, P. Biemer 1992. Audio computer-assisted self-interviewing: new technology for data collection on sensitive issues and special populations. Presented at the annual meeting of the American Statistical Association, Boston, Mass.

Pierzchala, M. 1992. Generating multiple versions of questionnaires. In *Essays on Blaise. Proceedings of the first international Blaise users meeting 1992*, S. Vogelesang (ed.), 131–45. Netherlands: NCBS.

Saris, W. E. & W. M. de Pijper 1987. *Computer assisted interviewing using home computers. SRF Research Memorandum* 860415, Amsterdam: SRF.

Schou, R. & M. Pierzchala 1993. Standard multi-survey shells in NASS. In *Essays on Blaise 1993. Proceedings of the second international Blaise users conference 1993*, T. Manners & J. Gray (eds), 133–42. London: OPCS.

Sperry, S., D. Bittner, L. Branden 1991. Computer-assisted personal interviewing on the current beneficiary survey. Presented at American Association for Public Opinion Research Conference, Phoenix, Ariz.

Statistics Sweden 1989. *Computer-assisted data collection in the Labour Force Survey: report of technical tests*. Stockholm: Statistics Sweden.

Weeks, M. F. 1992. Computer-assisted survey information collection: a review of CASIC methods and their implications for survey operations. *Journal of Official Statistics* 8(4), 445–65.

Wojcik, M. & R. P. Baker 1992. Interviewer and respondent acceptance of CAPI. Presented to Bureau of the Census 1992 Annual Research Conference, Arlington, Va.

CHAPTER 5

Statistical software packages

Clare Ward and Angela Dale

This chapter is concerned with software for the analysis of survey-type data. We start with the assumption that data have been collected – typically from a questionnaire – in a way sufficiently standardized to allow responses to be recorded using a common coding frame. Usually information will have been sought from a number of different individuals (or other units such as households), often sampled on a random basis, with the aim of understanding how particular outcomes or responses (e.g. amount of income earned, number of hours worked) vary in relation to a variety of other factors. Unless a very limited amount of information has been collected, it will be much quicker and easier to analyze the data using a computer than manually. As well as allowing large amounts of data to be handled with ease, computers also enable data to be edited as it is entered, by including checks for valid values and for consistency in responses.

Coded data, entered onto a computer, are held as separate "variables" containing information on, for example, the number of cars owned by a household or the occupation or income of an individual. Before the social science "story" held by the data can be unravelled, there are a number of steps which need to be worked through. First, the data must be organized systematically and efficiently; this is done by creating a database. Secondly, relationships within the data need to be understood. This is often a two stage process, with exploratory data analysis followed by confirmatory analysis. There are now many computer packages that support exploratory data techniques and allow graphical displays of the relationships in the data. Computers also allow relatively sophisticated statistical analyses to be conducted accurately and quickly; in particular, many modelling techniques allow successive models to be fitted until the one which most accurately reflects the data is obtained. Finally, one may want to display the results of analyses graphically, so that the reader is presented with an easy-to-understand visual image.

Some packages are written specifically for one or other of these stages, whilst others are wide-ranging and cover all aspects of data management, analysis and display. The kind of software required also varies with the size of the dataset and whether it is to be analyzed on a personal computer, workstation or mainframe. Whilst some packages appear almost identical in their use irrespective of the platform, others are only available on a personal computer, or have a substantially different mode of use on the different platforms. It is also important to draw a distinction between packages designed for Windows and non-Windows environments. Many PC-based packages are now becoming available in Windows versions; these usually provide a more flexible working environment, but they also require a more powerful PC.

In the rest of this chapter we discuss a variety of packages within a framework that distinguishes database management aspects from both exploratory and confirmatory data analysis. We highlight differences between PC and mainframe versions and outline the particular requirements of PC-based packages. We do not attempt direct comparisons between packages, but try to highlight those aspects of each which may be of particular value to the user and to indicate the various levels of expertise which are assumed by different packages. We do not give the prices of the packages discussed since these change rapidly and vary with the size and capacity of the computer used, and with whether the package is being purchased by the academic or non-academic sector. However, it is appropriate at times to indicate relative pricing of comparable products. At the end of the chapter we give the address from which further information on each package can be obtained.

Database management packages

As the name suggests, database management packages are designed primarily for data organization and handling. One of the most important packages for use with survey data is SIR (Scientific Information Retrieval). This is a relational database management system very well suited to handling hierarchical household-based information where one may be collecting information about the household, the family and the individuals living within the family. An example of very simple hierarchical data is shown in Figure 5.1. The household is the case, and each household contains a variable number of individuals. There is one record for each household and within each household there are separate records for each individual. There is no duplication of data; one can relate the household level data to any or all of the individuals living in the household without making a duplicate copy for each individual.

In general, SIR provides an efficient means of managing data where there may be a variable number of records. For example, an individual may hold a record for each visit to a doctor, and the number of visits may vary from none to many. Information may be collected on the number of burglaries recorded by a household or the case may be the firm with data held on each employee of the firm.

One of the more important aspects of SIR is its data dictionary, which stores the descriptions and definitions of the data. This can be used to provide a powerful edit check when reading in data, as well as in documenting the database. For example, valid values and valid ranges can be defined, as well as missing values, variables and value labels. Of particular importance in some social science applications is the fact that the database is designed to allow continuous updating; therefore, adding late responses from a survey, or from a second sweep of data collection, is relatively straightforward. The way in which data is organized into predefined record types makes the package particularly appropriate for use with household based surveys which often contain a number of discrete topics. It is often appropriate to use a separate record type for each topic, with a number of basic demographic variables held readily accessi-

household 1 record	001 12 34 54 67
person 1 record	001 01 67 1
person 2 record	001 02 66 2
person 3 record	001 03 21 2
person 4 record	001 04 19 2
household 2 record	002 12 35 45 67
person 1 record	002 01 34 1
person 2 record	002 02 23 2
household 3 record	003 13 33 56 98
person 1 record	003 01 20 2

Figure 5.1 A representation of a hierarchical database.

ble in the Common Information Record.

SIR provides a very flexible TABULATE procedure that can produce summary statistics such as means, medians, maxima and minima, quintiles and percentages based on any cell in a table. Multi-dimensional tables can be produced through nesting and concatenation. However, the package does not include procedures for statistical analysis (apart from univariate descriptive statistics), and therefore provides an interface to a number of well known data analysis packages, including SPSS, the SAS system, BMDP, MiniTab, Lotus 1–2–3 and Systat, all of which are discussed later in this chapter.

When do you need SIR?

For many relatively simple tasks the power of SIR is not required and packages discussed below, which combine some data management capabilities with data analysis, are quite adequate. SIR comes into its own for large and complex databases where the ability to make linkages across records, to compute complex new variables and to store data efficiently are of prime importance.

Availability

SIR is available on a variety of mainframe and workstation platforms with a range of operating systems. It is also available for personal computers but requires a maths co-processor to run. There is no appreciable difference in the mode of operation between the different platforms. The latest version (SIR version 3.2) provides the option of a Windows-oriented pull-down menu system. SIR is at the upper end of the market in terms of cost and, because of this and its rather specialist nature, it is not very widely available within the UK academic sector.

Analysis packages

There are many packages available for the statistical analysis of quantitative data in the social sciences. Some are multi-purpose, covering data management and manipulation as well as a wide range of statistical routines. Others are more specialized, covering a smaller range of specialist functions. This section covers two of the most widely used multi-purpose packages: SPSS and the SAS System. Both are powerful data management and statistical analysis packages available across a range of computers and operating systems and both offer versions for mainframes, minicomputers, workstations and personal computers, with a Windows version available for the PC.

A straightforward comparison between the two packages is neither possible nor desirable. Any decision over which to use will depend heavily upon the requirements of the user and available hardware. The decision will also depend on which, if any, packages are already being used by colleagues since the ability to exchange information and obtain help, either formal or informal, when it is needed, is a major benefit. In the following sections we provide an overview of the capabilities of each package in a social science context. We also consider the computing and statistical expertise required by the user, outline differences between the personal computer and mainframe versions of the packages and list the system requirements of the DOS and Windows versions.

Overview of the capabilities of SPSS and the SAS System

The basic building block of both packages is the "base product" which offers all the elements needed for basic data analysis including data management facilities, routine statistical procedures and facilities to display the data. The base SAS software provides elementary univariate and bivariate statistical procedures. More advanced statistical procedures in the SAS System are available in the SAS/STAT and SAS/INSIGHT software which are licensed as additions to the base product in both mainframe and personal computer versions. These provide procedures covering: regression, multivariate analyses, discriminant analysis, scoring analyses, analysis of variance, categorical data analyses, clustering techniques and survival analysis.

The SPSS base product provides statistical procedures from simple descriptive statistics such as frequencies, to regression and analysis of variance. More advanced statistical procedures covering multivariate techniques, log-linear analyses, logistic regression, life table analysis, factor, cluster and discriminant analyses as well as techniques for testing the re-

76

liability and validity of created measures are available in the advanced and professional statistics modules. These are included in the base system of most mainframe and workstation versions, but are optional in both the DOS and Windows versions of the PC based software.

Statisticians often prefer the statistical procedures and algorithms offered by the SAS System to those in SPSS but for the non-statistician the documentation, defaults and output offered by the statistics procedures in SPSS are more accessible.

Both packages provide a wide variety of additional modules designed to meet specific user requirements. These are shown in Table 5.1. The system requirements of the DOS computer and Windows versions of the packages are listed in Table 5.2.

Table 5.1   Features in SPSS and SAS.

SPSS	
Graphics	high quality graphics
Trends	forecasting and time-series analyses
Categories	evaluation of categorical data
CHAID	finds significant predictors and relationships between variables
DBMS/Copy	enables data to be transferred between a variety of sources and SPSS/PC+
Data entry II	easy and accurate data entry
Tables	produces high quality, camera-ready tables
Codebook	creates, maintains and presents documentation about every step of research project
LISREL7	linear structure models and simultaneous equations
Mapinfo	displays data across geographical regions
SAS	
SAS/ASSIST	provides a menu-driven, interactive interface to the package
SAS/AF	interactive applications development facilities
SAS/IML	high level language for matrix manipulation
SAS/GRAPH	high quality graphics including three-dimensional plots
SAS/OR	operational research routines
SAS/ETS	econometric routines
SAS/FSP	collection of interactive full-screen procedures for a variety of information processing tasks
SAS/INSIGHT	interactive tool for exploring and analyzing data visually. Includes three-dimensional rotating plots

Table 5.2 System requirements of personal computer versions of SPSS and SAS.

Requirements	DOS		Windows	
	SPSS (5.0)	SAS (6.04)	SPSS (6.0)	SAS (6.8)
Type of PC	286 or better	286 or better. Also runs on IBM XT machines running DOS 2.0 and later	386 or 486	386 or 486
Storage space*	Hard disc, with at least 11 MB of space	20 MB min, 40 MB would be good starting point	Hard disc, with at least 20 MB of space	120 MB good starting point
Memory/RAM	2 MB of RAM for extended DOS, including 1 MB of available extended memory. Version available for machines with 640 kB of RAM	640 kB RAM; 1.5 MB of expanded memory strongly recommended and necessary for some products	At least 4 MB of RAM min. 8 MB recommended	At least 6 MB, 8+ MB recommended
Version of DOS	DOS 3.0 or above	DOS 3.0 or above	DOS 3.0 or above	DOS 5 and later recommended
Version of Windows	–	–	Windows 3.1	Windows 3.1
Other recommendations	Maths co-processor highly recommended	Maths co-processor highly recommended	VGA monitor or Hercules™ graphics card. Windows compatible mouse. Maths co-processor highly recommended	Maths co-processor highly recommended

* Varies according to modules loaded. Figures are for base module.

Data management capabilities

Prior to most analyses, some manipulation of the data, such as recoding existing variables or creating new ones, is necessary. An important consideration is therefore the data handling/management capability of a package; for example, its ability to import, transform and restructure data as well as its programming capabilities. How, in other words, does the package handle complex file structures, store, retrieve, merge and restructure data files, select observations and variables for inclusion in the analysis, and modify, create and label variables?

The SAS System has more sophisticated data handling capabilities than SPSS although both provide powerful tools for merging and restructuring data files. The SAS System has greater scope for programming than SPSS, allowing users to write their own procedures for statistical analysis. The mainframe version of SPSS is more powerful in terms of programming capabilities than its DOS version whereas the Windows version of SPSS has the same power as the mainframe in programming terms. (See later section for a discussion of the personal computer versions of the packages.) Transformations used to manipulate the data are provided by both packages, although the range and complexity of functions provided by the SAS System is greater than that available in SPSS. The SAS System offers identical functionality on mainframe and PC systems running Windows.

SPSS and the SAS System in a typical social science analysis

A typical social science analysis is likely to involve some initial exploratory data analysis to identify patterns in the data, followed by more complex analyses to explain these patterns. The extent and nature of the further analysis will determine whether the base product is adequate or whether an optional module will be needed. For example, SPSS provides regression in its base module but this is not available in the SAS base software. Exploratory data analysis techniques are available in the base products of SPSS and the SAS System. SPSS has a procedure called EXAMINE to conduct exploratory data analysis. Similar analyses can be done in the SAS System using PROC UNIVARIATE. These procedures include stem-and-leaf plots, box plots and tests of normality. Other procedures provide further descriptive and univariate statistics and graphical displays such as the frequencies, means, summary, tabulate, correlation, chart and plot procedures in the SAS System, and crosstabs, frequencies, correlations, descriptives, means and plot in SPSS. SAS/INSIGHT software, which has to be licensed separately, enables interactive exploratory data analysis using powerful visual techniques.

Both SPSS and the SAS System enable tables to be produced in a variety of ways; basic tabulations can be generated using the crosstabs statement in SPSS and the frequency procedure in the base SAS software. In addition both packages offer the option to produce camera-ready tables either in the base software (the tabulate procedure in SAS) or as a separate module (SPSS/Tables). Both allow considerable flexibility in the content and layout of the table but the SPSS commands are considered by some to be more logical for the new user than those in the SAS System (Stemerdink 1988).

Computing and statistical expertise required by SPSS and the SAS System

The SAS System is a more complex package than SPSS, particularly in its data management capabilities, and so can be daunting for the inexperienced user. SAS/ASSIST software provides an interface that makes it easier to access the power of SAS software, with a minimum of knowledge. However, once learnt, new users have at their disposal probably the most comprehensive package of its kind with highly regarded data management and statistical facilities.

Both packages have extensive documentation. That produced by SPSS is clearly explained and is very accessible to the relatively inexperienced user. This is particularly apparent in the manuals produced specifically for students. The SAS System manuals are also very comprehensive, providing many examples of correct syntax and the application of the statistical procedures. The downside of the SAS System documentation for many users, however, is its size; four manuals are required to cover just the base product and SAS/STAT software. In general the SAS System manuals are more statistically technical and with fewer social science examples than those produced by SPSS. This may be less helpful for the non-statistician but preferable for the more competent user or statistician.

Personal computer versions

DOS *versions*

With the exception of its Windows version, the SAS System runs with the same look and feel across all operating systems with identical syntax and functionality. An integral part of the base software is the SAS Display Manager which provides a good user interface to the SAS System. This split screen interface provides three windows – the command window in which commands are written, the output window in which the output is viewed and the log window in which the log-file is displayed. The user can have all three windows visible or can zoom in on the window currently in use. The SAS Display Manager is available for all versions of the software although it is necessary to have the right terminal in order for it to work in the non-PC versions.

Until its most recent version (SPSS 4.0), SPSS looked and felt different on the personal computer and the mainframe. SPSS/PC+ has a split-screen user interface with pull down menus and can be used either through an editor or through the menus. The latest mainframe version, SPSS 4.0, also has a similar user interface called SPSS manager but the function keys for particular commands are not necessarily the same in the two versions. The menus in SPSS/PC+ make it easy to use but they quickly become cumbersome. Although the menus can be switched off, the default is to return to them following the execution of a command. It is necessary therefore to continually switch from one mode to another. Alternatively the menus can be turned off via the creation of an "spss-profini" file. This file can contain any defaults for the operation of SPSS/PC+ and runs automatically each time SPSS/PC+ runs. There are also some syntactical differences between SPSS and SPSS/PC+. Commands in the DOS version must end in a period whereas this is not necessary in SPSS. In addition DO LOOPS and vectors are not available in SPSS/PC+ which will be a restriction for users with more than basic data handling requirements.

Windows versions

SPSS 5.0 for Windows was recently awarded the editor's choice in *PC Magazine*. It was found to be easy to use, providing in-depth statistical procedures and high resolution graphics. Although the Windows version of SPSS needs a more powerful PC than the DOS version, it has a much wider range of functions. As well as being faster, it is able to handle hierarchical data, for it can aggregate cases, merge files and process DO LOOPS. It allows the user to move between a series of different windows: the syntax window displays the commands to be executed, the data editor window displays the data in the active file and the output window displays the output. Two further windows are available for using charts and graphs. Procedures can also be run via pull down menus and dialogue box selections. Care should be taken when leaving the package so that the active file is not overwritten unless this is required. SPSS 5.0 for Windows has easy-to-use graphics with bar charts, pie charts and line graphs that can be run by simply calling up variables from the menu. SPSS for Windows can use an unlimited number of variables. However, above 4,500 the dialogue boxes are not guaranteed and the user would need to write commands in the syntax window.

SAS for Windows is the same as the other versions of SAS with the exception of support for the Windows interface, including dynamic data exchange and object linking and embedding.

Using the SAS System and SPSS with hierarchical data

Both the SAS System and SPSS will handle hierarchical data of the kind described earlier. Using SPSS, if data are organized as person records within households, a system file can be set up which contains household data duplicated for each person in the household. As long as the data contain identifiers for each household and for each person within the household, then the AGGREGATE command can be used to group together all records in the same household. One might count the total number of people in the household with certain characteristics – for example the number of children, or the number of elderly. If a family number is available, then aggregations can also be made to the family level. Similarly, the age of the youngest dependent child can be derived by computing the age of each dependent child and then taking the minimum age of the dependent children in a household. Aggregated variables at the level of the household can also be distributed to each individual using the MATCH FILES command. For example, one could calculate the number of persons in a household with a limiting illness and then tabulate the age of each individual by the total number of people with a limiting illness in the household. Middleton (1993) provides step-by-step examples of these and other ways of using SPSS to handle hierarchies.

In the SAS System, hierarchical data may be handled by setting up two system files (datasets), one for the household records and one for the individual level records. These can be merged to provide a cross tabulation of age (individual) by tenure (household) for example. Aggregation and matching of files can also be used in the SAS System to create the variables discussed above with SPSS and worked examples are supplied by Middleton (1993).

Multilevel modelling

In much, if not all, social science data, the populations under consideration have complex, rather than simple structures; people live in households located in districts and children are educated in classes grouped in schools within local areas. Recognition of the hierarchical nature of much social science data, and the need to develop statistical models to handle this nesting, first arose in the context of educational research. Here it became evident that the achievement of children within a local area might be influenced not just by individual characteristics such as parental social class, but that different kinds of schools, and different teaching methods, might also affect the relationship between social class and educational achievement. If these higher level relationships are ignored, then the individual relationship between social class and educational attainment (typically measured by a regression model) is likely to be misleading. Models that can take into account the fact that schools may vary considerably in the class background of their pupils and that the relationship between parental class and educational achievement may vary between schools are therefore required.

In recognition of the natural clustering in much social science data and the need to explicitly model this clustering, statistical models and the software to evaluate them have been developed (Goldstein 1987). There are currently four packages available for multilevel analyses (Jones 1992). These are ML3 (Prosser et al. 1991), HLM (Bryk & Raudenbush 1986), VARCL (Longford 1986) and GENMOD (Mason et al. 1988). In the UK, regular training workshops funded by the Economic and Social Research Council are available for ML3. The address for obtaining further information is given in the final section of this chapter.

83

Spreadsheets and databases

Spreadsheets and databases have a variety of uses in the collection and production of information. Spreadsheets are often used in the analysis of administrative data; for example, the Office of Population Censuses and Surveys (OPCS) make available fertility and mortality data for local and health authority areas on floppy disk in a format that can be read directly into a spreadsheet package such as Lotus 1–2–3. The data can then be manipulated to calculate rates, or percentages, or to produce age-stand-ardized figures. If further analyses of already published data are required, then spreadsheets offer an easy way to accomplish this, particularly for the non-specialist or for those without access to more specialized statistical analysis packages.

Most spreadsheet packages offer good graphics facilities for use in the production of a final report or presentation. Data from most statistical analysis packages can be output to spreadsheets, and the graphs or charts produced by the spreadsheet can be easily integrated by most word processing packages. It may also be easier to do some data manipulations in spreadsheet packages than in specialist data analysis packages – for example, where one wants to divide one column by another, or to apply weights to particular columns. However, the inability of spreadsheets to deal with missing values can be a major problem (Chell 1992, Gray et al. 1992). Although data can be entered directly into spreadsheets and frequencies and other simple statistics produced, advanced statistical routines are not usually available. This is not, however, an insurmountable problem since data can often be transferred into other specialist packages for further analysis.

Data manipulation and management are important functions of databases and these have been discussed in an earlier section of this chapter. Relational databases such as R:Base, Dbase and Lotus 1–2–3 can also be used to store and provide easy access to metadata – that is, text data which describes survey data. A large complex survey may have several thousand variables; each variable may have a short description (for example, the variable label as stored by SPSS) and each may also have labels to describe the values of each category of a variable. It may also be appropriate to store additional information about each variable – for example, the way in which it was derived or edited. In some cases the survey may have been repeated several times over a number of years. For these large and complex databases it is often valuable to hold descriptive information in a relational database which is indexed to allow access through structured search facilities. Each variable may be referenced by a keyword that describes the topic; searches based on strings of text may be used to locate variables. For example, a researcher may wish to find out whether there is any information on the social class of a respondent. By searching for the words "social class" in the label describing the variable, all variables that relate to social class, whether of the respondent, partner, mother or father, should be located.

New advances in databases

In recent years there has been a growth in specialist tabulation packages specifically designed for the analysis of survey data by non-specialist users. Two such packages are QUANVERT and QuickTAB. In general these packages are primarily designed for the PC but QUANVERT also has a mainframe version. These packages all use "inverted data files" (see below) or relational databases to achieve considerable data compression and to provide very quick access to the data (Katz 1992, Roberts et al. 1992). Conventionally, data are held and accessed sequentially, starting with the first case and working through until the final case is reached. If one wishes to tabulate sex by marital status for people aged 16 and over, the computer has to read every case to extract the relevant information and process it into a table. By contrast, with an inverted file structure, data are held on a variable by variable basis and only those variables required for the tabulation will be referenced. Additionally, the data are organized so that where a number of individuals share the same characteristics, this is held as a single item of information. This releases disk space and leads to a reduction in computing time. For instance, the 1989 Family Expenditure Survey takes up 60 megabytes of space in a SIR database, but requires only 8.4 megabytes in QuickTAB. The General Household Survey reduces from 35 megabytes to 7.2 megabytes (Truscott 1992). Evaluation work (Roberts 1992) at the University of Manchester Computing Centre showed that QuickTAB and QUANVERT typically compress a raw data file by a factor of about three. Other packages such as SIR, SPSS and the SAS System, on the other hand, produce files that are only marginally smaller, and in some cases bigger, than the raw data. Similarly QuickTAB and QUANVERT take much less time than the other packages to run a comparable job. For example, SPSS on the PC takes roughly an hour to complete a job done by QUANVERT in five to six minutes and by QuickTAB in about two minutes. Once on the mainframe, differences in the time taken by the different packages are reduced.

QUANVERT and QuickTAB have both been developed for the market research industry, and are both premised on the assumption that they will be used by clients who need a quick and easy way to analyze their survey data. QUANVERT is designed to take data already processed and prepared by a parent product (QUANTUM) and a number of datasets frequently used by academics are now available in this format, for example the Labour Force Survey (LFS) and the newly available Samples of Anonymized Records (SARs) from the 1991 Census. The most distinctive feature of these packages is their ability to compress very large datasets into a size that can be held on a PC and which can be processed very quickly. Obviously this is of particular value to those who only have access to a personal computer. Since they hold large datasets in a very compressed form, many of the problems of importing and handling datasets which may be 50–100 megabytes when held by the SAS System or SPSS can be overcome. Although both packages can deal with hierarchical data, their statistical analysis facilities are limited. However, they do offer export routines which enable them to be used in conjunction with other packages such as SPSS and the SAS System. Subsets of data can be extracted from either QUANVERT or QuickTAB and then analyzed further with other statistical packages.

Other packages

There are a huge variety of packages available for data analysis and it is beyond the scope of this chapter to cover many of these in any detail. Of course, everyone has their own favourite and here we can only provide a brief outline of a few. Talking to other data analysts in the field provides an invaluable source of information for the potential user, particularly those with specialized data analysis requirements.

Systat provides statistics, graphics and data management facilities. It scores highly in various independent reviews including one carried out by the Software Digest Ratings Review in 1991 who, when comparing its PC version to those of Minitab, PC–90, SPSS, the SAS System and Statgraphics, rated Systat as providing "the best balance of power and usability".

BMDP is a collection of 42 statistical programmes often used by medical and epidemiological researchers. It has highly thought of statistical routines but its data handling facilities are weaker than those in many other packages.

Statgraphics is a PC based statistical graphics system which integrates statistical functions with high resolution colour graphics (Charles et al. 1990). A recent survey found it both easy to use and learn with high quality graphics. It is, however, less versatile, less powerful and more limited in its functions than other packages (Software Digest Ratings Report 1991).

MiniTab is a relatively cheap and easily used package, available on personal computers and mainframes and now at release 9. It uses a worksheet concept that makes it inappropriate for very large datasets but it is good for exploratory data analysis, simple statistics and regression and for graphical display. Although it lacks the more sophisticated statistical routines and many of the features available in other packages, MiniTab is good for simple analyses and teaching purposes since it is easy to learn and fast to use. A Windows version of MiniTab is now available.

STATA is a general statistics, data management and graphics package that can handle large datasets. It is available in both a PC and UNIX version. It is good for fast, straightforward analyses and modelling or as a preparatory package for more specialist econometrical packages (Banks 1992).

GLIM is a widely used package amongst statisticians. Version 4, available on both mainframe and personal computer, has recently been released by Lancaster University. Although not renowned for being user-friendly, GLIM allows the analyst a great deal of flexibility. As its name suggests (General Linear Interactive Modelling) GLIM is designed for interactive use and this provides the essential flexibility needed for statistical modelling, where the analyst usually wants to interact with the data and modify models in the light of results. It is not well suited to extensive data manipulation, so it is best to use another package for organizing the data. Neither is it designed to handle very large survey datasets; it is usually best to use another package to extract the subset of cases and variables needed for a particular analysis. It does, however, have excellent graphical and display facilities that can be very helpful in aiding the interpretation of analyses.

Conclusion

In the end, the choice of a package is likely to be determined by a number of factors including the needs of the user as well as the software and hardware facilities available at the site where the data are to be analyzed. If extensive database management facilities are required, then a specialist package such as SIR is recommended. For users with specialist data analysis requirements a variety of packages exist and specialist users are probably in the best position to advise on the package most suited to a particular type of analysis. If, however, wide ranging statistical procedures and data management facilities are required, then a multi-purpose package is likely to be most suitable. As we have pointed out, a vast range of such products exist, and if one is routinely used in your organization then this may well be your best option. If, however, you have a choice, then choosing the SAS System will mean that you have at your disposal a powerful program with enormous versatility but with a steep learning curve. Choosing SPSS means that you have access to the most widely used package in the academic community in the UK which, for the new user, is quicker and easier to learn. However, it may not meet all the needs of the more experienced user with more sophisticated programming needs.

Acknowledgements

We would like to thank Bruce Bovill at the SAS Institute and Ann-Marie Sharkey at SPSS for providing technical information for, and comments on, an earlier draft of this chapter. We would also like to thank Ed Fieldhouse of the Census Microdata Unit, University of Manchester for information on SPSS for Windows and all those who replied to our request through the electronic news groups comp.soft-sys.sas and comp.soft-sys.spss for views about the packages discussed.

Contact addresses for packages discussed in detail

SIR
Forvus,
53 Clapham Common, Southside,
London SW4 9BX.
Tel: 071-498 2602 Fax: 071-498 1939

The SAS System
SAS Institute, Wittington House,
Henley Road,
Medmenham, Marlow,
Buckinghamshire, SL7 2EB.
Tel: (0628) 486933 Fax: (0628) 483203

SPSS
SPSS (UK) Ltd, *SPSS* House,
5 London Street, Chertsey,
Surrey, KT16 8AP.
Tel: (0932) 566262 Fax: (0932) 567020

ML3
The Multilevel Models Project,
Department of Mathematics, Statistics
   and Computing,
Institute of Education,
University of London,
20 Bedford Way,
London, WC1A 0HL.
Tel: 071-621 6682 Fax: 071-612 6686

QUANVERT
Quantime Ltd, Maygrove House,
67 Maygrove Road,
London NW6 2EG.
Tel: 071-625 7222 Fax: 071-624 5297

QuickTAB
Forvus,
53 Clapham Common, Southside,
London SW4 9BX.
Tel: 071-498 2602 Fax: 071-498 1939

GLIM
The Numerical Algorithm Group Ltd,
Wilkinson House, Jordan Hill Road,
Oxford OX2 8DR
Tel: (0865) 511245 Fax: (0865) 310139

References

Banks, J. 1992. Software reviews: STATA. *The Economic Journal* **102**, 1581–8.
Bryk, A. S. & S. W. Raudenbush 1986. *Hierarchical linear models: applications and analysis methods*. New York: Sage.
Charles, B., A. Westlake, P. Rose 1990. Software for statistical and social survey analysis 1989–90 prepared for the Study Group on Computers in Survey Analy-

sis. *Computational Statistics and Data Analysis* 9, 317–40.

Chell, M. 1992. A comparison of some software packages for survey analysis. See Westlake et al. (1992), 385–94.

Evans, G. E. & W. A. Newman 1988. A comparison of SPSS PC+, SAS PC, and BMDP PC. *Collegiate Microcomputer* 6(2), 97–106.

Goldstein, H. 1987. *Multilevel models in educational and social research.* London: Charles Griffin.

Gray, W. A., N. J. Fiddian, E. W. Lawson 1992. Recent trends in database management and their effect on statistical computing. See Westlake et al. (1992), 439–48.

Jones, K. 1992. Using multilevel models for survey analysis. See Westlake et al. (1992), 231–42.

Katz, M. 1992. A review of the tools for secondary analysis. See Westlake et al. (1992), 289–96.

Longford, N. T. 1986. VARCL: Interactive software for variance components analysis. *Professional Statistician* 5, 28–32.

Mason, W. M., A. F. Anderson, N. Hayat 1988. *Manual for GENMOD.* Population Studies Center, University of Michigan, Ann Arbor.

Middleton, E. 1993. *An introductory guide to analysing the Samples of Anonymised Records from the 1991 Census.* Occasional Paper No.3, Census Microdata Unit, University of Manchester

Prosser, R., J. Rasbash, H. Goldstein 1991. *ML3: software for three-level analysis.* Institute of Education, London University.

Roberts, J. (1992) Unpublished report on "Software evaluation for the Samples of Anonymised Records", Manchester Computer Centre

Roberts, J., E. Middleton, K. Cole, M. Campbell, C. Marsh 1992. Software solutions for Samples of Anonymised Records. See Westlake et al. (1992), 305–16.

Software Digest Ratings Report 1991. *Statistical programs* Vol 8, 5 (entire report).

Stemerdink, G. J. 1988. Complex tables: a comparison of SPSS-X Tables and SAS Tabulate. Paper given to SPSS European User's Group in Amsterdam, 29–31 March 1988.

Truscott, P. 1992. Tabulate a million records a minute. See Westlake et al. (1992, 337–46.

Westlake, A., R. Banks. C. Payne, T. Orchard (eds) 1992. *Survey and statistical computing.* Amsterdam: North-Holland.

CHAPTER 6

Databases for ordering and referencing information

B. N. Rossiter

Introduction

What does a database help you to do? It gives a logical basis for the storage of information in a consistent manner with integrity. However, storage by itself is generally an inadequate motivation to justify the effort involved in preparing, checking and inputting data into a database. It would also be expected that: (a) the data could be reordered (sorted) on various attributes so that different perspectives can be gained on it; (b) different types of data, but with some information in common, can be merged to give an amalgamation of values; (c) reports can be produced to display in an elegant format and in some sensible order the contents of all or part of a database; (d) searches can be made to derive subsets of the database based on values for particular features defined in the schema; (e) data values can be readily changed during the lifetime of a database; (f) data values should be of high integrity, that is their accuracy should be as high as is possible with machine checking.

When should you use one? When you have facts that can be reasonably easily classified into a set of properties describing objects of interest. Thus data that is mainly full text is probably best input into specialized text based information retrieval systems (Bain et al. 1989). For small numbers of simple facts, say up to a few hundred, the use of database techniques may not be justified, because the effort expended in learning a database system and setting up a database will not be quickly repaid. However, for larger numbers of simple facts or smaller numbers of complex interrelated facts, the effort spent in developing a database system is soon repaid by the ease with which the data can be reordered, searched, printed and proved to be of high integrity.

Types of database

Databases are classified by the type of data model employed for defining data structures, for manipulating data and for establishing rules governing acceptable states. Any model takes a particular stance on how to represent reality. Models are always reductionist in the sense that they are incapable of capturing all the facets of the complex situations found in the real world. Models therefore do involve some information loss but their use is mandatory in the current state of computing science because they have associated implementation routes enabling practical systems to be built and used.

Today the main products used are based on the relational data model in which reality is viewed as a collection of tables with each table holding one particular kind of fact. All data are represented by values within the tables, hence the term value oriented is sometimes applied to this type of database system. There are no facilities for complex pointer or linkage constructions as employed in what are called object oriented models.

The relational model therefore possesses a very simple basis. In simple situations, a user may work with a single table holding one type of fact. However, a major advantage of the relational model is that data facts in different tables can be drawn together and the two related facts considered as one for the purposes of searching, reporting and storage. This latter property is particularly interesting: it means that new database tables can be readily constructed from other tables containing any logical subsets or combinations of other tables. Moreover, these tables rank equally with other tables already in the database as ordinary database tables.

The instructions for retrieval and storage of information in tables in a relational database are provided by a query language which is based on standard mathematics – set theory. The normal form of operation is that queries are typed in on-line and the system responds on the workstation screen with the results. However, with a bit more effort, it is possible to produce sophisticated systems with menu driven command facilities available to the user, with the course of events controlled by circumstances arising in the data and with complex reformatting of the data in

Structure for database: D:baptisms.dbf

Number of data records : 80

Date of last update : 12/26/93

Field	Field Name	Type	Width
1	SURNAME	Character	20
2	CHRISTIAN	Character	10
3	OCCUPATION	Character	15
4	ADDRESS	Character	15
5	DATE	Numeric	4
6	ORIGIN	Character	1
** Total **			66

Structure for database: D:burials.dbf

Number of data records : 763

Date of last update : 12/26/93

Field	Field Name	Type	Width
1	SURNAME	Character	20
2	CHRISTIAN	Character	20
3	OCCUPATION	Character	20
4	ADDRESS	Character	20
5	DATE	Numeric	4
6	ORIGIN	Character	1
** Total **			86

Structure for database: D:foreign.dbf

Number of data records : 150

Date of last update : 12/26/93

Field	Field Name	Type	Width
1	SURNAME	Character	20
2	CHRISTIAN	Character	20
3	OCCUPATION	Character	20
4	ADDRESS	Character	20
5	LITERATE	Character	2
6	STATUS	Character	10
7	DATE	Numeric	4
8	ORIGIN	Character	1
** Total **			98

** Total ** 36

Structure for database: D:hearth.dbf

Number of data records : 175

Date of last update : 12/26/93

Field	Field Name	Type	Width
1	SURNAME	Character	20
2	CHRISTIAN	Character	10
3	DATE	Numeric	4
4	ORIGIN	Character	1
5	NO_HEARTH	Numeric	2
** Total **			38

Structure for database: D:surradmt.dbf

Number of data records : 642

Date of last update : 02/09/94

Field	Field Name	Type	Width
1	SURNAME	Character	20
2	CHRISTIAN	Character	20
3	OCCUPATION	Character	20
4	ADDRESS	Character	20
5	PROPERTY	Character	30
6	STATUS	Character	3
7	RENT	Character	10
8	DATE	Numeric	4
9	ORIGIN	Character	1
** Total **			129

Structure for database: D:debt.dbf

Number of data records : 271

Date of last update : 12/26/93

Field	Field Name	Type	Width
1	SURNAME	Character	20
2	CHRISTIAN	Character	10
3	OCCUPATION	Character	15
4	ADDRESS	Character	15
5	PLEA	Character	20
6	SUM	Numeric	10
7	DATE	Numeric	4
8	ORIGIN	Character	1
** Total **			96

Figure 6.1 Table structures for 17th century reconstruction of Hexham.

an abstract manner.

Before reviewing the various types of relational databases, we look at a relatively straightforward example of a history database involving the construction of a number of tables to collect data which can then be brought together for a scholarly perusal of a report.

A historical application

The purpose of the application is to synthesize the known events in a town, in this case Hexham in Northumberland, over a period of about a hundred years from 1600–1700 to reconstruct the social and economic structure of the town and to identify those in control of the town. Basic information to be held is records on hearth tax, adult male burials, samples of baptisms, surrenders and admittances of properties, foreigners' bonds, and pleas of debts.

The structure for each of these classes of records is shown in Figure 6.1 and an indication is given of the current number of entries of each type. Figure 6.1 shows the schema for this database. A record is the unit of addition or retrieval from a table; each record comprises properties or descriptors appropriate for the table which are known as fields; each field is associated with a data type which indicates its permitted values.

There is clearly a relationship between the various tables in that the same people are involved in a number of different activities. However, with uncertainties in spelling and with some people having the same name, it is not possible for the computer to make a definitive match between persons in the different tables. What is needed is a method of synthesizing the information which produces a provisional ordering (sorting) of the data. The proposed relationships can then be examined, alterations made to the data and a new ordering generated. The power of the computer here is in being able to change quickly the perceived order of data: the view of the data is dynamic rather than static.

The above tables have been implemented with a database program, dBase, merged into a master table containing all information, sorted into an order by creating an index, and then printed in report mode to give output to the user. The order is determined by the indexing instructions and can be varied on demand. The most common order will be based on names and dates to identify the history of individuals as in Figure 6.2 but we could equally easily derive orders based on occupations or places. Note that the origin of all data is preserved in this report: no information should be lost if scholarly decisions are to be made on the connections between people in different events.

Subsequently, all corrections and additions of new data should be applied to the basic tables shown in Figure 6.1. The master table is always constructed by a complete merge of the basic tables achieved by the run of a short series of instructions. It is never updated in a piecemeal fashion as it represents a view on the basic tables. This discipline is necessary as performing modifications to either the master table or the basic tables on an *ad hoc* basis would lead to inconsistent values and a virtually useless database.

Figure 6.2 illustrates the use of the database in correlating the data on the name *Philip Jefferson* who appears frequently as a court official. At first glance, this appears to be facts concerning one person but on closer examination, we have two people of this name: one an illiterate glover buried in 1682, the other a literate tanner buried in 1700. Having established there are two Philips, we can proceed to examine the property

Record#	SURNAME	CHRISTIAN	ORIGIN	OCCUPATION	ADDRESS	PROPERTY	NO_HEARTH	STATUS	RENT	DATE	LITERATE	PLEA	SUM
989	Jefferson	Barbara	F		Gilesgate			wit		1703	n		
850	Jefferson	Philip	F					wit		1638	n		
879	Jefferson	Philip	F	glover	Merry Leazes			lan		1668	n		
1495	Jefferson	Philip	P	glover	Gilesgate	burgage		sur	6d	1669			
1605	Jefferson	Philip	P	glover	Gilesgate	burgage and land		sur	8d	1671			
1606	Jefferson	Philip	P	glover	Gilesgate Fields	2 acres		sur		1671			
844	Jefferson	Philip	O							1682			
929	Jefferson	Philip	F	tanner	Gilesgate			wit		1682	y		
852	Jefferson	Philip	O	tanner						1700			
1653	Jefferson	Phillipp	H				6			1664			
1040	Jefferson	Robert	P	gent	Hexham West Field	1 acre		sur	8d	1667			

Figure 6.2 Master table – amalgamation of underlying tables. Origin codes: F, foreign.dbf; P, surradmt.dbf; O, burials.dbf; H, hearth.dbf.

transactions and the foreigners' bonds. Note also the variable spelling for Philip indicating that some human interpretation is required to give a final ordering.

Another source of research is to produce subsets of the data in a form suitable for statistical analysis. For example, for different occupations, the inventories and hearth tax returns can be ranked and their correlation tested for significance using a test such as the Spearman rank.

This application shows the importance of ordering in handling real-world requirements in the humanities or social sciences, where the user must deal with uncertain information and a number of possible interpretations of the underlying data. All the systems to be introduced later can handle this type of problem as they all have some sorting facilities. However, the dBase approach has actually been used to handle the application because of its flexible indexing facilities and the ease with which new tables can be created from existing ones. In effect, we are seeking a dynamic semantic ordering of the data, not to be confused with the routine syntactic ordering found in commercial data processing systems. Hypermedia systems also provide semantic ordering (Hardman et al. 1994) but it is often more difficult to alter dynamically the order of a complete set of records than it is with a database system (Rossiter et al. 1990).

Before moving on to another example involving extensive cross-referencing of tables, we now examine the various types of relational software available.

Schools of relational thought

Whatever the type of relational database being used, the tabular structures should be the same. The difference between approaches lies in the manipulation techniques for querying and updating and in the user interface. Three main schools of thought, not completely distinct, dominate the relational database market at the present time.

The dBase school

This type of approach can be thought of as semi-relational in that it allows linking of tables through cross reference by value but there is a restriction to the linkage in that the mappings allowed are not completely general: if two tables A and B are cross referenced on a common attribute X, then each value for X in A may be linked to only *one* value for X in B, not *many* as is required for some applications. There is also the restriction from the purist's view that linkages require certain physical structures (indexes) to be established before they can be used. Ideally, linkages should be made between tables on demand by a user without any need for careful setting up of physical access paths.

The historical advantage of the dBase approach is that it does not require much memory when running. It can therefore be implemented on microcomputers with small memories. However, with microcomputers offering ever higher capability at lower cost, this advantage has been eroded to some extent.

Products in this school are dBase III and IV (Pendharker & Biegel 1994), Clipper, FoxBase and FoxPro. Later versions have enhanced front-ends giving user interfaces which hide some of the underlying complexity inherent in the linking methods. Facilities are also present in recent versions (e.g. dBase IV) for using, as an add-on feature, the language SQL which we describe in the next section.

The SQL school

For large relational databases, the Structured Query Language (SQL) has been a popular choice for a number of years. Systems such as Ingres, Oracle and Informix are all based on the SQL approach. There are a number of reasons for this:

(a) SQL is based on a series of international standards (ISO 1987–92) which are still under development. The major relational database vendors adhere reasonably closely to the standard giving portability of applications from one product to another.

(b) SQL is soundly based upon standard mathematics. It is "sugared" relational calculus, effectively calculus with mathematical symbols replaced by English words. The formal basis enables the scope of the language to be precisely defined and proved, gives the language an underlying consistency (Carter 1993) lacking in more *ad hoc* approaches and enables standards mentioned above to be developed.

With the development of more powerful microcomputers, it is now possible to use SQL systems on PCs. However, the interfaces to SQL systems have traditionally been lacking in slickness and are not easy to set up by the more casual user. There has therefore been some reluctance to migrate to the SQL systems in spite of their greater functionality and the existence of international standards. This course of events can be viewed as a reaction against the use of commands in tightly controlled format for instructing the database system (the syntax driven approach). However, newer releases are now starting to introduce more usable visual facilities as described below.

The query by example school

All contemporary microcomputer database systems are now based on WIMP approaches with windows, icons, mice and pointers. There still has to be an underlying model, typically relational, but the interface is based on visual techniques.

What can be regarded as a third school of thought in relational databases has therefore emerged, based on more natural interfaces. Systems in this school typically employ highly visual screen based techniques to encourage their use by non-programmers. The original example of this type of method was QBE (Query By Example) (Zloof 1975) which, for querying purposes, presents users with table templates on the screen. The users enter search values into the tables together with the required logical connections and the system responds with records that meet the user's request. Window based systems (DOS, Macintosh) facilitate the use of this type of database today: Paradox is a typical example of a QBE product taking full advantage of icons and mice.

The approach of Query By Example is currently being incorporated into all relational systems as an enhanced mechanism for interfaces to end-users. Thus SQL systems now typically have available a Windows interface and FoxPro is an enhancement of FoxBase to introduce Macintosh/Windows facilities (Lima 1993a). Another bonus, from the iconic approach, is the *pick* facility which enables, on data input, a list of possible values to be provided to the user, one of which is selected by a "click" on the mouse. FileMaker Pro is a good example of an easy-to-use simple system based entirely on iconic principles (Coulombre & Price 1993).

The QBE approach is ideally suited to the current generation of microcomputers and to users who dislike complex syntax but have a clear visual idea of the access paths through their data. Whether it is a complete solution to complex database problems is another matter: application code then needs to be written to handle database commands (Lima 1993b) and to drive the system, and the advantages of simplicity are lost.

A political science application

We consider here a politics example which is well suited to the relational model, showing the natural applicability and scope of the model in dealing with a number of distinct tables with logical links between them. We will compare the capability of the three schools of relational systems in handling this problem.

The problem concerns the storage, organization and retrieval of biographical and demographical background data relating to individuals in regional government throughout China (where one wants to examine patterns of career mobility among regional politicians). This type of application requires some forethought before rushing in to create tables, add data and manipulate the database. One of the standard techniques used is the Entity–Relationship (E–R) model developed by the computer scientist Chen (1976) where we work out the types of entity involved in our data and the relationships between them. Application of this model gives us Figure 6.3 comprising five entity-types: provinces, posts, biogra-

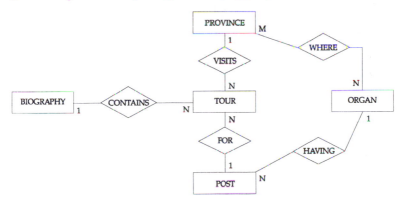

Figure 6.3 E–R model for tours by Chinese provincial politicians. Conventions: rectangles, entity types; diamonds, relationships; 1:N, one-to-many relationship; N:M, many-to-many relationship.

phies, organs, and tours of duty; and five relationships: visits, contains, where, having and for.

Two entity-types refer to province and position descriptions. The third on biographies holds, for each individual, personal information such as names and dates of birth and death, the fourth gives details of the tours of duty made by each person and the fifth gives the names of organs. The relationships indicate the access paths between the different entity-types. For example, there are paths from tours to provinces and posts and from posts to organs. By following tour $\rightarrow$ post, we find more information on post codes assigned to tours of duty. By following post $\rightarrow$ organ, we derive information on the organs associated with particular posts. Associated with the relationships is the form of the mapping expected between the entity-types. The 1:N mapping between, say, province and tour indicates that each province is associated with many tours but each tour involves only one province. The N:M mapping between province and organ indicates that each province is associated with many organs and each organ is associated with many provinces.

The next stage is to convert the E–R model into a relational model. There are standard rules for this mapping. The general rule is that each entity-type in the E–R model becomes a table-type in the relational model and each N:M relationship in the E–R model becomes a table-type in the relational model. We therefore end up with table structures and some illustrative data values as shown in Figure 6.4. The table structure (top row of each table) is the schema for our database.

Utilization of the information relies heavily on the manipulation of the dates at which positions were occupied and vacated by the politicians and on the use of codes to represent both the names of provinces and the descriptions of positions held. For the database to be effective, referential integrity must be maintained, that is any cross reference from, say, a province code in the tour table to a province code in the province table must succeed. This requires careful checking of input data to ensure, for instance, that a record of a tour is not added to the tour table with a province code that is not present in the province table. A feature of the tour table is the attribute service which is the difference between the start.date and finish.date. The value for service is calculated automatically by the system. No value is entered for it: it is a derived attribute.

Note the biography information is not shown in Figure 6.4 but is given in a separate figure – Figure 6.5. This holds data which, in terms of current relational systems, is difficult to handle because of the constraint

TOUR		post_	prov_			
tour.no	politician	code	code	start.date	finish.date	service
1	ABDULLA AHAGUAER	803	95	Dec 1949	Dec 1949	0.00
3	ABULIZI MUHEMAITI	553	95	Apr 1983	Nov 1985	2.07
4	AN LIN	423	4	Aug 1981	Mar 1983	1.07
5	AN PINGSHENG	323	62	Aug 1956	Jul 1961	4.11
6	AN PINGSHENG	502	63	Jul 1961	Jan 1967	5.06
7	AN PINGSHENG	543	63	Aug 1968	Sep 1975	7.01
17	AN PINGSHENG	500	63	Oct 1975	Feb 1977	1.04
18	AN PINGSHENG	540	63	Oct 1975	Feb 1977	1.04

PROVINCE	prov_code	province
	4	Hebei
	62	Inner Mongolia
	63	Xinjiang MR
	95	Xinjiang

POST	post_code	organ_code	post
	323	68	Dep Cmndr MR
	423	23	Vice Mayor
	500	14	1st Sec AR
	502	14	Sec AR
	540	34	Chmn ARR
	543	34	Vice Chmn ARR
	553	44	Vice Chmn ARPC
	803	22	Dep Sec Gen PPG

ORGAN	organ_code	organ
	12	Party Prov
	14	Party AR
	22	PGov Prov
	23	PGov Mun
	24	PGov AR
	34	Revcom AR
	44	PCong AR
	68	PLA MR

WHERE	prov_code	organ_code	organ_date_in	organ_date_out
	4	12	Oct 1949	Mar 1967
	4	12	May 1971	*
	62	14	Oct 1949	Apr 1967
	62	24	Oct 1949	Apr 1967
	63	68	Sep 1954	Jun 1985
	95	12	Oct 1949	Sep 1955
	95	14	Sep 1955	Dec 1967
	95	24	Sep 1949	*

Figure 6.4 Tables of data for Chinese provincial politicians.

NAME = AI DAYAN;
WG = AI TA-YEN;
MIN = 0;
BIRTHPLACE = Hebei Province;
SEX = M;
MISC.DI = 1949;
  MISC.DO = May 1950;
  MISC.POSTS = Deputy Sec-Gen., Beijing Military Control Commission.;
MISC.DI = May 1950;
  MISC.DO = Jul 1956;
  MISC.POSTS = Council mem., and concurrently Sec-Gen., Hebei PPG;
MISC.DI = Feb 1954;
  MISC.DO = *;
  MISC.POSTS = Dir., Administration of Students Studying Abroad, Ministry of Higher
Education;
MISC.DI = May 1954;
  MISC.DO = *;
  MISC.POSTS = council mem., Chinese People's Assn for Cultural Relations with Foreign
Countries.;
MISC.DI = Dec 1954;
  MISC.DO = Dec 1954;
  MISC.POSTS = mem., Chinese cultural delegation led by Hung Shen to East Germany to
sign China-Germany Cultural Cooperation agrreement.;
MISC.DI = Mar 1956;
  MISC.DO = *;
  MISC.POSTS = Deputy Dir., Bureau of Scientific and Technological Cadres, State Council.;
MISC.DI = Jul 1956;
  MISC.DO = Jul 1956;
  MISC.POSTS = mem., Chinese cultural delegation to USSR to sign Sino-Soviet Cultural
Cooperation Agreement;
;
―――――――――――

NAME = AN PINGSHENG;
WG = AN P'ING-SHENG;
MIN = 0;
BIRTHDATE = 1912;
BIRTHPLACE = Henan Prov '2' or Jiangxi Prov '40'.;
SEX = M;
ENTRY.DATE = 1932;
  POL.PARTY = CCP;
MISC.DI = <;
  MISC.DO = *;
  MISC.POSTS = Guangdong Prov Com, CPPCC.;
MISC.DI = <;
  MISC.DO = 1953;
  MISC.POSTS = Dep Dir Rural Work Dept, SChina Buro, CCP CC.;
MISC.DI = Dec 1955;
  MISC.DO = *;
  MISC.POSTS = Dir Office of Agriculture, Forestry and Water Conservancy, Guangdong
Prov Admin.;
MISC.DI = Jul 1956;
  MISC.DO = Feb 1958;

MISC.POSTS = Dir Rural Works Dept, CCP Guangdong Prov Com.;
MISC.DI = Apr 1960;
  MISC.DO = *;
  MISC.POSTS = Stdg Com CCP Guangdong Prov Com.;
MISC.DI = Dec 1973;
  MISC.DO = *;
  MISC.POSTS = Leading Mem Sino-Vietnamese Friendship Assn.;
  DUMMY;
MISC.DI = Dec 1977;
  MISC.DO = Dec 1979;
  MISC.POSTS = Chmn Yunnan Prov Com, CPPCC.;
MISC.DI = May 1979;
  MISC.DO = *;
  MISC.POSTS = Hd agricultural Deln to Japan.;
MISC.DI = May 1980;
  MISC.DO = May 1980;
  MISC.POSTS = Hd Friendship Delnnn to Romania, Switzerland and Malta.;
MISC.DI = Sep 1982;
  MISC.DO = Sep 1982;
  MISC.POSTS = Presm 12th CCP Nat Cong.;
  MISC.POSTS = Sec Gen Guangdong PPG.;
CRITICISM.DATE = Jan 1967;
  CRITICISM.TYPE = REMOVED;
COM.DI = Aug 1954;
  COMMITTEE = NPC;
  OTHER.COM = Dep for Guangdong.;
  CC.NO = 1;
COM.DI = Aug 1973;
  COMMITTEE = CC;
  CC.NO = 10;
COM.DI = Aug 1977;
  COMMITTEE = CC;
  CC.NO = 11;
COM.DI = Aug 1980;
  COMMITTEE = NPC;
  OTHER.COM = Presm;
  CC.NO = 5;
COM.DI = Sep 1982;
  COMMITTEE = CC;
  CC.NO = 12;
BIOGRAPHICAL = "Wife; Chen Ying.";
BIOGRAPHICAL = According to Radio Guangxi, removed from position of Sec CCP Guangxi Zhuang AR, but the news is not confirmed by Beijing, Jan 1967.;
;
_____

Figure 6.5   Biographical details for Chinese provincial politicians.

that every value must be atomic: each position in a table must be occu-pied by one undecomposable value. If a position in a table is occupied by a list or set of values, the table is not adequately normalized and there will be problems in searching and displaying information.

The data for the biography cannot therefore be held in tabular form with each row holding the name, birthplace, sex and a series of events: this construction breaks the normalization rule as each position in the events column holds a set of events, often called a repeating group. A possible solution is to store the information in two tables, one holding in each row the name, birthplace and sex; the other holding in each row the name and a single event. This decomposition of the structure, to ensure that every position in a table is single-valued, is called flattening. An al-ternative approach is to reduce the level of detail of the stored informa-tion by holding summary information only: some of the biography information could be held in paper form.

It is a limitation of current relational technology that unformatted data may need to be distorted from a natural representation for it to be held in an acceptable tabular form. There are systems using other models which can handle such data without the need for flattening, as for instance SPIRES (Rossiter et al. 1988) run by a number of North American univer-sities, and Advanced Revelation.

Another problem shown in the biography is the variability of the length of character strings as data values. Nearly all relational database systems have fixed length attributes which means that a fixed amount of space is reserved for each value irrespective of its actual length. Allowing for the longest value to be held can waste a great deal of disk space. SQL systems mitigate this problem by allowing compression techniques to be applied which remove unused space in the form of trailing blanks to data values.

For the purpose of this chapter, we assume the existence of biography in our table structure in a simplified form with attributes name, event and date_of_event.

An important aspect of our evaluation is the type of questions that can be readily handled. The type of questions that can be answered by a rela-tional system on the tables shown include the following:

(a) Which politicians have been posted to province number 4?
(b) Which politicians have been posted to the province called Hebei?
(c) Which politicians on tour in province Inner Mongolia were involved with the organ Party AR?

(d) Which politicians have only done tours of duty in the province Xinjiang?

(e) Which politicians have not done any tour of duty in the province Xinjiang?

(f) Which politicians have done different tours of duty in the same province?

(g) Which politicians have held posts in all provinces listed during their careers?

It is interesting to compare the strategies in our three schools for answering, say, question (b) which involves a *join* of two tables: cross referencing between PROVINCE and TOUR over values for PROV_CODE. There are two strategies in natural language terms:

(a) to locate "Hebei" in PROVINCE, determine its province code, look up this code in TOUR to find all occurrences and print out the associated politicians' names; or

(b) to examine each TOUR entry, look up each province code in PROVINCE, check whether the PROVINCE_NAME is "Hebei" and if so, print out the current politician's name in TOUR;

In dBase, the query is answered by the second approach (to give an N:1 mapping) with the sequence of commands (lower case = syntactical commands, upper case = names of tables, attributes, indexes):

```
select 1
use TOUR
select 2
use PROVINCE index PROV
select 1
set relation to PROV_CODE into B
display for B-$>$PROVINCE = 'Hebei'
fields POLITICIAN
```

The query assumes that an index PROV already exists on the PROVINCE table on PROV_CODE values. A relation is established from the first work area (selected as 1 – or A) into the second work area (selected as 2 – or B). This means that as you move through the TOUR file, a pointer also moves through the PROVINCE file so that the PROV_CODE values are equal in the two files. The query forces a complete pass through the TOUR file with records retrieved only when "Hebei" is the value for PROVINCE in the PROVINCE table.

Other relational systems allow a statement of what is wanted without a strategy being specified. So with SQL, the query is rather more simple:

> select unique POLITICIAN
> from TOUR, PROVINCE
> where TOUR.PROV_CODE =
> PROVINCE.PROV_CODE
> and PROVINCE = 'Hebei'

The system will decide itself which of the above search strategies to adopt, depending on which is the more efficient. Perhaps clearest of all is QBE as shown in Figure 6.6.

TOUR	tour.no	politician	post_code	prov_code	start_date	finish_date	service
		print		PC			

PROVINCE	prov_code	province
	PC	"Hebei"

Figure 6.6   QBE example.

The user, presented with empty table templates, has supplied the name of the province required "Hebei" in the appropriate column of PROVINCE, entered the *same* value for PROV_CODE in both tables (in this case PC but it could be any value at all), and indicated by the *print* instruction the information to be displayed.

Some of the above questions, namely (a)–(g), require a bit more thought to provide solutions, but there are standard ways of dealing with them in any relational language; see, for instance, Date (1990). Certain types of questions, however, pose problems for particular schools of the relational model. These include requests such as:

(a) Provide the complete biography and tours of all politicians with all codes transformed to their full name equivalents. This is easy enough in dBase but is difficult for the more fully set-based languages of SQL and QBE where we would perform a join of all the tables in the database to answer the query. If any facet of information is missing for a politician such as a biography entry, no information is produced for that politician at all. The difficulties arise from the loss of information when a join is not successful: information not matched in a join is discarded completely from the result. A new operator, the natural outer join, is being developed to solve this

problem which allows unmatched partial information to be retained.
(b) Find all the personal relatives (fathers, wives, father-in-laws, etc.) of a politician. This query requires a transitive closure in which step by step we navigate along a chain of records each time identifying a relative one step removed. In all types of relational database, this requires the repeated execution of a command to find each new relative. Artificial intelligence languages such as Prolog are more suited to this type of query, providing all solutions from one command.

Finally, how has this database been applied? The database actively supports academic research on the Chinese provincial leadership (Goodman 1986–7). In particular, the production of biographical texts has become a major use. The database also permits rapid answers to queries about Chinese personalities, from the media, publications like *Who's Who*, and organizations such as the Foreign Office.

Further applications

The relational model has been used in many other applications. For example:
(a) for managing a historical thesaurus – see Wotherspoon (1992) where the usage of both dBase and Ingres is discussed;
(b) for handling medieval texts – see Faulhaber (1991) where the package Advanced Revelation is used to add text facilities to the standard relational ones;
(c) for providing views of different versions of the same underlying text – see Heather & Rossiter (1990) where the bible is used as an example;
(d) for the integration of databases, expert systems and hypermedia, in the context of representing Shakespeare's works – see Neuhaus (1991).

Summary

We have examined two classical types of humanities database applications, one involving a dynamic semantic ordering of data, the other an extensive cross referencing of data. The relational model has undoubtedly produced useful results for both applications, whichever school of relational thought is followed: dBase, SQL or QBE.

There are, however, limitations to relational technology. Data which cannot be easily expressed in tabular form are difficult to handle and are often regrettably summarized when faced with the option of distorting the natural structure. In addition, the access paths that are explicit in the E–R model are only implicit in the relational model making searching routes less obvious to the user. Finally, some types of query lose information if standard joins are used and the execution of queries involving transitive closure is cumbersome.

Acknowledgements

I am grateful to David Goodman, formerly at the East Asia Centre, Department of Politics, Newcastle University, for use of the application on Chinese politicians, and to Anna Rossiter, Department of History, Newcastle University, for use of the application on seventeenth century records for Hexham.

References

Bain, M., R. Bland, L. Burnard, J. Duke, C. Edwards, D. Lindsey, N. Rossiter, P. Willett 1989. *Free text retrieval systems: a review and evaluation*. London: Taylor-Graham.

Carter, J. 1993. *Programming in SQL with Oracle, Ingres and dBase IV*. Englewood Cliffs: Prentice Hall.

Chen, P. P-S. 1976. The Entity–Relationship model: towards a unified view of data. *ACM Trans Database Systems* 1, 9–36.

Codd, E. F. 1970. A relational model for large shared data banks. *Communications ACM*, 13(6).

Coulombre, R. & J. Price 1993. *FileMaker Pro 2.0 for Windows, a practical handbook for creating sophisticated databases*. Reading, Mass.:Addison-Wesley.

Date, C. J. 1990. *An introduction to database systems*, vol. I, 5th ed. Reading, Mass.: Addison-Wesley.

Faulhaber, C. B. 1991. Philobiblion: problems and solutions in a relational database of medieval texts. *Literary and Linguistic Computing* 6, 89–96.

Goodman, D. S. G. 1986–87. *Chinese Provincial Leaders 1949–1985* [2 volumes]. University College Cardiff Press.

REFERENCES

Hardman, L., D. C. A. Bulterman, G. van Rossum 1994. The Amsterdam hypermedia model: adding time and context to the Dexter model. *Communications ACM* **37**, 50–62.

Heather, M. A. & B. N. Rossiter 1990. Syntactical relations in parallel text. In *Proceedings 15th International Conference of Association for Literary & Linguistic Computing*, Y. Choueka (ed.), 197–214. Jerusalem 1988.

International Organization for Standardization (ISO) 1987–92. *Database Language SQL*, Documentation: ISO/IEC 9075:1987; 9075:1989; 9075:1992.

Lima, T. 1993a. *Developing FoxPro for Windows applications*, Reading, Mass.: Addison-Wesley.

Lima, T. 1993b. *Developing Paradox 4.0 applications*, Reading, Mass.: Addison-Wesley.

Neuhaus, H. J. 1991. Integrating database, expert system, and hypermedia: the Shakespeare CD-ROM project. *Literary and Linguistic Computing* **6**, 187–91.

Pendharker, S. & R. Biegel 1994. *The dBase IV programming language: a building block approach*. Englewood Cliffs: Prentice Hall.

Rossiter, B. N., P. S. Davis, D. S. G. Goodman, M. K. Ward, M. A. Heather 1988. Generalised DBMS as a tool for research. *University Computing* **10**, 71–9.

Rossiter, B. N., T. J. Sillitoe, M. A. Heather 1990. Database support for very large hypertexts: data organization, navigation and trails. *Electronic Publishing: ODD* **3**, 141–54.

Wotherspoon, I. 1992. Historical thesaurus database using Ingres. *Literary and Linguistic Computing* **7**, 218–25

Zloof, M. M. 1975. Query by example: the invocation and definition of tables and forms. *Proceedings 1st International Conference on Very Large Databases*. Framington, Mass.

CHAPTER 7

Using computers
in ethnographic fieldwork

Michael D. Fischer

If computers are to act as an important tool for ethnographic research, the use of the computers must begin during fieldwork. As long as data are recorded in one form, only to be transcribed to another, preparing field data for computers competes with other tasks, such as indexing notes, transcribing audio and video tapes, and deciphering genealogies. One of the ways to diminish the "barrier" of preparation is to use computers throughout the research process.

Although easing the labour requirements of ethnographic research are important, these are not the most compelling arguments for using computers in ethnographic research, in the field or out, as Kippen remarks:

> ... I believe that the enormous potential of computers to improve the capacity of anthropologists to gather, store, and analyze information has yet to be demonstrated. Clearly, it is necessary to look beyond word processors and databases to other systems, such as knowledge-based systems, that have the power to change the ways in which we as researchers operate. (1988: 318)

To address the use of computers in ethnographic fieldwork we will examine the way computers can assist with "ordinary" ethnographic fieldwork, the capacity of computers to deal with a wide range of materials and media so as to extend the range of material we can consider as the ethnographic record, and how new field methodologies can be supported by field based computing. I conclude that computers in the field will lead not only to improvement in conventional field methodology, but will make possible some radical changes (and one hopes, improvements) in the fieldwork process.

Our most important goal in using computers as a tool for ethnographic research must be to do better, not simply more, ethnography. The best way to introduce computing into our research is to first replicate what we have done before, but greater benefits will come when computers are used to do things we could not do before.

Ethnographic fieldwork

Ethnographic fieldwork is the core method of data collection for many disciplines, and most social sciences include some researchers who use ethnographic methods. Increasingly, qualitative researchers from all disciplines are turning to ethnographic research as a core method, although ethnography is not limited to "qualitative" research. This multidisciplinary use has, of course, resulted in an explosion of conceptions associated with ethnographic fieldwork and related research methods such as participant observation and fieldnotes.

We can define four basic elements to ethnographic research: collection of information, analysis of that information, theory building and testing, and reporting the results. These are not sequential; because of the time invested in ethnographic research, these phases become intricately interwoven. Ethnographers have particular problems with respect to their data:

(a) Much of it is contained in fieldnotes, which are in chronological order rather than topic order, often irregular in structure, and contain many different topics distributed within.

(b) The investment in and intensity of most of the data collection effort, often over a period of months or years, demands a high "re-use" value. The same information may need to be reorganized in many ways to derive maximum value.

(c) For methodological, ethical, economic and practical reasons ethnographers can rarely perform experiments. Data is generally collected passively, often without any form of systematic sampling (other than "opportunity" sampling).

(d) The greatest strength and weakness of ethnographic data is its dependence on the researcher. Not only must we rely on the researcher to collect data in a satisfactory manner, but we depend heavily on the knowledge of the researcher to assess what the data are and their significance when applied.

Ethnography is not unique in this latter point – there are many research methods which depend on the subjective impressions of their practitioners. But it is only in ethnography that subjective knowledge is routinely taken for objective knowledge and where ethnographers are obliged, whether this be possible or not, to minimize the impact of their own biases and prior conceptions on this subjective knowledge. It is in this respect that computers may ultimately have the most impact.

Past and present feasibility of field computing

Early on, Weinberg & Weinberg (1972) and Brown & Werner (1974) attempted to shuttle information in and out of the field site for processing, but this was, understandably, not persuasive. The rapid development of microcomputers from the late 1970s – increases in power in conjunction with reductions in size and cost – has made the use of computers in the field not only practical, but also increasing numbers of ethnographers have taken computers into the field since the late 1970s (Tomajczyk 1985, Sutton 1984, Powlesland 1986, Guillet 1985, Dyson-Hudson & Dyson-Hudson 1986, Ellen & Fischer 1987, Agar 1983, Case 1984, Werner 1982).

These efforts were not without difficulties. Many of these systems weighed over 25 kg, and upwards of 50 kg with accessories, power supplies and spares. Equipment designed to operate at temperatures between 15°C to 27°C with relative humidity between 40 and 80 per cent (non-precipitating) found itself in temperatures from –10°C to 50°C and relative humidity of 100 per cent (precipitating), with wily ethnographers luring insects from the keyboard with peanut butter (Dow 1987). No-one who has participated has suggested it was not worth the trouble, but that it was trouble no-one would deny. Thus, for most ethnographers taking a computer to the field has become feasible only recently, not because it was technically impossible, but because the logistical difficulty of operating or accessing computers in most field situations was unacceptable.

Most of the problems with hardware are, if not solved, under control. Battery powered "notebook" computers the size of an A4 book, weighing

less than 3 kg, are capable of almost anything larger "desktop" computers can do, as are "palm top" computers, weighing less than 350 g, with
256kB+ RAM, powered for six weeks on two AA sized batteries, and a
non-volatile storage capacity equivalent to one thousand A4 pages on a
removable (and replaceable) 20 g wafer solid-state "disk". Interfaces for
direct entry via hand printing with a pen are available, which work
much like conventional paper pads, down to the ability to draw in the
margins. In short, an ethnographer can carry into the field more computing power and storage in a 350 g package the size of a tobacco tin than
was available in 1980 using a desktop microcomputer.

Computing aspects of written data produced during fieldwork

Most ethnographers find written records are the easiest to work with using conventional computing techniques. Almost any computer, of any
size, can be of some benefit to this process. In this section we shall look
briefly at the requirements of ethnography and how these can be recon-
ciled with computer based tools appropriate to working with written
materials. Ideally, in doing ethnography we would not be restricted in
any way in terms of the information we record and our subsequent access to this information. In practice the very tools used (the means of
writing and organizing this writing) encumber the process, not only because of the time required to create a record of our observations and experiences, but also because the volume of writing becomes so great that it
is difficult to keep an overall grasp of what has been recorded, much less
the detail. Part of this problem is our human inability to remember in a
non-selective manner (D'Andrade 1973), and part is technology, the pen,
paper and writing we use to improve our ability to remember. You can
use computer applications to address the technological problems as a
supplement to or as a partial or total replacement for conventional ethnographic technology. In applying computers to our research problems we
should consider Burnard's warning:

> ... users ... tend to see their information in terms of the particu-
> lar data structure in which it has previously been physically in-
> stantiated (index cards, ledgers, textual description, etc.). Even
> when computerization has been embarked upon specifically in

order to overcome some informational restriction inherent in the physical constraints of a manual system, it is not unusual to find users requesting that those very constraints should be eternally perpetuated in the very system which is supposed to do away with them. (1987: 65)

Types of written records produced during fieldwork

In terms of "conventional" ethnographic research, most data, and the most important data, are collected in the form of written records. Ellen identifies seven main types of written records produced during fieldwork.

Table 7.1   Types of written record produced during fieldwork.

Temporary notes
Conventional notebooks, general and specialized according to topic
Diaries, personal and register of events
Card indexes, such as name directory or dictionary entries
Questionnaire returns
Special records, e.g. register of taped material, special survey material, genealogical charts
Maps and diagrams

Adapted from Fig. 8.2, Ellen 1984: 282.

These forms of data, while not exhaustive, serve as a basis for discussing computer applications in the field, which must necessarily be oriented towards the overall fieldwork process.

In general, computers adapt very well to assisting in the collection and analysis of written materials, in part because humanities researchers have been active in devising methods of working with historical and literary texts, and in part because of the commercial "office revolution" in the 1980s which resulted in the widespread distribution of quality computer based tools for producing and accessing texts, as well as the provision of tools for representing complex information and facilities for making reports based on that information. Some of these tools can be applied directly to our material, with little accommodation on our part, some tools require that we structure data in ways which are otherwise unnecessary, and some tools require an entirely different conceptual basis to use effectively.

Temporary notes

Temporary notes are, currently, the least likely data to be entered onto computer in a form other than their contribution to the other types of written records. Most temporary notes are written into notebooks, and being temporary, there is little point for re-entry just for the sake of reproducing the notes. Some researchers, myself included, enter the temporary notes into a wordprocessor verbatim and then expand these, but do not systematically retain a verbatim computer copy (cf. Pfaffenberger 1988).

You can, of course, enter the temporary notes directly into a computer. Many ethnographers find taking notes on paper distracting to both themselves and their consultants. It is unlikely that a computer will be less so. In many cases there is so little "connected" text (as opposed to telegraphic prose, outlines, charts and drawings) involved in a day's temporary notes that there may be little value added if the presence of a computer is likely to detract at all. In my own fieldwork I have recently been taking some notes on a small handheld computer which is as unobtrusive as a pen and notebook (once I have initially demonstrated it to my informant). It saves no time whatsoever if I transfer these notes, unaltered, to my larger laptop computer later in the day, because the time required to set up the file transfer hardware and software takes about as long as typing the notes in (although with far less tedium). The major advantage is that I can partially fill the notes out on the handheld computer at odd times during the day, wherever I might be, which does save time, since otherwise I would be writing the expansion in the notebook, and retyping the expanded version later in the day. Also useful, I have all previous fieldnotes and card indexes (from current and previous research at the same site) on the handheld computer as reference for writing the expanded notes, as well as for preparing visits and interviews.

Conventional notebooks, diaries and interview transcripts

These materials are suitable for computer based entry in the field, using standard wordprocessors, hypertext editors for entry and/or simple textual database managers which are easily adapted by a casual user for these purposes. These are also the data from which much post-fieldwork benefit will come, since the preparation time will be considerably lessened for data which is among the more tedious and which requires the most sensitivity and specialization of knowledge to enter, information which should usually be entered by yourself on return.

The range of information which might be included within fieldnotes is quite diverse, ranging from notes on observations, interviews, house inventories and genealogical data to diagrams of house plans and the layout of agricultural plots (Ellen 1984: 282). I focus below on the use of computers to support the production and analysis of notes, interview transcripts and other textual documents – the textual components of fieldnotes. I have attempted to sidestep aspects of theory, focusing more on operations than the value of these operations, which is more or less dependent on the individual researcher. For a good overview of computer based textual methods for qualitative ethnographic research, you should consult Pfaffenberger (1988) and Fischer (1994). For a broader range of views Fielding & Lee (1991) is recommended.

Fieldnotes are, by their very nature, very cumbersome to use. They are a record of observations, narratives and new insights, primarily organized by chronology rather than topic. Indeed, a part of their value is in this order, recording the ethnographer's development of different ideas and lines of enquiry. Although difficult to use, the fieldnotes are usually the most significant source of information both in the field and out: constantly referred to, updated and cursed for incompleteness (cf. Jackson 1990). A conventional method to make fieldnotes more accessible is to produce indexes, based upon classification codes and keywords chosen by the ethnographer. Although indexing fieldnotes is a favourite activity for those times when you just cannot bear to face yet another difficult day, the notes are rarely indexed to satisfaction, since the indexing process itself is somewhat dependent on the stage of the investigation (Ellen 1984, Seidel 1991).

Computer programs can enhance the use and analysis of textual documents using methods such as automatic indexing, concordances and high speed search (see Hansen, this volume). The main drawback is that these documents must be available to the computer and its programs in "machine-readable" form; basically someone must type the manuscript into a computer. This is most easily done, of course, if a computer is available at the time of consolidating the notes or transcribing the interviews: in the field. However, paper notebooks are relatively cheap, portable, rarely malfunction and require little power. Computers are relatively expensive, generally less portable, occasionally malfunction and require rather more power. To justify these disadvantages, computers must yield significant benefits. For many ethnographers, a small computer might be justified in the field for no other reason than to enter notes using a wordprocessor. Writing or typing fieldnotes into triplicate notebooks, as Ellen suggests (1984: 282), is neither easy or fun. Once entered into a wordprocessor, or perhaps a specialized fieldnote application, as many copies as required can be printed, merged into other documents based on subject headings or copied onto diskettes for safe deposit or mailing.

Most ethnographers who have used computers in the field take most of their rough notes using paper, entering and consolidating these onto the computer in the evening. The simplest way to enter notes is to type the notes with a wordprocessor exactly as you would have written or typed them on a piece of paper. Even the most basic wordprocessor is useful for note entry. Unfortunately, there is little you can do with a wordprocessor alone, other than enter, edit, copy and review your notes. Pfaffenberger notes that wordprocessors were in part originally developed to "de-skill" typing, not for writing (1988: 18). Wordprocessors were certainly not developed to support ethnographic research. Other programs will be required for comprehensive search, access and analytic support. There are alternatives to using a wordprocessing program which may be advantageous. Text oriented database programs often have quite reasonable facilities for the entry and editing of text, and provide operations to assist in the organization of material such as fieldnotes, as well as incorporating many text oriented classifying, searching and collation operations.

The most basic, and common, use of a "computerized notebook" is to locate sections of the notes relevant to some topic of interest, replacing the more traditional indexing and eyes-over-pages methods. There are a range of partial computing solutions to these problems, some simple and some quite sophisticated. All are partial solutions, because no existing computer based method can refer to the meaning of the notes in any useful way (even two ethnographers can have difficulty in agreeing on this). Computer programs are restricted to referencing literal structural features of the notes (Pfaffenberger 1988: 41). If you type in the notes as you might with a typewriter, these structural features are limited to a model implicit in the technology of writing on paper: letters, words, lines, paragraphs, sections, pages and chapters. With such "raw" texts most contemporary computer software is incapable of identifying structures more complex than paragraphs, or even lines, unless user-defined boundaries are indicated.

The content of a text can only be referenced by most programs in terms of explicit lexical features (Pfaffenberger 1988). Most programs are limited to indexing, locating or counting specific words or phrases which appear in the notes. If you impose a more discrete structure, then more useful work can be performed by the computer with programs designed to exploit that structure. Additional structure can be as simple as including distinctive classification codes and keywords as you consolidate your notes, as is suggested for conventional fieldnotes (Ellen 1984, Sanjek 1990, Seidel 1991), or as complex as imposing direct links between entries that you judge to be related, or including formalized statements of content.

Fieldnotes serve another important purpose in ethnographic analysis: to contextualize other material collected in the field, and the writing we do based on our analysis of the fieldnotes. Other types of information are greatly enhanced if the note references relevant to the information can be easily retrieved. Computers are capable of representing almost all of the conventional forms of records that we make in the field; besides written records (and their structure) these include photographic material, video tape, audio tape, maps. High performance computer environments have operations which support all of these data types, not only for display, but as objects which can be interactively annotated and interlinked.

Card indexes

Card indexes are a common cellulose-based information technology (CBIT) for storing and accessing a variety of kinds of data in the field. Among the advantages of card indexes in the field are flexibility in inserting new material, and the option of sorting the cards into different orders for different purposes. Card indexes are particularly easy to implement using conventional computer programs. The type of program you should use depends on the kind of information, and how it is structured on the card equivalent.

To simply replicate the function and operation of a manual card index on a computer is very simple; you can enter the information using a basic text or wordprocessor, and use the "Find" operation of the editor to locate sections of the document by doing a word search, and, if desired, copy selected material into another document. This has the advantage of using a basic tool for two purposes, entry and retrieval, and permitting you to lay the information out in any way that you like that is compatible with the wordprocessor or text editor. Given that the more recent word-processors have the capability to store and display high quality images, and even video and sound, this can be a flexible structure indeed. However, there are severe constraints if your document becomes too large (and thus computer operation too slow) or if you want to process the information further.

If you want to automate storing the results of a word search, most text based computers have at least one program which will accept textual keyword(s) and search through your text file created using a text editor, displaying on the screen or printer, or storing in another text file, the lines in the source file which contain the keyword(s). If your card index is simple in structure, word lists or simple inventories, this may be adequate. If a single line is not adequate to represent the contents of your card index application, there are other programs which will work with larger sections, separated by some distinctive marker you type in after each entry. If you have stored the output of these searches in a new file, other programs can be used to count the number of lines or to sort these files into new orders.

Questionnaire and survey returns

Software for the analysis of survey data is perhaps the best known application of computers to social science research, for many the only known application. There is a broad range of applications for statistical analysis, questionnaire tabulation and generating tables for examination or publication. The kinds of program you require depend on the complexity of the survey instrument and the size of your intended sample. For surveys with mainly numerical data and where the number of cases is a few hundred, a spreadsheet calculator may be adequate. For more complex surveys, with linked or optional questions, a statistics program will probably be required. If the survey is especially complex, you may in addition need some kind of database management system (DBMS) which you can use to create simpler data structures for the spreadsheet or statistics program (see Ward & Dale, this volume).

The value of dealing in the field with questionnaire and survey returns depends on the use you intend for these while in the field, the sensitivity of their content and the means you have available to enter these into a computer. A problem, both in the field and out, is the preparation of survey data for the computer. If you intend to simply look over the questionnaires in the field, and you must enter these yourself from the paper forms, then it may not be a justifiable expenditure of valuable field time. If you think a particular questionnaire might be useful for planning further research while in the field, then it may be worth the time if you have an appropriate spreadsheet or statistical package. In many cases for planning field research an analysis of a relatively small sample (< 50) of the questionnaire or survey instruments will probably be adequate.

If you (or your field assistants) are filling in the questionnaires in the course of interviews, direct entry of the questionnaires into small notebook or handheld "palmtop" computers can be a productive option. A form representing the questionnaire can be "programmed" into the small computer and entries made and recorded quickly (see Martin & Manners, this volume). Green (1988) developed a program based on an expert system to assist in converting textual material such as interviews into questionnaire type data, by having the ethnographers develop a set of rules for answering the questions from a transcript and encoding these in the program. The program then asks the questions for each case, providing standardized assistance in classifying each case with respect to the question. This has the advantage that each questionnaire is produced in a consistent manner from relatively unstructured data.

Special records

Ellen (1984) includes in this category materials such as registers of taped material, special survey material and genealogical charts, and most other kinds of written data of a "special" sort. In the strictly written sense, most of these can be adequately dealt with using either textual databases or more structured database management systems, possibly in the case of genealogical data, and for special surveys which incorporate visual and aural materials a hypertext application. For many kinds of special records such as these it is sometimes useful to write a dedicated application for entry. This can be done with fairly limited programming skill using a hypertext editor program, most database management systems, or you can specify the function of the application to a programming partner. In both of these applications the data can be later output into more conventional forms if required.

Maps and diagrams

Most ethnographers seem to generate a lot of diagrams or other graphical representations while in the field, if with varying degrees of skill. For some kinds of research diagrams are essential; as an illustration of ethnographic detail (the placement of a decoration in a house), to denote certain kinds of relationships (genealogies), or for creating representations as an interviewing aid (drawings of material culture). Although the use of computers for making diagrams is of great value, especially in the presentation of ethnographic material, its use in the field very much relates to the role of drawings in your own fieldwork.

If rough diagrams begin life on paper, there may be little point to converting these to rough diagrams in the computer, except for the possible benefit of integration into your fieldnote database. You might, of course, want to catalogue references to these using a database. If you restrict yourself to rough diagrams, however, the effort is not very great. If you include an image scanner/digitizer in your hardware toolkit, the effort is rather less since you are not drawing but copying a drawing onto the computer. Quality problems in the field are of rather less importance than for published work.

I use a limited number of drawings as interview aids when discussing material culture, and find this very useful. From a printed copy I elicit "corrections" to my drawings, helping me to separate etic detail from emic detail. I attach the various responses to the computer based drawings (in a hypermedia program), using these as one means of access. It works well for me, especially given my limited skill in freehand drawing with pen and paper.

Special purpose graphic tools

There are an increasing number of programs which employ graphical tools potentially useful in fieldwork. These include programs for drawing and manipulating maps, programs for direct genealogical data entry in the form of diagrams, programs which can assist in the building and testing of taxonomies, based on recent work by geneticists on cladistics, and graphic editors for the direct input of musical notation, as well as facilities for playing back music in this form.

Maps, even rough ones, have considerable utility when on a computer (Gilbert, this volume). Drawing a good original map is difficult, even on a computer. But the sorts of rough maps (in appearance, not necessarily in accuracy) that are commonly used in the field are relatively easily entered. Use of maps in the field include monitoring cultivated areas, plotting social groups and kinship links, or other cultural variables, against the map, and tracking the coverage of surveys and questionnaires. Using a printer, the map can be reproduced in a variety of sizes, with different textual legends as required.

The value of graphical input of data in the field depends very much on your research. The strength is that the data input format (and thus at least one database record) is the same as the report or output format. If you tend to record genealogical relationships in diagrams in the field, then a genealogical editor may well make sense as a means of transferring data from notebook to computer, even more so if you intend direct entry working with an informant. The graphical structure of the data represents kinship structure as well, and this can help ensure that you have included everyone, and recorded all the relevant data. On the other hand, if you mainly record genealogical relationships in textual form (recommended in any case if you are recording genealogies of more than twenty or so people at a time), and mainly want to be able to see genealogical relationships between different groups and dwellings in a village or several villages, then other methods (Fischer 1994) will probably serve as well, or better, since genealogical diagrams of too great a scale tend to obscure relationships rather than bring these out. Certainly, as with any tools you intend to take to the field, you should learn and evaluate these well before depending upon them in a "live" situation.

Other types of data produced during fieldwork

In addition to the written data in Table 7.1, there are other common kinds of field data:

(a) photographs, cine film, video;

(b) audio recordings.

What most of these have in common is that, for most ethnographers, these are at present somewhat peripheral, if well established (Blacking 1984: 199). Even in the case of photographs, and to some extent audio recordings, which most ethnographers make, these are under-used for research, either in the field or out. On the other hand, most ethnographers I have spoken to are interested in using these materials, but have found them cumbersome in practice, so the material mainly sits in drawers.

Visual recordings: photographs, cine film and video recordings

If visual records are an important aspect of your research, there are many possibilities. The technical details of when, where and how to acquire images in the form of photographs or video and the basic methods of analysis and use are no different from more conventional media for representation. These issues are well covered in Collier & Collier (1986) and Jackson (1987), as well as briefly discussed by Blacking (1984). However, the range of analysis possible and the ease of access are more extensive. These range from text/code based computer assisted classification using authority lists (taxonomic thesaurus of classification terms for subject domains) to cross references between fieldnotes and people, places and events depicted in the records, to the incorporation of the images into a computer representation which can not only be accessed and viewed on screen from databases, but can serve as an interactive element for data entry relevant to the images and objects in the images. Images can be incorporated into most computer applications which operate on graphical operating systems, including wordprocessors and database programs. Images can be resized and otherwise manipulated using a paint program capable of editing colour images.

Although the technology is well established, at present the capability to digitize and incorporate digital images comes at a price, in both equipment and weight (and money, of course). Any notebook computer with greyscale or colour display can display images with adequate detail for most field use. There are, however, two basic problems with digital still images. First, devices for digitizing images are almost all larger than one would like for fieldwork. The best all around field solution is probably to use a video camcorder, with an attachment for slides and negatives if required. This camera, in conjunction with a video "frame-grabber" peripheral and associated software, will enable you to digitize stills directly from the camcorder. The frame-grabber should come supplied with software for this purpose. At present there are no frame-grabbing devices intended for portable use, but most can be coaxed to run off battery by a competent technician. In the very near future frame-grabbing capability will be built into more expensive notebook computers. Frame-grabbing also requires more memory than you would otherwise require. The second problem is storing the images on a disk. Even highly compressed, a full screen image will occupy about twenty to one hundred thousand bytes of memory (the equivalent of about five to twenty thousand words or twenty to fifty images per megabyte).

For video tape, support for partial or even full transcription at frame level is available, either through computer controlled players, or through direct representation on the computer. Indeed, full transcription may not be necessary in some cases because under computer control specific video frames or sequences can be displayed on the monitor as a response to database queries, along with notes and markings added by the researcher.

Because of current costs and limitations, using digitized video in the field has to be viewed in terms of application. For most researchers the principal applications of displaying or making video in the field include:

(a) *An interviewing aid.* This may require only the capacity to display video if you can prepare the materials in advance. Software required can be as simple as a wordprocessor, although special purpose applications exist for this purpose.

(b) *Interim analysis of activities with a visual element.* This will require facilities for producing video, although not necessarily of the highest quality. The kinds of analysis can range from frame by frame comparisons and documentation for interactional studies to creating video clips with very coarse temporal quality; rates as low as one or even one-half video frame per second can give a good overview of the structure of an event such as a ritual or other ceremony.

(c) *Data acquisition.* This will require facilities for producing video clips, though not necessarily of high quality. For example, with a temporal quality rate of one frame per minute or so you can record activity at a location for a day and analyze patterns of space use, traffic density or other periodic activity.

(d) *Indexing video tape.* This will require facilities for producing video clips, though not of high temporal quality. An index consisting of one frame per ten seconds for thirty hours of tape results in a computer document about forty megabytes in size. Time codes can be associated with the frames, which makes it very easy to locate sections of tape which you can watch using more conventional video equipment, including video decks which can be directly controlled by the computer.

In all cases video clips can be manipulated by other computer tools, such as database management systems or inserted into word-processing documents or hypermedia authoring systems, as well as specialized programs for working with video material. For example, a five minute video sequence can be broken into smaller and smaller sequences within an application such as a wordprocessor, where these can be documented, while retaining the entire clip for reference.

It is much simpler to display video clips (or still images for that matter) than to produce them while in the field. Any mid-range computer, notebook or desktop can display digitized video at some level using free or inexpensive system level software. It is important to have system level support for video, so that you can use video clips in your other programs which are not designed to support this kind of data. You can paste clips into wordprocessor documents and databases, as well as programs designed to use video directly. (For further discussion of digital video see Fischer 1994.)

Audio recordings

The range of options for audio recordings falls under similar lines as visual recordings. For the serious user of audio tape similar options for computer representation and control are available. Computer controlled audio decks can locate and play tape sequences on demand from either direct requests by the user, or as a result of searching a database or from a fieldnote reference. Audio of reasonable to high quality can be stored directly on disk, and a number of programs for editing and modification are available. Although the options are similar, digital audio recording directly to the computer poses few problems other than disk storage, and this is not of the scale of digital video. The equipment necessary for low to medium fidelity sound is quite inexpensive and trivial in weight, size and power requirements.

Sounds and audio clips can be manipulated by computer tools such as database management systems, or inserted into wordprocessing documents or hypermedia authoring programs, as well as specialized programs for working with audio material. Again, smaller clips can be taken from the original sound clips, regardless of what application they are embedded within, and installed into the same or another application. This is done by reference, rather than making a copy, so the new subclip does not add appreciably to the storage requirements. A twenty minute audio sequence can thus be broken into smaller and smaller sequences within an application such as a wordprocessor, where these can be documented, while retaining the entire clip for reference. Like video, in some cases there is no need to fully transcribe audio material in this form, since direct and immediate access to the audio clips can be directed from a computer based document, while retaining the context of the clip.

Conclusion

Most of this chapter addresses how conventional field materials can be created, stored and manipulated using readily available computers and software applications. We must recognize that much of the "traditional" method of ethnography is shaped by particular technologies, and new technologies open up new possibilities. What these new possibilities might be is not always self-evident – we, as practising ethnographers, must "discover" these. Based on my own ethnographic research, conducted with and without the assistance of computers, I have found that the use of computer based methods has the potential to reshape some of the objectives of ethnography (Fischer & Finkelstein 1991, Fischer 1994). The computer, if nothing else, provides a platform for manipulating symbols which permits us to extend our own symbol processing abilities. In particular, we can soon expect to use quantitative methods with more reference to context and idiosyncratic detail, and qualitative methods with more reference to systematic patterns and more meaningful constraints on interpretation.

Acknowledgement

The research and results in this chapter were supported by the Economic and Social Research Council of the UK under grants R000231113, R000231953, R000233509, R000233933 and R000234791, the Tri-Council HCI/Cog. Sci. Initiative (UK) under grant SPG8920734, and the Leverhulme Foundation grant "Enhancing the use of computers in anthropology in the UK and other European countries"

References

Agar, M. 1983. Microcomputers as field tools. *Computers and the Humanities* **17**, 19–26.

Blacking, J. 1984. Preparation for fieldwork: audio-visual equipment in general ethnographic studies. In *Ethnographic research: a guide to general conduct*, R. F. Ellen (ed.), 199–206. London: Academic Press.

Brown, J. A. & B. Werner 1974. An on-site data management system application in field archaeology. *Communications of the ACM* **17**, 644–6.

Burnard, L. D. 1987. Knowledge base or database? Computer applications in ethnology. In *Toward a computer ethnology*, J. Raben, S. Sugita, M. Kubo (eds), 63–97. Osaka: National Museum of Ethnology.

Case, R. P. 1984. Microcomputers in the field: practical considerations. *Byte* **9**, 243–4, 246, 248, 250.

Collier Jr., J. & M. Collier 1986. *Visual anthropology. Photography as a research method.* Albuquerque, N. Mex.: University of New Mexico Press.

D'Andrade, R. G. 1973. Cultural construction of reality. In *Cultural illness and health* L. Nader & T. Maretzki (eds). Anthropological Studies 9. Washington, DC: American Anthropological Society.

Dow, J. 1987. Hunting and gathering tales. *Computer Assisted Anthropology Newsletter* **2**(4), 42–3.

Dyson-Hudson, R. & N. Dyson-Hudson 1986. Computers for anthropological fieldwork. *Current Anthropology* **27**, 530–32.

Ellen, R. F. 1984. Producing data. In *Ethnographic research: a guide to general conduct* R. F. Ellen (ed.), 273–93. London: Academic Press.

Ellen, R. F. & M. Fischer 1987. Computers for anthropological fieldwork. *Current Anthropology* **28**, 677–9.

Fielding, N. G. & R. M. Lee (eds) 1991. *Using computers in qualitative research.* London: Sage.

Fischer, M. D. 1994. *Applications in computing for social anthropologists.* London: Routledge.

Fischer, M. D. & A. Finkelstein 1991. A case study in social knowledge representation: arranging a marriage in urban Pakistan. In *Using computers in qualitative research*, N. G. Fielding & R. M. Lee (eds). London: Sage.

Green, A. 1988. *The forms filling program.* Unpublished MA dissertation, University of Kent, Canterbury.

Guillet, D. 1985. Microcomputers in fieldwork and the role of the anthropologist. *Human Organization* **44**, 369–71.

Kippen, J. 1988. On the uses of computers in anthropological research. *Current Anthropology* **29**(2), 317–20.

Jackson, B. 1987. *Fieldwork.* Urbana, Ill.: University of Illinois Press.

Jackson, J. E. 1990. "I am a fieldnote": fieldnotes as a symbol of professional identity. In *Fieldnotes: the makings of anthropology*, R. Sanjek (ed.), 3–33. Ithaca, NY, and London: Cornell University Press.

Pfaffenberger, B. 1988. *Microcomputer applications in qualitative research.* Qualitative Methods Series 14. Newbury Park: Sage.

Powlesland, D. J. 1986. On site computing: in the field with the silicon chip. In *Computer usage in British archaeology: report of the joint IFA/RCHM working party on computer usage*, J. D. Richards (ed.). Birmingham: University of Birmingham.

Sanjek, R. 1990. A vocabulary for fieldnotes. In *Fieldnotes: the makings of anthropology*. R. Sanjek (ed.), 92–138. Ithaca NY, and London: Cornell University Press.

Seidel, J. 1991. Method and madness in the application of computer technology to qualitative data analysis. In *Using computers in qualitative research*. N. G. Fielding & R. M. Lee, (eds), 107–16. London: Sage.

Sutton, D. 1984. Field recording and computers at Pouerua, Inland Bay of Islands. *Newsletter of the New Zealand Archaeological Association* 27, 156–65.

Tomajczyk, S. F. 1985. Notes from the field: anthropologist uses Picocomputer. *PICO: The Briefcase Computer Report* 1, 17–20.

Weinberg, D. & G. H. Weinberg 1972. Using a computer in the field: kinship information. *Social Science Information* 11, 37–59.

Werner, O. 1982. Microcomputers in cultural anthropology: APL programs for qualitative analysis. Microcomputers aid in the study of Navajo and other cultures. *Byte* 7, 250–80.

CHAPTER 8

Computer assistance, qualitative analysis and model building

Wilma Mangabeira

Newly available computer packages for the analysis of qualitative data are an important innovation and bring many advantages to the traditional craft of analyzing qualitative data. Simply by reducing the amount of paper and the extent to which it needs to be shuffled, computer assisted qualitative data analysis software (CAQDAS) allows for a less tedious analytic process, saves time and offers the possibility of more refined and replicable analyses (Fielding & Lee 1991, Tesch 1989.) According to Drass (1989), besides other advantages, CAQDAS also produces potentially more explicit codification of qualitative techniques as researchers openly share data and results.

Despite these and many other advantages, this development should not be treated uncritically. For example, two specific problems can be readily identified. The first is that the sheer seduction of computer operations made possible through CAQDAS may easily divert attention from the logic of research design and the adequacy of the analysis. The second relates to the methodological and theoretical assumptions embedded in the software but rarely made explicit to the user.

This chapter will explore these two issues by concentrating on two "third generation" programs, i.e. those with model building capabilities: ETHNO and HyperRESEARCH. ETHNO is an MS-DOS application which also makes use of a rule-based system of production rules. (On production rules, see Heather & Lee, this volume.) HyperRESEARCH was developed as a HyperCard based Macintosh application. A run-time Macintosh version and a Windows version are now also available. The chapter also attempts to suggest how the software might be used with other methodological orientations such as Max Weber's ideal-type and the rational choice approach (see acknowledgements at the end of the chapter).

The advent of CAQDAS programs dates back to the beginning of the 1980s. Fielding (1993) has recently estimated that there are now available at least fifteen dedicated qualitative analysis programs. In terms of software development, it is possible to identify three types of program and their uses. The first group includes word-processors and utility programs which are potentially helpful as text analysis tools (Tesch 1991: 181–97, Heise 1992). The second group are dedicated qualitative analysis programs, which basically replace the manual "cutting and pasting" typical of much traditional qualitative data analysis. These programs allow the analyst to code and then search for coded segments of the text contained, for example, in interview transcripts. Among the more popular programs in this category is ETHNOGRAPH, developed by John Seidel. (For further detail on programs of this type, see Tesch 1990, Fielding 1993.)

The third group of programs, which I will call here "third generation programs", are those which have theory construction or model building capabilities and which make extensive use of knowledge based systems and artificial intelligence. Although these programs continue to treat qualitative data "in their own right", they offer the possibility that some testing of the research results might take place. Of course, the boundaries between the second and third groups are difficult to draw; almost all CAQDAS programs support description, interpretation and analysis. An alternative way to classify programs is to consider the *explicit intent* of the software designer/researcher and to look at the ways in which they have used their programs in concrete research.

The attempt to formalize research results through model building or the testing of qualitative data against a theoretical model is somewhat controversial. Such attempts have brought allegations that an essentially positivistic kind of reasoning is penetrating the qualitative sociological tradition through the use of third generation programs. Given the novelty and contested character which the third generation programs have brought to the debate, I will present information on how the program designers have used their software and discuss the methodological orientations implicit in them. I will also present, in an exploratory way, new possible uses, different from the ones envisaged by their original creators. I want to show that together with the ways the software designers have used their programs – Hesse-Biber et al. with the grounded theory approach (1991a) and Heise (1992) with a "production system model" – they can also be used with other sociological methodologies and with different models of reasoning about qualitative data. In particular, I will suggest that HyperRESEARCH fits well with an approach based on Weber's ideal-typical kind of reasoning, while ETHNO can contribute to empirical studies with a rational-choice/collective action orientation.

Third generation programs: HyperRESEARCH

HyperRESEARCH is a dedicated program for the analysis of qualitative data. It has three basic features. As with other programs in the second group outlined above, HyperRESEARCH replaces the manual "cutting and pasting" of segments of textual data and allows for the coding and retrieval of text segments. As with other programs, it performs boolean searches on any code or combination of codes through the use of AND, OR and NOT expressions. However, the program goes beyond these basic features and has a facility for creating propositions via procedural rules. It also goes a step further in comparison with second generation programs, since it can test hypotheses using artificial intelligence. This is done through the use of expert system software technology which uses production rules to create a semi-formal mechanism for theory building. Qualitative researchers may feel uneasy about this. Hypothesis testing and the building of formal or semi-formal models has not traditionally been a feature of interpretative sociology. Despite this possibility for discomfort, I will attempt to show that in fact what the program designers have sought to do is something exciting and promising since it challenges basic taken-for-granted assumptions of the qualitative paradigm and invites qualitative researchers to take a different, more explicit approach to the way in which they produce their research results. In fact, despite differences between the objectives and operation of both programs, HyperRESEARCH and ETHNO aid forms of testing for qualitative propositions by problematizing validation and by allowing greater replicability of the analytical process (Hesse-Biber et al. 1990a, 1992, Heise 1992).

In HyperRESEARCH research data are compared with a theoretical model through hypothesis testing. Hesse-Biber, one of the program's creators, has declared that the program's methodology is explicitly inspired by the grounded theory approach of Glaser & Strauss (1967) and concepts of "analytical induction" or "constant comparison" (Hesse-Biber et al. 1991a; see also Charmaz 1983, Corbin & Strauss 1990). (For an interesting discussion of how grounded theory has established almost a paradigmatic role among second generation programs, see Lonkila 1992.) In this analytical process, one codes categories deriving directly from or "grounded" in the data. These, in turn, orient the development of hypotheses which are then compared with the original data, in many cases leading to the addition or verification of the original codes. Hesse-Biber et al. stress how this process involves a cyclical movement of induction, deduction and verification as the refinement of codes and of the researcher's understanding of the relationship between them are refined (1991a).

Another important point made by the software creators is that to make efficient use of HyperRESEARCH, the researcher must make an effort not only to refine coding but also to introduce *directionality of codes*. (Although I will not develop the point here, it is important to consider how analytic induction attempts to break the traditional boundaries between qualitative and quantitative methodologies in which induction is regarded as exclusive to the first approach and deduction as exclusive to the second. See Popper (1959) for a classic discussion and Giddens (1976).) In automating theory generation (Hesse-Biber 1991), HyperRESEARCH allows researchers to code and retrieve in the traditional way and to create a set of production rules which allow working hypotheses to be tested. In programs of the second generation, code and retrieve is the most important aspect of the program's use. The researcher produces searches between codes, across the cases, informants or the events being analyzed. The use of the boolean search terms AND, OR, NOT allows one to test insights about the material by assuming that the presence and absence of a certain code in a particular search reveals hidden relationships not yet clear to the researcher. (On the use of boolean codes, see Richards & Richards 1991, Mangabeira forthcoming, Tesch 1990.)

In contrast to second generation programs, the creation of production rules and hypothesis testing in HyperRESEARCH comprises a further phase in the use of the software. According to the designers, the hypothesis testing mechanism is based on the building of a set of production rules, where the reasoning is as follows. The researcher identifies possible relationships between the data and elaborates these insights through a set of rules which make use of the codes already in the program. The production rules have the following structure: IF some set of codes is present THEN some set of conclusions is possible, or IF some set of codes is present THEN add a certain conclusion. In this context, production rules provide a "formal mechanism for describing the inference or thought process used to draw conclusions from the data". In other words, the creation of production rules describes the inference of one or more *new* codes, which were not derived *directly* from the data but *inferred* from the presence or absence of certain codes in the case being analyzed.

Taking Hesse-Biber's research on eating disorders (1987, 1991), we can illustrate the construction of a set of production rules, which will lead to the testing of a hypothesis about the research data. Hesse-Biber created two sets of production rules to test the extent to which a mother's damaging of her daughter's self image is an important proposition in explaining eating disorders among college females. (It is important to note that this hypothesis is only part of an overall explanatory pattern which is much more complex and multifaceted than can be presented here.)

The first production rule is as follows: IF the code "mother critical of daughter's body image" is present AND the code "mother and daughter relationship strained" is present AND the code "daughter is experiencing weight loss" is present THEN ADD THE CODE "mother's negative influence on daughter's self image".

The production rule above is only *one* of the many possible sets of production rules which the researcher could create and ask Hyper-RESEARCH to run. In terms of analytical reasoning, it implies the addition of new codes, given the presence of certain codes and not others. This procedure is in itself a theory building process. The researcher is moving away from the sheer handling of codes which are actually present in the data to the inclusion of new codes which are revealing a certain level of interpretation, of logic, about relationships between codes. The new code in our example above "evidence of mother's negative influence on daughter's self image" was not present in the informant's discourse and probably not self-evident to the researcher in the initial stages of the research. The discovery of a relationship between "critical body image" by the daughter, "strained relationship between mother and daughter" and daughter's "weight loss" is in fact the building of some sort of model which should be able to suggest propositions about relationships between codes and the research questions posed.

According to Hesse-Biber (1991), we could go on to develop this proposition further by creating a second set of production rules such as: IF "mother's negative influence on daughter's self image" AND "daughter dislikes daughter's appearance" THEN ADD "mother has damaged daughter's self image". This last CODE was created from the former reasoning and is to be the terminal rule against which the data will be tested.

When a set of production rules such as those presented above have been developed, a report is run to test the hypothesis against the actual data. At this point, the program executes these production rules against the knowledge base. HyperRESEARCH will report the success or failure of the two rules and whether the given hypothesis holds or not for each case in the study. If the hypothesis is not supported, the program will tell us why it failed. In other words, it will report for each case in the study if and how many production rules were found to be true in that case.

Having said this, it is possible to see the usefulness of Hyper-RESEARCH'S hypothesis testing facility, especially when the production rules are run *across* several cases or *across* several informants. At this point, the underlying links and relationships which were discovered for one or several cases and turned into an IF/THEN model will be tested *across* all available cases to see how strongly or weakly they will hold. In the running of the hypothesis tester, the researcher is testing for the occurrence or absence of the production rules which were previously formulated. The presence or absence of codes indicates a true or false value for that code, creating a "knowledge base". Indeed, the running of the report is the most important point of the program, when the absence or presence of production rules across cases *validate* or not the hypothesis created by the researcher.

It is important to note at this point how Hesse-Biber et al. view the utility of the hypothesis testing mechanism. As they put it, "in reaching overall conclusions regarding the validity of any hypothesis or set of hypotheses tested by the HyperRESEARCH system, the final decision is, of course, the researcher's. The conditions under which a researcher will 'accept' or 'reject' a given hypothesis or set of hypotheses will depend on the level of significance with which the hypothesis was held to be valid" (i.e. the number of cases for which HyperRESEARCH found evidence for the stated relationship) (Hesse-Biber et al. 1991a; see also Hyper-RESEARCH Manual 6–25).

In other words, what matters here is that the report points to the weakness of one's initial insights, formulated in the model, against an actual comparison with the data. The program orients the researcher to ways of re-examining the data. This can take place by recoding or checking whether some theoretical assumptions are erroneous. What matters to the researcher is that the understanding of where the reasoning breaks down or is inconsistent can lead to new ideas about the project. The major objective for creating such a system is to be able to refine the relationship between codes.

Hesse-Biber et al. see hypothesis testing as a cyclical process: "For researchers who use a grounded theory approach (constant comparison) to qualitative analysis, rules can be added as small relationships are located and coded in the data. Additional rules, which create relationships among the basic rules, can be added to construct a hypothesis. This hypothesis can then be tested, and additional coding can be performed to verify the validity of the hypothesis" (1991c).

It is very important to make a point about the underlying reasoning that is implicit in the program. Reasoning flows from directional coding to construction of production rules to the testing for the occurrence or absence of production rules against the data. Finally, it checks if and how the initial hypothesis is true or not and where it breaks down, for each case under study. Since production rules are statements of relationships between codes, the task of producing them is an invitation to the researcher to make his or her reasoning from the empirical data more explicit and to establish in an open way chains of thought and logical relations between, among and across the coded segments of text.

Having presented the methodological orientation underlying Hyper-RESEARCH and having discussed the most innovative features of the program – creating production rules and running them against the data to see whether the initial hypothesis holds or not – I would like to suggest an alternative mode of reasoning which can be supported by HyperRESEARCH. Taking the overall capabilities of the program, it is possible to suggest that the production-rule procedure and the hypothesis testing mechanism can be taken as a Weberian ideal-type.

Ideal-types and HyperRESEARCH

Max Weber's ideal-type methodology has long been admired for allowing the construction of general level concepts out of empirical and qualitative data, despite the never ending debates about Weber's methodology and despite questioning of the extent to which he fully adhered to his own methodological principles (see, for example, Scaff 1989, Jary & Jary 1991, Abercrombie et al.1984).

Weber emphasized in his work how sociology should attempt the development of formal models or ideal-types. Weber wanted to move away from simple descriptions towards theoretical propositions. Ideal-types are the way in which this objective might be achieved: "theoretical differentiation is possible in sociology only in terms of ideal or pure types" (Weber 1978), while "Ideal-types take traits, meanings in their essential features from the empirical reality of our culture and bring them together into a unified ideal-construct" (Weber 1949).

In *Economy and society* Weber justifies the creation of ideal-types in sociology as a way to formulate type concepts and "generalised uniformities of empirical processes" (Weber 1978). For Weber, ideal-types improve theoretical sharpness and help to reveal logical relations between social processes: "in order to give a precise meaning to terms . . ., it is necessary for the sociologist to formulate pure ideal-types of the corresponding forms of action which in each case involve the highest possible degree of logical integration by virtue of their complete adequacy on the level of meaning . . ." (Weber 1978). According to Weber, ideal-types are a way of introducing rigour in the sociological research: ". . . the more sharply and precisely the ideal-type has been constructed, thus the more abstract and unrealistic in this sense it is, the better it is able to perform its functions in formulation, terminology, classification and hypothesis" (Weber 1978).

Taking Weber's ideal-types and relating it with HyperRESEARCH, it is possible to see that both draw attention to the process of formulating general, abstract models out of empirical processes. While ideal-types are general conceptualizations or meaningful understandings of specific cases, HyperRESEARCH hypotheses are abstract logical propositions about social processes. A second significant aspect about ideal-types that suggests its productive use with HyperRESEARCH is the comparative status of the methodology. As pointed out by Scaff (1989), the unique heuristic significance of ideal-types is found when one uses them for comparison with reality. Although there is contention over the precise relationship between ideal-types and their empirical referents in Weber's work, ideal-types are ways for suggesting contingent "hypotheses" about social and historical relations that could be checked through investigation. Weber himself stressed this point when he claimed that "the construction of abstract ideal-types recommends itself not as an *end* but as a *means*. . . . Ideal-types have the significance of a purely ideal . . . with which the real situation or action is compared and surveyed for the explication of certain of its significant components" (Weber 1949). If we consider that the basic objective for constructing production rules in HyperRESEARCH is to establish inferred relationships out of research material and that hypothesis testing checks these propositions in comparison with the rest of the research data, it is possible to suggest that the final outcome in the program could be dealt with *as an ideal-type.*

This proposal is reinforced if we consider that ideal-types represent reality in an abstract, pure form. Although they are constructed out of empirical data, they do not exhaust reality nor do they correspond exactly to any empirical instance. As pointed out by Weber "in its conceptual purity, this mental construct cannot be found empirically anywhere in reality. It is an utopia" (Weber 1949). In a way this is precisely the idea behind HyperRESEARCH. As we have already seen, production rules work as models, which represent inference and abstraction from the empirical material.

If we think about HyperRESEARCH results as ideal-types, the objective of the program can be understood as aiming towards the creation of provisional theoretical models. The strength of the model is that it is to be compared over and over again with the empirical data. In this process, the model is refined and in this way gains greater levels of abstraction and explanatory power about social situations. Finally, once arrived at a reasonably sustainable conclusion, the researcher can present it as a mental construct, as an abstraction which might orient future research about a certain sociological question.

ETHNO

ETHNO is a program which deals with the modelling of events. In contrast to HyperRESEARCH, its source material is not textual data derived from people's actual discourse, representations or opinions but "verbally defined events" (Heise 1992) or "recorded event sequences" (Corsaro & Heise 1990). (Heise (1989, 1990) is clearly aware that the definition of "verbal sequences of events" is problematic, since sequences of events, the raw material for ETHNO, are themselves an interpretation.) The program can deal with written narratives, personal accounts, stories or novels and offers a principle for interpreting popular realities and reasoning (Heise 1992). The verbal content of the event is created by the interpretation of an "expert" (Corsaro & Heise 1990). According to Heise, the "expert" might be the researcher but also could be a "culturally competent" informant.

According to Heise, the program was designed for the modelling of the logical structure of events within happenings (Heise 1992). The analyst is responsible for defining the logical relations between each event, within a sequence of events. The program works in a two-step manner. First the researcher creates a diagram about the sequence of events. Once the diagram is ready, an "analyze a series" procedure is then run to see if the model logically accounts for the sequence of events in that happening according to a set of dynamic principles which will be shown shortly. As in HyperRESEARCH, once the abstract model is built, it is compared against the empirical event which was its source or against other similar events.

The theoretical and methodological roots of ETHNO are to be found in the general theory of production systems. Heise emphasizes two major points: (a) subjective realities are logical and thus have an underlying rationality; and (b) propositions have an IF:THEN structure. The idea that subjective realities are rational refers to the assumption that thinking is permeated by logic. People reason about things. They organize their reasoning into knowledge and whether this knowledge is correct or incorrect, scientific or commonsensical, it can be analyzed by logical principles (Heise 1989). The evolving postulate that people's conception of the world is logically structured is that action is also rational and that it unfolds within the constraints of performance principles. These principles are four-fold: (1) events have prerequisites; (2) an event cannot occur until all of its prerequisites have occurred; (3) the occurrence of an event depletes (uses up) its prerequisites; and (4) an event is not repeated until the conditions it created are used up by some consequence (Corsaro & Heise 1990).

The second fundamental regarding production rules is related to their structure as IF:THEN rules. We have already seen this IF:THEN structure in the discussion of HyperRESEARCH. Here, however, this principle is read as the following: IF a certain configuration of conditions arises, THEN a certain production occurs. Productions have natural consequences. They cause changes in conditions which can also be phrased as

IF:THEN rules; IF a given production occurs, THEN condition A changes from state X to Y.

Now that we know more about the theoretical principles, let us look again into the two step process of running ETHNO – the diagram and the "test". The construction of a diagram works in the following way. The user inputs the first "verbally defined event" and ETHNO provides the head of a diagram on the screen. The next steps consist of inputs of other "verbally defined events" in the sequence the researcher has decided to follow. The user will be asked by ETHNO to define the relations between each event as the model is built. ETHNO questions whether the following event in the sequence is implied in the predecessor event. The researcher builds up a model by answering yes or no to such questions and filling in the diagram. As the model is built, the program "learns" from the researcher's answers. As pointed out by Heise: "Once the program obtains some knowledge about the event under analysis, it does not query about logical relations it can infer on its own" (Corsaro & Heise 1990). The final diagram presents a sequence of events, points out the prerequisites of events and shows the logical constraints on how a given happening can unfold.

If, in the process of creating a diagram and answering questions, the program finds inconsistencies with the four principles outlined, it suggests to the user some ways out of the problem (Heise 1988). In the second step of the program, "analyzing a series", or "running a test", ETHNO "plays out" the event and reports a problem when an event is encountered which has been unprimed or unused. In this test, the program is posing two major questions: (1) does the logical structure (with the added assumptions) explain the sequence of events? (2) do we now have a grammar of action that accounts for event order? (Heise 1988). What ETHNO is doing at this point is testing the model, consisting of an implication structure and auxiliary principles, against the recorded sequence of events.

ETHNO has been used to analyze the folk-tale "Little Red Riding Hood" (Heise 1988), the routine interaction between professors (Heise 1989) and the study of "approach-avoidance play" in peer culture of nursery school children in the USA and in Italy (Corsaro & Heise 1990). To illustrate the use of ETHNO, I will present the nursery school children study. The basic issue of the research is centred on the observation that children are "frequently exposed to social knowledge and communicative demands in their everyday activities with adults that raise problems, confusions and uncertainties. These problems are later reproduced and re-addressed in the activities and routines that make up peer culture" (Corsaro & Heise 1990). The data were obtained from videotapes and fieldnotes of actual performances, of interactions between nursery school children. This material was later turned into "verbal codes" expressing the events which were analyzed (Corsaro & Heise 1990).

The actual use of ETHNO in this research involved the following steps: examination of the performance of the routines in great detail; creation of verbal expressions from fieldnotes and videotape; input of data on events of the actual performances; and creation of models by asking how each event relates to the subsequent and precedent event on the diagram.

As a result of these steps, two models of events were created, one for the "Walking Bucket" (the American case) and one for "The Witch" (the Italian case). Once these two models were ready, the researchers ran a series analysis. In this process the researcher verified the program's analysis of the actual performance. Research conclusions showed that in comparing the routines "Walking Bucket" and "The Witch", the researchers found some important differences between them. However, they also discovered that despite these differences, the two routines are basically the same. This was shown by an abstract ETHNO model of events, which represented the essential features present in both concrete models (Corsaro & Heise 1990). According to the authors, with the help of ETHNO they were able to successfully extract an abstract model that accounted for both events. They point out that the method enabled them to model actual performances of play and to interpret "its significance for peer culture without obscuring the complexity and meaning of the event from the children's point of view" (Corsaro & Heise 1990).

As a concluding remark, it is possible to compare the two model-building programs analyzed here. Although HyperRESEARCH and ETHNO base their principles on production rules, they use them differently and in contrasting ways. While ETHNO's typical application is the longitudinal examination of happenings, HyperRESEARCH involves the cross-sectional analysis of cases (Heise 1992). Another important difference is that while ETHNO models the data diagrammatically, HyperRESEARCH presents its model as sets of propositions. ETHNO wants to arrive at the structure of events showing the logical constraints on the unfolding of a certain happening. HyperRESEARCH arrives at a structure which reveals the levels and logic of implication between actual and inferred codes.

Having presented the underlying assumptions implicit in ETHNO and illustrated its use in concrete research, I will now suggest an alternative use for ETHNO, in a context quite different from the micro-sociological interactions in which the program has been used up to now. This alternative is linked to the rational choice paradigm in macro-sociological research.

Rational choice/collective action research agenda and ETHNO

Since ETHNO focuses on social happenings or events, it can theoretically be used both for micro and macro subjects. The suggestion that ETHNO might be useful as an automated tool for research within rational choice/ collective action research stems directly from the fact that both the collective action approach and ETHNO deal with the formal modelling of human action. Another shared assumption is that human action is rational. Although rational choice theory has long been present in sociological research through the works of George Homans and Peter Blau, its influence declined in sociology after the 1960s only to be renewed in the 1980s. According to Wallace & Wolf (1991), this re-emergence can be explained by the relative success of rational choice approaches in other disciplines, especially in economics and political science.

In very general terms, rational choice theory states that social life is principally capable of being explained as the outcome of the rational choices of individual actors (Collins 1991). As pointed out by Little (1991), in rational choice theory individuals are assumed to have a set of interests against which they evaluate alternative courses of action; they assign costs and benefits to various possible choices and choose an action after surveying the pros and cons of each. Rational choice explanations thus depend upon the "means-end" theory of rational action. The form of reasoning in this theory seeks to explain social outcomes as the aggregate result of large numbers of individuals, acting on the basis of rational calculations, given the circumstances of the social and natural environment within which they deliberate.

Within this general framework, rational choice has been notable for encompassing both micro and macro sociologies. It gives theoretical support both to studies of small scale interaction as well as to studies of large group collective movements. Within rational choice theory it is possible to find three sub-areas of applied research: decision making theory, game theory and collective action theory. I would like to focus on this last approach since I believe ETHNO could make a significant contribution to research on collective action. Collective action theory can be defined as a rational choice perspective on structural issues. This approach was generated by economists and centres on the understanding of collective behaviour within the public sphere. The theory suggests that there is a basic conflict between private rationality and collective action, between what would be rationally appropriate from the point of view of individual benefits and the types of actions required for the obtainment of public goods (Barry 1970). The basic presupposition behind this theory is that individuals are rational and motivated by self-interest. Within this view, individuals are always trying to maximize their own private interests while trying to minimize costs. (Some sociologists have criticized what they regard as an excessive focus of the narrow economic rationality of individuals in rational choice theory. See, for example, Little 1991, Wallace & Wolf 1991.)

The main question put forward by collective action theory is as follows: if rationally self-interested individuals are under an unavoidable incentive to take a "free ride" in circumstances of collective action, that is to refrain from contribution and hope that others make a contrary choice, under what circumstances will a group succeed in acting in concert to bring about its common interest? (Little 1991). Empirical research based on this approach has been used to analyze collective action of various kinds: strikes, rebellions and revolutions. (Classic discussions of this area can be found in Bowman 1982, Crouch 1982, Johnson 1988, Tilly 1979.)

The usefulness of ETHNO to research in the field of collective action can be understood if we look into its basic functions. As we have already discussed, ETHNO will take up segments of actions and events, organize them into a sequence in accordance with a set of logical principles, and then test how consistent was the model created against those principles. ETHNO shows the structure of events by pointing out the logical elements and constraints which were involved in the unfolding of a certain happening. By answering whether the logical structure elaborated explains the sequence of events and by showing a grammar of action that accounts for the order of events, ETHNO can significantly contribute to the improvement of the empirical base of rational choice theory.

This point has also been made by Fielding & Lee (1991) when they say that ETHNO might secure a more adequate empirical base for explanation and prediction in the rational choice approach. In fact, I would like to suggest that with the help of the ETHNO program, the collective action approach could deal with the major criticisms addressed to the theory: that it has been more successful in posing questions than answering them and that it has arrived at wide-ranging conclusions from a very small empirical base (Collins 1991, Little 1991, Wallace & Wolf 1991).

Conclusion

This chapter has discussed two third generation CAQDAS programs with model building features. Through a detailed explanation of the workings and capabilities of HyperRESEARCH and ETHNO, I have argued that their features can be seen as challenging and productive for sociological research. This chapter has shown how both HyperRESEARCH and ETHNO are based on production rule principles. It has also shown how HyperRESEARCH takes the constant comparison ideal from the grounded theory approach as its guiding methodology. The chapter has presented empirical research carried out by the software creators/researchers as a way of illustrating the programs' principles as well as demonstrating their potential.

Finally, this chapter has argued that HyperRESEARCH could be productively used within the framework of Weberian ideal-types and ETHNO could contribute to research on collective action. This use of ETHNO was justified by reference to its sharing of basic principles and a strong, systematic empirical basis for the overriding dilemma of collective action.

The ideas presented in this chapter are exploratory. I hope that they will be discussed by software designers and users in ways that can help develop a productive theoretical debate about the CAQDAS of programs of the third generation.

Acknowledgements

ETHNO was created by David Heise of the University of Indiana. HyperRESEARCH was designed by Sharlene Hesse-Biber, Scott Kinder and Paul

Dupuis at Boston College. The arguments presented in this chapter were developed during the course of a research fellowship, funded by the Fullbright Commission and to whom grateful acknowledgement is made, which permitted periods of close contact with the developers of both programs.

References

Abercrombie, N., S. Hill & B. Turner 1984. *The dictionary of sociology*. London: Penguin.
Barry, B. 1970. *Sociologists, economists and democracy*. Chicago: University of Chicago Press.
Bowman, J. 1982. The logic of capitalist collective action. *Social Science Information* **21**, 571–604.
Brent, E. 1984. Qualitative computing: approaches and issues. In *Computers and qualitative data*, P. Conrad & S. Reinharz (eds). New York: Human Science Press.
Brent, E. 1986. Knowledge-based systems: a qualitative formalism. *Qualitative Sociology* **9**(3), 256–82.
Brent, E. 1988. New approaches to expert systems and artificial intelligence programming. *Social Science Computer Review* **6**(4), 569–78.
Brent, E. 1989. Is there a role for artificial intelligence in sociological theorizing? In *New technology in sociology: practical applications in research and work*, G. Blank, et al. (eds). New Brunswick, NJ: Transaction Publishers.
Charmaz, K. 1983. The grounded theory method: an explication and interpretation. In *Contemporary field research*, R. Emerson (ed.), 109–26. Boston: Little, Brown.
Collins, R. 1990. *Sociological insight: an introduction to non-obvious sociology*. New York: Oxford University Press.
Conrad, P. & S. Reinharz (eds) 1984. *Computers and qualitative data*. New York: Human Science Press.
Corbin, J. & A. Strauss 1990. Grounded theory research: procedures, canons and evaluative criteria. *Qualitative Sociology* **13**(1), 2–21.
Corsaro, W. & D. Heise 1990. Event structure models from ethnographic data. In *Sociological methodology*, C. Clifford (ed.), 1–57. Washington, DC: ASA.
Crouch, C. 1982. *Trade unions. The logic of collective action*. London: Fontana.
Drass, K. 1989. Text analysis and text analysis software: a comparison of assumptions. In *New technology in sociology: practical applications in research and work*, G. Blank et al. (eds). New Brunswick, NJ: Transaction.
Fielding, N. 1993. *Social research update*. Surrey: University of Surrey.
Fielding, N. & R. Lee (eds) 1991. *Using computers in qualitative research*. London: Sage.
Gerson, E. 1984. Computing in qualitative research. *Qualitative Sociology* **9**(2), 204–207.
Giddens, A. 1976. *New rules of sociological method. A positive critique of interpretative sociology*. London: Hutchinson.

REFERENCES

Glaser, B. & A. Strauss 1967. *The discovery of grounded theory: strategies for qualitative research*. New York: Aldine de Gruyter.

Heise, D. 1988. Computer analysis of cultural structures. *Social Science Computer Review* 6(1), 183–96.

Heise, D. 1989. Modeling event structures. *Journal of Mathematical Sociology* 14(2–3), 139–69.

Heise, D. 1992. Computer assistance in qualitative sociology. *Social Science Computer Review* 10(4), 531–43.

Heise, D. & E. Lewis 1988. *Introduction to Ethno* (Manual). Ragleigh, NC: National Collegiate Software Clearinghouse.

Heise, D. & R. Simmons 1985. Some computer-based developments in sociology. *Science* 228, 428–33.

Hesse-Biber, S. 1987. *Eating patterns and eating disorders among Boston College students: a summary report*. Boston College.

Hesse-Biber, S. 1991. Women, weight and eating disorders: a socio-cultural and political-economic analysis. *Women's Studies International Forum* 14(3), 173–91.

Hesse-Biber, S. 1992. Unleashing Frankenstein's monster? The use of computers in qualitative research. ASA Meeting, Pittsburgh, August.

Hesse-Biber, S., P. Dupuis, T. Scott Kinder 1990a. HyperRESEARCH: a computer program for the analysis of qualitative data using the Macintosh. Paper presented at ASA Conference, Washington DC, August.

Hesse-Biber, S., P. Dupuis, T. Scott Kinder 1990b. HyperRESEARCH: a computer program for the analysis of qualitative data using the Macintosh. *Qualitative Studies in Education* 3(2), 189–93.

Hesse-Biber, S., P. Dupuis, T. Scott Kinder 1991a. HyperRESEARCH: a computer program for the analysis of qualitative data with an emphasis on hypothesis testing and multimedia analysis. *Qualitative Sociology* 14(4), 289–306.

Hesse-Biber, S., P. Dupuis, T. Scott Kinder 1991b. *HyperRESEARCH Manual*. Researchware. Randolph, Mass.

Hesse-Biber, S., P. Dupuis, T. Scott Kinder 1991c. HyperRESEARCH: a computer program for the analysis of qualitative data with an emphasis on multidata analysis and hypothesis testing. *Social Science Computer Review* 9(3), 452–60.

Hinze, K. 1987. Computing in sociology: bringing back the balance. *Social Science Microcomputer Review* 5(4), 439–51.

Jary, D. & J. Jary 1991. *The HarperCollins dictionary of sociology*. New York: Harper Perennial.

Johnson, J. 1988. Symbolic action and the limits of strategic rationality: on the logic of working-class collective action. *Political Power and Social Theory* 7, 211–48.

Little, D. 1991. *Varieties of social explanation. An introduction to the philosophy of social science*. Oxford: Westview Press.

Lonkila, M. 1992. When you have a hammer, all problems start looking like nails. Grounded theory as an emerging paradigm for computer-assisted qualitative analysis. Paper presented at the Conference on the Qualitative Research Process and Computing, University of Bremen, October.

Mangabeira, W. (forthcoming). Qualitative analysis and microcomputer software: some reflections on a new trend in sociological research. In *Studies in qualitative*

145

sociology 5: computers and qualitative research. R. G. Burgess (ed.). New York: JAI Press.

Popper, K. 1959. *The logic of scientific discovery*. London: Hutchinson.

Richards, L. & T. Richards 1991. The transformation of qualitative method: computational paradigms and research processes. In *Using computers in qualitative research*, N. Fielding & R. Lee (eds). London: Sage.

Scaff, L. 1989. *Fleeing the iron cage. Culture, politics and modernity in the thought of Max Weber*. Berkeley: University of California Press.

Schrodt, P. 1989. Artificial intelligence and formal models of international behavior. In *New technology in sociology: practical applications and research work*, G. Blank et al. (eds). New Brunswick, NJ: Transaction.

Seidel, J. & J. Clark 1984. The Ethnograph: a computer program for the analysis of qualitative data. *Qualitative Sociology* 9(2), 110–25.

Shelly, A. & E. Sibert 1986. Using logic programming to facilitate qualitative data analysis. *Qualitative Sociology* 9(2).

Taylor, M. 1988. *Rationality and revolution*. Cambridge: Cambridge University Press.

Tesch, R. 1989. Computer software and qualitative analysis: a reassessment. In *New technology in sociology: practical applications in research and work*, G. Blank et al. (eds). New Brunswick, NJ: Transaction.

Tesch, R. 1990. *Qualitative research. Analysis types and software tools*. London: Falmer Press.

Tesch, R. 1991. Software for qualitative data: analysis needs and program capabilities. In *Using computers in qualitative research*, N. Fielding & R. Lee (eds). London: Sage.

Tilly, C. 1979. *From mobilization to revolution*. Reading, Mass.: Addison-Wesley.

Wallace, R. & A. Wolf 1991. *Contemporary sociological theory. Continuing the classical tradition*. Englewood Cliffs, NJ: Prentice-Hall.

Weber, M. 1949. Objectivity in social science and social policy. In *The methodology of the social science*. New York: Free Press.

Weber, M. 1978. *Economy and society. An outline of interpretive sociology*. Cambridge, Mass.: Harvard University Press.

CHAPTER 9

Using information technology to analyze newspaper content

Anders Hansen

Introduction

The systematic analysis of media coverage of social issues, events and actors has long been a central component of both communications research and of sociology, linguistics and related disciplines. Traditionally, such analysis has been marred by the costly, and sometimes tedious, nature of large scale content analysis. Perhaps most frustrating is the effort, time and money spent on identifying relevant coverage (e.g. newspaper articles or television/radio programmes). Also frustrating is the energy that needs to go into the manual coding of relatively basic dimensions (such as time, place and size identifiers) of media texts before progressing to the coding and analysis of more complex and interesting dimensions (such as topic, thematic emphasis and inflection, vocabulary, ideological positions).

Systematic indexes of media material and well indexed archives have in the past been a useful resource and an alternative for researchers wishing to analyze media coverage, particularly where such analysis has been concerned with retrospective media coverage. Inevitably, however, indexes to media coverage often impose their own historically idiosyncratic categories and are too general for the examination of specific subjects of coverage. Even the clippings and video archives kept by newspapers and broadcasting organizations have, as noted by Withey & Hugget (1991) been notoriously idiosyncratic, and have worked well largely because of the exceptional skills of the librarians and other staff running them.

While good indexing and microfiche storage of, for example, newspaper text offered some advantages in the analysis of media coverage, the real revolution has come with the creation of electronic full text database storage of newspapers. Full text databases facilitate not only the easy, fast and reliable identification of "relevant coverage" and cut out some of the more tedious "book-keeping" aspects of analysis, but also offer scope for a much more dynamic analysis than that traditionally characteristic of content analysis. (See Holsti 1969, Krippendorf 1980, or Weber 1990 for full descriptions of the method of content analysis.)

The considerable potential of computer assisted content analysis was recognized as long ago as the 1960s (Stone et al. 1966). In the mid 1970s attempts were made to enhance the scope for computer assisted analysis of newspapers by converting the full text of newspapers to electronic storage (DeWeese 1976, 1977). The significant potential of such analysis was stated clearly by DeWeese:

> Content analysis exhibits promise as a complementary method to public opinion survey research. It overcomes several of the limitations of such research. Content analysis techniques can measure media emphasis, are unobtrusive, and can capture time changes: an investigator is limited only by the length of his data base in studying changes through time. Used together, content analysis of printed media and public opinion research might reveal interrelations between the media and public opinion.(1976: 93)

Despite the recognition of how computer assisted content analysis could help the enhancement of studies of media coverage as social and cultural indicators (see Weber 1984) or of the relationship between trends in media coverage and trends in public opinion (Janowitz 1976), the use of electronic news text in combination with computer assisted analysis has not been widely developed or used.

The aim of this chapter is twofold: to describe some of the main sources of electronic news text and to outline ways of enhancing traditional, "manual", quantitative content analysis of newspapers through the use of electronic text databases and computer software for the management and analysis of textual data. The chapter focuses exclusively on newspapers, rather than other mass media, for the simple reason that although well developed and well indexed video and broadcast archives exist, there are as yet no equivalents for broadcast media to the full text databases for newspapers. Using examples from press coverage of environmental issues and of "mad cow disease", the aim of the paper is to outline the steps involved in the computerized analysis of electronically stored newspaper text. (Mad cow disease is the term popularly used in the press and other media for bovine spongiform encephalopathy (BSE), a brain disease in cattle, first detected around 1986, and reported in the British national press from April 1988 onwards. Media coverage of the disease was at its peak during the spring and summer of 1990 when public fears that the disease might spread from cattle to humans resulted in a significant drop in beef consumption and widespread criticism of the government's handling of the problem.)

Content analysis: key steps

The key steps of any content analysis of media texts, whether "manual" or computer assisted, consists principally of three steps: (1) defining the research problem, (2) sampling and text retrieval, (3) analysis and interpretation. Defining the research problem is, of course, method-independent and applies to any type of research. The reason for listing it here is simply as a reminder that content analysis is not a theory, and thus, in itself, provides no pointers to *what* aspects of texts should be examined, or *how* those dimensions should be interpreted. Such pointers have to come from a theoretical framework, which should include a clear conceptualization of the nature and social context of the documents which are to be examined. In relation to the analysis of newspaper texts (and other media) this may concern questions about their production (e.g. the influence of ownership, commercial interests, editorial policies, journalistic practices, news sources) and/or their consumption (e.g. the role of news coverage in relation to social, political, ideological and economic processes, or in relation to individual audience/readership phenomena). It is in relation to the sampling/text retrieval step and the analysis step that computer assisted analysis differs in some ways, and in other respects greatly enhances, the method of manual content analysis.

Sampling in content analysis has traditionally been one of the most time consuming aspects of the method. A major virtue of content analysis (in contrast to, for example, semiotic analysis) is the ability to analyze large corpora of texts, but first texts relevant to the subject or issue being studied have to be identified and sampled. This involves the selection of: (a) a medium or media to be analyzed (e.g. newspapers representative of the national quality press, women's magazines, local radio); (b) a time period to be covered (this may be defined by particular events, or it may involve choosing a representative period to be analyzed); (c) genres and types of coverage within media (e.g. television soap operas, news programmes, documentaries, magazine advertising, newspaper editorials). Once (a), (b) and (c) have been defined and identified, there still remains the task of identifying, by applying some predefined selection criteria, texts or programmes which are about or refer to the subject matter to be analyzed (e.g. any article about "race or racial issues", any article mentioning "genes or genetics", any coverage of "terrorism", any coverage of "environmental pressure groups", etc.).

It is in relation to this step that the availability of on-line text databases and of newspaper text on CD-ROM (compact disc - read only memory) offers a major advance on traditional content analysis procedures. Where, in a conventional content analysis study, a large proportion of the research time (and funding) is allocated for several coding assistants to read or skim through hundreds of issues of newspapers to identify relevant articles, electronic full text databases enable (with the use of appropriate search terms) almost immediate identification and, if appropriate, retrieval of relevant articles. The ability to search for keywords anywhere in the full text of news articles ensures a flexibility and comprehensiveness not matched by traditional indexes or abstracts of news text.

The availability of electronic newspaper text

There are principally two ways in which newspaper text is currently available in electronic form: on compact discs (CD-ROM), and from commercial on-line databases which can be accessed from mainframe computer networks, or from desktop microcomputers with the help of a modem and a telephone line. Most British daily and Sunday quality newspapers are now available on CD-ROM. The current year issues are normally released for general purchase on a quarterly basis, cumulating onto a single disc for each newspaper for each calendar year. Having the news text on CD-ROM offers advantages in terms of unlimited use (once the disc has been purchased), unlike the use of on-line data-bases where usage is restricted by the cost of on-line time and the cost of lines of text read. Most of the newspapers on CD-ROM are available only from 1990 onwards thus restricting the degree to which they can be used for longitudinal retrospective analyses of press coverage.

The main on-line commercial database in Britain for accessing newspaper text is FT-Profile, provided by the Financial Times Group through its subsidiary The Financial Times Business Enterprises Limited (see Withey & Hugget 1991 for details of other on-line news services, including the main American source of on-line news text, NEXIS). FT-Profile holds a large array of different file types, including newspapers, news wires, magazines and journals, company and industry reports, reference and research publications. The focus here will be on newspapers only, although it should be emphasized that in media analysis terms, other files may equally be of considerable relevance. For example, an analysis of the British government press releases (Hermes) or of the Associated Press news agency releases may be useful in understanding both what newspapers choose to cover and the framing and nature of their coverage. (For examples of classic studies of the processes of news selection and news coverage see Tuchman 1978, Gans 1979, Golding & Elliott 1979, Fishman 1980, Ericson et al. 1987.)

All of the main British national daily and Sunday quality papers are available on FT-Profile. In addition, the tabloid papers *Today*, *The Daily Mail* and *The Mail on Sunday* and a number of regional newspapers are available. *The Washington Post* is also available. There is, however, considerable variation in how far back in time FT-Profile's logging of individual newspapers goes. Some, such as *The Guardian*, *The Financial Times* and *The Washington Post* are available from the first half of the 1980s onwards; others like *The Telegraph* and *The Independent* are available from around 1987–8, and others still have only been added much more recently (*The Observer*, for example, is available from October 1990 onwards, *The Daily Mail* and *The Mail on Sunday* from January 1993). In addition to variations in the length of time for which individual newspapers are available, there are also variations in the degree to which various sections and types of content are covered. Thus for some papers Letters to the Editor are included, for others they are not. These variations should clearly be taken into consideration whenever comparisons are made between different newspapers and their coverage of topics and issues.

Access, search and retrieval

While on-line searching and viewing of relevant information may be adequate for a wide range of business and information-seeking purposes, it will rarely be sufficient for social science analysis of news coverage. When the objective is *analysis* rather than merely *looking up information* it becomes imperative to see the use of electronic full text databases as essentially a two stage process, consisting of (1) search and retrieval, and (2) analysis of the retrieved textual material. If searching on CD-ROM, the relevant articles identified can be retrieved for analysis by simply copying them from the compact disc onto the computer's hard disk or onto a floppy disk. When accessing on-line databases retrieval is done by capturing the text as it is viewed on-line. Most communications programs for microcomputers have a facility for saving any text that scrolls up on the computer screen to a file on the microcomputer's hard disk.

While the search facilities available on an on-line database such as FT-Profile and those for CD-ROM differ with regard to particular refinements (e.g. the ability to search only particular sections of a newspaper such as editorials, obituaries or business news pages), the basic principles are very similar. Searching for articles relevant to the subject of analysis is done with keywords or combinations of keywords. Keyword searching can be done with boolean operators ("AND", "OR", "NOT"), with "wildcard" specifications (e.g. "genetic*" would find articles containing "genetic", "genetics", "geneticist", "geneticists" and any other words starting with "genetic"), and with word-proximity specifications (e.g. the keywords or search words must occur in, for example, the same paragraph). Searching can be further enhanced or restricted by specifying a particular date or date range, by narrowing the search to particular sections of a newspaper such as "editorials", and/or by restricting the search to particular parts of the article (e.g. the headline or the byline).

A search which looks simply for the occurrence of the specified string *anywhere* in the newspaper articles will almost invariably result in a large proportion of retrieved articles in which the search topic is mentioned only briefly and/or in passing. The ability to restrict the search to, for example, the headlines (or, in FT-Profile, to the headline and the first two paragraphs of the article) offers a way of retrieving primarily those articles where the subject is most likely to be of central significance.

Keyword searching is potentially a very powerful, efficient and reliable way of identifying relevant news coverage, but a keyword search is clearly only as good as the search terms used. Thus, for studies of press coverage of relatively narrowly defined issues, events or characters, the necessary keywords may be fairly simple and straightforward (e.g. a study of news coverage of the "greenhouse effect" (Wilkins & Patterson 1991); a study of news coverage of Hurricane Hugo and the Loma Prieta earthquake (Hornig et al. 1991); a study of news coverage of AIDS (Druschel 1991); of the Canadian "Seal War" (Lee 1989), or of the environmental pressure group "Greenpeace" (Hansen 1993)). Studies of more diffuse or broadly defined subjects, on the other hand, require rather more elaborate combinations of keywords, considerable familiarity with the range of terms and synonyms used by different newspapers, and perhaps the use of "successive filtrations" (Fan 1988) to filter out relevant coverage.

Text preparation

Having searched and retrieved the relevant textual material (the newspaper articles), the next step is to prepare the retrieved textual material for analysis. This task will clearly vary depending on the type of analysis to be carried out. There are, however, two organizing tasks that are useful almost regardless of how, or with what type of software, the textual material is to be analyzed.

The first of these is a "clean-up" operation which involves identifying and removing "irrelevant" articles from the retrieved text. "Irrelevant" articles are articles which contain the specified search term but are in fact nothing to do with the subject under analysis. The more narrowly defined the subject of analysis is, and the more unique and specific the search terms are, the less likely is it that the retrieved textual material will contain irrelevant articles. Conversely, the more general the terms are or where the search words may have multiple meanings, the higher will be the proportion of irrelevant articles in the retrieved material.

Irrelevant articles in the retrieved material can of course be identified by simply reading through all the material and removing inappropriate articles. But as the text is in electronic format there are much quicker ways of doing this. One is to use the "Find" facility of any good wordprocessor or text editing package, and read the context of each search term as it is found by the wordprocessor. A more efficient way to do this is to examine the retrieved text with the help of a concordance program or a program similarly capable of producing a listing of key words or phrases with their immediate context. A concordance is essentially an index of the words used in a body of text. (A widely used concordance program on mainframe computers is the Oxford Concordance Program (OCP). A microcomputer equivalent called Micro-OCP is available for IBM and compatible micros. Concordance programs for the Macintosh include Conc and Concorder.) From a key-word-in-context (KWIC) listing of the search terms used it is possible very quickly to identify uses (and articles) which have little relevance for the subject of analysis. These can then be checked in the full text, and the articles removed if appropriate.

The second preparatory task consists of extracting the "headline information" for each article from the full text and putting it into a separate data file. Electronically stored newspaper articles consist principally of "headline information" and "text body". The "headline information" part, in addition to giving the actual headline and byline of the article (as in the printed article appearing in a newspaper), also contains the name (in full or abbreviated) of the newspaper, the date-month-year and (in FT-Profile) a figure indicating the number of words in the article.

The headline information thus contains valuable descriptive information about the articles, information which lends itself well to immediate quantitative analysis to establish overall trends in the coverage of issues and topics. In order to take proper advantage of this information, it is useful to extract the headline information (which is in a relatively fixed format) from the rest of the text (which is in free text format and very variable in length).

Extracting the headline information from the full text, while leaving this intact, can be done in a number of ways. It can be done "manually" using the "cut and paste" facilities in a wordprocessor, but a rather more efficient way is to use a purpose-written computer program. Some wordprocessors and text editors have facilities for writing "find and replace" routines which will perform a task such as this, or it can be done with the file transformation facilities available in a statistical package such as SAS (Statistical Analysis System). With the headline information extracted from the full retrieved text, and organized into a separate data file, it is then possible to immediately proceed to producing descriptive trend analyses, examining the "ups" and "downs" in coverage over time and examining and comparing coverage in different newspapers.

Analysis of electronic newspaper texts

The analysis of electronic newspaper texts proceeds along broadly two different lines. The first of these is a straightforward quantitative analysis which utilizes the descriptive data contained in the headline information for each newspaper article. The quantitative analysis may further proceed, along the lines of conventional content analysis, through a systematic categorization of selected dimensions of the text (e.g. a categorization of types of newspaper article, of themes and types of sources mentioned, whether sources are quoted directly or indirectly, etc.).

The second line of analysis would normally be called qualitative, although it too may ultimately result in quantification of one kind or another. The main difference from the purely quantitative analysis is that the qualitative approach consists of uncovering and exploring patterns in the text through moving forwards and backwards between the text and the ideas or theories which circumscribe the analysis. When certain patterns begin to emerge, these may then be analyzed in more detail and perhaps subjected to various forms of quantification. A significant difference then is that where a traditional quantitative content analysis begins with the design of a coding schedule which is then applied to the text, a qualitative analysis offers greater flexibility in the sense that the content is not made to fit into predefined categories (the categories of a coding schedule). Instead, it allows new dimensions and aspects to emerge for further examination during the process of analyzing the text.

Quantitative coding and analysis of electronic newspaper text

In conventional content analysis of newspapers, much of the initial coding time is spent on the tedious task of coding basic descriptive or "indexing" dimensions of newspaper articles, such as date, name of newspaper, headline and size (normally measured in terms of column inches or column centimetres). Such information has to be recorded on content analysis coding sheets before the analysis can progress to the coding of particular variables relevant to or of interest to the study itself. These more interesting and more analytical variables would frequently include: themes, topics, sources/actors quoted or referred to, labels and vocabulary, positive/negative images and representations, and values.

In the analysis of newspaper text retrieved from CD-ROM or from an on-line database such as FT-Profile, the time-consuming task of manually coding the basic descriptive dimensions can be avoided altogether. The "headline information" contains most of this information, and can, with only very minor restructuring of the retrieved text, be subjected to immediate statistical analysis. Immediate analysis of the "headline information", whilst rarely a goal in itself, provides an overview of coverage. Principally, it is possible (with the help of appropriate statistical analysis software such as SPSS or SAS and associated graphics programs, e.g. Cricket Graph) to obtain an immediate overview of how the quantity of coverage changes over time and of differences between different newspapers in the amount of coverage they devote to the subject analyzed. While this type of analysis is rarely a goal in itself, variations in the quantity of coverage over time and between media often serve as an important component of agenda-setting research and social/cultural indicators analysis (see, for example, Beniger 1978, Brosius & Kepplinger 1990, Fan 1988, Funkhouser 1973).

Figure 9.1 offers an example from a study (Hansen 1993) of the coverage of the environmental group Greenpeace in a national broadsheet

Figure 9.1   Greenpeace in *The Guardian* and *Today*, 1986–1992.

156

newspaper, *The Guardian*, and a national tabloid newspaper, *Today*. The "raw" data for this analysis was the headline information extracted from the full text retrieved from FT-Profile. This was analyzed with SPSS and the graphs produced with Cricket Graph. The graphs show the number of articles mentioning "Greenpeace" in the two newspapers during each quarter from the second quarter of 1986 to the end of 1992.

The graphs give clear initial pointers both to differences between the two papers and to variations over time in the amount of coverage they give to Greenpeace. Following, for example, the bulge in coverage between the end of 1988 and the end of 1990, *Today*'s coverage of Greenpeace seems to have slumped back to its pre-end-of-1988 level, while *The Guardian* is maintaining its level of coverage. While the overall amount of coverage (as measured in terms of numbers of articles) is a relatively crude measure, it is useful for mapping differences between newspapers, agenda-setting processes, and the rise and fall of social issues over time.

With the "headline information" extracted and put into a separate computer file, one can proceed directly to the coding of further text dimensions of interest to the study in question. The coding of such variables can be entered directly into the file containing the headline information. As indicated earlier, this cuts out the rather tedious task of conventional manual content analysis where case identifiers such as "name of newspaper", "date", "headline" and "reporter" have to be copied onto printed content analysis coding sheets. With this type of information already set up directly from the retrieved text, it is possible to proceed to the coding of such variables as "themes", "topics", "sources quoted", or whichever dimensions are being examined by the study in question.

Qualitative analysis

The qualitative analysis of electronically stored newspaper text ranges from simple analyses of vocabulary and word occurrences to complex "tagging"/"coding" and analysis of textual segments and concepts. Although the approaches described below are normally considered as "qualitative approaches" in the research literature, what essentially makes them "qualitative" is the fact that they manipulate letters, words and strings of text rather than numbers. In many other respects, these approaches develop or aim in the direction of quantification even if they start out in qualitative and exploratory ways.

At the simpler end of computer assisted qualitative textual analysis are concordance programs, which are useful for examining vocabularies, word emphases, and selected key terms or concepts in their textual context. At the more complex end are programs for indexing, coding and retrieval of tagged or coded segments of texts. These text analysis programs, many of which developed originally out of ethnographic and participant observation research rather than textual analysis *per se*, include such programs as The ETHNOGRAPH, NUDIST, TextBase Alpha, and HyperQual. (See Tesch 1990, or Fielding & Lee 1991, for a comprehensive description of the range of programs available for computer assisted qualitative analysis.)

Examining vocabularies, word uses and word contexts

Almost regardless of what subject one wishes to analyze in newspaper coverage, a sensible starting point is to get some idea of the range of themes or issues or discourse clusters employed in the retrieved coverage. Concordance programs are eminently suited for this purpose. A concordance program can produce a list of all the words used in a body of text, ordered either alphabetically or by frequency. Most useful are concordance programs which can produce word lists showing not only the words themselves but also the frequency of each word in a body of text. Listing the words in order of frequency is a useful initial indication of the particular emphases of the news coverage under study.

Table 9.1 shows an excerpt from a listing, in order of frequency, of the words used in *Today*'s coverage of mad cow disease. This listing was produced with the Oxford Concordance Program and shows the most frequently occurring words together with the actual number of times each word appears in the text. Not surprisingly, "mad", "cow", "disease" and "BSE" (mad cow disease is variously referred to as "mad cow disease", "BSE" or "bovine spongiform encephalopathy") are among the top words. But the list also interestingly shows the prominence of the words "beef", "food" and "meat", and the words "pounds" (currencies are normally written out as words rather than symbols in electronically stored text, i.e. "pounds" rather than "£") and "government". In other words,

Table 9.1 The most frequently occurring words in *Today*'s coverage of mad cow disease.

disease	38	out	107	two	70	says	55
beef	336	Now	105	000	70	us	55
said	322	over	105	Britain	68	animals	54
mad	297	after	97	Ministry	68	cent	54
Today	275	Only	96	health	67	scare	54
cow	270	One	95	Even	66	banned	53
food	237	Gummer	94	night	65	fears	53
pounds	220	new	93	safe	65	sheep	53
British	184	farmers	90	1	65	before	52
90	182	Minister	89	sales	64	brain	52
bse	177	year	88	humans	63	David	52
meat	170	John	84	risk	63	time	52
Government	151	cows	77	per	62	like	49
cattle	146	infected	77	So	62	pet	48
May	134	years	77	still	62	action	47
no	129	yesterday	75	first	61	down	47
last	128	people	74	just	61	say	47
up	125	being	73	spokesman	59	human	46
Agriculture	122	million	73	eat	58	bovine	45
could	121	other	70	eating	55	market	44
ban	14						

there is a clear indication already here that the coverage focuses on: (1) the danger which this disease poses for a key component of the British diet, (2) on costs, and (3) on what the government is doing or should be doing about it.

By carefully examining the word list produced with a concordance program one can begin to identify the various discourses which come into play, and to identify their constituent vocabularies. Thus, in coverage of mad cow disease, there is, for example, a discourse concerned with *transmission* of the disease (words: infected, catch, symptoms, spread, link, caused, etc.), a discourse focusing on the *risk/threat* posed by the disease (words: safe, risk, scare(s), fears, safety, died, warned, danger, death, etc.), a discourse concerned with *science* (words: evidence, know, research, tests, report, veterinary, survey, inquiry, etc.), a discourse concerned with *food* (words: beef, food, meat, eat, offal, milk, sausages, organic, eggs, burger, etc.), and so on. Once such discourses have been identified, initially on the basis of a simple listing of the words used in a body of text, it is then possible to examine more systematically how prominent or otherwise each discourse is across time or across different newspapers. It is quite likely that what starts out primarily as a discourse about "disease", "transmission" and "science" becomes – over time – a much broader discourse about "food production practices", "animal welfare", "politics", "governmental action", "trade-regulations" and "individual personalities".

Just as it may be desirable to map, with the use of concordance programs, what the most prominent and frequently used words are in a body of text, so too is it often productive to study what the *least frequent* words are. The least frequent words in newspaper articles are a good indication of specialized or specialist terminology. They may give important indications of journalistic assumptions about who the readers are, of how new meanings are added to specific issues/problems over time (see Oehler et al. 1989 for a particularly interesting analysis of how "knowledge claims" are built in scientific literature), and of how new specialist concepts are introduced into the public sphere over time.

One of the key features of a concordance program is of course its ability to list keywords in context, which is itself a useful way of getting a first idea of how a particular issue, actor, concept or phenomenon is covered. While basic concordance programs can list keywords in their context in a number of ways, there are, however, text retrieval and analysis programs (for example Sonar Professional) which are more specifically designed for examining word contexts and complex relationships, and for finding and retrieving words or chunks of text.

The analysis of contexts and associated words

Much of the analytic approach outlined in the previous sections has focused on studying *what* and *how much* is covered in relation to selected topics in national newspapers. A further important component in most studies of newspaper coverage is to discover *how* issues, problems, actors, etc., are portrayed. In conventional content analysis the "how" of coverage is often studied by counting the specific terms used for describing and characterizing different types of actors or phenomena (see, for example, Van Dijk 1991), by coding the portrayal of key variables in terms of positive-neutral-negative, or by scoring key variables on a "semantic differential scale". (For a detailed description of these techniques, see Holsti 1969, Osgood et al. 1957, and Snider & Osgood 1969.)

In computer assisted analysis of electronic newspaper text, much can be learnt about how issues, actors and phenomena are portrayed through analyzing which words appear together or are "associated" with each other. Unlike the considerable resources and amount of coding that goes into analyzing the "how" of coverage in conventional content analysis, these dimensions can be analyzed – and re-analyzed as the "map" of how things are portrayed develops – very efficiently with text retrieval or analysis programs. Moreover, the computer assisted analysis is not as prone to variations in subjective judgement as conventional coding of value-dimensions is. It is, however, still important to emphasize that computer assisted analysis of value dimensions or "associated" words is only as valid as the rules by which it is guided or conducted. This is essentially the "old" problem that while a computer offers efficient means of finding patterns in a body of text, only the researcher can interpret the meaning of those patterns.

The analysis of how specified issues, actors or phenomena are portrayed starts with uncovering, and ranking in order of frequency, the words associated with their portrayal. Table 9.2 shows a listing in order of frequency of the words found immediately next to (either side of) three selected actors in *Today*'s coverage of mad cow disease. The three actors or actor groups are: the minister for agriculture, Mr John Gummer; scientists and experts; and the public. From the words most closely associated with these key actors, it is possible to get an immediate indication of how they are characterized and of the different rôles they play.

It is thus characteristic that both the government minister and the scientists are agents of discourse, while the public is the object of discourse. "Said" is thus closely associated with both the government minister and with the scientists/experts, but much less so with the public. "Said" is the word most often associated with the government minister, but also closely associated is a range of more distinctly aggressive/defensive verbs: "agreed", "accused", "admitted", "assured", "condemned", etc. While "say", "said" and "told" are similarly verbal-action verbs closely associated with the scientists, it is also clear that verbs of a more cautious kind than those associated with Gummer characterize this actor group, namely the verbs "believe", "fear", "warned". The further elaboration of an analysis of the verbs associated with key actors would of course need to be sensitive to word order (e.g. "Mr Gummer accused . . ." or "X accused Mr Gummer . . .").

The list of "associated words" further indicates a significant difference

Table 9.2 The words most prominently associated with Mr Gummer, Scientist(s)/Expert(s), and Consumer(s)/The Public in *Today*'s coverage of mad cow disease.

Gummer	Scientist(s)/ Expert(s)	Consumer(s)/ The Public
John	Government	health
s	food	British
said	top	groups
last	said	major
agreed	say	protect
accused	believe	fears
told	fear	Minister
90	until	fact
made	warned	although
admitted	Professor	champions
must	disease	confidence
appalled	after	like
assured	now	Today
didn	told	Britain
condemned	committee	champion
Cordelia	veterinary	exactly
comment	health	farmers
fed	independent	9
fights	last	first
assures	researching	fled
came	definitive	former
career	36	despite
insists	animal	choice
176	expertly	allay
180	advice	information
mad	farm	beef
hailed	Belfast	lobby
muffed	agriculture	courts
even	83	make
next	89	marketing

between the government minister and the scientists/experts. The words most closely associated with the scientists/experts are adjectives or noun-adjectives, which serve to characterize the scientists and experts. They are thus identified as "government" scientists/experts, "food" scientists/experts, "top" scientists/experts, etc. (other descriptors include: "veterinary", "health", "independent"). By contrast, John Gummer, the minister for agriculture, is characterized almost exclusively in terms of verbal-action and similar verbs.

This example focused only on the words immediately associated with a selection of key actors. It will often, however, be desirable to examine not just the most immediately associated words, but, for example, all the words that appear within a certain distance from the key search term, say within five or ten words of the search term. Text retrieval/analysis programs such as Sonar offer some very flexible ways of defining the "range" of associated words and of rank ordering such words according to their frequency of association with the search term.

The examination of "associated words" offers a good first insight into how key issues, phenomena or actors are characterized in the text. As with other approaches to the analysis of newspaper texts, the analysis of "associated words" lends itself well to comparisons between newspapers and over time. It further and almost invariably provides pointers to dimensions for more detailed scrutiny, for example by examining in quantitative terms how often certain actors or issues are described in a particular way.

While such an analysis could be simply a quantitative comparison of the number of times that two specific words appear together (e.g. "top" and "scientist", "government" and "scientist"), more usually the analyst would want to study the co-appearance of two sets: a particular class of descriptors and a particular class of actors. To achieve this, it is necessary to be able to create and use synonym lists in searches for the co-appearance of terms. An example of how this type of analysis can be done electronically can again be illustrated with mad cow disease coverage. The "associated words" listed above indicated that scientists and experts were often referred to as "top" scientists/experts. Cursory reading of the full text itself similarly indicated that when scientists or experts were referred to, the term scientist (or expert) was frequently bundled together with a seniority or authority reinforcing adjective such as "top", "leading", "senior". The cursory reading also indicated that this word combination might be more frequent in the tabloid paper (*Today*) than in the broadsheet papers. With the use of a text retrieval/analysis program (in this case, Sonar) this impression could quickly be tested as follows.

On the basis of alphabetically ordered lists (produced with a concordance program) showing the full range of unique words used in each newspaper, a synonym list was constructed of the general terms used in reference to experts knowledgeable about epidemiology, mad cow disease and cattle diseases more generally. The principal terms thus identified were "scientist(s)", "expert(s)", "researcher(s)", "vet(s)" and "doctor(s)". A search using these synonyms then extracted every occurrence of each of these "expert" terms together with their immediate context. From these extracts, another synonym list of "seniority-reinforcing adjectives" could then be compiled. The principal words in this list included "senior", "top", "leading", "distinguished" and "chief". Having constructed these two synonym lists, searches were performed on the texts of each newspaper to examine what proportion of total references to "experts" were bundled with a "seniority-reinforcing" adjective. Interestingly, this analysis showed that while "seniority" adjectives were used by all the papers, they were used relatively more frequently by the tabloid paper than by the broadsheet/quality papers. In other words, it seems more important for the tabloid paper than for the quality papers to emphasize, to its readers, the authority and legitimacy of the experts on whom it draws for statements about mad cow disease.

This need is partly explained by the fact that the tabloid paper on the whole provides far less information on the basis of which to determine whether individuals quoted in the coverage are suitably qualified for pronouncing on the subject matter. While the broadsheet newspapers often indicate more specifically what type of expert is quoted (e.g. microbiologist, epidemiologist, pathologist, neurologist, neuro-pathologist, biologist, neuro-surgeon, molecular biologist, neuro-physiologist), the tabloid paper tends to reference scientists using the non-specific expert terms indicated above in relation to the "expert" synonym list. In the absence of specific indications which may help the reader to assess the significance or importance which should be assigned to the statements of quoted experts, their legitimacy as authoritative sources has to be implied in other ways: for the tabloid paper, this is done principally through authority-reinforcing adjectives.

Conclusion

The example of authority-reinforcing adjectives illustrates one of the most powerful aspects of computer assisted analysis of electronically stored text compared with traditional content analysis. This is the ability to discover, elaborate, examine and re-examine textual patterns during the analysis process. Fundamentally, such analyses can be done manually, but unless the patterns examined had been built into a manual content analysis from the outset, their examination would constitute a pro-hibitive drain on time and resources.

One of the major weaknesses of conventional content analysis is the fragmentation of meaning and the decontextualization which inevitably follows when words, phrases and other chunks of text are "translated" into predefined codes and numbers. Important nuances and textual vari-ations thus often end up as shallow statements about relative emphases expressed in percentage figures. While this may be useful as a general first stage mapping of the content, it is also possible with computer analysis and handling of text to stay much closer to the text itself and to illustrate and substantiate the major points of the analysis by retrieving and electronically copying the relevant segments of newspaper text.

Unlike quantitative content analysis, the mode of qualitative analysis, with its origins in the humanities and in literary analysis, is one of ex-emplification or "showing by reference". The electronic storage of text, together with the use of text indexing and retrieval programs, make it possible comprehensively and systematically to identify segments of text exemplifying relevant points of analysis. This can be done infinitely faster than would have been possible by a "manual" search through printed text and it is less prone to selective representation of the original text.

There is, however, little to be gained from a sharp distinction between quantitative and qualitative approaches to the analysis of newspaper text. These are best thought of as complementary. With electronically stored text, and with appropriate text retrieval software, the analysis of newspaper text can proceed with a combination of quantitative mapping and qualitative exploration, which may itself in turn lead to quantitative re-examination. The particular advantages which computer assisted analysis offers over "manual" analysis are advantages of speed, reliabil-ity and flexibility – and of these, the *flexibility* to re-examine emerging patterns as the researcher works with the text is perhaps the single most important advantage that computer assisted analysis of electronically stored text holds over conventional content analysis.

Acknowledgement

This chapter is based on research funded by the Economic and Social Research Council, grant number A418254001.

Principal computer programs mentioned

Conc
Thompson, J. (1993). *Conc version 1.71 beta*. Dallas, Tex.: The Summer Institute of Linguistics (address: 7500 W. Camp Wisdom Road, Dallas, TX 75236, USA).
A beta-version concordance program for Macintosh computers.

Concorder
Rand, D. M. & T. Patera (1991). *Concorder version 1.1*. Montréal: Centre de Recherches Mathématiques, Université de Montréal. (address: C. P. 6128, succursale A, Montréal, Québec H3C 3J7, Canada).
A concordance program for Macintosh computers.

Cricket Graph
Rafferty, J. & R. Norling (1987). *Cricket Graph version 1.3.2*. Malvern, Pa.: Cricket Software (address: Great Valley Corporate Center, 40 Valley Stream Parkway, Malvern, PA 19355, USA).
Macintosh and Windows versions available; now marketed as CA-Cricket Graph by Computer Associates International, Inc. (1992).
CA-Cricket Graph III version 1.0. Islandia, NY: Computer Associates International (address: One Computer Associates Plaza, Islandia, NY, USA 11788–2000).

Oxford Concordance Program (OCP)
Hockey, S. & J. Martin (1988b). *Oxford Concordance Program version 2*. Oxford: Oxford University Computing Service (address: 13 Banbury Road, Oxford OX2 6NN, UK).
Concordance program for mainframe computers. The program is also available for IBM/compatibles as *Micro-OCP*: Oxford University Computing Service (1990). *Micro-OCP*. Oxford: Oxford University Press.

Statistical Package for the Social Sciences (SPSS)
SPSS Inc., 444 N Michigan Avenue, Chicago, Illinois 60611, USA. SPSS is a comprehensive system for statistical data analysis, available for IBM and compatible computers, for Macintosh computers, and for most mainframe computers.

Sonar Professional
Virginia Systems, I. (1991). *Sonar version 8.4*. Midlothian, Va.: Virginia Systems Software Services, Inc. (address: 5509 West Bay Court, Midlothian, Virginia 23112, USA).
Sonar Professional is a text retrieval and analysis program available for both Macintosh computers and IBM and compatible computers.

References

Beniger, J. R. (1978). Media content as social indicators: The Greenfield Index of agenda setting. *Communication Research* 5(4), 437–53.

Brosius, H.-B. & H. M. Kepplinger (1990). The agenda-setting function of television news. *Communication Research* 17(2), 183–211.

DeWeese, L. C. (1976). Computer content analysis of media: overview of a limited feasibility study. *Public Opinion Quarterly* 40, 92–100.

DeWeese, L. C. (1977). Computer content analysis of "day-old" newspapers: a feasibility study. *Public Opinion Quarterly* 41(1), 91–4.

Druschel, B. E. (1991). Sensationalism or sensitivity: use of words in stories on acquired immune deficiency syndrome by Associated Press videotex. In M. A. Wolf & A. R. Kielwasser (eds), *Gay people, sex and the media*, 47–62. Binghamton, NY: Haworth Press.

Ericson, R. V., P. M. Baranek, J. B. L. Chan (1987). *Visualizing deviance: a study of news organization*. Milton Keynes: Open University Press.

Fan, D. P. (1988). *Predictions of public opinion from the mass media: computer content analysis and mathematical modelling*. New York: Greenwood Press.

Fielding, N. G. & R. M. Lee (ed.) (1991). *Using computers in qualitative research*. London: Sage.

Fishman, M. (1980). *Manufacturing the news*. Austin and London: University of Texas Press.

Funkhouser, G. R. (1973). The issues of the sixties: an exploratory study in the dynamics of public opinion. *Public Opinion Quarterly* 37(1), 62–75.

Gans, H. J. (1979). *Deciding what's news*. New York: Vintage.

Golding, P. & P. Elliott (1979). *Making the news*. London: Longman.

Hansen, A. (1993). Greenpeace and press coverage of environmental issues. In A. Hansen (ed.), *The mass media and environmental issues*, 150–78. Leicester: Leicester University Press.

Holsti, O. R. (1969). *Content analysis for the social sciences and humanities*. Reading, Mass.: Addison-Wesley.

Hornig, S., L. Walter, J. Templin (1991). Voices in the news: newspaper coverage of Hurricane Hugo and the Loma Prieta earthquake. *Newspaper Research Journal* 12(3), 32–45.

Janowitz, M. (1976). Content analysis and the study of sociopolitical change. *Journal of Communication* 26, 10–26.

Krippendorf, K. (1980). *Content analysis: an introduction to its methodology*. London: Sage.

Lee, J. A. (1989). Waging the seal war in the media: toward a content analysis of moral communication. *Canadian Journal of Communication* 14(1), 37–56.

Oehler, K., W. E. Snizek, N. C. Mullins (1989). Words and sentences over time: how facts are built and sustained in a specialty area. *Science, Technology, & Human Values* 14(3), 258–74.

Osgood, C. E., G. J. Suci, P. H. Tannenbaum (1957). *The measurement of meaning*. Urbana: University of Illinois Press.

Snider, J. G. & C. E. Osgood (ed.) (1969). *Semantic differential technique*. Chicago: Aldine.

Stone, P. J., D. C. Dunphy, M. S. Smith, D M. Ogilvie (1966). *The general inquirer: a computer approach to content analysis*. Cambridge, Mass.: MIT Press.

Tesch, R. (1990). *Qualitative research: analysis types and software tools*. New York: Falmer Press.

Tuchman, G. (1978). *Making news: a study in the construction of reality*. New York: Free Press.

Van Dijk, T. A. (1991). *Racism and the press*. London: Routledge.

Weber, R. P. (1984). Content-analytic cultural indicators. In G. Melischek, K. E. Rosengren, J. Stappers (eds), *Cultural indicators: an international symposium*, 301–13. Vienna: Österreichischen Akademie der Wissenschaften.

Weber, R. P. (1990). *Basic content analysis*, 2nd edn. Newbury Park, Calif.: Sage.

Wilkins, L. & P. Patterson (1991). Science as symbol: the media chills the greenhouse effect. In L. Wilkins & P. Patterson (eds), *Risky business: communicating issues of science, risk, and public policy*, 159–76. Westport, Conn.: Greenwood Press.

Withey, R. & E. Hugget (1991). Fleet Street's second revolution: online technology in information gathering for newspapers. In S. Eagle (ed.), *Information sources for the press and broadcast media*, 134–56. London: Bowker-Saur.

CHAPTER 10

Expert systems
for the social scientist

Noel Heather and Raymond M. Lee

A graduate student in a social science discipline seeks help from an advisor about developing a sampling strategy. The interaction develops in a time-honoured way. The advisor asks questions about the purpose of the study, the population from which the sample is to be drawn, the likely analytic procedures and so on. The student supplies answers to the questions, clarifies points, makes decisions. Finally, a recommendation about an appropriate sampling procedure is made. Interactions like this are common enough. The difference in the consultation just described is that the advisor is not a human but a computer program – an expert system. Expert systems – a branch of artificial intelligence, a computer science specialism that seeks to emulate human cognitive processes – encapsulate the knowledge held by an expert in a precisely defined field or domain, and, in consequence, are sometimes called knowledge based systems. In the vignette above the expert knowledge encapsulated in the expert system is that of a statistician.

Expert systems have proved to be a useful aid to problem solving in a wide range of areas. The first expert system, DENDRAL, developed from the mid 1960s, was a chemical analysis program which efficiently identified organic compounds through analysis of mass spectrograms. In the following decade the much celebrated MYCIN expert system appeared as an aid to the diagnosis of meningitis and infections of the blood. MYCIN gives a judgement based on information gleaned from an interactive dialogue with a doctor about a patient's symptoms. Such a system is, of course, likely to be of most use at times and in situations where the knowledge and expertise of a consultant physician are not immediately available. Expert systems have since been employed in fields as diverse as the evaluation of mineral deposits, the design of integrated circuits, and advice on welfare, legal and financial matters.

This chapter describes a number of features of expert systems. First, a brief non-technical introduction to the topic is given. Then the use of expert systems to aid various aspects of the research process is explored. There then follows a discussion of the role of expert systems in teaching, together with a brief account of the processes and tools involved in developing an expert system.

How do expert systems work?

In very broad terms expert systems rely on three core mechanisms:
  (a) The knowledge base contains a representation of the expert knowledge in a defined field.
  (b) The inference engine provides a means of eliciting answers to problems based on the contents of the knowledge base.
  (c) The user interface facilitates the process of consultation by the user.

Attempts are made to represent knowledge in a variety of ways within artificial intelligence programs. In expert systems the method usually employed involves so-called production rules. These are based on an IF: THEN format which lists one or more premises together with their allied consequent or conclusion. To take a simple example, a expert system could, for instance, aid a railway traveller to chose the correct ticket. The system might contain the following rule, as one of many, detailing various options open to the traveller.

> RULE 1
> IF   Return = yes AND
> Month_stay = yes AND
> Advance_Booking >= 7 AND
> Changeable = no
> THENTicket = Advanced_Purchase;

This rule would be triggered (or "fired") when the traveller's answers match the four premises in the IF section:

Are you making a single or a return journey?   return
Are you returning in a month or less?   yes

How many days ahead will you be booking your ticket?   7
Is there a possibility you will want to change the ticket?   no
Another traveller with different requirements might trigger this rule:

RULE 2
IF   Return = yes AND
Month_stay = no AND
Advance_Booking < 7 AND
Changeable = yes
THENTicket = Standard_Return;

In accordance with this rule, a standard return fare would be recommended to an individual staying more than one month, who books at less than a week's notice, and who wants to retain the option of changing the ticket. The rules just used are very basic; working systems, however, may have many hundreds or indeed thousands of rules covering all sorts of eventualities. And the rules themselves, while retaining the "IF: THEN" format may each be quite complex.

Each rule in the knowledge base contains one or more facts and points to a conclusion which can be drawn about the relationships between the facts. Thus, in the example above, given the facts that a return journey is required and that the stay is less than one month etc., one can conclude or infer that an Advanced Purchase ticket is the most appropriate choice. Hence the name given to the mechanism which actuates the system, drawing the conclusions or inferences from the rules in the knowledge base: the inference engine, the second main component of an expert system.

The inference engine is at the heart of what an expert system is, and can be used to manipulate many different knowledge bases. How does the inferencing process take place? In the example given earlier, a query into the system might cause the program to begin to search for the goal associated with the variable "Ticket" in the knowledge base. In searching, the program comes to the first rule:

RULE 1
IF   Return = yes AND
Month_stay = yes AND
Advance_Booking >= 7 AND
Changeable = no
THEN Ticket = Advanced_Purchase;

and focuses on the possible solution contained in the conclusion to the rule "Ticket = Advanced_Purchase". The system then tries to determine whether this conclusion is valid by checking in turn to see whether all the premises in the first ("IF") part of the rule are correct. If each is successful, it confirms the conclusion of the rule. If one of the premises fails during the testing procedure, the system will leave that rule and search forward for the next occurrence of "THEN Ticket = . . ." as the conclusion of a rule. It then tests the validity of the premises in the "IF" section of that rule and so on.

This search strategy is called backward chaining, based on the principle that the system focuses on the conclusion, and checks back along the preceding sequence of premises to determine whether the conclusion is correct. This is sometimes referred to as goal driven reasoning. Expert systems may also use forward chaining which has the reverse perspective, and is said to be data driven. With forward chaining, the strategy is to match facts to rule premises ("if . . .") and work towards the final goal or conclusion. Many systems are able to use a combination of the two approaches.

The user interface of an expert system provides a range of facilities for supervising the way information is obtained from, and output to, the enquirer. Advice and explanation can, for example, be presented on the screen. Other functions include an on-screen help facility to explain terms used, and – increasingly – the possibility of setting up a graphical interface. The user interface will also normally offer a "what-if" option which allows the user to change the values supplied during the previous consultation. The impact of these alternative values can then be assessed. A system will also usually be able to display the series of steps through which it passed to reach the conclusion offered.

So far, expert systems have been discussed in which the individual possibilities are stated with complete certainty. There is no dispute, for example, about the conditions which make one ticket for a journey a more appropriate choice than another. But in some situations, there may be a level of uncertainty about the conclusion to be drawn. For example, in an expert system dealing with medical diagnosis a patient with symptoms X, Y and Z may be more likely rather than certain to have disease A, and disease A may be a more likely candidate then disease B. Within an expert system these probabilities have traditionally been dealt with in mathematical terms. The simplest method is one in which each rule can have an associated confidence factor expressed as a number from 0–100.

If no confidence factor is included, the system assumes a default level of 100 – absolute certainty. The usefulness of such features lies in the way that individual probabilities attached to different items can be combined mathematically to produce a number which represents a general, overall probability for a particular solution.

Rule based expert systems are usually presented to the developer in an English-like language which may be described as a knowledge representation (or specification) language. They may, however, be implemented in a programming language which encodes the knowledge in a more abstract logical form. This, for example, can be done in the PROLOG programming language. (The name PROLOG is derived from "programming in logic".) Expert systems which depend on this approach have a function which translates English-like language into PROLOG as a preliminary to an interrogation session.

Besides using an expert system shell which relies on PROLOG, it is also possible to develop expert systems directly in this programming language. In PROLOG, facts are declared about objects and their relationships, and rules are used to infer further knowledge based on these facts. The following are facts about objects:

```
female(mary).
male(peter).
```

Here female and male are predicates, and "mary" and "peter" are objects; thus in "female(mary)." female is a predicate with one argument. Relationships usually involve two or more arguments which are separated by commas;

```
daughter_of(mary,peter).
daughter_of(helen,tom).
son_of(alan,helen).
son_of(peter,helen).
son_of(edward,helen).
```

Based on this small database of facts, the user can make a query in PROLOG using a variable (which must begin with an upper case letter). (In the following examples, "?-" is the prompt used in PROLOG to make a query.)

```
?- son_of(X,helen).
```

would elicit responses covering the three possible solutions:

173

X = alan
X = peter
X = edward

By creating combinations of queries more advanced questions can be addressed. (Queries can be joined together with "AND", which is represented in PROLOG by the comma ",".) For example, the following would search out the granddaughter (variable Y) / mother (variable Z) / grandfather (variable X) relationships implicit within the database:

?- daughter_of(Y,Z), daughter_of(Z,X).

This should elicit the response:

Y = mary
Z = helen
X = tom

as mary (Y) is the daughter of helen (Z), AND helen (Z) is the daughter of tom (X). Finally, combined queries such as the above can be developed into a form which can be included in the actual program. They can be transformed into the PROLOG equivalent of an IF:THEN rule of the type "a if b,c." ("a:- b,c." in PROLOG syntax). The fact on the left-hand side of the rule (a) depends for acceptance of its truth on establishing the truth of the group of facts on the right-hand side (b,c.). In this example what were formerly combined queries become the items on the right-hand side of a rule for defining a grandfather relationship:

grandfather_of(X,Y):- daughter_of(Y,Z), daughter_of(Z,X).

This rule translates as: X is the grandfather of Y IF Y is the daughter of Z AND Z is the daughter of X. Once such a rule has been included in the PROLOG program, queries such as the following can be made:

?- grandfather_of(tom,Y).

By working through the rule the system should be able to respond:

Y = mary

PROLOG, then, can be used to support or directly create expert systems in which rules enable new facts to be inferred from other facts present in a knowledge base. PROLOG (as well as other programming languages) may also be employed to support another kind of expert system in which knowledge is represented in a more structured way. Data structures called frames are used to create stereotypical "packets" of knowledge which are linked together in a hierarchy or network. Take, for example, the way part of a bird taxonomy can be represented by related frames:

frame animal; default blood is warm.

frame bird is a animal;
    default skin is feather and
    default habitat is a tree and
    default motions are {fly}.

frame penguin is a bird;
    default habitat is the land and
    default motions are {walk and swim} and
    default size is medium.

frame thrush is a bird;
    default colour is brown and
    default size is small.

These lines represent the taxonomy animal-bird-penguin/thrush in frames written in the Flex knowledge specification language. Frames offer an economical way of storing knowledge. Generalized frames (an animal has warm blood, a bird flies) can be used to gather together general properties of the class in question. Thus, when specifying the features of examples in the instance frames, the developer does not have to redefine general properties (a penguin and a thrush have warm blood as they are animals). The instance frames are said to inherit the properties specified in the higher frames. Care has to be taken, however, to identify exceptions. In its present form above, the penguin frame inherits the "default motions are { fly } ." element of the bird frame. To rectify this anomaly the line "do not inherit motions" should be added to the penguin frame. The latter will not then inherit the property of flying from the higher frame. And the user of the expert system who asks which birds are capable of flight will not find the penguin included in the output list. (For an example of the use of frames to develop an expert system (described later in this chapter) for teaching aspects of the work of Erving Goffman, see Brent et al. 1989b.)

The use of expert systems in the research process

Expert systems are now beginning to have a role at every stage of the research process from the literature review to the analysis of data. For example, expert systems have a potential role as intelligent "front ends" for the on-line retrieval of bibliographic and other information, an increasingly important area for social scientists (Thomas, this volume). While some of the early promised breakthroughs in this area have not materialized (Drouth et al. 1991), systems are under development which will use, for example, knowledge about the characteristics of scientific networks to structure retrieval tasks (Ohly 1993). Beyond this, knowledge based systems have been put to three kinds of use in social science research: (a) as aids to developing theory, (b) as tools for providing advice about various aspects of the research process, and (c) as instructional devices. In relation to theory development expert systems have a variety of rôles. As shown by the illustrative examples given below, they have been used to examine the logical consistency and generative potential of specific theories, to model the dynamics of complex social systems, and to simulate historical events (Benfer et al. 1991).

Theory development

Sylvan & Glasner (1985) attempted to test Simmel's hypothesis that external conflict results in the internal cohesion of social groups. Rejecting existing attempts to test the conflict-cohesion hypothesis by statistical means, Sylvan & Glasner argue for a modelling approach which, in their view, remains closer to Simmel's conception of conflict and consensus as emerging social forms. They therefore translated a large number of statements relating to the conflict-cohesion hypothesis taken from Simmel's writing into LOGLISP, a powerful artificial intelligence programming language. Sylvan & Glasner argue that use of this strategy allowed them to assess the adequacy of Simmel's theory, both in terms of its logical consistency and its ability to generate extensions to the original proposition. According to Sylvan & Glasner, the modelling strategy they adopted was reasonably successful. Simmel's theory appears to be logically consistent. It also proved possible to specify some of the conditions under which the conflict-cohesion hypothesis holds, and to generate a number of further assertions consistent with the original theory. The writers conclude that a modelling approach based on formal logic of the kind they used is feasible, although they note the exercise revealed some limitations in the applicability of logic programming to the kinds of theoretical issues they wished to address.

Michael Fischer and Anthony Finkelstein have demonstrated the utility of computer based formal methods for the description of fluid and socially intricate behaviours (Fischer & Finkelstein 1991; see also Fischer, this volume). The substantive component of this work is based on Fischer's (1991) study of arranged marriages in urban Pakistan. Arranging such a marriage is a complex business involving the shifting preferences and actions of a multiplicity of actors over a period of time. An expert system for modelling this complex field of behaviour was developed using Modal [Action] Logic, a formal programming language well suited to "describing situations both in terms of structural relationships and in terms of the effects of actions by agents on those relationships" (Fischer & Finkelstein 1991: 125). Based on a cycle of development in which elaboration of the production rules for the expert system guided and were guided by recurrent periods of fieldwork, the expert system allowed the prediction of "good" and "bad" marriage choices. It also helped to broaden and deepen existing theoretical formulations and highlighted patterned deviations from customary practice.

Schrodt (1989) notes that work on expert systems in research on international relations has moved in the direction of simulation. This is perhaps hardly surprising. The decision making processes of interest to international relations specialists can fairly readily be represented as IF: THEN rules. Moreover, rule based simulation allows researchers to introduce counterfactuals – to look, in other words, at "possible worlds" (Thorsan & Sylvan 1982) in which decision makers face different though similar circumstances to those that actually happened. One intriguing example of this kind of approach is Thorsan & Sylvan's (1982) simulation of the Cuban Missile Crisis. Thorsan & Sylvan represented the decisions made by President Kennedy in the course of the crisis as a set of production rules. They then produced a number of "base-case runs" in which the program was run under conditions close to those obtaining at the time. Since the simulation produced outcomes not dissimilar to those which actually occurred, it could be regarded as having some validity. It was then possible to explore the counterfactuals by introducing different conditions to see how the crisis might have developed under different circumstances.

Data collection and analysis

Although they are still somewhat underdeveloped at the present time, expert systems have applications in the collection of social science data. For example, in anthropology expert systems combined with the use of small but powerful portable microcomputers (see, for example, Fischer, this volume) make possible member validation of ethnographic models. Kippen used an expert system to develop a formal model of the musical structures which underlie North Indian tabla drumming. The ability of the system to predict "correct and aesthetically acceptable . . . pieces of music" (1988: 318) could then be tested on local musicians, comments from whom could be used to refine and develop the basic model. In addition, as Fischer & Finkelstein (1991: 134) point out, gaps in a formal model which are revealed by consulting local informants in this way drive the search for new data by helping to target the researcher's efforts onto gaps in the existing knowledge base (see also Hesse-Biber et al. 1991). In survey research, Halfpenny and his colleagues (1992) have under development an expert system to aid in the design of questionnaires, while Tonn et al. (1993) have developed a prototype of an automated interviewing system. This system, which is written in LISP, is based, perhaps somewhat ironically, on a computer system originally designed for eliciting expert knowledge during the process of expert system development. The program treats survey questions as independent objects, allowing considerable flexibility in the development and maintenance of surveys as well as in the administration of the questionnaire in the course of an interview.

Developers in a number of countries have produced statistical support systems to aid researchers in making decisions about the use of particular statistical techniques (see, for example, Diesveld & van den Berg 1993, Brent 1989). Probably the most widely available of these systems is STATISTICAL NAVIGATOR which provides advice about the selection of statistics appropriate to a particular analysis. In addition, expert systems have found a place in the analysis of quantitative data and as analytic devices. For example, a difficulty in structural equation modelling lies in accepting a model on statistical grounds even though there may be many alternative models which meet the same criteria. TETRAD II attempts to provide automated techniques for the initial specification of causal models. Based on graph algorithms and on heuristic search techniques from artificial intelligence the program searches the complex set of possible

178

solutions to identify the best alternative elaborations. The program's developers claim that it provides more reliable model specification than conventional structural equation modelling programs (Spirtes et al. 1990). A number of writers have experimented with using expert system generators to induce sets of explanatory rules directly from data (Schrodt 1989, Garson 1987). The starting point for an analysis of this kind is that the relationship between the dependent variable and the set of independent variables for a given case in a data matrix can be thought of as an explanatory rule for that case. In a typical data set many such rules will be idiosyncratic, explaining only one or two cases. The expert system generator uses a classificatory algorithm to select a parsimonious set of rules which simultaneously explain a large number of cases. Using data from an existing study on the extent to which state legislators are satisfied with legislative outcomes, Garson (1987) compared this kind of approach with a regression analysis of the same data. Garson argues on the basis of this comparison that the rule based approach produced a more detailed and complex explanation of the sources of legislative satisfaction, and concludes that in particular the rule based approach is useful for generating hypotheses.

The program STATISTICAL NAVIGATOR mentioned earlier forms part of the "Methodologist's Toolchest", a suite of programs developed by Edward Brent, a sociologist at the University of Missouri, which use artificial intelligence techniques to assist researchers make decisions concerning various aspects of the research process. Brent has been assiduous in promoting the use of expert systems in the social sciences. He is a prolific software developer, distributing a number of expert systems for use in empirical research through The Idea Works, the software company of which he is president. (The Idea Works, Inc. is located at 100 N. Briarwood Lane, Columbia, MO 65202, USA; Tel: 314 445 4554.) As well as STATISTICAL NAVIGATOR the Methodologist's Toolchest comprises: DATA COLLECTION SELECTION, DESIGNER RESEARCH, EX-SAMPLE and MEASUREMENT AND SCALING STRATEGIST. DATA COLLECTION SELECTION provides advice on data collection methods potentially suitable for a particular research problem. DESIGNER RESEARCH helps in the design of experiments. EX-SAMPLE provides advice on selecting an appropriate sample size. MEASUREMENT AND SCALING STRATEGIST aids item construction in the design of survey instruments.

These programs illustrate well the advantages – as well as some of the limitations – of using expert systems to aid decision making in the research process. In each case the programs offer assistance with a complex task, the detailed exploration of which is tedious and prone to error, but where the consequences of error can be far-reaching. In EX-SAMPLE, for instance, the program determines the size of the proposed sample by systematically taking into account practical constraints like time, money and access to the population, methodological constraints such as response rates and sample mortality, and the requirements of particular analytic strategies. In responding to the program, one can make choices having varying degrees of certainty. Unlike a human expert the program itself is always available, tireless and methodical in its treatment of relevant considerations. Typically, the programs under consideration here output recommendations ranked in order of desirability.

Although the utility of such programs is undoubted, they have some disadvantages. First, the programs discussed so far are primarily oriented towards quantitative research. Secondly, in early versions of the programs making up the Methodologist's Toolchest the user interface could best be described as serviceable rather than friendly. In addition, when users requested elucidation of the questions asked by the program, they were in many cases faced with explanations which seemed unnecessarily terse. Just how important such features are can be seen if one compares early versions of STATISTICAL NAVIGATOR with its latest incarnation. The latter makes good use of colour, is under mouse as well as keyboard control and, perhaps most important, makes particularly effective use of hypertext. That is, the user confronted with an unfamiliar statistical term can click on it with the mouse to jump directly to a detailed explanation of its meaning. Thirdly, what is sometimes needed in research is the ability to reflect on a difficult research situation in an imaginative, playful, even fanciful, way (Webb & Weick 1983). Expert systems are usually not helpful in situations of this kind. To an extent, therefore, they might be seen as favouring essentially conservative solutions to research problems. Finally, for users outside North America, program assumptions about the nature of the researcher's social environment can sometimes be unrealistic. For example, naive users of DATA COLLECTION SELECTION not uncommonly find telephone interviewing recommended as a data collection strategy, something clearly inappropriate in countries where levels of telephone ownership fall below US levels.

Expert systems are beginning also to appear in qualitative research. For example, the qualitative data analysis program, HyperRESEARCH, allows working hypotheses, expressed as production rules, to be tested on any full or partial set of cases based on various kinds of qualitative data. (For more detail, see Mangabeira, this volume.) Carley (1988) has developed a two stage process for explicating the network of concepts and conceptual relationships within a verbal protocol. Coding a large number of protocols is tedious, time-consuming and prone to error. Although coding assistants can be employed, they rarely have sufficient background social knowledge to make fully explicit the definitions, connections and implications to be found within a protocol. However, provided this knowledge has been made explicit for some of the data it can be embodied within an expert system. In the first stage of the procedure Carley describes, assistants code protocols with the aid of a coding program, CODEF. An expert system, SKI, is then used to diagnose and correct errors and omissions in the initial coding produced by CODEF.

Intelligent computer aided instruction

There has been considerable scepticism about the use of computers for teaching. Rowntree, citing the cynical dictum, "Computer assisted learning is the medium of the future – and always will be" (1990: 261), argues that, far from exploiting the medium, developers of computer aided learning packages have too often produced what he calls electronic page turners. By contrast, writers like Woolf (1988) argue that expert systems hold considerable promise for improving students' learning. Such systems can reason about what students know on the basis of the responses they make, and can in consequence tailor teaching strategies to the individual needs of learners. (For an overview of computer aided learning, see Brent & Anderson 1990: Ch. 17).

The use of intelligent computer aided instruction (ICAI) or intelligent tutoring systems (ITS) is still uncommon in the social sciences. Brent and his associates have developed ERVING, an expert system for teaching students to reason sociologically using the dramaturgical perspective of Erving Goffman (Brent et al. 1989b). In ERVING students ask the computer questions about the actions of a variety of actors within a hypothetical social setting. The program not only answers these questions but provides its reasoning based on the dramaturgical perspective. Students then work through an assessment module in which they are questioned about what is going on in the setting. The program provides explanations of students' answers and summarizes their patterns of responses. In economics, ECONOMICS PC DISCOVERY WORLD, an intelligent tutoring system developed by Katz & Schultz (1989) helps students to develop their understanding of basic concepts in economics by allowing them to simulate the economy of an imaginary town. The program tracks the level of understanding students have through the choices and decisions they make in the course of the simulation. On the basis of this information the program suggests strategies of inquiry designed to improve students' comprehension and application of economic concepts. Both programs have received limited evaluation. It seems in general that students have favourable attitudes towards this mode of instruction. One interesting feature of ERVING, according to Brent et al., is that students felt use of the program allowed them to see more clearly the limits of dramaturgical theory – something, presumably, that might not be well conveyed by traditional teaching methods.

Some expert systems have been designed for dual use, as professional tools and as teaching aids. One example is the already mentioned suite of programs, the Methodologist's Toolchest (Benfer et al. 1991). In other cases, commercial products have been adapted for use in teaching, thus avoiding the lengthy and expensive process of producing custom-built software (Hayes & Acton 1991). Little attention has been directed to the use of non-dedicated expert systems in teaching. As Hayes & Acton point out, commercial programs often lack precisely those features of most use for teaching – fully developed help facilities and mechanisms for providing feedback on the learner's progress. In this situation, they argue, the onus is on the teacher to provide suitable problems, materials or scenarios for students to use with the expert system. Garson (1987) suggests that expert system generators could be used by students to produce a set of exploratory hypotheses. This would allow discussion of alternative rule sets as well as permitting comparisons with a rule set based on actual data.

It can sometimes be useful to combine the use of an expert system with more traditional approaches. For instance, experience with graduate students using the sampling design program, EX-SAMPLE, suggests that a three-way interaction between student, supervisor and program is often effective. Although this negates one advantage of using an expert system, the saving of staff time, it helps to deal with a number of problems. First, even though the program provides explanations for the questions it asks the user, these sometimes need further elucidation. Secondly, echoing a point made earlier, students from non-Western countries often detect assumptions about field conditions in the program that they feel to be inapplicable in their situation. Thirdly, some students seem to have particular problems in relating their substantive concerns to methodological issues. None of these problems makes the use of an expert system redundant. On the contrary, they allow the supervisor to target in a more systematic and effective way underlying problems that might otherwise have remained hidden.

Expert systems can themselves be used to teach students about the use of expert systems in the social sciences. For example, the authors of this article have successfully used DATA COLLECTION SELECTION, one of the programs in the Methodologist's Toolchest, to teach first-year undergraduates taking a course dealing with computer applications in the social sciences about the principles of expert systems and their utility in the research process. One advantage of this kind of strategy is that expert systems usually deal with substantive problems that are meaningful to students within a particular discipline.

A final point to make here is that expert systems are a "lumpy" technology, as Gum & Blank (1990) put it. For them to be used at all they require major changes which are themselves constrained by factors such as the cost and availability of hardware, the upward compatibility of software and so on. Moreover, as Gum & Blank go on to point out, the effective use of expert systems as instructional tools depends on their ability to go beyond the simple provision of advice. They need to provide to those who use them both a theoretical understanding of the topic of concern and the ability to demonstrate learned skills. Expert systems also become more effective where there exists a channel of feedback between users, developers and experts, and where learners can be helped to develop alternatives.

Acquiring knowledge and developing systems

The knowledge embedded in the rule set of an expert system is usually acquired from human experts. The process of acquiring such knowledge is problematic. Experts often operate on the basis of deep, complex and implicit procedures and structures. As a result, they are typically unaware of their own decision making processes. A detailed discussion of knowledge acquisition is beyond the scope of the present chapter. It is important to note, however, that the traffic between knowledge engineers and social scientists is "not a one-way street" (Read & Behrens 1989: 117). They go on:

> Much has been made of a knowledge acquisition "bottle-neck" in expert systems research. How can one elicit reliable knowledge from experts in the most efficient manner? It seems to us that anthropologists confront this problem every time they enter the field and, over the last hundred years of ethnographic research we have accumulated a vast tool kit for eliciting information from our "experts".

Making a similar point Benfer et al. (1991) describe a variety of methods of the kind used by cultural anthropologists which are useful in eliciting information from experts. These include sorting and ranking tasks, interviewing, the use of props and asking the expert to respond to scenarios. (Benfer et al. should be consulted for further details on the knowledge acquisition process including working with multiple experts and the testing and validation of knowledge bases.)

At one time developing an expert system was a costly and difficult exercise. Increasingly, however, expert system "shells" are available to facilitate development. An expert system shell is a software package which allows users having relatively little programming skill to set up an expert system in their own application area. Information on a number of available expert system shells suitable for social science purposes can be found in Brent (1988), Brent & Anderson (1990), Garson (1990) and Benfer et al. (1991). According to Brent & Anderson (1990) expert system shells may be rule based, language based, example based or fully integrated systems. (For a similar classification, see Garson 1990.) Rule based systems are generally inexpensive and easy to learn but often lack sophisticated features and in the case of some of the less developed systems are primarily useful for teaching and demonstration rather than development purposes. By contrast, Brent & Anderson suggest, language based systems, which are usually written in artificial intelligence languages such as LISP or PROLOG, are more difficult to learn and to use but are more powerful and more suited to developing complex applications than are rule based shells. In an example based system the rule set is generalized from examples provided by the user. Oriented to case based knowledge, these shells, it seems, are somewhat limited in their application. Brent & Anderson describe as integrated systems programs in which an expert system is combined with other applications, such as a spreadsheet or database. Although such systems are potentially powerful, they may be difficult to learn and may actually be too complicated to use for some kinds of fairly simple problems.

Developments and prospects

Attention so far has been directed at rule based systems. Such systems have many advantages. For example, Mills (1990) suggests that rule based systems are flexible both in terms of the way in which data can be handled and in their ability to deliver conclusions in a variety of different formats. In consequence, they may be particularly useful where one wants to move beyond the use of largely descriptive data but where statistical data are unavailable or quantitative analysis inappropriate. Mills (1990) suggests that in some situations rules are difficult to define. Like many other methodological strategies, rule based analysis is best used to analyze discrete events rather than long term trends. Used in some situations, without clarification of the broader complexities of an issue, rule based systems may produce rather simplistic results.

As indicated earlier, rule based systems typically represent knowledge in the form of production rules having the form "IF A THEN B". However, knowledge can be represented in a variety of ways, a number of which have found or are beginning to find applications in the social sciences. In the past few years neural networking has begun to attract attention from social scientists (Schrodt 1991, Kimber 1991, Garson 1991). Neural networks – the details of which lie beyond the scope of this chapter – are particularly useful for dealing with problems requiring complex classification procedures and where data suffer from high levels of "noise" in the form of ambiguous or missing data. Garson (1991) and Schrodt (1991) have both compared neural networks against a variety of multivariate statistical and artificial intelligence techniques for analysis of a given data set. In each case their evaluations suggest that neural networks perform at least as well as other techniques, and that their ability to deal with "noisy" data gives them considerable potential utility for the analysis of problems and data of the kind typically found in the social sciences.

Against this, some disadvantages have to be borne in mind. It is not always clear how neural networks arrive at the results they do (Garson 1990), and under some conditions they can provide results which are only partially accurate. Moreover, as Schrodt (1991: 376) points out, neural networks share with humans a tendency to over-emphasize the most frequent values in a dependent variable, making them unsuitable for the prediction of unusual cases.

Conclusion

The use of expert systems and other artificial intelligence techniques in the social sciences is not a panacea (Garson 1987: 13). They do, however, provide powerful tools which are likely to become increasingly important in the years to come. For a number of writers (Schrodt 1989, Mills 1993), there is an irony here. Computers which played such an important role in ensuring the diffusion of statistical methods in the social sciences now stand to overturn the statistical revolution. As Schrodt (1989: 125) puts it:

> When the mathematical social sciences developed in the late nineteenth and early twentieth centuries, first in psychology then in economics, it was the magnificent edifice of the mathematical physical sciences that served as a model . . .

Now, however:

> Problems that are intractable to algebra and calculus – large-scale memory, logical processing, learning – are easily, inexpensively and rapidly simulated in digital computers. These computational models are every bit as formal, unambiguous and testable as the mathematical models, but, also, they clearly are closer approximations to the capability of humans.

References

Benfer, R. A., E. E. Brent Jr, L. Furbee 1991. *Expert systems.* Newbury Park, Calif.: Sage.

Brent, E. E. 1988. Expert system shells for IBM-compatible microcomputers: a comparative review. *Social Science Computer Review* **6**, 143–53.

Brent, E. E. 1989. Designing social science research with expert systems. *Anthropological Quarterly* **62**, 121–30.

Brent, E. E. & R. E. Anderson 1990. *Computer applications in the social sciences.* New York: McGraw-Hill.

Brent, E., J. C. Spencer, J. K. Scott 1989a. EX-SAMPLE: an expert system program to assist in designing sample size. *Social Science Computer Review* **7**, 314–19.

Brent, E. E., J. Glazier, K. Jamtgaard, K. Wetzel, P. Hall, M. Dalecki, A. Bah 1989b. ERVING: a program to teach sociological reasoning from a dramaturgical perspective. *Teaching Sociology* **17**, 38–48.

Carley, K. 1988. Formalizing the social expert's knowledge. *Sociological Methods and Research* **17**, 165–232.

Diesvwld, P. J. M. & G. M. van den Berg 1993. The relevance of non-experts' knowledge in making a statistical support system. *Social Science Computer Review* **11**(3), 313–28.

Drouth, H., A. Morris, G. Tsenh 1991. Expert systems as information intermediaries. *Annual Review of Information Science* **26**, 113–54.

Fischer, M. D. 1991. Marriage and power: tradition and transition in an urban Punjabi community. In *Economy and culture in Pakistan: migrants and cities in Muslim society*, H. Donnan & P. Werbner (eds). London: Macmillan.

Fischer, M. D. & A. Finkelstein 1991. Social knowledge representation: a case study. In *Using computers in qualitative research*, N. G. Fielding & R. M. Lee (eds). London: Sage.

Garson, D. 1987. The role of inductive expert systems generators in the social science research process. *Social Science Computer Review* **5**, 11–24.

Garson, G. D. 1990. Expert systems: an overview for social scientists. *Social Science Computer Review* **8**, 387–410.

Garson, G. D. 1991. A comparison of neural network and expert system algorithms with common multivariate procedures for analysis of social science data. *Social Science Computer Review* **9**, 399–434.

Gum, R. L. & S. C. Blank 1990. Designing expert systems for effective delivery of extension programming. *American Journal of Agricultural Economics* **72**, 539–47.

Halfpenny, P., J. Parthemore, J. Taylor, I. Wilson 1992. A knowledge based system to provide intelligent support for writing questionnaires. In *Survey and Statistical Computing*, A. Westlake (ed.). Amsterdam: Elsevier.

Hayes, P. & M. Acton 1991. An exploration of the usefulness of a welfare benefits computer package in social work training. *New Technology in the Human Services* **5**, 2–14.

Hesse-Biber, S., P. Dupuis, T. S. Kinder 1991. HyperRESEARCH: a computer program for the analysis of qualitative data with an emphasis on hypothesis testing and multimedia analysis. *Qualitative Sociology* **14**, 289–306.

Katz, A. & J. Schultz 1989. A SMALLTALK/V intelligent economics tutoring system for microcomputers. *Social Science Computer Review* **7**, 192–99.

Kimber, R. 1991. Artificial intelligence and the study of democracy. *Social Science Computer Review* **9**, 381–98.

Kippen, J. 1988. On the uses of computers in anthropological research. *Current Anthropology* **29**, 317–20.

Mills, W. 1990. Rule-based analysis of Sino-Soviet negotiations. *Social Science Computer Review* **8**, 181–95.

Mills, W. 1993. The Methodology Tutor: an introduction to new social science methods. *Social Science Computer Review* **11**, 179–84.

Ohly, H. P. 1993. Knowledge-based systems: another data approach for social scientists? *Social Science Computer Review* **11**, 84–94.

Read, D. & C. Behrens 1989. Modelling folk knowledge as expert systems. *Anthropological Quarterly* **62**, 107–20.

Rowntree, D. 1990. *Teaching through self-instruction: how to develop open learning materials*, revised edn London: Kogan Page.

Schrodt, P. A. 1989. Artificial intelligence and formal models of international behavior. In *New technology in sociology: practical applications in research and work*, G. Blank, J. L. McCartney & E. Brent (eds). New Brunswick, NJ: Transaction.

Schrodt, P. A. 1991. Prediction of interstate conflict outcomes using a neural network. *Social Science Computer Review* **9**, 359–80.

Spirtes, P., R. Scheines, C. Gylmour 1990. Simulation studies of the reliability of computer-aided model specification using the TETRAD II, EQS and LISREL programs. *Sociological Methods and Research* **19**, 3–66.

Sylvan, D. & B. Glasner 1985. *A rationalist methodology for the social sciences*. Oxford: Basil Blackwell.

Thorsan, S. & D. Sylvan 1982. Counterfactuals and the Cuban Missile Crisis. *International Studies Quarterly* **26**, 539–71.

Tonn, B. E., R. Goeltz, T.-L. Chiang 1993. An object-based interviewing system. *Social Science Computer Review* **11**, 48–62.

Webb, E. & K. E. Weick 1983. Unobtrusive measures in organization theory: a reminder. In *Qualitative methodology*, J. V. Maanen (ed.). Beverley Hills, Calif.: Sage.

Woolf, B. P. 1988. Representing complex knowledge in an intelligent machine tutor. In *Artificial intelligence and human learning: intelligent computer-aided instruction*, J. Self (ed.). London: Chapman & Hall.

CHAPTER 11

Geographical computing for social scientists

David Gilbert

There has long been a close relationship between social science and the geographical representation of information. The nineteenth-century invention of the term social survey is in itself suggestive of the close historical relationship between cartography and social research. This relationship was more than simply metaphorical. Charles Booth's survey of London life and labour used coloured maps to show the complicated patterning of social class and poverty; these maps called into question simple generalizations about the social geography of the city. A map can often represent information more clearly than a number of tables or a written text, and will give extra information about the spatial attributes of that information. Many of the central issues for social scientists, such as social inequality, social stratification, and racial, ethnic and gender divisions within societies, are both expressed and to some extent constituted through geographical relations.

One of the most important and exciting recent developments in computing has been the combination of database and mapping technology known as geographic information systems, or GIS. GIS have been described as "the biggest step forward in geographic information since the invention of the map" (DoE 1987: 8), and they clearly have great potential for social science research. There can be few research projects currently using conventional non-spatial database technology which would not be enhanced by the use of GIS.

This chapter provides an introduction to GIS and explores their possible uses in social research. It looks in some detail at the UK 1991 Census and the use of geographical computing for the processing, analysis and presentation of small area statistics, and at the issues faced in linking census statistics with other spatial datasets. Spatial data have certain distinctive characteristics which can cause problems for statistical analysis, particularly where an attempt is made to make statistical inferences. These problems, such as spatial autocorrelation and the modifiable areal unit problem, are unfamiliar to most non-geographers and are therefore discussed here as issues which need to be addressed in research using GIS.

Despite their potential GIS should not be seen as exhaustive of geographical computing strategies. In the first place, even in a time of falling software and hardware costs, GIS remain relatively expensive and complicated. Using GIS is a commitment to a certain way of working. GIS must be seen as database systems involving a certain data management strategy, not simply as an add-on mapping package. In geographic computing as in other applications of information technology it is important to use the appropriate tools, and GIS are not the appropriate tools to use if all that is required is one or two thematic maps. These are best produced using drawing software, where the aim is to assist the cartographer in the production of a high quality map rather than to produce a large number of statistical maps automatically. This kind of computer assisted cartography is discussed in the next section of this chapter.

Secondly, arguing against some of the more aggressive claims made by advocates of GIS within the discipline of geography (see, for example, Openshaw 1991a), GIS is not exhaustive of what might be called the geographical imagination. There are other computing strategies which have potential for different kinds of geographical sensibility. The final part of this chapter suggests how other forms of computing, particularly developments in hypertext and multimedia, may be of use to some geographers, and to social scientists who share a concern for difference, diversity and particularity.

This chapter can be no more than a very brief introduction to geographical computing and, as with any written commentary on information technology, the situation described is changing rapidly. While certain products are mentioned in the text, the main focus is on the appropriateness and limitations of different approaches, rather than on the details of specific packages or equipment. The area of GIS is particularly well served by technical journals such as *Mapping Awareness and GIS Europe*, and also by an expanding technical literature. The discussion is largely restricted to British examples, although it is hoped that many of the themes are relevant in other situations.

Drawing maps with computers: computer assisted cartography

Using a computer to assist in the production of relatively simple maps has a number of important advantages over manual methods. Computer graphics packages can give a quality and consistency of line, detail and annotation even when used by non-cartographers. Maps drawn with a computer can be stored and readily altered. A computer can also produce a series of maps, showing perhaps changes over time, or patterns of different attributes. For most simple maps highly sophisticated geographical software is not required. (Indeed, Southall & Oliver (1990) argue that pen and paper may be more appropriate than the computer for some tasks, particularly where one simple sketch map is all that is required.) A social scientist, unlike a geographer or an archaeologist, is usually not producing a map directly from the results of topographical surveys or remote sensing (i.e. aerial photographs or satellite images), but is developing and annotating a base map to illustrate some aspect of an argument or analysis.

Computers can hold and manipulate graphical information either as raster images or as vector images. In a *raster image* (sometimes known as a bitmap) information is held as a grid of cells (or "pixels"), each with a particular colour assigned to it. At its most simple a raster image is built up from a grid of squares which are either black or white. A simple analogy of a computer raster image is a newspaper photograph; under a magnifying glass the photograph can be seen to be made up of discrete blobs of back or white. In a *vector image* information is held about the position, direction and length of lines. The production of any graphical image, including computer drawn maps, involves inputting information, manipulating and outputing, and usually storing the image for future use. At each stage either raster or vector techniques are used. Software packages which manipulate images using raster techniques are conventionally known as painting packages, those which use vector techniques as drawing packages. Although the work which can be done using raster techniques has improved greatly, vector techniques retain important advantages, especially that the image is independent of scale because it is stored as a set of mathematical relations and does not lose definition after repeated rescalings or manipulations.

Most university cartographic offices currently use a combination of a scanner, a personal computer equipped with a drawing package and a laser printer, and have access to an electrostatic typesetter. The current procedure in computer assisted cartography is that a base map is scanned into the computer as a bitmap image, which is then traced within a drawing package to produce a vector image of lines and areas. Once the base map has been created as a vector image, it can be shaded, annotated and manipulated using the tools provided by the drawing package. Specialized tools can be used for drawing straight and curved lines of a given thickness, for changing the shading of a particular area on a map, and for designing symbols to represent particular qualities. When completed the map can be printed. Laser printer output is of a quality suitable for most journal articles, especially if later photoreduced by professional printers, a process which tends to blur any jagged edges. Higher resolution images can be obtained from an electrostatic typesetter if required.

Computer assisted cartography is suitable for the production of simple reference maps, showing the location of places discussed in an associated text, with other geographic details such as rivers, coastlines, roads or railways to put these places in context. It is also suitable for producing certain forms of statistical thematic maps, particularly where only one or two of these is required. Distribution maps, showing the patterning of discrete examples of a particular event or phenomenon may be produced in this way, as may choropleth maps on which areas or regions are shaded, with the depth of shading representing variation in a particular quality. However, if more than one or two statistical maps are required, or if the spatial characteristics of the dataset under investigation form a significant part of the analysis, then the use of a GIS should be considered.

One important implication of the development of computer graphics applications which can be used to produce maps is that the design and production of maps is taken out of the hands of cartographers and others trained in graphic design. Modern computer graphics packages can produce high quality lines, shading and text for annotations, but this may only make it easier for the novice to produce badly designed maps. This is not the place to give detailed guidelines on the graphic design of thematic maps. Tufte's (1983) general recommendations on the graphic design of diagrams are well worth reading; Cuff & Mattson (1982) offer more specific advice about the visual logic and design of thematic maps.

Geographical information systems: spatial databases

As has been stressed already, the decision to use a GIS in a research project should not be taken lightly. Although GIS developed from earlier automated cartography systems which were used to produce maps from datasets, the modern GIS is a "multi-function, multi-purpose spatial data handling system" (Raper et al. 1992), and its use has wide-reaching implications for research. There are "almost as many different definitions of what a GIS is as there are actual software products on the market" (Heywood 1990), but it is perhaps best to think of GIS as a combination of different forms of information technology.

Although to most non-geographers the ability to produce maps is the most distinctive characteristic of GIS, they should be seen primarily as spatial databases, or more properly databases for the management of information with spatial and attributional components. Spatial data refer to the location of objects or phenomena; attributional data refer to the qualities of those objects. A grid reference or a postal code is an example of spatial data, while size of household or occupation of householder are examples of attributional data. The development of GIS owes as much to improvements in database management systems as it does to changes in graphical computing. Most GIS now use some form of relational database as their basis, and there is good compatibility between GIS and general database standards such as Structured Query Language (SQL).

Rather than thinking of GIS as mapping packages it is better to think of them in terms of the kinds of database query which they can answer, providing the response either graphically, as a computer generated map, or else as a numerical or textual dataset. Some GIS, such as those used in route planning, are concerned with queries about connectivity ("how far is it from A to B using motorways", "show me alternative routes out of West London"), but for most social research purposes the archetypal query asks for the specification of an area or areas with certain attributional characteristics ("show me all areas with male unemployment rates of 15% or more, and more than 10 infant deaths per 1000 live births"). This type of query is sometimes known as an overlay, as in pre-GIS times such problems were often approached by physically overlaying transparent maps of different distributions.

GIS derive their other functional characteristics from different kinds of computer software, particularly those most concerned with the capture, manipulation and production of digital graphical images. In this respect,

GIS can be seen as developing from computer aided design, automated cartography and the image processing software which was designed to handle data from satellite remote sensing. Like all graphical computing systems GIS hold images either as raster or vector systems. In the context of GIS each of these storage structures has strengths and weaknesses. Raster data structures facilitate overlay type queries, making the combination of area based data relatively fast and efficient. Vector data structures are more efficient for queries about connectivity and adjacency, have important advantages when images are manipulated and transformed, as was mentioned above, and generally take much less storage space (Raper et al. 1992). Most modern GIS support both kinds of spatial data structure, although most official and commercial digitized maps are in vector form.

There are a range of commercially available GIS packages which are suitable for social scientific research. The cheapest and most straightforward of these have developed directly from automated cartography packages, and their main function is to represent area based information and to produce good quality maps. Two examples of this kind of software are SPANS, which uses a raster spatial data structure, and MapInfo, which uses a vector structure. More expensive and complicated packages include GIMMS, which had an early lead in GIS work in British geography departments, and ARC/INFO, which is the current world market leader. These systems are capable of handling both vector and raster structures, offer more sophisticated database management languages and routines, and have more sophisticated spatial analysis functions. In Britain a number of these systems, including ARC/INFO, are available to academics at greatly reduced cost through CHEST agreements. As with the decision whether to use computer assisted cartography or GIS, there should be a strong sense that the technology is appropriate for the task required in choosing which GIS to use. Use of highly configured GIS like ARC/INFO involves not only substantial cost for software and hardware, but also a clear commitment to training and the development of new kinds of data processing skills. One of the small ironies of GIS development is that this inherently graphical form of computing has been relatively slow in making use of the types of intuitive graphical user interfaces which are now an established standard in Macintosh and Windows computing (see Raper 1991).

The complexity of GIS is reflected in the hardware required to run them. Like all types of computer applications, GIS have benefited greatly from improvements in performance and the falling costs of computing hardware. However, full GIS like ARC/INFO are really viable only on the fastest and most powerful of modern PCs (486 processor machines, with fast access hard disks). The natural habitat of GIS in the early 1990s is the workstation rather than the personal computer because of the superior processing power and graphics screens. Another important consideration in the use of full scale GIS is data storage. The datasets used by GIS are often very large, and even in a period when the costs of large hard disks are falling rapidly, storage costs are likely to remain a significant element in the cost of GIS hardware.

GIS: problems and practicalities for social research

The central problem faced by most social research applications using GIS is that of linking datasets. In a research context, the primary task of GIS is to merge and compare different data for the same location, and to analyze the relationships between the spatial patternings of different types of data. It is this characteristic of GIS which gives them such potential as integrators of information across traditional disciplinary boundaries. One good example is epidemiology, where health statistics can now be compared with socio-economic and environmental information for very small areas. Problems in linking datasets are not primarily technological, but are most often caused by differences in the spatial structure of datasets. For example, in Britain, even within government and public administration alone, there are a large number of different spatial units, such as electoral wards, parliamentary constituencies, census enumeration districts, health districts and so on. These do not all share common boundaries or nest into each other, and their boundaries may be altered for administrative reasons, making the analysis of time series difficult. Information from other sources may have still different spatial structures. For example, land use or environmental information often has a spatial structure which is defined with reference to the phenomenon being mapped, and this is very unlikely to be coincident with that of administrative boundaries.

There are very great problems in linking datasets where information is only available for relatively large areas. When working with larger aggregated spatial units, the researcher is usually forced to assume that there is a homogenous distribution of a particular quality within the area, and may also be tempted to make unsafe inferences from the relationships observed in aggregated data about individual experiences. To give a historical example, if statistics are available only at an aggregated level for towns or districts within towns, there is a clear relationship between rates of alcoholism and the number of adherents of Methodist churches in late nineteenth century Britain. To reason from this information that there is a relationship at the level of individuals and that Methodists were more likely to be alcoholics is an example of what geographers describe as the ecological fallacy (Harvey 1969, Martin 1992). This problem can be thought of as a spatial analogy of the limitations of the mean as a descriptive statistic.

The problem of the ecological fallacy is one of the reasons why it is important to have access to information in as unaggregated form as possible. This was one of the key recommendations to suppliers of data of the report of the Official Enquiry into the handling of geographic information chaired by Lord Chorley (DoE 1987, hereafter referred to as "the Chorley report"). From the perspective of the researcher, the ideal situation is that information is held at the level of the individual (whether person, household, firm, etc.), and that each individual has a geographical reference. For British information, the Chorley report recommended that a National Grid reference (rather than, say, latitude and longitude) be used as the common geographical referencing standard. However, it was recognized that the use of individual or household information was often incompatible with the need to ensure confidentiality. The Chorley report's main concern was therefore to provide some common geographical standard for the collection, storage and dissemination of data, and recommended that information be held and released on the basis of unit postcodes. The unit postcode refers to the full address code used by the Royal Mail in the delivery of post in Britain. In an effort to rationalize the spatial basis of British official statistics, the report recommended that in future the boundaries of administrative and electoral areas should not divide whole unit postcode areas.

This use of the unit postcode area as the basic building block of spatial statistics has a number of advantages for socio-economic research purposes. First, the unit postcode area is quite small. Within the UK there are around 1.5 million unit postcode areas, and most contain between 30 and 50 people. Secondly, postcode areas to some extent reflect the geography of population and economic activity. They make more sense as the building blocks for social research than using, say, grid squares of fixed size, with an arbitrary relationship to the patterns of human activity. Postcodes are also regularly updated to reflect changes in postal activity, and, more importantly, changes in the built structure of towns and cities. The Royal Mail keeps a central database of postcodes, known as the Postcode Address File (or PAF). This is available on CD, and is now updated each month. There have been problems in the adoption of the postcode as a common standard, particularly in the case of the 1991 census, which is discussed below.

Another practical problem in GIS computing is that GIS are notoriously data hungry. The cost of data is becoming an increasingly significant element in the budgets of GIS-based research projects. There are a number of reasons for this. First, by their very nature, GIS require unaggregated information, necessarily involving much larger datasets than those required for statistical analysis of aggregated information. Secondly, GIS require different kinds of information, most notably digitized boundary maps, which are often expensive to buy, or else very time-consuming to digitize as part of a research project. In Britain the Ordnance Survey (OS) is the main supplier of standard digital maps, and has made significant steps towards the provision of a national large scale digital map. At present the OS can offer complete coverage at a scale of 1:10,000, and coverage of populated areas at 1:1250 or 1:2500.

Unfortunately, the OS now has an explicit aim of recovering operating costs from revenue, and OS digital maps now involve considerable cost. This commodification of information is a process which is taking place more generally for both large official datasets and base maps, and has profound implications for the development of GIS research applications (Rhind 1991b). As is the case for other large scale database research technologies, the development of GIS is dependent on changes in research culture, and particularly in the credit given for placing information in the public domain (Gilbert & Southall 1991). However, as Heywood (1990: 850) notes: "The current climate of reduced research funding, near-market research, and competitive tendering for students is not one which encourages the sharing of ideas and information."

Spatial datasets and inferential statistics

The development of academic research using GIS has brought with it a growing awareness of the difficulties of working with spatial datasets. This is to some extent a rediscovery of issues and problems which were explored by some geographers during the 1960s and 1970s, when the discipline was heavily influenced by positivistic methods, and some attempted to recast the discipline as a science of spatial relations (see Livingstone 1993). One of the most serious technical problems faced by the spatial scientists (many of whom are now active researchers using GIS), was that many of the conventional techniques used by social scientists in the analysis of non-spatial datasets seemed to be severely flawed when used to analyze data with a spatial component. In particular, many of the assumptions made in drawing statistical inferences from linked datasets are usually violated by spatial datasets. The problem of the ecological fallacy has already been discussed; three other serious problems which are faced by researchers using GIS or spatial datasets more generally are the modifiable areal unit problem, spatial autocorrelation and the issues involved in spatial sampling.

The modifiable areal unit problem affects all statistical methods when applied to spatial datasets. The results of statistical techniques are influenced by the size, scale and configuration of the areal units chosen, usually to an unknown and unpredictable degree. The relationship between two variables can vary dramatically at different spatial scales, and the way that smaller units are aggregated to make larger ones can have a similarly important effect. Relationships which can be observed at a regional scale may not be evident at a local scale. One solution to this problem made possible by GIS is to repeat analyses many times, using a different spatial configuration each time. In a sense, the GIS is being asked to produce an "optimal" spatial arrangement of the data as a part of the statistical analysis. However, both the analysis of such procedures and the nature of the algorithms used in their computation remain controversial and require further research (Openshaw 1991b).

Spatial autocorrelation has long been recognized as a significant problem in applying inferential statistical procedures to spatial datasets. Most inferential statistical techniques have an underlying assumption of independence, and this is violated within spatial datasets where neighbouring or proximate data values are highly correlated. Most social datasets exhibit high levels of spatial autocorrelation. As for the modifiable areal unit problem, controversial procedures have been developed which attempt to make allowance for spatial autocorrelation, but as the Chorley report (1987) stated, the only simple remedy is "to avoid completely the use of inferential statistics".

Spatial datasets are also problematic in terms of research design, particularly when using sampling techniques. In a non-spatial dataset there are straightforward techniques for estimating the size of sample required to make inferences about the whole population; with a spatial dataset the issue becomes more complicated. First, there are difficulties in selecting the spatial arrangement of the sample, and the actual location of sampling points may be influenced by how accessible those points are. Secondly, sampling of a spatially distributed population requires a considerably larger sample if inferences are to be made about the distribution of a variable. For example, a sample size of around 1,000 is standardly used by opinion polling organizations to make predictions of each political party's share of the national vote in British elections. However, to produce predictions for each and every constituency with the same degree of confidence would require a sample of 100,000 or more.

GIS are primarily spatial databases rather than spatial analysis packages, and the main commercial packages contain very few tools or routines which are specifically designed to address the kinds of problems discussed here. This reflects both the main market for packages of this type, which is in the management of spatial information rather than its detailed analysis, and also the failure of statisticians to come up with easily operationable solutions to these problems. There are two possible responses to this situation. One response, particularly from those in the spatial science tradition, has been to call for a "spatial science research agenda" with the aim of providing spatial analysis tools for GIS (Openshaw 1991b). So far, however, twenty-five years of research into these issues have provided some insights into their scope and character, but little in the way of straightforward or reliable statistical tools. The alternative strategy is to be aware of the problems and limits of spatial statistics and to use them with caution. As with many other social science applications involving statistical analysis, there is much to be said for the careful, contextualized use of spatial statistics and the rediscovery of the usefulness and robustness of simple non-parametric descriptive statistics. Even without complicated statistical procedures GIS remain very powerful tools for the management and presentation of social research.

GIS and the 1991 Census

In Britain the decennial census is probably the most important single source of demographic and social information. Computer software packages designed to handle the 1981 Census data such as SASPAC were primarily designed to give access to Small Area Statistics (enumeration district level statistics, or SAS) in a form which could be used by standard non-spatial statistical packages, such as SPSS. Mapping of Census data was very much a secondary activity, using a specialized mapping package (Rhind 1983). GIS offer the possibility of a completely integrated approach to the collation of census results and their analysis and presentation. It is likely that by the time of the 2001 Census GIS or their successor technologies will be the dominant mode of access to census data. The 1991 Census is an important point on the way to that goal.

It was one of the primary recommendations of the Chorley report that the 1991 Census be produced with postcode areas as the basic spatial units. For previous censuses the smallest spatial unit for which information was available was the enumeration district. Each enumeration district is the responsibility of a single census enumerator, and in the past the boundaries of these have been drawn with the aim of making the enumerator's work as easy as possible. Although the boundaries of enumeration districts tend to follow streets (centre lines), railways, rivers and other obvious features, and where possible blocks of housing are not divided, the spatial structure of each enumeration district is to some extent arbitrary. In 1981 for England and Wales, there was close co-operation between the Office of Population Censuses and Surveys (OPCS) and local government in an attempt to construct areas which recognized specific local administrative needs (Denham & Rhind 1983). This meant that enumeration districts were more likely to reflect the underlying social geography; however, it also meant that the spatial structure of the census was fixed with certain issues and priorities in mind. As there is clear evidence from research into the modifiable areal unit problem that the scale and structure of spatial units selected for analysis has a powerful influence on what relationships are recognized between different variables, it is important that information can be accessed as flexibly as possible.

The use of postcodes in the census aims to achieve this greater flexibility of access to census data and to facilitate linkages with other types of data, especially at the most detailed level. From the point of view of researchers, the ideal form of access would be one in which aggregations of information could be produced for areas of any desired size and shape, built up on the basis of unit postcode areas (Rhind et al. 1990, Rhind 1991a). In principle this is already possible, as all individual census returns for 1991 were coded with the postcode. The adoption of this strategy is limited not by the technology, but by worries about breaches of the confidentiality of the census made possible by such powerful access to on-line information about very small areas.

In Scotland significant moves have been made towards making the postcode system the basis of census geography. In both 1981 and 1991, enumeration districts were based upon aggregations of unit postcodes. For research in Scotland it is now relatively simple to link postcoded information to census results, as unit postcode areas now form the basis for reporting SAS. The areas used for reporting in Scotland, known as "output areas" (OAs), are either unit postcode areas, or amalgamations of postcode areas. Areas larger than the unit postcode were required because of a statutory requirement that no OA should contain fewer than 16 households or 50 residents. The General Register Office for Scotland (the Scottish equivalent of the OPCS) publishes digital maps of these OA boundaries which can be used by GIS.

In England and Wales the situation is more complicated and less satisfactory. Enumeration districts were not adjusted to take account of the geography of postcodes, and in many places unit postcode areas straddle the boundaries of enumeration districts. Linkage of postcoded information with census SAS is much more difficult than in Scotland. The decision not to use the postcode areas for the 1991 Census was taken in 1986 because of the cost of producing digitized maps for over one million postcode areas in England and Wales. In view of the complicated strategies which have had to be devised to link postcoded data and SAS, this was clearly a false economy. For England and Wales, the link between postcodes and the census is provided by one of two strategies, both of which are organized around a linking gazetteer file, known as the ED/ postcode directory. Those wishing to relate the two geographies are faced either with using "part postcode units" or "pseudo-enumeration districts". Both of these strategies are compromise solutions to the problems of linkage, and both provide "new and complex possibilities for error propagation" (Martin 1992: 350). These strategies are discussed in detail in Martin (1992) and Raper et al. (1991). Unlike Scotland, the production of digital maps is also far less well organized in England and Wales. The OS has produced a set of digital boundaries for ward and civil parishes for England only, while various commercial organizations have produced digital maps of enumeration districts. The ESRC has acquired a digital map of enumeration district boundaries which is available at no cost for use in non-commercial research. This should be available in 1994. Researchers should be warned that this digital map is very large (around 250 MB), and potentially difficult to work with. Problems in linking the census with other datasets are mainly limited to detailed research involving the geography of very small areas. In analyses using basic spatial units larger than the enumeration district there are far fewer problems of linkage, although the analyst still faces problems inherent in statistical techniques for use with spatial data.

Specialist packages are available which can provide maps of various census categories rapidly and easily on a PC, although a full GIS is required for more detailed analytical work. These dedicated packages are worth investigating if all that is required is the production of choropleth maps of census information. SCAMP-CD and MAP91 produced by Claymore Services Limited provide census information and a mapping package which can be used on a PC with a CD-ROM drive. This system is capable of producing statistical maps down to enumeration district level for the whole of Britain, and contains information on over 200 census variables. This information can be downloaded for use in other applications.

Social research using GIS

The scope and scale of research undertaken using GIS has been influenced by a number of factors. First, the cost and complexity of GIS has limited academic research to a few major research initiatives. In Britain, the ESRC sponsored a number of centres of excellence in GIS-related research, known as the Regional Research Laboratories (RRLs). Secondly, both within the RRLs and within university departments of geography, research has tended to be concerned with planning and management applications of GIS. Thirdly, because most academic research using GIS has been undertaken by geographers, there has been an important and valuable emphasis on environmental issues and problems, often linking these to socio-economic datasets. Finally, a number of commercial organizations have developed GIS databases of social indicators for use in market research and in developing sales strategies. This type of activity has been christened "geodemographics" (Brown 1991), even though the type of information collected extends well beyond demographic information. Geodemographic databases may be of some use in academic social research.

The work undertaken by the RRLs is indicative of the range of academic work already done using GIS in Britain. The RRLs were set up by the ESRC in the late 1980s, and have become the main sites of academic research using GIS in this country, and are the obvious places to seek advice about GIS in social research. Much of their work has been very policy-orientated. Each of the RRLs have different substantive interests. For example, the South East RRL (based at Birkbeck College, London) has developed a GIS database of settlements and infrastructure for South East England (Shepherd 1991), and the RRL for Wales and the South West (at University College Cardiff) has undertaken research in the geography of housing, health and rural resource management.

An earlier research initiative by the Manpower Services Commission created the National On-line Manpower Information Service (NOMIS), which is based at the University of Durham. The NOMIS was one of the earliest integrated GIS in Britain, supplying information at a wide range of geographic scales about employment, unemployment and vacancies. This information is drawn from information supplied by the Department of Employment, and can be combined readily with SAS from the census. In its most basic form NOMIS simply produces tables of numerical and textual information, but the functionality of NOMIS is being improved so that on-line GIS-type queries or overlays can be made of the database (Blakemore 1990).

Although geodemographic databases have marketing rather than academic research as their main aim, they may be of some use either as a readily available source of information about the social characteristics of small areas, or as the basis for sampling in social surveys. In Britain there are a number of commercially available geodemographic databases. The best known of these is probably ACORN (A Classification of Residential Neighbourhoods) produced by CACI Ltd, although there are a number of other similar products, which include PiN, MOSAIC and Super Profiles (see Brown 1991 for further details of these products). All of these use census SAS and sometimes other variables to produce a classification of areas. For example, the Super Profiles system divides areas into 11 lifestyle types, 37 target market types and 150 area types, on the basis of clusters of census variables. Super Profile lifestyle A "is characterized by large, detached, owner occupied housing which accommodates highly qualified, multi-car owning, professional worker households with few children, in low density, suburban and semi-rural areas from which the majority of workers commute by car and train to office jobs" (Brown 1991: 227). Such categorization schemes are both somewhat subjective in design and clearly primarily designed for marketing purposes, but may save work in social research, enabling specific areas with specific characteristics to be targeted more easily. The Super Profiles dataset was developed directly from ESRC-funded work on area classification schemes in the early 1980s (see Charlton et al. 1985).

The limits of GIS and new forms of geographical computing

The current form and use of GIS has been criticized on a number of grounds. First, current social research using GIS has often amounted to little more than market research or governmental planning. As yet GIS have been under-used in more conceptual academic work or in more critical studies. Pickles (1992: 600) has called for a critical, socially aware reformulation of GIS to replace those current applications designed for "the totalizing gaze of the strategic planner, commercial manager, or military strategist". Secondly, GIS research applications have been insensitive about the social construction of data and have often shown an over-willingness to take official sources of information at their face value. This is partly a reflection of the need for large datasets to use with GIS, which are often only supplied by governments. When GIS-based research is heavily dependent on official sources, the geography of the investigation is often determined by the spatial extent of the data rather than of the social phenomena. Some GIS enthusiasts point to the global expansion of available digital information, but the development of such data is very geographically uneven, and for many issues electronic information is least available where it is most important. There is a danger that a GIS-led social research agenda will move interest away from those places poorly served with information. As Taylor & Overton (1991) succinctly put it, "good-bye tropical Africa: little data, little geography".

GIS-based research has also been criticized for showing a lack of concern for meaning and interpretation. This often manifests itself in a lack of awareness of the problematic relationship between GIS image and reality. Where GIS practitioners have shown any awareness of the nature of the activity that they are undertaking it has usually been a triumphant reassertion of the power and utility of positivistic method in social research. Heywood (1990: 850) has claimed that GIS have reaffirmed "the importance of the positivist approach to problem solving in the social sciences". Such statements have succeeded only in driving a wedge between GIS practitioners and social and cultural geographers who have become increasingly interested in the complex politics and philosophy of cartographic representations of the world. These social and cultural geographers have tended to reject GIS out of hand; one welcome consequence of an extension of GIS to social scientists outside of the geographic tradition may be a new impetus towards the use of GIS in more critical and contextually aware research.

A final criticism of GIS and their advocates has been the way in which they have represented GIS as exhaustive of geographical computing. Openshaw (1991a: 626) has even suggested that "GIS can provide an information system domain within which virtually all of geography can be performed." Cultural and social geographers who reject this view, and who are more concerned with the particularity of places and their social environments than with the construction of vast databases, are beginning to look at the expressive potential of information technology, and particularly its ability to create new textual strategies (Gilbert 1994). Some have pointed to the problems created by the sequential nature of writing for geographers, "when the concern is to convey, in 'thicker' ethnographic idioms, spatial simultaneity" (Livingstone 1992: 344). New ways of writing or making texts using the computer are able to create non-linear texts, generically known as "hypertexts". Recent years have also seen a growing concern for different forms of information in geography, most notably in the increasing importance given to the interpretation of visual information. Geographers are seeking to extend the textual range of their tradition to include, for example, oral history records and moving pictures, as well as extending and deepening their ways of reading visual sources. Multimedia technology, with its ability to juxtapose and to switch between different textual forms, clearly has some part to play in this widening of the textual scope of the geographic tradition, particularly when allied to the possibilities presented by electronic non-linear writing. Raper (1991) has used some of these hypertext and multimedia techniques to create a "hypermap", but this remains little more than a particularly interactive conventional GIS. One aspect of the recent cultural turn in the social sciences has been an increased concern and awareness of the differences that places make, and of the geographic imagination more generally. There is clearly great scope for collaboration between geographers and other social scientists in the development of new ways of representing the geographies of the social world.

References

Blakemore, M. 1990. The UK networked GIS (NOMIS) for monitoring and strategic planning. In *Proceedings of the first European conference on GIS (EGIS '90)*, 77–86. Utrecht: EGIS Foundation.

Brown, P. J. B. 1991. Exploring geodemographics. See Masser & Blakemore (1991), 221–58.

Charlton, M., S. Openshaw, C. Wynes 1985. Some new classifications of census enumeration districts in Britain: a poor man's ACORN. *Journal of Economic and Social Measurement* **13**, 69–96.

Cuff, D. J. & M. T. Mattson 1982. *Thematic maps. Their design and production*. London: Methuen.

Denham, C. & D. W. Rhind 1983. The 1981 census and its results. In *A census user's handbook*, D. W. Rhind (ed.), 17–88. London: Methuen.

Department of the Environment (DoE) 1987. *Handling geographic information: report of the committee of enquiry chaired by Lord Chorley*. London: HMSO.

Gilbert, D. M. & H. R. Southall 1991. Data *glasnost*: a user-friendly system for access to research databases across wide-area networks. *History and Computing* **3**, 119–28.

Gilbert, D. M. 1994. Between two cultures. The computer, geography and the humanities. *Ecumene* **2**.

Harvey, D. 1969. *Explanation in geography*. London: Edward Arnold.

Heywood, I. 1990. Geographic information systems in the social sciences. *Environment and Planning A* **22**, 849–52.

Lake, R. W. 1993. Planning and applied geography: positivism, ethics, and geographic information systems. *Progress in Human Geography* **17**, 404–13.

Livingstone, D. 1992. *The geographical tradition*. London: Blackwell.

Maguire, D. J., M. F. Goodchild, D. W. Rhind (eds) 1991a. *Geographical information systems, Vol. 1. Principles*. Harlow, England: Longman.

Maguire, D. J., M. F. Goodchild, D. W. Rhind (eds) 1991b. *Geographical information systems, Vol. 2. Applications*. Harlow, England: Longman.

Martin, D. 1991. *Geographic information systems and their socioeconomic applications*. London: Routledge.

Martin, D. 1992. Postcodes and the 1991 census of population: issues, problems and prospects. *Transactions of the Institute of British Geographers*, New Series **17**, 350–7.

REFERENCES

Masser, I. & M. Blakemore (eds) 1991. *Handling geographic information: methodology and potential applications*. Harlow, England: Longman.

Openshaw, S. 1991a. A view on the GIS crisis in geography, or, using GIS to put Humpty-Dumpty back together again. *Environment and Planning A* **23**, 621–8.

Openshaw, S. 1991b. A spatial analysis research agenda. See Masser & Blakemore (1991), 18–37.

Pickles, J. 1992. Review of David Martin *Geographical information systems and their socioeconomic applications*. *Environment and Planning D: Society and Space* **10**, 597–600.

Raper, J. F. 1991. User interfaces. See Masser & Blakemore (1991), 102–14.

Raper, J. F., D. W. Rhind, J. W. Shepherd 1992. *Postcodes: the new geography*. Harlow, England: Longman.

Rhind, D. W. (ed.) 1983. *A census user's handbook*. London: Methuen.

Rhind, D. W. 1991a. Counting the people: the role of GIS. In *Geographical information systems, Vol. 2. Applications*, D. J. Maguire, M. F. Goodchild, D. W. Rhind (eds), 127–37. Harlow, England: Longman.

Rhind, D. W. 1991b. Data access, charging and copyright and their implications for GIS. In *Proceedings of the second European conference on GIS (EGIS '91)*, 929–45. Utrecht: EGIS Foundation.

Rhind, D. W., K. Cole, M. Armstrong, L. Chow, S. Openshaw 1990. *An on-line, secure and infinitely flexible database system for the national population census*. Working report 14, South East Regional Research Laboratory. London: SE RRL, Birkbeck College.

Shepherd, J. 1991. Planning settlements and infrastructure. See Masser & Blakemore (1991).

Southall, H. R. & E. Oliver 1990. Drawing maps with a computer . . . or without? *History and Computing* **2**, 146–54.

Taylor, P. and M. Overton 1991. Further thought on geography and GIS. *Environment and Planning A* **23**, 1087–9.

Tutfte, E. R., 1983. *The visual display of quantitative information*. Cheshire, Conn.: Graphics.

CHAPTER 12

Using computer simulation to study social phenomena

Nigel Gilbert

This chapter introduces simulation as a tool for the investigation of social phenomena, focusing particularly on the methodology of simulation and on two approaches which have experienced a recent resurgence of interest: dynamic micro-simulation (DMS) and distributed artificial intelligence (DAI). Although the simulation of social dynamics has a long history in the social sciences (Inbar & Stoll 1972), the advent of much more powerful computers, more powerful computer languages and the greater availability of data about social phenomena have led to increased interest in simulation as a method for developing and testing social theories. (See Chapter 3 of Whicker & Sigelman 1991 for a historical review.) In the first part of this chapter, I outline some methodological principles common to most research using simulation. In the second half, I describe two approaches to simulation, both of which have become more prominent because of developments in computer science and information technology: dynamic micro-simulation and the use of distributed artificial intelligence techniques. There are several styles of simulation other than these two that have been used for modelling social phenomena, including discrete simulation modelling and using differential equation models, but these have already been well documented in the general literature on simulation and will not be considered further here (see, for example, Zeigler 1990, Doran & Gilbert 1993, Pooch & Wall 1993).

Simulation comes into its own when the phenomenon to be studied is either not directly accessible or is on too large a scale to observe directly. For example, I shall illustrate the use of DAI with an example of the simulation of social structure amongst hunter-gatherers in Upper Palaeolithic

France 20,000 years ago. Direct observation of such a society is obviously impossible. Instead of studying the society (the *target*) itself, it is often useful to study a *model* of the target. The model will be more accessible and smaller scale, but sufficiently similar to the target to allow conclusions drawn from the model to be (tentatively) generalized to the target. The model might be physical (for example, the London School of Economics has a macro-economic model consisting of coloured water flowing through an assembly of glass vessels), mathematical or symbolic (based on logic or a computer program). The important point about a model is that it must be designed to be similar to the target in structure and behaviour.

Generally, a model is defined in terms of a formal *specification* (Doran & Gilbert 1993). Sometimes it is possible to derive conclusions about the model analytically, by reasoning about the specification (for example, with mathematical proof procedures). Often, however, this is either difficult or impossible, and one performs a *simulation*. The simulation consists of "animating" the model. For example, if the model is expressed as a computer program, the simulation consists of running the program with some specified inputs and observing the program's outputs.

The basic method of simulation involves a number of steps:

1. Since no social phenomenon can be examined in its entirety, the first step is to select those aspects which are of interest. The selection must be influenced by theoretical preconceptions about which features are significant and which are not.

2. The modelling approach to be adopted is chosen. There are a number of different approaches applicable to the construction of models for social scientific problems. One approach is based on techniques drawn from operational research and uses ideas such as queues, random events and flows from sources to sinks as the building blocks of the model (e.g. Bulgren 1982, Gottfried 1984). Another approach is based on the construction of differential equations, relating the rate of change of quantities to other parameters (e.g. Spriet & Vansteenkiste 1982). A third approach uses symbolic logic or symbol manipulation as the basis of the model (Widman et al. 1989, Gilbert & Doran 1993).

3. Whichever approach is adopted, a further decision has to be made about the appropriate level of abstraction for the model. An important aspect of this is the level of aggregation selected for its units. For example, one might model the world economy using the major

power blocks, individual countries or (less practically) individual people as the units.

4. It is then necessary to select the form in which the model is to be represented. If the model is to be a computer program, the decision mainly concerns the choice of computer language, although there will also be choices about how the program should be structured.

5. Once all these preliminaries have been decided, the model can be constructed, the simulation run and the output examined. The model must then be validated. The main purpose of validation is to establish whether the model is a good model of the target. This means comparing some of the model's output against data collected from the target.

6. In practice, there is likely to be a period of modifying and testing gradually improving models. The simulation will be run a number of times, each time with a slightly "better" model.

7. Once the model is considered to be satisfactory, it is important to carry out sensitivity analyses. These examine the effect of small changes in the parameters of the model on its output. If small changes make large differences, one needs to be concerned about the accuracy with which the parameters have been measured; it is possible that the output is an artefact of the particular values chosen for the parameters.

The construction and validation of a simulation model is summarized in Figure 12.1.

The logic underlying the methodology of simulation is not very different from the logic underlying statistical modelling. In statistical modelling, a specification of a model is constructed (for example, in the form of

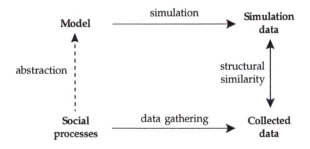

Figure 12.1 The logic of simulation.

a regression equation) through a process of abstraction from what are theorized to be the social processes that exist in the "real world" (Gilbert 1993). By means of some statistical technique (e.g. ordinary least squares), the model is used to generate some expected values which are compared with actual data. The main difference between statistical modelling and simulation is that a simulation model can be "run" to produce output, while a statistical model requires a statistical analysis program.

The benefits and problems of simulation as a methodology

Paradoxically, one of the main advantages of simulation is that it is hard to do. To create a simulation model, its theoretical presuppositions need to have been thought through with great clarity. Every relationship to be modelled has to be specified exactly, for otherwise it will be impossible to run the simulation. Every parameter has to be given a value. This discipline means that it is impossible to be vague about what is being assumed. It also means that the model is potentially open to inspection by other researchers in all its detail. These benefits of clarity and precision also have disadvantages, however. Simulations of complex social processes involve the estimation of many parameters and adequate data for making the estimates can be difficult to come by. For example, in simulating household decisions about whether to enter the labour market, it is necessary to model, among many other factors, the probability that a woman having a baby will decide to move to part-time work (Joshi 1990). Data on such transition probabilities are best derived from panel surveys and it is hard to obtain reliable figures.

Another, quite different benefit of simulation is that it can, in some circumstances, give insights into the "emergence" of macro level phenomena from micro level action. For instance, a simulation of interacting individuals may reveal clear patterns of influence when examined on a societal scale. A simulation by Nowak & Latané (1993), for example, shows how relatively simple rules about the way in which one individual influences another's attitudes can yield results about attitude change at the level of a society.

Simulation also has some disadvantages as a method. The difficulty of obtaining sufficient data to formulate the model with precision has already been referred to. Another problem often encountered in simulation

211

is that it can involve very considerable computational resources. A model based on simulating the actions of individuals over a period of time on the basis of some set of rules will consume computer resources proportional to the product of the number of individuals, the number of time periods through which the simulation is conducted and the number of rules. The runs required for sensitivity analyses also need to be factored into this product. As an example, the DAI based simulation to be described below typically involves 30 simulated individuals, 800 time periods and 60 rules, with the result that a single run on a workstation takes two or three days of continuous computation. This is not an extreme example.

A problem which has to be faced in all simulation work is the difficulty of validating the model. There is an understandable temptation to tinker with a model until it produces results which are close enough to those expected and then to conclude that the model is therefore valid. It has to be borne in mind, however, that even when a model has been successful in reproducing the behaviour of its target, it may still produce spurious behaviours in other conditions. Ideally, a simulation should produce behaviours which match those of the target for all possible inputs which can be envisaged to occur in reality, and should fail to produce output in all other circumstances. In practice, it is neither feasible to examine all input combinations, nor is it possible to assess whether the outputs from a wide range of inputs do indeed match the behaviours of the target, because the target may only be observable for some rather limited range of conditions. Sometimes a statistical solution to these problems is advocated (e.g. Bratley et al. 1983), but in practice it is hard to abide by the kinds of assumptions which conventional statistical tests require.

Two recent approaches to simulation

The above methodological points will be illustrated with examples taken from recent work with which I have been involved. The first uses an approach which has come to be called *dynamic micro-simulation*. Dynamic micro-simulation is used to simulate the effect of the passing of time on individuals and, often, on households (Harding 1990). Data from a large, usually random sample from some population (the "base data set") is used to characterize the initial features of the simulated individuals. For example, there may be data on the age, sex, income, employment status and health of several thousand people. A set of transition probabilities is used to simulate how the characteristics of these individuals will change over a time period such as one year. For instance, there will be a probability that someone who is employed at the start becomes unemployed during a simulated year. These transition probabilities are applied to the data set for each individual in turn, and repeatedly reapplied for a number of simulated time periods (years). In some simulations, it is also important to model births, i.e. the addition of new members to the data set, and marriage, death and the formation and dissolution of households, in order that the data set remains representative of the target population.

The adequacy and value of such simulation depends on the availability of two kinds of data: a representative sample of the target population to form the base data set, and a sufficiently complete and valid set of transition probabilities. In the simplest simulations, these probabilities consist of an array of constant values, each indicating the chance of some specific change occurring given the current state of an individual (i.e. first order Markov coefficients). In more complex models, the coefficients can be made to vary according to the situation of other members of the individual's household or the wider social context. For example, in a simulation designed to examine the relationship between family structures and the labour market, a model might include factors which relate the probability of a woman having a baby during a twelve month period to her age, her marital status, whether she has already had children (and if so, how many and of what ages), her current employment and earnings, and her partner's employment and earnings. The transition matrix would thus involve considering not only the individual's current characteristics, but also her biography and the characteristics of her household. The probability of the woman being in employment could in turn be modelled as a function of her age, education, qualifications, work history, husband's employment and earnings, and the number and ages of her children (at the individual and household level) and the state of the local labour market, the demand for full- and part-time labour and the demand for labour with particular skills (at the level of the social context).

One advantage of dynamic micro-simulation is that these very complex interrelationships can be modelled in a clear and precise fashion. The corresponding difficulty is that of estimating the required probabilities. The most appropriate way of doing this is to use data from panel studies, i.e. surveys of large samples which question the same sample at regular intervals over a period of several years. Unfortunately, such data are not common, although an increasing number of Western counties have started large panel studies recently (Rose et al. 1991). In the absence of suitable panel data, probabilities have to be estimated from cross-sectional data, which can yield biased results.

Validation of these models can be carried out by simulating through the past. For example, one can start with base data collected a decade ago, simulate the passing of ten years and compare the results with the current situation. Aggregate statistics from the simulation (e.g. the age profile, unemployment rates and income distributions) can be checked against the corresponding statistics from government sources or from current large scale surveys. Because the simulation is based on a sample, some difference between the results from the simulation and the actual situation would always be expected, no matter how good the model is. Unfortunately, however, it is difficult to quantify what is an acceptable difference in terms of confidence intervals because the statistical distributions of the parameters are not usually known (but see Pudney & Sutherland (1992) for some preliminary results).

Once the model has passed this kind of validation, it can be used to simulate developments in the future, for example to predict the age dependency ratio (the number of those retired compared with those in work), and to explore the long term effect of social policy options. Of course, the accuracy of such predictions depends on the adequacy of the model and the validity of the implied assumption of *ceteris paribus*, in particular that there will not be major social changes at the macro level.

In these simulations, the behaviour of each simulated individual is regarded as a "black box"; that is, behaviour is modelled by probabilities and no attempt is made to justify these in terms of individual preferences, decisions or plans. Moreover, each person acts individually without communicating plans or actions to others. The second approach to simulation to be described focuses specifically on the simulation of individual cognitive processes and on communication between people, using techniques drawn from artificial intelligence (AI). AI is a discipline devoted to the design and construction of computer software that has some of the characteristics commonly ascribed to human intelligence. Simulation based on *distributed artificial intelligence* uses many AI programs, each representing an "agent", which interact with each other and with a simulated "environment" (Bond & Gasser 1988).

An agent typically has three components: a memory, a set of goals and a set of rules. The memory is required so that the agent can remember past experience and plan ahead on this basis. The agent's objectives are defined by its goals, which may be as simple as to survive in a hostile environment in the face of depleting food or energy reserves, or may be more complex involving conflicts between alternative goals. The rule set defines the agent's behaviour and consists of condition-action rules. The condition part of each rule is matched against the contents of memory and input from environmental "sensors". If there is a match, the corresponding action is taken: this may be "internal" affecting only the state of the agent's memory, or "external" affecting the environment, for example the sending of a message through the environment to another agent.

The agents form part of a "testbed" which is also used to implement the simulated environment. Usually all agents share a common rule set and goals, but each has an individual memory. The testbed provides a rule interpreter which cycles through each agent in turn, collecting messages sent from other agents, updating the agent's internal state by firing any relevant rules, deciding on an action for the agent to take and finally communicating messages and the effects of the action to the environment. This is repeated for every agent and these cycles continue indefinitely until the simulation is stopped or all the agents have "died".

An example of a simulation in this style is work Jim Doran, Mike Palmer, Paul Mellars and I have done studying the "Emergence of social complexity" amongst hunter-gatherers in Upper Palaeolithic South-west France (Doran et al. 1993). Many archaeologists believe that at that time there was a change from an egalitarian, low density society in which people lived in small, migratory groups and there was little political organization and a simple division of labour by gender, to a somewhat more complex society, involving larger concentrations of people, some status differentials, role differentiation and more centralized decision making. Associated with these changes were changes in burial patterns and the emergence of cave art and various symbolic artefacts.

The question which the simulation explored is what caused this change. One theory centres on the effect of glaciation in concentrating food resources in particular locations (e.g. the migratory routes of reindeer) in a predictable annual cycle (Mellars 1985). As people gathered in these locations, there was "crowding", causing logistical problems and individual cognitive overload (Cohen 1985). The growth of what we have called social complexity was a solution to this, as means were found to schedule activities so that there were not too many people attempting to secure the same resources at the same time, so that there was an appropriate division of labour, and so that people could relate to other people through stereotypical rôles rather than on an individual basis.

We simulated this theory using a DAI testbed. The simulation included agents that have the ability to plan their actions depending on the situation they find themselves in, to recruit "followers" into groups and to communicate with other agents. The testbed also simulates the availability of resources of various types, some of which require several agents to be deployed before they can be "harvested". The simulation was used to investigate issues such as whether the formation of groups increases the chances of survival of the agents and reduces the cognitive processing that they need to engage in.

This simulation and others based on the same approach show that it is possible to build models of agents that communicate with each other and that act on the basis of quite sophisticated cognitive processing. However, this kind of simulation involves a great deal of computation as the simulated cognitive processes for each agent are complex and have to be activated on each round. Unlike dynamic simulation models, where the time period corresponding to a cycle can be as long as a year, DAI models typically use much finer-grained simulation, with time periods corresponding to minutes, hours or sometimes days. The computational load in carrying out a simulation is therefore much larger. This is exacerbated by the fact that simulating inter-agent communication means that as the number of agents is increased the amount of computation required goes up as the square of the number of agents, since each agent can potentially communicate with any other agent. Hence, DAI based simulations tend to involve rather few agents, often not more than about fifty.

Software

At present, programs to carry out the kinds of simulation discussed in this chapter have almost always been written specially by researchers using conventional programming languages. Dynamic micro-simulation programs are usually written in one of the standard languages, most often FORTRAN or C. It is also possible to use spreadsheet packages for fairly small and simple models (as the models become more complex, a spreadsheet becomes increasingly difficult to manage, and spreadsheets are not computationally efficient enough to support large datasets). And conventional statistical packages (e.g. SPSS) can also be used, albeit by having to adapt the features they offer towards the objectives of simulation.

It is possible that over the next few years, special programs designed for micro-simulation will become available. These would include a supervisory module to carry out the simulation work itself (creating random numbers, stepping through cases, and calculating changes and aggregating statistics about the changing sample) and facilities for users to define the transition probabilities and rules that specify how each individual in the sample is to be aged. An example of what could become a trend is Truscott's POM package, which simulates the effect of various tax and benefit policy options on household income, using a simulation based on a sample of 8,000 from the Family Expenditure Survey. The user is provided with the base data set, a special modelling language which makes it easy to specify tax and benefit rules, and a program that applies these rules to the data, summarizing the results by household type and aggregating to show the overall impact on Treasury expenditure (Truscott 1989).

DAI models tend to be written in the computer languages most frequently used by artificial intelligence researchers: PROLOG, LISP and Smalltalk. These languages are designed for tasks that involve manipulating symbols more than numbers. Although DAI simulations, as noted above, are usually run on a "testbed", these testbeds are almost always written specifically for the simulation and are not easily available to other researchers, nor easily adaptable to other related simulation problems. As the field matures, it is likely that this situation will change and, as with the case of dynamic micro-simulation, portable testbeds designed for particular types of simulation will appear.

Conclusions

The aims and methodological basis of dynamic micro-simulation and simulations based on distributed artificial intelligence have been reviewed in this chapter. Dynamic micro-simulation can be used to explore the long term macro consequences of individual social action. The life courses of a very large number of people are simulated according to individual, context-specific models of the probability of certain life events. The overall change over time is then assessed by aggregating the simulated individual changes. One advantage of dynamic micro-simulation is that the simulation starts with a detailed picture of current society, encapsulated in the base dataset. A disadvantage is the inadequate representation of individual action.

Artificial intelligence is concerned with achieving computational interpretations of aspects of human cognition such as memory, planning, learning and understanding. Distributed artificial intelligence investigates the properties of sets of communicating AI agents. Software testbeds have been constructed to provide a platform on which one can build and experiment with multi-agent systems, for example to model aspects of human societies. However, those DAI based models which have been built to date are rather abstract and difficult to relate directly to current sociological and policy issues.

The two approaches have evolved in almost total ignorance of each other and a synthesis might be valuable. A combination would be more powerful both for exploring important theoretical problems about the emergence of social phenomena from individual action, the current strength of the DAI approach, and for predicting the likely consequences of certain kinds of social policy change, the main value of the dynamic micro-simulation approach. Even if ways to effect this combination cannot be found, however, there is no doubt that the computer simulation of social dynamics will be increasingly important as a tool for social scientists.

Acknowledgements

I am grateful to Jim Doran for introducing me to DAI models and to my colleagues in the Social and Computer Sciences research group. This chapter is a revised version of a talk given at the SoftStat '93 conference, Heidelberg, March 1993.

218

References

Bond, A. H. & L. Gasser 1988. *Readings in distributed artificial intelligence*. San Francisco: Morgan Kaufmann.

Bratley, P., L. Fox, L. E. Schrage 1983. *A guide to simulation*. New York: Springer-Verlag.

Bulgren, W. G. 1982. *Discrete system simulation*. Englewood Cliffs, NJ: Prentice-Hall.

Cohen, M. N. 1985. Prehistoric hunter-gatherers: the meaning of social complexity. In *Prehistoric hunter-gatherers: the emergence of cultural complexity*, T. Douglas-Price & J. A. Brown (eds), 99–119. New York: Academic.

Doran, J. & G. N. Gilbert 1993. Simulating societies: an introduction. In *Simulating societies*, G. N. Gilbert & J. Doran (eds), London: UCL Press.

Doran, J., M. Palmer, N. Gilbert, P. Mellars 1993. The EOS Project: modelling Upper Palaeolithic change. In *Simulating societies*, G. N. Gilbert & J. Doran (eds), London: UCL Press.

Gilbert, G. N. 1993. *Analyzing tabular data: loglinear and logistic models for social researchers*. London: UCL Press.

Gilbert, G. N. & J. Doran (eds) 1993. *Simulating societies: the computer simulation of social processes*. London: UCL Press.

Gottfried, B. S. 1984. *Elements of stochastic process simulation*. Englewood Cliffs, NJ: Prentice-Hall.

Harding, A. 1990. *Dynamic microsimulation models: problems and prospects*. Discussion Paper 48, London School of Economics Welfare State Programme.

Inbar, M. & C. S. Stoll 1972. *Simulation and gaming in social science*. New York: Free Press.

Joshi, H. 1990. The cash opportunity cost of childbearing: an approach to estimation using British data. *Population Studies* **44**, 41–60.

Mellars, P. 1985. The ecological basis of social complexity in the Upper Palaeolithic of Southwestern France. In *Prehistoric hunter-gatherers: the emergence of cultural complexity*, T. Douglas-Price & J. A. Brown (eds), 271–97. New York: Academic.

Nowak, A. & B. Latané 1993. Simulating the emergence of social order from individual behaviour. In *Simulating societies: the computer simulation of social phenomena*, N. Gilbert & J. Doran (eds), London: UCL Press.

Pooch, U. W. & J. A. Wall 1993. *Discrete event simulation: a practical approach*. New York: CRC Press.

Pudney, S. & H. Sutherland 1992. The statistical reliability of microsimulation estimates: results for a UK tax-benefit model. In *Microsimulation models for public policy analysis: new frontiers*, R. Hancock & H. Sutherland (eds), 133–82. London: London School of Economics.

Rose, D., L. Corti, N. Buck 1991. Design issues in the British Household Panel Study. *Bulletin de Méthodologie Sociologique* **32**, 14–43.

Spriet, J. A. & G. C. Vansteenkiste 1982. *Computer-aided modelling and simulation*. New York: Academic.

Truscott, P. 1989. *A pluralist model of tax-benefit policy*. PhD thesis, University of Surrey.

Whicker, M. L. & L. Sigelman 1991. *Computer simulation applications*. Applied Social Research Methods Series. Newbury Park, Calif.: Sage.

Widman, L. E., K. A. Loparo, N. R. Nielson 1989. *Artificial intelligence, simulation and modelling*. New York: Wiley.

Zeigler, B. P. 1990. *Object oriented simulation with hierarchical, modular models*. New York: Academic.

Glossary

ASCII American Standard Code for Information Interchange, a list of standard codes used for storing text.

application A computer program designed to perform a particular task such as wordprocessing.

artificial intelligence (AI) The field of computing concerned with the design and use of computer programs capable of performing tasks commonly associated with human intelligence.

boolean operators The logical relations AND, OR, NOT associated with boolean algebra.

CAPI Computer assisted personal interviewing.

CAQDAS Computer assisted qualitative data analysis software.

CATI Computer assisted telephone interviewing.

CD-ROM Compact disc–read only memory. A storage medium which allows large quantities of digital material to be stored and easily retrieved.

central processing unit (CPU) The microprocessor and related circuits that perform the basic operations of a computer.

computer mediated communication (CMC) Generic term used to refer to electronic mail, computer conferencing, video conferencing, etc.

concordance A list of words in a text surrounded by the immediate context within which each one appears.

database A data file or files organized systematically to allow easy interrogation and retrieval.

desktop publishing (dtp) The use of computer technology to organize and present text and graphics in a form suitable for presentation or publication.

digitizing The process of converting information into a digital form for computer processing.

distributed artificial intelligence A system in which intelligent computer agents interact in complex ways to produce outcomes.

dynamic micro-simulation (DMS) A simulation technique which looks at long term macro level consequences of individual behaviour.

electronic mail   Messages sent from one user to another via a computer or network of computers.

expert system   A computer program which uses artificial intelligence techniques to emulate the performance of a human expert.

expert system shell   A computer program which allows a developer to construct an expert system.

floppy disk   A storage medium for microcomputers consisting of a magnetically coated surface in a protecting envelope.

frame-grabber   A device for acquiring a video image and inputting it for computer processing.

graphical user interface (GUI)   A way of interacting with the user of a computer based on windows etc.

hard disk   A rigid disk usually contained within the computer itself and capable of storing large amounts of data.

hypermedia   The integration and manipulation of various forms of media into a single digital form.

hypertext   A facility for organizing and linking documents in a way which allows the user to take multiple pathways through them.

inference engine   The part of an expert system where general rules of inference are used to reason from the knowledge base provided.

Internet   The system which connects multiple computer networks worldwide.

JANET   Joint Academic Network: the network used by academics in the United Kingdom.

knowledge acquisition   The process of acquiring from human experts the knowledge used by an expert system.

knowledge base   A file containing information and reasoning procedures for use in an expert system.

list server   A program for maintaining electronic mailing lists with facilities to allow users, for example, to automatically join or to control the messages they receive.

modem   Modulator-demodulator: a piece of equipment which allows a computer to communicate over telephone wires.

monitor   A device connected to a computer and used for displaying its visual output.

MS-DOS   MicroSoft Disk Operating System: a popular operating system for IBM microcomputers and compatibles.

network   A system of computers joined together so that they can share information.

neural networks   A machine learning technique the structure of which is analogous to the operation of the human brain and nervous system.

optical character recognition   A technique by which material is taken off the printed page and rendered into a computer-usable form.

PAPI   Paper and Pencil Interviewing.

PC   Personal computer.

production rules   A system of IF : THEN rules used in expert systems.

RAM   Random access memory: the area of computer memory available to be read and written to by programs.

GLOSSARY

string A sequence of characters.
user interface The means by which a computer interacts with the user.
windows Smaller screens which appear within a wider display.
Windows An operating system for IBM PCs and compatibles.

Index